RELIGION IN THE MIDDLE EAST

SUBJECT EDITORS

E. I. J. ROSENTHAL (JUDAISM)

M. A. C. WARREN (CHRISTIANITY)

C. F. BECKINGHAM (ISLAM)

Volume 1

JUDAISM AND CHRISTIANITY

RELIGION IN THE MIDDLE EAST

THREE RELIGIONS IN CONCORD AND CONFLICT

GENERAL EDITOR

A. J. ARBERRY

VOLUME I

JUDAISM AND CHRISTIANITY

CAMBRIDGE
AT THE UNIVERSITY PRESS
1969

Published by the Syndics of the Cambridge University Press
Bentley House, 200 Euston Road, London, N.W.1
American Branch: 32 East 57th Street, New York, N.Y.10022

Library of Congress Catalogue Card Number: 68-21187

Standard Book Number: 521 07400 2 (set of two vols.)

Printed in Great Britain
at the University Printing House, Cambridge
(Brooke Crutchley, University Printer)

CONTENTS

CONTENTS

PLATES

(Plates are near the end of the book, following p. 532)

PART 1: JUDAISM

PART 2: CHRISTIANITY

MAPS

NOTE. In view of the changing nature of Israel's boundaries with neighbouring states, the 1948 armistice boundaries have been used and are drawn in a fainter convention.

FOREWORD

Amongst the factors dividing and, to a certain extent, uniting the peoples of the Middle East, not the least interesting and noteworthy is the religions they variously profess and the sects within each religion by which they are further fragmented. The Middle East area (herein implying the lands of the Fertile Crescent, Arabia proper, and the territories to east and west, north and south affected by the Arab conquests and the spread of Islam) witnessed anciently, as is accepted for a commonplace, the rise of monotheism and its dissemination. Thereafter, and down to the present day, the three faiths predominantly concerned—Judaism, Christianity and Islam—have retained their separateness and have been in different degrees torn asunder by schisms; the "Two-and-Seventy jarring Sects" have long been distressingly notorious. Less well known, because less spectacular, has been the degree, admittedly modest, of co-operation between the three faiths and their multifarious sects, throughout history and even now.

What hopes can be entertained for a less turbulent future? The present symposium, conceived and planned before renewed crisis in the summer of 1967 rekindled always smouldering animosities, aims at giving a factual account of the three religions and their sects in this second half of the twentieth century. The table of contents is self-explanatory, and scarcely requires elucidation; experts from many parts of the world have written the individual chapters, and the whole work has been co-ordinated by a team of leading scholars. It should be said, however, that the writers in these two volumes were first invited to make their contributions in 1964 and had completed them by the end of 1966. At some points, recent developments in the Middle East might have led them to word some passages differently.

A very generous grant by the Spalding Trust underwrote a part of the expenses of this work. Cambridge University Press matched this grant by undertaking the costs of printing and publication. Grateful thanks is hereby rendered to both. G. M. Hinds of Cambridge University acted as the General Editor's assistant.

A few words are necessary to explain the system of transliteration employed. The editors have aimed at accuracy and consistency; it will be obvious, however, that complete uniformity, however desirable, remains unattainable, not least because of the great variety of source-languages involved. Contemporary proper names constitute a particular problem—Turkish proper names are a case in point, calling for more or less arbitrary decision; whilst the spelling of place-names is famously fraught with difficulty. A reasonable compromise has in practice been sought, as befits a work directed primarily at the general reader rather than the specialist.

A. J. ARBERRY

PART I

JUDAISM

CHAPTER I

JUDAISM TODAY

Judaism has never been a monolithic structure. Prophets and priests were at odds in biblical days. Pharisees, Sadducees, Essenes and a host of minor sectarian groups made up the composition of Judaism at the beginning of the Christian era when, in addition, there seem to have been considerable differences in approach between Palestinian Jews and the Jews of the Hellenistic–Roman Diaspora. There were, at that time, differences in religious observance between the Jews of Judea and Galilee in Palestine itself, just as, a little later, there would be differences between the Jewish communities of Palestine and those of Babylonia. Shortly after the rise of Islam, the Jews in the Muslim orbit were divided between Rabbanites and Karaites, the former upholding, and the latter denying, the validity of the rabbinic tradition. The later Middle Ages saw fierce conflicts between the Jewish rationalists and the Jewish anti-rationalists; and, while there had been a mystical undercurrent all along, the rise of Ḥasidism in eastern Europe in the eighteenth century led to open warfare between the mystical pietists and the more rationally inclined talmudic scholars—a conflict which, though no longer topical, has not altogether subsided even in our own period.

Attempts at fixing dogmas for Judaism have been extremely rare throughout Jewish history. The singling out of Deuteronomy vi. 4 ("Hear, O Israel, the Lord our God, the Lord is One") as the watchword of Israel's faith and the designation of him who denies the One God as a "denier of the Root", could be construed as dogmatic formulations in the early rabbinic period. The Talmud likewise stresses belief in the divine authorship of the Torah and in Resurrection—and that in a way which would entitle us to consider those beliefs as "dogmas" of rabbinic Judaism. Yet even here there was considerable leeway given to the Jew when it came to construing the details. Rabbinic Judaism, on the whole, operated within a certain "climate of belief", rather than within a rigid dogmatic structure. It was more interested in achieving uniformity in religious practice than in unanimity of underlying belief. Only the polemical and apologetic needs of Judaism in the

Muslim and Christian Middle Ages induced individual thinkers to draw up lists of Judaism's fundamental beliefs. Such enumerations of fundamental beliefs were the work of individuals. There no longer was a supreme ecclesiastical authority which, conceivably, might have been able to impose such creeds from above. Consequently, there were not only disagreements between the scholars about the precise number of fundamental beliefs deserving of such pre-eminence, but the creeds themselves never did achieve universal acceptance.

Still, in spite of all the sectarian divisions and in spite of the high degree of creedal flexibility, Jews, until the beginning of the modern period, did hold a number of very basic beliefs in common. Rabbanites and Karaites (as did Pharisees and Sadducees before them) might differ on the *contents* of Revelation. Did God reveal the written text of the Torah only, or did he also reveal the Oral Torah (part of which was later committed to writing in the Talmud and the Codes)? This, needless to say, was a very basic difference of opinion—with considerable repercussions in the area of religious life and observance. But it was a difference which was predicated upon the common acceptance of the *fact* of Revelation and of the divine character of—at least—the written Torah. Again, Maimonides and his opponents might differ sharply on the legitimacy of anthropomorphic concepts of God. Medieval Jewish philosophers might also disagree on the relative primacy of the "God of Aristotle" and the "God of Abraham". But all of those disagreements were predicated upon the common acceptance of the *fact* of God's existence. Moreover, there was never any doubt about the *fact* that the Jews were God's "Chosen People", the people bound to God by the "Covenant" which had never been abrogated, and the people which, though at present living "in exile", will ultimately be messianically redeemed.

Two further factors made for continuity and cohesion. One was the political status of the Jews in both Christian and Muslim society. Though they might enjoy greater or lesser degrees of toleration, depending upon a number of religious, economic and political circumstances, the Jews never enjoyed the status of full members of either Christian or Muslim society. Conversion to the dominant faith often (though not universally) brought with it the removal of any and all civil disabilities. But we are concerned here, not with those who left Judaism, but with those who were instrumental in maintaining it through the millennia. Always, to a certain extent, excluded from the society in whose midst they were living, the Jews were thrown on to their own resources. That meant, among other things, that they enjoyed (and were quite frequently compelled to enjoy) a considerable amount of self-government and legal autonomy. And the legal system which they employed was a system derived from the Talmud, which, in turn, was based upon biblical legislation—a legislation which claimed nothing less than divine sanction. Biblical legislation does not distinguish between civil law and religious law. It was designed for a theocratic society in which man serves God through political and civil life as much as through the cult, and in which there was no distinction between the national and the religious aspects of Israelite existence.

After the destruction of Temple and State, in the year 70 C.E., the pharisaic–rabbinic scholars were, of course, only too aware of the fact that the biblical "constitution" could no longer—in its entirety—be put into practice. They, therefore, distinguished between the commandments which were dependent upon the land of Israel and the commandments not so dependent. Only the latter were considered as binding now. Moreover, the Babylonian scholar, Samuel (third century C.E.), established the principle that, where it does not conflict with Judaism's religious demands, the civil law of the country in which Jews are living must be considered religiously binding for the Jew. With those modifications clearly understood, the biblical "constitution" and its rabbinic interpretations and amendments continued to be the legal system, the theology and the ritual code of the Jews until well into the eighteenth century. The levitical and agricultural laws were deemed to be temporarily suspended, but never abrogated. (They would be reinstated as part of the ultimate messianic redemption.) Thus, the catastrophic events connected with the destruction of Temple and State were painfully felt to limit the scope of the present applicability of Torah law. But they were not regarded as marking a final break. The legal system itself was viewed as an uninterrupted continuum. A legal decision rendered by Ezekiel Landau, in eighteenth-century Prague, would be regarded as a consequence of the Code written in sixteenth-century Palestine by Joseph Caro—the latter, in turn, claiming to have merely written a commentary on the Code of the fourteenth-century German immigrant to Spain, Jacob b. Asher, and so all the way back to the Talmud and the Bible itself! The legal autonomy which the Jewish communities enjoyed in Christian and Muslim lands made the existence of such a system possible.

At the same time, and here we come to the second factor, this externally imposed autonomy was made possible by—and, in its turn, it facilitated—the overwhelming victory of pharisaic–rabbinic Judaism over all other contestants. Sadduceeism, the outlook of the upper echelons of the priesthood and of the aristocracy, did not long survive the destruction of Temple and State. Karaism, a very serious competitor in the ninth and tenth centuries, ceased to be so after a while, and has lived on to this day as a numerically insignificant sect on the periphery of Judaism. Various sects of Judeo-Christians, disowned by the Synagogue and proclaimed heretical by the Church, disappeared by the fifth century. The revival of a quasi-Karaite approach briefly stirred the Jewish communities of the west in the seventeenth and eighteenth centuries. Spanish and Portuguese *marranos*, having secretly believed in a kind of scriptural Judaism, came to places like Amsterdam and London in order to profess Judaism openly. But the official Judaism they found was not "scriptural" at all. It was based on the rabbinic understanding of the Bible, rather than on the Scriptures directly. This led to attacks upon rabbinic Judaism of the kind made famous by Uriel da Costa in seventeenth-century Amsterdam. But those challenges were met. And where rabbinic Judaism proved to be an unsurmountable obstacle, Deism and various forms of Protestant Christianity already provided an alternative. The structure of Judaism itself, far more shaken at that time by pseudo-messianic and antinomian movements, remained intact.

All other spiritual battles were waged within the framework of official rabbinic Judaism itself. The rationalists and the anti-rationalists both represented legitimate versions of rabbinic Judaism, as did, later on, the Ḥasidim and their opponents. Rabbinic Judaism was broad enough to contain them all, even as it provided a high degree of flexibility in legal interpretation, and gave its sanction and recognition to divergences in liturgical practice which were due to local traditions and circumstances. A German or Polish Jew, for example, would not find his religious obligations sufficiently met by the ritual codes and the prayer manuals of the Spanish and Portuguese Jews and vice versa. Yet they both recognized the legitimacy of the other's procedure. They were both rabbinic Jews. They might differ in language, culture, custom and attire, but they lived in the same climate of belief, and they followed, in principle, the same ritual and liturgical provisions and they were governed by the identical system of jurisprudence.

In that sense, therefore, it can be stated that there was such a thing as a "normative Judaism", at any rate from about the second century of the Christian era until the beginning of modern times—a Judaism, that is to say, which had enlisted the allegiance of the vast majority of Jews and which looked upon itself as the uninterrupted continuation of biblical Israel and the rabbinic tradition.

Such was the Judaism which was lived and practised by people known as Jews, when in the larger world around them certain events took place which had their inevitable repercussion on both Jews and Judaism, and which set the stage for the various forms of Judaism with which we are familiar today. The events in question are the rise and spread of the Enlightenment and the Age of Reason, the American and the French Revolutions, the ideals of "liberty, equality, fraternity", carried through Europe on the banners of Napoleon's victorious armies, and the coming into being of the secular state. In one way or another, each of the above rocked the foundations upon which the fabric of Jewish society had traditionally rested. The Judaism of today is, therefore, as much the result of those environmental factors (and of the Jews' response to them) as it is a continuation of those features of the Jewish past which have retained their viability under totally changed circumstances. By the same token, however, the forms of Judaism today vary to the extent to which the lives of the Jews have been touched by the environmental factors which we have enumerated. The Jews of Westphalia, for example, gained their emancipation in 1808; the Jews of Prussia in 1812; in England the last disabilities were not removed until 1858. But in Russia the Jews were not emancipated until 1917; and in many of the oriental countries not at all.

Under the circumstances, it is easy to see that the problems faced by the German Jew in the nineteenth century were often of quite a different nature from those faced, at the same period, by the Russian Jew. To take but one striking illustration: the German Jew considered himself a German in nationality and in culture. The fact that his acceptance as a German by the other Germans may not always have been quite as complete or as wholehearted as he might have wished, that the emancipation of the Jews might have been more of a logical deduction from the axioms of Liberalism than a psychologically digested reality, is beside the point in this context. Even the last barriers to full integration fell away as soon as the German Jew gave up his Judaism and converted to the dominant Christian faith. In this way, and sometimes in this way only, he could obtain high positions in the universities, the judiciary and the civil service. Whatever, therefore, the attitude of the German non-Jew to the Jew, the German Jew did not have the slightest doubt about his own German-ness. If he nevertheless continued to regard himself as a Jew, then his Jewishness was a matter of religion only—completely devoid of national overtones. The question of Judaism, therefore, was purely and simply a religious question. In what form could Judaism continue to claim his allegiance, seeing that by nationality he was a German and by culture a European? What was there in the religious heritage of his ancestors that spoke to him in his present situation? Different answers were offered to those questions, as we shall have occasion to see—answers which were most clearly enunciated in Germany, though they were eagerly taken up in environments which provided a somewhat similar background to modern Jewish existence.

Quite different was the question of Judaism which faced the Russian Jew. As has been noted, he did not obtain his emancipation until 1917, so that, throughout the nineteenth century (a century which saw the Frenchman of the Jewish faith, the Englishman of the Jewish faith, and the German of the Mosaic persuasion) there was no such thing as a "Russian of the Jewish faith". There were Russian Jews, but no Jewish Russians, seeing that the Jewish masses of eastern Europe were never fully integrated into their environment. On the contrary, restrictive legislation even forced the Russian Jews into specifically designated areas of the "Jewish Pale of Settlement". The Russian Jews were, therefore, thrown back on to their own resources. They not only had their own religion, but also their own education system, their own literature and folk art, and even their own language, Yiddish. They were a distinct cultural group in eastern Europe.

Yet they did not altogether remain unaffected by the cultural and philosophical currents of the west. Positivism, agnosticism, socialism, and even atheism won their adherents among the rebellious youth of the East European Talmud academies. But because Jewish existence in eastern Europe was ethnic and cultural as well as religious, the Russian Jew who lost his religious faith did not, like his counterpart west of the Oder river, cease to be a Jew. He continued living within the Jewish environment and shared in those aspects of Jewish living which were not directly related to theological presuppositions. Still, such a Jew needed a theory, a philosophy to account for his Jewishness. With the demise of religious commitment, which saw Jewish existence in terms of a Covenant with God, such a theory was more likely to operate with concepts of culture and of nationalism. And, indeed, it was from the ranks of Russian Jewish youth that, in 1882, the first pioneer colonists went to Palestine—fourteen years before the Viennese Theodor Herzl published his blueprint of *The Jewish State*. It was among the Jews of Russia that the Hebrew language was reborn as a modern secular language, even as it was among them that various forms of Jewish nationalism were most fully developed.

Of course, we are speaking of representative trends. Herzl, as we have already indicated, was a "Westerner", and Zionism found some of its adherents among German Jews as well. Similarly, not all of the theories of Jewish nationalism developed in eastern Europe were irreligious or anti-religious. There actually were Russian rabbis like Samuel Mohilever (1824–98) and Isaac Jacob Reines (1839–1915) who favoured the colonization of Palestine on the basis of a religious version of Jewish nationalism—just as there were many Russian Jews who opposed the Zionist endeavour on religious grounds. The fact remains that the theoreticians of a purely religious Judaism arose within the German environment, whereas the major theoreticians of Jewish nationalism or secularist Jewishness were Russian Jews. Other Jewish communities made their transition to modernity to the extent to which they were indebted to the one or the other, or to both; or failed to make that transition if they had no contact with either.

Thus, Judaism in the United States in the nineteenth century was predominantly influenced by the German pattern of Judaism. At the turn of the century, however, American Jewry's ranks were greatly augmented by the waves of the Russian Jewish immigration which brought its own influences from the "old country". For about half a century the two types of Judaism existed side by side, sometimes in open conflict, at others in virtual ignorance of each other. Today, with the majority of American Jews born in the United States, the influences of both types are still being felt. But they are both contributing factors now to the formation of a distinct type of American Judaism which is evolving in response to the particular challenge of the American environment.

By way of contrast, the problem of Judaism in the State of Israel is immensely complicated by the fact that within the confines of what is meant to be a "Jewish" State, a confrontation is taking place between those Jews, mostly of East European provenance, whose Zionism derives from secularist ideologies, and those Jews, mostly of Asian and North African provenance, who, in their countries of origin, had been completely by-passed by either the West European or the East European transformations of traditional Judaism. The spiritual influence of the "western" Jews in the State of Israel has thus far been somewhat negligible.

It may, then, be said that the foundations of contemporary Judaism were laid in the nineteenth century both in Germany and in Russia. The twentieth century was to see the disappearance of both of those spiritual centres. Anti-Semitism, in its most virulent form ever, destroyed the former, anti-Judaism inhibited the latter. Judaism in the twentieth century seems to derive its inspiration from two major centres: the United States of America, with its five and a half million Jews, and the State of Israel, created in 1948. That both of these new centres are, in part, influenced by the ideologies developed in the previous two centres has already been hinted at, and will be made more explicit in the course of this presentation.

Moses Mendelssohn (1729–86) exemplifies the first stage of Judaism's entry into the modern west. Living before emancipation had fully been attained by any segment of western Jewry, and before the various schools of thought within modern Judaism had crystallized, Mendelssohn's career is paradigmatic for that of a whole generation. Child of a traditional Jewish environment in Dessau, he made his way to Berlin in search of learning and of culture. Never departing from the practice of traditional Jewish rituals, he became one of the most respected figures in German cultural life. Lessing and Lavater were among his personal friends. His popular philosophical writings were read with respect—not least on account of his perfect German style. Mendelssohn used the position he attained in German cultural life to work for the emancipation of his co-religionists. In his apologetic writings, he argued for the separation of Church and State. He argued on what he thought to be the basis of classical Judaism. His views on those matters were, in reality, influenced by the writings of Spinoza. But he did not share Spinoza's pantheism. Trying to influence the non-Jewish environment in favour of Jewish emancipation, he tried to influence his fellow-Jews in the direction of the Enlightenment. One of his aims in this sphere was to wean the German Jews away from the Judeo-German jargon of ghetto existence, and to make them adopt the German language of their time. A German translation of the Bible, undertaken by Mendelssohn and his collaborators, and published, at first, in Hebrew characters, was to serve that purpose. The Hebrew commentary appended to it favoured the classical Jewish exegetes as against the latter-day representatives of the *pilpul* ("hair-splitting") method, and it tended towards a rationalistic exegesis.

In his personal life, Mendelssohn set an example of how full participation in the cultural life of the environment can be combined with strict adherence to the traditional observances of Judaism. Yet that combination represented the personal equation of Mendelssohn's own character, rather than a reasoned position which, without revolutionary changes, could serve as a guide to succeeding generations. The fact that Mendelssohn, as it were, led the exodus of the Jews from the spiritual ghetto of the Middle Ages (even before emancipation had become a legal fact) enabled later Reform Judaism to regard him as one of its founders. The fact that Mendelssohn, however, adhered to strict traditionalist ritual practice made him appear to later Neo-Orthodoxy as one of its spiritual fathers.

Actually, of course, Mendelssohn was neither the one nor the other. Theologically he was a deist. The "eternal verities necessary for bliss" were not in need of any supernatural revelation. They are universally implanted in the human mind. It was not the purpose of the Revelation at Sinai to make known such religious doctrines. Yet Mendelssohn did not deny that the Revelation at Sinai took place. It was a historical event at which God revealed to Israel a system of legislation. That legislation is binding upon Israel—at any rate until such time as God will revoke it as impressively and as publicly as he had originally revealed it. When challenged by the competing claims of Christianity, Mendelssohn invoked the yardstick of Reason to defend his allegiance to Judaism. Judaism does not make as many demands upon man's credulity and, recognizing—as some of the ancient rabbis had put it —that "there are righteous men among the Gentiles who have a share in the world-to-come", it is far less "exclusivist" than Christianity and, therefore, more liable to be true.

Mendelssohn's championship of the Religion of Reason certainly fitted in with the needs and aspirations of the enlightened German Jews in the eighteenth century. His reduction of *torah* to a divinely revealed system of legislation binding only upon Jews was far more problematical. Many Jews at that time felt that, in order to deserve emancipation, they had to divest themselves of such "outlandish" practices as made the Jews appear like a foreign body within the state. But on any theory of a divinely revealed legislation, it was precisely those traditional Hebraic practices and customs which could not be tampered with. Besides, on Mendelssohn's own reading of the facts, the "eternal verities" existed quite independently of that legislation. They could be found in other religions as well. Mendelssohn's own descendants thought to have found easier access to them *via* the kind of liberal Christianity which was then prevalent in the Prussian capital. Mendelssohn's disciple and collaborator, David Friedländer (1750–1834), actually proposed a mass conversion to Christianity—on condition that the Jews who were going to be baptized would not be required to believe in the more pronounced *Christian* dogmas. Christianity, then, was merely regarded as one aspect of the total European culture; and those Jews who wanted to share in that culture to the fullest extent, and who equated the desired legal emancipation with the removal of any and all remaining barriers, were quite prepared to accept a nominal—though not a real—Christianity. Friedländer's proposal was emphatically rejected from the Christian side. His motivation, however, was characteristic of the age. In this connexion it should be remembered that some of the traditionalist rabbis in eastern Europe and in Hungary actually opposed the emancipation of the Jews—precisely because they, too, felt that Jewish participation in the dominant culture would inevitably lead to Jewish acceptance of the dominant faith.

The fact remains that, as far as the cultured and enlightened German Jews were concerned, the forms in which Judaism had been transmitted to them from the days of ghetto existence proved to be less and less attractive. Conversions to Christianity became more and more frequent; and in many instances the motivation for that step was utilitarian and aesthetic, rather than theological. The poet Heinrich Heine (1797–1856) called his own acceptance of Christianity an "entrance ticket to European culture", insisting, towards the end of his life, that, although he had been "baptized", he had never been "converted".

Those who were unwilling to accept Christianity for ulterior reasons continued to work for legal emancipation—and for a reformation of traditional Judaism which would make the expressions of the latter more in accord with the aesthetic standards of the environment. After his proposal of quasi-conversion had been rejected, David Friedländer threw himself into that work. He established a school for Jewish children in which secular subjects were taught. He argued for the substitution of German for Hebrew prayers in the synagogue service. In a German translation of the traditional prayerbook which he published (in Hebrew characters!) he did not modify any of the traditional prayers. But, separately, he argued (in 1812, the year of the emancipation of the Jews in Prussia!) for the omission of the prayers which deal with the messianic return to Zion. The Jew does not want to leave his German fatherland!

Meanwhile, the aesthetic, though not the doctrinal, reform of Judaism had found its first practitioner in Israel Jacobson (1768–1828). A wealthy layman, he established a school in Seesen (in 1801), to which he added a temple, in 1810. Services in that temple included German, in addition to Hebrew, prayers, and German hymns and chorales. Sermons were preached in German. The traditional chanting was abolished, and the singing was accompanied by an organ. It should be noted that Jacobson's reforms were all of an aesthetic character. He did not propound any theories of a doctrinal nature.

As long as those reforms were confined to the school's private temple, the opposition did not become too vocal. The situation was different once Jacobson moved to Berlin and tried to introduce such reforms on a larger scale, and when, in 1818, a temple came into existence in Hamburg in which Jacobson's kind of reforms was to be instituted on a permanent basis. At that stage, a traditionalist opposition began to crystallize. Even so, it should be borne in mind that, up to that stage, the reforms were characterized by two things: they were instituted by laymen; and they confined themselves to the aesthetic aspects of the Jewish divine services. As such, they could come into conflict with what had become traditional and accepted. But it is nevertheless noteworthy that, in 1818, at Jacobson's instigation, a collection of rabbinic *responsa* was published, in which those aesthetic reforms were shown to be in complete accord with the strict demands of the Talmud and the rabbinic codes. There was, then, as yet, no intention to depart from the "normative Judaism" of tradition, or to change and reform the doctrinal basis of the ancestral faith. It was all a question of making Judaism more "attractive", in order to retain the allegiance of the younger generation now educated to participate fully in the culture of the West.

The opponents of change did not see it that way at all. For them, the slightest departure from what had become customary in the externals of worship represented the thin end of the wedge which would split the entire traditional structure, leading to the demise of traditional Judaism as a whole. To a certain extent, the forebodings of the traditionalists were justified. The aesthetic reforms of divine service, ostensibly quite innocent in their aims and objectives, were but one aspect of a more thoroughgoing reformation which was indeed to mark a radical break with the past. The reforms instituted by well-meaning laymen were to be succeeded by reforms in practice and in doctrine, championed by a new type of rabbi who combined traditional Jewish learning with a doctorate from a secular university. And that new type of rabbi was himself made possible by, even as he contributed to, a new and unprecedented way of studying the documents of the Jewish past. We are referring to the *Wissenschaft des Judentums*, the "scientific study of Judaism".

The phrase was coined by Leopold Zunz (1794–1886) in 1823, when he published the *Zeitschrift für die Wissenschaft des Judentums*, a periodical issued by the "Verein für Kultur und Wissenschaft der Juden" (Society for the Culture and Science of the Jews). That society, in its turn, was founded in 1819 by men like Zunz, Eduard Gans, Heinrich Heine, and others. Its aim was the combination of the scientific study of Judaism with practical reforms in Jewish life which would maintain the allegiance of the enlightened and educated Jews. Through lectures and the publication of the periodical the former aim was indeed pursued. But, always confined to a meagre number of supporters, the society was unable to make much headway in the latter. In 1824 it disbanded, having failed to maintain the Jewish loyalty even of some of its leading members. Yet the "scientific study of Judaism" outlived the society which first promoted it. Leopold Zunz devoted his whole long life to its furtherance, being joined in this enterprise by the leading Jewish scholars of the nineteenth century—both west and east.

In order to understand both what the *Wissenschaft des Judentums* claimed to do, and what it actually did, we must call to mind what study in Judaism had been before the nineteenth century. Traditional Judaism had always assigned a very important role to study, even regarding it as a form of worship. Seeing that God's revelation had found its literary repercussion in a vast literature, only he could truly be pious who had mastered that literature. The Torah and its commentators, the Talmud and the Codes, thus formed the substance of both elementary and higher Jewish education through the centuries. But since that vast literature, in all of its parts, contained the Revelation of God—both in its original Sinaitic formulation and as refracted through the teachings of the later rabbis—external factors of history and of chronological sequence were of very little interest in the pursuit of the sacred studies, if they entered the picture at all. Rabbinic authorities separated by centuries were dealt with as contemporaries. Moreover, a casuistic methodology, developed in France and Germany in the thirteenth century, and brought to its full flowering in eastern Europe from the sixteenth century on, saw its *raison d'être* in the reconciliation and harmonization of all real and apparent contradictions within that body of literature. This method was pursued to such an extent that only he was regarded as a true "scholar" who had shown competence in all the highways and byways of that casuistry—far beyond the actual requirements of traditional Jewish practice.

That kind of traditional Jewish learning had little to commend itself to the young scholars who had left the confining atmosphere of the ghetto, and who were now throwing themselves enthusiastically into the historical study of the classics. One of the aims of the *Wissenschaft des Judentums*, therefore, was to make Jewish learning "respectable" in terms of the academic pursuits of the times. It began by applying the historical method to the study of the documents of the Jewish past. In this way it was hoped to gain a recognition for the Jewish contribution to civilization on a level with the recognition accorded to other ancient cultures. And, with such recognition obtained, it was likewise hoped that the western Jew would regain and cultivate his Jewish self-respect. The flowering of the *Wissenschaft des Judentums* coincided with the wave of Romanticism in the environment; and Romanticism had its share in motivating research into the Jewish past.

The employment of the historical method in studying the Jewish past, however, led to a picture of that past which was quite at variance with the way in which that past had been traditionally understood. Now it was no longer a question of reconciling and harmonizing real and apparent contradictions in the documents, but of evaluating those contradictions in their own right, of letting the sources speak for themselves within their own historical setting. What emerged from this approach was a picture of Judaism which was anything but monolithic. Judaism, it was found, had always been developing and had always been responsive to historical and environmental stimuli. The vast rabbinical literature was not all of one piece, after all; and religious practices and liturgical rites had always been products of evolution and development. That latter discovery was, of course, to furnish the theoretical justification for liturgical reforms in nineteenth-century Judaism, once rabbis trained in the *Wissenschaft des Judentums* took over from the laity the direction of the reform endeavours. Zunz's own *Die gottesdienstlichen Vorträge der Juden* (1832) demonstrated that the weekly sermon had been a constituent part of the Jewish divine service in the classical period of rabbinic Judaism. He thereby refuted the attacks against the "innovation" of the sermon which emanated from Jewish traditionalists and from conservative governments.

Within more recent years, the *Wissenschaft des Judentums* of the nineteenth century has been the recipient of much criticism. It has been pointed out that the so-called scientific study of Judaism had purposely been blind to certain crucial areas of Jewish history and literature. For example, the rationalistic bias of the nineteenth-century German Jew is said to have been responsible for the lack of attention which was paid the rather vital subject of Jewish mysticism, considering that, from the sixteenth century on, mysticism was a rather dominant theme in Jewish life. The *Wissenschaft des Judentums* has also been criticized for not dealing (except in one or two isolated cases) with the Bible itself. Its entire concern seemed to have been with post-biblical literature. It is possible that the founders of the *Wissenschaft des Judentums* were, for the time being, content to leave the scientific study of the Old Testament in the hands of Christian scholars who were, at that time, pursuing that study with great energy. It is, however, more likely that the men of the *Wissenschaft des Judentums* shied away from that particular area for apologetic reasons. Questions of personal religious belief, though not altogether irrelevant to the study of post-biblical Jewish literature, would very soon have put an end to the joint labours of conservative and liberal scholars if the problem of biblical revelation had been touched. The Bible, therefore, was taken for granted, and the scientific investigations began with what came after it. While that apologetic stance might be excused for pragmatic reasons, a more direct accusation has been levelled against the *Wissenschaft des Judentums* because it engaged in apologetics of a far more questionable kind. Its very founders regarded the *Wissenschaft des Judentums* as a means for the obtaining of Jewish emancipation. It is now being argued that no discipline which has so blatantly apologetic an aim could truly be considered either as uninhibitedly "scientific" or as properly "objective" in dealing with the phenomena it "investigates".

Be that as it may. For one thing, whatever faults the *Wissenschaft des Judentums* may have had in the nineteenth century, efforts are now being made in the institutions of higher Jewish learning in the United States and in Israel (themselves the products of that *Wissenschaft*) to rectify them. For another, *Wissenschaft des Judentums*, with all its advantages and disadvantages, is a basic constituent of the background against which the further development of Judaism in the nineteenth century must be seen.

A prayerbook for the Reform Temple in Hamburg was published in 1819. It was attacked by the traditionalists on legalistic grounds, and defended by the reformers with references to the identical legal sources. In spite of their efforts, the traditionalists were unable to prevail upon the Hamburg senate to close the new Temple. Members of that Temple continued to remain members of the Hamburg Jewish community, while they worshipped according to their own preferences. It was hardly a matter of more than local interest, though rabbis in other cities and countries were appealed to by both sides. But when, in 1841, a new edition of the Hamburg prayerbook appeared, the situation was quite different. This time the whole of German Judaism was involved, and the second stage of reform had been reached.

Though the traditionalist opposition was couched in the customary legalistic terms of prohibition and anathema, the attack was led by a man who himself represented the new type of rabbi. Isaac Bernays (1792–1849) became chief rabbi of Hamburg in 1821, among his qualifications being the fact that he had studied at the University of Würzburg in addition to having pursued the more traditional rabbinic studies. It was obviously felt by the traditionalists in Hamburg that only a man who himself had enjoyed the advantages of a modern education could lead the counter-reformation. Indeed, Bernays not only introduced the German sermon into the Hamburg traditionalist synagogue, he even refused to be known as "rabbi" because that title was no longer sufficiently respected. Though no Spanish or Portuguese Jew himself, he insisted on being called *ḥakham*, a title borne by the rabbis of the Spanish and Portuguese Jews. While Bernays' modern education did not affect the way in which he dealt with the Reform prayerbook, the fact that a man with that kind of education did occupy the position of chief rabbi in Hamburg at that time is worthy of note. That sort of thing was not yet universally taken for granted.

When, in 1839, another university-trained rabbi, Abraham Geiger, was elected as second rabbi of the Breslau Jewish community, the old rabbi of that community opposed that appointment, among other reasons, because Geiger was a university graduate. This led the supporters of Geiger, in 1842 and 1843, to publish a two-volume work, entitled, *Rabbinical Responsa on the Compatibility of Free Investigation with the Exercise of Rabbinical Functions*. Geiger, of whom more will be said later, ultimately succeeded in obtaining the Breslau appointment. For our present purposes it suffices to note that many of the respondents who affirmed the compatibility of free investigation with the exercise of rabbinical functions are also represented by their affirmative votes in a collection of *Responsa* which appeared in Hamburg, in 1842, defending the new edition of the Hamburg prayerbook against the attacks of Bernays and other traditionalist rabbis. Not all the respondents approved of all the changes introduced in the 1841 revision of the prayerbook. What they did affirm was the right of the Hamburg reformers to publish a prayerbook of that kind. And they denied the right of Bernays to attack with the weapons of anathema and prohibition. On the whole, they all found that the new prayerbook fitted the traditional requirements as they had developed. For that the prayerbook, in all its component parts, did not go back to hoary antiquity, that it, too, was subject to development and change—of that there no longer was any question among that group of university-trained rabbis, disciples of the *Wissenschaft des Judentums*. Nor was there any disagreement among them about the urgent need of a reform of Judaism in order to meet the exigencies of a new age. Where there might be disagreements was the area of application. On what basis was the much-needed reform to proceed? And what parts of the traditional law were to be reformed?

To solve those and related questions, the modern rabbis of Germany met at a number of rabbinical conferences—1844 in Brunswick; 1845 in Frankfurt on Main; 1846 in Breslau. At those meetings there was a general shying away from the discussion of underlying principles—which, on the one hand, made it possible for rabbis of different orientations to work together, and which, on the other hand, occasionally resulted in the discussions getting somewhat disorganized. But the rabbis managed to agree among themselves: that certain traditional prayers ought to be omitted; that some of the sabbath restrictions ought to be abolished; that the Scripture pericopes read on the sabbath ought to be abbreviated; that prayers for the messianic restoration of the sacrificial cult should no longer be recited; that the Jews were loyal citizens of the fatherland and did not look forward to a personal return to Palestine; that Jewish marriage and divorce law was in urgent need of reform, and that a committee should be elected to look into it; that the organ accompaniment of synagogue services was not against Jewish law; and that German prayers were admissible. It was only when they tried to agree on what prayers were to be recited in Hebrew, and what prayers in German, that no unanimity could be achieved. And when, at the Frankfurt conference of 1845, the rabbis voted that for the time being the retention of Hebrew was advisable, but that—and this was carried by a very narrow margin—there was no "objective necessity" for the retention of Hebrew, one of the rabbis, Zacharias Frankel, demonstratively left the meeting and proceeded to the founding of what was later to be known as Conservative Judaism.

It was one thing to decide matters at the rabbinical conferences. It was quite another to carry out the decisions at the local level. The rabbis gathered in conference did not represent Reform congregations, but only themselves. To the extent to which they held rabbinical office, they were in the service of various German Jewish communities; and those communities were guided by the desires of the majority of their members. The rabbi who wanted to reform the existing pattern first had to convince the council and officers of his own community. Some of them were not so easily convinced. Many of the German Jewish communities were proud of their history of several centuries—of their history and of their liturgical pattern. It seems likely that well into the middle of the nineteenth century the majority of German Jews were quite content to leave traditional usage untouched and unreformed. Only in Hamburg and in Berlin had places of worship been founded on a declared Reform platform; the former, as has already been noted, in 1818, and the latter, on a far more radical basis than the Hamburg Temple, in 1845. Even so, the members of those two Reform congregations continued to be members of the local Jewish communities. In all other instances, the battle for liturgical reform was fought within the existing structure itself, leading to a variety of compromise solutions.

While the rabbinical conferences mainly dealt with practical questions, individual rabbis worked out their own particular philosophies of Judaism which, in the course of time, developed into distinct schools of thought within German Judaism. Two of them, Abraham Geiger and Samuel Holdheim, had been leading participants in the rabbinical conferences. A third, Zacharias Frankel, had left the Frankfurt conference in protest against the negative vote on the "objective necessity" of Hebrew. The fourth, Samson Raphael Hirsch, a disciple of Isaac Bernays in Hamburg, and an erstwhile fellow-student of Geiger at the university, had never participated in the rabbinical conferences.

Abraham Geiger (1810–74), rabbi in Wiesbaden, Breslau, Frankfurt on Main, and Berlin, contributed equally to the *Wissenschaft des Judentums* (he was one of the very few to approach even the Bible scientifically) and to the application of the results of *Wissenschaft* to the practical task of reforming Judaism. His reforming zeal went far beyond the details of the synagogal liturgy. It was a reformulation of Judaism as a whole which he had in mind. His historical studies indicated to him that Judaism had always been involved in the process of change. Rabbinic Judaism was quite different from biblical Judaism; and modern Judaism, in its turn, could not be identical with rabbinic Judaism. Yet far from rejecting Tradition, Geiger saw in Tradition itself the very stuff and the dynamics of change. Only Judaism's monotheistic idea and its ethical commandments were eternal. Ceremonies were important; but they were to be retained only as long as they actually expressed a living religious idea. Nor must it be overlooked that religious observances also reflect the political status of the Jews at any given time. While, in antiquity, there was such a thing as a Jewish nation, the Jews are a nation no longer; and they do not hope to be reconstituted as a nation in Palestine. Only the universal aspects of the old messianic hope have retained their validity. The dreams of a messianic return to Palestine were nurtured by centuries of persecution. But the Jews are now no longer living "in exile". Even the idea of Palestine as the "cradle of our faith" must not be overly romanticized. The task of the Jew was in the here and now. Withal, the Jews are God's "Chosen People", though the fact of the choice must not lead to invidious comparisons with others—particularly since the Christians in whose midst we live are not identical with the idolaters against whom our ancestors had to contend. And there is such a thing as Revelation, though, for Geiger, "Revelation" had resolved itself into the fact of the peculiar Jewish *genius* for religion. God also manifests Himself in the spirit of the times; and that spirit was discerned as a rather rationalistic one by Abraham Geiger.

Geiger's views were proclaimed in sermons and in many scholarly volumes and pamphlets. He also edited theological periodicals and two editions of the Jewish prayerbook, reformed in accordance with his views. Geiger's prayerbook became a model which was emulated by many of the other reformed liturgies in Germany and abroad. Yet Geiger always saw himself and his task within the totality of Judaism. He wanted to reform Judaism from inside, and not as the leader of a schismatic group. That desire made Geiger far more conservative in actual practice than one would have expected him to be on the basis of his published theories alone. It also made him turn down the suggestion that he minister only to the reform-minded segment of the Breslau Jewish community. He insisted on being known as a rabbi of the total Jewish community. Similarly, it made him refuse to accept the position offered him by the radical Berlin Reform Congregation.

Samuel Holdheim (1806–60) accepted that Berlin position. Beginning his career as a strictly traditionalist rabbi, he was ultimately to jettison even those conservative restraints by which Geiger was still guided. At the rabbinical conferences, and as rabbi of Schwerin, Holdheim had already shown himself a champion of radical Reform. The Berlin Reform Congregation, founded on a radical basis, afforded him the opportunity of putting his reforming zeal into practice. Here, sabbath services gave way to Sunday worship, Hebrew was almost totally eliminated, and many other far-reaching reforms were instituted. Though Holdheim held many beliefs in common with Geiger, he did not share Geiger's view that change must be gradual and organic. Holdheim distinguished between the religious laws of the Bible and its "political" laws, that is, the whole system of agricultural, cultic and ceremonial laws which were meant to be obeyed in the theocratic state envisaged by the Bible. Though both sets of laws were God-given, only the purely "religious" ones had eternal validity. The others were time-bound, connected with the superseded national period of Jewish life. When God let Temple and State be destroyed, He clearly indicated that, by His will, the national and theocratic phase of Israel's existence was to be terminated. Holdheim was highly critical of rabbinic Judaism because it endeavoured to maintain the fiction that the old theocratic constitution was still in force. The distinction made by Holdheim between the "religious" and the "political" elements of the Bible may be seen in his attitude towards the traditional Jewish sabbath. To observe one day in seven as a day of rest, that, according to Holdheim, is a "religious" law and eternal. To make that day Saturday rather than any other day of the week, that was purely "political", that is, part of the exigencies of the ancient Israelite State. Since the "political" aspect, however, has no further validity, the German Jew must live by the political provisions of his modern state; and those include Sunday as the weekly day of rest! Altogether, the rabbis must be deprived of any of the juridical functions which they had still retained. They are to be spiritual leaders, not judges. Even those aspects of the old ceremonial law which could not properly be classified as "political" were attacked by Holdheim. Ceremonies speak the language of symbol; but modern man has a different mentality and no longer understands that ancient symbolical language. Moreover, many of the ritual provisions had the function of keeping the Jew apart from the Gentile. This was indeed justified in the period of Israel's infancy, when God had to wean the Jews from pagan influences. But our monotheistic neighbours are not pagans. The Talmud itself contemplates the abolition of the ceremonial law in the messianic age; and Holdheim felt sure that, with the emancipation of the Jews, the messianic fulfilment of history was at hand. The need of the hour, therefore, was for more contact with others, and not for ritual separation.

Holdheim, through his writings, and through his active participation in the rabbinical conferences, succeeded in making his position one to be reckoned with. His was the extreme "left wing" of German Reform Judaism. But, in practice, his style of Reform remained confined, within Germany, to his own Berlin Reform Congregation. His views were elicited by a short-lived radical Reform congregation in Budapest. However, it was in America, as we shall have occasion to see, a land without an entrenched traditional pattern, that Holdheim's views and ideas found more pronounced echoes.

Zacharias Frankel (1801–75), Chief Rabbi of Dresden and, later, first director of the newly established Jewish Theological Seminary in Breslau, was traditional in religious observance, but had also aroused the ire of some traditionalists through his historical approach to the sources of rabbinic Judaism. Mention has already been made of the fact that he attended the Frankfurt Rabbinical Conference of 1845, and that he had left that Conference in protest against the vote which determined that there was no "objective necessity" for Hebrew in the synagogue service. Frankel, of course, knew that, according to the Talmud itself, prayer can be offered in the language understood by the worshipper. What annoyed Frankel was the mere fact that a body of rabbis should formulate a question of that kind. Judaism, according to Frankel, was indeed constantly involved in the process of change. But traditions which have lost their meaning die of their own accord. It should be the function of the rabbis, not to abolish things, but to preserve traditions as long as possible. The people as a whole, through their observance and their non-observance, decided what parts of the tradition are dead and what parts alive. Frankel, who had made important contributions to the *Wissenschaft des Judentums*, and who felt that any reforms in Jewish life must be in accord with the results of that *Wissenschaft*, was far from being opposed to free scientific inquiry. But he disliked the *tendenz* of the work of men like Geiger and Holdheim. In contrast to their "critical-historical" approach, Frankel championed the "positive-historical" view. This amounted to an intermediate position between unchanged traditionalism on the one hand, and Geiger's brand of Reform on the other. That position became known as Conservative Judaism, and was very influential among German Jews—even as, in a somewhat modified form, it was later to become very significant in American Judaism.

Geiger, Holdheim and Frankel, in spite of their different views and emphases, were all at one in their recognition of the changed circumstances of Jewish life, and of the need of some kind of reform in order to adapt Judaism to those changed circumstances. They also believed in the value of the *Wissenschaft des Judentums*. All three had their followers among those educated, middle class and upper middle class, urban Jews who, by training and social position, shared their recognition of the changed situation of Jewish life, and their desire to make Judaism viable for nineteenth-century German Jews. They had little effect, however, upon the growing number of the "indifferent", that is, those educated Jews who were nominal Jews only, and who, without necessarily denying their Jewish origin, had little interest either in synagogal reforms or in theological speculation. Nor did they wield any influence upon the rural Jews, mainly of southern Germany, who continued to be averse to any change whatsoever. Not that such Jews necessarily had a well-defined theological position, or that they, to any extent, engaged in polemics and apologetics. The traditional belief that God was the author of the entirety of codified Jewish law served as a sufficient rationale. Moreover, the—mainly Roman Catholic—environment did not present the kind of challenge which would make them give up the implicit philosophy of "what was good enough for my father is good enough for me".

However, the coming of emancipation, with the wider economic opportunities it offered the Jews in the larger cities, brought about an influx of rural Jews into the urban communities, and the consequent confrontation with the intellectual world of the nineteenth century. Within that framework, traditionalism was in need of a philosophy which could compete both with the lure of the non-Jewish environment, and with the moderate or radical Reform approaches to Judaism. The man who supplied that need was Samson Raphael Hirsch (1808–88).

Combining the traditional rabbinical training with a modern university education, Hirsch had been rabbi in Oldenburg, Emden, Nikolsburg, and Frankfurt on Main. Proclaiming the motto of *torah 'im derekh ereṣ* (which literally means, "The Combination of Torah with a Worldly Occupation"), in the sense of "strict adherence to traditional Jewish law combined with full participation in western culture", Hirsch welcomed the benefits of emancipation. *Vis-à-vis* the Reformers, however, he denied that a full participation in modern life necessitated any changes in traditional Jewish law. That law, in all of its component parts, was divine and, therefore, as unchangeable as nature itself. The canons of literary and historical criticism, as utilized by the *Wissenschaft des Judentums*, simply do not apply to the study of the literary sources of Revelation. The sole purpose of studying those sources was to discover their inherent meaning and purpose. Greatly influenced by contemporary German Romanticism, Hirsch proceeded to give a symbolical interpretation to all provisions of Jewish law. Hirsch's interpretations were based on the belief that Hebrew was the original language of mankind, and on a kind of philology which was unacceptable to any but his own devoted followers. For his part, Hirsch rejected the rationalistic approach of which, in the Middle Ages, Maimonides had been the outstanding representative.

According to the scheme mapped out by Hirsch, mankind as a whole was to be educated, on the basis of their own experiences, to a recognition of God and a love for the fellow-man. This educational process was to be guaranteed by introducing into the world a single people, Israel, which, in its life and destiny, represented the Only God as the sole ground of being, and the fulfilment of His will as the sole purpose of life. In order to fashion this "Chosen People", it was necessary that, for a time, it occupy its own soil. But the possession of the Jewish State was not the aim of the Torah; merely a means of obeying it. Indeed, obedience to the Torah was the pre-condition of Israel's possession of the Promised Land. When Israel failed to live up to its responsibilities, it lost its State. Yet the special position of Israel within the divine economy is indicated not least by the fact that Israel's survival through the millennia was quite independent of the possession of a national state. At that point, Hirsch was in virtual agreement with his Reform opponents: Israel is not a nation, but a union of the faithful, a religious community. Unlike the Reformers, however, Hirsch believed that, at the time of the messianic fulfilment (but only then!), Israel would again assume national status. Meanwhile, it was the function of Israel to work for the advancement of all mankind—one of the aspects of that work being the faithful adherence to all the testimonies, statutes and commandments of the divine Revelation.

Hirsch expressed all of this in a poetic German style which he employed in the pulpit and in his voluminous writings. He favoured such aesthetic reforms of the Jewish divine service as could be accomplished without infringing the most minute rubric of the traditional code. In practice, he demonstrated that the traditional synagogue service (with choir, but without organ accompaniment; with German sermon, but without liturgical abbreviations) need not offend the aesthetic susceptibilities of the cultured German Jew. He also established elementary and high schools where equal stress was laid on secular and religious studies.

While it is true that in some of the congregations he served, Hirsch himself, on account of the minor aesthetic reforms he had advocated, was suspected of being a "reformer", it was he who succeeded in making traditional Judaism respectable within the world of nineteenth-century German Jewry. Hirsch supplied the rationale for what came to be known as Orthodoxy. Hirsch himself disliked that term, and preferred the phrase, "Torah-true", instead. But since the adjective, "orthodox", was also applied (wrongly, for "ortho*prax*" would have been more correct) to those traditionalists who rejected Hirsch's positive stance on western culture, Hirsch's brand of Judaism also became known as "Neo-Orthodoxy".

Many observant German Jews who considered Frankel's "positive-historical" approach too radical found in the system of Hirsch a religious view which answered their spiritual needs. But not all observant Jews who were in sympathy with Hirsch's general theological position were able to follow their master along the road of congregational politics. For Hirsch did not strive to get a hearing for himself within the Jewish community structure, but outside of it. One of the reasons why Hirsch disliked the adjective, "orthodox", was the implication that Orthodoxy was one form of Judaism, and that there were others. For Hirsch, however, there was only one legitimate form of Judaism—his own. As far as he was concerned, Reform and Conservatism were not Jewish. Yet German law, at that time, made it mandatory for all Jews to belong to their local Jewish community. Only those who were willing to declare their resignation from Judaism were permitted to leave the local Jewish community.

We have already touched upon this subject in connexion with the Reform rabbis who were compelled to win adherents to their cause within the existing community structures, a state of affairs which necessitated many compromise solutions. The latter, in the larger cities, might take the form of having one and the same community maintain a synagogue with the unchanged traditional ritual, and one with the reformed ritual, and to employ rabbis of different schools of thought. In the smaller communities, where only one synagogue was available, the character of that synagogue would be determined by the majority of its members, with various concessions being made to the minority. Just as the Reformers of Hamburg and Berlin, while remaining members of their local Jewish communities, had established separate Reform houses of worship, so a number of Orthodox groups, without ceasing to be members of the local Jewish communities, had set up separate synagogues for the purpose of conducting strictly traditionalist services.

Hirsch was not satisfied with that arrangement. It irked him that such Orthodox Jews, by means of communal taxation, were involved in supporting many local Jewish communities—some of them with a Reform majority—which, by Hirsch's standards, were no longer Jewish. He therefore agitated for a change in the German law, so that observant Orthodox Jews might leave their local Jewish communities without, at the same time, having to declare their resignation from Judaism. Through the good offices of the parliamentary deputy Lasker, Hirsch succeeded in having that change in the law approved, in 1876. Several Orthodox groups followed the example of Hirsch's own Frankfurt congregation in availing themselves of that new law. In this way, the adherents of "Neo-Orthodoxy" constituted a "Separatist Orthodoxy". In a number of cities, those Separatist congregations established their own institutions (hospitals, schools, cemeteries, etc.) to parallel those of the original Jewish community. Yet the number of Separatist congregations remained relatively small. The majority of German Orthodox Jews, though approving of Hirsch's interpretation of Judaism, preferred to work for the cause of Orthodox Judaism within the existing Jewish Community—particularly since their religious needs were being met even in communities which were led by the sympathizers of Reform. Hirsch's call for Separatism, presented as an absolute religious demand, was to lead to an internal struggle within the ranks of German Orthodoxy itself.

By the time the nineteenth century came to an end, the fiery debates which had marked the beginning of that century had died down. Congregations taking their spiritual direction from Holdheim and from Hirsch stood at the respective extremes of the religious spectrum. The religious views of Geiger were more prevalent, though they often were combined with a conservatism in practice more directly related to the position championed by Frankel. This refers to the synagogal cult. In their personal observances, in matters like the donning of phylacteries and the keeping of the dietary laws, most German Jews were far more lax. Intermarriage, too, was on the increase; and the "indifferent", who were to have been won over by the Reform endeavours of the early part of the century, continued to be indifferent. Many Jews, without denying their origin, continued to be uninterested in liturgical questions, or even in the findings of the *Wissenschaft des Judentums*.

On the other hand, without raising questions of synagogal reforms, and, therefore, on a non-party basis, attempts were repeatedly made to restate the "essence of Judaism" in terms both borrowed from and acceptable to the current philosophical universe of discourse. Particularly the philosophy of Kant, either in its original formulation, or in the Neo-Kantian version propounded by Hermann Cohen (1842–1918), was utilized in this connexion. A rare and largely ignored voice was that of Salomon Ludwig Steinheim (1789–1866), who polemicized against the contemporary attempts to identify the contents of Religion and Philosophy. For him, the very "shibboleth" of the truth of

Revelation was that it does *not* coincide with man's normal rational awareness. Steinheim, however, was anything but an observant Orthodox Jew, so that even the Orthodox circles, by temperament most disposed towards such a view, remained oblivious of it. (It was left to twentieth-century religious Existentialism to rediscover Steinheim.)

German Jews of all shades of belief and practice co-operated in the maintenance of communal philanthropic and welfare institutions, and even in the sphere of religious education there was a great deal of co-operation. After all, German Jews were proud to be both German and Jewish. In the face of rising anti-Semitism, from the last quarter of the nineteenth century on, they never missed an opportunity to reaffirm their German patriotism. The Jews, admittedly, may not be a Teutonic tribe, but they were descendants of a noble Jewish tribe which, alongside the Teutons, went into the making of the German nation. Not all German Jews were members of the "Central Association of German Citizens of the Jewish Persuasion" (founded in 1893), but those who were represented a true cross-section of the total Jewish population—irrespective of religious orientation.

That Judaism was a religious denomination and not a matter of nationality, on this all sections of German Jewry agreed, Orthodox and Reformer alike. Moses Hess (1812–75), who had come to a position of Jewish nationalism via his espousal of socialism, found no followers among German Jews in his day. The Jewish press of Germany reacted negatively towards his *Rome and Jerusalem* (1862). Theodor Herzl (1860–1904) encountered the opposition of the German rabbinate, both Orthodox and Reform, when he planned to hold the first Zionist Congress in Munich.

Here and there, however, after the turn of the century, individual German Jews were won over to the cause of Zionism. The factors responsible for that were various. There was, to begin with, a gradual influx into Germany of Jewish immigrants from eastern Europe; and, as we shall have occasion to see, eastern Europe was the native soil of any number of Jewish nationalist theories. More important, perhaps, was the fact that even in the west, and in spite of emancipation, anti-Semitism showed no signs of subsiding. Theodor Herzl, the founder of political Zionism in its world-wide organized form, was himself a western and assimilated Jew who, at the time of writing *The Jewish State* (1896), had as yet been unaware of the existence of Jewish nationalist theories in eastern Europe. Herzl, assigned by the Vienna *Neue Freie Presse* to cover the Dreyfus trial in Paris (1894), was led to Zionism by the shocked realization that anti-Semitism was possible even in France, the birthplace of Jewish emancipation.

Herzl, basically accepting some of the presuppositions of anti-Semitism, argued that the Jews were "a people, one people". As such, they were a foreign body among their "host peoples", inciting animosity through economic competition. There was no other solution to the problem of anti-Semitism than the total removal of the Jews from the lands of the non-Jews to a country of their own. For, wherever else Jews settle in appreciable numbers, they bring the seeds of anti-Semitism with them. Since anti-Semitism is an unsettling political disturbance, it would be in the interest of the non-Jewish nations themselves to help the Jews establish their own state. Palestine figured in the search for a suitable territory, but not exclusively. For a time, Herzl was willing to entertain the idea of a Jewish settlement in Uganda; but he was outvoted by the majority of the world's Zionists.

Other German Jews welcomed Zionism as a substitute for the Jewish religion. No longer believing in the doctrines of Judaism, or observing its traditional rites, they nevertheless still felt themselves to be Jewish. By a process of reasoning quite similar to that followed by the East European Jewish nationalists, they arrived at a secularist rationale for Jewish existence and became devotees of Zionism—particularly in its cultural aspects.

All told, however, Zionism or Jewish nationalism remained a minority movement among German Jews. It was not until the thirties of the twentieth century, under the impact of the Nazi persecution, that larger sections of German Jewry began to see in Palestine the solution of "the Jewish Problem".

On the other hand, already before the catastrophic end of German Judaism was in sight, a revived interest in Judaism had become noticeable among German Jews, and a veering away from the nineteenth-century positions had taken place. Some German Jewish soldiers, encountering the East European Jew for the first time during their war service in Poland, were impressed by the unapologetic and "natural" manner in which the eastern Jew carried his Judaism. They contrasted this with what they now thought to be the somewhat artificial constructions of Judaism as a "religious denomination" which they had inherited from the nineteenth century. One of those

German Jewish soldiers was Franz Rosenzweig (1886–1929). He had, however, already prior to this encounter, broken with German idealist philosophy (which was still the matrix in which modern Judaism was presented), and with the "polite" form of Judaism he had known in his home background—a *noblesse oblige* avoidance of baptism, without strong religious commitments.

In his major work, *The Star of Redemption* (1921), Rosenzweig introduced the approach of religious Existentialism into the world of modern Judaism. Considering God, world and man to be separate and distinct entities, he found them to be related through Creation, Revelation and Redemption. He was equally opposed to Reform Judaism's attempt to reduce Judaism to a number of abstract principles and to the Neo-Orthodoxy of Samson Raphael Hirsch, in which he saw an imposing but ugly (because artificial) edifice. Nor did he approve of Zionism, since, for him, the Jewish people stood above history, awaiting, without getting involved in the historical process, the messianic fulfilment. Above all, he rejected the alternative of "all or nothing" in the realm of Jewish observance. The modern Jew must make the Jewish heritage his own—gradually and at his own pace.

Translating the Hebrew Bible into German, Rosenzweig collaborated with Martin Buber (1878–1965). Buber, a native of Vienna who had spent his childhood in Galicia, lived in Germany where he achieved fame as the philosopher of "dialogic thinking" (*Ich und Du*, 1923; and numerous other writings). Buber, a "cultural Zionist" and a religious but ritually non-observant Jew, opened up the world of Ḥasidism (i.e. the East European mystical Jewish movement which originated in the eighteenth century) to the western Jew. Like all mystical movements, Ḥasidism had been largely ignored, if not misrepresented, by the *Wissenschaft des Judentums*; and German Jews had been aware only of its apparent obscurantism and its failure to live up to western standards of decorum. Buber did not undertake to fill in that lacuna of the *Wissenschaft des Judentums*. That task was left to Gerhard G. Scholem (b. 1896) who laid the foundations of the scientific and unprejudiced study of the various mystical movements in Judaism. But Buber presented Ḥasidism as an exemplification of the "life of dialogue", of religious inwardness and of the social dimensions of the religious commitment. He did so by retelling, in his own literary German, the tales of the Ḥasidic masters.

Both Buber and Rosenzweig exerted a great influence upon German

Jewry in the period before its final destruction. Both of them were deeply rooted in German culture and spoke the language of the German Jewish intelligentsia. They shared a common universe of discourse with many religiously alienated German Jews who were seeking ways in which to return to the sources of their Jewishness. No less influential in his own way was the last great representative of the German–Jewish synthesis, Leo Baeck (1873–1956). Himself a significant contributor to the *Wissenschaft des Judentums*, Baeck, though sympathetic to traditional practice, stressed the changing and developing character of Judaism, seeing in ethics its permanent element. But, unlike the great theoreticians of the nineteenth century, Baeck was able to appreciate the religious paradox in Judaism, as between universalism and particularism, mystery and commandment, etc. Though never a Zionist, he refused to join his fellow rabbis in protesting against Herzl's plans to hold the Zionist Congress in Munich. The leading thinker of German Liberal Judaism, he was personally observant. His broad perspective and wide sympathies gained him the confidence of all sections of German Jewry. In the hour of its greatest crisis, Baeck was entrusted with the organizational leadership of the totality of German Judaism. He kept that trust—even to the extent of refusing to emigrate as long as any Jews would remain in Germany. Miraculously he survived the Theresienstadt concentration camp; and, after liberation, he resumed his teaching activities both in England and in the United States, transmitting the heritage of the German–Jewish synthesis. The modern period in German Judaism thus began with Moses Mendelssohn and ended with Leo Baeck.

It was Baeck who summed up the various endeavours leading to the emergence of the modern forms of Judaism as attempts to create the "piety of the individual". The Jew who had stepped out of the ghetto, who could no longer take the Jewish environment for granted, was in need of a form of Judaism which would enable him to lead a life of Jewish piety within a non-Jewish setting. Baeck contrasted that particular need with the "piety of the environment", a piety which, while making maximum demands in matters of religious observance, involves the individual far less in terms of personal conviction and individual choice. When the "piety of the individual" became a necessity for the Jew of the west, the Jew of the east still retained the "piety of the environment".

A few figures will help us to visualize the density of the Jewish populations which were involved both east and west. At the turn of the century, there were 586,948 Jews in Germany; 235,000 in England; 103,988 in Holland; and 86,885 in France. As against this, there were 3,872,625 Jews in Russia; and 1,316,776 in Poland. Moreover, those figures were established after the mass Jewish emigration from eastern Europe to the United States had already been in full progress for a number of years, so that many of the 1,500,000 Jews described as then living in the United States had really been part of East European Jewry somewhat earlier in the nineteenth century.[1]

In view of the numbers involved, and in view of the fact that the Jewish masses of eastern Europe lived without benefit of emancipation, it is easy to see that the questions facing the German Jew and many of the answers he proposed, were of a kind to which the Jews living in eastern Europe often remained deaf. And here, of course, we are speaking of the majority of East European Jews in the nineteenth and early twentieth century. There was indeed a small minority of Russian Jews who were striving for "Russification". But the vast majority was neither predisposed by temperament and culture nor fitted by social and economic standing to think in terms of assimilation, or to regard themselves as "Russians of the Jewish faith".

Traditional Judaism, in its strict rabbinic formulation, continued to function for most Russian Jews in the nineteenth century, even as it had done in earlier centuries, as the criterion of Jewish self-identification. No secular categories were invoked to account for Jewish existence. Such divisions as there were, such as between mystics and rationalists, were divisions within the framework of rabbinic Judaism. Both sides acknowledged the authority of the same classical religious texts; and both sides lived within a community structure where the authority of the rabbinate was unquestioned. By and large, modern knowledge was frowned upon; and even the very clothing worn by Russian Jews for a number of centuries was invested with religious significance.

All of which is not to say that the light kindled by Mendelssohn in Germany was altogether invisible to the Jews of Russia. Dedicated to the German language though the men of Mendelssohn's circle were, they saw in the revival of the classical Hebrew language a suitable medium through which modern culture and enlightenment could be

[1] Figures taken from *The Jewish Encyclopaedia*, vol. XI, pp. 531–2.

brought to the Jewish masses. Thus, between 1784 and 1811, Mendelssohn's disciples published the Hebrew periodical, *Ha-Me'asseph* (lit. "The Gatherer"), which first came out in Königsberg and later in Berlin, Breslau, Altona and Dessau. The society which sponsored the publication of *Ha-Me'asseph* called itself, "The Society of the Friends of the Hebrew Language". But when, in 1787, the society changed its name to "The Society of the Friends of Goodness and Virtue", the true aims and objectives became apparent. Moreover, after a while, there was no further need to propagate the ideals of enlightenment among German Jews in the Hebrew language. The spread of enlightenment ideals and of assimilationist and reformist tendencies had actually exceeded the rather modest aims of the *Ha-Me'asseph* contributors; and the periodical ceased publication.

However, being written in Hebrew, and published in Königsberg, close to the Russian border, *Ha-Me'asseph* had found both readers and contributors among Russian Jews and had given rise, among Russian and Galician Jewry, to a movement known as *Haskalah* (i.e. "Enlightenment"). Long after Hebrew had ceased to be a medium of communication among enlightened German Jews, the *Haskalah* writers of eastern Europe were engaged in the task of creating a modern Hebrew literature. That literature included poetry, drama and the novel. All of them, together with the modern Hebrew essay, sounded the call of rebellion against the unnatural kind of Jewish existence (cultural, economic, religious and vocational) which was lived by the East European Jews. It challenged the stringencies of rabbinic law—without, however, advocating all the liturgical reforms which were then being fought for in Germany, and without attempting, as the German Reformers did, to rid Judaism of its "particularism". It opposed the domination of the rabbis and particularly the Ḥasidic suppression of secular learning. Drawing upon itself the ire of the rabbinate, *Haskalah* literature was, on occasion, led to adopt an anti-religious stance, though the literature as a whole cannot be said to have been anti-religious. It did, however, evidence some strong secularist tendencies. There was also the hope, both explicit and implicit, that a Russian Jewry become adept in modern culture and Enlightenment would make a more favourable impression upon the Russian government, and thus "merit" emancipation.

There were indeed vacillations in the attitudes which the Russian government took towards the improvement of the position of the

Jewish population. More liberal approaches alternated with more reactionary repressions. But full emancipation was never granted; and actual physical persecutions, pogroms, were on the increase towards the end of the nineteenth century. To the extent to which the Russian Jews did not suffer this fate docilely—and many of the pious did indeed regard the new persecution merely as a further instalment of "exile" history—there were two major forms which were adopted to deal with the problem. One was emigration. Despairing of any improvement in the situation, thousands—ultimately, millions—sought their fortunes across the seas. The greatest number went to America. A few went to Palestine as colonists. The other form of Jewish reaction to the worsening of the Russian Jewish position was the socialist movement. The "Jewish Problem" was seen as but one aspect of the present corrupt social system. It would be solved once the government was in the hands of the proletariat.

A number of Russian Jews joined the Russian socialist movements. Others, however, were too deeply rooted in their own language, Yiddish, and in their own Yiddish culture to forego their own cultural heritage in striving for the socialist solution. Jewish socialist movements, therefore, came into existence—movements, that is to say, which envisaged a socialist solution of the political problem, while envisaging the continuation of a distinctive Jewish group. Since, however, socialism in general was decidedly anti-religious, the Jewish socialists saw the constitutive elements of Jewish life in terms of culture and language, rather than in religion.

Both in connexion with Jewish socialism and independently of it various theories of Jewish nationalism were being propounded, accepting the secular basis of Jewish existence for which the groundwork had already been laid by the *Haskalah*. However, Jewish nationalism did not necessarily imply emigration to Palestine or other countries. Thus, Simon Dubnow (1860–1941), who saw Jewish history as a succession of autonomous centres of Jewish national creation, advocated a "Diaspora nationalism" in terms of cultural autonomy and "minority rights" to be granted to Jews wherever they may be living. In fact, for Dubnow, the Jews constituted one of the peoples of Europe! Leon Pinsker (1821–91), on the other hand, insisted upon a "territorial solution" of the "Jewish Problem". The Jews would have to leave Russia! But Pinsker left it an open question, whether the Jewish territory was to be established in Palestine or in the Argentine. Once

Theodore Herzl's Zionism got to be known in eastern Europe and Russian Jews began to take an active part in the world Zionist movement, the establishment of a "Jewish national home in Palestine" gradually replaced the aims of other territorial solutions. Nevertheless, as we have already noted in a different context, Herzl himself had not originally been convinced that Palestine was the only possible solution. When the British government, in 1903, offered Herzl the territory of Uganda for Jewish settlement, he was prepared to accept it. But Herzl was outvoted at the Zionist Congress—particularly by the Russian Zionists. Though, at that time of increased pogroms, they were most in need of a place of refuge, they were too deeply rooted in Jewish tradition to consider any place but Palestine as the locale of a future Jewish State.

Different theories of Jewish nationalism were competing for the allegiance of the Russian Jew. Pinsker, a physician, had spoken in terms of the psychopathology of anti-Semitism. Nations, he wrote, respect one another only so long as they can anticipate reciprocity in the extending of hospitality, that is, as long as they all have a Homeland of their own. The anomaly of the Jews consists in their lack of a Homeland. As a nation without a Homeland, they create a ghost-like impression among their host-peoples. By not having a country of their own they are completely unlike the other nations. And there is a general fear of ghosts, a universal dislike of the unlike—which, *vis-à-vis* the Jews, manifests itself in the phenomenon of anti-Semitism. Let the Jews, therefore, acquire a Homeland of their own and thereby become like all the other nations; and anti-Semitism will be deprived of its cause.

Quite other was the approach of Asher Ginsberg (1856–1927), who is known by his pen-name, Ahad Ha-am (*aḥad ha-'am*, "one of the people"). Ahad Ha-am saw the dissolution of traditional religious ties—he himself was an agnostic—and he despaired of the possibility of creating a secularized Jewish culture either in eastern Europe (where the Jews were too poor, too persecuted, and too demoralized), or in the west (where the Jews were already far too assimilated to non-Jewish culture). There remained only one hope: to establish a spiritual, or cultural, centre for world Jewry on Palestinian soil, where the Hebrew language could be revived and where a Hebrew culture could come into being. This aspiration did not necessarily envisage any large-scale immigration of Jews into Palestine, or the dissolution of the Jewish communities in the Diaspora. In fact, Ahad Ha-am was highly critical of Herzl's political Zionism, even as he was one of the very few Zionists in those days to draw attention to the fact that Palestine already had an Arab population. It was rather to be the function of the Palestinian Spiritual Centre to help in the revival of Jewish culture elsewhere. The imagery employed was that of a circle, with its centre and its periphery. It was Ahad Ha-am who voiced the opinion that one Palestinian centre of higher Jewish learning was of greater importance than a hundred agricultural settlements there.

Ahad Ha-am, who had given up the religious basis of Jewish life, found his Jewish nationalism grounded in the quasi-biological "will to survive" of the Jewish people. He also found the Jewish national genius expressed in a particular approach to ethics. Jacob Klatzkin (1882–1948), on the other hand, denied the dependence of Jewish nationalism on any particular spiritual values, of either the religious or the ethical kind. What makes a nation is land and language. The Jews must therefore return to Palestine, argued Klatzkin, and learn to speak Hebrew again. Neither Ahad Ha-am nor Klatzkin coupled their ideal of the national restoration with any specific social system which is to be introduced in Palestine. Yet several other Zionist theoreticians did. Among them was Ber Borochov (1881–1917), one of the founders of Labour Zionism. Borochov felt that the Jewish worker was unable to participate fully in the class struggle as long as he does not live in a Jewish country. What was needed, therefore, was for the Jews to have a country of their own, in which the Jewish working class can establish the socialist society.

It was, then, for a variety of reasons that Jews left Russia for Palestine. Some, having despaired of any improvement in the political situation of the Jews in Russia, looked for the solution of the "Jewish Problem" in the creation of a Jewish State on the ancestral soil. Then there was the striving for a "return to the soil" as such, for greater contact with Nature—of a kind made impossible by the restrictive Russian legislation governing Jewish settlement. Life in agriculture promised a "normalization" of the economic and professional structure of Jewish society. One of the chief apostles of this doctrine of the "return to the soil" and of the "religion of labour" was Aaron David Gordon (1856–1922) who became associated with the first Palestinian *kibbutz*. Still others saw in the return to Palestine an opportunity of putting into practice their Marxist ideology.

Yet, when all was said and done, most of the Jews who emigrated from Russia did not go to Palestine at all, but to the United States of America. Bringing with them their own East European Jewish culture and their various religious and non-religious ideologies, they were to change profoundly the whole character of American Judaism and of the American Jewish community which, in the twentieth century, was destined to become the largest Jewish community in the world.

German Judaism provided the ideologies and the religious reforms which enabled the western Jew, *qua* Jew, to enter the world of modernity. Russian Judaism maintained the reservoir of traditional Jewish learning and practice, and evolved theories of nationalism, which ensured the survival of the corporate form of Jewish existence. But it was in America that the Judaisms of West and East were given an unhindered opportunity to test their mettle and their ability to adapt themselves to unprecedented circumstances. For, from the perspective of the millennial history of the Jew, the circumstances of Jewish life in America were quite unprecedented. "Congress shall make no law establishing an official church or prohibiting free exercise of any religion." Thus begins the First Amendment to the Constitution of the United States. In Russia, the Jew had been exposed to government-sponsored discrimination. In Germany, even after the emancipation, the government continued to be involved in the Jewish community structure and supervised the communal taxation. In the United States of America, however, religious affiliation was a purely voluntary matter in which the government took no interest. Jews desiring to establish Jewish congregations were free to do so. Jews who wanted to sever their ties were likewise not prevented by the government from carrying out their designs. Nor would the government be in any way responsible for the maintenance of Jewish communal institutions. In other words, the Jew who wanted to be a Jew was left entirely to his own devices, and there was no legal backing of the rabbinate, as, in many instances, there had been throughout the European phase of Jewish history.

So much for the external aspect of the situation. The internal Jewish situation was quite different, too. The Jewish communities of Europe were old-established communities, some of them looking back upon a history of many centuries. We have noted, in describing the Reform attempts in Germany, that the Reformers had to work within the existing structure—a state of affairs which of necessity slowed down too great a radicalism, and ultimately caused Reform to flow in more conservative channels. No such considerations applied to the development of Judaism in America. Here, congregations were started *de novo*, and no attention had to be paid to old-established local traditions. One of the characteristic American contributions to Jewish life, therefore, is the creation of an organizational structure which guaranteed the maintenance of Jewish life within that atmosphere of freedom.

The other contribution, likewise characteristic of the American setting, is the mentality of "peaceful co-existence" and even of co-operation between various Jewish groups differing widely in ideology and religious orientation. Not only did the state exclude the possibility of an "established church", Jewish life in America, too, did not allow the development of a rigid ecclesiastical structure or of institutions like a chief rabbinate. All of which is not meant to imply that, from time to time, there have not been bitter religious struggles in the evolution of American Judaism. But only that, in the long run, it was always the typical American pragmatic approach which won out.

Under the circumstances, the history of American Judaism is mainly one of the organizations created to maintain Jewish life in America, and of the men who called those organizations into being. In turn, both men and organizations were the joint products of the American environment on the one hand, and of the various European "waves of immigration" with their own particular traditions on the other. A few figures will be needed to clarify the demographic aspect of this situation.

Twenty-three Jews settled in New Amsterdam, in 1654; and their arrival marks the beginning of North American Jewish history. They were Sephardi (i.e. Spanish and Portuguese) Jews who had come from South America after the Portuguese had won a victory over the Dutch in that part of the world, and the Inquisition was going to catch up with the Jews in the New World. Those twenty-three were followed, in the course of time, by other Sephardi Jews and, here and there, by a sprinkling of Ashkenazi Jews, that is, Jews from Germany, Poland, and other European countries. After the American Revolution, in 1776, the Jewish population was estimated at about 3,000. The figure given for 1840 is 15,000.[1] The dominant influence on that "wave of immigration" was exerted by the Sephardi Jews.

[1] See Lee J. Levinger, *A History of the Jews in the United States* (Cincinnati, 1932), p. 142.

By 1858, however, the estimated number of Jews in the United States had reached the 200,000 mark.[1] The "wave of immigration" responsible for that increase was mainly one of German Jews. They had come in large numbers during the forties of the nineteenth century —partly to escape the restrictive measures which were still imposed by the government particularly on the Jews of southern Germany, partly to seek more promising economic opportunities and partly out of despair over the failure of the Liberal revolutions in Europe.

The third "wave of immigration", set in motion by the Russian pogroms of 1881 and the restrictive Russian legislation of 1882, brought some 2,000,000 East European Jews to the United States, between 1881 and 1920.[2] And by 1928, there were some 4,200,000 Jews in the United States, of whom 3,500,000 were of East European birth or descent.[3] In 1964, the Jewish population of the United States was estimated at 5,500,000, or about 3 per cent of the total American population.[4]

The pattern of Judaism established by the first "wave of immigration" was that of the Sephardi kind. It was strictly traditional, but also decorous. Sephardi congregations in Europe exercised considerable control and discipline over their members, imposing fines for the infraction of rules. Attempts were made to establish that discipline in America as well, to outlaw the breaking of the dietary laws, for example, or intermarriage. But the American climate was against such authoritarian measures and the attempts to impose them were ultimately given up. Intermarriage did deplete the numbers as far as the families of the original settlers were concerned. Religious instruction was of a rudimentary character; and, until the forties of the nineteenth century, American Jewry did without the leadership of a properly ordained rabbi. However, the lay prayer-leaders of the Sephardi congregations gradually developed into "ministers" of the Protestant prototype. The early Sephardi settlers were mainly merchants, many of them attaining positions of wealth and leadership. Though a certain laxity in ritual observance came about in the course of time, the Sephardi Jews felt sufficiently secure within the total American setting to obviate the necessity of a consciously undertaken "reform" of Judaism to meet the exigencies of the times.

[1] See Ismar Elbogen, *A Century of Jewish Life* (Philadelphia, 1946), p. 116.

[2] Levinger, *op. cit.* p. 265.

[3] *Ibid.*

[4] See Oscar I. Janowsky (ed.), *The American Jew—A Reappraisal* (Philadelphia, 1964), p. 29.

An exception was the case of "The Reformed Society of Israelites" which, in 1824, was organized by Sephardi Jews in Charleston, South Carolina. Under the influence both of the prevalent Deism and of the liturgical example set by the Hamburg Temple in 1819, those Jews demanded some minor liturgical reforms, the inclusion of English in the synagogue service, and a sermon in the vernacular. When these demands were refused, they organized their own services, and produced a manifesto in which they publicly declared their rejection of rabbinic Judaism. However, the Society disbanded again in 1833, the members rejoining the old congregation, which, at that time, was ready to introduce liturgical reforms and to install an organ. The Charleston attempt at reforming Judaism was to remain without imitators among American Sephardi congregations. But the procedure adopted of establishing a reformed manner of worship was, as we shall have occasion to see, repeated many a time in the creation of American Reform Judaism.

Ashkenazi Jews who, in increasing numbers, came to the United States even before the second "wave of immigration", adapted themselves to the prevailing Sephardi pattern of synagogal life. The Westphalian Isaac Leeser (1806–68) became minister of the important Sephardi Mikveh Israel Congregation of Philadelphia, in 1829. Yet in 1802 an Ashkenazi congregation had already been established in the same city—the first such congregation on American soil. A congregation of East European Jews was established in Buffalo, N.Y., in 1848; and the first such congregation in New York City was organized in 1852. On the whole, however, Ashkenazi Jews began to make up an increasing proportion of the membership of the Sephardi synagogues.

That situation was to change with the coming of the second "wave of immigration", which began in 1836 with a mass exodus of Jews from Bavaria. These Jews established their own congregations wherever they went and, as traders and pedlars (which most of them became), they were soon to be found in all parts of the expanding country. As we have already pointed out in a different context, the Jews of southern Germany were, for the most part, strict traditionalists and the Judaism they brought with them was of the traditionalist and largely unsophisticated kind. However, even more than in the case of the well-to-do Sephardi merchants, the strict demands of traditional Judaism often came into conflict with the life of the Ashkenazi Jewish peddlers and small business men. Sabbath and dietary observances were often compromised, even though the synagogue ritual remained untouched.

But, included in the second "wave of immigration" and following in its wake, there were several rabbis who had already taken an active part in the struggles which led to the creation of German Reform Judaism. Some of them, like David Einhorn (1809–79) and Kaufmann Kohler (1843–1926), had already shown themselves to be too radical to find and to hold rabbinical positions in Europe. Others were attracted by the unlimited opportunities which America seemed to offer for religious development. Still others combined a political with their religious liberalism, and left Europe for America in search of freedom.

Before long, the weakening of the hold of Jewish law on the German immigrants combined with the theoretical justifications for reform, preached by the immigrant Reform rabbis, to lead to the establishment of congregations with an avowed Reform programme. There were various ways in which a Reform congregation could come into existence and the ease with which it could happen points up most clearly the unique character of the American environment. A traditionalist congregation might of its own accord, slowly or rapidly, make innovations of a kind at variance with the traditional pattern; for example, abbreviated synagogue services, the installation of an organ, mixed seating for men and women, prayers in the "vernacular" (which for most German Jewish congregations in America at that time meant German), the removal of head coverings for men, etc. Many congregations which were founded by strict traditionalists developed in that direction.

In some of them, such innovations led to the secession of a traditionalist minority which, in due course, established its own traditionalist synagogue (in which as often as not the story of reform and traditionalist secession might repeat itself). In other instances it was the Reformers who seceded—sometimes, as in the Charleston prototype, to rejoin the older congregation once their Reform demands were being met, at other times to found their own permanent Reform synagogue. Still other congregations came into existence as Reform congregations from the very beginning—usually preceded by a society aiming at the creation of such a place of worship. Withal, the lines were not yet too clearly drawn. Men like Marcus Jastrow (1829–1903) and Benjamin Szold (1829–1902), who are now reckoned among the founders of what became Conservative Judaism in America, actually produced reformed liturgies which, in some respects, were more radical than the liturgical productions of some of their Reform contemporaries.

And, through the third quarter of the nineteenth century, there was still the constant hope that all American Jewish congregations would unite.

One of the major advocates of such unity was the minister of Philadelphia's Mikveh Israel Congregation, Isaac Leeser, whom we have encountered before. Leeser was a champion of traditional Judaism and a fierce opponent of Reform. Yet he was also the first Jewish minister in America who combined the office of precentor with regular sermons in English. As founder and editor of a newspaper, as Bible translator and as voluminous writer, he tried to establish American Judaism on a solid foundation and in accordance with the needs of the environment. And he sounded the call for a union of all congregations, for joint educational enterprises and for the establishment of an American seminary for the training of rabbis.

To achieve these objectives, he was even willing to make common cause with his counterpart in the Reform camp, Isaac Mayer Wise (1819–1900), who, for his part, was willing to make any number of concessions—even to the extent of recognizing the Talmud as the sole legitimate interpretation of the law of the Bible. (Throughout his life, even after departing from this concession, Wise was striving to "legitimize" Reform by showing its relatedness to the talmudic development of Judaism and by having it "authorized" by a body of rabbis or a synod. This, however, was not the path which American Reform Judaism was ultimately to take.)

The hope for union remained unrealized. But what Leeser and Wise were unable to achieve for the totality of American Jewry, Wise succeeded in creating for its Reform wing. Establishing the "Union of American Hebrew Congregations" in 1873, he founded the "Hebrew Union College" for the training of rabbis in 1875, and the "Central Conference of American Rabbis" in 1889. Wise had meant to have the whole of American Jewry served by those institutions. For reasons to which we shall return, this was not to be. But the pattern created by Wise was, in due course, adopted by the other wings of American Judaism. To correspond to the "Union of American Hebrew Congregations", the Orthodox founded the "Union of Orthodox Jewish Congregations" in 1898 and the Conservatives established the "United Synagogue of America" in 1913. To correspond to the "Hebrew Union College", the Conservatives established the "Jewish Theological Seminary of America" in 1887 and the Orthodox, in 1896, founded the "Rabbi Isaac Elchanan Theological Seminary", which has since developed into the "Yeshivah University". Finally, as a counterpart to the "Central Conference of American Rabbis", the Conservatives, in 1900, established the "Rabbinical Assembly of America" and the Orthodox, in 1935, founded the "Rabbinical Council of America". We shall come back to these various institutions within their proper historical setting. For our present purposes it suffices to note that the pattern established by Wise was so suited to the needs of the American scene that the other branches of American Judaism could not improve on it.

Wise himself was born in Bohemia and came to the United States in 1846. After serving as a rabbi in Albany, N.Y., he came to Cincinnati, Ohio, in 1854, making Cincinnati the headquarters of his manifold activities. In terms of the Reform endeavours on the European continent, Wise was a radical. He abolished the covering of the head, instituted mixed seating, introduced the organ and abbreviated the liturgy. But, in terms of what was taught and preached by other American Reformers at that time, Wise's position was distinctly conservative. Though he advocated doctrinal reform (he did not believe in the personal Messiah, in the return to Zion, in the restoration of the sacrificial service and in the physical resurrection of the dead), Wise championed even more the idea of a unified American Israel. Reform, he thought, would take care of itself once such a union was effected and would, by sheer force of numbers, represent the "orthodoxy" of American Judaism. Above all, Wise was concerned with adapting Judaism to the American environment and with the "Americanization" of the American Jew. In most of the German congregations in America German was the language of the sermons, of the vernacular prayers, of religious education, and of the periodical literature. Wise wanted to see English take the place of German. For that reason, too, he was so eager to have American rabbis trained in America, instead of importing them from Germany, as was then the custom. Yet the immediate influence of Wise was confined to the Jewry of the American Middle West.

In the east of the United States quite a different kind of Reform Judaism was being preached, particularly by David Einhorn. For Einhorn, Reform Judaism and German language and culture were inseparable. Besides, while Wise endeavoured to make Reform a mass movement, Einhorn and his followers were quite content to let

Reform Judaism remain the religion of an intellectual Jewish élite. They drew the full logical consequences from the Reform presuppositions first enunciated in Germany, and particularly from those associated with the name of Samuel Holdheim (see above, pp. 21–2). They felt completely unhindered in America by the limitations of environment and tradition which had been imposed upon the full unfolding of radical Reform Judaism in Germany.

In this connexion it should be noted that some of the problems which agitated the Reformers in America were problems of German provenance, rather than of American origin. There had never been any question about the American patriotism of the American Jew; and, until the arrival of the German rabbis, it had not occurred to anyone to make a public declaration to the effect that the Jews were a religious community, rather than a nation. In fact, America has always prided itself on being a "nation of immigrants", and foreign antecedents were not felt to be a hindrance to full participation in American political life. Yet the German Reformers imported their *problematik* to the United States and found it necessary, again and again, to stress the universalistic character of Judaism and the fact that the Jews were not a nation. At the same time, the Reformers firmly believed in the "Mission of Israel" (i.e. the task of the Jewish people to spread the knowledge of ethical monotheism among all mankind), and for that very reason David Einhorn was vociferously opposed to intermarriage. (Holdheim, in Germany, had solemnized such unions.) The Jewish people, God's "priest people", must be kept intact—for the purpose of fulfilling its universal mission. But only the pronounced "religious" elements of the Jewish past were to be retained. Whatever was associated with the ancient Hebrew commonwealth had outlived its usefulness.

In 1869, thirteen of the German Reform rabbis met in conference in Philadelphia. There they adopted seven principles which asserted: (i) that the messianic aim of Israel was not the restoration of the old Jewish State under a descendant of David, but "the union of all men as children of God in the confession of the unity of God"; (ii) that the destruction of the second Jewish commonwealth was not a punishment for the sinfulness of Israel, but the result of the divine purpose which consists in the dispersion of the Jews to all parts of the world, to lead the nations to the true knowledge and worship of God; (iii) that the Aaronic priesthood and the Mosaic sacrificial cult were preparatory steps for the real priesthood of the whole people, which began with the dispersion of the Jews; (iv) that every distinction between Aaronides and non-Aaronides, as far as religious rites and duties are concerned, is consequently inadmissible, both in the religious cult and in life; (v) that the selection of Israel as the people of religion shall only be mentioned with full emphasis laid upon the world-embracing mission of Israel and the love of God for all His children; (vi) that the belief in bodily resurrection has no religious foundation, and the doctrine of immortality refers "to the after-existence of the soul" only; (vii) that, important as the Hebrew language is, it has become unintelligible to the vast majority of our co-religionists and must therefore, under existing circumstances, make way for intelligible language in prayer "which, if not understood, is a soulless form".[1]

The above sentiments were reaffirmed when, in 1885, the Reform rabbis met again (this time there were nineteen of them) in Pittsburgh, Pennsylvania, and adopted the so-called "Pittsburgh Platform". Like its Philadelphia predecessor, the Pittsburgh gathering concentrated on spelling out its departures from the Judaism of tradition. It noted *inter alia* that "all such Mosaic and rabbinical laws as regulate diet, priestly purity and dress, originated in ages and under the influence of ideas altogether foreign to our present mental and spiritual state. They fail to impress the modern Jew with a spirit of priestly holiness; their observance in our days is apt rather to obstruct than to further modern spiritual elevation." The "platform" went on to say:

> We recognize, in the modern era of universal culture of heart and intellect, the approaching of the realization of Israel's great Messianic hope for the establishment of the kingdom of truth, justice and peace among all men. We consider ourselves no longer a nation, but a religious community, and, therefore, expect neither a return to Palestine, nor a sacrificial worship under the sons of Aaron, nor the restoration of any of the laws concerning the Jewish state.

Indicative of the great interest which the Reform rabbinate was to take in the realm of social justice was the eighth and last "plank" of that "platform":

> In full accordance with the spirit of Mosaic legislation, which strives to regulate the relation between rich and poor, we deem it our duty to participate in the great task of modern times, to solve, on the basis of justice and righteousness, the problems presented by the contrasts and evils of the present organization of society.[2]

[1] See the full text in *Yearbook of the Central Conference of American Rabbis*, vol. I (1891), pp. 117 ff.

[2] See the full text, *ibid.* pp. 120 ff.

Isaac Mayer Wise was a member of both the Philadelphia and the Pittsburgh conferences and, as such, signed both documents. Just as he had previously been willing to reach a compromise with Leeser's traditionalism, so he was now ready, the earlier compromise having failed, to concede to Einhorn and the other Reformers of the East. At the same time, Wise insisted that the "Pittsburgh Platform" represented the views of the rabbis who attended that conference without binding either the Union of American Hebrew Congregations or the Hebrew Union College. Moreover, since the Pittsburgh conference antedated the formation of the Central Conference of American Rabbis (1889), the "platform", according to Wise, was not even authoritative for that rabbinical body.

But the "platform" did crystallize the Reform position. It did legitimize the abrogation of dietary and other ritual laws and the virtual elimination of the Hebrew language. And it did lay the theoretical foundations of a Reform Jewish opposition to Jewish nationalism and Zionism, which was to remain the characteristic Reform posture for many a year to come. This was not lost on some of the more traditionalist congregations who had been constituents of Wise's Union of American Hebrew Congregations and who now terminated their membership. Together with the serving of ritually forbidden food at the Ordination banquet of the first class graduated from the Hebrew Union College in 1883 (i.e. at a time when Wise still hoped to train rabbis for all American Jewish congregations, and when some of the more conservative rabbis were still actively participating), the "Pittsburgh Platform" induced rabbis like Sabato Morais (1823–97) and H. Pereira Mendes (1852–1937) to form the Jewish Theological Seminary Association in 1886. In 1887 the Jewish Theological Seminary began to conduct classes. Alexander Kohut (1842–94), who became Professor of Talmud at the Seminary, outlined its ideology as follows:

> The hope is based upon the assumption that in the new Seminary a different spirit will prevail, different impulses will pervade its teachings and animate its teachers. This spirit shall be that of *Conservative Judaism*, the *conserving* Jewish impulse which will create in the pupils of the Seminary the tendency to recognize the dual nature of Judaism and the Law; which unites theory and practice, identifies body and the soul, realizes the importance of both matter and spirit, and acknowledges the necessity of observing the Law as well as studying it.[1]

[1] Quoted in Moshe Davis's *The Emergence of Conservative Judaism* (Philadelphia, 1963), p. 239.

While the "Pittsburgh Platform" did indeed chart the course on which American Reform Judaism was to sail for another generation, it was more in the nature of a summary of the underlying beliefs and assumptions of the German phase of American Jewish history than a signpost for the future development of American Judaism as a whole. For that German phase, with its radical Reform Judaism, its hospitals, its lodges, its charitable and philanthropic institutions (all of them founded and financed by German Jews in America), was fast coming to an end. The Pittsburgh conference took place in 1885. But the third "wave of immigration", bringing millions of East European Jews to the United States, had already started in 1881 and was just then gathering momentum. In less than half a century, the East European Jews were to achieve an overwhelming numerical domination of all facets of American Jewish life.

The East European Jews were bringing with them both their religious practices and institutions, and their secularist and nationalist ideologies. To the extent to which they were religious, they were untouched by the modernization attempts which had been made in nineteenth-century Germany. Nor did they have any use for what they found on the Jewish religious scene in America. They therefore founded their own synagogues in America, duplicating as much as possible the institutions they had left behind in eastern Europe, even congregating together in groups coming from the same East European towns. Some, however, who had been religious in eastern Europe, far from continuing in their old Orthodoxy jettisoned religion altogether. America represented a new environment, and Judaism was bound up with the old environment. It was one of the logical consequences of the "piety of the environment" that the piety should be forsaken together with the environment—just as, on the other hand, those who were eager to maintain that piety were striving for the recreation of the old environment on American soil.

Others, of course, had already forsaken religion while still in eastern Europe. In dealing with Russian Judaism, we have had occasion to note the existence of various secularist ideologies which were developed there, ideologies of nationalism and ideologies of socialism and ideologies which combined both. Those ideologies, too, were transplanted to America. Socialism in particular found a fertile soil, since most of the East European immigrants were reduced to a proletarian form of existence, trying to make a living as unskilled workers in the new country. The economic expansion westward, which had facilitated the economic and social rise of the German Jewish immigrant, had come to an end by the time the Russian Jews arrived.

Philanthropically, the Jews who had already established themselves in America did much to aid the new arrivals. But they were also bothered by the way in which the new immigrant might possibly affect the image of the Jew. The American Jew of German provenance, be he Reform or traditionalist, had no use either for the ghetto form of religious Judaism which the East European had brought with him, or for his Jewish nationalism and socialism. Steps were taken, therefore, to "Americanize" the East European immigrant. Such steps included the provision of English language classes, of youth centres with cultural and educational activities, and the creation of the Jewish Theological Seminary.

For the "Pittsburgh Platform" and the breach of the dietary laws at the Hebrew Union College banquet were not the sole causes of the establishment of that Conservative institution. The new Seminary was largely financed by prominent members of Reform congregations who also served on its board, and the establishment of the Seminary has, therefore, been regarded as a conscious attempt to provide the East European immigrants with an "Americanized" religious leadership. The Reform Jews involved in this project realized that the Jews they wanted to "Americanize" had no point of contact with Reform Judaism. Hence this institution was to be founded on a more traditionalist basis.[1]

For a while, the attempt backfired. In 1898 the Union of Orthodox Jewish Congregations was founded both for the purpose of supporting the Seminary and in order to provide constituents to be served by the rabbinical graduates of that Seminary. But when the East Europeans achieved numerical superiority in that organization, they refused to recognize the Seminary graduates as proper rabbis. They gave their allegiance to the graduates of the Rabbi Isaac Elchanan Theological Seminary (founded in 1896 on a strictly traditionalist basis) instead. In other words, though the Jewish Theological Seminary was to have its success with East Europeans and particularly with the succeeding generations, it was still not sufficiently "right wing" to appeal to those who, fresh from eastern Europe, were seeking to perpetuate their ancestral faith. Those, therefore, who stood to the right of American Reform Judaism were themselves divided into a Conservative and an

[1] Cf. Nathan Glazer, *American Judaism* (Chicago, 1957), pp. 73 ff.

Orthodox movement. And even that Orthodox movement appealed only to those East Europeans who had made their peace with the English language and an American education. To this day there are Orthodox congregations in America which neither belong to the Union of Orthodox Jewish Congregations nor accept the leadership of the rabbis trained at Yeshivah University (which is what the Rabbi Isaac Elchanan Theological Seminary became in 1928). By the side of the more "Americanized" institutions of traditional Judaism, Orthodox congregations and Yiddish-speaking rabbinical schools of an East European type have continued to exist and to be replenished by immigration after the Second World War.

But, regardless of the success or lack thereof with which it met at first, the Jewish Theological Seminary was to achieve a position of great significance when, in 1902, it was reorganized under the presidency of Solomon Schechter (1850–1915). Schechter was born in Rumania and educated in Vienna and Berlin. Before being called to the presidency of the Jewish Theological Seminary of America, he had served as Reader in Talmudic and rabbinic literature in the University of Cambridge and as Professor of Hebrew at University College, London. His international reputation as a scholar was established by his identification of a *Geniza* fragment as a part of the Hebrew original of Ecclesiasticus and by further *Geniza* discoveries and scientific editions of ancient texts. Apart from his academic scholarship, Schechter had also made known his views on contemporary Jewish issues. He was a man who could appreciate the emotional warmth of Ḥasidism as well as the scientific approach of the *Wissenschaft des Judentums*. He was in favour of Zionism, yet deplored its secularist factions and firmly believed in the permanence of Judaism in America. A traditionalist in sentiment and practice, he yet found it possible in 1913, as President of the Jewish Theological Seminary, to give an address at the dedication of the new building of the Hebrew Union College—an address in which he expressed his pleasure at being able to participate in those exercises.

> Probably you all know [he said on that occasion] the way in which some English statesmen speak of their opposition in the Parliament, referring to them as His Majesty's Opposition. This sounds like a paradox, yet it contains deep truth, implying as it does that both His Majesty's Government as well as His Majesty's Opposition form one large community, working for the welfare of the country and the prosperity of the nation. The same principle may also be applied to theology ...

He continued by saying:

> Opposition there must be, owing to the difference of temper and temperament, the difference of training, the difference of surroundings which no process of schooling can entirely obliterate, and the difference of opportunity. Of course, it will always be a question as to which is which; we Conservatives maintaining that we are His Majesty's Government and you His Majesty's Opposition.[1]

Best of all, however, Schechter preferred to avoid "denominational" labels within Judaism altogether and to speak of what he called "Catholic Israel" in all its manifold variety.

Only a man of Schechter's knowledge and broad sympathies (he liked the analogy of the English "Broad Church") could stand at the head of an institution which was to occupy a position midway between radical Reform and uncompromising Orthodoxy. In fact, it was Schechter who gave the Seminary a direction which placed it in line with the "positive-historical" school of thought founded by Zacharias Frankel in Germany. Under Schechter, the Seminary stood for free inquiry and loyalty to Jewish tradition and practice, allowing for such changes as circumstances made necessary. It was in this spirit, too, that, in 1913, Schechter founded the United Synagogue of America as the congregational body to support, and to be served by, the Seminary. The Rabbinical Assembly of America, the rabbinical association of the Conservative wing, had already been founded in 1900, prior to Schechter's arrival in the United States.

The United Synagogue, the Jewish Theological Seminary and the Rabbinical Assembly are the three major institutions of what has come to be known as Conservative Judaism. Ideologically, that movement has not yet given a full definition of itself, though its spokesmen resent being described as holding a midway position between Orthodoxy and Reform. Conservatism does stand for progress and change—but *within* the framework of traditional Jewish law. Changes in the traditional pattern for which the Reformers had to fight bitterly half a century before are taken for granted in Conservative Judaism. They include, as far as many Conservative congregations are concerned, mixed seating, the use of an organ for worship, the ceremony of confirmation for boys and girls, the inclusion of English prayers, etc. Yet, in matters of ritual observance, the Conservative movement has both its "right

[1] Solomon Schechter, *Seminary Addresses and Other Papers*, 2nd ed. (New York, 1959), pp. 240 ff.

wing" and its "left wing", even as in theology it allows for the greatest variety of belief. Its membership includes those who are traditional in belief and sentiment but somewhat lax in practice, as well as those who are attached to traditional ritual while holding radical views in matters of theology. Conservative Judaism had its greatest appeal for the second and third generation American Jew of East European descent. In fact, Conservative Judaism has always stressed "Jewish peoplehood". Its espousal of Hebrew and its sympathy for Zionism have made it attractive to those whose Jewish commitment is as much ethnic as it is religious.

It was one of the professors of the Jewish Theological Seminary, Mordecai M. Kaplan (b. 1881), who proclaimed religion to be but one of the aspects of Judaism. In his book *Judaism as a Civilization* (1934), Kaplan criticized the existing schools of Jewish religious thought: Orthodoxy for its supernaturalism; Reform for its anti-nationalism; and Conservatism for its apparent indecision. Kaplan himself is a "religious naturalist". He rejects the Personal God of tradition—God, for him, being "a process". Salvation, for Kaplan, is "this-worldly", and he denies the doctrine of the "Chosen People", a doctrine which he considers to be irreconcilable with democracy. Yet the traditional customs and ceremonies of Judaism should be perpetuated as much as possible. They are subject to such changes as may be necessary and new forms are likewise to be created; for, while the customs and ceremonies can no longer be regarded as divine commandments, they are the "folkways" of the Jewish people which help it survive. Palestine is to be the centre of Jewish civilization, from which all the dynamic forces of Judaism are to radiate. Religion, as has been noted, is but one aspect of that civilization. Others are culture and ethics. It is, therefore, quite possible for a Jew who has no religious belief to participate in those other aspects of Jewish civilization. While Palestine is to be the centre, Kaplan does not deny the viability of American Jewish life. In fact, the American Jew has the task of living in two civilizations, the American and the Jewish. To facilitate this, Kaplan advocates the creation of the "organic Jewish community", somewhat along the lines of the old European Jewish community—but, of course, without government control and interference. That community must provide for all the manifestations of Jewish life, make allowance for the varieties of religious expression, and cater to the cultural and artistic needs of Jews. Jewish education is to be undertaken on a community-wide basis, the Hebrew language is to be fostered and the building of a Jewish Homeland in Palestine is to be supported as that activity which, by involving the participation of all Jews, will lead to the renaissance of the Jewish spirit.

In 1935 Kaplan founded the Reconstructionist movement to promote his ideas. A few congregations have since been established on a Reconstructionist basis, but Kaplan did not intend Reconstructionism to become a fourth "denomination" within American Judaism. He and the majority of his rabbinical followers have not left the Conservative Rabbinical Assembly of which they represent the "left wing", even as others have remained members of the Reform Central Conference of American Rabbis. His lay following has mainly been among intellectuals who have found difficulties with the traditional Jewish God concept, but who also want to maintain their Jewish identity. Yet, his own theological views aside, Kaplan's practical suggestions have touched many a responsive chord and the field of Jewish education, youth work and Jewish educational and recreational centres has been greatly influenced by Reconstructionist ideas.

However, changes in Jewish orientation were taking place also in other quarters. For one thing, Jews of East European descent had by now obtained leading positions in all areas of American Jewish life—including the rabbinical and lay organizations of Reform Judaism. For another, the rise of German anti-Semitism gave American Jews pause to think. The slogans of the nineteenth century just no longer seemed appropriate to the needs of the twentieth. The Reform Central Conference of American Rabbis devoted several annual conventions to a reappraisal of the "Pittsburgh Platform" and, in 1937, adopted a new set of "Guiding Principles of Reform Judaism", the so-called "Columbus Platform" (on account of the city, Columbus, Ohio, in which the Conference met when the "Guiding Principles" were adopted). The new "platform" reaffirmed Reform Judaism's belief in progress and change. But it also affirmed the reality of Jewish peoplehood.

Judaism is the soul of which Israel is the body. Living in all parts of the world, Israel has been held together by the ties of a common history, and, above all, by the heritage of faith. Though we recognize in the group-loyalty of Jews who have become estranged from our religious tradition a bond which still unites them with us, we maintain that it is by its religion and for its religion that the Jewish people have lived.

Further on, the "platform" declared:

In the rehabilitation of Palestine, the land hallowed by memories and hopes, we behold the promise of renewed life for many of our brethren. We affirm the obligation of all Jewry to aid in its upbuilding as a Jewish homeland by endeavouring to make it not only a haven of refuge for the oppressed, but also a center of Jewish culture and spiritual life.

Also noteworthy in the "Columbus Platform", by way of contrast to its Pittsburgh predecessor, is the following paragraph:

Judaism as a way of life requires, in addition to its moral and spiritual demands, the preservation of the Sabbath, festivals and Holy Days, the retention and development of such customs, symbols and ceremonies as possess inspirational value, the cultivation of distinctive forms of religious art and music, and the use of Hebrew, together with the vernacular, in our worship and instruction.[1]

To understand the significance of the "Columbus Platform", one must bear in mind the extremely negative approach which Reform Judaism had always taken *vis-à-vis* the phenomenon of Jewish nationalism. As a matter of fact, the Reform opposition to Zionism even antedates Zionism's own appearance as a world-wide political movement. Herzl's *The Jewish State* appeared in 1896, and the first Zionist Congress met in Basel, in 1897. But the German Rabbinical Conferences had already rejected the nationalist interpretation of Judaism in the forties of the nineteenth century and the Philadelphia and Pittsburgh conferences in America, in 1869 and 1885 respectively, had gone on record against the hope of a return to Zion. And when the first Zionist Congress met in 1897, the Central Conference of American Rabbis, urged by Isaac Mayer Wise himself, unanimously condemned Zionism. This was to remain the official policy of American Reform Judaism until 1935, when the Central Conference of American Rabbis rescinded the 1897 resolution and voted that:

Whereas we are persuaded that acceptance or rejection of the Zionist program should be left to the determination of the individual members of the Conference themselves, therefore be it resolved that the Central Conference of American Rabbis takes no official stand on the subject of Zionism.[2]

[1] For the full text of the "Columbus Platform", see *Yearbook of the Central Conference of American Rabbis*, vol. XLVII (1937), pp. 97 ff.

[2] *Yearbook of the Central Conference of American Rabbis*, vol. XLV (1935), p. 103.

The 1935 and the 1937 positions were, of course, adopted because, the 1897 resolution notwithstanding, Zionism had already made heavy inroads into the ranks of the Reform rabbinate. In fact, American Reform rabbis had been associated with the Zionist movement from the very beginning. Gustav Gottheil (1827–1903), who began his rabbinical career as an assistant to Holdheim in Berlin and who, in 1873, became rabbi of New York's Reform Temple Emanu-El, was also a vice-president of the Federation of American Zionists. Bernhard Felsenthal (1822–1908), rabbi of a radical Reform congregation in Chicago, had always espoused an ethnic interpretation of Jewish life and, in his later years, he became active in the Zionist movement. David Neumark (1866–1924), a former collaborator of Ahad Ha-am's, who later became Professor of Jewish philosophy at the Hebrew Union College, had argued for the compatibility of Reform Judaism and Zionism on the ground that both represented a humanistic reinterpretation of the traditional messianic hope. There were others, of whom only two should be mentioned here, because they became world leaders of Zionism: Stephen S. Wise (1874–1949) and Abba Hillel Silver (1893–1963). Wise was so dissatisfied with the official anti-Zionism of Reform Judaism that, in 1922, he founded his own rabbinical seminary, the Jewish Institute of Religion, seeing that at the Hebrew Union College in those days Zionism was but barely tolerated. (In 1949 the Jewish Institute of Religion was merged with the Hebrew Union College.) Silver is credited with an important rôle in the political activities which led to the establishment of the State of Israel in 1948.

However, for most of the Zionist Reform rabbis, as for American Zionists in general, Zionism was primarily a philanthropic endeavour. A haven of refuge had to be established for persecuted brethren. That is why the change of the official Reform position coincided with the rise of German anti-Semitism. Regardless of the nationalist theories of East European provenance which continued to be expounded in the Yiddish and Hebrew press of New York, the native variety of American Zionism never contemplated the dissolution of the American Jewish community and large-scale American emigration to Palestine. There was even a pronounced reluctance to apply the concept of "exile" to America. That is why, after the creation of the State of Israel, American Zionist leaders have been living in a constant feud with former Israeli Prime Minister Ben-Gurion. The latter was always trying to confine the name "Zionist" to those who were personally committed to emigration to Israel. The vast majority of American Zionists have no such commitment and are content with supporting the State of Israel financially.

But, in 1942, dissatisfied with the Central Conference's abandoning of its stand of "neutrality" *vis-à-vis* Zionism and disturbed by the participation of the Central Conference in Zionist political activity, a few Reform rabbis and laymen founded the American Council for Judaism. That Council is not opposed to philanthropic activity, even in Israel. But it upholds the religious interpretation of Jewish existence espoused by the early Reformers, as against the tendency, now common even in Reform ranks, to regard the Jews of America as belonging to the same "nation" as the Israelis. The American Council for Judaism represents a small minority of American Jewry. Yet the problems to which it drew attention in the forties are problems of which American Jews are becoming increasingly aware now that the State of Israel is engaged in the pursuit of its own interests, which do not necessarily always coincide with those of American Judaism. Ben-Gurion's constantly reiterated call for immigration from America, a call which continues to fall on deaf ears, is perhaps even more of a challenge to the American Zionists than the views of the American Council for Judaism. It compels them to find a new *raison d'être* for the Zionist movement, one which would have to depart quite radically from what Zionism has traditionally been understood to mean.

Before the Second World War, Zionism in America fulfilled a function for which it no longer seems to be needed. In those days, American Judaism had its three major synagogal organizations: the Union of American Hebrew Congregations (Reform); the United Synagogue of America (Conservative); and the Union of Orthodox Jewish Congregations (Orthodox). The latter was, in theory, close to the kind of combination of strict ritual observance with general culture envisaged, a century before in Germany, by Samson Raphael Hirsch. Yet the majority of American Jews belonged to none of those organizations. The existence of non-affiliated small Orthodox synagogues of the East European type is only a small part of the reason. A more significant number of Jews simply had no religious commitments whatsoever. Some had just drifted away from Judaism—in part as a rebellion against the "foreign ways" of the parental home. Others were identified with the various secularist Jewish movements which the East European socialists had established. There was even a network of non-religious "folkist" Jewish schools, in which the language of instruction was Yiddish. American society was seen as one of "cultural pluralism", in which the Jewish ethnic group would continue to exist and to flourish side by side with the many other ethnic groups which made up the American population. Within such a constellation, Zionism provided a common meeting-ground for Jews of various religious persuasions or of none.

Since the Second World War, however, that picture has changed. Sociologists now realize that America is neither the "melting pot" nor the "cultural pluralism" which earlier analysts had seen in it. Ethnic groups do not find acceptance *qua* ethnic groups in the long run. American society still allows for variety, but it is a variety of *religious* denominations. To be a good American, one is either a Protestant, a Catholic, or a Jew. That is to say, religious affiliation through *any* of the three categories is not only tolerated, but practically mandatory. But cultural differentiations on a secular basis are ruled out. Whether this analysis will hold in the long run remains to be seen. For the present, it seems an adequate description of the contemporary American mood.

Under the circumstances, even Jewish secularists in America have begun to realize that "Jewish survival" is possible only through the synagogue. Besides, the anti-religious orientation which was appropriate to the socialist stance of a proletarian generation of immigrants is somewhat out of place now that the children and grandchildren of those immigrants are members of the professional and middle classes. Usually, with a move to a house in the suburbs, membership in a synagogue is bound to follow—if only in order to give the children a Jewish education. There has, therefore, been a considerable increase in synagogue membership and in the building of new synagogues since the late forties. By 1964 about three-fifths of all American Jews were said to be affiliated with a synagogue.[1] True statistics are hard to come by; but Conservatism and Reform account for about a million each and Orthodoxy for slightly more, though that includes many Jews who are only nominally Orthodox.

The three synagogal organizations and the three rabbinical bodies co-operate in the "Synagogue Council of America" (founded 1926) in all matters affecting Jews and Judaism as a whole. Although the East European trained Orthodox rabbis are suspicious of their American

[1] Janowsky, *op. cit.* p. 101.

trained colleagues and although, from time to time, even some of the English-speaking Orthodox rabbis withhold their support, the relations and the co-operation between the three "wings" of Judaism in America, particularly on the local level, have been cordial and of mutual respect. Moreover, it is quite common for American Jews to hold membership in more than one synagogue at one and the same time—an anomaly which helps to break down quite a few barriers. There have been occasional explorations of the possibility of a merger between the Conservative and the Reform groups. So far, however, such a merger has been found to be premature. But areas of co-operation are increasing—in spite of vested institutional interests; and there are predictions that the future will see a unified "American Judaism" which will make allowance for variations in the degree of personal religious observance. American Conservative and Reform institutions now opening branches in the State of Israel have already found that, both in relation to Israeli Orthodoxy and in relation to Israeli secularism, the two American religious movements are occupying more or less the same ideological ground. It is, however, still too early to make exact predictions about the future structure of American Judaism.

Meanwhile, there is evidence in all quarters of a dissatisfaction with yesterday's answers to today's problems. Among the Orthodox, who have pioneered an elaborate school system, there is a serious striving to come to terms with the modern world of science and technology. The Conservatives are grappling with the problems of sabbath and dietary observance, with the difficulties of the traditional Jewish marriage and divorce law and with the definition of their own ideological position. The Reformers are busy implementing the "Columbus Platform", intensifying Hebrew and religious education, and seeking ways of relating themselves to the tradition of Jewish law. And then there are the theological questions which are being debated within and across the "denominational" lines: The Personal God, Revelation, the Covenant, the nature of Israel, and the problem of Theodicy in the light of recent Jewish experience. While nineteenth-century religious Liberalism still has its spokesmen, and while Mordecai M. Kaplan's type of "religious naturalism" still has its followers among rabbis and laymen, a group of the younger American Jewish theologians is bringing the insights of Martin Buber and Franz Rosenzweig to bear on the problems of American Judaism. Also transcending the inner

Jewish "denominational" lines are the joint efforts in the cause of social justice (i.e. civil rights, the integration of the American negro, etc.) and participation, together with Christian clergymen, in meetings to further the "Christian–Jewish Dialogue" in an atmosphere of complete frankness and freedom.

Different, therefore, as was the Russian environment from the German environment, so is the American environment different from both. Yet each Jewry has made its distinct contribution to that totality which we call "Judaism Today". It is a totality made up of the interaction between historical and environmental factors and the heritage of the millennial Jewish tradition.

CHAPTER 2

JUDAISM IN ISRAEL

INTRODUCTION

Jewish population of Palestine in the nineteenth century

The late Professor Martin Buber wrote eloquently of the unique attachment of the Jewish people to the land of Israel, which stretches back nearly 3,800 years to the era of the Patriarchs Abraham, Isaac and Jacob. Though the Hebrews, and later the Jews, were the ruling people of the country for only 1,400 years before the Romans destroyed the Temple and the City of Jerusalem and laid waste the land, the generations in dispersal to the ends of the earth continued unbrokenly to regard the land promised to their ancestors in antiquity as their spiritual home. It was the goal of their hopes and aspirations, and destined to be again in the fullness of time their national centre. They carried with them into exile a spiritual fatherland, and it was a fundamental part of their religious faith that they would return. Israel was "a nation dwelling by itself, not counted among the peoples" (Num. xxiii. 9), and the territory of Israel was set apart from other lands and not counted among the countries.

The love for the country appears over and over again in quaint rabbinical maxims, such as: "He who has walked four cubits in the land of Israel is sure of a place in the next world" (B.T. *Keṯuboṯ* 111*a*). The Jewish prayers and ceremonies have the return to the land as their constant theme. There is not a religious service or occasion on which the prayer is not uttered; morning and evening, work-day and sabbath, fast and feast, at marriage and death, in the home and in the synagogue. From time to time, a leader claiming to be the Messiah would arise and proclaim that he would lead the people back; and mystic—kabbalist—sages pondered over the interpretation of the sacred words in the hope of hastening the messianic coming. There was indeed no time when the continuity of Jewish life in the land was completely broken, not even in the days of the massacres by the Crusaders and the Mongols. Nor were practical efforts wanting to place Jews in the towns and on the soil, whenever Christian or Muslim rule allowed. So, after the expulsion

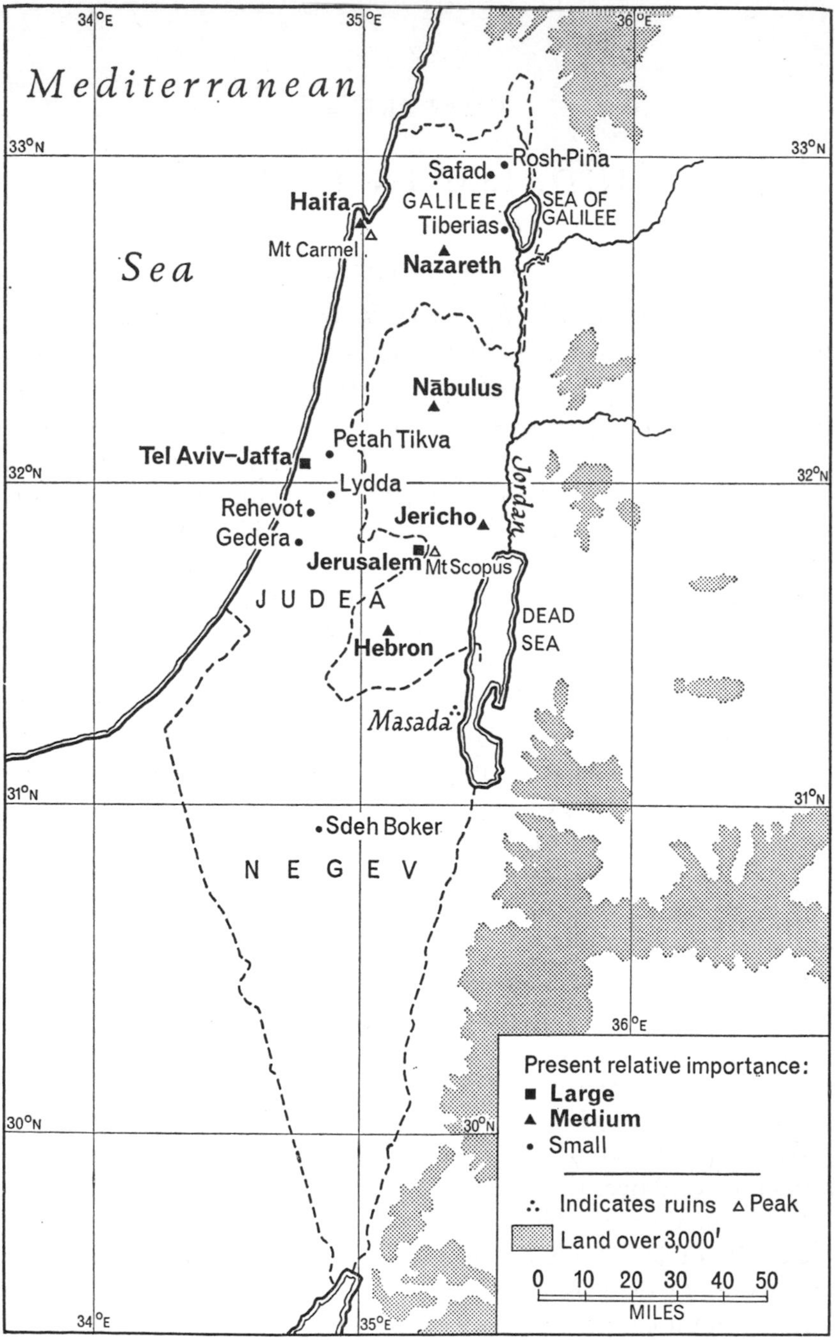
34°E
35°E
36°E
Mediterranean
Sea
33°N
32°N
31°N
30°N
Rosh Pina
Safad
Haifa
GALILEE
SEA OF GALILEE
Tiberias
Mt Carmel
Nazareth
Nābulus
Petah Tikva
Tel Aviv–Jaffa
Lydda
Rehevot
Jericho
Gedera
Jerusalem
Mt Scopus
Jordan
JUDEA
DEAD SEA
Hebron
Masada
Sdeh Boker
NEGEV
Present relative importance:
Large
Medium
Small
Indicates ruins
Peak
Land over 3,000′
0 10 20 30 40 50
MILES

Israel.

from Spain and Portugal in the fifteenth century, a remnant found a home in Palestine, then part of the Ottoman Empire. During the 400 years of Ottoman rule—1517–1917—while the country was sadly neglected, the Jews were a continuous and definite element of the scanty populations and a few inhabited agricultural villages in the Galilean Hills.

At the end of the eighteenth century a famous sage of Vilna, the Gaon (i.e. the exalted) Rabbi Elijah, revived an ancient practice of collecting sums of money in the synagogues of European communities for the purpose of maintaining Jewish scholars in the four holy towns: Jerusalem and Hebron in Judea, Tiberias and Ṣafad in Galilee, where the congregations of mystics had their schools. In this way he was able to settle some thousands drawn from Russia and Poland, Galicia and Germany, Holland and Hungary. Each community maintained its own scholars so that they might devote themselves to the study of the Torah. The system was known as *ḥaluqqah*, the Hebrew word for distribution (of alms). It became subject to abuse, because many officials who collected and administered the funds disbursed a large part to their own family or friends; and the amount of the distribution for the scholars varied according to the benevolence of each community and the number of its scholar beneficiaries. The petty jealousies and intrigues, such as Trollope described in his *Barchester Close* in England, were multiplied in the Palestine ghettos, and pauperism became a skilled profession.

The European movement of nationalism in the nineteenth century, which led to the liberation of Greece and the Balkan States and Italy from foreign rule and to giving the people independence, influenced the Jewish national leaders. But Zionism had deeper roots than any of these national risings; and it received a fresh impetus from the frustration of Jewish life in eastern Europe. The Jew was a member of the oldest and most distinctive nationality, in the sense of a group dispersed over the world but united by a common cultural heritage. Judaism, the religion, was indissolubly bound up with the nationality, so the return to the land was from the outset associated with the fulfilment of Judaism. A rabbinical saying about the messianic hope, that God will not come to the heavenly Jerusalem till Israel has come to the earthly Jerusalem, inspired the movement.

The first agricultural settlements in Palestine were founded before 1880. They were Petah Tikvah—meaning the Gate of Hope—in the plain of Sharon north of Jaffa, and Jaouni, the future Rosh-Pina—

meaning the Corner Stone—in northern Galilee near Ṣafad. The spiritual leader of the small band which founded Petah Tikvah, though an observant and religious Jew, was excommunicated (put into *ḥerem*), by the orthodox rabbis of Jerusalem, because it was heresy for Jews to redeem the soil and so to anticipate the Messiah. But this particular excess of obscurantism did not prevail for long; and some leading rabbis of eastern Europe were enthusiastic supporters of the colonizing movement.

Socialist Zionists were divided from the outset between two movements: the Workers of Zion (*p̱oale Zion*), who accepted the Marxian dialectic and regarded Zionism as a means to the Socialist society; and the Young Workers, who placed Zionism, the Jewish ideal, first and stressed its spiritual aspects. The new society in the land of Israel must be based on the ideals of the Prophets, justice and equality. The numbers of each section were very small in these early years. The first Workers Conference, 1901, was attended by only 150.

The Jews of western Europe and of America in the first half of the nineteenth century were engaged in the struggle for civil emancipation as it was called, that is, civil and political rights in the country of their sojourn. They had little concern about Palestine. An English Sephardi Jew, however, Sir Moses Montefiore, the first to hold municipal office as Sheriff of London and a prince of philanthropy, had a creative vision. It was to persuade the Jews in the four holy cities to leave their narrow ghetto and work on the soil, as their biblical ancestors had done. To this end he visited the country seven times between 1827 and 1876, when travel in the Orient was not lightly undertaken, and he became a legendary figure to the whole Jewish world. On his first Jewish pilgrimage he met the Egyptian conqueror of Palestine, Ibrāhīm Pasha, son of the famous Pasha Muḥammad 'Alī, and negotiated with him a project for Jewish colonization on a large scale in the deserted plains and mountain valleys. But before the plan could be started Ibrāhīm had been compelled by the Great Powers to renounce his sway over Syria and Palestine and restore the province to the Ottoman Sultan, his overlord. No negotiation was possible at that time with the Turks, and for the rest of his long life Montefiore had to be content with the betterment of the conditions of a few thousand Jews living in the country, almost entirely in the towns. Yet in the year of his centenary, 1884, a conference of Lovers of Zion from many countries was held in Polish Katovice and resolved to pursue the plans for "colonization"

—as it was called in that age of innocence. Already a few hundred of the old urban dwellers, supplemented by an immigration or *aliyah* (a movement upwards to the land of Israel) of a few score from Russia and Rumania, had started the work of redemption. The fulfilment of prophecy had begun. The idealists who came from Europe called themselves the Bilu, that name being the initial letters of the biblical verse "House of Jacob, let us be up and going" (Isa. ii. 5). The love of Zion, *ḥibbat Zion*, henceforth was a permanent motive in the Jewish communities alike of Europe and the Orient. It began to transform the life of the Jews in the land of Israel and to create islands of colonization in the Judean hills and the coastal plain of Sharon.

Of the small band of Bilu, numbering twenty-five members, only ten remained to found in 1884 the colony of Gedera, south of Jaffa. Prophetically they inscribed on a shield of David flag their motto: "The small one shall become a thousand, and the youth a mighty nation" (Isa. lx. 22). A small group of Russian peasants who had adopted Judaism were among the earliest settlers.

The Jewish population of Palestine during the nineteenth century rose gradually from about 10,000 to 60,000–70,000 in 1900. The larger part resided in the four holy towns, and in Jaffa, which was the centre of commerce and the port of Jerusalem. Small groups, also, were in other port towns, Ghazza (Gaza) in the south near the frontier of Egypt, and Haifa, which was also a commercial town and the terminal of the railway to Damascus, and the historic port of 'Akkā (Acre). During the last twenty years of the century, the agricultural settlements attracted the new type of the Jewish farmer and the Jewish agricultural worker. They were most generously assisted by the head of the French House of Rothschild, Baron Edmond de Rothschild, on whom the mantle of Moses Montefiore fell.

The modern Zionist movement was launched by Dr Theodor Herzl, the Viennese playwright and visionary statesman, who, in his book *Der Judenstaat* (The Jewish State) published in 1896, defined its object as the establishment of a Jewish home in Palestine assured by public law. Israel a Nation was the new rallying cry. It gave a fresh impulse to what had been largely a philanthropic activity, inspired by national-religious faith and converted it to a world political movement, organized by a Zionist International Congress or Parliament meeting annually and by national federations of Zionist Societies.

Before the outbreak of the First World War, which was to change the destiny of the Jews and of the land, forty Jewish villages or settlements had been founded in all parts of the country with a total population of 12,000. They were inspired by the idea of auto-emancipation, self-government in a Jewish home, which took the place for them of emancipation of the western Jews, their claim to take part in the civil and political life of the gentile state. These earliest pioneers were for the most part scholarly and pious Jews, who often had graduated from the Talmudic College, *Yeshivah*; and they combined *derekh ereṣ* (literally, "the way of the land"), with *talmud torah* (the study of the law). The Russian–Jewish philosopher, Asher Ginsberg—known by his pseudonym Ahad Ha-am—who inspired this *aliyah*, taught that the essential task of the National Home was to revive Judaism rather than save homeless or persecuted Jews. Zionism could not be just a secular national movement. It must be the expression of Jewish culture. In the land of the prophets the ideals of justice within the nation and between nations must be fulfilled. The synagogue was the central building of the village, and next to it the children's school was conducted usually in Yiddish or French—the language of the administration set up by the princely philanthropist, Edmond de Rothschild—but, in latter years, sometimes in Hebrew. An agricultural college, founded by the French *Alliance Israélite Universelle*, with the name *Mikveh Israel*, near Jaffa, gave boys and girls instruction in modern scientific cultivation.

It was a fortunate factor of the Ottoman rule that these agricultural settlements and also the Jewish communities in the towns, like other non-Muslim communities, could enjoy *de facto* a large measure of self-government. The non-Muslim community was a *millet*, that is, a recognized religious society with jurisdiction over its own members in matters of personal status (marriage, divorce, succession, etc.). It gave Jews the right of establishing schools in their own chosen language. The *millet* had power also to organize itself for religious worship and religious practices, such as the ritual slaughter of animals for food and the baking of unleavened bread for the Passover. An elected *va'ad*, committee, existed in each colony. The early settlers indeed went further in the way of autonomous organization. All disputes between them were normally submitted to the rabbi or to a voluntary peace tribunal, *mishpaṭ shalom*, for adjudication according to Jewish law or natural justice, and the colonist did not have resort to the government courts, even if one of the judges might be a Jew. Moreover, transactions in land or immovable property were regularly registered not with the government office—for that was notoriously corrupt and inefficient—but with a secretary of the community who kept the land-books and whose certificate of ownership or tenancy was authoritative in the *yishuv* (the name of the whole Jewish population in the land). With government acquiescence they maintained their own police force for the protection of their villages or fields against marauders. The colonies were then a National Home on the way, and the religious requirements of Judaism could be freely carried out.

At the turn of the century a second wave, or rather a rivulet, of immigration came from eastern Europe, moved partly by the "love of Zion", and partly by the ideal of "back to the land" and manual labour. They were influenced as much by Tolstoy's teaching of regeneration through simple productive work as by the Zionist aim.

The second *aliyah* was largely composed of ardent Socialists who had imbibed the teaching of Karl Marx and accepted the doctrine of dialectical materialism. They were in revolt against the strict Jewish ritual and observance based on the belief in divine revelation, which they did not regard as in conformity with modern science and the theory of evolution. The leader of the Labour group was a Russian-Jewish writer, Aaron David Gordon, who came to the Land at the age of forty-eight and inspired the first collective community, *kibbutz*, planted at the southern end of the Lake of Galilee. He was a religious Jew himself, but he believed that productive work was the service of God: the Hebrew word for work and worship is the same. Like the early Hebrew Christians, who inhabited the same region, the members shared their slender property and eschewed private possessions. The collective form of settlement, *kibbutz*, means simply a gathering. The other form of gathering is the *moshav*, where the family has its separate residence and smallholding where no hired Jewish or Arab labour is introduced, and where the whole economic life is conducted through co-operative societies.

The economic maxim of the *kibbutz* was "from each according to his capacity, to each according to his need". Jews returning to the soil must redeem it with the work of their own hands and not by the work of others. The Hebrew word for reclaiming the land, *kibbush*, means literally subduing, and most of the "workers of Zion" started their life in Palestine by breaking stones and making roads. Ramsay MacDonald, the future British Socialist Premier, after his visit to Palestine in 1922, recorded: "These pioneers are men who subdue both heaven and earth." Martin Buber, who was the spiritual father of the movement among the youth in central Europe, pointed to the new Jewish character who was being created, the *ḥalutz*, or pioneer, living together on a basis of justice. Their Socialism was spontaneous and voluntary, not imposed by a government from above. In this it was contrasted with the Russian agricultural collective *kolkhoz*. In the forefront of their mind was the creation of a national society in which social justice should be realized.

The migration (aliyah) *to Palestine–Israel 1920–66*

After the establishment of the British Mandate over Palestine in 1920, with the trust to facilitate Jewish immigration and settlement in the land, a steady flow of immigrants came from Europe, mostly from Poland and Rumania. It reached in 1925 the high figure of 35,000, being nearly one-third of the existing Jewish population of the country. Thereafter it fell steeply, because of economic depression in Poland; and it was not till 1932 that it rose again to comparable numbers. The fresh impetus came from the virulent growth of anti-semitism in Europe and in 1935 the intake reached 65,000. The Jewish population during the thirty years of British rule—including the two years of military administration, 1918–20—was increased nearly tenfold, from 70,000 to 650,000. Of that total about one-fifth were living in rural villages and engaged in agriculture.

The emigration, *aliyah*, from Germany, Austria and Czechoslovakia, which turned to Palestine in large numbers after 1933, the year Hitler and the Nazis seized power, made a signal contribution to the youth movements and the *kibbutz*, and also to the academic, scientific, and economic manpower of the country. Both classes of immigrants from central Europe brought method and a sense of order, qualities less characteristic of the East European Jews then at the head of the *yishuv*. The German immigrants were known as *yekke*, which was a half-humorous synonym of reliability and thoroughness which sometimes seemed excessive. The *yekke* and the *ḥalutz* were two contrasted ideal types which complemented each other.

A few German Jews with these qualities had been prominent in the Zionist movement from the beginning of the century, particularly as directors of the agricultural settlement and also in the first appointments of professors and lecturers at the Hebrew University. A small band of Zionist pioneers, young German-Jewish men and women seeking a better and more adventurous way of life than was led by the assimilated solid Jewish bourgeoisie in Germany from generation to generation, had come to Palestine in the 1920s and settled in co-operative or collective agricultural villages. But only few of them were able to adjust themselves to the hard conditions and the others drifted to the towns or returned to Europe. Now, however, those who left central Europe under the pressure of persecution had prepared themselves for the new way of living before they immigrated and they were readily integrated. The first fifty youths arrived in 1934, and were apprenticed in a collective settlement. The German-Jewish youth favoured particularly the *kibbutz*, which was their principal nursery, while they were the principal reservoir. They were normally mixed in the new settlement with pioneers from eastern Europe and with native-born boys and girls of the *yishuv*. What turned the development of the *kibbutz* from experiment to achievement was the combination of ideal and practical necessity. It proved to be the most effective instrument for creating an agricultural society out of inexperienced young people without material capital, but possessed of enthusiasm and skill.

German-Jewish teachers were also the chosen directors of a special educational institution devised for the reception and integration of the young immigrants. There were children's villages in which the pupils spent half the day in study and half in fieldwork under the guidance of trained leaders. It was education in the community by the community for the community. At first designed particularly for the youth from central and eastern Europe, it was expanded during and after the Second World War to rescue and redeem an *aliyah* from Asia and Africa. A spectacular group of over a thousand boys and girls were rescued in 1943 from Tehran. They had escaped with or without their parents from the Nazi holocaust of eastern Europe, wandered through Asiatic Russia, and were finally gathered near the Caspian Sea by emissaries from Palestine.

Most of the youth were from observant families, and most of the children's villages were conducted in accord with religious tradition. But the most renowned of them, Ben Shemen, was the creation of a dedicated German-Jewish educator, Dr Siegfried Lehmann, who belonged to the Reform wing. At the end of the First World War he founded an original institute in Kovno (Kaunas) for the redemption of homeless waifs and strays from Lithuanian ghettos. After some years he realized that Palestine was the place for his experiment. He had original ideas of the rôle of music in education, of inculcating reverence for the wonders of nature, and of fostering practical friendship between young Jews and Arabs. Yet the master-mind of the education for a new life, deriving sap from the soil and a spirit from the Bible, was not the German educator but an American Jewess of genius and saintliness, Henrietta Szold, who, when past her seventy years of devotion to medical and social work in Palestine, became the mother of all the child immigrants.

The migration from America and the British Commonwealth, which is perversely called Anglo-Saxon, is quantitatively small but in quality important. The United States, which has far the largest Jewish community in the world—more than double that of Israel, sends only a few hundreds a year, and Great Britain much the same number, but relative to the size of the community a much bigger proportion. The British immigrants have included a class of higher civil servants of Israel and also several of the religious leaders, notably, the second Ashkenazi chief rabbi, Dr Herzog, and the third, Rabbi Unterman. The Americans have included many doctors, welfare workers and skilled industrialists.

Jews from America have made another distinct contribution to the religious development. A few rabbis of the Reform or Progressive movement (see below) came from the United States, and a Jerusalem branch of the Reform Seminary, the Hebrew Union College in Cincinnati, is a link between Israel and Liberal Judaism in America. At the same time the Jewish Theological Seminary of America, the citadel of Conservative Judaism (which is midway between Orthodox and Liberal), has its branch in Jerusalem, a hostel where its graduates stay for a year's study at the Hebrew University.

From the other and smaller West and North European countries, France, Belgium and Holland, and Scandinavia, the *aliyah* has been limited. France is the classic country of assimilation; and the established Jewish families, in spite of the suffering of Jews in France during the Second World War, feel themselves integrated Frenchmen. Of the vast new Jewish population, which was part of the exodus of French citizens from Algeria to the metropolitan country, some movement to Israel may be expected. But the effort of the major Jewish philanthropic body, the *Alliance Israélite*, which has many schools in France and the Orient, is rather to "Frenchify" the pupils than to prepare them for migration to the Jewish State. From the terribly reduced community of the Netherlands after the war, the Jewish contingent that has made its way to the National Home is for the most part combined with the "Anglo-Saxon" settlers.

Since the Soviet Revolution of 1917, which almost coincided with the issue of the Balfour Declaration by the British government, the immigration of Jews from Russia has been extremely limited. The Communist State, which claims to have given Jews equal citizenship and opportunity, while it narrowly restricts the right of the Jews to have any distinct cultural activity, is utterly opposed to their emigration and to their association with Israel or Israelis. So the community which took the lion's share in the first steps to the foundation of the Jewish National Home, has been deprived of the power to participate in the upbuilding of the State. Such immigration as has been permitted is limited mainly to aged individuals who have a family or kith and kin in Palestine–Israel. Moreover, Soviet policy in the Middle East is to support the Arabs and to convince them that the Russians are their friends and are unfriendly to the Jews and the government of Israel, who are alleged to be the agents and stooges of Western Imperialism. The one important cultural contribution of Russian Jewry, since the British Mandate for Palestine was conferred, was the *Habimah* dramatic company who came to Palestine in 1928 and, in 1931, resolved to settle there. They were reorganized by the government of Israel as the Israel National Theatre.

The other creative aspect of the *aliyah* from central and western Europe was the reinforcement of the intellectual and artistic contribution of the National Home. The sudden exclusion by the Nazis of thousands of scholars and scientists in German universities because of their Jewish origin led to a migration of scholars, doctors, lawyers, musicians, and artists, unparalleled in modern history. These refugees were distributed to all parts of the world, and a relatively large portion came to Palestine to be absorbed in the Hebrew University and other institutes of higher learning, or to carry on their profession in new conditions. Eminent among them was a group of teachers of Judaism from the German and Austrian "High Schools" (or seminaries) of "Jewish Science". They made Palestine a principal seat of Jewish learning, and later a principal intellectual centre of Jewry. So, too, in the world of music and the visual arts the immigrants from Germany and Vienna brought high standards. The German–Austrian–Czech migration to Israel was culturally the most important in the last thirty years.

Numerically, however, the flood which came from eastern Europe—Poland, Rumania, Hungary, Bulgaria and Yugoslavia during the first years of the State, when the gates of the National Home were at last opened wide, and the steady stream that came in the last decades, far exceeded it. They brought the intense sectional and party feeling which was nurtured in the ghetto. One section was composed of religious fanatics and another, moved by the Communist doctrines, had an almost equal anti-religious bias. But the masses were readily absorbed, and they provided a large proportion of the professional class and the skilled workers.

The main migration, however, after 1951, has been of Jews from the oriental countries, the ancient diasporas of the Yemen and Iraq, and after the Suez affair, 1956, the mainly commercial Jewish population of Egypt. From Yemen and Iraq it was a mass movement, so that few Jews were left in the countries in which Jewish life has been continuous from the Babylonian Captivity. Many came by airlift, Magic Carpet and Ali Baba, thus, as the simple thought, fulfilling the prophecy that they should be borne on eagles' wings. Compared with the Jews of central and eastern Europe they were educationally backward and religiously conservative. The next wave of immigrants, also of oriental Jews, was from North Africa, and the mass again was educationally backward, but loyal to the Jewish tradition. Save that they had a simple belief in the messianic age, they were ill-prepared for the utter change of the way of life and of their environment. They were sensitive of their minor part in the administration of the country, in its economy, in secondary education and institutes of higher learning. They tended to ascribe to an Ashkenazi bias against the Sephardi what was essentially due to their inferior qualifications. The government and public bodies have been at pains to raise their level of education and their standard of life; and slowly and systematically the effort for a coherent national society makes an impact. Yet there is still much leeway to make up. In central politics they for the most part adhere to the major parties, but in local government elections they tend to vote for ethnic lists. Religiously they strengthen the synagogal tradition and many are devout mystics. Broadly they maintain and cherish the family unit, and few can be persuaded to be members of a collective *kibbutz*. So far as they are planted in rural setlements they adopt the co-operative form, the *moshav*, in which the family has its own home and preserves its identity. It is notable that, though the large majority of the Oriental Sephardim are religiously observant, they do not vote for the lists of the religious parties in the elections to the *knesset*. Within a generation the "Oriental" Jews will be the major part of the population, and Israel an "Oriental" country.

The Sephardi immigrants, with a few exceptions, have not yet had sufficient opportunity to rise to high office. But the young generation, born in Palestine or Israel of Sephardi parents, have equal opportunity and equal achievement with those of Ashkenazi parentage. They are equally *sabras*—the name given to native Israelis, which is also the name of the fruit of the cactus plant, and indicates their prickly exterior. The *sabra* is a new type of young Jew, self-confident and enterprising, without inhibitions and self-consciousness, independent of his parents, and somewhat contemptuous generally of Jews of the dispersion and their Zionism.

The early *aliyah* to Palestine before the First World War was not only from Europe. Throughout the nineteenth century there was a trickle of Oriental Jews from Muslim countries, Persia and Bukhara, Morocco and Tunisia, Yemen and Egypt. They were classed together as Sephardim in the major division between Ashkenazim and Sephardim, but each national group had their own synagogue and ritual and a *beth-dīn*, a tribunal for matters of personal status. Officially, in relations with the Ottoman government, the Sephardim were the established and privileged community. The chief rabbi of Jerusalem, *ḥakham bashî*, was always chosen from them, and the council was composed mainly of Sephardi representatives. Each of the two main communities had its separate supreme rabbinical tribunal.

The gathering of the "exiles" has embraced also small communities and groups of Jews in different parts of the world who were regarded as heretics. In the first place there are the Karaites, who in the early Middle Ages were cast out of the major community because they rejected the rabbinical commentaries on the Torah and observed only the written law enshrined in the Books of Moses. For centuries these puritans were a powerful element. But in modern times they have greatly declined in numbers. They awaited the restoration to the land of Israel no less ardently than the majority. In the nineteenth century a small Karaite congregation was living in Jerusalem; other congregations were in Egypt and in the Russian Crimea. The Russian consulate protected those in Palestine, but the Soviet government's antipathy to religion and the Egyptian government's revengefulness against Jews in their country after the Suez affair in 1956 led to a complete exodus of the Karaites from the two states. They came to Israel, took readily to agriculture, and are settled in the Ramla–Lydda region. The Rabbinate was more tolerant of them than of several other redeemed tribes and permitted their marriage with other Jews. Whether the puritanical heresy will survive as a living doctrine remains to be seen.

A still smaller remnant, but with an almost unbroken foothold in the land since the first captivity, is now divided between the territory of Israel and of Jordan. They are the Samaritans, claiming descent from the Hebrews who founded the Kingdom of Israel after the schism on the death of Solomon, and who were taken captive by the Assyrians in the seventh century B.C. They have conserved their historic attachment to Shechem, the former capital of the Kingdom of Israel and now called by the Arabic name Nābulus (corruption of Neapolis), and look upon it as their religious centre. They have also conserved the ceremony of the sacrifice of the paschal lamb at the Passover festival on Mt Gerizim near Nābulus. Today, they are almost a museum minority. For they number only a few hundred, divided geographically between the two states. They, too, have attained partial recognition as Jews, from both State and Rabbinate. For them, too, the query arises as to whether they will keep for long their ritual separateness or be integrated into the people of Israel. Their abundant lore and religious literature, which have long engaged the attention of a few scholars, are now studied with fresh zest.

Yet another lost tribe which is represented, though in very small measure, is the Falasha tribe of Ethiopia. They are an ancient Judaized element in a Christian country. They still preserve a primitive form of Judaism and the hope of migrating to the land of Israel, and they call themselves Beth Israel. Only a few, however, have been able to migrate. Recently a fierce controversy arose over the intended marriage of a Falasha man with an Israeli Jewess. The Rabbinate refused to celebrate the marriage unless he would undergo some ritual immersion, and that he refused to do.

Another remnant of the early pre-Christian dispersal lived in the Crimea and was rescued at the end of the Second World War. The Krimchaks traced their origin from a migration of the second century B.C. when the country had a Hellenistic culture. The Greek translation of the Old Testament (known as the Septuagint), the Apocryphal books, and the Greek Allegories of Philo of Alexandria, were included in their scriptures. Only some 500 survived the Nazi massacre of the Jews in the Crimea and were brought to Israel.

Two branches of an early dispersion in India, which were almost lost tribes, the *Bney Isrā'ēl* of the Bombay province and the Cochin Jews of the south, who included white, black and brown, i.e. half-caste elements, were also moved by the messianic hope. They came to Israel in considerable numbers during the early years of the State, bringing their special rituals and language to the ingathering. They were traditional and pious Jews, and some of them were gravely disappointed when they found that their neighbours were not observant of the Torah. They demanded a return to their former home, and some of them went. It was another disappointment—or worse—when the Rabbinate required those who wanted to marry Israelis of a different origin to undergo some form of ritual habilitation. Their ancestry, they claimed, was as good as that of the Ashkenazi of Europe or the Sephardi of Iraq.

One lost tribe of Jews has not yet had any part in the return. They are the *marranos*, or Crypto-Jews, of Spain and Portugal, whose ancestors adopted Christianity under duress at the time of the expulsion of the Jews from the Peninsula and have secretly kept some Jewish practices. A few of them have visited Israel, expecting to find paradise and the Messianic Age established. They, too, were disappointed and did not stay.

THE JEWS AND JUDAISM IN MANDATED PALESTINE

It was in July 1920 that the British mandatory government for Palestine came into being, with a Jew, Sir Herbert (later Viscount) Samuel, as the first High Commissioner. Though the terms of the mandate concerning the Jewish National Home were not confirmed by the council of the League of Nations till 1922, and did not formally operate till a year later, the High Commissioner took early steps to regulate the organization of the Jewish community as well as of other religious *millets*. A commission of inquiry was appointed, and after its report an assembly of rabbis and lay representatives (with a lay majority, and presided over by the Jewish attorney-general of the government) drew up a regulation for the election of a unified rabbinical council for Palestine, with two equal chief rabbis, Ashkenazi and Sephardi, six associate rabbis for each community, and three lay councillors. They proceeded to the election, and the saintly Rav Kook, at that time the spiritual head of a pious congregation in London, and Haham Meir, formerly head of the Salonica Jewry, were respectively the Ashkenazi and Sephardi choices. The differences between the two communities were only on small points of ritual.

It was beyond hope that all the congregations would accept the authority of a united Rabbinate. Some fundamentalist congregations, formed of the old *ḥaluqqah* groups, challenged its fitness and maintained their own tribunal (*beth dīn*) and their own ritual killing. Though they were not recognized by the government as a second official community, they were allowed to keep their separate institutions. Some years later, after Field-Marshal Lord Plumer had followed Samuel as the High Commissioner, comprehensive regulations of the Jewish community were approved by the government and given legal effect. They provided liberally for a lay as well as a rabbinical authority. An elected assembly of seventy-one members, the number of the ancient *sanhedrin*, met once a year and decided policy. It elected also an executive national council which was in constant session. Judicial bodies, central and local, dealt with ritual questions and matters of personal status. The Jewish *millet* was recognized as a *knesset*, later to be the name of the permanent legislative assembly of the State of Israel. Its organs, subject to government supervision, could levy rates on Palestinian Jews who did not contract out of the community for religious needs, education and other social services. Arbitration committees, too, were appointed, with rabbis or elected or nominated lay members, to adjudicate on general civil disputes.

Though the regulations were made under an Ordinance concerning a religious community, they were in fact designed as the autonomous constitution of the National Home, and the executive body, the *va'ad leumi*, was a national council not only in name. It was essentially secular, but provided the means for the religious authorities. For the election of the general assembly and of the local councils women had the vote on the same terms as men. The rules for the election of the Rabbinate and the defining of its functions have remained in force in the State of Israel with little amendment. But the provisions for the organization of the Assembly, *knesset*, and the National Council have naturally lapsed with the establishment of the State which has sovereign powers. The *knesset* and the *va'ad leumi* achieved their purpose when they participated in the proclamation of Independence, 1948, and they were merged in the provisional council of the government of Israel then established. The religious-national community was transformed overnight into an independent state, a republic.

The Chief Rabbinate and Rabbinical Council of Israel are generously housed in Jerusalem, thanks to the munificent gift of Sir Isaac Wolfson, originally of Glasgow, who is the President of the United Synagogue of Great Britain. In a commanding building that dwarfs the head office of the Jewish Agency for Palestine, there are a synagogue and a large assembly hall, a library, study rooms for the rabbis, and court-rooms for the rabbinical tribunals which are more spacious than those of the civil courts of the government. That, perhaps, is intended to be symbolical of the authority of the religious law in the State. It offers a contrast to the lowly accommodation of the Rabbinate in the period of the British Mandate. It is notable, however, that in the long Israeli Declaration of Independence the only reference to divine help is in the last paragraph, and uses a nationalist term for God: "With trust in the Rock of Israel we set our hand to this Declaration." The contrast is marked with the American Declaration of Independence where reliance on God is repeated time and again.

Zionism in Russia started as a revolt against the conception of Judaism as the passive faith of the people living in exile and held together by a peculiar way of life that separated them from their neighbours. Anatole France, in his historical romance *Le Procurateur de Judée*, puts into the mouth of Pontius Pilate the remark about Judaism that it is not a "religion", meaning literally a force that binds together, but an "abligion", a force that separates. That was also the feeling of some of the Russian-Jewish intelligentsia who were revolutionary Socialists and also Zionists.

Enthusiastic for the Hebrew language, they were passionate opponents of Jewish religious observance, which in their opinion menaced the national existence. Judaism in the land of Israel should shed practices which were designed in the Dark Ages and the Middle Ages as a "hedge" of the Torah, to preserve the integrity of scattered Jewry in the dispersion. On the other hand, many urged that the restoration of the Jews to the land should be a prelude to the messianic fulfilment and enable Jews to uphold the prophetic ideals of peace, social justice and the unity of mankind. Judaism in a Jewish land must determine the life of the individual and the community, and recover the sense of destiny. Ahad Ha-am's notion of the spiritual centre was a synthesis of the two poles. Judaism was not just a religion or a culture, but the national creative power of the people, which expressed itself in the form of a culture of essentially religious character. In the land of Israel it would be regenerated as a civilization in which religion would have a leading part. The Judaism of the dispersion would be transformed in the way of life of Israel. A professor of the Hebrew University, Dr Jacob Talmon, has put forward another aspect of the same basic conception, that religion is not the sole test of Judaism. The Jews are a community of fate, the product of history crystallized round the nucleus of race and religion.

The Jews of Israel have recovered the Hebrew scriptures. The awareness of the relevance of the Bible to present-day life permeates the schools of all sections and moulds their thought and expression. On the other hand, the influence of the Talmud may diminish, though it is also a compulsory subject in the programme of all the public schools. While the Bible represents the history and the thought of the biblical period, with which modern Israel feels a close affinity, the Talmud represents the thought of the exile, with which she has not an equal affinity.

The Judaism of isolation accentuated the ceremonial side of Jewish life and crystallized itself into a mode of separate living. The modern phase of Judaism, both in Israel and in America, tends to emphasize the cultural aspects more strongly. The importance of worship in the synagogue was derived from the dispersion. Because the Jews could not lead a full Jewish life, they multiplied the "hedges" and compensated themselves by dreaming of the coming of the Messiah. Following the civil and intellectual emancipation in the nineteenth century, the isolated Jewish way of life became untenable. When the individual Jew could take part in the life of the general society the sense of the rules of separation was lost. A few among them in eastern Europe came to Palestine to formulate a new and free Jewish life.

Among the early pioneers from Russia and members of a *kibbutz* were the future founders of the State of Israel: David Ben-Gurion, first Prime Minister and Minister of Defence; Isaac Ben-Zvi, the second President of the Republic; and Moshe Shertok (Sharett), Foreign Minister and, for two years, Prime Minister. The *kibbutz* in the period of the British Mandate was the conscience of the nation. Where did the members of the *kibbutz* and the *moshav* stand in relation to traditional Judaism? Broadly, they wanted a new religion with freedom of thought as part of a new social life. The meticulous ordering of the individual's whole activity, which was observed in the ghetto, was out of keeping with the effort for freedom and self-expression in a young society. Its philosophical basis in the dogma of the divine revelation to Moses of the law of conduct in all its details was unacceptable, not only to the Marxists among them, but to all who believed in free will and evolution.

At the same time, they had a strong national consciousness and a will to preserve as a national institution the sabbath day of rest and leisure. But the sabbath was made for man, not man for the sabbath (see *Mekhilta*, ed. J. Lauterbach, vol. III, p. 198), and the essential idea of a holy day was not maintained. The mandatory government, in accordance with the terms of the Mandate, made the sabbath an official day of rest for Jews who could enjoy it the more fully because the public services on that day were conducted by the non-Jews. In the mandate period there were no troubles about sabbath-keeping.

The Jewish population, religious and non-religious, also celebrated as national and nature holidays the religious festivals of Passover, Pentecost (in Hebrew, the feast of the First Fruits), and Tabernacles, the feast of the vintage. But the association of Pentecost with the revelation of the Torah to Moses on Sinai is lost or omitted. They attached a fresh significance to the Feast of the Maccabees, which commemorates historical events of the period of the Second Temple and the struggle against the pagan Hellenistic kings; and to the Feast of Esther, which is based on a romantic story of the Jewish dispersion in Persia, and traditionally was a welcome day of fun and carnival in a calendar studded with memories of calamity and persecution. Since the State was established, a new festival has been added, the Day of Independence. It is celebrated with ardour and dancing and fun on the eve and the day in the Hebrew Calendar which corresponds with the anniversary of the Declaration in 1948. It has not yet received regular religious expression, but on the eve there is a home service, including the reading of the narrative of the Jewish struggle, a *haggadah* on the lines of the *haggadah* of the Passover, the narrative of the exodus from Egypt.

Not all the pioneers of the second *aliyah* were rebels against the Judaism of the ghetto. In the third *aliyah* which began, at the end of the First World War, to stream to Palestine (then under British administration), many remained faithful to the Torah. They were drawn from eastern Europe and subsequently from Germany and Austria, when Hitler's persecution threatened to ruin catastrophically the most intellectual and—it was thought—the most integrated Jewry of the west. They were ardent to combine the religious law with the Socialist way of life and the pursuance of social justice. For them Socialism could not be a substitute for Judaism, but only an integral part of it. Their religious *kibbutz* and their *moshav* gave a full place to the synagogue and the talmudic study-room. Their members included a substantial element which came to Israel by way of Great Britain and the United States, where they had made their preparation for their new life, and they drew material and moral support from those countries. In the War of Independence, 1948–9, they were amongst the bravest and most steadfast, holding their outposts in the Judean hills and the Jordan valley against tremendous odds with a sense of dedication like that of the martyrs in the long medieval darkness, and, what was new, with a resolve to fight till they fell at their posts.

We have traced the enlargement and transformation of the *yishuv* during the last fifteen years of the British Mandate and the first eighteen years of the State of Israel. The Hitler persecution, culminating in the effort to exterminate European Jewry, brought to Palestine a new religious element which consisted of the assimilated members of the Reform and Liberal synagogues and which did not exist previously in Palestine. It brought also a great accretion to the extreme right wing of fundamentalist rabbis and students from the famous schools of Talmud and mysticism. Then the struggle for independence between Israel and the Arab states caused a spectacular mass migration of Jews living in the Arab and other Muslim states. The Arab–Israeli war in Palestine involved the whole Arab people, and to a less extent the other Muslim peoples. The Jews found their life precarious in the countries which took an active part in the war; Iraq, Syria, Lebanon, Trans-Jordan (later the Hāshimite Kingdom of Jordan) and Egypt. The Arab solidarity movement involved also Yemen and Aden, where the conditions of the Jews had been growingly unstable. A few years later it affected Jews also in countries which had been under French and Italian rule and were now independent, the ancient dispersion in Morocco, Algeria, Tunisia and Libya. The Muslim Arab population became strongly conscious of the Arab heritage and antipathetic to minorities.

At the same time, the religious appeal to the Jews in those lands to migrate to the State of Israel was strong, and in their simple faith was the prelude to the messianic redemption. They arrived in Israel by ship and by plane in their tens of thousands. And they changed the balance of the population between the keepers of the tradition and the revolutionary freethinkers. Smaller groups came from other Muslim countries, Persia and Turkey, not on account of any religious persecution, but because they too were drawn by the messianic magnet. Others again came from the distant congregations in India, Afghanistan and Kurdistan, whose origins stretched back to a misty past, to have their part in the redemption. The Kurdish Jews preserved the Aramaic language in which much of the Talmud was written. So in the first eighteen years of the State of Israel, 1948–66, the Jewish population was more than trebled—from 650,000 to 2,250,000—and formed a microcosm of the Jewish people.

The supreme problem of Judaism in Palestine and Israel is to find the unifying force, in addition to the political state, for the diverse mass. At the laying of the foundation-stone of the Hebrew University of Jerusalem in 1918, Dr Weizmann declared: "The soul of the Jewish people which has wandered for centuries will find a home here." The Hebrew University would be an instrument for the bond of the Hebrew language. In the period of thirty years of British administration of Palestine the University achieved a unifying influence by making Hebrew the national language, replacing a Babel of tongues. The mandatory government gave encouragement by including Hebrew as one of the three official languages with English and Arabic. That language, it was said, was the best student of the University. It learned how to formulate vocabularies for the expression of every aspect of human thought, science and learning. The Institute of Jewish Studies, the most complete school of Judaism in the world, embraced Bible and Talmud, history and philosophy, philology and sociology. It moulded the general humanities in the light of Hebraic thought; and Judaism itself, as studied there, was not just a remnant of antiquity, but a living tree striving upwards for wholeness and completeness.

There is no religious or national test for teachers or students, and no attempt to restrict freedom of Bible criticism. There is no school of theology as such, but the Department of Comparative Religion is devoted to the study of the relations of Judaism to Christianity, Islam and the Eastern religions, with a view to finding the common ethical principles. The University has also inaugurated a special department for the study of the development of contemporary Jewry. That is the one institute in the world where the aspects of Jewish life in the dispersion are examined, recorded and classified, and where the interaction of the State and the dispersion is under constant observation.

Lord Balfour, the signatory of the declaration of the British government about the National Home, when opening the University in 1925, declared his supreme confidence that the Jewish people would make there a creative contribution to learning and science and the things of the spirit and that Hebrew was an instrument capable of adaptation in every realm of knowledge. Sir Herbert Samuel, then the High Commissioner, remarked that the University of Jerusalem would combine with the whole body of knowledge the search for the spiritual, which is indigenous to the soil of Palestine. Both were proved right.

The first President of the University, Dr Judah Magnes, who had been a Reform—and later a Conservative—rabbi in America, gave his vision of the Hebrew University at the opening of the Institute of Jewish Studies.

> We want the University to be a place where Judaism in all its phases can be studied, but where at the same time it is possible to study the humanities and that which constitutes our modern civilization. Not here Judaism, and there humanity, but rather fusion of the two into a harmonious whole, an enriched and enlarged Judaism, an enriched and enlarged humanity. It is our purpose to reverse the social process of a past century, not assimilation among the peoples, but the absorption into Judaism of mankind's spiritual treasures. We want, with the aid of a scholarly research, to look on humanity through our own eyes, unblinded by a bondage to its machinery and its material achievement.

That was one conception of the University. There was the other, of a University which should be a general institution of higher learning, dealing with the natural sciences, the economic and political sciences, medicine and law and all the subjects of a modern university, with Hebrew as the medium of instruction. Both are on the way to fulfilment and the University "gives spirit to those who live in the land".

One aspect of historic Judaism is strikingly manifested in the University: the love of learning, which has been an instrument of Jewish survival. The demand for higher education and adult education strains the capacity of the teachers. Characteristically, the heads of the military forces who have not had the opportunity of a university education, retire in order to study and obtain an academic degree. The same desire holds for those in the diplomatic or civil service who are not university graduates.

In the early years of the State a university, named after a religious leader, Bar-Ilan, was founded by the religious party, the Mizrachi, near Tel Aviv on a religious basis. Teachers and students are required to be observant Jews, and every student is required to include in his course Jewish studies. The multiplication of talmudic schools (*yeshivot*) in the land has been remarkable. The destruction of the seats of Jewish learning and mystical contemplation in central and eastern Europe induced the surviving teachers and disciples to come to Israel and renew the ancient tradition with little or no incursion of modernity. The number of students is not less than that of the scholars in the secular universities together. And the *yeshiva* not less than the University prepares teachers of Judaism for the dispersion. Its students are an aristocracy of the old religious learning.

The principal cultural contribution of Palestine Jewry, after the University, in the period of the mandate was the development of the Hebrew school and the system of Hebrew education. Hebrew was not just another idiom added to those in which Jews of the dispersion had developed their culture: Yiddish, the German dialect, which was carried in the Middle Ages from western to eastern Europe and in modern times to America; Ladino, the Spanish–Castilian dialect, which was carried by the expelled Sephardim in the fifteenth century to the countries of the Levant; and Judeo-Arabic, which was developed by a large part of the oldest dispersion in countries under Muslim rule and was the literary language of the Golden Age of Jewish–Arab civilization. Hebrew was both the expression and the instrument of the renaissance, and the Hebraization of the schools was a first step in that renaissance.

The struggle for its acceptance as the main language of instruction in primary and secondary schools began indeed some years before the First World War. It was conducted by a handful of enthusiasts led by the single-minded Ben Yehuda, an immigrant from Russia, for whom the language was life. It was waged against the foreign Jewish philanthropic bodies, the *Alliance Israélite* of France, the *Anglo-Jewish Association* of Britain, and particularly the *Hilfsverein der Deutschen Juden* of Germany who together were responsible for the principal secondary schools in the towns. Each of these educational agencies wanted their schools in Palestine to give a large part of the general education in its respective language—French, English, German. The latest in the field, the *Hilfsverein*, was the most insistent on this condition. As the authority for the direction of the first polytechnic, at Haifa—commonly known as the Technion—it resolved that German should be the language of instruction for both technical and general subjects. Their resolution led to a strike of the Palestine teachers in all their schools and to a determined effort to establish independent Hebrew high schools. The polytechnic itself, boycotted by the students, was an empty fabric till the events of the Second World War resolved the struggle between the Teutonizers and the latter-day Maccabees. The rebels aspired to a Hebrew-speaking people, nurtured in a Hebrew foundation and conscious of a national unity through the common language, instead of a collection of Russian, French and German Jews. They prevailed and illustrated the truth of Herzl's maxim: the return to Judaism—or Jewishness—must precede the return to the land. At least it must coincide with it.

Another early institution of the Hebrew renaissance was the Hebrew secondary school in Tel Aviv which started in 1909 as the all-Jewish suburb of Jaffa. Tel Aviv quickly became the largest town in Palestine and Israel, and it was notable that the first building of the suburb, and for fifty years its principal public and cultural institution, was the "gymnasium". It was the gift of an English Zionist. The outlook and curriculum of the school were secular but the Hebrew Bible provided the foundation of their studies. If its first teachers were almost aggressively non-religious, the influence of the Bible could not fail to stir a fresh feeling for Judaism, different from that of the traditional ghetto school.

The Hebrew basis and Hebrew influence were immensely expanded in the schools during the period of the British Mandate. It was a great help that the British administration, like the Ottoman, left the provision for education to the autonomous Jewish community, exercising only broad supervision and inspection, mainly by Jews, and making a modest grant-in-aid to the budget. In the early years of the British regime the main financial help came from the Jewish Agency for Palestine, representing the Jewish communities of the world and invested by the Mandate with the right and duty to co-operate with the government in building the National Home. After the responsible National Committee, elected by the Jewish community, was firmly established, the primary responsibility devolved on it and was executed by a national education committee. The religious and secular parties of the population were fairly represented. The budget of the primary schools was mainly met by rates levied on the local Jewish communities. The budget of the secondary and vocational schools, on the other hand, continued to be contributed by foreign Jewish bodies, but with a growing recognition of Hebrew and the national spirit.

With the talent for sectional and party division, which is endemic in the Children of Israel at this stage of transition, the education soon developed four distinct and competing "trends", as they were called, in the Jewish public system. The General Trend, which was the largest, provided for secular education without political or religious bias. The Labour Trend was directed to inculcating knowledge of the Socialist movement and its principles. The Mizrachi, or Religious, Trend laid emphasis on the traditional religious teaching and inculcated religious observance. The schoolday must begin with prayer, the teachers must be observant and believing Jews, and a large part of the lessons must be devoted to Talmud and the subjects of traditional learning in the old ghetto schools. Lastly the Agudah Trend emphasized still more the traditional learning. Each Trend had its own administrative staff and its own inspectors. For good measure a fifth section was recognized, the No-Trend, which was eclectic. Near the end of the Mandate the British government appointed a committee to survey the Jewish education system and report on its possible unification. The committee recommended the abolition of the trends, but the Mandate came to an end before the report could be implemented.

It was left to the sovereign government of Israel in 1950 to legislate for a simplified system of public education which recognized a division into general and religious public schools, and provided that one-quarter of the school time might be given optionally either to rabbinical or to socialist studies. The public school system comprised two parallel streams: state education, and state-religious education, each with its own educational staff. A law of 1952 abolished the Trend system and the affiliation of schools to political parties, and allowed the parents to choose the type of school. The fundamentalist Agudah group contracted out of the public system and conducted their schools on strictly orthodox lines.

Some years later the need was recognized for introducing in the general schools a subject, Jewish consciousness, which was designed to give knowledge of the principles and development of Judaism as a religion and a way of life as well as of post-biblical Jewish history from the destruction of the State by the Romans to the present century. Responsible leaders in Israel were worried by the growing estrangement of the Israel youth from the youth of the dispersion. The aim of the pedagogic innovation was to strengthen the moral attachment of the youth to Jewry through appreciation of the common destiny and the historic continuity which has united Jews the world over in all generations and in all countries. For Jews, more than for any other people, past and present cannot be dissociated. The boys and girls who were not brought up as observant Jews in their home should at least know about the religion and why Jews were a religious people. The practical experience with the subject hitherto has not been altogether encouraging. Many of the teachers were ill-trained in the subject, and some of them had an anti-religious bias. But the need for teaching about the Jewish heritage is acknowledged.

Israelis as well as Jews of the dispersion must intensify the consciousness of the Jewish heritage, of the common destiny that unites all sections, and of the vision of the redemption of Jews and humanity. The integration of Israel with the outer Jewish world is a primary aim. What the grandparents knew, and the parents try to forget, the grandchildren of this generation should recall. Moreover, the introduction of the subject of Jewish consciousness into the schools should help to build a bridge between three groups in Israel: the religious, those with a secular outlook, and the children of the Oriental communities with their attachment to tradition.

An ideological conference was held in Jerusalem in 1957, on the initiative of Mr Ben-Gurion, head of the government. The wise men of Jewry from many countries were invited to consider the broad issues arising out of the unity of the Jewish people. Ben-Gurion, opening the conference, suggested that all sections regard the return of Israel as a messianic movement fulfilling the mission of Israel's Hebrew prophets. The heart of Israel's faith and the source of its brimming constructive energy was the messianic hope that is not purely religious. The conference resolved that every loyal Jew must know Hebrew, which will become the common language between Israel and Jews outside Israel, and he must be Hebraized by the influence of the Hebraic renaissance. The spreading of Jewish day schools using Hebrew in the dispersion is remarkable.

We have seen that an original constructive educational inspiration distinguished the schools of the *aliyah* of Children and Youth, which were spread over the country after 1933. That enterprise of child rescue was designed to bring to the land of Israel the young Jewish generation of Germany and central Europe who were faced with frustration and discrimination in their native country, and bring them up for a productive life with emphasis on cultivation of the soil. It was extended to cover the under-privileged children coming from all countries, and by the thirtieth anniversary of its foundation had rescued and absorbed 120,000 young persons from all parts of the world and from all classes, and converted a large part of them to be pioneers for whom Judaism meant a productive way of life. The call "Save the Children" went home to the Jewish people everywhere. The funds for the large continuous operation of rescue came in large part from their contribution. Before the State of Israel was established, the Zionist Organization, the *yishuv* of Palestine and the philanthropic bodies and communities of the Diaspora were partners in the building of the National Home, the settlement of immigrants on the land, and the cultural renaissance. The issue of the religious education of the immigrant children, which involved the relation of State and Synagogue, caused the break-up of the first coalition government of Israel in 1951 and the dissolution of the first Assembly. Yet, whatever the differences between the parties about the choice of religious or less religious schools, the common aim accepted by all was to create a generation of productive workers. When the British Mandate came to its end in 1948 half the Jews in Palestine were engaged in productive enterprise. The foundation of the National Home was well and truly laid.

CIVIL AND RELIGIOUS LAW IN ISRAEL

The law of Israel is still in large part the law of mandated Palestine. The first legislative act of the Provisional Council of the State of Israel, in May 1948, laid down: "The law which existed in Palestine on 14 May 1948, shall remain in force in so far as there is nothing therein repugnant to this Ordinance, or to the other laws which may be enacted by or on behalf of the Provisional Council." The law of Palestine under the British Mandate was itself a mixture of the Ottoman law, which was in force at the time of the British occupation, and legislation modelled on English statutes. The ultimate source was the substance of the English common law and the doctrines of equity. The English administration left in force the Ottoman code of civil law known as the *mejelle*—meaning a code—which embodied Muslim religious norms and contained the rules about contracts, sales, and the like, but not about matters of personal status, which are governed by the laws of the different religious communities. It was an example of British conservatism that the *mejelle* remained in force throughout the period of the mandate, though in the Muslim-Turkish State of Atatürk it was replaced by a modern Europeanized code.

The Ottoman law with regard to land also remained in force, during the mandate period, with some substantial amendments. The criminal law, commercial law, civil and criminal procedure, and the rules of evidence, which had been prescribed in "Frenchified" codes, were replaced by legislation on English lines. And many principles of the English common law and equity were introduced in Palestine by judgments of the Palestine courts over which British judges presided, sitting with Arab and Jewish members, or by the Judicial Committee of the Privy Council of England, which was the ultimate Court of Appeal. Broadly, Palestine became a member of the great family of the common law.

The creation of the State of Israel was bound to affect the fundamental issue of the law of the land and the religious law. In the mandate period, Jewish law—in Hebrew *halakhah*, which means the right way—was applied by rabbinical tribunals, in accordance with the terms of the mandate and of the constitution of Palestine in certain, but not in all, matters of personal status of Palestinian Jews. It covered particularly marriage and divorce, and wills and charitable trusts drawn up in Jewish form. It could be also applied, with the consent of all parties concerned, to other matters of personal status, such as succession, and to matters of personal status affecting Jews who were foreign subjects, but with the exception that a rabbinical tribunal could not grant a divorce by Jewish law to such persons. Civil marriage was possible where one party or both were foreign subjects, by a ceremony at a consulate. And, as in Ottoman times, a rabbi or a religious arbitration tribunal, with the consent of both parties, could decide disputes in general civil matters between Jews.

The jurisdiction of the official Rabbinate in personal status was made more exclusive in the State than it had been under the mandatory government, by an agreement between the religious and the secular parties of the coalition government. The kernel of the coalition government has always been the secular Mapai, the party from which the Prime Minister and the other principal ministers are regularly drawn. It was agreed with the religious parties in the coalition that the rabbinical law of marriage should apply to all Jews resident in Israel, whether Israeli citizens or not. The effect was to make it impossible for an Israeli Jew to marry a non-Jew since the rabbinical law forbids such a union. No civil marriage has been introduced, and the rabbinical authorities refuse to recognize the validity of a civil marriage of a Jew celebrated abroad in a country where such marriage is valid. They reject the application of the rules of Private International Law generally accepted by the comity of Nations, because the Jewish law, as they hold, is divinely revealed, and absolute, and therefore cannot be modified by secular legislation. It applies to Jews wherever they are. In this extreme attitude they are not supported by the civil courts of Israel, and inevitably conflict arises. They are adamant against the introduction of civil marriage in Israel. That would lead to the restriction of marriage between religious and non-religious, and to intermarriage of Jews with Christians or Muslims.

On the other hand, a law of the *knesset* about women's equal rights in all legal matters (succession, guardianship of children, etc.) which is expressly to be applied by the religious as well as by the civil courts, runs counter to the rules of the *halakhah*. It was forced on the government by the weight of Socialist ideology; but the religious parties secured that the law should not affect any prohibition or provision relating to marriage and divorce. Another law, related to it and required by modern social principles, abolished the exemption from a charge of bigamy, accorded in the mandatory government's penal code in favour of members of religious communities which allowed polygamy. They include certain oriental Jewish communities as well as the Muslims. The validity of the law was tested in the supreme court by a Muslim on the ground that it violated freedom of religion. The plea was rejected on the ground that the Muslim religion did not require polygamy, but only permitted it.

The residuary source of law for the courts of the mandatory regime, where Ottoman or Palestine statutes gave no guidance, was the substance of the common law of England and English doctrines of equity. That is no longer the exclusive source, and the courts are entitled to look to the principles of Jewish law in the Bible or later texts. It is remarked, however, that the common law derives its fundamental conceptions, e.g. about human rights and individual freedom, from that very source.

Israel has not a full-fledged constitution or organic law, corresponding with the Palestine Order-in-Council (1922) of the mandatory government, which defined the rights and duties of the organs of government and the fundamental rights of the citizens. It was at first proposed, in accordance with the provisions of the resolution of the United Nations Assembly of 1947, to hold a constituent assembly for that purpose; and a draft constitutional law was published for comment. But after the first *knesset* was elected in January 1949, the Prime Minister, David Ben-Gurion, convinced his Cabinet that Israel should follow the English principle of letting the constitution grow empirically. The religious parties and the Rabbinate were opposed to a constitution that was not based on the religious law (*torah*).

One major decision followed at the end of the same year, that Zion (i.e. Jerusalem) was, and always would be, the capital of the State of Israel. That was in reply to a resolution of the United Nations Assembly to establish an international administration of the city. It was an article of the religious faith shared by all sections. Then in 1950, the fundamental Law of the Return confirmed simply the right of every Jew to return to the country and receive an immigrant permit, which implied the right to settle and become a citizen. Soon that law provoked the question, "Who is a Jew?". It was first raised before the civil courts in the case of a Polish-born Jew who had become a Roman Catholic monk, but was an ardent Israel patriot, and wished to make his home in the land. His claim to registration as a Jew under the Law of Return, and to receive Israel citizenship immediately, was contested, and a majority decision of the High Court rejected his plea. A religious renegade was not a Jew in the common opinion. The term connoted, at least negatively, a person who had not repudiated the religion.

Similar questions arose about the Jewishness of children of a Polish Jew and a Roman Catholic mother who had not been received into the Jewish community in accordance with the stringent rules of the *halakhah*. The rabbinical authority was not prepared to modify the restrictions in the interest of the State or out of consideration of humanity, and the religious parties upheld their attitude.

That intractable issue in the coalition government between the majority of the ministers and the representatives of the religious parties (about the registration of the children of mixed marriages on their arrival as immigrants) arose in 1958. The issue was deemed to involve the relation of the State to the religious law. The Ministry of the Interior, in registering newcomers, prescribed that they should state whether they were Jews. An instruction was issued that an adult or child should be so registered if he declared himself, or was declared by his parent, to be a Jew, and was not a member of another religious creed. If both parents declared that their child was a Jew, that should be regarded as though it were a legal declaration of the child.

Among those who arrived from Poland and Hungary were hundreds of children of mixed marriages, and the mother being Roman Catholic was not, and was not willing to be, received in the Jewish community. The father, however, declared that his children were Jews because he felt himself a Jew and wished his children to be so registered. By the rabbinical law, the child of a non-Jewish mother, who had not been received into the community, was not a Jew. The ministers of the Religious party resigned in protest against the Ministry's instruction, and the Rabbinate denounced it in the most violent terms. It would disrupt the community; and any differentiation between a Jew for secular purposes and a Jew for religious classification would imperil not only Israel but the whole of Jewry. In face of the storm the Prime Minister, Ben-Gurion, decided to postpone the administrative order while he consulted with the rabbinical and lay leaders in, and outside, Israel. He pointed out in his memorandum to those consulted that the law of Israel forbids discrimination between one person and another on account of differences in nationality or religion; but Jews enjoy a special privilege by virtue of the Law of the Return, and for this purpose religion and nationality were separable. The consultation of the sages produced no certain result, and the issue was temporarily avoided.

Since the election in 1949 of the first *knesset*, every government has had to be a coalition, built around the central Labour party, Mapai. The system of proportional representation by *scrutin de listes*, treating the whole country as one constituency, has the inevitable result of making it impossible for any one party to have a majority over all the others. Ben-Gurion, Moshe Sharett, Levi Eshkol, the three heads of Mapai who have held the office of Prime Minister, have had to negotiate, after each general election, about the terms on which they could establish a government with the religious parties. Originally, there were four parties—Mizrachi and their Labour wing, Hapoel Ha-Mizrachi, and Agudat Israel and its Labour wing. For the purpose of some elections they have combined as one bloc and combined in accepting office in the Cabinet. Generally, however, the Agudat Israel, which is the most extreme in its demands for the enforcement of religious rules and practices, has stood out of the coalition. Recently, the two sections of the Mizrachi have coalesced into one party, while the Labour section of the Agudat Israel has been more conciliatory than the other, and has entered the coalition. The condition of entering and supporting the government is always subject to a concession by the more secular-minded Mapai, who must give effect in legislation to some religious demand.

One of the principal controversies between laymen and rabbis arose over the requirement in the law of National Service, 1951, that unmarried women as well as men should be conscripted. The Agudat Israel protested against the application of the law to young women of religious and fundamentalist families, on the ground that it was contrary to the Jewish religious law and threatened the sanctity of the home and the family. The two chief rabbis gave the weight of their authority to support the dissenters. The government first contested the objection on grounds of national security; but when a second coalition was formed by Mapai with the religious parties, a compromise was found and accepted by all but the extreme fundamentalists. A girl or woman of a religious family would do social service in a religious village or district and would not be required to do any military exercises or live away from home. For the irreconcilables the way-out was tacit exemption.

Another fundamental controversy about the relation of Synagogue and State is in regard to legislation. The draft constitution, which was sidetracked, included a vague article providing that new legislation must be in conformity with the basic teaching and ideals of the Mosaic tradition. The religious parties in the State stood for the implementation of the principle. Their demand was that the law should be radically changed to be Mosaic and not *a*mosaic. Some zealots wanted the immediate application of the corpus of rabbinical law compiled in a code and embodying the *halakhah* concerning all the topics of civil law besides personal status. A great part of the religiously observant immigrants, particularly of the Oriental communities, were indifferent about a matter which they hardly understood; and the large majority of members of the *knesset*, including the central and left Labour parties, the Liberals, and the right-wing Nationalists, were united against such a radical measure. Influences from abroad also opposed a sudden and radical change. The existing *halakhah* did not envisage the reality of an independent Jewish state, and made no provision for a secular Jewish government. On the one hand, the religious Jew cannot accept the completely secular basis for a Jewish state, and on the other, he has accepted for centuries the governing axiom that the law of the government is the law. Hitherto that norm has applied to the law of a Gentile country in which Jews lived. But now it is made applicable to the legislation of a Jewish republic.

There is a paradox about the American complaint of a theocracy in Israel. The secular Israeli parties help to maintain a measure of the religious law as part of the state system, while the American–Jewish religious bodies demand in Israel an American pattern of the separation of the Church or Synagogue and the State. Many individuals and groups in Israel stand indeed for ethical standards of Judaism in political and international relations. Several Hebrew journals and one English, the *New Outlook*, are devoted to this theme. And several intellectual leaders of the highest stature, such as Professor Buber, and his disciples Hugo Bergmann and Ernst Simon at the Hebrew University, and the late Dr Judah Magnes, the first President of the Hebrew University, were protagonists for an ethical and altruistic nationalism. The conscience of Israel has been strong in the academic circle. A political group, also, composed of immigrants from Germany, Austria and Czechoslovakia, supported an ethical policy on humanitarian, if not religious, grounds. So also did a non-religious group of *kibbutzim*, the Young Guard, which was attached to the Left Labour wing, Mapam.

Martin Buber posed the dilemma. Can Israel hold faithfully to Jewish moral principles and drive the plough-share of ethics into the hard sod of political fact? The problem of Israel is similar to that of the Indian nation, which professes devotion to the moral principles and peaceful ideals of Gandhi, but cannot apply them in her international relations with her nearest neighbour.

The conflict between the secular and the religious standpoint is fundamental. The religious elements hold to the rabbinical maxim: Israel is a nation only through the Torah. The strictest religious party, the Agudat Israel, questions whether it is legitimate to participate actively in the government of a Jewish State which deviates from the principles of Jewish law. The other religious parties, however, have accepted a *modus vivendi*, by which the application of Jewish law in family matters is assured to those who want it, and as regards marriage and divorce is imposed on all Jews resident in the country, while in other matters the existing law, based on western norms, is temporarily maintained. Although the prevailing principle in Israel is that everything should be done at once, it is generally recognized that the problem of secular and religious law cannot be solved in one generation.

A spokesman for the radical introduction of Jewish law in all civil matters, Professor Leibowitz of the Hebrew University, where he has a Chair, not of Law or Jewish Studies but of Chemistry, urges the development of a new *halakhah* which will be derived from the principles of the existing Jewish law, but will befit an independent Jewish State. He is critical of the standpoint of the present Rabbinate who insist on applying that law rigorously. And he is equally critical of the present compromise, by which Jewish law is the law of the land only in a very limited field.

The young generation should be prepared and trained in *yeshiva* and university for the task of formulating religious laws to govern the nation's policy, as well as the individual's life. That sounds unrealistic, but it is significant as the extreme faith of a Puritan, which may be adapted in time to the reform of the law of the State and of Judaism. It is remarked that the Torah cannot go forth from Zion, unless it has entered Zion.

A small but very vocal dissenting sect, which is not represented in the *knesset*, denies altogether the authority of the secular state. They call themselves "the Guardians of the City", *neturei karta*, and they refuse to do any national service, military or social, because they repudiate a non-religious Jewish authority. They have applied to the United Nations for the establishment of a trusteeship over the territory which is now Israel. Some of them took violent action against those who in their eyes desecrate the Sabbath Day rest by driving a motor vehicle in the Holy City of Jerusalem between sunset on the Friday and sunset on the Saturday. Even if the driver and the passengers are not Jews, they are treated as sinners and transgressors and may be stoned. The administration has sought a way of avoiding grave breaches of peace by closing to traffic on the sabbath certain areas where the "Guardians" live or where there are synagogues. While not prohibiting, by legislation, the use of private transport on the Sabbath Day, it enforces the closing of shops and industries and the stoppage of public transport by sea or air.

As regards public motor-transport, it leaves the regulation to the municipal authority; and in Haifa, where the residential areas extend over the steep Carmel heights, and where the local religious party is small, buses are permitted on the sabbath. The State also prohibits the import of any meat which is not of an animal ritually killed (*kāshēr*) and it prohibits the breeding of pigs and the selling of pig-food by Jews. In the army camps and barracks, the navy and air force, the feeding is ordered according to Jewish law. Israel is not then a completely secular State; but its Parliament has regard to religious institutes which have the sanction of history.

Like Great Britain, Israel favours a pragmatic mixture. It would be inconceivable that Judaism, which has kept the Jewish people alive, united them through the centuries, and is a strong link today between Israel and the Diaspora, should have no place in the constitution of the State and be regarded purely as a matter for the individual. The dissociation of religion from the State would be fundamentally opposed to the spirit of Judaism, which repudiates the distinction of religious and secular. There is in fact a compromise between two schools.

Besides the driving of motor-cars in Jerusalem on the Sabbath Day, another head of offence for the Rabbinate was the opening in Jerusalem of a mixed bathing pool for males and females. The pool was attached to a hotel which professed to be "religious", and the rabbis threatened to cancel its certificate of fitness for observant Jewish visitors. In view of that threat the proprietor had to compromise and fix different times for men's and women's bathing. Recently, too, there has been agitation by the religious parties over the use of corpses for study of anatomy in the medical schools. A bill was submitted to the Israel *knesset* designed to put restrictions on the practice; but so far no law has been enacted.

Jewish law lost touch with reality in the nineteenth century, after the civil emancipation of the Jews, by which they became subjects of the civil law of the country where they lived. The attempt must now be made to bring it in touch with reality once more. A systematic digest has been undertaken by the Institute of Research for Jewish Law, attached to the Law Faculty of the Hebrew University. The reform of the Law of Israel is to be made piecemeal, starting with the replacement of the Ottoman code of civil law with its Muslim basis.

The Israeli legislator is thoroughly eclectic in his models, which may be English, European, or American, as well as Jewish, but the two main sources are Jewish law and English law, the one for national, the other for historical reasons. The process of gradual reception of English law, which marked the period of the mandate, has been checked by Israel's independence, but the norms of the common law have taken root and cannot be suddenly discarded. Jewish law at present is fully applied only in matters of personal status, and even there the civil authorities keep it within bounds and in matters of marriage make it subject to rules of the civil law involving public policy. Thus the marriage of a girl below the age of seventeen is made a criminal offence, though the rabbinic law allows a younger girl to be wedded. The Dean of the Law Faculty of the Hebrew University has pointed out that in an indirect way Jewish law constantly influences the Israeli legislator. In the first place he borrows from the Talmud and the *Responsa* his vocabulary and style. Hebrew, and also Aramaic, the language of much of the Talmud, are admirably suited to the concise formulation of legal norms. So Jewish law "exercises an influence beyond its immediate usefulness; and pragmatism yields to the appeal of National sentiment" (see Ginossar, "Israel Law", in *Israel Law Review*, 1966, p. 380).

The government has contrived to avoid an out-and-out conflict (*Kulturkampf*, as it is called) with the religious parties and the religious authorities. It has made these concessions to the public opinion of a large section of the nation for the enforcement of practices which are both national and religious. On the other hand, the restrictions on marriage and divorce and on Sabbath transport, are attacked by a section of non-religious citizens forming a league against religious coercion, as well as by bodies in the dispersion, claiming to be upholders of Judaism. They demand the separation of Synagogue and State on the American pattern, regardless of the essential character of historical Judaism. Josephus, the Jewish historian of the first century, proudly asserted that the Jewish State was a Theocracy. They are regardless also of a fundamental distinction of Judaism, that it covers the whole of life, moral, social and national.

Paradoxically, the recognition of Jewish law remains much as it was under the British Mandate. What is novel is that the Rabbinate and the local religious councils are State institutes, supported by State funds, instead of being the institutes of an autonomous religious community within a gentile State. Individual Jews, moreover, may no longer contract out of the jurisdiction of the religious authority in these matters of personal status.

As in the mandate time, the civil courts execute the judgment of the religious tribunals. That gives them the opportunity to control the rabbinical judges, if there has been an excess of jurisdiction by them. On the other hand, the civil authority may come to the help of the religious and enforce a decree in a matter of personal status. So, if a man party to a divorce suit refuses to carry out the order of the rabbinical court to give a bill of Divorcement—*get*—to the wife, which by Jewish law is an essential procedure, the Attorney-general of the government may apply for a warrant of arrest and get an order for his imprisonment for contempt of court till he obeys. That should be a more effective measure of execution than the old practice before the establishment of the State, by which the rabbinical authority could excommunicate the recalcitrant party.

Israel maintains a Ministry of Religions which is responsible for seeing to the religious requirements of the Jewish population, rabbis, synagogues, and ritual equipment. The rabbis, *dayyānīm* (judges of the rabbinical tribunals) and other religious officials are paid by the Ministry. The judges are appointed by the President of the State, on the recommendation of a panel comprising rabbinical and lay members. The Jewish section of the Ministry is closely associated with the Jewish religious parties, and broadly supports their claims. It is a consequence of the political system, which also has come down from the mandatory regime, that the battle about religious values is fought in the Israel political arena by parties which are secular or religious, and are concerned over political rather than philosophical or theological issues. The reproach is levelled by both sides that the fundamental questions are not argued out fundamentally, but for the most part are decided empirically, and sometimes for reasons of political expediency.

Outside the sphere of ritual observance and personal status, Judaism in its ethical aspects of social justice has a growing and less controversial influence on the life of the people. A chief motive of the return to the land and of the establishment of the National Home was to form a society where ideals of social justice, prominent in the Torah of Moses and the books of the Hebrew prophets, would be more fully realized than in existing national states. A step was taken towards that goal in mandatory Palestine when the biblical law about the land being owned not privately, but on behalf of the nation, was applied voluntarily by the Zionist movement's governing bodies. They carried out the command in Leviticus: "The land shall not be sold for ever, for it is Mine, saith the Lord, and ye are sojourners with Me." The Jewish National Fund, *keren kayemeth leisrael*, which was instituted in the early years of the century to acquire land in the country or in town for settlement, afforestation, and cultural institutions, was the largest landowner. It granted leases for a period up to forty-nine years to individuals or groups, and provided an effective system of the voluntary nationalization of land. The State of Israel, by a statute on the law of land and land administration, has given legally binding effect to the principle which is now applicable, first to all lands of the Fund that is still maintained, and then to the land owned by government, including former Arab agricultural areas which it sequestrated. Another statute of the *knesset*, which imports into the welfare state a principle derived from the rabbinical development of charity, places the responsibility on the family for the well-being of its members even to distant relations, and goes far beyond normal family liability.

A third statute, the Wages Protection Law 1958, designed to ensure prompt payment of the worker's salary, was clearly inspired by a command of the Mosaic law: "The wages of a hired servant shall not abide with thee all night until the morning" (Lev. xix. 13). It is put still more strongly in Deuteronomy: "Thou shalt not oppress the hired servant that is poor, whether he be of thy brethren or of the sojourners that are in thy land within the gates. In his day thou shalt give him his hire, neither shall the sun go down upon it" (Deut. xxiv. 14).

A major statute on a matter of personal status, replacing both the religious law and the civil law of succession after death, was enacted by the mandatory government. It is the outcome of many years' discussion in and out of the *knesset*; and it is a characteristic mixture of Jewish, English and Continental legal ideas. The purely religious law of succession may still be invoked if all parties concerned in the succession and having legal capacity consent, but that will be rare. A far-reaching family law, embracing other incidents of personal status, like the guardianship and adoption of children, has also been presented for years to the attention of a legislative committee of the *knesset*, but is not yet ready for enactment. The *knesset* is adopting parts of it in stages. In these matters the *knesset* acts on the maxim, hasten slowly. The Ministry of Justice includes a special department of research in Jewish law, which was created for the purpose of tracing principles in rabbinical *responsa* that may be suitable for projected legislation on all manner of subjects. The Faculty of Law of the Hebrew University likewise includes an institute for projects of research in the *mishpaṭ 'ibri* (Jewish Law); and every student in the Faculty is required to study Jewish law throughout his four years' course.

From its establishment in 1948 the Supreme Court of Israel has regularly included one or two masters in the rabbinical jurisprudence who can enlighten their brothers on the bench when some gap in the law appears, and the claims of the English common law, the Roman system, and the Jewish system to close the gap must be weighed. The earliest of them, Rav Assaf, was at that time Professor of Medieval Jewish Jurisprudence and also Rector of the University; he had been formerly head of a *yeshiva* in Russia. He made a distinctive contribution to supplement the references to the British judicial precedents by quoting rules on the subject in the rabbinical law. The preparation for the introduction of rabbinical law, and the ethic embodied in it in the civil law are sufficiently safeguarded. Of greater moment is the extent to which the biblical ideas of social justice, which are an unfailing theme for perorations of speakers, are actually effective in the policy of the State. As regards internal affairs the record is encouraging. As regards external relations with the Arab peoples, however, the paramount need for survival and the intransigence of the Arab rulers have hitherto prevented the application of the ethical law of Judaism. During the thirty years of the British Mandate, many earnest attempts were made on the Jewish side to get together with the Arabs. The Jewish protagonists, led by Dr Magnes and Martin Buber, endeavoured to establish personal friendships with moderate Arab leaders. In the first decade of the mandate the Society called *brit shalom*, the Covenant of Peace, which included several leaders of the *yishuv*, seemed to be making progress. But the grave disturbances of 1929, of which the immediate cause was a dispute about the Jewish right of worship at the Wall of the Jerusalem Temple, put the clock back and led on to the Arab revolt of 1936–9. Another earnest effort was made during the Second World War by a Society, *iḥud* (meaning Unity), which included a few leading Arabs as well as the Jews who led the earlier effort. Their programme was a bi-national Jewish–Arab State as an alternative to partition of the little country. But that, too, failed. It was not found possible to raise political differences to a higher religious or spiritual plane. The crucial question was a limit to the number of Jewish immigrants, which might give assurance to the Arab majority of the inhabitants of Palestine that they would not become a minority, and then gradually be dispossessed of their land, which was a genuine fear. Finally came the decision of the Assembly of the United Nations for partition, and during the last six months of the British Mandate a state of civil war and terrorism broke out, culminating in the invasion by the Arab armies of the territory allotted to Israel. Bitter fighting was accompanied by the flight of the larger part of the Arab population who were seized with panic.

It was a tragic irony that the return of Jews to their historic land, which was associated in the prophet Isaiah's vision with the establishment of peace on earth and the coming of the Messiah, has been in fact accompanied by the misery of the former population and a continuous cold war. George Eliot, the first famous Christian writer of the English-speaking world to herald the return, writing some ninety years ago, saw "...the new Judea, poised between East and West, as a covenant of reconciliation and a halting-place of enmities". That seems today *sancta simplicitas*. The rabbis of the Rabbinical Council in Israel, who might be expected to be the "spiritual spokesmen", and who are profoundly concerned over small points of the Torah, had no message about the Arab refugees, based on the Hebrew Ethic. The moral aspect of a vast human problem was sounded in Israel by lay individuals and groups, and was not a matter affecting the public conscience. However, the journal of the *iḥud* Society, named *ner* (Light), though with little support, keeps up the struggle. Some of those who urge the adoption of Jewish law, and notably Professor Leibowitz, have been outspoken in protesting against the policy of reprisals on Arab villages.

In Israel the battle is joined in the minds of responsible leaders, educationists and teachers, between the particularist and universalist conception struggling for supremacy. Stress is laid now on national aspects and now on universal. Inevitably, the national aspect has been strong in this period of cold war between Israel and the Arab States.

Israel's statehood has had a revolutionary effect in the way of law, the administration of justice, social life and, most acutely, defence. The necessary conditions for the rebirth of ethical Judaism will be created when the ideas and ideals of the religion are put to the test of political reality demanding political responsibility. An American sociologist observed that the State of Israel has not yet cherished the moral and spiritual values which distinguished the Jews when they were a minority people in dispersion, and when they were building up the National Home under the rule and protection of England. As an independent State, they have, like other national states, placed national security above other considerations. Yet it would be premature to dismiss the messianic hope after less than two decades of Israel's statehood. Israel must, as a primary aim, pursue peace with her neighbours for realistic, no less than idealistic, reasons. As soon as the opportunity is given, it may set the example of altruistic nationalism, which aims to apply the principle of loving thy neighbour in international as well as in internal relations. Israel may provide the seed-ground from which a great religious leader may spring and give fresh inspiration to Israelis, and through them to humanity. If only she can find a way of understanding with the Arabs, it may usher in "the time of the Jews".

ISRAEL AND THE DISPERSION: RELIGIOUS STIRRINGS

There is a religious stirring today among Jews in all the countries where they form a considerable community, but especially in Israel. The accent of the religion has shifted from Torah and ritual to the social sphere. In the little land they have created new social institutions. The most notable of them is the *kibbutz*, which has gained a fresh appeal from the discovery, soon after the foundation of the State, of documents from a buried monastery by the shores of the Dead Sea, dating probably from a century before the Christian era. They indicate that the communal way of life was pursued by a Jewish sect 2,000 years ago; and that gives to the present-day development the *aura* of history for a history-conscious nation.

No fresh formulation of belief and religious practice has yet been adopted in Israel, but it is significant that Professor Arnold Toynbee, who, in his *Study of History*, was highly critical of the narrowness and exclusiveness of Judaism, has had a change of heart since the Nazis' mass murder of the Jews and the attempt of genocide on the one hand, and the establishment of the Jewish National Home on the other, caused a fresh dispersal and a fresh concentration. Judaism can no longer be dismissed as a "fossil of Syrian civilization". Toynbee himself suggests that, just as the Jews returning from the Babylonian captivity to Judea were conscious of being the bearers of a universal religion and carried it to the peoples of the Persian and later the Hellenistic and Roman empires, so the Jewish survivors of the Nazi holocaust in Europe, and Jews from the oriental countries emigrating to Palestine, may again be conscious that they have a spiritual message for mankind, hungry for it in a materialistic and distracted age. Toynbee stresses, indeed, that, in order to carry out their destiny as carriers of a universal monotheist religion, Jews must abandon nationalism and independent statehood. He stresses also that Israel has been established wrongfully at the expense of the former majority of the inhabitants of Palestine, the Arabs. Events have moved fast, and his vision of a denationalized missionary Jewish people seems unreal. The Jews from all parts of the world are being steadily welded into a nation living in free conditions, as they have not been for nearly 2,000 years. And they will surely not give up this freedom.

They are conscious, too, of a mission to other developing nations in Asia and Africa, with whom they multiply contacts by educational and social missions. It is striking that Theodor Herzl, the founder of the modern Zionist movement, in his novel *Alt-Neuland*, which is a picture of what the National Home should be, foresaw that the Jews would take a lead in helping the cultural development of the African negroes. The African and Asiatic nations, which look to Israel for technical and social know-how, have been particularly impressed by the social philosophy of the *kibbutz* which liberated the young generation from the thraldom of money. Some of them have sent youth parties to live for a period in a *kibbutz* and bring back the fruit of that experience to their country.

A special development of the *kibbutz* is inspired by Ben-Gurion, the Prime Minister for sixteen years, who has retired to a settlement in the heart of the arid Negev. Here he has established a college and attracts to it some of the best of the Israel-born youth. They train to be teachers who will go to the frontier settlements where life is rough and hard, or to developing countries, or to Jewish communities abroad. He believes that the desert Negev turns an ordinary person into a creative being. The College of Sdeh Boker will prepare an élite of emissaries or apostles of the new way of life.

One branch of the *kibbutz* movement, while sharing the Socialist faith, exemplifies a trend back towards traditional Judaism. It is called *Bachad*, being the initial letters of the Hebrew words for "League of Religious Comrades". The members are observant Jews, combining Socialist conduct with cultivation of the soil and Jewish studies and faithfully carrying out the practice of traditional Judaism. Their motto is Torah—the religious teaching—and '*avodah*—physical labour;

and their aim is a religious life rooted in the soil and taken to the factory and the field. Torah is the way of life, including the life of agricultural pioneers. At the same time they are in the vanguard of those who want reform of the Jewish law, or widening of its scope, to suit the conditions of the modern State.

In the latter years of the British administration of Palestine the Jewish struggle for independence was itself the religion of a large part of the young people. After independence was won and the State established, many found that nationalism was not enough. They needed a more universal idea for a philosophy of life, and sought it in a harkback to fundamental ideas of Judaism. Neither nationalism nor socialism in the long run is a substitute for religion.

It would be a false picture to suggest that Judaism, the religion, is being revived everywhere in Israel. It is indeed in a state of flux and many old, as well as new, controversies have yet to find a solution. In western Europe and in America, the Orthodox and the Reform congregations during the early years of the twentieth century were engaged in a constant struggle for the soul of the Jewish emancipated population from eastern Europe. The Orthodox rabbis strove to maintain the hold of the Torah and the *halakhah*, with the "hedges" erected round the Mosaic law to protect it. They held also to the faith in the restoration of the Jewish people to the land of Israel, but did little about it. The Reform and Liberal rabbis were strongly international and claimed that the Jews were a purely religious brotherhood who by their dispersion had an ethical mission to the world; but they did little about the mission. The attitude of both Orthodox and Reformers changed when the mandate for the establishment of the Jewish National Home in Palestine was conferred on Great Britain by the world society of the League of Nations, and later, when Hitler's persecution intensified the desperate need for a country of refuge. Both sections strengthened the Zionist following, and many Zionist leaders in the United States were rabbis of the traditional synagogues and Reform temples. Only a small clique, with the deceptive title of the "American Council for Judaism", sustained a bitter opposition to the Zionist movement.

The controversies of the former generations of Jews in the Diaspora about the ritual, the form of synagogue worship, or the national character of Judaism have today resumed their relevance and their tensions. The present issue concerns mainly the form of synagogue worship, but it may open up more fundamental aspects. Many of those who have come to Israel from western Europe, the British Commonwealth and America, have been used to a Sabbath and festival service which, though based on the tradition, is more selective and in many details differs from it. They are repelled by a lack of order and decorum in the old-fashioned and un-Reformed congregation. They permit also the seating of men and women together, and the use of instrumental music. Their minister, when they have one, is less exacting in the admission of proselytes and about certain marriage practices such as the levirate, the rule requiring a childless widow to marry the deceased husband's brother, unless he renounces his right. Some of the new congregations are Conservative; some Reform. The official Rabbinate, supported by the religious parties in the government, has hitherto refused to recognize the Reformed congregations as Jews. They have withheld from several of the Reform rabbis a licence to celebrate marriages of their members; and they have put obstacles in the way of the Reformers obtaining rooms for their service, and even building a hall of their own. Freedom of religious worship, by a strange paradox, is denied to an earnest body of Jews in Israel, because they diverge a little from the narrow way.

The Rabbinate, which rigidly rejects any religious diversity, is fighting a rear-guard action. The groups which want a Reform ordering of public worship steadily grow, and not only among the western Jews. Some groups of Oriental Jews are antagonistic to the Rabbinate, because of its refusal to accept their capacity to marry Jews of other communities save after individual inquiry. They have applied for affiliation to the Progressive Synagogue whose attitude is more humane. What makes the Progressive programme more significant in Israel is that it is an honest seeking for an acceptable form of synagogue worship, which is not induced by any desire to imitate the form of worship of a non-Jewish environment.

The clash over the right of Reform and Progressive rabbis in Israel to celebrate a marriage of their members was extended, and became an international question, by the refusal of the Rabbinate of the Establishment to recognize as valid marriages of Jews celebrated abroad by such rabbis. That action was calculated to estrange the sympathy of a large section of the American and other English-speaking Jewish communities. If persisted in, it would probably have meant a serious reduction of the material support from those countries for Israel's needs. In fact, the

Rabbinate, while making no formal abandonment of its attitude, has not sought to press it. However unyielding the Orthodox rabbis may be in their professions, they have, as established officials of the State, to take account of the necessity for the Israel government to retain the goodwill and practical help of all sections of Jews of the Diaspora, including the Progressives.

Mr Shalom Ben-Horin, originally from Germany, was the pioneer of the "progressive" Jewish service. He was a student of the Hebrew University of Jerusalem and found a response first among the students, and then among a few older members of the *yishuv*. He began by conducting the services in Hillel House, the students' club, and after a year or so it was possible to form a small congregation in Jerusalem and obtain a permanent building, and add to the services lectures and social gatherings. Hebrew is the language of all the service, including the sermon. The Jerusalem congregation in the latter years has had a regular minister. The first was an Algerian Jew who had been the leader of the Progressive movement in Paris. The example of Jerusalem has been followed in Tel Aviv, Haifa, the new Jewish quarter of Nazareth, and the township of Kfar Shmaryahu in the plain of Sharon north of Tel Aviv.

At Haifa, also, a religious secondary school on the lines of Progressive Judaism flourishes. It is called after Rabbi Leo Baeck, the saintly spiritual leader of German Jewry in the terrible period of Nazi persecution.

Professor Mordecai M. Kaplan, founder of the Movement of Jewish Reconstruction in America, who was for many years a teacher at the Hebrew University of Jerusalem, has commented on the inflexibility of the Israel Rabbinate in its interpretation of the *halakhah* for the reborn Jewish Nation, which might hope for mitigation of the ghetto strictness. His own movement in America has the aim of bringing Judaism to terms with the revolutionary advance of natural science. Israel is focal in the reconstruction of Judaism, and indispensible as the centre of Jewish civilization. At present, however, Israel is suffering from a retarded spiritual development, which is the harder to bear because the people—in their economic, political, and cultural development—show outstanding powers of growth and progress. If we want Judaism to be again a universal faith, its religious civilization must be relevant to the present world situation and climate of opinion. The Jewish people, he holds, can reform their way of life in the land of

Israel only in such a way as to make it acceptable to the communities of the dispersion; and he himself is a mediator between Israel and American Jewry.

The demand is raised from various sources for the convening of a *sanhedrin*, or a rabbinical council representing all sections of Jewry, such as the *sanhedrin* which, in the days of the Second Temple, guided the religious life and in the autonomous Jewish communities of the Middle Ages in the Christian and Muslim realms gave rulings on religious problems. The last *sanhedrin* was the historic assembly of French and Alsatian Jews, convened on the orders of Napoleon Bonaparte to answer questions affecting the civil and political emancipation of the Jewish population. Its complacent answers, repudiating Jewish nationalism, prepared the way for the acceptance of the Jews as citizens and for the assimilation of the life and culture of their Gentile neighbours, which in the nineteenth century marked the Jewish population of western Europe. An Israel *sanhedrin*, if and when it is assembled, would have a very different task. It would be asked to propose modifications of the *halakhah* which would adapt it to modern thought and to the actual conditions of life in Israel. But in view of the existing outlook of the Rabbinate, the time is perhaps not quite ripe for such an assembly in this generation. The present heads of the rabbinical hierarchy are still tied to the old dogmas.

Rav Kook, the first Ashkenazi chief rabbi of Palestine during the British Mandate, and himself both profound scholar and devout mystic, had a more constructive perception of the need for development of the *halakhah* than his successors in that office. A story is told that a delegation of rabbis came to him sorely troubled that the Jewish boys were playing football in public places on the sabbath afternoon. They begged him to issue an order denouncing the desecration of the sabbath. He gently reproached them and told how, in the days of the Temple, the workers who were repairing the structure were allowed into the Holy of Holies. So these youths, who were working to rebuild the National Home, should be allowed to transgress the *halakhah* concerning permitted and forbidden work on the Holy Day, so that they might enjoy their day of leisure. That is the spirit which, it may be hoped, will inspire those who are searching for the reconciliation of the *halakhah* with modern life.

If a *sanhedrin* is not convened to reform the *halakhah*, it is likely that a religious section will be formed which, while rejecting the present rabbinical insistence on the existing *halakhah*, will seek to formulate a way of life more in accord with the conditions of our day. One grave defect of the *halakhah* is the discrimination against the Gentile in the Jewish law, as it was developed in the harsh circumstances of the Roman and Christian persecutions. The failure of the Rabbinate and the religious political parties to oppose the reprisal policy of the government against Arab guerillas may be due in part to their acceptance of two standards of conduct, to Jews and to Gentiles.

The religious reformation which will be inspired in Israel in due course, will not be an assimilation of Judaism to the faith and practices of the non-Jewish environment, as it was largely in Europe and America, but a creation of a more natural form of worship and ceremonial, in accord with the life and thinking of a diverse and free people. It is likely to include a return to some of the traditional institutions which were hastily rejected by the early pioneers afire with the spirit of revolt.

A growing regard by the young generation for traditional ceremony is illustrated in the Passover Eve service, the *seder*, as it is celebrated now by a section of the Leftist Mapam group in the communal dining-room of the *kibbutz*; the whole collective society is gathered together for the ceremony. For untold generations the central feature has been the recital of the *exodus* of the Children of Israel from Egypt. In the pioneering period that recital, known as the *haggadah*, was replaced by a topical story of the *exodus* of the pioneer members of the *kibbutz* from Europe to their present home in Israel. Today most of the traditional *haggadah* is recited; the unleavened bread is eaten; the four cups of wine prescribed by immemorial custom are drunk—but without the traditional blessing of God. The narrative of the present-day adventure has been omitted. At the same time, some of the innovations of the communal *seder* make the evening memorable. The choir of the *kibbutz* sings passages from the Song of Solomon and poems by Bialik, the laureate of the Hebrew renaissance. One can feel the birth of a freer and gayer tradition. The religious stirring is more manifest in the idealist and close-knit society of the *kibbutz* than in the big urban masses. It is strongest naturally in the religious *kibbutz*.

It is another example of the return to the tradition that in some children's villages and *kibbutzim* the religious maturity of a boy when he becomes *bar-mitzvah*, a responsible Jew on completing his thirteenth year, is celebrated with a religious service. For years that was omitted, and in place of it a mere registration took place. Besides the ceremony, the occasion is marked by the giving of presents. A corresponding ceremony is introduced for the confirmation of a girl when she becomes *bat-mitzvah*, on the completion of her twelfth year.

The religious stirring is also manifest in the institutions for the rescue and integration of children and youth by training in agricultural villages. Here, too, there is a division between the strictly religious villages and the rest. In the former, synagogue worship is an integral part of the life. In the latter, while part of the ceremonial of the Sabbath and the festivals is preserved, prayer and public worship are not part of the school programme. In recent years, however, the desire for traditional prayer and ceremonial has come from part of the youth, largely of Oriental families who have kept more steadfastly to the tradition than the young generation of Europe. Several new villages, though not classified as religious, contain a synagogue where worship is optional. The oldest of the secular villages, Ben Shemen, is to be equipped with a synagogue building. Meantime, through the influence of a deeply religious teacher of Bible, services are held on the sabbath in the room of the agricultural college which is named after Albert Einstein, and prominently bears his motto: "Science without Religion is Blind, Religion without Science is Lame." The tendency today is towards the tradition, even among the groups who profess to be followers of Karl Marx and his dialectical materialism.

The Jew of modern Israel nearest to prophetic stature was the late Martin Buber, who lived in Jerusalem from 1938 till his death in 1965 and wrote many books of religious philosophy. He made a big impact on both Jews and Gentiles; and he gave to the voice of Jerusalem a spiritual quality. He belonged to that generation which conceived as a major aim of Zionism the creation of a spiritual centre in the Jewish Homeland, from which would radiate religious and cultural influences to all parts of the dispersion. Judaism and Zionism were indissolubly linked. Buber regarded the Israel *kibbutz*, of which he was a chief sponsor, as an experiment that had not failed, in contrast with the *kolkhoz* of the Soviet Republic, which had failed.

A large part of Israel's population, particularly of those living in agricultural villages, are classified as "non-religious", because in the technical sense they do not observe all the ritual rules. On the other hand they emphasize the moral rules of man's relation to his neighbour, aiming at a society of equals without difference of class. That was, and is, an essential part of Judaism. It is often overlooked that the famous Rabbi Hillel, a contemporary of Jesus, when challenged to give the essence of Judaism while standing on one leg, remarked that the command "to love thy neighbour as thyself is the whole Torah. The rest is commentary".

A member of a religious *kibbutz*, Eliezer Goldman, has recently written a booklet, *Religious Issues in Israel's Political Life*; and pleads that the "non-religious" should face up to the essential religious issues of personal faith in, and personal commitment to, the one God. The character of the *ḥalutz* of the *kibbutz*, which dominated the *yishuv* in the mandate period, was both collective and austere. That character and particularly its austerity, is no longer dominant in the State of Israel. A new focus of dedication with a fresh content is required; and it may come from the religious *kibbutz* where the faith in divine guidance is strong.

The common faith of the founding fathers of the modern Zionist movement, Herzl, Weizmann and Buber, was that the Israel part of the Jewish nation would be again a chosen people, chosen to give fresh life to the dispersion. It is the function of the Israeli Jews to show that the Children of Israel have survived through centuries of suffering and persecution in order to live freely and be masters of their soul, and have not lived painfully in order merely to survive. Judaism should have a fresh life as a universal religion, emphasizing the ideas of a single moral law and a single human brotherhood. In the land of Israel it will be again a religion of this world, an integral part of everyday life.

It is too early to expect the fulfilment of this vision; and Israel has been forced, from the establishment of the State, to live dangerously and to place survival in the forefront of its political activities. But there are few places where the fundamental issues of religion and ethics are more sincerely examined. Many groups are searching for a fresh religious expression. Among them is a body of teachers inspired by Hugo Bergmann, formerly Professor of Philosophy at the Hebrew University and a devoted colleague of Buber. From a different approach Professor Urbach, the Professor of Talmud at the Hebrew University, has formed a group of Searchers for Truth, whose aim is to choose elements of *halakhah* which have relevance and significance in the new conditions of the Jewish people.

The creators of the State of Israel, who were mainly secularists, did not accept the principle of unity between the State and the Jewish religion. At the same time they practised toleration towards the diverse communities within its territory and recognized the right of Jews to be non-religious. The State wishes to be in close relations with the Jewish dispersion and recognizes that that aim cannot be achieved simply by material bonds, but must have a cultural and spiritual basis. It has recently founded to that end, with the World Zionist Organization, an institute for cultural activity in the Jewish communities abroad, which sends teachers to spread the knowledge of Hebrew and of Israel. Hitherto Israel has not found a way to translate Judaism into a way of social life that can be meaningful for other Jews. But a modern Isaiah, who would inspire Israel, requires a certain moment of time.

A small but influential group of native-born Israelis, calling themselves the Canaanites, plead not for a complete break with traditional Judaism, as did some of the rebellious poets and novelists among the early Russian Zionists, but for a return to the simple way of life of the Hebrews in the days of David and Solomon. Their idealistic picture of the Children of Israel in that age is a romantic dream; but their governing purpose is clear, to get away as far as possible from the development of the Jewish religion in the exile. That period in their reckoning dates from the destruction of the First Temple by the Babylonians. Back to nature and to the strong men, Gideon, Saul, David. It is another romantic dream of the Canaanites that they can come to terms with the Muslim Arabs because of their common attachment to the land. Their maxim is: "Think not of what was."

Golah or *galuth*, the Hebrew term for dispersion (literally meaning exile) is not so much a geographical term as a spiritual concept of limitation caused by exile from the land of Israel. A saying runs: "*Golah* is the place for the study of Torah, Israel the place of its fulfilment." It is the special function of the restored nation of Israel to realize the ethics of Torah. The State is not an end in itself. The secularization of life has inevitably affected Judaism in Israel. The mass of Oriental Jews are rooted in traditional Judaism and maintain its observance; but for many western Jews who have abandoned traditional Judaism, there is a lack of a focal point for the orientation of their lives. Aristotle taught that man is a social animal. He is also a religious creature, and must find some concept of the universe to give him a vision of the whole of creation and his place in it.

It is obvious that we cannot treat Israel, with its population drawn from all parts of the world and comprising all sections of religious and non-religious Jews, as a uniform, integrated society. That miracle could not be achieved immediately anywhere, even in Israel. There is a variety of groups distinguished by ethnic origin and cultural environment, as well as by their religious heritage. Yet they all feel themselves good Jews and good Israelis. Some may repudiate the one God of the Bible and the observance of the sabbath. They would accept, however, Ben-Gurion's epigram that "true realism requires the belief in miracles". It is said of the Marxist Left Labour party, Mapam, that they accept God *de facto* but not *de jure*. Jewish culture matters for them more than ritual law as the national bond. But for all Israelis Jewish culture has its deep roots in the Hebrew Bible. They are indeed the people of the Book, and the Bible is the book of the people. The broadcasting programme of "the Voice of Israel" begins each day with the recitation of a Psalm, and in the evening before the news a chapter of the Bible is recited. The daily speech of the Israeli is full of the language of the Bible. The Book is the supreme source of the nation's history and the supreme literature. Knowledge of it is a proud distinction. An annual Bible quiz, open to all-comers, is held in Jerusalem and is a national event, generally attended by the President of the State and the Prime Minister. It gives the Jews everywhere pride and self-respect that they have a living language and literature.

Amanah is the name of a group of over a hundred members, mostly teachers from all parts of Israel, who meet periodically in order to discuss the problems of religion and its implication for life in Israel today. They took their name (meaning covenant), from a verse in the Book of Nehemiah, chapter x. Just as Ezra and Nehemiah realized that the return from exile in Babylon was meaningless unless accompanied by a return to the Torah, and prevailed on the leaders of the community to sign a covenant to follow the Torah, so today Israel, if it is to be significant, must symbolically sign a covenant to revive the Torah.

The group has a national gathering once or twice a year for three or four days, usually in one of the *kibbutzim* or children's villages. There they live together and pray together and talk. They are conscious of the grave harm done because many religious Jews and Jewesses could not find contentment of heart and mind in Judaism and turned to other religions. They are conscious also of the frustration of Judaism in the dispersion where it cannot develop freely. Now at last Jewish religious youth have the opportunity to live a full Jewish life. What that life should be is at present a matter for their experiment. Some seek to live in the way of that Jewish monastic sect commonly identified with the Essenes of the period before the Destruction of the Temple, whose records have been so amazingly found among the Dead Sea Scrolls. Some want a return to the traditional *halakhah* combined with the mystical contemplation of the *Ḥasidim*. The importance of the movement is not in the pamphlets which they issue from time to time, but rather in the example of searching for a living religion. They are seeking forms of religious practice which, while rooted in the tradition, will be appropriate to the free conditions and creative spirit in the land of Israel. All of them know the Hebrew Bible and must be influenced by it. The revival of Hebrew leads to a revival of Hebraism.

More recently, in 1966, a group of earnest educators launched a determined attempt to enrol in a new society those who feel the need for a religious life but do not accept the Orthodox test of observance of the 613 precepts included in the sixteenth-century Code of the oral law of Judaism. Belief in God is an essential element of the religion; as are the observance of the sabbath and the festivals, and brotherly conduct towards all neighbours.

Dr Joseph Schechter, principal of a teachers' training college at Haifa and a member of *Amanah*, who exercises a strong influence over his students, calls on them to live a full Judaism, combining the mystic contemplation of the *Ḥasidim*, of which Martin Buber was the enthusiastic interpreter, with the *halakhah*, the legal institutions. He teaches also that they must exercise the same brotherly love to the non-Jew as to the Jew. He is opposed to modern science and does not contemplate the harmony of science, religion and philosophy. On the other hand he introduces the teaching of the present-day existentialist philosophy. A day at the college opens with prayer, and the students are encouraged to revive the traditional forms of Judaism. Dr Schechter inspired the group which settled in a *kibbutz* in the Negev, between the Dead Sea and Elath, in the region where the Essenes dwelt.

The immediate aim of the *Amanah* group is to form like-minded cells in different parts of the country in a *kibbutz*, *moshav*, or town. Some years ago, a number of students who were inspired by them formed themselves into a society, the *mitnadvim* (meaning volunteers), who give service and friendship to groups of backward immigrants from the oriental countries.

The revived Judaism of Israel as a way of life begins to penetrate to the mass of the Jews outside Israel—the Jews for whom Judaism has meant a cycle of ceremonies and rules more or less observed, but with little effect on daily conduct. The most decisive impact is made by Israel's recovery of the Hebrew Bible as a living oracle. The dramatic discoveries by archaeologists of the Hebrew University, Yigael Yadin, Benjamin Mazar, Yohanan Aharoni and others, give a fresh reality to the ancient written record and link the present and the past. They give, too, roots in the land for the ingathering.

Before the Balfour Declaration about the Jewish National Home, the philosopher of Zionism, Ahad Ha-am, said that in the land of Israel there would be a miniature of what Jews can be and should be. The Jewish population there is no longer a miniature, but rather a new image of the Jew. It is also a new unifying force surmounting the barriers of space. The fragmentation of the Jewish people, which was threatened in the period of assimilation of the nineteenth and twentieth centuries, has been averted. Another unifying feature, which every year grows stronger, is the pilgrimage to the land, especially at the festival seasons. In the days of the Second Temple that pilgrimage to Jerusalem, known as the *regel*—literally the foot—was a religious duty of the Jews in the Diaspora, just as the *ḥajj*, the pilgrimage to Mecca, has been a binding duty of the Muslims all over the world. Today air communications make it much easier than it was before. The Jewish pilgrims come in their hundreds of thousands, and their contact with the country and its citizens must ultimately strengthen the feeling of unity. In addition, Jewish youth groups in Europe and America are encouraged and assisted to visit Israel and to spend a year of service there; conversely, thousands of young Israelis go abroad to those continents every year.

The invigoration of Judaism in Israel and abroad is not exclusively inspired by the life of the *yishuv*. Dr James Parkes, in his book *The End of an Exile*, distinguishes five roots of the tree of Israel: Judaism as the religion of a living and free community, the messianic hope, the history of the experiences of the nineteen centuries of dispersion, the continuity of Jewish life in Palestine during those centuries and finally, the relationship between the Jewish community of Palestine and the rest. The dispersion, in his view, has an essential part to play in the revival of Judaism and the fulfilment of the messianic hope. Only together can Israel and the free Diaspora express to the full the reason for the survival of the Jewish people.

In the land of Israel, therefore, not only the people but the religion, Judaism, promises to be reborn. What was called Palestine is again to the Jew, anywhere in the world, the Israel of his dreams and his history. It offers a spark in the present to rekindle the fires, and gives a modern ideal and purpose to the people in dispersion. The little nation gives hope of enriching the larger human community with social and religious values. By her social institutions she begins to be a light to the nations. The National Home forges a fresh spiritual bond for communities which were threatened with disintegration. Albert Einstein pointed out that for centuries what united the Jewish people was their law of conduct embodied in their dearly guarded tradition and the thought of the past. That bond of the community was weakened in the last century. It is being reinforced in the spiritual centre. Zionism and Israel, it has been said, are the expression of a national will to live, which transcends the traditional orthodox religion.

In Israel there are signs that the leaders of Judaism and its offspring, Christianity, will get together with the purpose of reaching mutual understanding and reconciliation. Living in the land of Israel where Jesus lived and ministered, many of the young generation are anxious to know about his teachings. They read carefully the New Testament; and the first Professor of Jewish History of the Second Commonwealth at the Hebrew University, the late Joseph Klausner, wrote in Hebrew a *Life of Jesus* and a *Life of Paul*, which in translation made a notable impact on both Christian and Jewish opinion. Writing from an ardent nationalist standpoint, he yet recognized that Jesus was one of the major prophets.

The Department of Comparative Religion in the Hebrew University, headed by Professor Werblowsky, gives particular attention to the study of Christianity. While Islam was studied from the early years of the University in the Arabic and Oriental Institute, Christianity was not a subject of academic discipline till the Department was founded. At the same time the expansion of Asian Studies at the University encourages an intensive searching into the Eastern religions, Hinduism and Buddhism.

The first steps to understanding between the two religions are likely to be taken by individual scholars, and not by the official heads of the communities. In Jerusalem an Inter-faith Council was established a few years ago with representatives of the three monotheistic creeds,

Judaism, Christianity and Islam. Hitherto it has not been very active or constructive. A more active and constructive group of a few Jews and Christians meet regularly and discuss the approach of the church and the synagogue to moral problems. It is known as the *Rainbow*, and it includes the Anglican Archbishop of Jerusalem (who crosses from the Arab section of the city for the meetings), Roman Catholic monks, the President of the Hebrew University, and the Professor of Comparative Religion in the University. It may be the forerunner of a more sustained effort of "dialogue", to bring about co-operation and united action in the major international problems of the Middle East. At present there is little hope of Muslim co-operation. In Israel itself there are few Muslims who have the scholarship and the knowledge to take a lead in discussions, and the Muslim leaders in the Arab States are precluded from meeting with Israel's scholars by existing political conditions.

It is possible that meetings of Jews and Buddhists in Israel will be achieved. Some Buddhists of Burma have been singularly sympathetic to Israel, and Ben-Gurion is known to be a profound admirer of Buddhist teaching and to practise yoga. Jerusalem would be an appropriate meeting place for a congress of faiths. And an ideal site would be the original building of the Hebrew University on Mt Scopus, facing the city of Jerusalem. That site has been inaccessible for its cultural purposes since the War of Independence; but we may contemplate its reoccupation by a branch of the Hebrew University devoted to the cause of international and inter-religious understanding and open to students and teachers of all countries without discrimination.

The Israel Ministry of Religions has functions in relation to the non-Jewish minorities in Israel which are less controversial than its function in relation to Jews. They are to assure the execution of the pledges in the Declaration of Independence, "to guarantee freedom of religion, conscience, education and culture, and to safeguard the holy places of all religions". In practice it has maintained the old *millet* system of communal autonomy in religious matters. The Ministry is concerned also to foster co-operation between the State and the Muslim and Christian populations. For the Muslim community, which is the largest religious minority, it has helped to re-establish the religious courts (*shar'ī*) presided over by *qāḍīs*, who are paid by the State, and to appoint leaders of prayer and worship. It has special care for the preservation of the mosques and the cemeteries in places where the Muslim community has disappeared. In recent years it has established a mainly Muslim committee to deal with the administration of the Muslim charitable foundations (*waqfs*) and to use the income for the benefit of the Israeli Muslims. The Ministry publishes a bulletin in three languages (Hebrew, Arabic and English) on current Muslim affairs, not restricted to developments in Israel.

The relations with the Christian communities are more diplomatic than executive. The Ministry deals with the responsible ecclesiastical officers of the many Christian bodies in Israel. It constantly consults the spiritual heads, some of whom are not resident in Israel, and it has restored to the bodies concerned the ecclesiastical properties which were occupied by the military forces of one side or the other during the War. It has also carried out repairs on religious buildings which were damaged in the fighting. It facilitates Christian pilgrimages to the Israel section of the Holy Land, and the visits of Christians living in or visiting Israel to the Holy Places at Nazareth, and at Christmas and Easter to Bethlehem and the Old City of Jerusalem, which are in the Arab State. It issues a bulletin, *Christian News from Israel*, not only in the two official languages, but also in English, French and Spanish, giving information about the Christian communities, so that the many Christian bodies interested in Israel may know what is happening. Each issue contains authoritative articles on the latest archaeological discoveries, which interest the general public not less than the Israelis.

The Ministry sets an example of tolerance and puts no obstacles in the way of Christian missionary activities. The Baptists, whose congregations are made up from members of many nationalities, including Russian, Polish, American and Arab, have established a collective settlement near Tel Aviv on the model of the *kibbutz*. The Ministry does not oppose the settlement in Israel of Christian converts from Judaism, though it cannot prevent popular prejudice, which may stand in the way of employment. It welcomed a group of converts to Judaism from a village in Italy who arrived after the foundation of the State and was settled in a *kibbutz* in Galilee. However, many of the converts left Israel after a few years and returned to Apulia. A number of young Finns, male and female, came for a sojourn of a year or more in the *kibbutzim*. Some of the girls have married Israeli boys, having first been admitted into the Jewish community. It seems likely that the

Jews in Israel, having re-established their nation, will attract proselytes as they did 2,000 years ago.

Within the territory of Israel there are 160 churches, 50 Christian schools—many conducted by missionary bodies—and over 1,000 clergy. One major Christian construction has been completed by the Franciscan Order, the vast new Basilica of the Annunciation at Nazareth. The Christian communities which have congregations in Israel include the Greek Orthodox, Greek Catholic, Latin, Russian Orthodox, Armenian, Coptic, Ethiopian, Anglican, Scotch Churches, and the Baptists. A Scandinavian theological college of the Evangelical Church is established in Jerusalem, in the Street of the Prophets. Stress is laid on Hebrew and rabbinical literature, and on the life and culture of Israel today. The students learn modern Hebrew, as do many of the monks whose monasteries are in Israel. Some smaller Christian groups, both Roman Catholic and Evangelical, have come from Germany to live in Israel and help the immigrant Jews, with the purpose of making atonement for the Nazi crimes against the Jewish people. One group has its centre in the village of Zichron Yaacov, south of Haifa, and brings there students from Germany for a few months of service. Another group, headed by a Sister Gabrielle, has its home in Galilee; and the nuns work for all who turn to them.

Another peculiar religious minority with a secret creed and with a community in Israel is the Druze population, whose main centre is in Syria. The Israeli section is in the northern district and consists mainly of peasants. They are sturdy and warlike, and in the War of Independence they fought on the side of Israel; and they have thrown in their lot with Israel. Though Arabic speaking, they were not on happy terms with the Muslim Arabs and lived apart. In the Ottoman and mandate periods they were not recognized as a community having jurisdiction in matters of personal status. The Israel government has conferred this right on them, and the elders form a tribunal. The Ministry issues for them yet another bulletin in three languages about their affairs in Israel, including reports of the judgments of the tribunal; and most of the articles are written by heads of the community.

A smaller sect, of Persian origin, but having its religious and spiritual centre in Palestine since the beginning of this century, is the community of the Bahā'īs, or Bābīs. They were formed during the nineteenth century in Persia where a religious reformer claimed to be the forerunner of the Muslim Messiah, and assumed the title of *Bāb*, i.e. the gate, because he was the gate to the new era. He was executed, and one of his Persian disciples who preached his universal religious teaching was exiled from the country and took refuge in Turkey. The Sultan, alarmed at the spread of the new creed, imprisoned him in the fortress of 'Akkā (Acre) in Palestine, but after some years he was released and made his home first in that town and later in Haifa. Bahā' Allāh continued to preach the brotherhood of men, and his son 'Abbās, who succeeded him, spread the doctrine to America. Father and son are buried in the beautiful garden above Haifa on Mt Carmel, which has become a place of pilgrimage for all Bahā'īs in the world. The head of the community, at the time of the establishment of the State of Israel, was the grandson of 'Abbās. He died in 1956, and no member of the Persian family has taken his place. The Bahā'īs have their tribunal for matters of personal status recognized by the Government. The direction of the community, which is spread over the world, and particularly in North America, is now exercised by an international spiritual board with its seat in Haifa.

When peace is made with the Arabs, as it will be in time, the status of Jerusalem may have to be reconsidered. The Jewish part of the town will surely remain the capital of the nation. Its impressive civic centre, with the Parliament House, the government offices, the buildings of the Hebrew University and of the National Museum, is a kind of acropolis. The conception of a Greater Jerusalem as a *corpus separatum*, under the trustee administration of the United Nations, which was prescribed in the resolution of the United Nations for partition of Palestine in November 1947, has been shattered by events. But part of the project, the demilitarization of the area and the appointment of a United Nations Commissioner to assure the protection of the Holy Places of the three faiths, full freedom of worship for all, and the preservation of the unique character of the city, may be renewed in some form, and then implemented. It may be, too, that time, the great healer, will make it possible for another part of the original United Nations project to be salved. That is the establishment in Jerusalem of the centre of an economic union between Israel and Jordan, and, looking further ahead, the centre of a Middle East confederation of states.

The buildings of the Hebrew University on Mt Scopus (meaning the watchman) will surely be restored to their original purpose. Since the summer of 1948, when an agreement for the demilitarization of the area was made through the good offices of the United Nations mediator, and despite clear provisions in the armistice agreement between Israel and Jordan, they have not been available to the University. The area has been an Israel enclave in the territory of Jordan, occupied by a small force of Jewish police and the road to it from the city, passing through Arab quarters, is barred against access.

Recently a foundation for the advancement of peace in honour of Harry Truman, the former President of the United States, has been inaugurated in Jerusalem and attached to the Hebrew University. It is fitting that such a foundation should have its seat in the city of Isaiah and Jesus, and the hearth of the three monotheist faiths. The programme of the foundation is still indefinite, but it may be hoped that it will foster specific fields of research, such as Afro-Asian studies, which may serve the cause of international co-operation and peace, and help to bring about a peaceful confrontation of Israel and the Arab nations. The idea of a world academy is engaging; but what is most wanted is positive action to bring the peoples of the Middle East together, and to find a way of co-operation through the common ethic of the three universal religions.

Judaism in Israel should have something to say on the spiritual issue of the revolution, the third of modern times, and the first world revolution of all time, which has been bound up with the two World Wars. In the rabbinical phrase "if not now, when?", it should emphasize the idea of a single moral law and a single human brotherhood. The first intellectual and spiritual revolution of the modern age was that which we know as the Reformation and the Renaissance. Jews played their part in preparing for it by the preservation of the Hebrew Bible; but they had no share in the enlightenment that was brought to the people of western Europe. The second, the French Revolution, 180 years ago, gave to mankind a watchword: liberty, equality and fraternity. The Jews were among the beneficiaries, receiving civil and political rights in the West European States; but they were passive. Today Judaism, revived in Israel, should be regarded not as the peculiar teaching of a small separate people, but as the source of moral principles which are at stake everywhere. It will renew its ideal of the universal teaching which characterized it in the age of the Hebrew Prophets.

In his last book, *A Threefold Cord*, the late Viscount Samuel, who had been High Commissioner for Palestine, recorded that in Palestine there were engendered spiritual and cultural movements of supreme value to humanity; "I held the belief, which I still hold, that Palestine, in the latter days, might add a third to the religious revolutions of 4,000 years and 2,000 years ago". The Jews in Israel today, when another civilization is in dissolution, may have a contribution to make to a peaceful order, some fresh religious teaching derived from the experience and vision of the free people in the Bible land.

CHAPTER 3

THE ORIENTAL JEWISH COMMUNITIES[1]

HISTORICAL INTRODUCTION

A survey of the Jewish communities in the Muslim Middle East, such as they still exist, or existed until the middle of the twentieth century, is fittingly preceded by a historical sketch of developments from the Arab conquest in the seventh century until the Ottoman conquests. Though it cannot be said that the Arab conquest had revolutionary consequences for the religious life and general history of the Jews in the region, it is nevertheless true that quite far-reaching changes took place in every sphere and, above all, that the pattern of existence that evolved many centuries ago has still not lost its effectiveness.

The sketch outlines the rise, decline and eclipse of the Jewish communities parallel to the developments in the Muslim countries.

The political, legal and social situation

In our survey of the history of the Jews in the Asian and African territories of the caliphate we should bear in mind a number of facts pertaining to the long period of earlier Jewish history in that region; they greatly influenced the shaping of political and social relations between the Arab conquerors and their successors on the one hand and the Jewish population on the other. Many developments and changes of attitude are only intelligible by reference to the situation in the Arabian peninsula in the pre-Islamic past and in the lands conquered by the Arabs during the final period of Byzantine and Persian rule.

Reliable historical traditions, supported by early inscriptions, attest that hundreds of years before the emergence of Islam, Jews were to be found in South and North Arabia. These traditions become clearer and more precise as we approach the fourth and fifth centuries C.E. The information conveyed by South Arabian votive inscriptions mentioning kings of Ḥimyar, the inscriptions of Beyt̲ She‘ārīm near Haifa, the

[1] This chapter has been prepared for *Religion in the Middle East* from material gathered for a *History of the Jews in the Middle East*, a project being carried out at Bar-Ilan University (Israel) with the aid of the "Memorial Foundation for Jewish Culture".

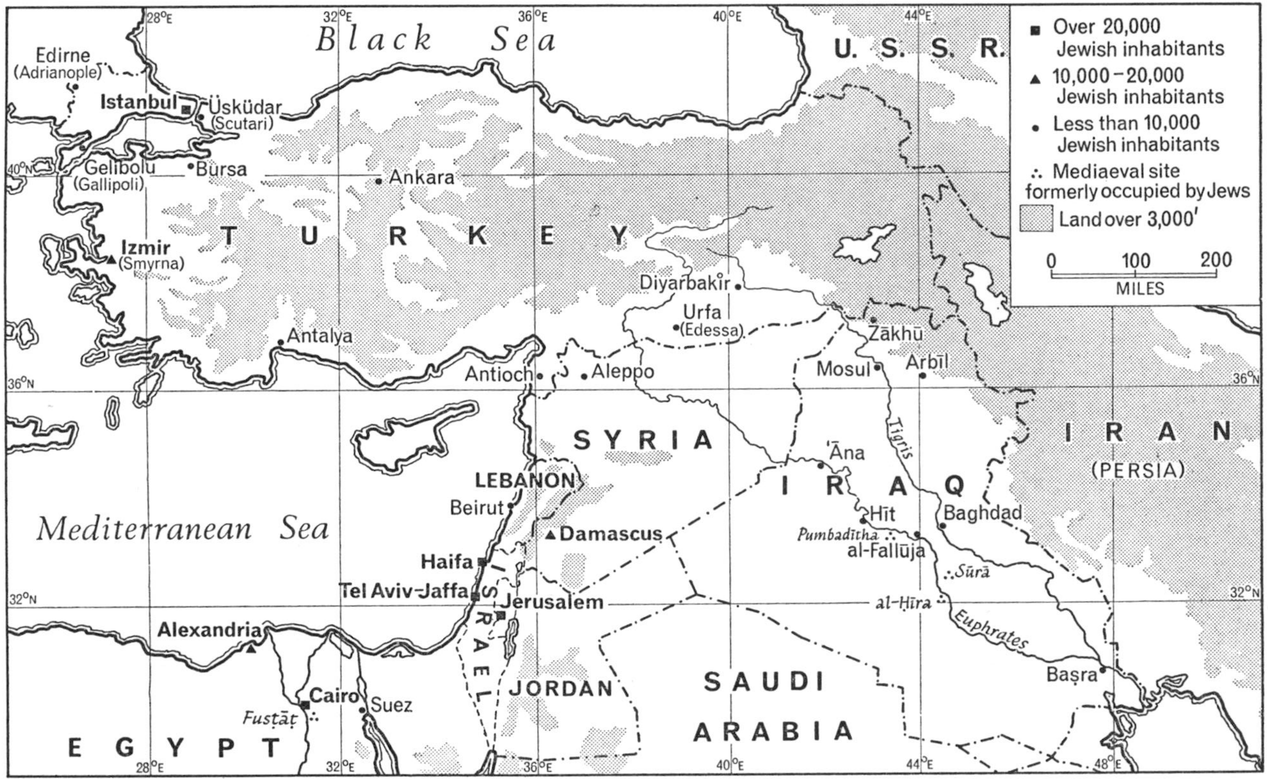

Jewish Communities in Turkey, the Fertile Crescent and Egypt, from A.D. 600 to the present day.

stories of Christian ecclesiastical writers, and the traditions preserved in North Arabian literature combined, present an interesting picture: by the side of Jewish communities trying to stem the spread of Christianity we find Judaizers among the South Arabian tribes and even among the kings ruling them. Almost all scholars agree that the "monotheistic" inscriptions were written by Jews, converts to Judaism or Judaizers, at any rate not by Christians.

Two inscriptions discovered not long ago, put up by the army leader of King Yūsuf Ash'ar—the Yūsuf Dhū Nuwās of Christian and Arab sources—during the war against the Abyssinian invaders and their helpers, the Christian rebels in Najrān (521–5), complete and confirm the long-known reports.[1]

Immediately upon his accession in 518, the Emperor Justin delegated his powers to his nephew Justinian, who succeeded to the throne after his uncle's death. Justinian at once embarked upon an energetic policy against Persia, drawing Abyssinia which had won victories in Ḥimyar, to his side. With Byzantine aid Abyssinia might perhaps have succeeded in subduing South Arabia and thereby promoting a change in the balance of forces also in North Arabia as early as 521. However, the throne of the Tubba' was then ascended by the Jewish king Dhū Nuwās, a notable statesman and general who realized the danger threatening his country and began to mobilize resources within and allies without, in opposition to Abyssinian and Byzantine expansionism.

The war between the Jewish king and the Negus of Abyssinia is described in almost all available sources which mention relations between rabbis, especially those in Tiberias, and Dhū Nuwās and their activity during the war.

In the meantime Yūsuf mobilized the South Arabian tribes in order to repel the Abyssinian attack. The Jewish king vanquished the Abyssinians and forced them to retreat to the coast and thence to their own country.

The operations against the inhabitants of Najrān are known from Christian sources. The vengeance wrought by Yūsuf, who could not forgive the townspeople for their treachery, so angered the Byzantines that they helped the Abyssinians to invade Ḥimyar a second time. Yūsuf had to meet a double threat: the Abyssinian attack from without and the defection of several tribal chiefs from within. He was, however, unable to prevail against the traitors. His forces were insufficient to

[1] Cf. G. Ryckmans, "Inscriptions Sud-Arabes", in *Le Muséon*, LXVI (1953), pp. 284–303.

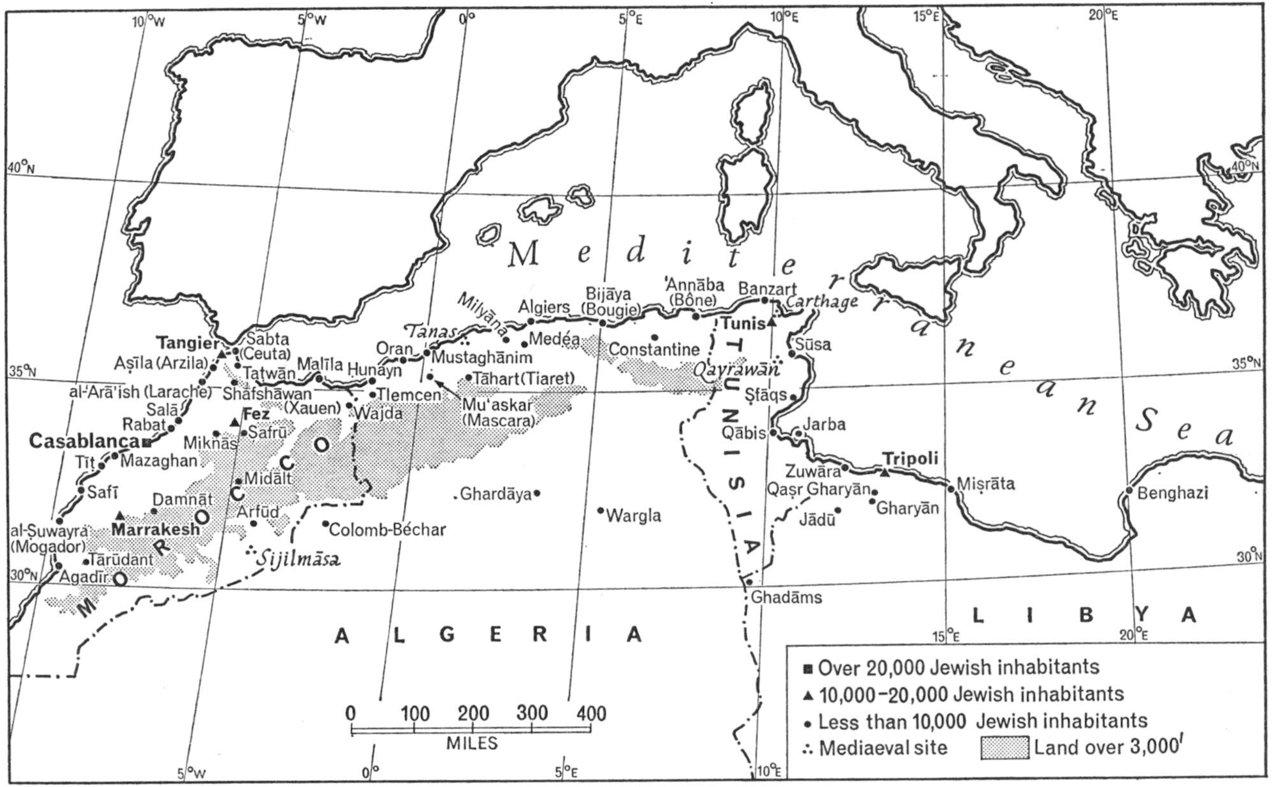

Jewish Communities in North Africa, from A.D. 600 to the present day.

ward off their three-pronged thrust. He fell in battle, along with those tribal chiefs who had remained loyal to him. An Arab legend has it that he leapt into the sea with his horse and was drowned.[1]

Yūsuf was the last Jewish king of Ḥimyar. But Jewish communities continued to exist in the country at the time of the persecutions and in the Islamic era, when the Christians emigrated or embraced Islam. Arab historians report that many Judaizers among Bedouin tribes adopted the new religion. Through them, it seems, Jewish beliefs and biblical legends penetrated into Islam. We may suppose that Jews by descent were also converted in some cases, but the majority of them remained Jewish. They stayed in the country until the early twentieth century when large groups of Yemenite Jews began to emigrate to Palestine and finally to Israel in 1949–50 in a massive exodus.

The settlement of many Jews in the north of the country was no less important, even though it lacked the glory of the "Jewish kingdom" of Ḥimyar. We find them in the fertile oases and along the *wādīs* through which caravans moved from the ports at the southern end of the Arabian Peninsula towards Palestine and Syria, carrying valuable Indian and Chinese products: frankincense, perfumes, spices and silk. They engaged in agriculture, supplying the needs of the caravans, and in handicrafts, making implements and ornaments for the Bedouin and their women and especially arms and armour which were renowned for their quality and beauty. The Jews thus contributed to the economy of Arab society which was based on camel-breeding, the carriage of goods and the provison of escorts for traders. The Jews in North Arabia also played an important rôle in imparting religious concepts. There is evidence of Jewish influence on the *ḥanīfs*, the God-seeking contemporaries of Muḥammad, and especially on their foremost representative, Umayya b. Abi 'l-Ṣalt.[2]

Contrary to the view once widely held by European scholars that early Arabic literature reflects contempt of the Jews, it contains numerous testimonies of good relations between Jews and Arabs. We find expressions of respect for the Jews and praise for their great virtues, their generosity and hospitality. Their loyalty was, in fact, proverbial. Numerous reports of Judaizing important South Arabian and Ḥijāzī tribes likewise show that there can be no question of contempt of the Jews.

[1] Cf. H. Z. (J. W.) Hirschberg, *Israel in Arabia* (Hebrew) (Tel-Aviv, 1946), pp. 76–111.

[2] Cf. J. W. Hirschberg, *Jüdische und christliche Lehren im vor- und frühislamischen Arabien* (Krakow, 1939), pp. 32 ff.; E. I. J. Rosenthal, *Judaism and Islam* (London, 1961), pp. 1 ff.

Jewish Communities in the Balkans from A.D. 600 to the present day.

The good-neighbourly relations between Jews and Arabs in Yathrib ceased soon after Muḥammad arrived there, due to the inevitable contest between Muḥammad and the Jewish tribal chiefs, and subsequently between a developing and increasingly institutionalized Islam and Judaism. The result was growing enmity between Muḥammad and the devotees who had followed him from Mecca and his "helpers" in Medina on the one hand and Yathrib Jews on the other. Hostilities opened with the charge against the Jews of falsifying the Torah (Qur'ān, ii. 83) and making additions to it (iii. 72); they were said to hate the believers (v. 85). Moreover, Muḥammad degraded the Jews by the obligation of poverty (ii. 58; iii. 108). Massacres followed. Two tribes—first the weak Banū Qaynuqā', then the Banu'l-Naḍīr, one of the *kāhinān* (priestly) tribes—were expelled, and the other *kāhinān* tribe, the Banū Qurayẓa, was exterminated.

The expulsion of the Banu'l-Naḍīr, one of the major Jewish tribes in Medina, was openly regretted by their Arab neighbours. Some Arab poets bemoaned the departure of their Jewish friends; 'Abbās b. Mirdās's farewell lines are most moving. But there were also those who said that the Jews had deserved their fate: they were enemies of the Prophet and Islam; therefore they and their property were denied legal protection. Muḥammad's utterances in the Qu'rān and those attributed to him and his close associates by oral tradition naturally had their effect, and Muslim writers used them to stir up hatred of the Jews and to poison the atmosphere in fanatical Muslim circles.

On the other hand, however, a different set of facts has to be taken into account. Muḥammad himself, at the end of the war against his Jewish neighbours in Medina, established another practice during the fighting against the Jews of Khaybar, and in the terms of surrender agreed with them and with the Jewish settlements in northern Ḥijāz and on the Palestinian border. These terms—the same for Jews and Christians—served as binding legal precedent for all agreements with both in conquered territories. The *jizya* (poll-tax payable by non-Muslims) is imposed by the Qur'ān itself (ix. 29), and the protection of the *dhimmī*, the *jizya*-paying subject, was incumbent on the authorities and on the individual.

In their victorious campaign after Muḥammad's death the Bedouin tribes found in almost every country large or small Jewish communities, established in the region for many centuries past. The political and social status of the Jews declined since Christianity became the dominant religion in Asia Minor, Syria, Palestine, Egypt and the Maghrib. The Emperors issued ordinances and regulations prohibiting Jews from holding public office, as this would give them authority over Christians, and from erecting new synagogues. In Africa Justinian even ordered the demolition of existing synagogues (*novella* 37); he also forbade the study and teaching of the Oral Law (*novella* 146). Needless to say that the Jew tax (*fiscus judaicus*) of the days of the Destruction of the Temple was enforced; it had become a poll-tax.

It was little comfort to the Jews that the non-Orthodox Christians also had their share of molestation at the hands of the fanatical clergy in Constantinople and its willing tool, the secular authorities.

The situation of the Jews in Persia was not favourable either. During the last 150 years of the Sāsānid dynasty Babylonian Jewry underwent severe crises which weakened its religious and administrative institutions. Almost simultaneously with Muḥammad's appearance in Mecca the Persians launched a powerful offensive against Byzantium and penetrated deeply into its territory. The Jews of Antioch revolted against the Byzantines, killed the Patriarch and thereby indirectly facilitated the city's capture by the Persians. Upon the Persian invasion of Palestine and occupation of Jerusalem the Jews were permitted to return to that city from which they were banished in the time of Hadrian. But the hopes for the rebuilding of the Temple were disappointed. The Persian Army, whose victorious advance suddenly turned into a hasty retreat, was forced to abandon Palestine. The Christian clergy took revenge upon the Jews, although the Emperor Heraclius promised them pardon.

Not only Christian sources but also the Arab historian al-Balādhurī make much of the assistance extended to the Arabs by the Jews during the conquest. His confidence in the Jews caused Muʿāwiya to settle some of them in Tripoli. On the other hand a Syrian chronicle reports that in 634 poor Jewish villagers fought on the side of the Byzantines in a battle with the Arabs twelve miles east of Ghazza (Gaza). The story of the *Kāhina*, the woman who, as the leader of the Judaized Berbers, fought the Arab conquerors in Africa, is likewise characteristic, even if legendary. Later Jewish sources, including an almost official one of the end of the tenth century, reflect a favourable view of the attitude of the first caliphs towards the Jewish authorities in Babylonia.

The accounts of Jewish co-operation with the invading armies appear generally correct, though perhaps not free from exaggeration. After all, even Christian sources admit that those Christians in Syria and Egypt who did not belong to the ruling church regarded the Arabs as deliverers from severe masters and heavy taxation. It soon became known that the Arabs scrupulously adhered to the undertakings given by them upon the surrender of the population, which was excellent propaganda for their cause.

At the end of the Umayyad period relations between the Muslim authorities and the *dhimmīs* seem to have deteriorated, due to a variety of causes, some of which will be discussed presently, while the economic aspect will be dealt with later.

The Caliph ʻUmar II (717–20) emphasized the religious principle, though he himself was fair and just in his personal relations with Jews and Christians. Increasing religious zeal led to intolerance, alien to the early Umayyads. They were secular rulers, targets of the propaganda of the ʻAbbāsids and of the Shīʻīs.

A second factor was the improvement of the cultural and technical standards of the Arabs who felt that they were able to manage the affairs of state themselves, without Christian officials. At the same time, the *dhimmīs* became increasingly assimilated to the Arabs by adopting their language, dress and customs. This, to the exponents of religion, seemed rather dangerous. A certain incident led to the enactment of discriminatory regulations designed to check those frowned-on tendencies. These regulations appear to go back to ʻUmar II and are called *shurūṭ ʻUmar* (ʻUmar's regulations). Their attribution to ʻUmar I is erroneous.

ʻUmar II ordered provincial governors to remove the *dhimmīs* from government posts and warned them not to become friendly with the "unbelievers". ʻUmar's regulations imposed no restrictions on economic activities, but the appointment of "unbelievers" to high public office, giving them authority over Muslims, was rejected as contrary to the Qur'ān (cxiv. 3; liv. 5). ʻUmar also prescribed special dress for the *ahl al-dhimma*, lest they be mistaken for Muslims. Christians had to wear special girdles and trim their hair at the forehead; Jews were subject to other restrictions in their attire. In time, clothing regulations were tightened up. Turbans of special colour were prescribed for each community—blue for Christians, yellow for Jews, red for Samaritans—as well as special shoes, saddles, etc. The prohibition of erecting buildings higher than those of the Muslims is first mentioned by an author who died in 1058. However, the ban on the construction of new synagogues and churches and the repair of existing ones was not taken seriously. Al-Maqrīzī admits that all the synagogues in Cairo were undeniably built in the days of Islam, and does not even try to explain the contradiction between this fact and 'Umar's regulations. Still, sometimes when Muslim popular passions were inflamed, these regulations were a pretext for the destruction of synagogues—which the authorities subsequently permitted to be rebuilt.

In actual fact most of the special laws concerning Christians and Jews were at first almost ignored. From time to time devout, zealous caliphs confirmed their validity, as they were apt to be quickly forgotten. The caliphs themselves infringed the prohibition of admitting "unbelievers" to high government office, and the latter did not willingly submit to discriminatory measures. Only when cultural standards declined and fanaticism among the masses and ignorance among the rulers increased did these measures penetrate the consciousness of the people and become part of their religion. From then onwards the life of the *dhimmī* was very hard indeed.

The nearer we come to the sixteenth century, the more is the fanaticism of the Muslim *qāḍīs* and *muftīs* reflected in the treatment of non-Muslims, due to changes in the structure of Muslim society. The rule of mercenaries recently arrived from central Asia, or of emancipated slaves newly converted to Islam, weighed heavily upon the veteran residents of the state, and the more the established population was exploited and humiliated, the more it practised oppression and intolerance towards the *dhimmīs*. The expulsion of the Muslims from the Spanish provinces reconquered by the Christians was a further stimulant to fanaticism. A change for the worse is particularly noticeable in the Mamlūk period, when rioting mobs attacked Christian quarters. When a Christian wished to go out into the street, he would borrow the yellow turban of a Jew which would shield him against attack. In 1354 the Mamlūk Sultan al-Malik al-Ṣāliḥ issued a decree re-stating 'Umar's regulations.[1] In countries where Islam was the official religion, non-Muslims did not need to seek special privileges in order to settle in a conquered territory or in a newly built town or to follow any calling not involving authority

[1] Concerning the status of the *dhimmīs* cf. A. S. Tritton, *The Caliphs and their non-Muslim Subjects* (London, 1930), *passim*; A. Mez, *The Renaissance of Islam* (London, 1939), *passim*; L. A. Mayer, "The Status of the Jews under the Mamlūks" (Hebrew) in *Magnes Anniversary Volume* (Jerusalem, 1938), pp. 161–7; E. Strauss, "The Social Isolation of the *Ahl Adh-Dhimma*", in *P. Hirschler Memorial Volume*, pp. 73–94; S. D. Goitein, *Jews and Arabs* (New York, 1955), pp. 62–88.

over Muslims and to have their privileges renewed by every successive ruler.

The right of residence of Jews and Christians was based on the Qur'ān. Therefore, in order to justify the expulsion of Jews and Christians from Ḥijāz, the exponents of the *ḥadīth*, in addition to the *ḥadīth* reporting Muḥammad's command "that there shall not be two religions in Ḥijāz", invented another *ḥadīth* to the effect that the peace treaty with the people of Khaybar contained an article permitting Muḥammad to expel the Jews whenever he wished. In fact, in Muslim countries the Jews did not feel like strangers since most of them had been there even before the arrival of the Arabs.

At the same time, the isolation of the religious communities from one another should be noted. No one familiar with the Jewish sources of the period will be surprised that they contain almost no reference to personal relations between the Jews and the non-Jewish society within which they lived. Similarly, Arab-Muslim writers almost completely ignore the existence of non-Muslim communities, mentioning them seldom and only incidentally. This attitude is a true mirror of reality. Such was the way of life of medieval man in the East. Relationships of blood, origin, and religious and communal affiliation were paramount, and only what went on within their purview was of real interest. Even important political events were passed over in silence if they did not affect members of the group.

We hear no actual complaints of violence, coercion and malice at the hands of the authorities. Only incidentally, when we learn of the effectiveness of an army commander's promise not to touch the women on entering a town, do we gather how the soldiery sometimes behaved. Another time we are told that somebody "is grievously punished by the authorities; they trouble him, and sometimes his wife is seized in his stead". The incarceration of women was apparently not unusual.[1]

If matters of this kind were not mentioned, established customs (familiar for generations) were certainly not thought worthy of note. People in those days saw nothing humiliating in certain regulations that to us seem utterly degrading. Both those who made them and those who suffered them regarded them as the logical outcome of a factual situation which evolved over the ages. Naturally, it seemed

[1] J. Mueller, *Responsen der Lehrer des Ostens und Westens* (Hebrew) (Berlin, 1888), §47; A. Harkavy, *Responsen der Geonim* (Hebrew) (Berlin, 1887), §346 (addressed to Qayrawān); and cf. Hirschberg, *A History of the Jews in North Africa* (Hebrew), 2 vols. (Jerusalem, 1965), I, p. 145. (An English edition is to be published by E. J. Brill, Leiden.)

desirable to evade some of these regulations, to ensure that they fell into oblivion, to pay bribes to achieve impunity for offenders, but no need was felt to denounce them as new vexations. Some of them, such as the poll-tax and the restrictions on public worship, legal competence and civil rights, had their roots in the remote past prior to the Arab conquest. It should be noted in this context that Arab historians regarded the Christian Romans resident in Africa as aliens (*'ajam*), while they described the Jews as *ahl al-dhimma*, protected people.

In the large towns the Jews undoubtedly lived together in separate quarters. This is apparent from a letter about the disaster of the Qayrawān community which states that the *ḥāra* (the Jewish quarter) and *al-miqdash al-jalīl*, its magnificent synagogue, were laid waste.[1] But the concentration of the Jews in a separate quarter, and even its assignment to them in early Muslim times should certainly not be regarded as an oppressive measure. Rather was it a voluntary concentration for reasons of convenience. We know that the Jewish tribes in pre-Islamic Yathrib each inhabited a region of their own. When the Arab conquerors came to areas under Persian rule they found there *maḥallāt al-Yahūd*, Jewish quarters. The delimitation of a Jewish district did not prevent the settling of non-Jews in it, nor the establishment of Jews in other quarters. We find Muslims living among Jews and Jews renting dwellings in Muslim neighbourhoods.[2]

But even under those conditions of discrimination and restrictions the attitude of the Muslim authorities towards the *dhimmīs* was generally better than that of the Byzantine authorities towards Jews and Muslims and even towards Christians who did not belong to the official church, which is why such Christians, too, preferred to be protected persons under Muslim rule rather than persecuted citizens in the Byzantine state.

True, the Muslim rulers introduced humiliating restrictions and disabilities for the "unbelievers" and practised blackmail on behalf of the Treasury in various ways. But religious law set a limit to greed: the estate of a Jew or Christian who died heirless at his place of permanent residence devolved upon the community to which he belonged; only in the Mamlūk period was it assigned to the Treasury. Also, the law voided the right to succession of a convert, indiscriminately—even if he had become a Muslim.

[1] J. Mann, *Texts and Studies in Jewish History and Literature*, vol. 1 (Cincinnati, 1931), p. 246 and n. 17.
[2] B. Spuler, *Iran in früh-islamischer Zeit* (Wiesbaden, 1952), p. 216.

In the long medieval history of the Jews in Muslim countries we know of only one instance of organized forced conversion on a mass scale: that of Maghrib Jewry under the Almohads (*al-Muwaḥḥidūn*) whose declared aim was to purge Islam of every deviation from the belief in the oneness of Allāh, as Muḥammad had demanded. This demand was originally addressed to the Muslims themselves, and the campaigns of the *tamyīz* (purge) organized by the disciples of Ibn Tūmart at first affected Muslims, thousands of whom were killed. The attacks against Jews and Judaism were probably less severe than those against Christians and Christianity, whose last vestiges then disappeared from North Africa.[1]

Those forced conversions and expulsions are not comparable in intensity, thoroughness and duration to similar measures in Europe. Arab historians accept the presence of Jewish communities in the state of the Almohads and their successors as a matter of course, not requiring any explanation. Yet the statement made in 1224 that there is not a single synagogue in the whole of the Maghrib may be correct. The Jews were no doubt still wary of building synagogues which might inflame the passions of their enemies and preferred to hold their prayer meetings unobtrusively.

In 1231 Yaḥyā, Muḥammad al-Nāṣir's son, descended from the mountains, captured Marrakesh, destroyed the Christian church, killed a great number of Jews and Banū Farkhān, looted their property and entered the *qaṣba*, or citadel. Just as the author who gives this information meant the church of the Christian garrison in the capital, so he clearly referred to Jews who professed their faith openly and not to crypto-Jews. The discriminatory measures imposed by the Almohads against the new Muslims, i.e. the forcibly converted Jews, naturally had a destructive effect.

Once the Jews were again permitted to practise their religion in public, most of these measures lapsed automatically. However, the clothing regulations continued in full force, even though details of cut and colour were changed. In contrast to the pre-Almohad period, the *ghiyār*, discriminatory signs, are now mentioned in Tunisia (1199) and Spain; on the initiative of Maghribi fanatics they were reintroduced in Egypt. An author of African origin who lived in Spain in the late Middle Ages describes the duty of the *muḥtasib* (an official with judicial

[1] Cf. *Documents inédits d'Histoire Almohade*, ed. E. Lévi-Provençal (Paris, 1928), especially pp. 109–12 and 181–5.

powers in charge of markets, manners and *dhimmīs*); he had to enforce the discriminations imposed on the *dhimmīs*.

The degrading conditions under which the Jews in North Africa and Yemen lived for centuries undoubtedly had a very adverse effect on their development. In a way their consequences were more serious than expulsions and bloody persecution.[1]

The Middle Ages also saw voluntary defections from Judaism. The motive was mostly material—the desire to escape onerous taxation. However, the new Muslim lost his house and land, which remained the property of his former community, and paid the *kharāj* (land tax); he retained only his personal property. Islam was not interested in winning believers and thereby losing revenue.

A general survey of Jewish, Christian and Arab sources reveals that in the Middle Ages the situation of the Jews under Arab rule was generally better than that of the Christians, and incomparably better than the situation of the Jews in the Christian countries of Europe. True, more Christians than Jews served in high government posts, but precisely this made the Jews less vulnerable to persecution. Their behaviour did not arouse popular hatred and anger as much as did that of the Christians who were arrogant and domineering.

This outline of the political status of the Jews, of their legal rights and obligations, does not reflect all the developments and changes which occurred during roughly nine hundred years in the states arising in the territories of the Umayyad Caliphs. Within a general framework of tolerance towards the *dhimmī*, based on the Qur'ān and the *Ḥadīth*, we find a wide gamut of nuances—from near-equality with Muslims in everything not specifically religious, to the status of lowly subjects, tolerated but completely ignored.

This may be illustrated by one example. It is well known that sectarian Islam, the Shī'a, was more fanatical than the Sunna, and that the position of non-Muslims under Shī'ī rule was more difficult, so that eventually the only Shī'ī territories where Jews were still to be found were Yemen, wide stretches of Persia and North Africa. On the other hand we know that precisely in the areas of certain sects, such as the Khārijīs, the Ibāḍīs, and the Fāṭimids, conditions were exceptionally favourable to the development of non-Muslim communities.

[1] Cf. Hirschberg, *History*, vol. 1, pp. 145–51.

Social and religious trends

The Jewish society immediately before, and at the inception of, the Islamic period, was neither homogeneous in its composition nor orthodox in its beliefs. True, its concepts and views were mainly based on the Oral Law, but as this had not yet crystallized in all its tenets, it did not repudiate ideas that it did not regard as a threat to its existence.

Jewish influence was considerable in many countries situated on the periphery of the new regional entities then taking shape: as a result, whole, or large sections of Gentile tribes were attracted to Judaism, to the point of adopting various Jewish customs or even converting outright. This cannot have been due to political or economic power. Nor can we suppose that a particular institution existed—comparable to certain agencies of the Church—that concentrated on spreading Judaism. There can thus be but one explanation of those undeniable facts: the personal influence of one individual upon another, of members of a particular community upon their neighbours which—by its cumulative effect—led to the conversion of certain persons of royal lineage in South Arabia, to Judaizing tendencies among several tribes, to the conversion of the Khāqāns in the Khazar country, to the adoption of Jewish customs by Berber and Negro tribes in North and central Africa, and to all those individual instances of conversion in the Christian world which went down in history through the stir they created. In determining the causes of the interest in Judaism we cannot ignore the superstitions and magic practices rampant in late antiquity which involved the use of Jewish holy names in incantations; one of the features of Judaizing was the use of the tetragrammaton. Incidentally the belief in (holy) "names" and the urge to use them for magic purposes were not confined to adherents of "primitive" religions. We find them in Jewry as well.

The *midrashim* originating in that period are in part fraught with messianic tension, reflecting the hope of redemption then widely cherished. We certainly cannot say that messianic hopes were the monopoly of one section of the Jewish people, but it is a fact that the tension they generated led to serious upheavals in peripheral Diasporas, in Jewries whose ties with the centres of Jewish learning were not sufficiently strong. Active messianic movements had at all times something heterodox about them and were therefore disowned by rabbinical authorities, and their end usually proved their heretical implications.[1] For example, a simple, ignorant Jew named Obadiah, known as Abū 'Īsa 'l-Iṣfahānī, regarded himself as the Messiah or harbinger of the Messiah for his people. He lived in the Umayyad period. Another messianic movement, probably predating Abū 'Īsā, that of Serenus-Severus (Suryānī, Zonoria), led to the formation of a heretical sect in Jewry. The report of the appearance of the Messiah reached Spain, which proves both the strength of the movement at the time and the ties that existed already at the beginning of Arab rule in Spain between the Jewish communities in the eastern caliphate and those in its extreme west. One of the *geonim*, on being asked what attitude should be adopted towards that sect, displayed the utmost tolerance towards those who had followed Serenus and who (or whose children) wished to return to Judaism.

In his book *Kitāb al-anwār wa 'l-marāqib*, al-Qirqisānī mentions several sects that broke away from Judaism after Abū 'Īsā. But in his time, mere remnants were left of all of them—a small group of supporters of Abū 'Īsā, living in Damascus.[2] While these sects were short-lived, an important part was played by the Karaite movement, which opposed the ruling Rabbanites—adherents of the Oral Law—and wished to base Judaism exclusively on the Written Law. Its founder, 'Anan b. David of the family of the Exilarchs (second half of the eighth century), was to have succeeded to the exilarchate after the death of his uncle, but the scholars of the Babylonian Talmudical academies (*yeshivot*) took exception to his views and elected his younger brother instead. 'Anan took advantage of anti-Oral Law trends that still existed centuries after the disappearance of the Sadducees and brought about a split in Judaism. His views found favour, especially in places remote from the Babylonian *yeshivot*. Benjamin al-Nihāwandī and Daniel al-Qūmisī, the heads of the new sect, which called itself Karaites (sons of Scripture), came from such places.

Al-Qirqisānī stresses the differences between 'Anan's teachings and those of later Karaite leaders, in particular the wide divergences in religious practice as a result of the liberty granted to every person to

[1] Messianic trends in pre-Islamic Arabia are analysed in H. Z. (J. W.) Hirschberg's "Footsteps of the Messiah in Arabia during the Fifth and Sixth Centuries after the Destruction of the Second Temple" in *Memorial Volume for the Vienna Jewish Theological Seminary* (Hebrew) (Jerusalem, 1946), pp. 112–24; *idem*, *Israel in Arabia* (Hebrew), pp. 175–6.

[2] Cf. S. W. Baron, *A Social and Religious History of the Jews* (Philadelphia, 1957), vol. v, pp. 182–97 with notes.

interpret the Law according to his own lights. Possibly because of that liberty, Karaism spread among Jewry throughout the Mediterranean area, including North Africa and Spain. At its apogee (ninth to eleventh centuries), the sect constituted a serious threat to Rabbanite Judaism. Jerusalem was the seat of *nesī'īm* or the House of 'Anan and of anti-Rabbanite scholars. The general decline of Palestine in the second half of the eleventh century and the destruction of the Jewish population of Jerusalem by the Crusaders eliminated that centre, whereas *gaon* Saadia's persistent struggle against Karaism diminished its influence in Iraq. Although the centre of gravity shifted to Byzantium, important Karaite communities survived in Egypt, Syria and Iraq—even in Spain, but they were no longer a threat to Rabbanite Jewry. The tension that had prevailed during the first few centuries following the split had largely abated.[1]

After describing the heterodox trends in Judaism, we are able to appreciate the normative centres striving to consolidate Jewry into a single entity. During the first four hundred years these were the *yeshivot* in Babylonia and Palestine in which the most active and fertile brains were concentrated, radiating their spirit near and far.

The foremost task of these *yeshivot* was the teaching of the Law, and it is hard to overestimate the decisive rôle of the two ancient Babylonian *yeshivot* of Sūrā and Pumbadītha which renewed their activity under the caliphate after periods of oppression and paralysis; they contributed enormously to the development and fixing of the *halakhah*. Scholars flocked to them for intensive research—from Byzantium, Egypt, Africa, Italy and Spain, and even the son of one of the Palestinian *geonim* came.

In Palestine, on the other hand, the emphasis lay on the emotional, reverential, irrational aspects of religion. Pilgrims visited the country in fulfilment of the sacred duty of "going up" to Jerusalem. On *Hoshana Rabba*[2] the pilgrims would assemble on the Mount of Olives to pray and earn blessings through the prayer of the Palestinian *gaon*, to hear his proclamations on matters of *halakhah* and the dates of next year's festivals, and the curses uttered against the Karaites. On

[1] Abraham b. David, the Spanish-Jewish historian (middle of twelfth century), regards them as a small, insignificant minority; cf. his *Book of Tradition* (Hebrew), ed. A. Neubauer, *Mediaeval Jewish Chronicles*, vol. 1 (Oxford, 1887), pp. 78–9. Cf. also Simon b. Ṣemaḥ Duran, *Magen Aḇōṯ* (Livorno, 1785), 31*a*; Abraham Zacuto, *Liber Juchassin*, ed. H. Filipowski (London, 1857), p. 115. The testimony of these two authors does not extend to Byzantium and eastern Europe.

[2] I.e. the seventh day of the Feast of Tabernacles.

returning to their own countries they would bring with them something of the sanctity, poetry, and craving for redemption of the Holy Land.[1]

The Babylonian *yeshivot* did not only provide oral instruction. The teaching and guidance in form of the answers (*responsa*) to inquiries addressed to the *geonim* were far more important. In addition to manifold practical questions aimed at guidance in the everyday affairs of the individual and the community—regarding the relationship between man and God and between man and man—we frequently find theoretical questions concerning the interpretation of some biblical passage or talmudical term, the use of some astronomical instrument or some abstract problem of religious belief. Transport and communication facilities made it advisable to ask a number of questions at a time, and we accordingly meet with whole tracts each containing a group of *responsa* addressed to the same place.[2]

The *geonim* and Exilarch had power to appoint *dayyānīm* (judicial officers) in their respective districts and to supervise the administration of justice. Each of the two Babylonian *yeshivot* had a *beyṯ dīn gāḏōl* (High Court) beside it, headed by a president (*aḇ*), who acted as deputy to the *gaon* and sometimes succeeded the *gaon* after his death.

Litigants from other countries could, by mutual consent, bring their cases before the *geonim* for an opinion. Moreover, by means of the *responsa*, the *geonim* exerted great influence over the organization of lawcourts, procedure and uniformity of jurisdiction. We cannot deal here with the rôle played by Maimonides during his residence in Cairo in the development of Rabbanite Judaism, nor with his son, Abraham, and his descendants—five generations in all (until the end of the fourteenth century)—who were the *negīdīm* (government-approved secular leaders) of Jewry in Egypt and its dependencies and, at the same time, spiritual leaders consulted on all matters of religion and law. (Incidentally, the Egyptian *negīdīm* were also in charge of the quite large Karaite and Samaritan communities.) The spread of magic beliefs among the people was paralleled by an increase of mystical tendencies. There is evidence of cosmogonic speculation and a yearning for nearness to God in talmudical literature and ancient *midrashim*. But now these subjects are taken up in special *midrashim* and tracts on *The Mysteries of the Creation* and *The Mysteries of the Chariot*. The exact

[1] Cf. the "Letter of Ben Meir, the Palestinian Gaon", ed. A. Guillaume in *JQR*, N.S., vol. v (1914–15), pp. 552–4; Abraham b. David, *Book of Tradition*, p. 79.

[2] A classical example is the collection of *Responsa*, ed. A. Harkavy, *Responsen der Geonim* (Berlin, 1887).

date of the composition of these works is difficult to determine, but, as far as we know, their popularity did not precede the inception of Islam.

The autonomous administration

By unanimous Jewish testimony the Caliphs 'Umar and 'Alī were sympathetic towards the representatives of the supreme institutions of the Babylonian Jewish community: the Exilarch and the head of the *yeshiva* of Fīrūzshāpūr whither the sages of Pumbadītha had repaired when the religious and administrative organization of the Jews was shaken by social upheavals besetting Persia. The position of the Jews had then been weakened in every respect. Now, following the stabilization of Arab rule which did not interfere with the internal affairs of non-Muslims, a period of renewal and flowering set in. A state of peaceful coexistence developed between the Muslim authorities and the autonomous institutions of the non-Muslims so that the Jews were able to reconstitute a system of self-government.[1]

The head of the "secular" autonomous administration was the Exilarch. His office originated in Parthian times and continued under the Sāsānids. The Exilarch was of Davidic stock; his office was hereditary. After a period of instability, Bustanai was recognized as Exilarch and transmitted the office to his sons by his Jewish wife and by a Persian princess. The hereditary and elected representatives of Iraqi Jewry were charged with the administration of all taxes to be levied from Jews, with the representation of Jewry before the Muslim rulers, with autonomous judicial functions, the enactment of communal regulations and the supervision of the *yeshivot*, etc.[2]

The traveller Benjamin of Tudela who visited Baghdad about 1168, gives an eyewitness account of the honour and splendour surrounding the Exilarch Daniel b. Ḥasdai (1150–74) at the caliph's court. He was received by the caliph every Thursday in official audience when all Muslims and Jews had to stand before him; he sat beside the caliph while all the Muslim dignitaries remained on their feet. Another Jewish traveller, Petaḥya of Regensburg, reports that the heads of the Jewish community in Mosul punished offenders even if the other party to the case was a Muslim. (There was a Jewish prison in the city.)

[1] Cf. H. Tykocinski, "Bustanai The Exilarch" (Hebrew), *Debir*, vol. I (1923), pp. 145–79; A. Marx, "Der arabische Bustanai-Bericht und Nathan ha-Babli" in *Livre d'hommage à la mémoire du Samuel Poznanski*, pp. 76–84.

[2] A colourful description of the Exilarch's office is given by Nathan b. Isaac in *Seder 'Olam Zuṭā*, ed. Neubauer, *Mediaeval Jewish Chronicles*, vol. II, pp. 83–6.

Petaḥya also notes that the Jews did not pay taxes direct to the caliph, but paid one gold dinar *per annum* to the Exilarch. When the Mongol Khān, Hülegü, conquered Baghdad (1258) he did not harm the Jewish community nor the Exilarch, Samuel b. David. Jewish leaders of the House of David continued to reside in Baghdad until the days of Tamerlane (1401).

During the decline of the 'Abbāsid caliphate, when control was passing to the Seljuks, minor governments sprang up in Mosul, Damascus, and Aleppo. Scions of the families of the Babylonian Exilarch settled in those cities and obtained important positions which were confirmed by the governments. So dear was the memory of the Davidic Kingdom to the people that the descendants of David were received everywhere with great honours. They were given the title *nāsī*. Their dynastic origin placed them automatically at the head of the community as its recognized representatives. This splitting-up of the exilarchate into different territorial units began in the eleventh century. The *nesī'īm* collected tithes, poll-tax and other imposts, appointed communal officials and judges and sat in judgment themselves.[1]

In contrast to the general silence of Arab sources about other communities generally and the Jews in particular, the Exilarch is repeatedly mentioned by them.

Our knowledge of the development of Palestine in the first few centuries of Arab rule is scanty. It derives from certain apocalyptic *midrashim* and some fragments from the *Geniza*. It seems that the dualistic method of *sārīm* (princes) whose main functions were representation before the authorities and the collection of taxes, and *rāshey yeshiva*, heads in charge of learning, religion and law had not penetrated to this area.

We know more about the forms of organization of Egyptian and North African Jewry which were different from those so far described. For political reasons the Fāṭimid Caliphs in Egypt did not want the Jewish communities in their domains, which extended as far as present-day Morocco, to be subject to Jewish authorities located outside their realm. Like the Umayyad rulers of Spain and part of Morocco, they therefore encouraged the separation of local Jewry from the Babylonian

[1] *The Itinerary of Benjamin of Tudela*, ed. M. N. Adler (London, 1907), Hebrew text, pp. 39–40, transl. p. 39; *Tour du Monde ou voyages du Rabbin Péthachia*, ed. E. Carmoly (Paris, 1886), pp. 18–21; J. Mann, "The Office of the Exilarch in Babylonia", etc. in *Livre d'hommage à la mémoire du Samuel Poznanski* (Hebrew Part), p. 24; *idem*, *Texts and Studies*, vol. 1, pp. 394 ff.

centre. Several versions of letters of appointment of *negīdīm* in Egypt have come down to us. They show that the *nagīd*'s functions were similar to those of the Exilarch in Babylonia: he represented all the Jews and was their religious guide and judge; he drew up deeds of marriage and divorce and saw to it that prayers were said while facing Jerusalem, in contrast to Samaritan custom; and he was responsible for the implementation of the special measures applying to the *dhimmīs*.

Palestinian and Syrian Jewry was headed by a local *nagīd*, subordinate to the *nagīd* in Cairo, whose deputy he was supposed to be and without whose permission he could not be appointed. Apart from the *nagīd* two other functionaries represented the community: the minister (*ḥazzān*) and the prayer-leader (*shelīaḥ ṣibbūr*).

The office of *nagīd* existed in Egypt until the conquest of that country by the Turks (1517) and was abolished shortly after. On the other hand, the office of the *nagīd* in Morocco (similar offices existed in Algeria, Tunisia and Tripolitania) was restored in the sixteenth century.

Influence of economic factors

The Arab conquest tore down the political and economic barriers separating Persia and Byzantium, and Byzantium and Visigoth Spain, so that all subjects of the caliph—without discrimination—were able to exert their initiative and abilities in the vast area extending from the approaches of India to the domain of the Frankish kings.

Simultaneously, as if by magic, administrative centres and capital cities began to spring up, some nominally subject to the caliphs, but actually semi-independent, others founded by sectarian, Shī'ite dynasties. They included *inter alia* (in geographical order, from east to west): Ahwāz, Tustar, Kūfa, Baghdad, Ramla, Fusṭāṭ, Cairo, Mahdiyya, Qayrawān, Ashīr, Tāhart, and Tlemcen. By and by these places became also centres of commerce and seats of scholarship and religious instruction. The phenomenon of rival twin cities, known from antiquity (e.g. Jerusalem-Caesarea), repeated itself. New cities developed at the expense of older ones. Cases in point are Lydda-Ramla, Ctesiphon-Bagdhad, Bābilyūn (Egypt)—Fusṭāṭ-Cairo. The new cities attracted many of the inhabitants of the older ones which became depopulated and sank to the level of provincial towns or suburbs. The ninth century saw a change in the function of ports in the Muslim part of the Mediterranean, especially in the western sector. The Arab navy grew strong and enabled the Arab armies to attack Byzantine positions in

Cyprus, Crete, Sicily and southern Italy. This development was especially advantageous to North Africa. The Mediterranean became an Arab sea, and the Byzantine fleet ceased to play an effective rôle in the trade of the area. The importance of North Africa as a link in maritime trade communications between east and west, south and north increased. Muslim merchantmen began to sail from western Tripolitania, from Mahdiyya, and later also from Bijāya (Bougie), Sabta (Ceuta), and Salā (Salé). They went in three directions: east to Egypt and Syria, north to Sicily and southern Italy, and west to Spain to load and unload goods brought from far away. The southern route via the Red Sea towards the Indian Ocean was not yet open to water-borne traffic, and goods had to be taken from Alexandria to the Red Sea ports and vice versa by a combination of different means of transport. Hence the decisive importance of Fusṭāṭ-Cairo.

These changes in the distribution and economic structure of the population had far-reaching effects on Jewish society. In the early days of Arab rule there were probably still a not inconsiderable number of Jews in the villages of Palestine and Babylonia. Our sources suggest that also in North Africa and Spain Jews tilled the soil, planted gardens and orchards and bred cattle. But it seems that most of the Jewish population in those days subsisted by handicrafts and itinerant trading. Muslim sources tell us that most of the Jews in Syria are dyers, tanners, barbers, cooks, or *jahābidha*, a term whose meaning we shall discuss presently. On the other hand, most physicians and clerks in government service were Christians. An order by the Caliph al-Muqtadir (908–32) restricts the employment of Jews and Christians in government jobs to physicians and *jahābidha*, but this order was not strictly enforced so that we find them also in other positions.[1]

In the countries of Islam, Muslims were practically forbidden to work in gold and silver. Islamic law regards the wage received for work in precious metals as usurious profit and lays down that no more may be charged for gold and silver articles than the metal value (by weight if payment is made in the same metal), that is to say, without remuneration for the work and without compensation for wastage. This restriction was accepted by Muslims and accounts for the fact that in most Muslim countries the trades connected with the fashioning of precious metals became a monopoly of non-Muslims. These trades included not only gold- and silversmiths, but also the *jahbadh*, i.e. the

[1] Ibn Taghrībirdi, *al-Nujūm al-ẓāhira* (ed. Cairo), vol. III, p. 165 (ed. Juynboll, II, p. 174).

tester of precious metals; the moneychanger (who was at first also the moneylender); and the collector of taxes and customs dues who had to be conversant with the different kinds of coins current in the world, capable of calculating their value according to the percentage and price of the precious metal contained in them and, moreover, to keep books properly—an art not at first met with among the Bedouin. Initially these occupations were closely related or even identical, and in more advanced stages of economic development some of them were called by the same name so that it is sometimes difficult to decide which of them is meant in a particular case. Thus Persian *jahbadh*, which originally meant a person who understands and discerns, came to denote a moneychanger, coin tester, tax-collector, banker, etc.[1]

That Muslims refrained from working in gold and silver was the reason that mints in Muslim countries were operated by Christians and later also by Jews. Though exact information concerning the early period is lacking, we know that mints in the territory of the Aghlabī dynasty were operated by Christians. Later the mint in Egypt was run by Jews, and Jews also minted the coins in Yemen and North Africa.[2]

But the view that Jews were mainly members of menial, despised occupations—moneychangers, tanners, shoemakers, dyers, weavers, masons—has likewise been refuted. In the *Geniza* materials we find them as dealers in linen and silk, perfumes, pearls and corals, that is, as highly esteemed businessmen engaged in luxury trades. Arab sources contain short notes on Jewish wholesale merchants, toll-farmers and bankers at the court of the caliphs in Baghdad. This is confirmed through Jewish sources.

We know of a Baghdad merchant who attained the exalted position of vizier in the Fāṭimid administration in Egypt. Ya'qūb b. Killis, a native of Baghdad and according to tradition a descendant of al-Samaw'al b. 'Ādiyā', the famous Jewish poet who lived in the Arabian Peninsula in the generation before Muḥammad, was at first a "merchants' warden" in Ramla, that is, the official representative and trustee of the Jewish merchants in this important administrative and commercial centre. He enjoyed the confidence of Kāfūr, the Ikhshīdī ruler of Egypt, and was appointed director of revenue of the *dīwān* in Egypt and Syria. However he aroused the envy of the Muslim vizier, and after

[1] Cf. W. J. Fischel, *Jews in the Economic and Political Life of Mediaeval Islam* (London, 1937), pp. 2–8.

[2] Cf. A. N. Poliak, "The Jews and the Mint in Egypt under the Mamlūks" (Hebrew), *Zion*, vol. I (1936), pp. 24–36; S. Asaf, *ibid.* p. 256; Hirschberg, *History*, vol. II, p. 48.

Kāfūr's death was compelled to flee Egypt for Qayrawān. He is said to have, with the help of Jews at the court of the Fāṭimid Caliph al-Mu'izz, entered the service of that ruler who was then about to march on Egypt. According to Arab sources, Ya'qūb effectively assisted al-Mu'izz's army commander during that campaign. He rose very high at the Fāṭimid court, was appointed vizier, and laid the foundations for a public tax-collection system in that country (he died in 991). Although he embraced Islam, he remained friendly with the Jews and posted some of them as his representatives in Egypt and Syria in the tax-collection and intelligence services.[1] One of them, Manasse al-Qazzāz, i.e. the silk merchant, was the Fāṭimid commissioner in Syria and continued in this task when 'Īsā b. Nestorius, a Coptic Christian, was appointed vizier.[2]

After the convulsions in the reign of the Caliph al-Ḥākim (996–1021), the founder of the Druze sect, we again find Jews at the court of the Fāṭimid Caliphs in economic and administrative jobs. The sons of the merchant Sahl al-Tustarī, i.e. members of a family originating from southern Persia, were especially prominent. Tustar was an important commercial centre in the tenth century, and its Jews had a large share in its prosperity. Copious data on the firm of the sons of Sahl have been preserved. The sources stress their trade in precious stones which led to their becoming court purveyors of other goods as well. The trade in precious stones launched them in international business and they carried on a correspondence with many countries. It is hardly surprising that their economic position made its impact on political affairs. The Persian traveller Nāṣir-i Khusraw and the Egyptian writer al-Maqrīzī admiringly describe the wealth of the sons of Sahl.[3]

Fusṭāṭ was the natural meeting-place for Jewish traders from the Maghrib, Sicily and the East (from the Indian Ocean to China). We therefore find in Fusṭāṭ, apart from the Babylonians (*'irāqīs*), Palestinians and Syrians (*shāmīs*), a great number of emigrants from the Maghrib who had either settled or were staying there for long periods on business. The influx of immigrants into Egypt increased from the second half of the eleventh century following political upheavals in the west and east.

The first half of the twelfth century saw a great increase of Jewish

[1] Cf. Fischel, *op. cit.* pp. 45–68; Hirschberg, *History*, vol. 1, pp. 74, 153.

[2] Cf. Mann, *The Jews in Egypt and in Palestine* (Oxford, 1920), vol. 1, pp. 19–22.

[3] Cf. Fischel, *op. cit.* pp. 68–89.

trade between Egypt and India by the land-and-sea route passing through South Arabia. A fairly clear picture of the situation emerges from a preliminary survey of the *Geniza* material which puts in relief the large share of Maghrib Jewry in that important economic activity. The cause of this phenomenon is not far to seek. In addition to general factors, above all the Crusades, it was prompted by a powerful local motive: the decline of the Maghrib compelled its traders to seek new sources of livelihood.[1]

Important political and economic events—the Crusades, the Almohad conquests and the attendant tribulations, the rise of the Italian seaports (Venice, Pisa, Genoa) and of Marseilles, and the Mongol incursions—began to make their impact on the Muslim East and its trade. They also affected the position of the Jews who were compelled to adjust themselves to new conditions.

A turning-point in the social status of the Jews is already noticeable in the thirteenth century. Even the communities in Egypt (then the richest Middle Eastern country) became impoverished, although they were still better off than those in other countries of the Middle East. The pedlars and craftsmen already met with in previous centuries now formed the majority of Jewish breadwinners and barely made ends meet. The system of state monopolies in various branches of commerce reduced the share of the Jews in these. Trade with India declined owing to European competition which had found new ways of access. Religious fanaticism debarred all but a few Jews from government service. They were fewer than in the earlier period, and there was always the danger of a renewal of the ban which had been issued from time to time. On the other hand, there existed apparently a relatively large number of Jewish physicians, including famous specialists who continued the tradition of Maimonides.

On the whole, it may be said that the nearer we get to the end of the Middle Ages the smaller becomes the number of skilled craftsmen and the larger that of wretched, poverty-stricken pedlars. Simultaneously, we observe a decline of the merchant class due to the economic instability prevailing in Egypt and the remainder of the Mamlūk territory extending as far as the centre of Asia Minor.

[1] Cf. S. D. Goitein, "The Main Industries of the Mediterranean Area" in *Journal of Economic and Social History of the Orient*, vol. IV, part II (1961), pp. 168–97; "La Tunisie du XIè siècle..." in *Études d'Orientalisme dédiées à la memoire de Lévi-Provençal* (Paris, 1962), pp. 559–79; "Letters and Documents on the India Trade..." in *Islamic Culture*, vol. 27 (1963), pp. 188–205.

WAVES OF IMMIGRATION: REVIVAL AND NEW TRENDS

Immigrants from Europe

The characteristic feature of the Jewish communities in Middle Eastern countries at the end of the Middle Ages was a general decline—religious (in piety and learning), social, economic and numerical. This process had begun already at the time of the disintegration of the ʿAbbāsid caliphate. It was at first not conspicuous since attempts were made from time to time to arrest it. From the fourteenth century on, however, the marks of decline were obvious. The Oriental countries from Persia, Mesopotamia, Syria, Palestine and Egypt to the outermost Maghrib in part became emptied of their Jewish communities. For Persia and Mesopotamia, we possess no information at all, which is not a favourable sign. The emigrants from the East went to Europe, first of all to those countries which at the beginning of the second millennium were partly under Muslim rule (Spain, southern Italy); from there they moved on to Christian Europe.

The numerical decline of Jewry in Palestine, Egypt and North Africa owing to emigration and forced conversion was in part set off by natural increase which has always been high in the Middle East. In the middle of the twelfth century a numerically small return movement to the East set in, which imparted new energies, a fresh impetus and new religious ideas to the communities there. Individuals and groups from the Maghrib settled in Egypt and Palestine as a result of the policy of the Almohads. A large group of rabbis from France immigrated to Palestine in the thirteenth century. From the fourteenth century on immigration from Christian-dominated countries spread over the whole Muslim East. At first merely symbolical, it became in time a real movement and in the late fifteenth and early sixteenth centuries assumed truly significant proportions. It never ceased from then onwards. Most of the immigrants were "returnees" (sometimes after centuries) from countries where they had been persecuted (Spain, Hungary, Ukraine), but many came from countries where their lives had not been in danger (Italy, western Europe). The settlers from Europe radically changed the numerical and qualitative composition and organizational structure of the Jewish communities in the countries where they established themselves.

It is worth noting the motives which impelled Jews in Christian Europe to migrate to North Africa, to Asia Minor and to Syria-

Palestine. Three successor dynasties carved up the Almohad state between them and in the middle of the thirteenth century set up three states very roughly coinciding with the areas now known as Morocco, Algeria and Tunisia. The three countries abrogated the disabilities inflicted by the Almohads on Muslims who did not accept their doctrine and partly also on non-Muslims—i.e. Jews, for they alone had remained.

Even before religious oppression began to afflict the Jews of Spain and the Spanish-controlled islands, many of them settled in Algerian coastal cities. This was due not only to geographical proximity, but also, and mainly, to a tradition of close cultural, economic and political ties between North Africa and Muslim Spain, jointly designated as "the West" (Maghrib).

Most of those expelled from Spain and the Balearic Islands in 1391 likewise settled in the Algerian seaports: Ḥunayn, Oran, Mustaghānim, Tanas, Brishk, Algiers, Bijāya (Bougie); also in Tunis and in cities not far from the sea: Tlemcen, Milyāna, Medéa and Constantine.

Those expelled in 1492 settled in Fez, Marrakesh and Shafshāwan (Xauen) in the interior of the country, in the Atlantic cities of Aṣīla (Arzila), al-ʿArāʾish (Larache), Azammūr, Tīṭ, Mazaghan, Safī and Agadīr, and in the Mediterranean ports of Sabta (Ceuta) and Bādis (Velez) which the Spaniards left untouched in deference to existing agreements.

A third wave of emigrants reached this area (except Morocco) from the late sixteenth century onwards. They were the *Gornim* (the people from Livorno, in Hebrew sources called Ligorna), mostly descendants of expellees from Spain, but including also Italian Jews and North Africans. Long after they were given the right to settle in that port city (which Medicean rulers had begun to develop) they struck out for the southern shores of the Mediterranean. They are first attested in Tunis and Tripoli and later also in Algiers.[1] Jews from central Europe (Ashkenazim) did not yet come to the Maghrib.

We now pass to the eastern part of the Middle East where a shift in the balance of forces set in already in the second half of the fourteenth century. From then onwards the military might of the Ottoman Turks increased and Ottoman expansion reached its peak in the days of Süleyman the Lawgiver and Selim II. These conquests brought many Jewish communities under Turkish sway, both in hitherto Christian-

[1] Cf. a *Responsum* of the sixteenth century (R. Simon b. Ṣemaḥ Duran, *Responsa*, vol. IV, §21); also Hirschberg, *History*, vol. II, pp. 49, 53–5, 120, 185.

ruled areas and in Muslim countries threatened by Spanish invasion; they could then breathe freely. But this was not all. Towards the end of Meḥmed the Conqueror's reign (1451–81), a German Jew resident in Adrianople earnestly appealed to his brethren in Germany and Italy to settle in Turkey: "... Under Ismael, every man dwells safely under his fig tree and under his vine ... Not so the German lands and all their surroundings. No Jew in all the cities there wears green or red." The epistle concludes with a call for immigration to the land of Israel.[1]

In the fifteenth and sixteenth centuries we indeed find Ashkenazi and Italian communities in several cities of the empire: Constantinople, Adrianople, Salonica, Sofia, Pleven, Vidin, Trikkala and Arta. The Ashkenazim came from Germany, France and Hungary, the Italians from Sicily (then under Spanish rule), Apulia, Otranto and Calabria.

But those expelled from Spain and Portugal in the years 1492–7 played the decisive rôle in shaping the character of the Jewish communities in the Ottoman Empire. Although they do not seem to have numbered more than 7–8,000, they in time set their imprint on all the other Jews, both the veteran residents in the Arab and Byzantine areas (the latter called Romaniots) and the Ashkenazi and Italian immigrants. They arrived in the days of Sultan Bayezid II (1481–1512), who opened the gates of his country wide to the Jews.[2]

The newcomers naturally preferred places with a Jewish population which had mostly settled earlier than the ruling majority groups (Turks, Mamlūks, Arabs). Their establishment in places with no existing Jewish community—such as the Atlantic ports of Morocco—was exceptional. The veteran communities called themselves, and were called by the immigrants, by different names: in Africa, they were "the residents" or "turban-wearers" (from their headgear, which was similar to that of the Muslims, in contrast to the garment of the Jews from Spain called in Hebrew sources *capos* or *caperon*).[3] In Egypt, Palestine and Syria the old-established Jews were called *musta'rabim*, i.e. speakers of Arabic (compare the name Mozarabs for those Christians in Spain who assimilated to the Arabs, adopting their language and

[1] In A. Jellinek, *Zur Geschichte der Kreuzzüge* (Hebrew) (Leipzig, 1854), p. 21. Cf. also the "Epistle from Salonica 1550", ed. I. Loeb, in *REJ*, vol. xv (1887), pp. 270–2.

[2] Cf. S. Usque, *Consolaçam ás tribulaçoens de Israel* (Ferrara, 1553), ff. 207–9. I. Aboab, *Nomologia o discursos legales compuestos* (Amsterdam, 1629), p. 195; *The Chronicle of Joseph Sambari* (completed 1672), ed. Neubauer, *Med. Jew. Chronicles*, vol. 1, p. 138. Cf. p. 148 below, with p. 185 n. 2. for *Romaniots*.

[3] Cf. R. Salomon b. Simon Duran, *Responsa* (Livorno, 1742), §413.

customs). Travellers from Italy called them Moriscos.[1] The Jews living in the territories of the former Byzantine Empire were called Romaniots or Gregos, from (eastern) Rome and the Greek language, which they used in everyday speech. Small Karaite and Samaritan communities also existed in the former Byzantine territory and in Egypt and Syria.

The impression which the first expellees from the affluent European countries received upon meeting the "residents" in North Africa was dismal in every respect. R. Isaac b. Sheshet Perfet, an eminent rabbinical scholar from Spain, describes their grave material condition in one of his *responsa* thus: "The inhabitants of this country can hardly afford a modicum of bread and water. They sleep on the ground or on carpets of animal skin and cover themselves at night with their daytime clothes. Their garments are all in patches and most of them go barefoot."[2]

Their spiritual condition was even worse. Books, which were then very expensive, and even Torah scrolls for use in the synagogue were lacking. The persecutions during the Almohad era and the cessation of relations with communities in other countries arrested their development. Maimonides' great treatise was the only halakhic work in their possession. In the opinion of refugee scholars ignorance was rife among the masses and the religious leaders.[3]

R. Obadiah of Bertinoro, who immigrated to Palestine in 1488 and settled in Jerusalem, describes the utterly wretched condition of the inhabitants of that city. He found there some *marranos* who had returned to Judaism—surely immigrants from Spain. R. Obadiah preached in the synagogue twice a month in Hebrew. He had two Spanish disciples who studied regularly with him. His efforts led to a great improvement of the situation a few years later.[4]

However the immigrants did not always maintain satisfactory moral and religious standards. R. Isaac Perfet tells about a Mallorcan refugee who vilified him, the aged and distinguished scholar, but he would not let the community outlaw the man. According to R. Isaac Perfet, the Muslim governor of the city permitted refugees to land without payment until that Mallorcan Jew induced him to impose a tax of one doubloon on them. Furthermore, the local *qāḍī* rejected

[1] Cf. B. Lewis, *Notes and Documents from the Turkish Archives* (Jerusalem, 1952), p. 5; R. Mosheh Bassola, *A Pilgrimage to Palestine* (Hebrew), ed. I. Ben-Zvi (Jerusalem, 1938), pp. 36, 43.

[2] Perfet, *Responsa*, §153.

[3] *Idem*, *Responsa*, §5; R. Simon b. Ṣemaḥ Duran, *Responsa*, vols. III, §49; II, §75.

[4] Cf. *Letters from Palestine* (Hebrew), ed. A. Ya'ri (Jerusalem, 1943), pp. 142, 157.

complaints by Muslims that the influx of refugees caused food prices to rise. But when one day a group of *marranos* arrived, that Mallorcan tried to persuade the community to put pressure on the governor not to admit them.[1]

The immigrants from the Iberian Peninsula included a percentage of *marranos* who managed to escape to Muslim countries where they could openly return to Judaism. This percentage increased as the condition of the *marranos* deteriorated, especially after the establishment of the Inquisition. Already in the fifteenth century many third-generation *marranos* decided to leave Spain. So long as Jewish communities existed in Spain and Portugal the *marranos* were able, to a certain extent, to preserve Jewish traditions and to live clandestinely according to Jewish law. But it became difficult, indeed almost impossible, for them to do so after the 1492–7 expulsions and after the Inquisition functioned in Portugal as well.

Many doubts arose about the position of the *marranos* in the religious and social spheres and especially as regards their personal status. Rabbinical literature time and again discusses the question whether the *marranos* were to be regarded as defectors reverting to Judaism or as strangers who wished to embrace the Jewish faith. While in the first generation it was easy to ascertain whether a *marrano*'s wife was a Jewess and whether the marriage rites had been duly performed, the inquiry became complicated and its results doubtful in the case of children and grandchildren born as Christians. The status of members of the priestly class (*kōhanīm*) enjoying certain privileges, but for that very reason subject to special obligations, was of particular importance.

Some rabbis favoured a rigorous attitude towards those *marranos* who had neglected opportunities of escape and thus remained voluntarily in the countries where they turned renegade; they were therefore to be regarded as real Christians. But most religious authorities were inclined to be lenient, to regard the *marranos* as Jews and to enable them to return to Judaism without much difficulty even in the second, third, or fourth generations.[2]

Complaints of a different kind were voiced against the immigrants from Spain by R. David Kohen, a Romaniot rabbi who lived in Constantinople about the time of the expulsion. He accused them of

[1] Perfet, *Responsa*, §61.

[2] Cf. H J. Zimmels, *Die Marranen in der rabbinischen Literatur* (Berlin, 1932), pp. 12 ff.

ignorance in religious matters, the reading of apocryphal books, and neglect of the *Torah* and said that they were not god-fearing. All, he said, thought themselves very clever; and as they did not recognize the ordination of rabbis (which had then been introduced with the Ashkenazim) in Italy and with the Romaniots, every one of them regarded himself as competent to make decisions and issue instructions in matters of Jewish law.[1]

R. Eliyahu Mizraḥi, one of the most prominent Romaniot rabbis in those days, known as a modest and conciliatory person, uses rather sharp language about the immigrants: "If it happens in my lifetime that people rely on their own opinion to justify desecration of the Sabbath . . . what will happen after my death? Who ever heard or saw such a thing? People who have never seen the light of the Torah issue faulty instructions contrary to religion on their own authority. . ."[2]

The "residents" also complained about material disadvantages caused to them by the immigrants. To attract wealthy merchants from Spain, experienced in international trade, Algerian rulers in the fifteenth century agreed to grant them substantial concessions in regard of the payment of poll-tax. R. Simon b. Ṣemaḥ Duran (a contemporary of R. Isaac b. Sheshet Perfet) reports that "as the newcomers did not accede to the veterans' demand to equalize the payment, the veterans agreed between them to separate from the immigrants . . . not to eat the meat of animals slaughtered by them, not to drink their wine, not to visit their sick and not to circumcise their sons; at the time fixed for their sacred studies, no veteran settler was to remain in the synagogue, and when it was the turn of one of them to lead in prayer, no veteran settler was to stand up and read lessons."[3]

Apart from the above-mentioned attempt of the Mallorcan Jew we know of no action by Jews residing in Muslim countries to prevent the settlement of Jewish immigrants from Europe. This is due to the right of free economic activity and unrestricted settlement enjoyed by Jews and Christians in those countries—except for the general prohibition of settling in Ḥijāz and two or three cities sacred to Islam.

If, in summing up, we evaluate the characteristics of the new immigrants, we must admit that their sense of intellectual pre-eminence and superior economic ability was certainly justified. At the same time we cannot overlook their conceit and vanity which may be the result of

[1] David Kohen, *Responsa* (1734), §12.
[2] Mizraḥi, *Responsa* (1561), §87.
[3] Duran, *Responsa*, vol. III, § 46.

their close contact with the Arabs and Spaniards, two peoples noted for their lofty pride.

As a result, the immigrants from Spain and Portugal organized themselves everywhere in separate communities, called *kehalīm*. They maintained synagogues of their own with rabbis, religious educational establishments (such as Talmud schools), charitable institutions and separate taxation. The *kehalīm* were not a transitory feature which ceased or became blurred and unimportant in time as was the case in the Maghrib. In Tunis we indeed find a deterioration of relations between the *Touansa* and the *Gornim* in the eighteenth century leading to the establishment of a separate office of a *qā'id* for the *Gornim*. The separation between the two communities lasted until the 1940s. Although the differences in language, culture, economic circumstances and religious customs which justified the existence of a separate organization of the immigrants immediately after their arrival became obliterated, the original dividing walls did not disappear, due to a tendency to sectionalism and fragmentation among the Sephardim. Evidence for this is the formation of separate communities according to regions, even cities of origin and subdivisions within these communities as a result of debilitating internal squabbles. Things went so far that regulations had to be issued forbidding the withdrawal of members from their communities, accession to other communities or combination into new ones.[1]

Their legal and social status

Until the mid-nineteenth century no change occurred in the legal position of the non-Muslim subjects of Muslim rulers. The special tax laws and the restrictions regarding the erection of new synagogues and the shape of the existing ones (i.e. the decrees forming the hallowed tradition based on 'Umar's regulations) remained in force. The Muslim authorities strictly enforced the *ghiyār*, the distinctive dress and footwear, and the segregation in special quarters. True, in the Asian and European areas of the Ottoman Empire (except Yemen) the Jewish quarter had not always the character of a ghetto.

The sympathetic attitude of the rulers towards the immigrants from Christian Europe did not exempt them from the application of 'Umar's regulations, nor give them a status similar to that of the

[1] Cf. for the Spanish–Portuguese exiles J. Caro Baroja, "Minorias israelitas en el Occidente europeo durante la edad moderna", in *Rapports du XIIe Congrès International des Sciences Historiques* (Vienna, 1965), vol. I, pp. 151–9.

Muslims. Sometimes such immigrants were exempted from certain obligations or obtained certain concessions, but these were passing phenomena. More frequent were cases when certain individuals, such as court physicians, were exempted by special order (imperial *ferman*) from the payment of taxes and the *ghiyār* and were permitted to ride horses. Persons in the service of the representatives of European powers which had capitulation treaties with the Ottoman Empire likewise enjoyed certain privileges and were exempt from wearing special dress.[1]

Just as the Jewish sources were silent about 'Umar's regulations during the caliphate they ignored personal discriminations and restrictions so long as they did not go beyond accepted custom. The immigrants from Christian Europe likewise saw nothing unusual in them, since they were accustomed to similar afflictions in their countries of origin. The particulars of the clothing regulations are mostly known to us from the reports of Christian travellers who immediately perceived the difference between the status of Muslims and non-Muslims so strikingly demonstrated by their outward appearance.

The situation of the Jews and the legal status of the Jewish religion in the Ottoman Empire were generally not different from those of Christians and Christianity, although the veteran Jewish residents could not claim the protection of the European powers which regarded it as their sacred political and religious duty to assist Christians and Christianity in Muslim countries.

The poll-tax. The *jizya* (also called *kharāj* or *jawālī*) was generally collected, as of old, from the small income earners, the middle group and the well-to-do at the ratio of 1 : 2 : 4 in the local currency. We have seen above, though, that the expellees sometimes enjoyed reductions, and it also happened that the "merchants", i.e. *marranos*, were completely exempted from or succeeded in evading the tax, but these were isolated cases.

Under the capitulation agreements interpreters, agents or others employed by the embassies and consulates of European powers were completely exempt from poll-tax or enjoyed a substantial reduction. Owing to abuse of this privilege by the ambassadors, the number of persons exempt from tax and enjoying a certain legal immunity

[1] Cf. A. Galanté, *Documents officiels turcs concernant les Juifs de Turquie* (Istanbul, 1931), pp. 194–7; also the *berat* (letter of appointment) of the Chief Rabbi of Egypt of 1892 which contains the passage: "No military (officer) shall interfere with horses or mules of the Chief Rabbi or his people" (*idem, Appendice à l'ouvrage "Documents" etc., ibid.* (1941), p. 8).

increased, which is why the power of foreign representatives to employ clerks was severely curtailed.

By ordinances of the years 1855 and 1856 the poll-tax was replaced in Turkey by a military service exemption tax for non-Muslims (*bedel-i ʿaskerî*). This tax was abolished only in the Young Turkish revolution, when non-Muslims were also made liable to military service by a law of 1909.[1]

The Tunisian constitution of 1857 still contains a clear reference to the *jizya*. Exemption from personal taxes is mentioned in capitulations concluded in the second half of the nineteenth century between Morocco and European countries; the poll-tax must consequently have still been in force there. In the amirate of Bukhara *jizya* was collected from the Jews, but not from the Russian Christians. This and all the other forms of discrimination continued after Bukhara had become a Russian protectorate.[2]

As already stated, no complaints were voiced about the poll-tax as such. On the other hand there were numerous complaints about the manner of its collection and the imposition of other taxes not based on Muslim religious legislation: charges, fines and one-time levies. But this was a feature endemic in all the Muslim states, causing hardship to the entire population without distinction of creed.

Restrictions on the building of new synagogues. Non-Muslims knew how to circumvent the regulation which forbade them to construct new buildings for religious worship and thus restricted them to the use of those built prior to the Arab conquest. In actual fact many hundreds of houses of worship were erected in cities founded under Islam such as Qayrawān, Baghdad, Fez and Cairo; they included large and sumptuous ones, as we may conclude from a letter describing the destruction of the Jewish community of Qayrawān.[3] Naturally things were not the same all the time.[4] According to Obadiah of Bertinoro, the Jew

[1] Cf. A. Galanté, *Histoire des Juifs d'Istambul II* (Istanbul, 1942), pp. 12–15; B. Ch. Nedkoff, *Die Gizya* (Kopfsteuer) *im osmanischen Reich* (Leipzig, 1942), *passim*, esp. pp. 23–4, also the facsimile of a *jizya* ticket (*adnā*, lowest rate) issued in Jerusalem for the year 1832–3 in Hirschberg, *Israel Exploration Journal*, vol. II (1952), p. 244; cf. J. Karabacek, *Fuehrer durch die Ausstellung Erzherzog Rainer* (Vienna, 1894), p. 177 and figs. 1–2. For the *bedel* cf. B. Lewis, *The Emergence of Modern Turkey* (London, 1961), pp. 114, 331.

[2] J. Chalom, *Les Israélites de la Tunisie* (Paris, 1908), p. 25; F. Rey, *De la Protection Diplomatique et Consulaire dans les Echelles du Levant et de Barbarie* (Paris, 1899), pp. 514–19; F. H. Skrine and E. D. Ross, *Heart of Asia*, p. 380.

[3] Cf. p. 130 above.

[4] Joseph Sambari, *Chronicle* (ed. Neubauer, *Med. Jew. Chronicles*, vol. I, p. 136) reports that during excesses against Jews and Christians in Egypt, the Jews proclaimed the antiquity of their synagogues.

of his period (late fifteenth century) was forbidden "to rebuild his house and yard (in Jerusalem) without permission, even if they were falling down, and the permit was sometimes more costly than the rebuilding itself".[1]

Such was the situation in Jerusalem which was then under Mamlūk rule. At approximately the same time the Ottoman Sultan Meḥmed the Conqueror forbade the construction of new synagogues, but permitted the use and repair of old ones. A generation or two later R. Jacob b. Ḥabib, a scholar of the first generation of refugees from Spain, describes conditions in Turkey: "We are not permitted to obtain permanent quarters for a synagogue, let alone build one; we are compelled to hide underground, and our prayers must not be heard because of the danger."[2]

Zealous officials and fanatical *qāḍīs* and *muftīs* used these regulations to harass the Jews. But the facts prove that many synagogues were also built during the Turkish period, thanks both to tolerance and venality on the part of the administration.

When in 1584 a complaint was lodged with the Sublime Porte about the multitude of synagogues in Ṣafad, the following decree was issued:

20 Dhu'l-qa'da, 992. Given to the person who brought the petition.

Order to the Beglerbeg (and) the *qāḍī* of Damascus:

The *qāḍī* of Safad sent a letter to My Threshold of Felicity and reported that in the Town of Safad there are only seven sacred mosques. And the Jews (who) in olden times had three synagogues (*kenīsa*) have now thirty-two synagogues, and they have made their buildings very high. And they have bought much real estate and constituted it as pious foundations (*waqf*) for their synagogues. (Thereby) they have given much annoyance to the Muslims.

I have therefore ordered that you shall personally investigate the said matter and report. . . . Are the above-mentioned synagogues ancient synagogues which have remained (in existence) since the Inspired Conquest, or newly established synagogues? If they are new, how (and) when were they established?[3]

The results of the inquiry and the action taken to "remedy" the situation are unknown. The matter may have been disposed of by a bribe.

[1] Cf. *Letters from Palestine*, ed. A. Ya'ri, p. 130.

[2] Ben Ḥabib's statement quoted by R. Joseph Caro, *Beyt Yosef* to *Ṭūr Oraḥ Ḥayyim*, §154; cf. Galanté, *Documents*, pp. 50–4, 124 ff.

[3] U. Heyd, *Ottoman Documents on Palestine, 1552–1615* (Oxford, 1960), p. 169.

Such restrictive and vexatious practices by the authorities continued until the middle of the nineteenth century. Every major or minor repair required a bribe for the functionary who had to express an opinion on its necessity. Synagogues in Jerusalem were in a dilapidated condition, and a change occurred only during the liberal regime of Muḥammad 'Ali. Muḥammad's son, Ibrāhīm Pasha, permitted two of the important synagogues in the Old City to be repaired and enlarged.[1]

Eventually even the Turkish Government could not ignore a situation which bred corruption. The *berat* of the *ḥakham-bashis* (chief rabbis) stated that the reading of the Scroll of the Law (during services) at the house of the *ḥakham and in other houses* was in accordance with Jewish religious practice, and that it was permitted to hang veils and candelabra in the places where it was performed. Synagogues and their property were henceforth immune; they must not be damaged nor held (confiscated) as security for debts.[2]

In most other Muslim countries we hear nothing of harassment in respect of the construction of synagogues, since the Jews took care to build them from the outset in such a way that they were inconspicuous. Moreover, as the Jews in those countries lived in special quarters, the Muslims had not even the semblance of a reason for claiming that their feelings were hurt. The expellees do not seem to have encountered any difficulties in establishing their synagogues in North Africa. Still, d'Arvieux, French Consul in Algiers in 1674 and 1675, says in his memoirs that the Turkish rulers will not permit the Jews of Algiers to build additional synagogues unless the latter pay them substantial bribes.

A few years earlier during the Sabbatian upsurge in Morocco, when members of that movement were persecuted, synagogues were closed in several towns. In Marrakesh prayer meetings of ten persons (*minyanīm*) were only permitted in private houses.

Not infrequently savage, incited Muslim mobs or mutinous troops vented their wrath upon synagogues. Chronicles tell of desecrated Torah scrolls, stolen devotional articles, burnt furniture and buildings. However, these occurrences had no direct connexion with 'Umar's regulations—on the contrary, they violated them. When the troubles sub-

[1] Cf. the *ferman* of 1825 for the repair of a synagogue in Constantinople; Galanté, *Appendice*, pp. 9–13; Hirschberg, "Ottoman Rule in Jerusalem", in *Israel Exploration Journal*, vol. II (1952), p. 243 and n. 12.

[2] Cf. the *berat* of 1841 of the first Chief Rabbi of Jerusalem appointed by the Sublime Porte (Hebrew translation by D. Yellin) in *Jerusalem*, vol. IV (1892), pp. 186–217.

sided, the Muslim authorities would sometimes help to repair the damage.[1] After the persecutions of 1790–2 in Fez a *qāḍī* asked that the mosque built in the Jewish quarter be demolished, and Mawlāy Sulaymān gave orders to this effect.

The Jewish district in oriental towns became the "Jewish quarter" in a derogatory sense when it was surrounded by a wall and its gates were bolted at night. From then onwards the inhabitants of the *madīna*, the (Muslim) city, no longer permitted Jews to live in their area, while they themselves would not settle in the Jewish quarter. The assertion that the walls served to protect the Jews against mob violence was incapable of divesting this segregation of its humiliating character which was also not lessened by the fact that not only the Jewish quarters in the major towns were surrounded by walls. A wall of contempt separated the "quarter" from the "city" even where no actual walls existed.

The term by which the Jewish quarter was known was not in itself derogatory. In Morocco it was called *mallāḥ* (a word of uncertain etymology) while literary sources also use the term *massūs*, now fallen into oblivion. In the other Maghrib countries the Jewish quarter was described as *ḥāra* (also *shāra*), i.e. quarter, or *zanqa* (street, alley). In Yemen its designation was *qāʿa* (open space, square), *sharḥa* or *masbata* (place where keepers of the Sabbath live), and in the Balkans, Persia and Kurdistan it was *maḥalla* (quarter, camp).

Descriptions of Middle Eastern Jewish quarters are frequent in European travel literature from the sixteenth century onwards. They say a great deal about overcrowding and poor housing conditions and repeatedly mention the indifferent state of health of the inhabitants which they attribute in part to inferior sanitation and the dirt filling the narrow lanes. It should be noted, however, that such unfavourable accounts are not always sufficiently objective. The special dress of non-Muslims in the East (*ghiyār*) is described in detail by European tourists. Jewish sources generally do not mention the *ghiyār*, but are more interested in cases of deviation from regulations, whether expressly sanctioned by the authorities or tolerated owing to a lax application of the law.

The commonest and most striking feature was the difference in dress. As already mentioned the expellees from Spain in Algiers wore the

[1] L. D'Arvieux, *Mémoires du ... envoyé extraord.* (Paris, 1735), vol. v, p. 230; G. Vajda, *Un Recueil de Textes Historiques Judéo-Marocains* (Paris, 1951), pp. 46–7, 81, 83, 94, 97.

capos or *caperon* and thereby differed from the veteran residents whose head-dress was the cap (*shāshiyya*). The *capos*, too, was a sign of the Jewishness of its wearer because the Muslims did not wear European garments and there were as yet no Christians in the region. In the late fifteenth century the Chief Rabbi of Constantinople forbade the wearing of the *caperon*, the cloak of the Sephardi *ḥakhāmīm*.[1] The difference in dress between veteran residents and descendants of immigrants from Europe continued for centuries. D'Arvieux describes in detail the clothing of Jews in Algiers: "the residents wore a burnous over a black shirt of light-weight tissue and covered their heads with a black woollen *shāshiyya*; those from other Muslim countries wore a turban of different shape, ending in a tassel descending upon the shoulders; all wore sandals without stockings. Livornese and Alexandrian Jews wore hats and clothes like the Italians or Spaniards whose customs they even preserved in their homes."[2]

The archives in Constantinople contain a number of orders, issued in the years 1568–1837 to the *qāḍī* of Istanbul, to the officer in charge (*muḥtasib*) of non-Muslims and, in one case, to a chief rabbi, concerning the headgear and clothes of Jews and Christians. These orders lay the emphasis on the headgear, and so did the clothing regulations for Jews in Persia in the seventeenth and eighteenth centuries. The headgear of the non-Muslim became such an established characteristic that its replacement by the turban of the Turks was deemed evidence of a change of religion.

The Jews generally had to wear dark clothes. Light or coloured clothes were only permitted on sabbath and religious festivals within their own districts. The authorities seem to have been particularly strict about the prohibition of green (a green headgear was a sign of descent from the Prophet Muḥammad) and purple. But there is evidence that the aforementioned Ottoman decrees were not rigidly applied. According to eighteenth-century sources many Jews in Constantinople wore green turbans and the same type of shoes as the Turks. Among the Jews themselves doubts arose whether this kind of dress was permissible from the halakhic point of view, and a discussion of this question is preserved in rabbinical literature. The strict prohibition to wear green and purple clothes issued in Morocco by Mawlāy Yazīd in 1790–2 (and revoked by his successor Mawlāy Sulaymān),

[1] Cf. Schechter, "Notes sur Messer David Léon", in *REJ*, vol. XXIV (1892), p. 137.
[2] D'Arvieux, *op. cit.* p. 288.

shows that the prohibitive decrees were not rigorously implemented in the Maghrib either.[1]

The *ghiyār* are mentioned in official Turkish sources until almost the mid-nineteenth century. A decree of 1837 says that Jews and Christians permitted to wear the *ṭarbūsh* must provide it with special marks so as to be distinguishable from Muslims. The *berat* issued to the first *ḥakham bashī* of Jerusalem in 1841 says that his official emissaries are exempt from the *ghiyār* in order that they may be able to travel unmolested. They were also permitted to carry arms in order to defend themselves if attacked.[2]

Open rebellion against the *ghiyār* first broke out in Tunis and, as it sheds light on the situation of the Jews in various respects, it seems worthwhile to dwell on it at some length.

The victories of Napoleon I in Italy strengthened the position of the *Gornim* who, by virtue of their Italian origin, considered themselves entitled to the protection of the French government. They began to wear the French coat-of-arms on their clothing which Ḥammūda Bey, the ruler of Tunisia who regarded them as his subjects, forbade. When a *Gorni* once appeared before him with the French emblem on his lapel, he ordered him to be burnt alive, though eventually he contented himself with having him whipped.

This was the first signal of new developments; the actual issue was not settled this time. The next stage was the "European hats" affair in 1823, which almost led to the severance of diplomatic relations between Britain and Tunisia. Although the incident itself may seem trivial and ludicrous, it was characteristic of the state of mind then prevailing among Tunisian Jewry.

The *Touansa* were still subject to the regulations concerning distinctive clothing. They wore a long blue outer shirt without collar or sleeves, stockings only in winter, and black sandals. On their shaven heads they had a small black cap wound round with a blue silk kerchief. They were forbidden to wear other colours. The *Gornim* wore European clothes like the Christians and wrapped themselves in a burnous or *ḥā'ik*, which also covered the head. Jewish merchants who went to Europe on business wore European hats during their travels and

[1] Cf. Galanté, *Documents*, pp. 112–27; *idem*, *Appendice*, pp. 21–3; S. A. Rosanes, *Histoire des Israélites de Turquie* (Hebrew) (Sofia, 1937–8), vol. v, p. 7. For Morocco see Vajda, *op. cit.* pp. 86, 95.

[2] Cf. Galanté, *op. cit.* pp. 119–21. For Persia in 1897, 1907, cf. N. Leven, *Cinquante ans d'Histoire* (Paris, 1911). vol. I, pp. 372, 375–87.

continued to do so after their return to Tunisia. This *de facto* abolition of a notable discriminatory feature did not at first provoke any unfavourable reaction on the part of the authorities. But when more and more subjects of the Bey, not entitled to consular protection, wore hats to get rid of the humiliating Jewish headgear, an order was issued that every Jew, even if he was a foreign national or under consular protection, had to wear the Jewish cap. A Jewish agent born in Gibraltar and thus a British subject, who had just arrived in Tunisia and refused to obey the order, was arrested by the authorities and thereupon complained to his consul. The latter lodged a strong protest with the ruling Bey Maḥmūd (1814–24) demanding the release of the prisoner and the exemption of British subjects from the order. The Bey's refusal was no less peremptory. The consul thereupon threatened to leave his post, i.e. to bring about the severance of diplomatic relations between his government and the Bey, but Maḥmūd merely reiterated his instructions that the order was to apply also to foreign Jews and to those under consular protection. The British Government thereupon ordered its Mediterranean fleet to sail for Tunis. When this became known, one of the Bey's ministers called upon the consul and promised that the order would not be applied to British subjects. About that time some of the *Gornim* received permission to wear white turbans instead of black caps.

The arrest of two Jews of Tuscan nationality for wearing European hats caused great excitement among the Jews of Tuscany and led to the intervention of the Dutch Consul-General Nissen who was at the same time the representative of Tuscany, Austria, and Russia. Nissen, who was on good terms with the Bey's court, succeeded in freeing the two men.[1]

Only a small section of the population was involved in this emancipation of the outer man, represented by the shedding of the *ghiyār*. The overwhelming majority of the Jews of Morocco, Tunisia and Tripolitania, of the "Old Yishuv" in Palestine and of the Jews of Yemen, Kurdistan, Persia and Afghanistan retained their traditional garb until quite recently.

Finally we mention a few other restrictions and discriminatory practices applied to non-Muslims. Ottoman decrees of the sixteenth century repeatedly forbid Jews and Christians to buy male and female

[1] Cf. Hirschberg, *History*, vol. II, pp. 142, 144 and nn. 21–2, and for the distinctive headgear, below, p. 200.

slaves lest they lure them away from Islam. At that time Jews or Christians were no longer in government service. But the Muslim authorities in Damascus still employed in their offices a number of Samaritans—regarded as members of the Jewish community. A decree of 1570, addressed to the *qāḍī* of Damascus, notes that the service of Samaritans who could read and write Arabic in government posts was apt to cause unpleasantness to Muslims. Invoking both religious and secular law as well as an imperial order already issued in this matter, the decree forbids the employment of Samaritans in government posts. We have here to do with a last echo of the centuries-old fight for the removal of non-Muslims from government posts, a fight directed mainly against Christians, Karaites and—in its last stage—Samaritans.[1]

A special instance of humiliation of the Jews was the order issued by the authorities in Constantinople in 1821 to throw into the sea the body of the Greek Patriarch Gregory who was executed and left hanging for three days in punishment for the Greek revolt in Morea. We know that at the other end of the oriental area, in Morocco, Jews had to collect the heads of executed persons and rebels fallen in combat, salt them in order to delay putrefaction and hang them on the gates of the city for all to see. This custom existed there as late as the beginning of the twentieth century. The practice of employing Jews as executioners is attested in the Byzantine Empire in 1073, and in Crete and Tripoli in the late Middle Ages.[2]

Our last example is a feature which in Muslim countries occurred only in the Ottoman period and in areas where Jews and Christians lived in proximity to each other: the blood libel. From 1530 to the end of the nineteenth century we hear again and again the charge that Jews use blood for the preparation of *matzah* and kill Christians and Muslims for that purpose. The number of such accusations was particularly large in the nineteenth century, though only the one brought in Damascus in 1840 became widely known. From the seventies to the end of the nineteenth century blood libels were increasingly frequent throughout the Empire: in Egypt (Alexandria, Port Saʿīd), Palestine (Jerusalem 1870, 1871 and 1896), Syria (Damascus, Beirut), Asia Minor

[1] Cf. the *fermans*, in Galanté, *Documents*, pp. 121–4, 170–1; *idem*, *Appendice*, pp. 23–4.

[2] Cf. M. Franco, *Essai sur l'histoire des Israélites* (Paris, 1897), p. 132; Galanté, *Histoires des Juifs de Rhodes, Chio, Cos, etc.*, pp. 101–2; for Crete and Byzantium cf. S. Asaf, "Jewish Executioners" (Hebrew), in *Tarbiz*, vol. v (1934), pp. 224–6; J. Starr, *The Jews in the Byzantine Empire*, pp. 22–3. Hirschberg, "The 'Mellaḥ' or 'Mesoos'—the Jewish Quarter in Morocco", in *Erets Yisrael*, vol. iv (1956), p. 229.

(Smyrna) and European Turkey (Constantinople, the Dardanelles area). The *ferman* issued to Sir Moses Montefiore and the proclamations of Orthodox metropolitans and patriarchs were of no avail. Needless to say that such slander had an adverse effect on the attitude to the Jews and their religion.[1]

Religious and intellectual life

The profound changes which occurred at the end of the Middle Ages on the threshold of the Modern Era manifested themselves in the religious and intellectual spheres more intensely and conspicuously than in other fields. For many generations the religious life of the well-established communities in the areas of Muslim rule followed a fixed pattern. Reverence for the sages of earlier generations and their teachings hindered the quest for new ways of studying Torah, and scholars were content to rehearse the decisions embodied in ancient literature. When the storm over Maimonides' philosophical writings had abated no fresh impulse animated religious thought. It was the great merit of the immigrants from Spain, Italy and other European countries to have injected some new ideas. The blows of fate which shook occidental Jewry from the Crusades onwards (and even before) and the successive crises and disasters which visited the Jews of Spain and Portugal activated religious and intellectual trends that hitherto hardly found expression in official religious literature.

The immigrants from central Europe brought with them moral concepts, modes of study and legal methods which developed in France and Germany in the course of centuries and from there spread to Italy and finally to Poland.[2] The veteran residents came into contact with rabbinical scholars from Germany (pupils of the Talmud commentators of the Franco-German school) such as R. Benjamin Halevi Ashkenazi, who settled in Salonica, R. Eliyahu Halevi b. Mosheh, the teacher of R. Eliyahu Mizraḥi of Constantinople, leading rabbi of the city, and, most important of all, R. Jacob Pollak, the originator of the *pilpul* (subtle argument) method, a native of Prague and rabbi in Cracow who was forced to emigrate to Turkey because of certain

[1] Cf. Galanté, *Documents*, pp. 157–61, 214–40; N. Leven, *Cinquante ans*, pp. 388–92; U. Heyd, "Ritual Murder Accusations in 15th and 16th Century Turkey" (Hebrew), in *Sefunot*, vol. v (1961), pp. 135–49; J. M. Landau, "Ritual Murder Accusations and Persecutions of Jews in 19th-Century Egypt" (Hebrew), *ibid.* vol. v (1961), pp. 415–60; E. Sternberg, "A Document of a Blood Libel in Jerusalem in 1870" (Hebrew), in *Yoseph Y. Rivlin Memorial Volume* (Jerusalem/Ramat Gan, 1964), pp. 160–6. Cf. also p. 212, below.

[2] On the new trends in central Europe cf. Y. F. Baer, "The Religious–Social Tendency of 'Sepher Ḥassidim'" (Hebrew), *Zion*, vol. III (1938), pp. 1–50.

disputes, and many more whose teachings were sometimes steeped in popular mysticism. These new influences were mostly transmitted by scholars from Italy or the Venetian-controlled Greek islands who studied at central European *yeshivot*.

The problems preoccupying the immigrants from the Iberian Peninsula went very deep, and their impact upon the veteran settlers increased steadily. Three or four generations of Spanish Jewry in the fifteenth century saw their material and political existence crumble, their philosophy collapse and their hope for redemption evaporate in the terrible catastrophe of 1492. The expellees never ceased brooding over their fate and sought to detect its meaning. The numerous *marranos* among them were harassed by the thought that they or their fathers had sinned by changing their religion and deeply repented their opportunist behaviour. This mood finds faithful expression in Samuel Usque's *Consolaçam ás tribulaçoens de Israel* written in Portuguese and first printed in Ferrara in 1553. But even those who had not defected were remorseful. A historian at the time of the expulsion writes:

Our sins grew over our heads and our guilt piled up to heaven. But God has not dealt with us according to our sins. According to the wickedness, the misdeeds and the great pride that spread all over Spain we would, but for his mercy and the righteousness of our fathers which he remembered, have been almost like Sodom: "Behold, this was the iniquity of Sodom, pride, fullness of bread" (Ezek. xvi. 49). But worse than this the Torah was almost abandoned in Israel for worldly learning "because by them their portion is fat" (Hab. i. 16). Only the poor observed the Oral law.[1]

Some regarded the calamities as a portent of the Messiah. An author living on the island of Rhodes writes in 1495: "I think that the troubles that befell the Jews in all the kingdoms of Edom from the year 1490 to the year 1495 are a succession of visitations for Jacob from which salvation will come to him; they are the birth-pangs of the Messiah."[2]

This explanation especially kindled the imagination of the kabbalists and created favourable conditions for trends combining messianic hopes with mystic leanings. An exponent of these trends can be found in Palestine already in the early sixteenth century. He is R. Abraham b.

[1] Abraham b. Solomon of Torrutiel in Neubauer, *MJC*, vol. I, p. 111. Still harsher are the strictures of Joseph Yabeṣ, *Or Haḥayyim* (ed. Lublin, 1910), pp. 26, 64. Cf. also H. H. Ben-Sasson in *Zion*, vol. XXVI (1961), especially pp. 34–64.

[2] *Sepher Hapeliah*, MS. Vatican 187, as quoted by G. Scholem, *Shabbetai Zvi* (Hebrew) (Tel-Aviv, 1957), vol. I, p. 15, n. 1. For 1530 as the year of the redemption cf. M. Lattes, *De Vita et Scriptis Eliae Kapsalii* (Hebrew) (Padua, 1869), pp. 90 ff.

Eliezer Halevi who lived and worked in Jerusalem prior to its occupation by the Turks. Kabbalistic books now began to spread among the common people who did not understand them nor were conversant with the Oral Law. Many began to hope that the coming of the Messiah could be hastened by asceticism, meditation and the "improvement of the soul". These dreamers also included eminent halakhic scholars. At the same time, there were men like R. Yosef Yaḇeṣ, the author of *The Light of Life*, a work directed mainly against the "sect of philosophers" and dissociating itself from both extremes in Spanish Jewry: rationalism and mysticism.[1]

Distinguished halakhic scholars felt that they had to mend existing defects due not only to neglect of talmudic studies, but also to apostasy and forced conversion and especially to differences in custom between one place and country and another and the lack of binding decisions concerning a uniform way of life. R. Joseph Karo hears a heavenly voice saying: "Many will repent because of you and you will go up to the Land of Israel."[2]

As stated on p. 146, a large proportion of the exiles from Christian Europe concentrated in areas conquered by the Turks in the fifteenth century: the Balkans and Constantinople, captured about forty years before the expulsion from Spain. Hither flocked those who wished to throw off the mask of Christianity and live openly as Jews. Scholars who later won fame as leaders of their generation and teachers of Jewry to the present day, such as R. Joseph Karo, R. Levi b. Ḥaḇiḇ, R. Shelomo Alqabeṣ and many others first settled in Adrianople, Nikopoli, Trikkala and Arta.

The most important centre was Salonica which became a predominantly Jewish city surnamed "Little Jerusalem" on account of its many scholars, synagogues and houses of study. In spite of natural disasters that visited this community, it made an earnest appeal in 1550 to the Jews of Provence to leave their country before catastrophe overtook them and to settle in Salonica.[3]

A few years after the Ottoman conquest of Palestine Ṣafad, a city without any Jewish antecedents, became an important religious centre repaired to by large numbers of eminent scholars. It is difficult to accept

[1] Cf. n. 1, p. 161 above.

[2] *Maggīd Mēshārīm*, ed. Zolkiew (1770), 56*b*.

[3] Cf. S. Usque, *Consolation for the Tribulations of Israel*, transl. by Martin A. Cohen (Philadelphia 1965), pp. 211, 212; I. Loeb, "La Correspondence des Juifs d'Espagne", in *REJ*, vol. xv (1887), p. 272.

the explanation that it was Ṣafad's economic prosperity that tempted them. The *beyṯ midrash* of R. Jacob Beyraḇ, an expellee from Spain who settled here after some wanderings in North Africa, was founded soon after the Ottoman conquest, and it was as his residence that Ṣafad first became famous. His great learning drew many students to the city and, in addition to Ṣafad's record as an administrative centre in Mamlūk days, attracted many expellees and members of other Diasporas. Then came practically minded people who used the existing favourable conditions for the development of the clothing industry that became the basis for Ṣafad's economic progress.

The school founded by Beyraḇ comprised all Ṣafad's scholars, some of whom were the colleagues of the school head. They dealt with all matters collectively, wrote *responsa*, and issued decisions. Here the idea of the revival of ordination (*semīkhah*) arose, which would invest qualified rabbis with some of the powers of the *sanhedrin*, the central religious and legal body that existed in Palestine at the time of the Second Temple and was abolished during the first centuries of Roman rule. R. Levi b. Ḥaḇiḇ, rabbi of Jerusalem and Beyraḇ's strong opponent, accused him of secretly planning to establish a *sanhedrin* in Ṣafad. He regarded Beyraḇ's attempt to revive the ordination of the Ṣafad scholars as a first step in this direction. R. Levi also charged Beyraḇ with coveting the office of president of the *sanhedrin*. In his attempt to revive ordination, Beyraḇ relied on Maimonides' Mishnah Commentary and passages in his *Mishneh Torah* which was regarded as most authoritative in the post-talmudic era; the dispute originally revolved on the interpretation of Maimonides' words. In 1538 Beyraḇ ordained some of his companions. Although the first holders of ordination in turn ordained their disciples, the idea was doomed to failure through the vigorous opposition of R. Levi b. Ḥaḇiḇ and ultimately abandoned.[1]

Beyraḇ's most renowned colleague was R. Joseph Karo, also an expellee from Spain who settled in Nikopoli after a period of wanderings and tribulations in Europe, but whom his mentor angel (*maggīd*) instructed in 1521 to move to Adrianople. Here he began to write his

[1] Cf. H. Z. Dimitrovsky, "Rabbi Jacob Beyraḇ's Academy" (Hebrew), in *Sefunot*, vol. VII (1963), pp. 41–102; J. Katz, "The Controversy on Semikha (Ordination) between Rabbi Jacob Beyraḇ and the Ralbaḥ" (Hebrew), in *Zion*, vol. XVI (1951), pp. 28–45; M. Benayahu, "The Revival of Ordination in Ṣafad" (Hebrew), in *Yitzḥak F. Baer Jubilee Volume* (Jerusalem, 1961), pp. 248–69. Cf. also A. Epstein, "Ordination et autorisation", in *REJ*, vol. XVI (1903), pp. 197–211, dealing with this question in talmudic literature.

outstanding commentary on *Arba'at ha-ṭūrīm* (*The Four Columns*), a digest of accepted rules of the Oral Law. In this commentary *Bēyṯ Yoseph*, Joseph Karo traces every legal provision from its roots in the Bible through all the stages of its development down to his own time. Karo continued to work on his commentary during his stay in Greece and subsequently in Ṣafad where he joined Beyraḇ's *yeshiva* and, though certainly not inferior to him in learning and wisdom, called him "our great teacher". The huge task was completed after thirty years' research and careful consideration of all the sources. Shortly afterwards Karo wrote the *Shulkhan 'arūkh*, first printed just over 400 years ago in Venice (1564–5). The author intended to provide observant Jewry with a practical religious code, comprising all spheres of life. This code, with the glosses and commentaries of later rabbis, has remained binding to this day.

R. Joseph Karo was one of the four rabbis ordained by R. Jacob Beyraḇ in 1538. When Beyraḇ failed in the attempt to revive ordination on an all-Jewish scale, Karo continued to hope that the venture would succeed, as his "mentor angel" promised him.

Despite Ṣafad's importance as a halakhic centre for sixteenth-century Jewry, especially in the Ottoman Empire, another feature in its religious life had a significant impact on future generations: the revival of the Kabbalah.

Joseph Karo himself had mystical leanings, as evidenced by his book *Maggīd mēshārīm* ("Declarer of Things That Are Right"), the identity of whose author had indeed been in dispute until Werblowsky recently established it.[1] Joseph Karo's disciples included some like R. Mosheh Cordovero and R. Shelomo Alqabeṣ who devoted themselves to the mysteries of the Kabbalah. These three initiated the pre-Lurianic Kabbalah in Ṣafad. The most notable in the field of theoretical Kabbalah was Cordovero who first tried to describe the process by which the ten spheres emanate from God's hidden abode. He interpreted the emanations as degrees of divine existence, and his book *ha-Pardes* attempts to give the Kabbalah a logical explanation.[2]

The Kabbalah attained its peak with R. Isaac Luria Ashkenazi. He was born in Jerusalem in 1534 and died in Ṣafad in his thirty-eighth year, two years after the death of his teacher Mosheh Cordovero who died aged forty-eight. Luria, surnamed Ari (an acrostic of the Hebrew

[1] R. J. Zwi Werblowsky, *Joseph Karo, Lawyer and Mystic* (Oxford, 1962), pp. 126 ff. about ordination.

[2] Cf. *EJ*, vol. v, cols. 662–8.

words Ashkenazi (or *elohī* "divine") Rabbi Isaac),[1] was the exact opposite of Cordovero. Of all the books and tracts known as *The Writings of Ari* only one, a commentary on the *Book of Concealment*, was written by him. But his personality made a very deep impression on his disciples. His teachings are known to us from tracts and commentaries written by his disciples, the most famous of whom was Ḥayyīm Vital Calabrese.

This is not the place to expound Luria's kabbalistic system.[2] Suffice it to quote some passages from G. Scholem: "... Parts of the Lurianic Kabbalah undoubtedly represent the greatest victory which anthropomorphic thought has ever won in the history of Jewish mysticism... The conception of man as a *micro-cosmos* and of the living God as a *macro-anthropos* has never been more clearly expressed and driven to its farthest consequences."[3]

Luria's activity in Ṣafad lasted no more than three or four years (1569–72). Shortly after his death, the people began to weave a wreath of fact and fiction round his impressive personality, and in the following generation these stories were collected in the *Shibḇhey ha-arī* (Praises of the Lion).

G. Scholem regards the Lurianic Kabbalah as a mystical interpretation of Exile and Redemption. Its aim is to end the Exile through the *tiqqūn*, the restitution of all things in God, the re-integration of Israel. It is not surprising, therefore, that Ḥayyīm Vital Calabrese (and a later writer) saw in Luria the Messiah b. Joseph who died before the Redemption expected for the year 1575. Vital subsequently thought of himself as the Messiah b. Joseph or at least as a forerunner of the Messianic Age.[4]

It is usually believed that mystical preoccupations weaken religious observance. But this was not the case in Ṣafad. The founders and principal exponents of the new kabbalistic trend were all rabbinical scholars, strict upholders of tradition and distinguished halakhists, chief among them Joseph Karo.[5]

[1] *Arī* as a word means "lion"; Luria's disciples and followers were called "lion whelps".

[2] Cf. G. Scholem, *Major Trends in Jewish Mysticism* (New York, 1961), pp. 244–86; cf. also *EJ*, vol. x, cols. 1198–1212.

[3] *Op. cit.* pp. 268 f.

[4] Cf. Scholem, *Shabbeṯai Zvi* (Hebrew), vol. I, pp. 21, 43, 55; D. Tamar, "Luria and Vital as the Messiah b. Joseph" (Hebrew), in *Sefunot*, vol. VII (1963), pp. 167–77.

[5] Cf. S. Schechter's "Safed in the Sixteenth Century—a City of Legists and Mystics", in his *Studies in Judaism* (Philadelphia, 1938), vol. II, an excellent picture of religious life in that town.

The Lurianic Kabbalah spread very quickly, at first by oral transmission and from the seventeenth century in print. Its influence on Jewish society increased and it began to dominate its whole life. It struck deep roots among the expellees from Spain whom bitter experience disposed to mysticism, asceticism and lyrical pessimism.[1]

Other factors made for the penetration of the Kabbalah into broader strata. These found in it ideas that stirred their hearts. Religious life, based on the observance of prescribed practice, was greatly influenced by Luria's additions to the existing liturgy and ritual: special days of fasting, prayer, and uplift; study on the night preceding festivals; study of Mishnaic passages for the happiness of the souls of the dead. All these were accepted and became an organic part of the people's religious life. The mysteries of the *Zohar* and other kabbalistic works produced in Ṣafad were at first the patrimony of a select few. They were studied by distinguished halakhists, recognized authorities on religious law and religion. But not long after Luria's death they percolated through various channels to the consciousness of a wider public and were shared by all and sundry, according to each person's understanding. This phenomenon is less apparent among the Jews of Christian Europe. Here, far from the centre of the Kabbalah, its influence was limited to smaller circles. The masses of Polish and Russian Jewry were only affected in the eighteenth century when a new religious movement, Ḥasidism, arose, which in turn produced a counter-movement, the *Mitnagdim* which opposed the form in which kabbalistic ideas were presented.

The people were especially captivated by the messianic element in Luria's teachings. Here was the mystic outlet for a yearning whose beginnings in the Middle Ages can be found in Arabia before the appearance of Muḥammad and which expressed itself in a succession of Messiahs and announcers of the Messiah in the Islamic East. The expectation of the early coming of the Messiah merged with the earnest desire for the *tiqqūn* of the individual, the moral regeneration of man.[2] This phenomenon to some extent explains the events of the time of Shabbeṭai Zvi.

Halakhic and kabbalistic writings also spread in the Islamic East by means of printed editions, as mentioned. Striking proof of this intellectual alertness of the expellees is that only two years after the

[1] A. Castro, *The Structure of Spanish History* (Princeton, 1954), pp. 551 ff., notes that these ideas of Jews and converts and their descendants left their imprint on Spanish literature.

[2] Cf. G. Scholem, *Shabbeṭai Zvi*, vol. 1, pp. 44 ff.

expulsion *Arba'at ha-ṭūrīm* was printed in Constantinople. During the subsequent centuries (sixteenth to eighteenth), printing presses in Constantinople, Salonica, Smyrna, Ṣafad and Fez (only in the sixteenth century) turned out a series of most important halakhic, aggadic, historical and kabbalistic works. The first polyglot Jewish Bible was printed in Constantinpole in 1546. When these printing presses ceased to operate, others were established in Baghdad, Calcutta, Poona and eventually also on the island of Jarba (South Tunisia), in Tunis, Sūsa, Algiers, Oran and, in the twentieth century, in Casablanca. It should be noted that a large proportion of the works published during the past hundred years are kabbalistic books, especially popular prayer-books, Bible commentaries, *midrashim*, and various tracts dealing with practical Kabbalah. They were printed in Ladino (the Spanish dialect of the Sephardi Jews) or in the Jewish–Arabic dialect, just like various folk-stories, abridgments of French novels and periodicals written in North Africa.[1] The names of the authors and titles of the books printed are further proof that hardly any clashes occurred between the two trends, the nomistic, and the mystical and messianic.

This harmony was disturbed in the middle of the seventeenth century upon the rise in the Muslim East of Sabbatianism, a religious movement sparked by the ideas of the Lurianic Kabbalah and especially by its Messianic hopes. That movement presently changed its character, and members of its extremist sections, upon instructions from the movement's founder, Shabbeṯai Zvi, began to break the laws of the Torah in public. Sabbatianism eventually led to defection from Judaism when a part of its adherents—following the example of Shabbeṯai himself—embraced Islam. An offshoot of the movement which developed in Poland about 100 years later under the leadership of Jacob Frank (1726–91) ended up with the conversion of thousands to Christianity—again following the example of the leader. But we are here only concerned with the activities of Shabbeṯai Zvi himself, his earliest disciples and the spread of his movement in the Middle East.[2]

[1] Lists of books printed in Turkey will be found in M. Franco, *Essai sur l'Histoire des Israélites de l'Empire Ottoman*, *passim*, and S. A. Rosanes, *Histoire des Israélites de Turquie* (Hebrew) (Tel Aviv/Sofia, 1930–8), vols. I, pp. 63, 316–26; II, pp. 15, 16, 73, 230–40; IV, pp. 389–97; V, pp. 346–64; A. M. Habermann, *The Jewish Press in Ṣafad* (Hebrew) (Ṣafad, 1963). On printing-presses and prints in Baghdad and India cf. D. S. Sassoon, *A History of the Jews in Baghdad* (Letchworth, 1949), pp. 200, 214, 216. Concerning North Africa cf. Hirschberg, *History*, vol. II, pp. 159–61.

[2] On Shabbeṯai Zvi and his disciples, the author follows G. Scholem. Cf. the Eighth Lecture ("Sabbatianism and Mystical Heresy") in his *Major Trends in Jewish Mysticism*, and the relevant Bibliography and Supplement (*ibid.* pp. 441, 442).

Shabbetai Zvi (1625–76), a native of Smyrna, was from his youth subject to psychic conditions bordering on mental illness. He studied Jewish law in the traditional manner and also the books of the Lurianic Kabbalah. His morbid fancies of being the Messiah who would redeem his people from exile, though causing him to clash with the local rabbis and to leave his native city, would hardly have led to the convulsions which Jewry endured on his account but for the activities of his "prophet", Nathan b. Elisha ha-Ashkenazi (1644–80), usually called Nathan of Ghazza (Gaza). The latter studied Jewish law in Jerusalem and after his marriage settled in Gaza. Here he began to occupy himself with the Kabbalah. He read the *Zohar* and the writings of Luria and his disciples. He engaged in *tiqqūnīm* (moral purification exercises and meditations) and asceticism. Once after a spell of fasting he felt imbued with the spirit of prophecy and had a vision of the Messiah. About that time (1665) Shabbetai Zvi, after spending some time in Egypt, arrived in Gaza and there proclaimed himself openly as the Messiah. Nathan became his prophet and devoted all his ability, energy, and fervour to make propaganda for him. Although Shabbetai first appeared in a small community in Palestine which was not the centre of Jewish life in those days and met with hostility from Jerusalem's scholars, his fame spread throughout the East from Morocco to Persia. In Tripoli (Africa) he had a very active supporter in the physician Abraham Miguel Cardozo (1627–1706/7), a Spanish *marrano* who reverted to Judaism in Livorno and became a leading theorist of Sabbatianism. The reports evidently reached Italy at an earlier date. From there, again, they penetrated to other European countries. Hopes were kindled everywhere for the ingathering of the exiles and rumours were abroad of imminent redemption and of the rediscovery of the Ten Tribes who were said to be preparing to join their brethren in the return to Zion.

Shabbetai meanwhile went back to his native Smyrna where he began to rally "believers", as they called themselves, who were ready to do whatever he told them. He displayed royal pomp and solemn ceremonial as befitted the King Messiah. At the same time he engaged in strange practices: he publicly contravened Jewish law, both Written and Oral. He desecrated the Sabbath, ate forbidden food, changed the liturgy and abolished fasts commemorating the destruction of the Temple and Jerusalem; his behaviour with women was also talked about. Moreover, he became interested in the figure of Jesus. Shabbetai assured his supporters that all his doings were aimed at overcoming the hosts of Satan, and they believed him. Some scholars, headed by R. Aaron Lepapa, one of the local *dayyānīm*, indeed tried to stop his activities, but R. Aaron was swept from office, and R. Ḥayyim Benveniste, a prominent halakhist who was thereupon appointed sole *dayyān*, became a Sabbatian.

Trading and industry in Smyrna, which had developed into an important commercial centre, were suspended. All the local Jews celebrated and held mass processions shouting "Long live the King Messiah! Long live the Sultan Zvi!" At the same time, by order of the "king" they held penitential exercises. When the news of these events reached Constantinople, the Ottoman authorities—anticipating civil disorders—sent appropriate instructions to the local administration. This seems to have been one of the reasons why Shabbeṯai and some of his followers left Smyrna late in 1665 for Constantinople. The Jewish population of the capital city was divided in its attitude. Many feared that Shabbeṯai's appearance would provoke the central government into punitive action against all Jews. Others were carried away by the upsurge of messianic enthusiasm. Shabbeṯai was arrested by the authorities before he set foot in Constantinople. He was detained at the fortress of Gelibolu (Gallipoli) where he continued to hold court because his guards had been bribed into permitting his followers to visit him. When Sultan Meḥmed IV, then in Adrianople, heard of these goings-on, he ordered Shabbeṯai to be brought before him. In Adrianople Shabbeṯai and several of his followers were converted to Islam in September 1666.

This step dumbfounded the Jewish world. Shabbeṯai's opponents warned of the danger threatening Judaism should others follow his example, but many of his adherents regarded his conversion as the acceptance of suffering for the purpose of hastening redemption. They were particularly numerous in Morocco where Cardozo's propagandistic assertion that Shabbeṯai's apostasy held a profound mystery was widely believed. Cardozo was most active in offering this explanation, spreading it also among the communities of Turkey and the Balkans. He, the *marrano* who had left Madrid, developed the theory that all Jews had been doomed to forced conversion and a life of *marranos*, but that Shabbeṯai had taken upon himself the suffering of the people, and that this proved his messianic mission.

Shabbeṯai's opponents were likewise deeply perturbed and were not sure how to react to the propaganda of the movement. The first to raise his voice was R. Jacob Sasportas, a native of Oran, successively a *dayyān* in Tlemcen and Salā, who was in Hamburg at the time. Sasportas' utterances against the Sabbatians, collected in his *Ṣīṣat nobel ṣebī* (A Fading Flower is Beauty) are the principal source on the Sabbatian propaganda conducted by Cardozo in the Maghrib.[1]

A most revealing story is that of Joseph b. Ṣūr of Miknās. After the hopes for the coming of the Messiah in 1672 had been disappointed, they were revived by a simple man to whom his mentor angel (on the eve of the New Year 5434 (1673)) had foretold the coming of the Redeemer, Shabbetai Zvi, for the eve of Passover 5436 (1675) after the removal of the leaven. Nathan was said to be his prophet, whereas he, Joseph b. Ṣūr, was said to be the Messiah b. Joseph. The news spread, and scholars and kabbalists from Fez, Taṭwān, Salā, Qaṣr al-Kabīr and other places in Morocco came to see and acclaim Joseph. To convince them of the truth of his claims, he suggested: "If you agree I am willing to walk through the streets of the city proclaiming Shabbetai Zvi as the prophet of Israel, and you will see that no harm will come to me or to you or to anyone in Israel." This suggestion proves that the public demonstrations of Shabbetai's adherents caused much trouble to the Jews in the past. When Joseph b. Ṣūr's predictions did not materialize the Sabbatians believed that the Redemption would come in 1676; and especially the *marranos* in the Maghrib did penance.[2]

We advisedly described in detail the manifestations in Morocco of belief in a second appearance of Shabbetai as Messiah a few years after his conversion. Similar phenomena occurred at the other end of the Islamic world: scholars in Kurdistan composed songs in honour of Isaac Luria and Ḥayyīm Vital and tracts and poems on Sabbatian themes. We possess a letter of a Sabbatian emissary urging strict observance of the customs introduced by the master. Another document combating the influence of Sabbatian emissaries by refuting their views shows that the belief in Shabbetai's Messiahship was very widespread in Persia in 1674.[3]

[1] R. Y. Sasportas, *Sepher Ṣīṣat Nobēl Ṣebī*, ed. Y. Tishbi (Jerusalem, 1954).

[2] Cf. Hirschberg, *History*, vol. II, pp. 257, 258. G. Scholem gives other versions.

[3] Cf. W. J. Fischel, "The History of Persian Jewry under the Sefevid Dynasty" (Hebrew), in *Zion*, vol. II (1937), pp. 289–91; M. Benayahu, "Sabbatian Liturgical Compositions and Other Documents", from a Persian MS. (Hebrew), in *Sefunot*, vols. III–IV (1960), pp. 7–38.

Shabbeṯai Zvi died in 1676—almost exactly ten years after his conversion—in the fortress of Dulcigno (Ulcinj) at the southern end of the Dalmatian coast where he had been deported four years previously from Adrianople. After his death Sabbatian legend and propaganda initiated traditions that he did not die, but merely vanished. A myth was created concerning the deification of the Messiah and the incarnation of the Godhead in him. This development is strongly reminiscent of the Druze doctrine of the fate of the Caliph al-Ḥākim who did not die, but vanished on Mount al-Muqaṭṭam. It is interesting that more parallel features exist between these two religious movements, separated by an interval of 650 years, although this is surely accidental: antagonism and rebellion against the religious law; concealment of membership of the sect by those who outwardly adhered to Islam, Judaism, or Christianity; marriage only within the sect; stories of a "Night of Errors", of orgies at which the sectaries exchange wives.[1]

The foregoing applies especially to the Doenme sect, descendants of the 300 Sabbatians who were converted to Islam in Salonica in 1687. They subsequently split into three sub-sects, differing in customs and beliefs. They maintained their (secret) racial and religious identity until the time of the Second World War, although their strictness concerning custom and endogamy relented already after the First World War. Some of their poems and songs, which are almost all in Ladino, were published.[2]

Large groups of Sabbatians remained within the Jewish fold as a kind of voluntary *marranos* revealing their convictions only to fellow "believers". They brought forth the "Holy Societies" who emigrated to Palestine in the years 1700 to 1702 under the leadership of Yehuda Ḥasīd, Ḥayyīm Mal'akh and Abraham Rovigo; they came from Poland, Germany, and Italy to await the early coming of the Sabbatian Messiah in the Holy Land.[3]

Another violent tremor shook eastern European, and especially Polish and Bohemian, Jewry in the days of Jacob Frank (1726–91),

[1] Cf. the author's contribution on the Druzes, below (vol. 2, pp. 330 ff.).

[2] "Doenme" in Turkish means a convert to Islam. Christians who had changed their religion were also called thus; cf. H. Vámbéry, *Meine Wanderungen und Erlebnisse in Persien* (Budapest, 1867), p. 8. On the conversion of the Sabbatians cf. Rosanes, *op. cit.* vol. IV, p. 219. Much historical and ethnographical material on the Doenme was collected by I. Ben-Zvi and published in his *Studies and Sources* (Hebrew), pp. 526–51. Some of their poetry has been published by M. Attias, *Poems and Hymns of the Sabbatians* (Hebrew), 1948.

[3] See M. Benayahu, "The 'Holy Brotherhood' of R. Judah Ḥasīd and its Settlement in Jerusalem" (Hebrew), in *Sefunot*, vol. III–IV (1960), pp. 131–82.

who was regarded as the reincarnation of Shabbeṯai Zvi and the continuator of his Messianic mission in Poland. We mention this episode because Frank undoubtedly obtained his ideas in Sabbatian circles which he frequented in the Balkans. His activities and those of his followers proved extremely destructive. They did not shrink from using the blood libel against their Jewish brethren. In 1759 almost 1,000 men, women, and children embraced Christianity—almost all of them simple folk, inhabitants of towns and villages of eastern Galicia. Frank explained to them that by doing so they were following in the footsteps of Shabbeṯai Zvi.[1]

This is the story of the extremist Sabbatian groups. But Sabbatian ideas found access also to Orthodox Jewish circles. Even some distinguished rabbis fell in with them or were at least suspected of doing so. This dichotomy could not but have an adverse effect on spiritual life.

Unconscious Sabbatian influences are discernible in certain Jewish circles in the nineteenth and even in the twentieth century. A Tripolitanian author on the threshold of the twentieth century mentions a folk-song in honour of Shabbeṯai Zvi which women were singing quite innocently until—in 1860—a *dayyān* stopped them. He also mentions two Sabbatian converts to Islam who came to Tripoli where they gained fame by their holiness among both Jews and Muslims. Their graves were sacred to the Muslims, and the Jews voluntarily lit candles on these graves on Friday nights "for the time being".

S. Rosanes reports that at the time of writing (1934) Nathan of Gaza's tombstone was still to be seen at the Jewish cemetery in Skopje (Yugoslavia) and that the local Jews had formerly marked the anniversary of his death by prostrating themselves on his grave, reading the *Zohar* and the *Tiqqūnīm* (biblical passages, kabbalistic comments, prayers and liturgical poems) and holding joyous celebrations; the Doenme would send representatives to that festival. This custom ceased only upon the disintegration of Turkish rule in the Balkans.[2]

The assumption is almost inevitable that the example of the new sect of voluntary or involuntary *marranos*, i.e. crypto-Sabbatians posing as observant Jews, and of the Doenme crypto-Jews, influenced—though perhaps unconsciously—*marranos* of Mas͟hhad in Persia (in 1839) who used Muslim first names in public and Jewish ones among

[1] On the connexion between that movement and Sabbatianism see Scholem, "The Sabbatian Movement in Poland" (Hebrew), in *Beyt Yisraēl be-Pōlin*, vol. II, pp. 36–76.

[2] Cf. Hirschberg, *History*, vol. II, p. 188; Rosanes, *op. cit.* vol. IV, pp. 444, 445.

themselves, attended mosque and recited Jewish prayers at home, drew up marriage contracts according to the precepts of Islam and gave their wives *keṯubbōṯ* (marriage contracts) as required by Jewish law. Another effect of Sabbatianism may have been the success of the Bahā'ī movement with part of Persian Jewry who perhaps sought to escape persecution by pretending to be members of the new Muslim sect.

We close the discussion of Sabbatianism with the following remarks of G. Scholem: "Its heretical mysticism produced an outburst of more or less veiled nihilistic tendencies among some of its followers. Finally, it encouraged a mood of religious anarchism on a mystical basis which, where it coincided with favourable external circumstances, played a highly important part in creating a moral and intellectual atmosphere favourable to the reform movement of the nineteenth century."[1]

We now come to developments among the communities of the Muslim East after the fever of Sabbatianism and the sharp polemics about it had subsided. At the beginning of the eighteenth century life seemed to resume the course it followed a whole generation earlier: a fusion of the nomistic and the mystical trend—study of the Oral Law and rabbinical literature and meditation on the mysteries enshrined in the writings of the Kabbalah. It was only at the beginning of the twentieth century that the *dōr dē'ah* (Generation of Knowledge) movement arose in Yemen which meant to base the values of Judaism on the Talmud and the decisions of Maimonides whose *Mishneh Torah* was always regarded as binding by observant Yemenite Jews.[2]

At the same time the fight against Sabbatianism and its literary expression did not remain without untoward consequences. Many books showing Sabbatian influence appear to have been discarded or destroyed. Only this can account for the fact that in North Africa, where, as we have seen, the ascendancy of Sabbatianism in its heyday was very strong, almost no books of that period have been preserved.

It is impossible to adduce the development of rabbinical literature as evidence for the renewal of intellectual activity in the eighteenth century and we confine ourselves to the testimony of Ḥayyīm Joseph David Azulay, a famous rabbi and author of the second half of the eighteenth century who toured the East and Europe as an emissary of Palestinian communities. He was born in Jerusalem and died in

[1] Cf. G. Scholem, *Major Trends*, p. 299.

[2] Cf. E. Brauer, *Ethnologie der jemenitischen Juden* (Heidelberg, 1934), p. 350. This movement is not comparable with nineteenth-century European *Haskalah*.

Livorno. Azulay is our principal source for intellectual activity in Tunisia which he visited in the years 1773–4. It consisted almost exclusively in the study of the Talmud and the exploration of the mysteries of the Kabbalah. We may have to accept Azulay's statement that it began only two or three generations prior to his visit, in the early eighteenth century. Cazès asserts that Tunis was known as a centre of learning already in the seventeenth century, but this is hardly more than hearsay; at any rate, he is unable to give any names or indicate works written in that period—possibly, indeed, because they were committed to oblivion on suspicion of Sabbatianism.

According to Azulay's information "there are at present nearly 300 scholars in Tunis. I have also seen boys of fourteen display the utmost subtlety at study (*lit.* hit a hair)...The notables cherish learning and their fondest wish is to have scholarly sons. They are charitable, honour the Torah and study it very assiduously."

This testimony is the more significant since the Tunis community was not large; it was never noted for an important centre of learning like Algiers, Fez, Cairo and Smyrna. In those days benefactors—individuals and whole communities—made generous contributions to the maintenance of *yeshivot*, especially in the "four holy cities" in Palestine: Jerusalem, Ṣafad, Hebron and Tiberias. All communities, large and small, had rabbis and scholars of more than local repute. However, the process of renewal was slow and the standard of the *yeshivot* was lower than that of the Polish and Lithuanian ones in the nineteenth century. Literary activity was mostly confined to *responsa*, Bible and Talmud commentaries of medium calibre and homiletic books of a popular standard. We know from Azulay's travel memoirs of persecutions in Tunis to which people who concerned themselves with the Kabbalah or were said to be secret devotees of Sabbatianism were subjected.

The powerful *qā'id* of Tunisian Jewry, in whose house Azulay enjoyed generous hospitality, relentlessly persecuted the Livornese Freemasons and mystics. They were apparently considered non-observant and crypto-Sabbatian. Azulay naïvely refers to a brother of the *qā'id* who boasted "that he was a prophet, a spark of Jeremiah and Ezekiel, full of mystic insight; and all this because of the pride that was in him until he became mad and spurned all the sages of Israel".[1]

Assessing the effect of the fusion of the two religious trends—the

[1] Cf. Hirschberg, *History*, vol. II, pp. 136, 156–9.

nomistic and the mystic—on the broad strata of Jewish society in the East, we note both positive and negative features which persist to the present day.

The messianic element in the Lurianic Kabbalah kindled a spark of hope and cheerfulness under circumstances which, objectively speaking, were sometimes beyond endurance. Prostration on the graves of "saints", patriarchs, prophets and sages, an age-old practice deprecated already by a tenth-century Karaite writer, was given a fresh stimulus by the strolls outside Ṣafad, dedicated to contemplation and marking of saints' graves introduced by the Ṣafad Kabbalists, especially Luria. This led to the arrival in Palestine of individuals and groups who wished to settle there and live near the holy places or at least to make a *ziyāra*, a visit and joyful religious celebration, once in a lifetime. As the inhabitants of distant Diaspora countries were unable to visit the Holy Land every year, they would visit—at least once a year, but mostly several times—graves of prophets and sages and reputedly ancient synagogues in Babylonia, Persia and Africa, including the grave of Nathan of Gaza. These occasions, which imparted something of the atmosphere of the Holy Land and a taste of the freedom of the Messianic age, were a source of contentment and encouragement for the whole year.[1] They also provided an opportunity to pray for the sick and the barren, to purchase amulets, to fulfil vows and bestow charitable gifts pledged during the year. Naturally, stories were current among the people of miraculous recoveries of incurable sufferers or barren women giving birth, especially to male children. These stories strengthened a natural tendency, extremely prevalent in all strata of eastern Jewry, even among those enlightened and educated in other respects, to believe in the power of the practical Kabbalah. Hence the large consumption and wide distribution of a popular "literature", especially in the languages of the common people, based on the application of the practical Kabbalah and dealing with the interpretation of dreams, the casting of lots, etc. Needless to say that the borderline between faith and superstition was blurred.

[1] Antoninus Martyr (sixth century) mentions pilgrimages to the tombs of the Patriarchs and of David (*Palestine Pilgrims' Text Society*, vol. II, pt. 4, pp. 23, 24). Cf. the Letter of Sahl b. Maṣliaḥ (tenth century), ed. S. Pinsker in *Liḳḳūṭēy Ḳadmōnīyōṯ* (Hebrew) (Vienna, 1860), Appendices, p. 32. For the tombs in Morocco cf. especially L. Voinot, *Pèlerinages judéo-musulmans du Maroc* (Paris, 1948). The present writer saw many of these places during his visit to North Africa in 1955 and took part in several pilgrimages; cf. his *Inside Maghrib* (Hebrew), pp. 151–60; cf. also I. Goldziher, *Muhammedanische Studien*, vol. I (Halle, 1889), Excursus II, pp. 229–63.

The love for the Holy Land was greatly enhanced by emissaries whom Palestinian Jews sent to collect donations for Talmud schools and their students and who were a living link between the land of Israel and the Diaspora. The common people regarded these emissaries as messengers of God and turned to them with difficult religious problems. In several instances, the grave of an emissary who died in the Diaspora became an object of *ziyāra* and prostration.

The Lurian Kabbalah introduced the study of Mishnah passages for the happiness of the souls of the dead and inserted short extracts from the *Zohar* into the prayer-book. The following generations did not content themselves with these things. They chose passages from the *Idrās* (tracts of *Zohar* literature) as "study material" for the happiness of the dead, to be recited on every occasion, and would memorize large portions from other *Zohar* books, sometimes without understanding them. However well-meant, these innovations hardly contributed to the intellectual improvement of the masses.

Many of those beliefs and superstitions are still the spiritual property of the people who regard them as an integral part of their religion. At the inception of large-scale immigration to Israel, following the establishment of the State, notes in Hebrew script were often found during repairs to tombstones in the old Muslim Mamilla Cemetery in Jerusalem which apparently were of recent date and which contained incantations in Judeo-Arabic.[1]

At the same time it is clear that the intellectual revolution and political changes which began in the nineteenth century and extended to all spheres of life of the eastern nations, wrought many changes in the religious and intellectual life of Jewry as well. These will be dealt with in the last part of this chapter.

Religious and secular administration

Characteristic of the management of the Jewish community in medieval Muslim Iraq and its dependencies, was bipolarity in the division of functions and powers between essentially secular and essentially religious and academic authorities which generally persisted until the beginning of the second millennium. Afterwards it not infrequently happened that the secular head (Exilarch) was called upon to head also the Academy and the Great *beyṯ dīn* attached to it.

[1] For the custom of placing incantations on the tombs, cf. E. Doutté, *Magie et Religion dans l'Afrique du Nord* (Algiers, 1909), pp. 225 ff.

Very little is known of the situation in the eastern part of the Islamic world from the beginning of the Mongol invasion in the second quarter of the thirteenth century onward. From the sources in our possession we can only assume that until the stabilization of the Ottoman power in the fifteenth century, each community managed its affairs as best it could. On the other hand much information is available about conditions in the Mamlūk state until its conquest by the Turks.

Likewise, we are extremely ill-informed concerning events in the Maghrib during the two centuries following the accession of the Almohads. The form of the organization of communities in that region is known to us from collections of *responsa* of Maghrib scholars beginning with the first expellees who reached Algeria in 1391; from a collection of regulations (*Sēpher ha-taqqanōṯ*) of Fez, the first of which were enacted one or two years after the expulsion from Spain (1492); and from local chronicles. They differ from those in the East (European and Asian Turkey and Egypt). The communal courts were particuarly well organized and highly respected. As the expellees and the veteran residents had different matrimonial laws they maintained separate courts, but all public affairs were regulated by agreement and co-ordination. An exception was the conflict mentioned above, between the *Touansa* and the *Gornim*, which affected the status of the courts and the apportionment of secular functions, but not the prestige of the *dayyānīm* of the two communities.

A small community of Spanish Jews existed in Algeria already before the 1391 expulsion, headed by R. Saul Astruc Hakohen, scholar and physician to the ruler Abū Ziyān the Second at whose court in Tlemcen he wielded some influence. He was the spiritual leader of his community, to whom religious and legal matters were submitted for decision. However, when Mallorcan and Spanish scholars arrived in Algeria, including the wise old R. Isaac b. Sheshet Perfet, Astruc saw to it that the ruler of Tlemcen appointed Perfet sole *dayyān* of the community. The intervention of a Muslim ruler in internal Jewish affairs drew sharp protests from other scholars and the community at large. The chief opponent was R. Simon b. Ṣemaḥ Duran who feared that the intervention of an alien potentate and the conferment of wide exclusive powers on a single *dayyān* might shake the foundations of Jewish society; at the same time he showed great respect for Perfet as a person and a scholar. The original project failed because Perfet agreed to the appointment of other *dayyānīm* by the community. When after Perfet's death Duran was himself elected *dayyān* by the community he promised not to seek approval from the king and his ministers. A logical consequence of this attitude was Duran's demand that the communities should provide scholars and *dayyānīm* with a decent livelihood in order to enable them to fulfil their duties without pressure from any side.

From then onwards, Muslim rulers in the Maghrib did not interfere in the appointment of *dayyānīm* or otherwise in the internal religious affairs of the Jews, although a Moroccan ruler once forced the scholars to permit expellees to take two wives, contrary to what was already prescribed in Spain.[1]

It appears that the Jews who served in various capacities at the courts of Maghrib rulers (commercial and diplomatic agents, physicians, treasurers, etc.) were at first also the natural spokesmen and representatives of their brethren. Other expellees besides R. Saul Astruc succeeded in consolidating their positions at the court of the Ziyānids and thereby to impose their authority on the Jewish population. R. Abraham Sasportas was known to be very influential at court, and Perfet asked his intercession in seeking customs exemption for the books he saved from Spain. Prominent among the Mallorcans was the Shulal family (Solal in the pronunciation of Algerian Jews) which provided the last *negīdīm* in Egypt prior to the Ottoman conquest. However, none of its members held an official position at the Tlemcen court.

In the middle of the fifteenth century the status of Hārūn (Aaron), a Jewish courtier of 'Abd al-Ḥaqq, the last of the Banū Marīn kings in Morocco, was different. He and his master perished through the machinations of political opponents who used the well-tried device of stirring up religious fanaticism. This story is told in several sources; almost direct testimony is contained in the diary of 'Abd al-Bāsiṭ, an Egyptian merchant and writer who stopped in Tlemcen during a tour of Africa and Spain because unrest in Fez prevented him from proceeding thither. His remarks reveal various aspects of the position of Jewish official and unofficial representatives in the Maghrib, of relations with the authorities and of the attitude of the Muslim public. 'Abd al-Bāsiṭ took advantage of his stay in the capital of the Ziyānids in order to study medicine with a famous Jewish physician who granted him the *ijāza*, i.e. authorization to practise the profession. He is full of

[1] Cf. Perfet, *Responsa*, §61; Duran, *Responsa*, vol. 1, §§158–62. For the salaries, see *ibid.* §§142 and 147.

praise for his teacher Moses b. Samuel b. al-Ashqar, an expellee from Malaga, noting that he never saw a *dhimmī* of such excellent intellect and character. Moses' prudence, he says, kept him from meddling with state business. At the same time he notes that Hārūn had been a clever man and that if his master had listened to his advice he would no doubt have saved both his own life and that of his adviser. ʿAbd al-Bāsiṭ relates that a Jew-baiting preacher in Fez had great influence on the local populace, whereas a famous Muslim theologian in that city only agreed under duress to the massacre of the Jews. Events of this kind occurred several times during conflicts among the Muslims; the Jewish representatives were the first victims of the attendant agitation.[1]

Our sources do not describe Hārūn as an official representative of the Jews. Only from the sixteenth century onwards regulations, chronicles of Fez, and *responsa* mention the *nagīd*, Jewry's official representative and spokesman at the court of the ruler. The *nagīd* was probably chosen by the ruler from among the persons who had dealings with the court, by agreement with the Jews. The office was frequently hereditary within families. Besides the *nagīd* in Fez (or, sometimes, in Marrakesh, the original capital of the Saʿdīs), we find a *nagīd* in Miknās during the reign of Mawlay Ismāʿīl who rebuilt the city and made it his capital. Other *negīdīm* resided at Ṣafrū and Salā. Ṣafrū as the seat of a *nagīd* is accounted for by its nearness to Fez from where the centre of activities sometimes shifted, usually because of disturbances which were frequent in Fez. The *nagīd* in Salā (Rabat) probably represented Jewry with the independent *shaykhs* and pirates in control there. Presumably *negīdīm* were in other cities as well. In addition to the *nagīd*, there were usually seven notables (*ṭobey haʿīr*) concerned with the manifold needs of the community. Regulations required the consent of the rabbinical courts and the entire community. Although the influence of the Spanish expellees is usually evident, there were certain deviations due to political conditions and to the need for a system also acceptable to the veteran Jewish residents.[2]

The autocratic status of the Dey of Algeria affected the position of the Jewish representative at his court who was known as the *muqaddam*. In pre-expulsion Spain, this title was borne by a member of the manage-

[1] R. Brunschvig, *Deux Récits de Voyage inédits en Afrique du Nord* (Paris, 1936), vol. I, ʿAbd al-Bāsiṭ, *passim*.

[2] Cf. G. Vajda, *Un Recueil de Textes historiques Judéo-Marocains* (Paris, 1951), *passim*; J. M. Toledano, *La Lumière du Maghrib* (Hebrew) (Jerusalem, 1911), *passim*; Hirschberg, *History*, vol. II, pp. 272–3.

ment of the community and it seems that in Algeria too, there were at first several *muqaddams* who looked after the affairs of the community; they are mentioned in a *sharī'a* document of the early eighteenth century in connexion with the purchase of land for a cemetery. But in 1735 a change was introduced in the management of the community, and from then onwards increasing reference is made to the *muqaddam* as the sole representative of the community with the Dey. That post was henceforth a monopoly of two or three families: the Boucharas and subsequently the Busnachs and Bacris (who were related) and the famous Durans. Their activities at the Dey's court were internationally noted, especially from the early nineteenth century onwards.

After the conquest of Algeria by the French in 1830, one of the principal measures of the military administration in respect of the Jews was to curtail the powers of their communal courts. This was done systematically by several decrees, issued between 1830 and 1842, which gradually restricted their jurisdiction in matrimonial matters to the holding of merely symbolic ceremonies and the tendering of advice and written opinions; most matters were transferred to the jurisdiction of the French civil courts. The French policy-makers were assisted in their efforts by the influence, encouragement and co-operation of Jewish religious institutions in France and French-Jewish citizens who settled in Algeria.[1] Throughout the French era, until they regained full independence in 1962, Algerian Muslims jealously guarded their position as an autonomous community, not subject to French law in matters of personal status.

The fate of the *muqaddam*, described by Christian writers as "king of the Jews", was similar to that of the rabbinical courts. On 16 November 1830 Jacob Bacri was appointed *muqaddam* and empowered to supervise all Jews in town, execute judgments and collect taxes. In the following year he was given three advisers, and after him Aaron Mu'atti was appointed head of the Jews. But after five years the *muqaddam*'s title was changed to Deputy Mayor for Jewish Affairs. He became a French official drawing a salary from the Government.[2]

The head of Tunisian Jewry was known as the *qā'id*. His position was very strong, since as tax- and toll-gatherer and, in the capital Tunis as treasurer as well, he played an important part in the Bey's adminis-

[1] Cf. p. 208, below.

[2] Cf. I. Bloch, *Inscriptions tumulaires des anciens cimetières israélites d'Alger* (Paris, 1888), p. 11; M. Rosenstock, "The House of Bacri and Busnach", in *Jewish Social Studies*, vol. 14 (1951), pp. 343–64; Hirschberg, *History*, vol. II, pp. 62–80.

tration. Azulay gives some idea of the wealth, prestige and autocratic ways of the *qā'id* Joshua Ṭanūjī. Some other *qā'ids* he mentions belong to the class which rules supreme in the religious and wordly affairs of the community.

An exact definition of the functions and powers of the *qā'id* is given in the following words of a Tunisian rabbi:

It is the custom in this country . . . that a Jew who serves the royal house by collecting dues for the king's court appoints the *dayyānīm*, the scribes and the seven *ṭōḇey ha'īr*, each to his particular task, so that all kinds of communal services are regulated by him and nobody disobeys him, because the king has given him authority to rule the people as seems right to him and to appoint whomsoever he pleases at his discretion. Even if the seven notables and the *beyṯ dīn* have agreed to sell any communal property they can do nothing, great or small, save after obtaining permission from the ruler of the city (*sar ha'īr*, i.e. the *qā'id*); he signs at the top, and if ever he does not sign, the deed is endorsed with the remark: "And all this is done with the consent of the ruler of the city." Such has been the custom from time immemorial.

The dependence of the *qā'id*'s office upon the Bey sometimes led to its becoming hereditary in a family. Mutually independent sources attest that the powers of the *qā'id* as head of the community were very wide, that all matters of religious leadership and the management of communal property were decided by him.[1]

The powers of the *qā'id* were not appreciably curtailed until the second half of the nineteenth century. D. Cazès knew matters from personal observation; he says that the *qā'id* is the representative of the state authorities *vis-à-vis* the Jews; that the *qā'id* proposes to the authorities, or himself appoints, the *dayyānīm*, the seven notables, the persons in charge of certain departments, the notaries and the scribes. His signature appears first on official documents, even before that of the chief rabbi. Nothing is done in the community without his consent because he has a veto against all decisions of the *dayyānīm*, the seven notables and the managers of the community. Every document, whether public or private, has to bear his signature or the remark that it has been drawn up with his consent. The *qā'id* is also in charge of the administration of justice among the Jews on whom he may impose fines, whipping and imprisonment. The city authorities have to lend him their assistance, and the chief of police must carry out his judgments.

[1] Cf. also p. 174 and n. 1, above.

A decree of 1876 concerning the organization of the Tunis Relief and Charity Fund (the official designation of the body carrying out in Tunisia the functions of the community in the spheres of religious services and social welfare) prescribed that it should be headed by the *qā'id*. The chief rabbis should be subordinate to him. After long negotiations between subjects of the Bey and persons under consular protection—on the distribution of the income of the abattoir among the needy—it was agreed that the committee dealing with the distribution should be headed by the *qā'id*. A decree of the Bey confirmed the agreement, of which one copy was delivered to the *qā'id* and another to the French consul. Beylical decrees issued up to 1898 concerning various communal matters still reflect the status and powers of the *qā'id* as evolved in the course of many generations.

Only after the death of Rabbi Elie Borgel in 1898 did a fundamental change in the powers of the head of the community occur. A decree of 1899 concerning the organization of the Tunis Relief and Charity Fund mentions (in article 4) a president elected annually by the members of the board.[1]

The Jews of Tripolitania refer all the "administrative usages of the community" to Simon Lavi. The sources yield almost nothing concerning these usages. It may be assumed that, as in all the other eastern countries, the community was headed by a *shaykh* (an elder or chief) like the *qā'id* in Tunisia. But we do not know whether this *shaykh* performed the same functions of financial agent and treasurer at the court of the Pasha in Tripoli as were associated with the office of the *qā'id* in Tunisia or the *muqaddam* in Algeria. We have to be content with information supplied by a late chronicler on the basis of ancient material. According to him the names of the leaders of the Jews, "both the new ones and the old ones", were not mentioned in the prayer for the dead on the Eve of the Day of Atonement with the names of the *dayyānīm* because they were no scholars. "Only a rich man who was not a scholar was elected to be the intermediary between the Jews and the Government, and on his orders the *beyṯ dīn* would inflict the punishment of whipping on evildoers. He would, moreover, send to prison those who refused to accept his judgment or failed to pay their share of the poll-tax."

[1] Cf. D. Cazès, *Essai sur l'histoire des Israélites de Tunisie* (Paris, 1888), pp. 109–10, 162–3, 206–8; *idem*, *Notes Bibliographiques* (Tunis, 1893), pp. 121–2; R. Arditti, *Recueil des textes concernant les juifs de Tunisie de 1857 à 1913* (Tunis, 1915), pp. 1–2, 11–12, 55, 65, 149.

Another time he notes:

The *shaykh* collects the money of the poll-tax from the Jews for transmission to the Government treasury. He receives no remuneration for this labour except that he is exempt from poll-tax. Nevertheless people go to enormous expense in order to obtain that office because they are ambitious, for the *shaykh* imposes and releases from imprisonment; he also has a fixed place among the governors in the council chamber where he is consulted like the other notables, and in most cases his advice is taken.

The chronicler's language indicates that he is referring to things of the present or the recent past. The *shaykh*'s main function is the collection of the poll-tax, and he has power to send defaulters to prison. He also carries out judgments, and the *beyṯ dīn* inflicts whipping on his orders. He is proud to belong to the Council of Notables, an advisory body to the Pasha (*majlis shūrā*), consisting of representatives of the population whose task it is to advise the administrative authority on everything pertaining to taxes and charges and to the maintenance of correct relations between it and the governed.

Published extracts by Abraham Khalfon mention several members of his family as heads of the Tripoli community. Abraham himself headed the community from 1778 to 1781. After him his brother held the post for five years. Under Burghul Pasha the head of the community was Raḥamīm Barḍa. The best-known of the *shaykhs* in the nineteenth century was Shalom Tito. These extracts show that the office of head of the community was not held for life.

The creation of the post of *ḥakham bashī* in the second half of the nineteenth century no doubt impaired the powers of the *shaykh* and lowered his prestige with the authorities. From then onwards the *ḥakham bashī* was the recognized intermediary between local Jewry and the provincial governor and his assistants.[1]

The duties of the recognized leaders of the community in the Maghrib, especially those of the *qā'ids* and *muqaddams*, were not easy. We know from reliable evidence that they included men of high moral calibre, eager to be of service to their brethren. As regards those accused of abusing their position, it should be remembered that all communal leaders in these countries—especially in Algeria—were agents of the local rulers, in whose name and for whose benefit they engaged in a variety of sometimes doubtful business. All were the first target of the ruler's anger or of incited mobs who held them responsible

[1] Cf. Hirschberg, *History*, vol. II, pp. 197–8.

for every injustice in connexion with taxes and toll-duties, farming of government monopolies (*iltizām*) and various transactions with foreign states at the expense of the population; particularly shocking was the fate of the *muqaddams* of the Busnach-Bacri family in the early nineteenth century.

Nor was their position easy with their co-religionists. They were responsible for the collection of the poll-tax, whether it was imposed on each separate individual or whether an aggregate amount was fixed for the community, leaving it to the latter's representatives to apportion it among its members. They also had to ensure the payment of every fine or special charge the ruler saw fit to collect from the Jews. To protect themselves against serious personal loss they made the community promise in writing to bear those disbursements. It was of course not pleasant, either, to have to impose internal taxes to finance the requirements of the community, although the necessary means of enforcement were available. The commonest tax of this kind was the *gabella*, an excise duty on meat, wine, etc. In Tripolitania, this name was given to an internal tax (at the rate of 2–3 *per mille*) on imported goods. This latter impost, known also as *khābā*, served to maintain children of destitute parents at religious schools.[1]

In sum we may say that the wide jurisdiction of the secular authority is an outstanding feature of the Maghrib. The secular functionary appointed the *dayyānīm* or, if they were elected by the people, confirmed their election (incidentally, the people's right to elect *dayyānīm* was limited, since according to hallowed tradition religious offices were hereditary in a few families). The *nāgīd* in Morocco and the holders of parallel positions in the other Maghrib countries were responsible for the conduct of the affairs of the community with the outside world.

We know much less of the religious and secular administration in the East. At the time of the extension of Ottoman rule over the Near East and Europe in the fifteenth and the sixteenth centuries, the following picture presents itself in the light of the available sources.

According to Sambari, Sultan Meḥmed the Conqueror (1451–81) assigned three seats on his Imperial Divan to official religious functionaries: The Muftī, the Patriarch, and the Rabbi. The aged Rabbi Moses Capsali was appointed head of the Jews. Sambari continues: "And

[1] On the collection of the *jizya* cf. Perfet, *Responsa*, §132; Duran, *Responsa*, vol. III, §254; on the payment of a fine by the community, Vajda, *Recueil*, p. 23; on import duties and the internal tax, Hirschberg, *History*, vol. II, p. 198. Cf. also Léon l'Africain, *Description de l'Afrique*, ed. A. Épaulard (Paris, 1956), p. 401 (the *gabella* of Jarba).

Sultan Meḥmed imposed taxes on the whole country in the manner of kings: *kharāj*, *'awāriḍ* and *rab̲ akchesi*. And all the Jewish communities were assessed for tax by the said rabbi, and it was collected by him and delivered to the Treasury. And the Sultan loved all the Jews."[1]

According to Conforte (a contemporary of Sambari), Moses Capsali was appointed also rabbi and chief of the *dayyānīm* of Constantinople. "He was rabbi of the Romaniots, who were resident in the city in the time of the Greeks and exercised jurisdiction over all Jews of the city by the Sultan's command. And the *ḥakhāmīm* of the city in his generation were all submissive to him because of fear of the authorities and they had no power to speak to him about any matter or any decision he gave that did not commend itself to them."[2]

The usual version in historical works and encyclopaedias that Capsali was appointed *ḥakham bashî* resulted from a combination of these two reports. The title *ḥakham bashî* is not mentioned in any form in the Hebrew or Turkish sources of that period and it is nowhere stated that Capsali was given jurisdiction over all Jews in the Ottoman Empire and appointed chief of all *dayyānīm* and *ḥakhāmīm*. Sambari and Conforte can thus not be quoted in evidence of the early establishment of the office of a *ḥakham bashî* for the whole Empire. The silence cannot be accidental, for the same situation is reflected in the sources dealing with Eliyahu Mizraḥi who succeeded Moses Capsali after his death.

Sambari exaggerates with regard to the three seats reserved on the Imperial Divan to the representatives of the three religions. In point of fact, even the *sheykh ül-Islâm* (Grand Muftī of the Empire) who ranked equal with the Grand Vizier was not a member of the Divan. But it seems that the Orthodox Patriarch was given the honorary rank of "Pasha with the rank of Vizier" (three *tughs*), and it may be assumed that Rabbi Capsali was given similar status; at any rate Sambari thought so on the analogy of the status of the Christian representative.[3]

Sambari's statement that Capsali was the recognized head of the Jewish community, responsible to the authorities for its affairs and

[1] Extracts from Joseph Sambari's chronicle (Hebrew) in A. Neubauer, *Mediaeval Jewish Chronicles*, vol. I, p. 138; cf. also *ibid.* p. 153. The Turkish technical term is not *ḥakham akchesi* or *ḥ. Yahudiyan*, but *rab̲*. ...

[2] D. Conforte, *Qōrē ha-Dōrōṯ* (Hebrew) (Berlin, 1846), ed. D. Cassel, 28*b*. Conforte mentions the Romaniots also *ibid.* 48*b*. Sambari, *op. cit.* p. 153, calls them *benē rūmāniya* (children of Rumania).

[3] Cf. H. A. R. Gibb and H. Bowen, *Islamic Society and the West* (Oxford, 1950–7), vol. I, pt. II, pp. 86, 216, and *ibid.* pt. I, pp. 139, 140.

especially for the payment of taxes, appears to be correct. From other sources we know that after the capture of Constantinpole (1453) Meḥmed the Conqueror granted official recognition to the *millet* (the religious communal organizations of non-Muslims in his state) and conferred wide powers on their religious leaders. This does not contradict the assumption that a Jewish communal organization was already in existence for some time in the areas occupied by the Turks in the fourteenth and earlier fifteenth centuries. Sambari and Conforte emphasize that Capsali was old at the time of his appointment by Meḥmed and had previously (perhaps at the time of the capture of Constantinople) headed the Constantinople Romaniot community.[1]

Capsali's successor was Rabbi Eliyahu Mizraḥi, a noted scholar and the author of astronomical and mathematical works. According to the sources and his own testimony he had jurisdiction "over the whole city of Costantina" for more than forty years (he died in 1526). In exercise of this power he once convened the Sephardi *dayyānīm* of all synagogues in Constantinople and forbade them to wear their distinctive Sephardi clothing. The administrative and geographical definition "the city of Costantina" seems roughly to coincide with the definition "city people" in the description of Capsali's powers having regard to the increase of the Jewish population of Constantinople during almost seventy years since the conquest and its spread to the suburbs of the capital. This assumption is confirmed through Mizraḥi's judgment in the "*Kâkhyalîk* case".[2]

Capsali's wide and exclusive powers as chief of the *dayyānīm* met with opposition from the Ashkenazi and Italian rabbis in Constantinople who requested the intervention of a noted rabbi in Italy in the matter of a judgment believed by them to be erroneous. This happened a considerable time before the expulsion from Spain. The settlement in Greater Constantinpole of *ḥakhāmīm* from Spain—unwilling to accept Mizraḥi's authority—led to tension between Romaniots and Sephardim who also did not recognize the form of authorization of rabbis practised in Byzantium.[3]

The Jews in the Byzantine Empire adopted the authorization of

[1] Cf. *ibid.* pt. II, pp. 216–19, 221 n. 4, 225–6; Sambari and Conforte, *loc. cit.*

[2] Cf. Conforte, *op. cit.* 31*a–b*; and especially a *responsum* of Messer David Léon, ed. S. Schechter (*REJ*, vol. XXIV (1892), p. 137), quoted by R. Ḥayyīm Benvenishti, *Kneseṯ ha-Geḏōlah, Oraḥ Ḥayyīm*, §301.

[3] Cf. Conforte, *op. cit.* 28*b*–29*a*; Sambari, *op. cit.* 153*a*. Mizraḥi and contemporary non-Sephardi rabbis complain of the state of affairs in their *responsa*; cf., e.g., *REJ*, vol. XXIV (1892), p. 137, and p. 185 n. 2 above, with pp. 188–9 n. 1, below.

rabbis "according to the custom of France and Germany" at the end of the fourteenth century. This was not ordination such as Jacob Beyrab intended to reintroduce[1] and which had a religious and charismatic significance, but the award of a certificate by which a distinguished rabbi and teacher attested that the bearer was conversant with the religious law. It was similar to the *ijāza* in Islam, a certificate granted by a recognized authority to a student who passed the prescribed course of study or oral examinations to the satisfaction of his master. The purpose of this authorization was to prevent ignorant or morally unworthy persons from giving religious and legal decisions as *dayyānīm* or rabbis, thus leading the people astray. The certificate was not in itself sufficient to secure its holder the position of rabbi or *dayyān*, because these were elected by the people, although only on the strength of a certificate. Authorization was not adopted in Spain because it did not conform with the requirements of halakhic tradition. When the Spanish expellees arrived in Turkey, the Romaniot rabbis not seldom denied both the moral and formal academic qualifications of the latter's *ḥakhāmīm* and *dayyānīm*. On the other hand the Spanish scholars, conscious of their intellectual superiority and general education, looked down on and refused to acknowledge the authority of the Romaniot rabbis. This dispute, which found its expression in questions of the overall administrative organization of the Jews in a city or the whole country, was—perhaps unconsciously—one of the factors which prompted Beyrab's unsuccessful attempt to revive ordination. As the expellee *ḥakhāmīm* refused to recognize the substitute devised in Europe, the claim of the leading Romaniot rabbi on the office of chief *dayyān* of Constantinople lapsed after Mizraḥi's death.[2]

In Ṣafad, too, where the most prominent halakhists were concentrated a few years after Mizraḥi's death, no single person was formally entitled to head the local *dayyānīm* and rabbis. Yet there was a council of *ḥakhāmīm* which met from time to time to co-ordinate important matters of general interest.[3]

Apparently Rabbi Eliyahu Mizraḥi was never charged with assessing and collecting government taxes. Rabbi Capsali may have carried out

[1] Cf. p. 163 n. 1 above.

[2] Cf. Perfet, *Responsa*, §271; Messer David, *Kebōd Ḥakhāmīm* (Hebrew), ed. S. Bernfeld (Berlin, 1889), Introduction, pp. x–xii; text, pp. 53–4, 62–3. On the decline of the Chief Judgeship in Constantinople cf. Rosanes, *Histoire* (Hebrew), vol. 1, pp. 126 ff.

[3] Cf. Mosheh b. Joseph of Trani, *Responsa*, vols. I, §106; II, §§115 and 131. Even J. Karo's halakhic authority as decisor was accepted only after a prolonged struggle; but cf. Werblowsky, *Joseph Karo*, pp. 126–7.

these functions so long as the number of Jews under Ottoman rule was small, and internal discipline—the fruit of long tradition—was still effective. But the increase of the Jewish population and the crystallization of different elements which settled throughout the Empire, made the task too burdensome. The improvement of the Ottoman administrative machinery upon the completion of the great conquests in the fifteenth and early sixteenth centuries enabled taxes to be collected more efficiently through general channels: a secular bureaucracy, *qāḍīs*, market supervisers, etc.

The situation in the Constantinople Jewish community may be gathered from a judgment rendered by Rabbi Mizraḥi in the "*Kâkhyalîk* case" (in 1520), restoring the rights of the *kâkhya* She'altiel[1] of which he and his sons had been deprived one-and-a-half years previously. Many Jews were in the service of the sultan or powerful viziers and pashas as commissioners of revenue and expenditure, superintendents of the mint, toll and customs farmers and, very importantly, farmers of monopolies on certain exported and imported goods. From the recital of the facts it appears that the *kâkhya*, the official spokesman and intercessor with the authorities in all matters affecting the Jews of the city—especially in the matter of tax collection—would accept monetary and other gifts for perverting the course of justice. The representatives of the various congregations complained bitterly to Rabbi Mizraḥi, and in their presence and with their consent he deprived the *kâkhya* and his sons of all the rights enjoyed by them—at the end of 1518. Moreover, a severe ban was imposed on him and anyone who might apply to him in those matters. This judgment was subsequently reversed, and he was restored to his position, but only after he had promised "to do nothing, great or small, in any public matter, with the government, the (secular) judges, the *qāḍīs* or any dignitary whatsoever, save with the permission and on the advice of persons appointed by the congregation from among themselves; nor to intervene between two litigants—helping one and opposing the other—save with the permission of the representative of his congregation, and to do good to the Jews to the best of his ability".

In this judgment, Rabbi Mizraḥi figures as the chief *dayyān* of the city conducting a trial affecting all Jews and strictly adhering to customary procedure. Nevertheless, the judgment caused dissatisfaction among the

[1] *Kâkhya* is the Jewish–Turkish version of the Persian *katkhudā* (= major-domo). Cf. A. Galanté, *Documents officiels turcs*, etc., pp. 135 ff., 199–205.

Sephardi *ḥakhāmīm* who, in Mizraḥi's words, were "inadequate scholars who wish to impress the ignorant and their fellow townspeople, who presume to sit in judgment and to lay down the law in Israel; they increase strife in Israel, they destroy the world and extinguish the light of the Torah".[1]

R. Eliyahu Mizraḥi, as rabbi, clearly had nothing to do with the collection of taxes and the representation of the Jews with the various authorities. That the collection of taxes was not the concern of the official representatives of the *millet* is confirmed by many sources. In fact, the opposite is true: the various tax-collectors, toll-farmers, cashiers and bankers of pashas, in so far as they were non-Muslims, were the natural spokesmen of their communities by virtue of these functions and their influence at court.

A similar situation prevailed in Egypt under Ottoman rule, though here the tradition of the *negīdīm* was still alive. Sambari indeed gives the title of *nagīd* to Abraham Castro, who was "governor of the mint" in Egypt during the first years of Ottoman rule and through whom Süleyman the Lawgiver rebuilt the walls of Jerusalem. But the description "governor of the mint" indicates that Castro was a kind of *kâkhya* of the sultan and did not enjoy the status held by the *nagīd* in Mamlūk Egypt. Conforte adds that Castro was in charge of the customs, but he calls him *sar* (high dignitary), a quite indefinite designation. Elsewhere, Sambari indeed says when "the light of the Ottomans began to shine, the office of *nagīd* reverted to him who was worthy of it because of his wisdom, activities and wealth, and the people of Costantina, with the consent of its *ḥakhāmīm*, *sārīm* and advisers, would send a wise and esteemed Jew to judge the people justly, and he punished, fined, whipped and excommunicated as was necessary". But these vague remarks merely confirm that the *nagīd* was sent by the government authorities in Constantinople. Sambari, moreover, contradicts himself when he says that in the middle of the sixteenth century after thirty years of Ottoman rule in the country, the rabbi of the community excommunicated the *nagīd* sent from Constantinople for having slighted him; the *nagīd* complained against the rabbi to the Muslim governor, which shows that he was not empowered to anathematize him. The dispute ended with the expulsion of the *nagīd* from Egypt. Sambari concludes: "And from that day onwards, he (the Muslim ruler) made it a law in Israel that no Jew who came from

[1] Eliyahu Mizraḥi, *Responsa*, §15.

Costantina should be called *nagīd*, but that he should be called *chelebi*; and this has been the law for Israel to this day."[1]

Later sources indicate that the titles *chelebi*, *bazargan* and *mu'allim*, still in use in early nineteenth-century Constantinople, were given to a prominent Jew who performed the function of official intercessor by virtue of his position in the financial and economic administration of the Egyptian rulers. Jewish dragomans in seaport towns likewise had influence with the authorities and used it for the benefit of their co-religionists.[2]

Rabbi Eliyahu Mizraḥi's judgment in the case of *kâkhya* She'altiel repeatedly mentions the representatives of the congregations in Constantinople. "Representative" (*memunneh*, *lit.* "appointee") is one of the titles designating the persons elected by the congregation to manage its affairs. Other titles are *parnās*, *bārūr*, *qāṣīn* and the ancient collective designation *ṭōḇey ha'īr*. The powers, number, manner of election and period of tenure of these functionaries varied greatly. Their main task was the colletion of communal taxes (especially the *gabella*), which were used to maintain the children of the needy at school and to finance charitable purposes. The mode of imposition and amount of the taxes were also different; as a rule, the consent of the whole congregation or at least of the tax-payers was required. The congregations of expellees and immigrants from Europe usually retained the practices they had followed in their countries of origin.

The veteran residents likewise maintained their ancestral tradition according to which public affairs were looked after by the elders, the heads of the prominent and influential families.

This situation lasted for centuries, continued after the introduction of reforms in the organization of the *millet* in the nineteenth century, and its remnants exist to this day.[3]

[1] Cf. Sambari, *op. cit.* pp. 145 and 116–17, Conforte, *op. cit.* 33*a*; also p. 139, above.

[2] Turkish *chelebi* (Arabic *shalabī*) means gentleman (of fashion); Arabic *bazīrkān* is a loanword from Persian *bāzargān* "merchant"; *mu'allim* (Arab.) means teacher, master. Cf. also Galanté, *op. cit.* pp. 176–8(*ferman* concerning Jewish and Christian dragomans in the service of foreign powers). Cf. also Franco, *Essai...*, p. 134; B. Lewis, *Middle Eastern Studies*, vol. I (1965), p. 289; and for the *bazargan-bashî* (purveyor of textiles to the Palace) cf. M. D'Ohsson, *Tableau Général de l'Empire Ottoman*, vol. III (Paris, 1820), p. 290.

[3] Cf. M. S. Goodblatt, *Jewish Life in Turkey* [in XVI c.] (New York, 1952), pp. 61 ff.; Galanté, *op. cit.* pp. 75–92; *idem*, *Appendice à l'ouvrage "Documents officiels turcs"*, pp. 15–20.

CHANGES IN LIFE AND ATTITUDES

Political changes

On the threshold of the nineteenth century an ever-increasing urge for change pervaded society. Political upheavals, revolts and civil disobedience were much in evidence in the border areas of the Empire inhabited by non-Turkish and non-Muslim populations. There was growing tension between the Ottoman authorities and these citizens. The powers intervened in favour of the subject Christian peoples from motives of Christian love and brotherhood and in the interests of undisguised imperialist aspirations. Sultan ʿAbdülmejid, in the "Noble Decree" (*khaṭṭ-i sherif*) of 1839 and the "Imperial Decree" (*khaṭṭ-i hümayun*) of 1856, guaranteed the right of non-Muslims to religious freedom, civic equality and fair taxation, but those decrees were issued under pressure from the powers whose intervention obviously intensified the suspicion, hatred and fear in which the internal enemy was held.

Egypt's political status was a special one. The processes of its detachment from the Ottoman Empire and subjection to British political ascendancy were different from the corresponding processes in other countries. French cultural influence there established itself already in Napoleon's time and determined the character of the social élite. It also lent a particular quality to the Jewish communities.

The changes in the territorial set-up of the Near and Middle East are the most striking result of the political, cultural and ultimately military struggle waged for the right of religious and national minorities to freedom and sovereignty. The many changes in the East obviously had a tremendous impact on developments in the intellectual and religious life of the Jewish communities. The Balkan communities were now hemmed in by political boundaries which weakened their traditional relationships, and French influence in Algeria (and, to some extent, in northern Tunisia) radically changed the attitude of most of the Jewish inhabitants to the values of Judaism.

As a result of increasing interest in Middle Eastern affairs and of the changes occurring in that region, the Jewish communities in Iraq and the Persian-speaking territories emerged from oblivion. Centuries of the history of these areas are known to us, if at all, only by vague and fragmentary reports. Their integration into the general picture makes it necessary to describe their past in order the better to understand their situation.

From the middle of the thirteenth century Iraq had a chequered history. For about a hundred years, Iraq remained a bone of contention between the Ottoman sultans and the Persian kings, until in 1638 the Ottomans succeeded in finally annexing Baghdad and the rest of Iraq to their state. At the same time the rule of the pashas was more independent in Baghdad and Mosul than in other districts.

The Jewish population—once so important and distinguished in all respects—had to adapt itself to the special political circumstances. Baghdad, once the capital of a world power, was now the seat of the pasha of a remote province impoverished by frequent wars and even more by its severance from the great international trade routes. The Jewish traveller Zekharya al-Ẓāhirī, a native of Yemen, who visited Baghdad in the second half of the sixteenth century, says little about its scholars. But he mentions the famous graves in Iraq of the Prophet Ezekiel and Ezra the Scribe. The lack of competent scholars in Baghdad forced the community to address questions on religious matters to the rabbis of Aleppo; some Aleppine scholars indeed settled in Baghdad. Communities in those days were headed by *nesī'īm* who sometimes conducted their affairs in a high-handed manner.[1]

Particular importance attaches to the commercial activity of Baghdadi and Baṣran Jewish traders who began to emigrate to India in the late eighteenth century. A sizable British-protected Jewish colony came into being in Surat. It traded with cities in Iraq and on the Persian Gulf. From the early nineteenth century onwards the importance of Surat decreased, and the Baghdadi merchants thereupon moved to Calcutta, Bombay and Poona. Among the founders of these communities the Sassoon family deserves special mention because it had a large share in their religious and intellectual development. These Iraqi Jewish colonies maintained close contact with Far Eastern markets and with London, the commercial and political metropolis. Relationships formed in India between erstwhile Baghdadi Jews and the British trading companies which also performed governmental functions and had considerable influence on relations and contacts within Iraq itself during the British Mandate.[2]

[1] Cf. D. S. Sassoon, *A History of the Jews in Baghdad* (Letchworth, 1949); A. Ben-Jacob, *A History of the Jews in Iraq* (Hebrew) (Jerusalem, 1965) and *Kurdistan Jewish Communities* (Hebrew) (Jerusalem, 1961).

[2] Cf. W. J. Fischel, "The Immigration of Arabian Jews to India in the Eighteenth Century", in *Proceedings Americ. Ac. Jew. Research*, vol. XXXIII (1965), pp. 1–20 and *The Jews in India* (Hebrew) (Jerusalem, 1960), esp. pp. 176–203.

In India, the Iraqi immigrants came upon two groups of communities whose origin and historical past are still not clear. The members of the larger group call themselves *Bney Isrā'ēl*. In the mid-nineteenth century they were estimated at 5–6,000 persons. They claim descent from the Ten Tribes, but there is reason to assume that they are the remnant of immigrants who came to India from one of the Arab countries, perhaps from South Arabia. The centre of the *Bney Isrā'ēl* was in Bombay and the villages of the Bombay District, and here the Baghdadis met them. They speak Marathi and English. Their neighbours call them *shanwar tellis*, i.e. "Sabbath-observing oil pressers", as they refrain from work on that day. They keep the holy days and the commandments of the Written Law, but it seems that until the arrival of the Iraqis they never heard of the Oral Law or of the customs and rules which spread after the conclusion of the canon of the Hebrew Bible. The *Bney Isrā'ēl* have always preserved their religious identity and kept apart from the Indian population. There is also a small group of "Black *Bney Isrā'ēl*", apparently the offspring of intermarriage with the Indians.

The other, smaller, group which never exceeded 2,000 was concentrated in the south of the peninsula in the city of Cochin and the cities of the Malabar Coast. Their past is likewise controversial. In any event it is certain that they have been settled in Cochin Province for at least 1,500 years. A decree—apparently of the fifth century—engraved on copper tablets indicates that the ruler of the state of Kranganur granted them various rights, such as exemption from taxes and recognition of their leaders who had the rank of high dignitaries. The Portuguese dislodged the Jews from the coast and forced them to concentrate in the city of Cochin, but here, too, they suffered at the hands of the conquerors. During that period new immigrants, expellees from Spain and former inhabitants of Germany, joined the communities. From then onwards there were two strata: "white" Jews and the dark-skinned veteran settlers, augmented by the "freedmen" who had been the slaves of "whites" or veterans. All these spoke Tamil or Malayalam, but at the same time they had poems and ditties in Hebrew. Their ties with Jewish custom and tradition were incomparably stronger than those of the *Bney Isrā'ēl*, no doubt owing to their contact with Middle Eastern Jewry and immigrants from Europe.[1]

Our knowledge of Persian Jewry shows a gap which until the sixteenth century extends to Persia proper and until the nineteenth century

[1] Cf. Bibliography.

comprises also the areas under Persia's political and cultural influence: Transcaucasia, Georgia and Armenia.

A Christian traveller reports the existence of Jewish communities in the days of Shah 'Abbās I (1587–1621). He puts the number of Jews at 8–10,000 families (about 50,000 persons) scattered all over the country. A Jewish source of the second half of the seventeenth century mentions eighteen localities where Jewish communities existed; a few more might be added on the strength of other sources. These communities extended in the northern region from Qazwīn in the west to Khurasan in the east and Jewish settlements straggled south as far as Lār and Kirmān. We also find Jews in the southern seaports of Bandar 'Abbās and Hormuz. Jews engaged in all crafts and in commerce. Many made a living by the manufacture and sale of alcoholic liquors. Moneylenders were not lacking. There were a great number of witch-doctors and soothsayers and women mixers of love-potions. A European traveller who toured the country in the seventeenth century noted that the Jewish population was poor.

Persian Jewry's belief in witchcraft prompted a Jewish renegade to allege that they used the formulae of the books of the practical Kabbalah in order to harm the Shah, whereupon a decree was issued in 1620 for the confiscation and destruction of these and many sacred books. The opposition of the Iṣfahānī community to the destruction of the books led to an order for the forced conversion of the heads of the community subsequently extended to all its members. This measure remained in force until 1628. Further persecutions occurred under 'Abbās II (1642–66). They began with expulsion from Iṣfahān and eventually all Jews in the country were ordered to adopt Islam (1656). The contemporary author Bābay b. Luṭf, a native of Kāshān, wrote a poetical chronicle of these events in which he says: "The rule of every king brought us fresh troubles. But this disaster was worse than all. Our heart was torn into a hundred pieces. When a calamity befell us at other times it affected our wealth, our money. But under this government we became as dust, for our religion was lost together with our wealth."

The forced converts were called *jadīd al-Islām* (neo-Muslims). They were freed from the poll-tax and the duty to wear special dress and received gifts of money. However, they remained Jews in their hearts. Five years later they were permitted to revert openly to Judaism on condition that they returned the gifts of money, paid the poll-tax for the time they had been exempt from it and again wore distinctive clothing.[1]

The persecution of Persian Jewry reached another peak in 1839 with the forced conversion of the community in Ma<u>sh</u>had, the capital of the district and one of the holy cities of the Persian Shī'īs. A Persian youth accused a Jewish woman of vilifying the Shī'ī faith on the day of solemn mourning for the murder of al-Ḥusayn, Muḥammad's grandson. A fanatical mob, excited by the account of al-Ḥusayn's sufferings, demanded the death or forced conversion of all Jews. Thirty-five Jews were killed in the ensuing disturbances and the others were forced to embrace Islam. The shocking spectacle of the *jadīd al-Islām* now repeated itself—this time without their being able to return to Judaism—in Ma<u>sh</u>had or some other Persian city even years after the disturbances had died down. The account of J. Wolff, a missionary of Jewish extraction who was in Ma<u>sh</u>had several years after the events, reflects the wretched condition of the converts. Wolff advised them to apply to Sir Moses Montefiore in London for help. For three generations the community had to pose as Muslims while secretly observing the Jewish laws. Many of them, indeed, succeeded in crossing into neighbouring countries, especially Afghanistan, thus strengthening the small communities in Kabul, Herat and Balkh, a certain percentage of which were probably refugees or emigrants from Persia who arrived in the preceding centuries. It should be noted that the Ma<u>sh</u>had *marranos* established a community of their own in Jerusalem, which still maintains two synagogues in the Bukharian Quarter.[2]

Isolation from the communities outside the Persian-speaking area, recurrent persecution, the hostility of the Shī'ī population and fanatical clergy, but perhaps most of all the abandonment of the communities by their spiritual leaders, indelibly marked the religious life of Persian Jewry. Biblical learning, Hebrew—the language of the ancient prayers—and Aramaic—the language of the *Zohar* and other kabbalistic books, extracts from which were still recited by rote—fell into oblivion. The link with the spiritual treasures of Judaism was preserved through a translation of the Bible into the Persian-Jewish dialect, liturgical

[1] W. Bacher examined contemporary Jewish sources (see Bibliography). For material from travellers' books see W. J. Fischel, "The History of the Persian Jews during the Sefevid Dynasty" (Hebrew), in *Zion*, vol. II (1937), pp. 273–94; and I. Ben Zvi, "New Sources on the History of Persian Jewry" (Hebrew), in *Sefunot*, vol. II (1958), pp. 190–213.

[2] Cf. J. Wolff, *Narrative of a Mission to Bokhara* (London, 1845), vols. I, p. 240; II, pp. 169–76; W. J. Fischel, "The *marrano* Community in Persia" (Hebrew), in *Zion*, vol. I (1936), pp. 49–74. Cf. also p. 172 above.

poetry (*piyyūṭīm*), popular literature, and ritual observances. Conditions thus created were favourable to the influence of various religious trends, such as the Bahā'ī Movement which won adherents among the Jews, and to Jews joining Ṣūfī orders. The author of this chapter met in Tehran in 1942 a Jew who was the *murshid* (leader) of a local Ṣūfī sect.

To complete the picture we must mention the Persian-speaking communities in Uzbek territory: Bukhara, Tashkent, Samarkand, and Kokand. In the first half of the nineteenth century Bukharian Jewry is said to have numbered over 5,000. In the second half of the nineteenth century these communities came under Tsarist rule. They all preserved strong ties with Persian Jewry through a common language and literature.[1]

Impact of new factors

The influence and impact of new factors arising during that period are noticeable in three fields: (1) communal organization; (2) the struggle for the security of the individual; (3) changing values in religious and intellectual life.

Communal organization

At the end of 1836 or the beginning of 1837 the Ottoman authorities confirmed Abraham Levi as *ḥakham bashi* in Constantinople. According to a report in the Official Gazette of the Empire this gesture was made at the request of those members of the community in the capital who were subjects of the Sultan. They had no Christian European powers behind them and were jealous of the honour of official confirmation accorded by the government to the Greek and Armenian patriarchs. This was in fact a turning-point in the policy of the Ottoman authorities, which hitherto did not interfere in the internal affairs of the Jewish community and for centuries past gave no official status to its representatives. The original copies or authentic texts of the *berat hümayun* (imperial confirmation of appointments) occurring from 1836 onwards, which were also granted to *ḥakham bashis* in Adrianople, Salonica, Izmir, Bursa and Jerusalem, show that here was indeed a policy the significance and consequences of which went beyond mere confirmation of appointments. Implicitly it contained an official recognition of the Jewish *millet*.[2] A *berat* was concerned with three interrelated matters.

[1] J. Wolff, *op. cit.* vol. 1, p. 14, puts the number of Jews in Bukhara at 10,000.

[2] Cf. M. Franco, *Essai*..., pp. 151 ff.; A. Galanté, *Documents officiels*..., pp. 32–50; *idem*, *Appendice*..., pp. 5–8.

Religious powers of the ḥakham bashî

Within his area of jurisdiction the *ḥakham bashî* was the supreme authority in all religious matters and in charge of all *ḥakhāmīm* and heads of the community. He alone was authorized to ban and excommunicate offenders and prohibit their religious burial. The person and official residence of the *ḥakham bashî* enjoyed immunity which extended also to the *ḥakhāmīm* and officials subordinate to him. Disagreements on religious questions between *ḥakhāmīm* and the local Muslim authorities were to be settled before the supreme authorities of the Empire in Constantinople.

Powers as representative of the government

The *ḥakham bashî* was responsible for the collection of government taxes; government officials had to lend his officials every assistance in performing this task and place guards at their disposal. To protect his officials from molestation and restrictions when travelling they were excused from wearing distinctive Jewish clothing and permitted to carry arms. They were thus exempt from two important provisions of 'Umar's regulations. By an order of 1850 the religious heads of the four *millets* must collect the poll-tax.[1]

Permission to read the Torah

The intention to grant rights to the community as a whole is conspicuous in a clause figuring in all *berat* texts declaring that the reading of the Torah in the house of the *ḥakham and in other houses* is permitted in the Jewish religion, as is hanging veils and candelabra where such reading takes place. This declaration was tantamount to a permission to establish permanent synagogues and constituted an ingenious circumvention of a prohibition contained in 'Umar's regulations that was a source of many difficulties and an occasion for incessant extortion.[2] We read of the founding of a synagogue in Jerusalem in the early nineteenth century:

When the Muslims heard that the Ashkenazim had established a place of worship they became very angry, attacked the congregants and tried to take away the only Torah scroll they had. Only by weeping, entreaties and a gift of money did the worshippers save the scroll. They had to promise

[1] Franco, *Essai...*, p. 146.

[2] Y. Goldman, *Ha-Asif* (5647; 1886/7), p. 72; B. Klar, *Rabbi Ḥayyīm ibn Aṭṭār* (Hebrew) (Jerusalem, 1951), pp. 37–8; cf. also p. 154 n. 2, above.

the Muslims that they would never again pray in that place. From then onwards the scroll was kept at the house of one of the members of the community. A hole was made in the wall of the house and whenever Torah readings were in progress four children functioned as lookouts, and as soon as they reported that the Muslims were approaching, the scroll was removed through the hole to the roof of the house. In this way the Ashkenazim went through a long period of trouble and vexation. More than once they were in mortal danger when the Muslims took them by surprise and found them praying fervently...[1]

The *berats* issued in provincial towns to *ḥakham bashîs* state expressly that they were granted upon the recommendation of the *ḥakham bashî* of Constantinople who was thus the head of all the rabbis in the Empire. This was why, in the event of a disagreement among the members of a community concerning the appointment of the local *ḥakham bashî*, the disputants would try to influence the *ḥakham bashî* of Constantinople. His decision was not infrequently based on other than objective considerations. From certain (especially Tripolitanian and Iraqi) sources it appears that a *ḥakham bashî* was sometimes sent from the capital without the local community having been consulted.

At the same time it is clear that while the *ḥakham bashî*'s official functions enhanced his importance and prestige they were not in themselves sufficient to grant him supremacy in the field of *halakhah* and religious jurisdiction. In fact, this post was sometimes assigned to a simple schoolteacher. Besides the *ḥakham bashî* who was described in French as *chef temporel* (a translation of the Arabic–Turkish term *shaykh zamanî*), we find *ḥakhāmîm* bearing the designation *rab̲ hakōlēl* or *chef spirituel* (*shaykh rūḥî*). Naturally sometimes a *ḥakham bashî* who had resigned or been deposed subsequently served as *rab̲ hakōlēl*, just as a *rab̲ hakōlēl* was occasionally appointed *ḥakham bashî*. The powers vested in the *ḥakham bashî* show that the Ottoman authorities regarded him as their representative *vis-à-vis* the Jewish population, who performed official functions on behalf of the Jews, and so he was regarded by the Jews themselves. His situation was further complicated by dissensions between strictly traditionalist, anti-modernist members of the community and those favouring a general education and reforms in communal affairs. All this accounts for the fact that of the five *ḥakham bashîs* officiating in the years 1836–63 three were deposed by the community and one was dismissed by the government because of his non-Turkish nationality. Three continued in office in the post of *rab̲ hakōlēl* which

---

[1] See p. 197 n. 2.

seems to indicate that their deposition had been brought about by clashes between the different trends within the community.[1]

The affairs of the Constantinople community had generally become unsettled. The prominent Jewish families in the capital, the Gabbays, Carmonas and Ajimans maintained close relations with the Janissaries and their official positions as bankers and tax-farmers assured them of the leadership of the community. The massacre of the Janissaries in 1826 was followed by the execution of the principal representatives of these families which thereupon lost their influence in Jewish society. In the thirties leadership passed to Abraham de Camondo, a member of a respected family of scholars and wealthy merchants. Camondo became influential in official circles, and the confirmation of the appointment of the first *ḥakham bashî* of Jerusalem in 1841 goes to his credit. He headed the faction which tried to strengthen the position of the community in its economic competition with the Armenians and Greeks. For decades past these groups had had the upper hand, especially because of their superiority in general education, their readiness to accept European influence and through their connexions with court circles, although the latter viewed the Greeks with suspicion after Greece achieved independence. Correspondingly, the Jews lost their traditional economic positions and their influence with the authorities. Camondo was impressed by the winds then blowing in Europe which he knew from his great commercial and financial experience and his travels. He inspired the establishment of a modern-oriented school in the capital and bore half of the cost of its maintenance. At the same time we clearly discern the influence of the *khaṭṭ-i hümayun* of 1856 which led, not long after the establishment of the school, to the constitution of a "committee of notables" (*lit.* functionaries, *wa'ad peqīdīm*, *majlis gashmī*) consisting of wealthy progressive-minded persons under the chairmanship of Camondo. The formation of this body in 1860 in which members of the Carmona, Hamon and Ajiman families also took part, was a somewhat irregular response to the appeal directed by the *khaṭṭ-i hümayun* to the non-Muslim communities to submit to the Sublime Porte proposals for their reorganization in accordance with the spirit of the times. A serious rift developed in the Jewish community between progressive-minded notables and conservative religious circles. The conflict sharpened as a result of the establishment of the school where French was taught, and of the attempt to avoid elections to the govern-

[1] Franco, *op. cit.* pp. 151 f., 161 f.

ing bodies by the establishment of a Rabbinical Grand Court and a secular "committee of notables". The *ḥakham bashî* of the day, Rabbi Yaakov Avigdor, attended all the meetings of the committee.

Some of the committee's regulations—in part trifling but characteristic of the spirit which prevailed in it, e.g. concerning the wearing of the fez which in 1829 was proclaimed obligatory for every Muslim Turk—incensed the orthodox. Anti-Camondo propaganda, conducted by Yiṣḥaq 'Aqrish and Shlomoh Qamḥi, alleged that the school sponsored by Camondo encouraged children to become Christians. This accusation was more likely to inflame the common people than abstract charges of modernism. Camondo was excommunicated and, in reply, Yiṣḥaq 'Aqrish was imprisoned by order of the *ḥahkam bashî*, but he was released by order of the Sultan 'Abdülaziz after demonstrations by his supporters. To assuage feelings, the Grand Vizier convened a special rabbinical court, consisting of the *ḥakham bashîs* of Salonica, Adrianople and Izmir, to hear the claims of the two parties—the opponents of *ḥakham bashî* Avigdor who demanded his removal and the notables supporting him. The court cleared Rabbi Avigdor of all charges and threatened to excommunicate whomsoever repeated them. Camondo and Carmona were also cleared and their detractors ordered to apologize. But Avigdor could not continue in office as *ḥakham bashî*; he was deposed in the following year (1863), though he served for another eleven years as *rab̲ hakōlēl*.[1]

These events delayed the submission of proposals for the reorganization of the Jewish community (*Yahudi milleti*) as required by the *khaṭṭ-i hümayun*. The regulations of the Greek community (*Rum milleti*) were finally drafted and approved in 1862, those of the Armenian community (*Ermeni milleti*) in 1863. Only six months later was the *ḥakham bashî* of Adrianople appointed as successor of the deposed *ḥakham bashî* of the capital and instructed to draft immediately regulations for the community (*niẓam-name*). It is difficult, therefore, to blame the jealousy of the Greeks or Armenians for the delay in the confirmation of the regulations which took place only in May 1865 after minute examination and the introduction of certain changes. Friction within the community was well known. An objective observer writes: "A partir de 1859, des

[1] Franco, *op. cit.* pp. 132–40, 161–6; Galanté, *Documents*, pp. 8 and 9; B. Lewis, *Middle Eastern Studies*, vol. I (1965), pp. 288 and 289. On the family Camondo cf. Franco, *op. cit.* pp. 246–8; S. Rosanes, *Histoire des Israélites de Turquie* (Hebrew), vol. v, pp. 143 and 144. In modern Iraq the *sidāra* has been accepted as the national headgear also by the Jews; cf. A. Ben-Jacob, *A History of the Jews in Iraq*, p. 250.

dissensions produites comme chez les Grecs et les Arméniens par l'antagonisme de l'élément clérical et de l'élément laïque portèrent le trouble et le malaise au sein de la communauté qu'elles partagèrent en deux camps, bouleversant les anciennes institutions sans donner aux nouvelles le temps de s'asseoir, et créèrent pourtant un provisoire qui dure encore."[1]

The "Organizational Regulations of the Rabbinate" (*ḥakham-khane niẓam namesi*) fall into five chapters. (*a*) The status of the *ḥakham bashî* as the head of Jewry in the Empire; his qualifications and election (clauses 1–4). (*b*) His powers and his replacement in the event of resignation or removal from office (clauses 5–15). (*c*) The "General Committee" (*mejlis 'umumî*), its election and powers. It consists of eighty members and is presided over by the permanent deputy of the *ḥakham bashî*. Sixty secular members are elected by the inhabitants of Constantinople according to city districts and they, in turn, elect twenty rabbinical members. These eighty members elect the seven rabbis forming the Spiritual Committee (*mejlis ruḥanî*) and the nine members of the Secular Commitee (*mejlis jismanî*). These elections require the approval of the Sublime Porte. At the election of the *ḥakham bashî* for the Empire, the General Committee is temporarily reinforced by forty members summoned from eight districts where they officiate as provincial *ḥakham bashîs*: Adrianople, Bursa, Izmir, Salonica, Baghdad, Cairo, Alexandria and Jerusalem (clauses 16–19). It should be noted that clause 16 fails to prescribe the Committee's term of office; only in 1910 was it fixed at ten years. (*d*) The powers of the Spiritual Committee. The seven rabbis are to concern themselves with religious and other matters referred to them by the *ḥakham bashî*. The Committee must not prevent the publication of books or the spread of science and art unless it is prejudicial to the government, the community or religion. The Committee supervises the activities of the city-district rabbis (*marey de-athrā*), who act under its instructions. The Committee is headed by a president, who is also the head of the Rabbinical Court; he has two deputies (clauses 20–38). (*e*) The powers of the Secular Committee as regards the management of communal affairs and the carrying into effect of government orders. It apportions the communal impost and ensures the integrity of the property of orphans and endowments (clauses 39–48).

[1] F. Van den Steen de Jehay, *De la situation légale des sujets ottomans non-musulmans* (Brussels, 1906), pp. 67, 95, 348. Franco, *op. cit.* pp. 167 f.; Galanté, *Nouveau recueil de nouveaux documents*, etc., pp. 34,6 7; A. Ubicini and Pavet de Courteille, *Etat présent de l'Empire ottoman* (Paris, 1876), p. 205.

The tenor of the regulations reveals a desire to limit the powers of the clergy which was naturally the general tendency of the regulations of all the communities. They remained in force so long as the Ottoman Empire existed; only under the Republic did they lapse *de facto*—without being officially replaced.[1]

Iraq

The severance of Iraq from the Ottoman Empire and the establishment of the British Mandate at first brought no change in the organizational structure of the Jewish community. Baghdad Jewry was presided over by "the Deputy *ḥakham bashî* of Baghdad and spiritual head", and the performance of religious-legal and social functions was entrusted to two committees—as under the Imperial regulations. The Jewish Community Law enacted by the Iraqi Parliament in 1931 did not materially change the pattern of management of the important communities of Baghdad, Baṣra and Mosul. But Iraqi Jewry filled this framework with living, vigorous content. The contacts established for decades past by Iraqi immigrants in India now bore fruit. The Baghdad and Baṣra communities prospered. The munificence of wealthy families and prominent businessmen enabled the establishment of a number of charitable institutions and hospitals and a network of schools which were among the best in the Middle East. All these were, in one way or another, under the control of the community committee.

This prosperity could not fail to have its effects, especially so long as the British mandatory administration was the actual government, as is noticeable in the development of the community. The course of events after the termination of the mandate does not concern us here. The new reality of a small group of only a few thousand members is reflected in the Community Law of 1954.[2]

Organization in the three countries of the Maghrib

Political circumstances caused far-reaching differences in the development of each of the Berber countries conquered by the Ottomans in the sixteenth century. In 1835 Tripolitania came again under the direct rule of the Sublime Porte which introduced the same order here as existed throughout the Empire. A special position in the life of the

[1] Cf. G. Young, *Corps de Droit Ottoman*, vol. II, pp. 148–55; Galanté, *Documents*, pp. 10–27; *Jerusalem* [*Yearbook*] (Hebrew), 5652/1891–2, pp. 188–202.

[2] A. Ben-Jacob, *A History of the Jews in Iraq* (Hebrew), p. 267.

community was occupied by the chief rabbis, who were appointed by imperial *ferman* and popularly called *ḥakham bashîs*. In earlier generations the *ḥakham* recognized in the town was referred to as *harab̲ hakōlēl* and does not seem to have been traditionally vested with permanent judicial functions. He was the religious and spiritual leader of his community; "matters of permission and prohibition" were brought before the *ḥakhāmīm* whose status was lower than that of the *dayyānīm* and was equal to that of the clerk to the court, while the *rab̲ hakōlēl* ranked higher than an ordinary *dayyān*. As far as we can gather from the sources the *rab̲ hakōlēl* had no connexion with the authorities. This was the prerogative of the head of the community, the *qā'id*.

In 1874 Rabbi Eliyahu Ḥazan was appointed *ḥakham bashî* by imperial *ferman*. The title *ḥakham bashî* became so common in those days that the head of every small community was designated by it. Rabbi Eliyahu Ḥazan was the emissary of Jerusalem in North Africa in the years 1872–74. During this period he wrote a book *Zikhrōn Yerushalayim* (*The Memory of Jerusalem*) in the form of a debate held in Tunis between the *gēr* ("sojourner", Rabbi Ḥazan) and the *ezraḥ* ("native-born resident", described as *maskīl*, educated, enlightened). The book is divided into sixteen "days" and deals with religious questions, civil marriage, and problems of the coming of the Messiah. Joining in the debate are the *nāsī* (chief), the *qāṣīn* (official), a student, the *melīṣ italkī* (Italian spokesman) and the *melīṣ ashkenazī* (Ashkenazi spokesman). The author was obviously aware of the trends prevailing in certain Maghribi Jewish circles as a result of French influence. "Therefore I felt prompted to compose this little tract in order to awaken the love of the Holy One, blessed be He, summon the attention of the sons of our people and their chiefs, judges and leaders...I have called this tract *The Memory of Jerusalem*, for my love of Zion, the desire for Yeshūrūn, my domicile, has given me a pure heart...May all enemies of Zion be shamed and draw back, may they become like nothing and perish..."[1] The line of rabbis appointed by the authorities continued till 1908.

Immediately after the occupation of Tripolitania by Italy, representatives of Italian Jewry visited the country. In 1917, during the First World War, the Grand Council of the Jewish community was set up in Tripoli. It was elected under a decree issued by the Italian Government in 1916 concerning the organization of the Tripoli Jewish community.

[1] Eliyahu Ḥazan, *The Memory of Jerusalem* (Hebrew) (Livorno, 1874), Preface. Cf. also p. 183 above.

It was headed by an executive committee consisting of a president, a vice-president, an honorary secretary and four other members. From 1920 onwards chief rabbis sent from Italy under appointment by the authorities officiated in Tripoli. The main function of all chief rabbis during the Turkish period and after the annexation of the country by Italy was representation *vis-à-vis* the authorities. The people regarded them as heads of the community—similar to the *qā'ids*—rather than as religious leaders.[1]

In Tunisia, owing to the influence of its western neighbour, changes were introduced in the powers and structure of Jewish religious courts even before France had assumed the protectorate of the country. The Bey Muḥammad al-Ṣādiq who organized civil courts for all his subjects restricted the competence of the rabbinical courts to matters of personal status. In a decree of 1872 he says: "It has come to our knowledge that the rabbis of Tunis, Sūsa and other cities in our state deal with civil and commercial matters of their co-religionists. As this practice is contrary to the rules concerning the judicial power, the said rabbis are hereby forbidden to deal with those matters and to adjudicate disputes other than those relating to the personal status of Jews." By order of the Bey the Jewish religious court in Tunis was reorganized in 1898 in respect of its composition and jurisdiction.

The new composition of the court was as follows: The Chief Rabbi of Tunisia—honorary president; one rabbi—presiding judge; two *dayyānīm*; two deputy *dayyānīm*; one clerk. The sessions of the court were held in public under the chairmanship of the presiding judge with two *dayyānīm* or deputy *dayyānīm* as assessors. The jurisdiction of the court was extended over the whole country, and it was possible to bring any matter, from anywhere, directly before it or to appeal to it from a judgment given by a *dayyān* in a provincial town. It was thus a kind of rabbinical grand court in the Geonic tradition. On the other hand the court was denied the right to deal with matters of personal status of Algerian Jews since these were French nationals, and of persons under the protection of a foreign state. The salaries of the chief rabbi, of all the *dayyānīm* belonging to the court and of the clerk were paid out of the Bey's treasury.

The Chief Rabbi of Tunisia was at first given wide powers with regard to communal organization and religious life. According to the beylical

[1] H. Nahum, *Discorso inaugurale del nuovo gran consiglio della Communità israelitica* [di Tripoli] (Tripoli, 1917), pp. 6–29; Hirschberg, *History*, vol. II, pp. 202–6.

decrees concerning the organization of the committees of the "Assistance and Charity Funds" (*Caisses de secours et de bienfaisance israélite*)—the official designation of the Jewish communities in Tunisia—in several provincial towns, he proposed the members of some of them and submitted their financial reports to the Prime Minister. Elsewhere this right was reserved to the "civil Controller" (*Contrôleur Civil*), i.e. District Governor. The chief rabbi granted *qabbālōṯ*, i.e. certificates of competency to ritual slaughterers and licences to communal notaries. These powers extended over the whole country except for the towns where they were expressly vested in the local rabbi. The chief rabbi presided over the Rabbinical Council attached to the chief rabbinate and the board of examiners for notaries.

The Rabbinical Council was set up under a beylical decree of 1922. It consisted of six members appointed by the Prime Minister upon the proposal of the chief rabbi for a period of one year (the appointment was renewable). The Council was to advise on all religious matters of Tunisian Jewry. Its meetings were attended by a representative of the government as an observer.

In the major provincial centres, such as Sūsa, Ṣfāqs and the island of Jarba, there were chief rabbis vested with certain official powers: to serve as *dayyānīm* on the Rabbinical Grand Court; to grant *qabbālōṯ* to ritual slaughterers; and to supervise the work of the notaries in their respective localities. The salaries of these rabbis were paid by the local committee.

The change in the status of the Bey and his principal officials in the provincial centres entailed the abolition of an important part of the functions of the Jewish *qā'id* in Tunis and other cities and ultimately his disappearance from the public scene. The Tunisian authorities now found it necessary to entrust public bodies in each locality with the management of Jewish religious affairs: synagogues, burial societies, charitable and benevolent funds. These bodies were organized, under beylical decrees issued for each locality separately, in the form of committees of "Assistance and Charity Funds" whose task was to manage all local religious affairs in co-operation with the rabbinate. The "Assistance and Charity Funds" aided the traditional educational institutions—*talmūdey tōrāh* and *yeshivoṯ*—and the schools of the *Alliance Israélite Universelle* in Tunis, Sūsa and Ṣfāqs. The revenue of the committee was mainly derived from the *gabella*; gifts and subscriptions; funds and immovable property. The Tunis and Sūsa communities had a monopoly on the baking of *matzot*, and Tunis was empowered to levy a charge on the importation of flour for *matzot*. Apparently because of the financial straits of the communities in question, worship in private synagogues, i.e. synagogues established as family endowments, was in some places allowed only after payment of an annual fee of an appropriate amount to the local committee. A provision to this effect was contained in the beylical decrees for Munastīr, Sūsa, Ṣfāqs, Qayrawān and Nābil.

Each locality had a single Fund Committee for the *Touansa* and the *Gornim*. But the antagonism between the two groups in Tunis was so great that some of their services and institutions continued to function separately. To satisfy their requirements in this respect, the *Gornim* (who were in the minority) received a certain percentage of the revenue of the unified Fund from charges for slaughtering and *matzot*. A representative of the civil authority participated in every committee in order to supervise financial affairs and the management of immovable property (endowments, cemeteries, etc.). The influence of these official representatives within the committees became so great that the latter were regarded as tools of the authorities. This increased their political ascendancy, but at the same time lowered their moral stature.

A law promulgated by the President of the Tunisian Republic, Ḥabīb Bourguiba (Abū Ruqayba), in July 1958 dissolved the Community Council of Tunis. On the same day the Department of Justice summoned eight Jewish notables in order to appoint them as a "Provisional Committee for the Management of the Jewish Religion". The main task of the committee was to prepare elections for the leadership of the religious society which was to take the place of the Tunis community. The law provided that "religious societies" of the district should be managed by an administrative council elected by all Jews of the district of either sex who were Tunisian nationals and had completed their twentieth year. Every administrative council was to consist of five to fifteen members, depending on the size of the society. Every district was to have not more than one religious society, and there might be one society for several districts.

In an address to the members of the Tunis Provisional Committee on their assumption of office, the Secretary of State for Justice explained the purpose of the law—which was to adjust the representative bodies in charge of Jewish religious affairs to the requirements and aspirations of independent Tunisia—to which the previous bodies were not adapted.

The religious societies were to confine their activities to strictly religious matters: the organization and maintenance of synagogues; ritual slaughtering; burials; and the supply of *matzot*.

The Provisional Committee replacing the "Assistance and Charity Fund" in the Ṣfāqs district was appointed by the District Governor in November, its counterpart for Qābis (Gabes) in December 1958. These Provisional Committees are still functioning because the elections provided for by the 1958 law have not yet been held. In the meantime, changes are taking place which may rob the law concerning the Jewish community in Tunisia of all real significance.[1]

A different development took place in the Jewish community of Algeria which from 1830 was a part of France. A decisive rôle was here played by the Jews of French nationality who began to stream into the country after the occupation. They did not content themselves with the restriction of the powers of the rabbinical courts and the abolition of the office of *muqaddam*, but wished to organize the community on the model of the *consistoire*, the political and religious body of French Jewry established by Napoleon I and based on the principle of priority of the obligations towards the state.

In 1840 a committee was set up to draft rules for the religious organization of Algerian Jewry. However, despite the efforts of the members of the Marseilles *Consistoire* (many of whom were of North African origin) the proceedings at first made no headway at all. The leaders of the Marseilles *Consistoire* went to Algeria to study the problem at close quarters. They tried to set up progressive Jewish schools as a first step towards emancipation after earlier attempts in the educational field had come to nought.

The mission suffered complete failure in its main purpose—partly owing to the opposition of French army circles who did not wish to antagonize the Muslims by granting rights to the Jews. It was only when it was joined by Albert Cohn, orientalist and adviser on philanthropic affairs to the House of Rothschild, that it overcame the obstacles, especially the rigid attitude of Marshal Bugeaud, Governor-General from 1840 to 1847, who was known as an anti-Semite. Bugeaud repeatedly expressed unfavourable views on Algerian Jewry and would not have the Paris *Consistoire* supervise Algerian Jewish affairs and thereby infringe the exclusive authority of the army.

[1] Cf. Hirschberg, *History*, pp. 347 ff. with notes 39–41, 43. Cf. also A. (R.) Haṭal-Attal, "The Jews in independent Tunisia" (Hebrew), in *Bi-Tefūṣōt ha-Gōlah*, vol. VIII (1966), pp. 87–96.

The active participation of A. Crémieux—who from 1843 was concerned with Algerian–Jewish affairs—in the rules committee was very important. At last in 1845 the regulations for the organization of the Algerian *consistoires* were published and their functions defined as (*a*) to ensure the orderly conduct of communal affairs; (*b*) to supervise the school attendance of the children; (*c*) to encourage Jews to engage in useful crafts and (*d*) to supervise endowments and charitable funds. After the coming into force of the regulations *consistoires* were established in Algiers and Oran in 1847 and in Constantine in 1848.

Already before the establishment of these bodies great tension existed within the community between the French Jews and the indigenous Jewish population which lived its traditional life and was joined by many former inhabitants of Tunisia and Morocco who had settled in Algeria. M. Weill, the principal of the Jewish schools, a French national and a militant assimilationist who was appointed Chief Rabbi of Algiers, staunchly opposed democratic elections to the public bodies lest the orthodox gained control. After the 1848 revolution the influence of these circles increased, and in order to combat these dangerous tendencies Weill and other assimilationists suggested placing the *Consistoire* of Algiers under the supervision of the *Consistoire Central* in Paris. In 1867 a decree was in fact issued which imposed the authority of the *Consistoire Central*, the supreme religious body of French Jewry, upon the three Algerian *consistoires*.

From that time on and especially after the promulgation of the Crémieux decree conferring French citizenship upon the Jews of the three northern departments of Algeria (Algiers, Oran and Constantine) in 1870, the status and organization of the Jews inhabiting these areas resembled more and more those of the Jews in France. The Crémieux decree did not apply to the military region in the south (*territoires du Sud*), and so the Jewish communities in Mīzāb (Mzab) and several other oases retained their traditional structure and organization. This split had an influence on the religious life of Algerian Jewry which developed along two different paths.[1]

Morocco retained its sovereignty until 1912. The events of the First World War slowed down France's military efforts to gain control of the interior and of the south of the country (where the occupation and the subjection of the free tribes were completed only in the mid-1930s).

[1] Cf. the monograph by Lloyd Cabot-Briggs and Norina Lami Guède (listed in the Bibliography).

Nevertheless, the French administration drafted two decrees (*ẓahīr*) which were published in May 1918 in the name of the Moroccan ruler and with the signature of the French High Commissioner. One of them dealt with the organization of the Jewish communal courts and the other with the organization of the Jewish communities.

At first seven rabbinical courts (*tribunaux*) of first instance, each consisting of three *dayyānīm*, were set up in Casablanca, Fez, Mogador (al-Ṣuwayra), Miknās, Marrakesh, Wajda and Tangier. In 1953 such a court began to function also in Rabat.

Simultaneously a High Court of Appeal was established in Rabat with a bench of three: the chief rabbi as president and two judges. The dispersal of the Jewish population over a wide area necessitated the appointment of *rabbins-délégués* for provincial towns where no courts existed. Their powers were less than those of the full-scale courts.

In a later period a court of a special kind was set up which, to my knowledge, had no parallel in any country. In Morocco certain prominent families had a vested right in the positions of *dayyānīm*, rabbis, ritual slaughterers, prayer-leaders, synagogue wardens, etc. All these posts were hereditary. In the course of time sharp disputes over the conferment of such offices were so frequent that in our generation the need arose to set up a "hereditary offices court" (*Tribunal de la Serara*) for the settlement of such matters. Its members were rabbis who themselves enjoyed no *serārāh* rights.

The social position of all *dayyānīm-rabbānīm* was a highly respected one. Their salaries and those of the secretaries were paid out of the Sharīfian treasury. This gave them a feeling of independence which enhanced their prestige. Administrative supervision over the working of the courts was exercised by the Sharīfian Bureau for the Supervision of Jewish Institutions. With the Bureau's sanction the *dayyānīm-rabbānīm* in 1947 formed a *Conseil Annuel des Grands Rabbins du Maroc*, which had to meet once a year to discuss the religious situation and make regulations for the administration of justice and the improvement of the religious situation. The members of the *Conseil* were the members of the Rabbinical High Court and the presidents of the rabbinical courts in the various cities, but the High Court could add rabbi-assessors of the courts and *rabbins-délégués*. The meetings which in fact took place only once in two years dealt with matters of personal status, religious education, Sabbath observance and dietary laws and passed resolutions binding upon the rabbinical courts. It was the declared object of the *Conseil* to unify the principles of court decisions which until then were based on local custom and to issue regulations answering current needs.

During the last few years, with the Jewish population of Morocco dwindling to one-quarter of its previous size and many communities disappearing completely, numerous posts of *rabbins-délégués* ceased to exist, and so did—in 1965—the High Court of Appeal.

The other decree issued in May 1918 dealt with the organization and powers of Jewish community committees in Moroccan towns. These committees were to consist of the president of the rabbinical court or the *rabbin-délégué* and notables—chosen by the Grand Vizier from a list submitted by the communities—whose number varied according to the size of the Jewish population; in 1945 this choice of notables was replaced in theory by the election by secret ballot of candidates from among whom the authorities were to select the members of the committees. The term of office of the members was four years. The functions of the committees were: (*a*) to maintain religious services; (*b*) to assist the needy; and (*c*) to administer endowments (immovables, or rights therein, acquired with moneys of charity funds and pious contributions).

A decree promulgated in 1945 established a Council of Jewish Communities which had to co-ordinate the activities of the communities. It consisted of the heads of the various communities and met once a year in Rabat under the chairmanship of a representative of the Directorate of Sharīfian Affairs. These meetings dealt with matters of budget, housing, education and hygiene. The question of a permanent representation of the communities was also mooted. In the early fifties a permanent bureau was set up under a secretary-general. The bureau was to guide the community committees in preparing budgets, operating services and providing education in *talmūdey tōrāh* and evening classes. Most of the revenues of the communities came from charges on ritual slaughtering and the sale of *matẓot* as well as from the management of public endowments, which were not many since most endowments were family ones. The Council sent six delegates to the Moroccan (natives) Committee of the Council of Government. It published a four-page monthly under the title *The Voice of the Communities*.

Upon the reinstatement of Sultan Muḥammad V in 1958 and the rise to power of the nationalist *Istiqlāl* party, the composition of the community committees was changed by appointing persons acceptable to the ruling group. They now lost what little independence and initiative they possessed and became tools of the government.[1]

The struggle for the security and social betterment of the individual

In what preceded we have seen how the demands of the non-Muslim communities for autonomy were met in a manner consonant with ancient Islamic traditions regarding the status of "the people of the Book".

From the early nineteenth century on, the demand for equal rights for non-Muslim subjects in all spheres of life was growing, and the European powers lent full diplomatic support to this demand. At the same time a surprising change for the worse in the personal safety of non-Muslims occurred. The first to be affected were the Jews who experienced waves of pogroms in all Middle Eastern countries from 1805 onwards. However, the number of Christians killed in obedience to orders in Anatolia in 1916 and in Iraq in 1933 was a thousand times greater than the number of Jewish victims in Middle Eastern countries during the past century and a half. Outbreaks of such intensity and savagery were not known before in the history of the Muslim countries. Similarly, the number of Greek Orthodox who left the Turkish Republic for Greece after the First World War was twice as great as that of the Jews who left Muslim countries from 1948 onwards and partly settled in Israel, or of the Palestinian Arabs who left for the neighbouring Arab countries in 1948.

The first anti-Jewish excesses occurred in Algiers in 1805. Incitement against the Jews was in part prompted by their pro-French attitude which became apparent in Africa during Napoleon's invasion of Egypt when Muslim crowds demonstrated their anger against France and the French. France enjoyed the sympathies of the Jewish merchants in the ports as the veteran European power protecting the rights granted to foreign nationals in the Ottoman Empire by the capitulation treaties. Napoleon may have deliberately encouraged pro-French feelings by vaguely promising the establishment of a Jewish state in Palestine. At any rate, his policy of granting the Jews equal rights and integrating them into French society impressed the Jews living in areas under French influence.[2]

[1] Cf. A. Chouraqui, *La condition juridique de l'Israélite Marocain* (Paris, 1950), *passim*; Hirschberg, *Inside Maghrib* (Hebrew), pp. 146–8.

[2] Cf. p. 157, above.

The difficult over-all situation of North African Jewry in those days made it unlikely that it would initiate the struggle for the advancement of the Jewish individual either theoretically or practically. Almost naturally this task at first devolved upon certain prominent French and British Jews: Sir Moses Montefiore whose family hailed from Livorno—the literary centre of Mediterranean Jewry where almost all its books were printed—and who was himself born there and remained all his life attached to the local community; A. Crémieux, an advocate and politician who took an active part in French public life; Albert Cohn, the official representative of the Paris Rothschilds in matters of charity; and Baron M. Hirsch, a prominent businessman and philanthropist. After a time special societies were set up for the purpose of improving the political and intellectual situation of the Jews in Africa, Asia and eastern Europe. The *Alliance Israélite Universelle* was established in France in 1860, the *Anglo-Jewish Association* in Britain in 1871; the latter undertook activities abroad which until then were to some extent carried on by the Board of Deputies, the central body of British Jewry. These societies enjoyed the moral and material support of their co-religionists in France and Britain and used their extensive contacts with the authorities in order to influence political protagonists at international congresses and enlist the support of the diplomatic and consular representatives of their countries in the Orient. Finally, in 1901 the *Hilfsverein der deutschen Juden* was established in Germany with the object of promoting German influence, culture and political aims among the Jews of the Orient. Only a few of the activities of all these organizations can be touched upon in this context.

The *khaṭṭ-i sherif* of Gülhane (1839) solemnly proclaimed the following principles: (*a*) security of life, honour and property; (*b*) orderly imposition and collection of taxes; (*c*) orderly enlistment for and fixing of length of military service; (*d*) fair public trial of all accused persons; (*e*) equality of the members of all religions before the law. However, these principles did not stand the test of reality when the ill-famed blood libel was uttered against Damascene Jewry a few months later and a similar charge was made on the island of Rhodes. To protect the Jews from slanderous accusations Montefiore, Crémieux and the well-known orientalist, S. Munk, travelled to Constantinople and in October 1840 after an audience with the Sultan obtained a *ferman* which could be regarded as a bill of rights for the Jews. It stipulates that in conformity with the *khaṭṭ-i sherif* the Jewish nation shall possess the same advantages and enjoy the same privileges as are granted to the numerous other nations who submit to the Sultan's authority. The Jewish nation shall be protected and defended. To accomplish this object the most positive orders have been given for the protection of the Jewish nation dwelling in all parts of the Empire.

The presence of Jewish refugees from Morocco in Algeciras and Gibraltar in 1860 was the occasion for the first intervention of European Jews in the relations between the Moroccan authorities and their Jewish subjects. A Jewish committee set up in Britain (apparently at the instigation of the Board of Deputies) sought to obtain assistance for Moroccan Jewry. Montefiore's visit to Morocco early in 1864 was a continuation of these activities. He was received by the Sharīf Mawlāy Muḥammad in his capital, Marrakesh. In an address to the Moroccan ruler he mentioned the *ferman* he received in Constantinople in 1840 and which was reaffirmed by the Sultan 'Abdülaziz in 1863.[1] Montefiore was famous among the Jews of Bukhara, Samarkand, Balkh and Kokand. J. Wolff repeatedly stressed that Montefiore's letters to the Amir of Bukhara concerning the Jews, sent through the British representative, did not reach their destination. These letters seem to have contained, *inter alia*, a request for indirect action on behalf of the Mas͟hhad forced converts. About the situation in Persia generally, we know that Montefiore was prepared to visit Persia in 1865 in view of a worsening of conditions there. But as the British Government did not approve of the trip he had to content himself with an audience with the Shah in London in 1873. Following that audience the Persian minister in London promised on behalf of the Shah that the Jews would be safe from injustice and hardship.[2]

In the parts of the Ottoman Empire directly controlled by the Sublime Porte the Jews enjoyed, at least on paper, the same rights as the other non-Muslim subjects. The position was different in the independent principalities of Serbia and Rumania. Here the *Alliance Israélite Universelle* and the *Anglo-Jewish Association* had a wide field for their work. Jews were expelled from their places of residence in Serbia. The situation was particularly grave in Shabaz which was the centre of anti-Jewish activities. In 1865 several Jews were murdered there and a sixteen-year-old girl was abducted from the house of her widowed

[1] Cf. for the *khaṭṭ-i sherif* Ubicini and Pavet de Courteille, *op. cit.* pp. 231–3. Both *fermans* appear in Galanté, *Documents*, pp. 158–61; cf. also above, p. 160 n. 1. On Montefiore's mission to Morocco cf. H. Guedalla, *Refutation of an Anonymous Article* (London, 1880), esp. p. 35.

[2] Wolff, *Narrative*, vols. I, pp. 242, 255, 293; II, pp. 29, 178.

mother and baptized. The sufferings of Serbian and Rumanian Jewry were described in a memorandum of the *Alliance Israélite* to a conference of representatives of the Great Powers which met in Constantinople late in 1876.[1]

Discrimination against non-Muslims did not really cease in the Ottoman Empire in spite of the most solemn declarations and the provisions of the capitulations.[2] The only way to escape the arbitrary and unjust practices of the local authorities was by obtaining the protection of one of the European states under the capitulation treaties which gained in importance during the nineteenth century. New nations such as the United States, Greece and Belgium also concluded such agreements with the Sublime Porte. Fourteen states participated in a conference in Madrid in 1880 to regulate protection under capitulations in Morocco. In the agreement signed on that occasion Morocco granted the participating states the same rights as were enjoyed by France and Britain.

According to the capitulation treaties (which were not identical in every particular), government officials were forbidden to proceed against the person or enter the houses of foreigners or foreign-protected residents, or prosecute any of them without permission from their consuls. In Egypt, foreign nationals were tried by "Mixed Tribunals" which were only abolished in 1949. Protection was granted to persons employed by consulates and embassies as well as to brokers and agents employed by foreign merchants. It conferred exemption from personal taxes and imposts not only upon the protected person himself, but also upon the members of his family who lived with him.

Whereas in the eastern part of the Mediterranean basin most of the holders of these rights were Christians of all denominations, in the western part they were mostly Jews. France was the principal protecting power, both for reasons of tradition and in the interests of her position in the Mediterranean area. Her chief rivals were Russia and Austria in the Ottoman Empire, and Spain and Italy in the Maghrib. A paradoxical situation sometimes arose when the representatives of Tsarist Russia protected the Jews of the Ottoman Empire and claimed rights for them that were denied them in Russia. The Ottoman Government naturally tried from time to time to put an end to the capitulations, and especially to the plentiful granting of letters of immunity by ambassadors and

[1] I. Loeb, then Secretary-General of the A.I.U., prepared the memorandum and subsequently enlarged it into a book (see Bibliography). [2] Cf. p. 150, above.

consuls. The attempts were unsuccessful. Morocco tried to restrict these rights at the Madrid Conference with the support of Britain who hoped to check French influence.

The capitulation system was abolished some fifty years ago, but its consequences were felt until quite recently when tens of thousands of Jews in all eastern countries, but especially in Egypt and the Maghrib, still held some foreign nationality acquired in the past century. Among 75,000 Jews or so living in Egypt in 1950, 30,000 were of foreign, chiefly French, but also Italian, British or German nationality. About 5,000 had Egyptian nationality and nearly 40,000 were stateless, belonging in their majority to the old-established population.

New trends in education and in religious and intellectual life

On p. 155 we saw the Jewish communities in their isolation from the outside world. The society in which they lived was stagnant and no longer able to exert any influence, and this determined the situation of the established Jewish population in Oriental countries. Jewish-Arab co-operation in the sphere of the sciences and the humanities, which existed in the Middle Ages, now ceased completely. The Jews continued to use their special Arabic (or Persian-Jewish) dialect which developed in the Middle Ages and which sufficed for everyday conversation and commercial or professional dealings, but nothing more. The successive waves of expellees and emigrants from Europe moved away from its spiritual domain as well. They indeed retained a certain knowledge of European languages (in their late medieval stage) and developed special Jewish dialects: Ladino and Yiddish. Moreover, a small class of merchants and agents in the coastal cities cultivated a knowledge of western European languages enabling them to carry on foreign trade or to act as interpreters of Muslim rulers, or as diplomatic agents of European countries. But the knowledge of these languages entailed no contact with European intellectual life.

Changes in this sphere first became noticeable in the second half of the nineteenth century. The outstanding Jewish philanthropists in Europe such as the Rothschilds, Sir Moses Montefiore, Baron Maurice de Hirsch and Abraham de Camondo in Constantinople, anxious to better the condition of Middle Eastern Jewry, regarded the raising of their general educational standard as a lever for the attainment of their goal. Although utilitarian considerations were foremost in the establishment of schools with instruction in French and many general subjects—with the addition of several hours for religious education—we cannot overlook the ideals of enlightenment which inspired the work of principals and teachers. The tendencies then prevalent in western Europe particularly affected the *Alliance Israélite Universelle* which adopted the spread of European education as one of its main objectives. The first school was opened in Taṭwān in 1861. Funds for the establishment of schools were at first provided by individual philanthropists, the British Board of Deputies and communities desirous of possessing educational institutions. When the *Alliance* was consolidated organizationally, it continued its work with its own resources, viz. contributions obtained from its members in various countries and in certain centres with the help of the *Anglo-Jewish Association.*

The establishment of French-language schools met with strong opposition in wide circles who feared that European education might adversely affect the attitude towards traditional religious values and sacred customs. They anxiously watched the religious reformism of French Jews, their critical attitude, faintly echoed in the Orient, towards the sources of Judaism and the resulting great number of defections from the faith. The most sensitive area in which relations between the "keepers of the walls of Judaism" and the advocates of progress and reform became strained was that of religious education. It was no accident that the conflict between Camondo, the President of the Committee of Functionaries, and orthodox circles in the Constantinople community sharpened over that matter. Camondo assumed in 1858 the moral and material patronage of a school established by the community several years previously and struggling hard for survival.[1] The issue was that now teaching French was introduced. Rabbis ʿAqrish and Qamḥi threatened to excommunicate parents who sent their children to that school and in 1862 they excommunicated Camondo.

Strong opposition was also at first encountered by the schools established by the *Alliance* in Baghdad, Damascus, Kurdistan, western Tripolitania, Tiberias and Greece. Though incidents like those in Constantinople did not occur, many of the schools were closed for lack of pupils and reopened only several years later when feelings had calmed down.

Fifty years after the establishment of the *Alliance Israélite Universelle* the network of schools maintained by it—sometimes in partnership

[1] Cf. pp. 199–200, 215, above.

with the *Anglo-Jewish Association*—covered all the eastern countries where Jews lived, from Morocco to Persia, including the Balkans.[1] The only country where the *Alliance* did not succeed in establishing a single school was Yemen.

Algeria's political status as a part of France affected Jewish education. Government schools were subject to the law for the separation of church and state, and religious instruction was therefore prohibited in them. Some Jewish children acquired the elements of reading Hebrew prayer-books in supplementary lessons organized by the communities during school holidays with the assistance of the *Alliance*, which participated in the cost of their maintenance and the recruiting of teachers. Other children received no religious instruction at all. Only a steadily dwindling minority of parents, chiefly in the departments of Constantine and Oran, tried to give their children a proper Jewish education.

It redounds to the credit of government education in Algeria that it generally imparted French cultural values to no lesser extent than schools in Metropolitan France, and that its talented graduates attained respected positions in French society.[2] But the emigration to France of superior intellectual manpower—a common feature throughout Algeria—led to a lowering of the cultural standards of the Jewish population. While the movement of Frenchmen to the mother country was in some measure offset by the transfer from France to Algeria of young people who took their first steps here in various fields, no corresponding phenomenon existed in the Jewish sector.

The *Alliance* in its educational work used the method of acculturation. Not only were all subjects in its schools taught in French, but its entire education was imbued with a French spirit. This was understandable in countries under direct French influence (Tunisia, Morocco) and was not officially discouraged in the Ottoman Empire or even in Iran. An *Alliance* teacher, in a book on the history of Turkish Jewry (1857), ingenuously points out in praise of the *Alliance*, that the 300,000 Jews of the Ottoman Empire include between 80,000 and 100,000 men and women who speak French and hardly 1,000 who understand Turkish.[3]

[1] Cf. N. Leven's second volume of his *Cinquante ans* (Paris, 1920), and A. Chouraqui, *L'Alliance Israélite Universelle et la Renaissance Juive Contemporaine 1860–1960* (Paris, 1965), *passim*.

[2] Chouraqui, *op. cit.* p. 346, notes that at least sixty-five Algerian Jews were on the teaching staff of Paris University in 1962, some of them in leading positions.

[3] Franco, *op. cit.* p. 249.

Objections to the *Alliance*'s acculturation tendencies were raised among the Jews themselves, first, as already mentioned, by the orthodox and subsequently by German Jews who regarded the *Alliance* as a tool for strengthening French influence. Under the inspiration of the German Government the *Hilfsverein* was set up.[1] Upon the increase of Hebrew consciousness, Zionists—not content with the religion lessons provided until then—demanded the introduction of modern Hebrew into the curriculum.

After the First World War the problem of the *Alliance* schools became acute at a high political level when the national states of Bulgaria and Greece and afterwards Turkey and Iran demanded that instruction be given in the language of the country and that the study of French be confined to the upper forms. After a time demands were made in Bulgaria and Greece that the ownership of the school should pass to the government. In 1932 the schools in Turkey passed to the communities and, in keeping with the secular character of the state, religious instruction was forbidden. In Iran, too, a change in the attitude of the authorities was noticeable.

In contrast with these restrictions the activities of the *Alliance* expanded greatly in Morocco after the Second World War. Schools were established in new places and existing school buildings enlarged to absorb more pupils.

To adapt itself to the changed conditions the *Alliance* started to teach the language of the country and also English. In the countries where the authorities permitted it, attention was now also given to the teaching of Hebrew as a living language.

When, as a result of mass emigration in the years 1956–63, the schools in Morocco had become depleted, the government nationalized about one-third of them for general educational purposes. In 1962, following legislation restricting education in private institutions, the schools and all the other assets of the *Alliance* were transferred to the *Ittiḥād-Maroc* society headed by a Moroccan national. In 1963 the number of pupils dropped to about 12,000, i.e. one-third of the figure for 1955.

According to reports published recently the *Alliance* still maintains more than ninety educational institutions, ranging from elementary schools to two teachers' training colleges (in Paris and Casablanca). Secondary schools in French cities (Paris and Nice) were lately added for the children of new immigrants from North Africa.

[1] Cf. p. 212, above.

It is estimated that in the course of a century the *Alliance* schools were attended by about 600,000 boys and girls who by acquiring the French language and a general education were given many opportunities to improve their economic status, to rise socially and thereby to advance in their private lives.[1]

In contrast to the work of the *Alliance* in the field of education and acculturation, hardly any impact was made by the independent activities of the *Anglo-Jewish Association* which established or maintained only a few schools and generally worked together with the *Alliance*. Nor had the *Alliance* a real competitor in the *Hilfsverein*, though the latter set up—between 1901 and 1931—some thirty educational institutions, ranging from kindergartens to the Haifa Institute of Technology (1914, though teaching did not then begin owing to the war, and at the end of the war the management passed into other hands). Despite all our appreciation of the rôle of these educational institutions in the Europeanization of Middle Eastern Jewry we cannot overlook a series of undesirable features connected with that process.

In any case this school network comprised only a part of the youth of compulsory education age. Another part, in some areas the majority, continued to be educated in the traditional *ḥadarīm* and *talmūdey tōrāh* which devoted the same amount of time to secular studies as the *Alliance* schools did to religious instruction, viz. theoretically very little, practically none at all. After the Second World War the centres of religious Jewry in the United States and Israel made great efforts to enhance the standards of teachers and pupils and improve conditions in traditional education in Morocco, Tunisia and Iran through the establishment of special religious schools.

It should further be noted that the secular national and cultural movement which did so much for the revival of the Hebrew language—turning it into a language of everyday speech, journalism and science—did not succeed in establishing a single school in the whole of the Muslim East, though in Palestine (and between the two World Wars in eastern and central Europe) it established a network of schools and scientific institutions with Hebrew as the language of instruction, ranging from kindergartens to universities and academies of humanities and sciences. On the other hand, efforts to revive the Hebrew language were successful in the case of persons without a secular education. The traditional upbringing they had received, however scanty (a knowledge of

[1] Chouraqui, *op. cit.* pp. 168–70; 353, 498–504.

the prayers and an understanding of the weekly Bible portion by means of a translation), enabled them to speak the sacred tongue—a very basic Hebrew. In the case of the women who generally received no religious instruction spoken Arabic was the stepping-stone.

Education in European-Jewish institutions—mainly in the *Alliance* schools—within the general framework of a society with a pronounced and most vivid religious and communal consciousness produced a type of person uprooted from the spiritual soil of his community who had not properly received the French (or English) cultural values imparted to students at government schools in Algeria or at European-American colleges; moreover, the tenuous link his father and grandfather had with the Muslim environment was cut as a result of his pseudo-European superiority, and thus arose the type of the Levantine Jew lacking a spiritual homeland and in many cases a definite legal nationality as well. All this made for his increased mobility. We find *Alliance* graduates emigrating to overseas countries and acclimatizing themselves thanks to their knowledge of European languages. Those remaining in their countries of residence found employment in government offices, foreign commercial companies and agencies. The Muslim population needed this *petit bourgeois* intermediate class of clerks and agents who knew both the language of the country and the European languages. *Alliance* graduates usually provided teachers and the members of the professions, especially doctors, but not the more prominent specialists who were mostly European Jews practising in those countries.

The nationalist-Zionist movement for settlement in Palestine and the establishment of a Jewish state, which started in eastern Europe in the 1880s and thence spread to western Europe and the United States, made very little impact in the Middle East. Although Messianic hopes and the yearning for Zion, the most characteristic features of Middle Eastern Jewry, were still alive, the drive for emigration to Palestine had weakened in the East, except for Yemen and Bukhara, during the last few generations. Thus, among the Jews of the Maghrib, where it was very considerable, emigration dwindled to very modest proportions. (Official statistics show that between 1919 and 1948 only 0·9 per cent of the Jews settling in Palestine—4,033 out of 482,857—came from Africa, including Egypt and South Africa, while 9·5 per cent (40,776) came from Asian countries.) This was due to the fact that a society which in its overwhelming majority continued its traditional way of life was not yet interested in a modern national movement.

One may compare the fact that among the peoples of the Near East the national movement began only in the early twentieth century, while in Africa it has only recently gained its full momentum.

On the eve of the Second World War the general picture was rather dismal. In a religious and social respect the communities were in a state of inefficacy. Their unity was shaken by the penetration of new trends and educational influences from Europe. The generation or generations who had been brought up the new way had no longer a common language with the representatives of the old generation who just marked time. Nazi propaganda was spreading everywhere, boding evil for the Jews. Moreover, the Jewish-Arab conflict in Palestine sharpened, casting its shadow over both individuals and the whole group.

Epilogue: collapse and winding-up of the communities after the Second World War

We cannot here discuss the events that occurred in the Middle East during the present generation and directly and fatefully affected the Jewish communities. We still lack the perspective making possible an objective evaluation of all the data, especially as the documents kept in the various archives are not yet available for research. At the same time it is obvious that since the 1920s the population of the entire region has been in a state of growing ferment and tension and the crystallization of a new society is still far off.

The traditional cosmopolitan Muslim state assigned definite spheres and duties to the non-Muslim communities. The new Muslim states, even those claiming to be secular and socialist, have little understanding for their non-Muslim citizens. The concept of the *millet*, the separate non-Muslim community, is ineradicably fixed in the consciousness of the Muslim public.

There is no reason to suspect the various national governments of harbouring any pronounced anti-Christian or anti-Jewish feelings. It is only natural, however, that they should care for their own co-religionists first. They are bound to expend their efforts upon rehabilitating the backward Muslim citizen before devoting their attention to those who are much better off economically and educationally.

A few examples may illustrate this. The Turkish Republic, the creation of Kemal Atatürk, is surely the prototype of a Muslim state turned national and secular. In this state, however, the term "Turk" denotes only a Muslim and is on no account applicable to a member of another religion who is at most a Turkish citizen. The consistency of the governments of republican Turkey in drawing conclusions from this classification in their policy towards non-Muslims is evidenced, for instance, by the capital tax (*varlik vergisi*) approved on 11 November 1942 and put into force the following day. This tax which was directed against those who made great profits during the Second World War, passed over the Muslim farmers who enriched themselves, but utterly impoverished the Greeks, Jews and Armenians, especially the poorer ones. The quotas were imposed arbitrarily and collected ruthlessly by means of arrests, confiscations and deportations to labour camps.[1]

The same communal consciousness exists in the new Arab states. Even the Christian Arabs in Lebanon, Syria and Egypt feel the social cleavage between them and the Muslim population. Obviously, communal segregation in Arab states was practised especially towards the Jews. While in Arab states with an Arabic-speaking Christian minority the majority is prepared, with certain reservations, to accept the former as (Christian) Arabs, the term (Jewish) Arab, i.e. Arab of the Jewish persuasion, does not exist. Arabic-speaking Jews in Arab countries are described as Iraqi or Syrian Jews, etc. The feeling that the Jew is not an Arab, although his ancestors lived in the country even before its conquest by the Arabs, is old. The *Alliance* education, especially the *présence française* in the Maghrib and its influence in Egypt, widened the existing gap in the economic and political respects.[2]

This gap has certainly acquired a most negative connotation in the national states which tend towards total uniformity. In the struggle for independence and sovereignty Jews and Christians and naturally all foreigners were suspected of aiding international—French, British, American—imperialism, and incited mobs drew the practical conclusions by resorting to violence. At the same time laws and regulations were enacted for the purpose of bettering the condition of the population, but the immediate—sometimes unintentional—effect was to harm the Jews. Two instances of fundamental significance may illustrate this. In 1956 Egypt abolished the religious courts of all communities, and the matters which were under their jurisdiction were now transferred to

[1] B. Lewis, *The Emergence of Modern Turkey*, pp. 8, 15, 291–4, 350 f.

[2] Chouraqui's opinion, *Alliance*, p. 240, that the "présence française" gave the Jews in the whole of North Africa conditions of freedom they had never enjoyed before and that the departure of France caused the mass exodus of the Jews, cannot be accepted unreservedly; it is only valid for Algeria.

the civil courts. This measure raised the level of justice for the Muslims, did not affect the status of the Christian clergy, but destroyed the religious and communal autonomy of the Jews. In 1960 the Moroccan Government nationalized about one-third of the *Alliance* schools in order to give Muslim children an elementary education. But the result for the Jewish children was a lowering of educational standards.

A number of publications give detailed accounts of the following:[1] the removal of the Jews from their economic and official positions in Iraq after its attainment of full independence in 1932 and in Egypt after the emergence of a generation of intellectuals capable of performing the functions until then carried out by Jews; the pogroms in Constantine in 1934 and in Baghdad during the pro-Nazi revolt and as a result of Nazi propaganda in 1941; and other similar occurrences preceding or immediately following the UN resolution of 29 November 1947 for the establishment of a Jewish state in Palestine.

It is impossible to pronounce finally upon this period of the history of Asia and Africa before all the forces then at work in the area have been traced. However, it is certainly permitted, even necessary, to point out the practical conclusions drawn by the Jews there. The number of Jews in Asia (except Palestine) and North-west Africa dropped from 950,000–1,000,000 at the end of the Second World War to a quarter of that number in 1965. The others left the countries where their forefathers lived for hundreds or even thousands of years. The rich and the well-to-do mostly succeeded in transferring their property or a great part of it before they themselves left. The poor—they were the overwhelming majority—carried their paltry belongings with them.

This phenomenon of Jews leaving their countries of birth in Asia and Africa where they were never subject to Nazi or Fascist terror, deserves a thorough and detailed study, exceeding the scope and dimensions of this survey. We have here a combination unique in world history of irrational and rational motives, of objective and subjective factors which prompted members of communities scattered over a vast area to act alike. We should therefore not be content with stating the bare facts, ignoring the complex reality behind them and—in the wake of a certain superficial propaganda—regarding the establishment of the modern Jewish state as the only stimulus.

[1] Cf. e.g. A. Ben-Jacob, *A History of the Jews in Iraq*, pp. 228–67; Landshut and Robinson (mentioned in the Bibliography) and *The Treatment of Jews in Egypt and Iraq* (published by the *World Jewish Congress*, December 1948).

We should note, first of all, that only two-thirds (about half a million) of those who left their countries of residence migrated to Israel, while one-third scattered all over the world, though the great majority of them settled in France. According to available data some 125,000 Algerian Jews of French nationality went to France in 1962, and likewise about 100,000 Jews from Tunisia and Morocco (the former including many French nationals). Several thousand Moroccan Jews settled in Spain, chiefly in Madrid and Barcelona; there were no Jews in Spain from the expulsion in 1492 until the establishment of a small community in Barcelona in the early twentieth century and the arrival of a number of refugees from central Europe during the Second World War.

We may confidently affirm that no Zionist political propaganda reached the broad strata of the Jewries of Yemen, of the interior of Morocco and of "Kurdistan" (certain parts of Iraq, Iran and Turkey), which constitute the overwhelming majority of those who emigrated to the State of Israel. The leaders of those communities at times complain and express indignation that the Zionist movement ignored them and made no efforts to win them for the idea of a national rebirth. The European-educated and well-off among those Jewries whom Zionism tried to enlist usually proved unresponsive and, when leaving their countries of residence, went to Europe or to North or South America. This was partly due to the fact that in their case alien cultural influences prevailed over the religious link with the Holy Land. Moreover, their choice was prompted by important practical considerations: the possession of French or some other European nationality and the wish for freedom of economic enterprise.

In the communities under review the messianic attachment to the Holy Land has always been strong, and emigration to Palestine has been on a larger scale than in the European communities (except the Italian). The statistics of the British mandatory government concerning immigration to Palestine in the years 1919–48 show that the influx from those countries declined during that period. This may have been due to the severe restrictions imposed on immigration by the government, but it also seems that the active interest in the Holy Land lost in intensity even in the lower strata of society. It would be rather paradoxical to suppose that the establishment of a secular state was in itself capable of stirring up messianic feelings and so inducing emigration.

Clearly the above-mentioned political changes and developments in intercommunal relations contributed to provide solid grounds for the exodus. But in addition we may be faced here with irrational impulses which it is hard to explain. Oriental Jewry became aware that they were no longer able to exist in Muslim lands either as a separate group or as Jewish individuals, and most of them drew the only possible conclusion. Part of them felt that, as a group, they were deprived of their legal status, stripped of the framework to which they were accustomed, bereft of the right to react like any other community. Some, again, realized that if they remained they would never be accepted as equals in Arab society; besides, they had been taught to regard the cultural and social level of that society as lower than theirs.

Objective expert observers, far removed from Jewish national ideologies, predict that a great part of those still remaining in comparatively large concentrations in Morocco and Tunisia, even in Turkey and Iran, will emigrate to countries willing to admit them, leaving behind only those who for various reasons are unable to go. Several tens of thousands of Jews will doubtless continue to live among hundreds of millions of Muslims, but the time of organized, autonomous Jewish communities in Muslim countries is drawing to a close, however much we may regret this from a historical and human point of view. On the other hand we should note the fact that upon the completion of one cycle in the life of Middle Eastern Jewry a new cycle has opened in the State of Israel which seeks its place and way among the peoples of Asia and Africa.

CHAPTER 4

THE JEWS OF YEMEN

The main body of the Jewish community is not divided into denominations adhering to opposing dogmas, as Christianity. Rather, not unlike Islam, it is composed of "rites", differing from each other in liturgy, ceremonial matters and partly also in religious law. The rites normally were to be found in different geographical areas and developed under the impact of the specific historical conditions which prevailed in those regions. The Yemenites, or Jews of Yemen in south-west Arabia, represent such a rite and a very distinctive one indeed. After the establishment of the State of Israel in 1948, the whole Jewish community of Yemen was transferred to the newly founded state, a process completed in 1962. Thus, the Yemenites who themselves form a very composite and variegated society can be studied in full in Israel, where, however, they are undergoing a rapid and profound transformation. Sporadic Yemenite congregations are to be found also outside Israel, e.g. in New York. The present-day Yemenites constitute the remnants of a previously far more numerous population and at present count not more than about one hundred and fifty thousand souls, i.e. they are a community approximately of the size of the Islamic sect known in the West as the followers of the Āghā Khān.

Why should such a small community, coming from a backward country, lay claim to the attention of the historian of religion? A glance over the history of the Yemenites will show that their study may promise rewarding results in more than one respect.

The Yemenites claim that their forefathers emigrated from Palestine to Yemen prior to the destruction of the first Temple. In view of the maritime undertakings of King Solomon and other Judean kings in the Red Sea, it is not far-fetched to assume that some Judeans settled in Yemen in that early period. However, no historical record of such settlements, if they existed, has been found thus far. The presence of Jews in Yemen is attested for the centuries immediately preceding Islam by Islamic and Christian literary sources, as well as by local inscriptions written in the Ḥimyarite language. The joint testimony of these sources shows that the Jews in Yemen were in close contact with their co-religionists in Palestine and proselytized vigorously in their country of adoption. The last Ḥimyarite king, Yūsuf Ash'ar Dhū Nuwās (died A.D. 525) followed the example of some of his predecessors and adopted a certain form of Judaism. Inscriptions dedicated by some of his noblemen prove that the All-merciful (*Raḥmān*—the talmudic name for God) was worshipped in shrines originally sacred to local gods, as was the case with the Ka'ba of Mecca later in Islam. The same inscriptions contain also the first occurrence on Arab soil of the idea of the Holy War fought for God.

The religion of the Ḥimyarite noblemen, as it appears to us in their inscriptions, should not be taken to represent that of their teachers, the Jews of Yemen. The latter's beliefs and practices may best be reconstructed from the copious notions about Jews and Judaism found in the Qur'ān and early Islamic traditions, for the biography of Muḥammad shows that the Jews of Ḥijāz, with whom the Prophet had so many dealings, were closely connected with those of Yemen. Judaism, as reflected in the Qur'ān and early Islamic traditions, was of the talmudic type, i.e. based on an elaborate oral law, which widely expanded the biblical injunctions.

The flourishing Christian element in Yemen disappeared entirely under Islamic rule, while Judaism stood firm throughout the chequered history of that country. This difference is perhaps to be explained by the fact that the Christians were a predominantly urban population whose wholesale expulsion constituted no grave administrative problem once it had been decided to realize the dictum ascribed to Muḥammad that in Arabia there should be no religion other than Islam (the Muslim sources speak only about the expulsion of the Christians from Najrān, the seat of a bishop). The Jews then as later, probably, were widely dispersed all over the country, less conspicuous and, as we shall see, difficult to replace, because they formed a large section of the country's caste of artisans and craftsmen. The fact that the Jews were scattered in many small places in Yemen is evident from the letters addressed to them in the ninth or tenth century by the head of a Jewish academy in Iraq, from letters preserved in the Cairo *Geniza* and from Maimonides' references to them. In 1950–2, when the present writer made a survey of about forty-five thousand immigrants to Israel from Yemen, he discovered that they had come from about one thousand and fifty different places. This high degree of dispersion must have had a considerable assimilatory effect. On the other hand, the tenacity with which, under such circumstances, these tiny communities adhered to their faith, bears witness to the strength of their religious convictions and the solidity of their communal ties.

It is indeed the preservation of a very ancient type of a religious group which makes the Yemenites so valuable for the historian of religion. When Islam emerged, the Jews of Yemen were cut off from the rest of the Jewish people, for the Ḥijāz, through which the caravans to the Mediterranean countries had to pass, became closed to non-Muslims. For some time, the land route to Iraq and Iran remained open, but, owing to the state of lawlessness which returned to the Arabian peninsula after a few centuries of comparative order, this outlet, too, was shut. The sea remained open. The sea route was effective for commercial and spiritual contacts, for the conveyance of goods, books and ideas, but was not suitable for population movements. The Yemenite community is the only one that remained practically unaffected by inner-Jewish migration. Moreover, it could not admit any proselytes, for Islam put the death penalty on apostasy. The present writer does not share the widely held belief that the Yemenites are mainly or largely the descendants of pre-Islamic Ḥimyarite proselytes. The type of religion developed by a foreign population won over to Judaism may best be studied in the Falashas, the so-called Jews of Ethiopia. Their beliefs and practices have very little to do with Judaism. On the other hand, the Yemenites may be called the most Jewish of all Jews, so that it is rather unlikely that all or even most of them should be the offspring of Ḥimyarites, for Judaism used to be essentially the religion of a people, not one adopted by conversion. Anyhow, this question of the racial origin of the Yemenites shrinks into insignificance in view of the fact that during the last thirteen hundred years this Jewish population, although much reduced by forcible conversion and natural catastrophes such as famines and plagues, was not augmented at all by proselytes and only very sporadically by a few immigrants coming by sea.

What, then, is the type of religion represented by the Yemenites? In a nutshell: they, more than anyone else, have preserved rabbinical Judaism, familiar, to a certain extent, to the Christian reader from the New Testament. This is a world centring around the synagogue, where simple people, craftsmen and labourers, are versed in religious lore and are able to follow arguments based on the Scriptures. The great majority of the Yemenite Jews were craftsmen, providing the population of the country, which consisted mainly of farmers, with the implements necessary for their work and home, with clothing and ornaments and partly also with weapons. The very existence of the Yemenites was based on the specific rôle they fulfilled in the economy of the caste-like society of Yemen, before the twentieth century changed everything.

Economically and socially, gold- and silversmiths were the leading craftsmen. There were no savings banks in Yemen. A woman carried her possessions on her body in the form of jewellery. A man's pride was in his daggers, swords and flintlocks. Expensive ornaments were designed to enhance the prestige which such weapons bestowed on their bearers. The Jewish artisans preferred gold- and silversmithery to other crafts, because it left mouth and mind free for the discussion of religious topics. The holy texts were mostly known by heart and, if not, a boy would read from a book while the artisans were working. The same applies to the second largest industry of Yemenite Jews: weaving. Weaving occupied in Yemen, in particular in the country-side, a place different from the one it fills in modern society. The cut of a garment was simple. One ordered one's dress not from a tailor, but from a weaver. There were Jewish villages inhabited exclusively by artisans exercising this craft, while the Muslim villages surrounding it served as their customers. A third industry of great diffusion was the embroidery of women's trousers. (In Yemen, women, not men, wear this piece of clothing. Of an effeminate man they would say: "He wears the trousers." The ornaments reached from the knee to the ankles.) Every Muslim district and often even every village had its own patterns for the decoration of the women's trousers, and many Jewish men earned their livelihood by creating these works of art. Incidentally, at the other end of the Arab world the students of the Qarawiyyīn (the Muslim religious college of Fez, Morocco) derived their sustenance from the same occupation. Primitive as life was in Yemen, there were about seventy different arts and crafts in which the Jews were engaged. The present writer knew well a blacksmith (who also was a good Hebrew scholar) who produced with his own hands not only ploughshares and other agricultural and domestic implements, but also simple nails. This vital rôle of the Jews in the economy of the High Yemen explains two aspects of their existence: their wide dispersion—they were needed everywhere—and their comparative safety in an otherwise lawless and turbulent environment. A

Jew was addressed as *uṣṭa* (derived from classical Arabic *ustādh*) which means "master", and he and his family usually were attached to a tribe or a clan which was prepared to go to war to redress an injury inflicted on unarmed persons under their protection.

Much has been written about the humiliating position endured by the Jews in Yemen. However, one has to keep in mind that Yemen used to be a country strictly governed by Islamic religious law; the disabilities and discriminations often referred to were nothing but provisions of that law—a situation for which the Yemenite Jews themselves had much understanding. Visitors from Europe were outraged by conditions with which they were not familiar, because the Muslim countries more exposed to western influence had abandoned them long ago. In certain respects, though, conditions in Yemen differed. The highland of Yemen is occupied by the Zaydī sect, and sects are prone to develop discriminatory laws of their own. One such law was the forcible conversion of Jewish orphans to Islam. This cruel practice, which often tore families apart, seems to have had its basis in a famous dictum ascribed to Muḥammad: "Every one is born in the natural religion (i.e. Islam); only his parents make him a Jew, a Christian, or a Zoroastrian." This was interpreted to mean that a child who had lost his father (the mother does not count as an educator in religion) had to be raised in Islam. The hunt after orphans (even after they had become adults) was one of the main reasons for the emigration of Jews from Yemen in the twenties and thirties of this century.

On the other hand, the Zaydī environment constituted a positive influence on the religious life of the Jews. The Zaydī persuasion emphasizes very much the study of the holy texts. The *imām*, or ruler of Yemen, is expected to be a scholar, and many *imāms* have indeed written learned treatises. A Muslim merchant, studying a manuscript on Zaydī law in his shop while waiting for a customer, was a common sight in the bazaars of Ṣan'ā'. This atmosphere was extremely conducive to the preservation of that popular rabbinical Judaism which is basically the type of religion represented by the Jews of Yemen. They were spared that dichotomy of spiritual life which so often was the lot of the Jewish Diaspora. Moreover, since four-fifths of Yemen's Jews, whose males were largely or completely literate, lived in villages surrounded by a predominantly illiterate Muslim rural population, the minority took pride in a more devoted observance of the ideals which it shared with the ruling majority.

This situation also had a deep impact on the Jewish women. Seemingly, a bottomless chasm separated the world of the bookish, "learned" Jewish men from that of their women, none of whom was taught to read and to write. (It was perhaps different in the Middle Ages. A trustworthy visitor to Yemen saw a Pentateuch copied in the fourteenth century by a woman excusing herself for possible mistakes by her pregnancy.) Women, though they patiently listened to the synagogue service for hours, did not know how to pray, since prayers were said exclusively in Hebrew. Once, the present writer asked a Yemenite girl, whether her mother prayed. "Yes," the girl answered, "but she says to God what *she* wants" (i.e. unlike the father who says only what is written in the books). The women bore Arabic names, not those of the heroines of the Bible, for, with a few exceptions, the women did not know the biblical stories. While the men's poetry and songs were exclusively religious and in Hebrew or in a pseudo-classical Arabic, the poetry and the songs of the women were secular throughout and in colloquial Arabic of varying degrees, depending on the type of poetry cultivated. Yet, the women identified themselves entirely with the values of their men. Their songs expressed pride in their learned men and it was they who often fought with their husbands for the continuation of their boys' studies, when the former wanted to take them out of school in order to have them contribute to the earnings of the family. The reason for this attitude is to be found in the fact that the society in which the Yemenite women lived was dominated by the belief that the pursuit of religious study was the highest merit a man could obtain.

There is one strange aspect of the traditional world of the Yemenites whose consideration is essential to an understanding of their spiritual culture: their excessive devotion to the study of the *sheḥīṭā*, the ritual killing of animals and the subsequent examination of their carcasses. While in other communities the study of this subject is more or less confined to specialists, in Yemen it was, so to say, the main content of secondary education; everyone aspiring to an educational status higher than the elementary stage studied this subject. The knowledge of the anatomy of animals and the countless questions of ritual connected with it, possessed by ordinary Yemenites, often astounded (and put to shame) the present writer. During the last eight hundred years there has scarcely been a Yemenite author of consequence known to us who has not written a book or a treatise on *sheḥīṭā*. There were also hotly discussed local divergences in the theory and practice of this ritual. All this seems to be a relic of the ancient Near East, where the examination of the carcasses of sacrificial animals was one of the major religious sciences. On the other hand, it reflected the mood of a time that expected the reconstruction of the Temple of Jerusalem with its elaborate service of sacrifices to take place in the immediate future.

The term rabbinical Judaism, used above to characterize the religiosity of the Yemenites, now needs to be examined more closely. Elementary education in the Yemenite community consisted of the memorization of those books and sections of the Bible which, in one form or another, constituted a part of the synagogue service. Likewise, their Targum or Aramaic version was studied to the extent that these versions were read in the syngagogue. Of the Talmud, only the Mishnah was learned, partly in school, but more thoroughly in the synagogue after or between services. This basic study was complemented by two other branches of rabbinical knowledge—codified law and ethical expositions. The *Gemārā*, or learned discussions of the Talmud, which in eastern Europe formed the main content of Jewish education, was left in Yemen to scholars found only in the capital and a few other places.

This syllabus of religious education was by no means particular to the Yemenites. It was the one in vogue from the early post-talmudic period down to the eleventh century approximately. The peculiarity of the Yemenites consists in the pure conservation of this early type of education. Memorizing the biblical texts while paying meticulous attention to the correct pronunciation of every sound (including the musical intonation) had been vital so long as oral tradition alone was the means of preservation of the correct reading of the unvowelled texts. After the invention of the vowel signs and musical notation and their introduction into general use (sixth to ninth centuries), these efforts were largely redundant, but were continued. (As it often happens in education, studies are pursued after the aim for which they have been created has ceased to exist.) Still, the great efforts made by the Yemenites throughout their lives to master the biblical text and its Targum with precision not only rendered them excellent Hebraists, but had also a strong disciplinary effect on their whole mental frame.

From the foregoing remarks one should not conclude that the Yemenites became mentally fossilized in the tenth century. On the contrary. With one exception, they took part in all the spiritual movements of the main body of Judaism. To be sure, they did so in their own way. Long before Maimonides they had adopted codifications of religious law compiled in Iraq and in Morocco. But even Maimonides who became their main lawgiver was not accepted without local modifications. To the sixteenth-century codifier Joseph Caro also only qualified homage was paid. Theological studies were pursued by Yemenite scholars in the manner of various Islamic schools of thought, again with some characteristic local specialities. Eventually, Maimonides' influence became paramount in this field too. More than anything else it was ethical pietism, as developed by some Mediterranean Jewish thinkers under the impact of Ṣūfism, which affected the whole religious life of the Yemenites. The reading of edifying pietist literature became a regular part of the synagogue service. Hebrew religious poetry, as cultivated in Spain, was adopted by the Yemenites enthusiastically, since it was congenial to the new pietist mood and based entirely on biblical Hebrew. From the second half of the sixteenth century, the Kabbalah, especially in its Palestinian version, became a strong force among the Jews of Yemen. It tinged their religious poetry which was of considerable merit and which, albeit not admitted to the synagogue service, used to be sung for many hours at wedding celebrations, circumcision meals and other semi-religious gatherings. Magical beliefs and practices which had led an uneasy existence during a more rationalistic period, now became sanctioned by a theosophical substructure. Printed prayerbooks, compiled according to kabbalistic views, were imported into Yemen from Palestine and other countries and caused a real schism. The congregations adopting them were called *shāmī* (from *al-shām*, the Arabic name of Palestine), the others—*baladī*, which means adhering to local custom. The history of this schism, which persists to the present day even in small Yemenite settlements, has not yet been completely clarified. Ḥasidism, which affected East European Judaism so much, seems to have had no repercussions in Yemen. That movement did not produce a single great work in Hebrew and had no real function in Jewish Yemen, which anyhow was pervaded by a strong spirit of popular pietism. Some of the Hebrew publications of nineteenth-century East European "Enlightenment" did reach Yemen. It is not sufficiently known, however, how far they contributed to the latest schism dividing Yemenite Jews: that between "Rationalists" called in Hebrew *dōr dēʿah* (*dör deʿō*), "Age of Reason", from which an Arabic plural *darādʿāh* is formed) and conservatives (called by their opponents *'iqqĕshīm* "the crooked" or "obstinate ones"). This split, which is not a simple continuation of the ancient rift between the adherents of the Kabbalah and their opponents, became particularly acrimonious during the last twenty-five years of the life of the leader of the *darād'äh*, Yiḥyā' Qāfeḥ, who died in Ṣan'ā' in 1932 at the age of eighty-two. As is often the case with divisions over religion, communal and even personal antagonisms were involved. In any event, the *darād'äh* had a leavening influence on the Yemenite community and served to a certain extent as a preparation for the greatest revolution in its life: the wholesale transfer into a thoroughly westernized society.

The grandson of the originator of the *darād'äh* movement, Joseph Qāfeḥ (spelled also Kafih), is the Yemenite member of the Rabbinical Supreme Court of Israel, the highest religious dignity after that of the two chief rabbis. He is an extremely knowledgeable man, having to his credit sixteen printed volumes, mostly learned editions of medieval authors, but also a valuable illustrated book on the manners and customs of the Yemenites. Still, in true Yemenite fashion, he exercised the craft of silversmithery not only in Ṣan'ā', but also in Palestine, whereto he emigrated in 1943, until he was called upon to devote all his time to the rabbinate. The Israeli Yemenites' vivid interest in the study of their past and the important contributions they have made in this field are truly remarkable. Special mention should be made of Y. Ratzaby, an M.A. of the Hebrew University, whose contributions are of a strictly scientific nature.

The Yemenites more than any other Jewish group have developed a folk art of high quality, especially in the fields of silversmithery, embroidery and basket-work. Their songs and sacred dances are also of very considerable artistic merit. It is therefore not surprising that they have made characteristic contributions to art life in Israel. These activities, however, lie outside the scope of this study.

A visit to a synagogue of Yemenites in Palestine in the forties of this century, when it still was possible to observe them in a relatively unspoiled condition, gave an impression of utmost antiquity. As in talmudic times, the pulpit on which the Torah was read was a mobile piece of furniture, not a fixed structure. The holy ark occupied almost the whole eastern wall. The congregation was seated on the floor. No rabbi or precentor officiated, but, as in ancient times, the "head of the synagogue" (the "archi-synagogus" of antiquity) apportioned to various members of the congregation the solo chanting of the prayers and the reading of the weekly portion from the Bible. The biblical texts were translated verse by verse into Aramaic, mostly by boys reading with breathtaking rapidity. The head of the synagogue had the privilege of opening the recitation of the sections chanted by the congregation, which then broke in with a deafening polyphonic performance. Everyone, including the little boys seated before their fathers, knew these texts by heart. As impressive as the thunderous sound of the congregational chantings was the absolute stillness which prevailed during silent prayer. Despite the many children present not a sound would be heard or a movement seen. (Unlike the Ashkenazim, the Yemenites are completely motionless during silent prayer, but make vehement jerking movements during congregational chantings.) Thus the Yemenite service combined the decorum of the Sephardim with the fervour of Ḥasidism. It fully complied with the admonition so often heard from the lips of Yemenite preachers: "Rejoice with trembling" (Psalm ii. 10).

PART 2

CHRISTIANITY

CHAPTER 5

CHRISTIANITY IN THE MIDDLE EAST: SURVEY DOWN TO A.D. 1800

INTRODUCTORY

Like its great rivals Judaism and Islam, Christianity is a revealed religion taking its rise in the Middle East. In this work devoted to the study of the situation in recent times it is not necessary to give more than the briefest survey of the growth of the Church in the first four centuries.[1] For this great formative era of Christian history the student has to hand a wealth of material contributed by scholars from nearly all parts of the globe. Even so, to understand the position occupied by the Churches in the Middle East in our own day a few of the classic landmarks of that period must be recorded. The New Testament story ends with Paul's arrival in Rome, *circa* 60, but the fall of Jerusalem in 70 ended all hopes of winning Jesus' homeland for Christianity. Indeed it delayed its mission eastward toward the great centres of Jewry at Babylon and elsewhere in Parthia and among the Syriac- and Aramaic-speaking peoples of Mesopotamia for over a century.

Instead, Christianity became a western religion and the main language of its mission was Greek. While gradually freeing itself from a legacy of Jewish apocalyptic preserved in Matthew and Mark and in some sub-Apostolic writings, Christians were confronted by the need for interpreting the Bible message within the framework of current Greek philosophic thought. How was the Holy Trinity in whose name the convert was baptized, to be understood? In what way was Christ to be thought of and worshipped as God? The attempt to formulate basic christological truths begun by the Apologists in the mid-second century was continued by the Alexandrians, Clement and Origen. It was impossible, however, to find a solution acceptable even to a majority of Christians. By the end of the third century Rome, Antioch and Alexandria all represented different and not easily reconcilable standpoints.

[1] See for instance, B. J. Kidd, *A History of the Church to 461*, 3 vols. (Oxford, 1921) and H. Lietzmann, *Geschichte der alten Kirche*, 4 vols. (Berlin, 1937–42; Eng. trans. by B. Woolf, 1952).

Meantime, the rapidly increasing number of Christians was confronting the Church with difficulties as well as opportunities. After a century of sporadic persecutions by the Roman authorities, an attempt was made by the emperor Decius in 250 to force the Christians to join with their fellow-provincials in a general act of sacrifice for the well-being of the empire. This failed, and in the next decades continued disasters coupled with increasingly severe extortions and taxation seem to have convinced a large number of the rural provincials in North Africa and in the eastern provinces of the Empire that the old territorial gods had failed them, and that both earthly and heavenly salvation was to be sought from the Christians. Christianity was no longer confined to Greek or Latin speaking town-dwellers, and among the rural converts it began to take on new forms, such as the monastic movement associated with the Copt, St Antony (*circa* 270).

The failure of the final effort of the Roman Empire to crush the Christians during the Great Persecution of 303–12 and the conversion of Constantine introduced the factor of Imperial policy into what previously had been purely theological matters. Constantine summoned the Councils of Arles in 314 and Nicaea in 325, and he and his successors strove to bind Church and State together on the basis of the largest amount of doctrinal and disciplinary unity within the Church. It took, however, fifty-five years of almost incessant discussion and controversy before the Creed of Nicaea defining the Son as "Consubstantial with the Father" was accepted by the Church in both the East and the West, a warning of the difficulties which any attempted imposition of formulae of doctrinal orthodoxy would be likely to meet.

Meantime, Constantine's shift of the capital from Rome to Constantinople had raised for the Church grave problems of organization and precedence. Did its position as imperial city entitle Constantinople to ecclesiastical precedence after Old Rome? In 381, however, this had been conceded at the Second Ecumenical Council at Constantinople. It was challenged by Rome and Alexandria, both deeply aggrieved by the decision. For the next seventy years the history of the Church is dominated by a fierce struggle fought over matters of doctrine and discipline involving the four great patriarchates, Rome, Constantinople, Antioch and Alexandria.

Throughout most of this period Rome and Alexandria were acting in concert against Constantinople. The patriarchs of the capital, John Chrysostom and Nestorius, were driven into exile, and Alexandria seemed about to dominate the Church theologically. At the Council of Ephesus in 431 Cyril with the aid of Pope Celestine secured the rejection of the rival theology of Antioch and the downfall of Nestorius.

Cyril's successor Dioscorus however was not content to let well alone. Cyril's christology based on his profound belief in the unitary character of Christ's personality and of the perfection of his deity was just within the acceptable canons of orthodoxy. Any slight exaggeration which could be interpreted as tending to eliminate the human nature of Christ might be regarded as heresy. Dioscorus, sure of the support of fanatical Egyptian monks and aiming at complete ecclesiastical supremacy, recklessly upset this delicate balance. At the Second Council of Ephesus in 449 he humiliated once again the patriarchs of Antioch and Constantinople and defied the Roman see.

The ensuing Council of Chalcedon in 451 is one of the landmarks of Christendom. Amid frenzied scenes, the *Tome* of Leo declaring that the Son existed "in Two Natures", God and man "without confusion or change" was accepted as the faith of the Church by the sentence of more than 500 bishops. Though Nestorius remained condemned, other champions of the Antiochene "Two Natures" Christology, Theodoret of Cyrrhus (d. 466) and Ibas of Edessa (d. 457) were vindicated. Dioscorus was condemned and sent into exile. Constantinople, Rome and Antioch were once more united in doctrine and sentiment.

Now, however, the popular character of the Christian movement demonstrated its importance. Egyptian monks had already played a considerable part in the scenes that had characterized the Church councils of the first half of the fifth century. By 451 doctrinal differences were corresponding with great territories and linguistic and cultural areas. "The valiant Dioscorus" was all-powerful among the Copts in Egypt but Syriac-speaking Christianity of eastern Syria and Persia tended to support Nestorianism, while Leo was the undisputed spokesman for the Latin West. Chalcedon was accepted by Constantinople and the Greek-speaking provinces of the empire in Asia and Europe. Within a few years the Copts had murdered Proterius their "Chalcedonian" patriarch and moved irrevocably along the path of the Monophysite "One Nature" christology. Christianity now expressed deep-felt material as well as spiritual aspirations of the native inhabitants of the Empire and beyond.

In the next 150 years successive emperors strove to restore religious unity between the four great patriarchs, now joined by Jerusalem.[1] Zeno (474–91) and Anastasius (491–518) favoured the Monophysites, and the *Henotikon* of Zeno promulgated in 482 in stating that the Son was "one and not two" turned its back on Chalcedon and by implication condemned the *Tome* of Leo. The result was the Acacian schism, and for more than thirty years Rome and Constantinople were not in communion with each other.

This schism had a profound effect on the development of Christianity in the Middle East. There was no counterweight now to the forces tending towards Monophysitism in the eastern half of the empire. Under the leadership of Severus, Patriarch of Antioch 512–18, and Philoxenus, Bishop of Manbij (Maboug) (d. 523) the Monophysites gained the upper hand in Syria, and in 491 the council of Vaghapat also accepted Monophysitism as the faith of the kingdom of Armenia. At the other end of the Christian world, Ethiopia moved in the same direction. On the other hand, Nestorianism, expelled from Edessa, its last stronghold in the Empire, in 489, consolidated its grip on Christianity in Persia.

Justin and his nephew Justinian came from the outlying Latin-speaking province of the empire. Under them links with Rome were restored, but all attempts to coerce the Monophysites into accepting Chalcedon failed. Justinian's concession in the condemnation of the Three Chapters embodying the remnants of Antiochene theology (544–53) failed to satisfy them, while persecutions began to build up a legacy of bitterness against the imperial government which was to bear fruit in the next century.

After Justinian's death in 565 his successors attempted to continue his policy, but no formula could bridge the differences of ecclesiastical thought and outlook that now divided the Latin and Greek worlds and within the latter, the "Chalcedonians" from the "Monophysites". The latter gained more ground through the missions of James Baradaeus (d. 579) in Asia Minor and eastern Syria and among the Arab tribes on the borders of the empire and Persia, and by the missions originally promoted by Justinian's Monophysite empress Theodora (d. 548) down the Nile Valley into Nubia. By 600, Monophysitism claimed the allegiance of the native populations of a vast area extending from the Black Sea to the sources of the Nile. It was the third religious

[1] For this period see L. Duchesne, *L'Eglise au VIème Siècle* (Paris, 1924).

force embracing a greater area than either its Chalcedonian or Latin rivals.

The catastrophe which befell the empire and ultimately Christianity in the Middle East in the seventh century must be considered within this context. Even before the civil war between the adherents of Phocas and Heraclius (608–10) and the great Persian invasion of the eastern provinces of the empire that followed, eastern Christians were divided into two camps between whom the deepest mistrust prevailed. Under the Persian occupation of Antioch and Egypt (612–29) the Monophysites had prospered and in 619 a formal act of dogmatic union on the basis of the teaching of Severus of Antioch had been achieved by the Churches of Alexandria and Antioch. Heraclius' restoration of the imperial fortunes was not welcome, no more than was his final effort to square the circle once more by the *Ecthesis* propounding the doctrine of the One Will as the christology of the Empire. Before this had been promulgated in 638, however, the battle of the river Yarmūk had been fought and Heraclius had bidden his "long farewell" to Syria. Not surprisingly the native inhabitants were welcoming the Arabs as liberators.

THE CHURCHES UNDER ISLAM 641–1800

The Syrian Churches

With Heraclius' death in February 641 one can no longer follow the history of Christianity in the Middle East as a single theme. By 646 Egypt had joined Syria and Palestine irrevocably among the lost provinces of the Empire, and by the end of the century all North Africa lay outside its frontiers. The old imperial provinces follow the destinies of their new overlords. Syria was at first the most favoured. The Umayyads chose Damascus as their capital and Syria benefited from the flowering of the rich Greco-Arabic culture associated with their name. Moreover the Arab conquest swept aside the old frontier between Rome and Persia and enabled the Mesopotamian Monophysites to enter into direct contact with their Syrian brethren. But on the fall of the Umayyad dynasty in 750 and the removal of the caliphate to Baghdad by their supplanters the 'Abbāsids, stagnation and decline set in. Syria and Palestine became badly administered provinces lying between the two main centres of Arab power at Baghdad and Cairo. In the tenth century Egypt assumed the leadership of the Arab world with the Fāṭimid empire stretching from Cairo to the Atlantic ocean, and in the European Middle Ages, while Baghdad fell to the Mongols in 1258, the Egyptian sultans won more fame by their defence of the whole western Islamic world first against the Crusaders and then against the Mongols themselves.

For the Christians, however, these struggles were struggles which concerned their masters or foreigners. At no point from the seventh century onwards do the Coptic or Syrian Christians play a decisive part in the history of their own territories. Theirs was a culture in isolation and decline, and the interest of the story lies both in the extraordinarily fateful consequences of the decision of their leaders to welcome the Muslims as liberators, and thereafter their dour struggle for survival. In spite of the fact that millions of Christians were to live in close contact with Muslims, no organized churches composed of Muslim converts to the Christian faith emerged. Failure and ineffectiveness have been complete.

Meantime, though strong cultural links continued to bind the Monophysite churches to Byzantium, ecclesiastical and political links were broken. The condemnation of Monothelitism by the Sixth General Council in 680–1, ended all reasonable hope of compromise with Orthodoxy, though when the Byzantines reconquered northern Syria in the tenth century there were again fruitless efforts in that direction. All attempts to find a basis of agreement between Constantinople, Alexandria and Rome had failed, and the emperors were rewarded for their continuous and not wholly unimaginative efforts with the worst of all worlds.

At first, the Muslims did not seek to propagate their faith among their subjects except those of Arab race, a fact important for consolidating the existing religious pattern in Syria and Palestine, and ultimately for the survival of Christianity there. Indeed, for seventy years after the Muslim conquest the Syrian Christians appeared not to have done badly by the exchange of Muslim for Byzantine masters. In this great period of Muslim expansion the subject peoples were left much to their own devices and in return the Christians were loyal. One interesting sidelight on the religious situation in Palestine is provided by a Western pilgrim, the Gallic bishop Arculph, whose account of what he saw in the years 680–3 has been recorded by Adamnan the monk of Iona.[1] Arculph shows how Christianity and Judaism remained the religions of the vast majority of the inhabitants of

[1] Adamnan's *De Locis Sanctis* (ed. D. Meehan, Dublin, 1958).

Palestine and the parts of Syria which he visited. He mentions the existence of "Saracen churches" in Damascus and on the site of the temple at Jerusalem, but these did not impress him.[1] He also records how the Caliph Muʿāwiya decided a dispute between Christians and Jews in Jerusalem over the possession of the Holy Shroud in favour of the Christians.[2] No hint of Arab persecution of the latter is to be found in Arculph's work, which may perhaps reflect the period of tolerance that followed the signature in 678 of the treaty between Constantine Pogonatus and the Caliph which ended the first attempts by the Arabs to destroy Byzantium.

Muʿāwiya's successor Yazīd I (680–3)[3] was also tolerant, but ʿAbd al-Malik (685–705) was less friendly to the Christians.[4] In Egypt ʿAbd al-Malik's *amīrs* were to be responsible for an increasingly suspicious attitude towards the Coptic Patriarch. The renewal of war with the Byzantine empire led to the expulsion of the Orthodox Patriarch from Antioch in 702, a ban which lasted for forty years. In 705, however, the caliphate passed to al-Walīd who left the reputation of "hating the Christians and demolishing their churches".[5] In the first year of his reign the Church of St John at Damascus which hitherto had been divided between Christians and Muslims was taken over entirely by the latter. In other ways he showed that he intended Islam to be a conquering religion as well as the religion of conquerors. Greek began to be superseded by Arabic as the language of the administration. Arab script appears on the Umayyad coinage.[6] Arab tribes who had remained Christian were now pressed to convert to Islam, and the first of a series of financial exactions designed to humiliate the Christian population was enforced. In Egypt al-Walīd's measures were reflected by those of Umayyad officials against the Copts. Monks, who had hitherto been exempted from the poll-tax were now forced to pay, and some Coptic churches were stripped of their carved pillars and

[1] *Ibid.* II, 28 (Damascus) and I, 1 (Jerusalem).

[2] *Ibid.* I, 9. Muʿāwiya had himself married an Arab Monophysite Christian.

[3] Yazīd was described in the *Continuatio Byzantino-arabica*, as "jucundissimus et cunctis nationibus regni eius gratissime habuit...cum omnibus civiliter vixit". He was, however, responsible for the first attacks on images which would ultimately have embroiled him with his Orthodox Christian subjects (see Adamnan, *loc. cit.* p. 119 n.).

[4] For the conversion of many of the inhabitants of Aleppo to Islam in this reign, see M. Sobernheim, "Ḥalab", *The Encyclopaedia of Islam*, vol. II, pt. 1, p. 229.

[5] Michael, *Chron.* XI, 17 (Chabot, p. 481). He remained, however, on reasonably good personal terms with the Patriarch Mar Elias (*ibid.*).

[6] Michael, *Chron.* XI, 16 and cf. also, *ibid.* 17. About the same time a census in Egypt was drawn up in Arabic (*History of the Patriarchs* (ed. B. T. A. Evetts), *P.O.* vol. V, p. 67; cf. Hitti, *op. cit.* pp. 472–3).

marble decorations for the benefit of mosques.[1] al-Walīd's policy was continued by 'Umar II (717–20) and less vigorously by Yazīd II (720–4), and though Michael the Syrian claims "the Christian leaders still directed the affairs of the government in the cities and the countryside", a shock had been administered to the Church's self-confidence.[2]

The advance of Islam now began to be felt seriously among settled Christian communities. This development may have influenced the rise of the major movement which affected the eastern Christian churches in the eighth and ninth centuries. It has been pointed out that the Iconoclast emperors came originally from Melitene on the borderland between the Byzantine and Arab empires, and that in the case of Leo III, the influence of his adviser Beser, a one-time convert to Islam, should not be discounted. Again, Michael the Syrian comments "Leo ordered the removal of images from the walls of churches following the example of the Arab king".[3] This cannot be proved, but Muslims had been arguing in Islam's favour both its unity as against Christian discords, and its refusal to represent Divine things in pictorial form.[4]

As was to be expected, Leo's Iconoclast decrees of 726 and 730 caused most stir among the Orthodox. These produced a notable champion, Yaḥyā b. Manṣūr (John of Damascus, *c.* 670–753), the son of a civil servant who had been treasurer to the Caliphs Mu'āwiya and 'Abd al-Malik. Between 726 and 730 he wrote three treatises against the Iconoclasts. He followed these with a continuous series of systematic doctrinal and apologetic works restating and elaborating the faith of Chalcedon and extending its implications to themes such as the nature of the Virgin Mary. The best known of these are *The Fount of Wisdom* which included one of the most comprehensive statements of Orthodox doctrine ever attempted, and the *Sacra Parallela*, a vast compilation of scriptural and patristic texts on Christian moral and ascetic life.

John had written impartially against Muslims, Monophysites and Nestorians, but now in the heart of the Orthodox camp itself had arisen a school of thought which was to affect permanently Church life in Syria. The Maronites trace their origin to the anchorite Maro who flourished near Apamea in the Orontes valley in the early fifth century.

[1] *History of the Patriarchs*, pp. 67–8.

[2] Michael, *Chron.* XI, 16 (Chabot, p. 474). 'Umar's proseletysing zeal, *ibid.* XI, 19.

[3] *Ibid.* XI, 19 (Chabot, p. 491).

[4] *History of the Patriarchs*, pt. I, ch. XVI (Evetts, pt. III, *P.O.* vol. V, p. 35). "For the Muslims said the Christians were in error, giving God a wife and a son, and uttering many falsehoods in their religion, and the Amir rebuked their want of agreement in the doctrines of religion." This incident appears to have taken place in 695.

A great monastery was founded in his honour and became one of the main strongholds of Orthodoxy against Monophysitism in Syria. In the last year of the reign of Anastasius the monks were in touch with Pope Hormisdas and were represented at Justinian's anti-Monophysite council held by the Patriarch Menas at Constantinople in 536. The Arab conquest still saw them on the Orthodox side and the record survives of a disputation between the monks of the monastery of Hagios Maro and the Monophysite Patriarch held in 660 at Damascus before the Caliph Mu'āwiya. Despite everything, however, Heraclius' final effort at reconciliation between the warring religious factions of the empire, embodied in the *Ecthesis* had some success. Monotheletism struck a responsive chord and for all their dislike of the Monophysites, the monks of Hagios Maro seem to have been prepared to accept the emperor's compromise, and once accepted they stuck to it. The condemnation of Monotheletism in 680 passed them by, and when in *c.* 702 they decided in the absence of any Orthodox Patriarch of Antioch to elect their own patriarch and bishops, it was to the Monothelete creed they subscribed.[1] Moreover, as the plains of Syria became less and less secure, the Maronites tended to emigrate into the high valleys of the Lebanon. Maronite communities were established there, and henceforth Syrian Christianity contained the three main groups of Orthodox, Monophysites and Maronites.

During the eighth and ninth centuries the Monophysites continued to maintain their position of strength. Such favour as the Caliphs granted to the Syrian Christians they granted to them. In *c.* 720 the first Monophysite church was built in Antioch itself. Six years later, the synod of Dvin brought about union with the Armenian Christians. The great monasteries continued to produce men of learning, such as the chronicler James of Edessa (d. 707), but the Umayyads fell in 750, and under the 'Abbāsids Christians were often a prey to hostile measures.[2] Thus we hear of 5,000 men, members of the last Christian Arab tribe, the Banū Tanūkh, being forcibly converted in a district near Aleppo on

[1] Referring to a brief persecution at the hands of the Chalcedonian patriarch Theophylactus bar Qanbara in 736, Michael records that they accepted the one will of Christ, and the Monophysite *trisagion* with its addition "who was crucified for us", but they also accepted the Council of Chalcedon. *Chron.* XI, 22 (Chabot, p. 511).

[2] An example of the tendency of Arab tribesmen, now Muslim, to pay off old scores against Christian townsfolk, is given by Michael, *Chron.* XII, 9. The people of Edessa who complained of depredations by one of these tribes were told by its representatives that in the times of the Romans they had been forced to scratch a living in the desert, but now that the Romans had been defeated the Edessenes must pay tribute.

the orders of Caliph al-Mahdī (775–85).[1] There was always the danger, too, that some local fanatic might invoke the *sharī'a* as an excuse for destroying Christian churches, allegedly built after the date of the conquest.

The Monophysites of Syria were not, however, to suffer the same disastrous decline that befell the Copts during the ninth century. Conversions to Islam among their leaders were in particular discouraged by the Caliphs themselves, as Ignatius, Metropolitan of Takrīt found to his cost in 1016.[2] Instead, this seems to have been the great era for monastery building in eastern Syria and north-western Iraq, and there ground was gained in the latter area at the expense of the Nestorians. Internal disputes in the Church such as over the precise wording of the Eucharistic invocation, if long standing, were rarely dangerous.

During the middle of the ninth century Christians in Syria and the Lebanon were under considerable pressure. Already in 807 Caliph Hārūn al-Rashīd had ordered the destruction of all churches built since the Muslim conquest and prescribed distinctive garbs for Christians and Jews. Between 850 and 854 his grandson al-Mutawakkil revived these orders and added further instructions designed to humiliate and ridicule the Christians. Many now gave way and accepted Islam. In addition the now Islamic Banū Tanūkh Arabs began to carve for themselves principalities in the Lebanon, thus increasing Muslim influence in that area. Arabic, too, was gaining on Syriac and Aramaic as the language of common use, and without the Byzantine revival in the tenth century Christianity in Syria might have been seriously menaced.[3]

All this time, the 'Abbāsids ruled in Baghdad and an assortment of amirs and petty chiefs governed the territory stretching from the Euphrates to the Egyptian frontier. There were border wars between Muslims and the Byzantines, but nothing decisive was gained by either side. Then, in the 940s, the Byzantines began to take the offensive and in the course of a generation reconquered Cyprus, Cilicia, Syria, the Lebanon and Phoenicia. In 944 the city of Edessa had been forced to hand over its precious Christian relic, the miraculous image of Christ imprinted on cloth, and this had been transported in triumph to Constantinople. The Muslims were pressed back from the Taurus

[1] Michael, *Chron.* XII, 1.

[2] He quarrelled with his people and became a convert to Islam. He was despised by the Caliph Michael, *Chron.* XIII, 5.

[3] See P. K. Hitti, *A History of Syria* (London, 1957), pp. 543–5.

passes and Armenia. Crete after 130 years of Muslim occupation was reconquered in 961, and then successively Tarsus, Mopsuestia, the coast of Syria, and finally in October 969 Antioch was betrayed to the forces of Nicephoros Phocas.

For the next three centuries (969–1268) Antioch was under Christian rule, except for thirteen years 1085–98 when the Turks held it. The campaigns of Nicephoros and his successor John Tzimisces (969–76) were as much inspired by the crusading ideal as those of the Crusaders themselves. Nicephoros saw himself as freeing Jerusalem and marching on to Mecca! In his letter to the king of Armenia describing his campaign of 975 John Tzimisces wrote, "Today all Phoenicia, Palestine and Syria are freed from Mohammedan yoke and recognize the authority of the Byzantine Greeks". Again, "our desire is to free the Holy Sepulchre from the outrages of the Muslims",[1] and but for a check before Tripoli on the coast, he might have achieved this aim. When the era of Byzantine reconquest ended in 1001 with the treaty between Basil II and the Fāṭimid Caliph, the frontier between the two empires was stabilized on a line that left western and northern Syria and the Lebanon in Christian hands. Phoenicia and eastern Syria remained debatable land.

The era of reconquest emphasized the role of the Byzantine emperor as the ultimate protector of all Christians in the Middle East. The treaty signed in 970 with the Amir of Aleppo which turned his territory into a Byzantine client state indicates the sort of religious settlement which the Byzantines would have imposed on the Muslims had they carried their conquests further. The Arab historian Kamāl al-Dīn (thirteenth century) records that now it was the Muslim population who had to pay the taxes whereas the Christians were freed. All churches destroyed by the Muslims were to be rebuilt and there was to be freedom of conversion from Islam to Christianity.[2] The boot was on the other leg.

Even so, the Christians were not completely masters of the situation. Basil II was unable to intervene to prevent the fanatical outbursts of Caliph al-Ḥākim against the Christians in Palestine and Egypt. In 1009 he ordered the destruction of the Church of the Holy Sepulchre, revived the discriminatory measures of al-Mutawakkil against Christians and instituted acts of petty persecution against the pilgrims. In Egypt it is said that nearly 3,000 churches were destroyed and many

[1] Cited from S. Runciman, *A History of the Crusades* (Cambridge, 1951), vol. I, p. 33.

[2] Cited from A. A. Vasiliev, *History of the Byzantine Empire* (Madison, 1952), p. 309. Cf. Runciman, *Crusades*, vol. I, p. 31.

terrorized into conversion to Islam. The storm however was brief, though the effects on Western Christian attitude towards Muslim control of the Holy Places was to be lasting. al-Ḥākim had abandoned his policy before he died in 1021, and after another flurry on the frontiers in which the Byzantines lost control of Aleppo in 1031 but captured Edessa the next year, Michael IV concluded an important treaty with the Fāṭimid Caliph in 1036. The Church of the Holy Sepulchre was to be restored, but at Byzantine expense. Christians might rebuild all destroyed churches, and the emperor from now on took over the Caliph's right to appoint the Orthodox Patriarch of Jerusalem. Ten years later, the Persian traveller Nāṣir-i Khusraw commented on the splendour of the restored Church of the Holy Sepulchre.[1] At last it seemed that an equilibrium between the two great empires and faiths had been reached.

The disturbers of the peace were not to be the Arabs. For some decades groups of tribesmen of Seljuk Turkish stock had been moving westwards from the central Asian steppes towards the boundaries of the Arab and Byzantine empires. Many had been taken into the service of the caliphs, and this fact as well as long association with Muslim ways had turned them from leanings towards Nestorian Christianity into zealous if unconventional followers of the Prophet. Already during the first decades of the eleventh century a great Muslim Turkish empire had extended from central Persia to Lahore and north as far as Bukhara. From Persia raiding bands struck northwards into Armenia. The Byzantines were gradually forced out of the province, and in 1071 the effort by the emperor Romanus IV to reconquer lost ground was disastrously defeated by the Turkish leader Alp Arslan at the battle of Malazgint near Lake Van. The eastern frontier of the empire lay wide open to the advance of Turkish nomad bands. Farther south, Antioch fell to the Seljuk Amir Ortok in 1085. The Fāṭimids, however, were not to escape the emergence of this new power in the Middle East. Between 1065 and 1085 Turkish marauders swept over southern Syria and Palestine. In 1070 Jerusalem fell to them, and though their wrath was directed impartially at Muslim and Christian, tales of horror and desecration were brought back by pilgrims from the West to the courts of France and the Empire. This time they were hearkened.

The Crusades brought Eastern and Western Christians into close contact for the first time since the era of Justinian. The result, however,

[1] *Diary of a Journey through Syria and Palestine*, ed. Le Strange, p. 59.

was the permanence of schism. This was the product far more of increasing mutual antipathy than a quarrel over doctrines and rites.[1] No Byzantine emperor could ever concede that a Frankish chieftain was sovereign of Jerusalem and Antioch, and that Latin bishops should lord over Orthodox clergy.

At first, however, things went more smoothly than either Pope Urban or the emperor Alexius could have anticipated. Common hatred of the Turks and their allies welded the clergy and fighting men from East and West together. In Jerusalem the Crusaders found no Orthodox patriarch or higher clergy when they stormed the city in July 1099, and the Orthodox Christians were prepared to accept a Latin patriarch. In Antioch, however, relations were less harmonious. The Orthodox patriarch, John the Oxite, had stuck to his post throughout the siege and neither he nor his congregation were prepared to accept the presence of a Latin patriarch. When the Latins established their own bishopric in the captured town of Atbara suspicion of the motives of the Crusaders grew. It was still further increased by the proliferation of Latin bishoprics in Cilicia and Syria. Runciman has shown that the expulsion of the Patriarch John from Antioch by Bohemond in 1100 was "the first turning point in the general schism" between East and West.[2] It added fuel to the distrust already aroused by the presence of warrior bishops and arrogant feudatories in the crusading host. The continuance of high-handed and ultimately unsuccessful efforts of the latter to enforce Latin rites and Latin superiority in areas conquered from the Turks rendered division permanent.[3]

Further south, however, the rapprochement between Crusaders and all traditions of eastern Christians lasted longer. Western pilgrims had been for centuries a familiar sight in Palestine, and now a western army had expelled the Muslims. The establishment of the Kingdom of Jerusalem brought about an immediate improvement in the position of the native Christians. Many Muslim communities emigrated, and in the Crusader-held areas the Christians once more became a majority

[1] S. Runciman, *The Eastern Schism* (Oxford, 1955), p. 168. "The tragedy of the schism was that it was not a matter of superficial jealousies and conflicting ecclesiastical traditions. It went deeper; it was based on mutual dislike that arose out of political events of the eleventh and twelfth centuries." The Orthodox Patriarch did not return to Antioch until after the city fell to Sultan Baybars in 1268.

[2] S. Runciman, *The Eastern Schism*, p. 94.

[3] See H. J. Magoulias, "A Study in Roman Catholic and Greek Orthodox Church Relations on the island of Cyprus 1196–1360", *The Greek Orthodox Theological Review*, vol. x, pt. 1 (1965), pp. 75–106.

of the population.[1] Baldwin I brought in Syrian Christians from Transjordan to colonize the city.[2] But the old historical divisions persisted. Latin Jerusalem never saw a Greek Patriarch, and for their part the Monophysites hated the Orthodox more than the Muslims.[3]

In the second half of the twelfth century we become aware again of a tendency on the part of the Christians to take precautions against the ultimate failure of the Frankish kingdoms. Grievances, particularly in the Kingdom of Jerusalem, began to be felt more keenly. Here the Crusader clergy had been tempted to assimilate the native "heretical" Christians to the Jews and Muslims and to tax them heavily.[4] In 1169 there was another visit by the Monophysite leaders to Constantinople, but no progress was made towards healing the schism. During Ṣalāḥ al-Dīn's (Saladin) victorious counter-attack against the Crusaders culminating in the battle of Ḥiṭṭīn and the capture of Jerusalem (October 1187) the Monophysites remained passive, while the Orthodox seem to have been hostile to the Crusaders, though neither escaped the consequences of the fall of the Kingdom. By this time relations between Latin and Orthodox had soured irredeemably. Mutual exasperation was well expressed by a Cypriot monk, Neophytos, who wrote shortly after the failure of Richard Coeur de Lion to recapture Jerusalem in 1191, "No, it did not please Divine Providence to chase out the dogs from the Holy City in order to put wolves in their place".[5]

Moreover Latin relations with the local Monophysites were never cordial. Gradually, despite personal friendships like that of the Latin Patriarch of Antioch, Amaury of Limoges, with Patriarch Michael (1166–99) native Christian opinion hardened against the Franks. In 1217 James of Vitry sent by Pope Honorius III as Bishop of Sidon reported that the Christians hated the Latins and preferred Muslim rule.[6] Twelve years later, when Frederick II entered Jerusalem he found that the native Christians held aloof fearing the restoration of Latin rule.[7] Though in 1245 Patriarch Ignatius received a Papal

[1] S. Runciman, *The Crusades*, vol. II, p. 295.

[2] J. Prawer, "The Settlement of the Latins in Jerusalem", *Speculum*, vol. XXVII (1952), pp. 490–503, quoting William of Tyre, XI, 27 (*Pat. Lat.* 201, col. 515).

[3] For instance, reproaches by Dionysius Bar Ṣalībī (d. 1171) against the "Chalcedonians" in his letter to Rabban Ishro (ed. R. Harris and A. Mingana, "Woodbrooke Studies", *John Rylands Library Bulletin*, vol. XI (1927), pp. 110–71), and the Patriarch Michael's description of the flight of the Monophysites from Melitene to Amida in 1033 to avoid living under Byzantine rule, *Chron.* XIII, 7.

[4] S. Runciman, *The Crusades*, vol. II, p. 299.

[5] *Ecclesia Graecae Monumenta* (ed. J. B. Cotelier, Paris, 1677–92), vol. II, p. 457.

[6] S. Runciman, *The Crusades*, vol. III, p. 146.

[7] *Ibid.* p. 188.

emissary at Mardin, his main residence, and discussed union with him, the negotiations had no lasting result.[1] The native Christians had come to prefer minority existence under Muslim rule in which they had a recognized status and often manned influential professions to association with fanatical barbarians who knew no law but the sword, or the Greeks whom by long tradition they hated and despised.

The thirteenth century was a century of disaster for Christianity in the Middle East. The disgraceful climax of the Fourth Crusade, the Latin capture and sack of Constantinople in 1204 shattered for centuries all hope of co-operation between Eastern and Western Christians. The Latins now treated the Orthodox as heretics. In Cyprus Orthodox monks were cruelly put to death for refusing to use unleavened bread in the performance of the Eucharist, and an all-out but disastrous attempt was made to convert the islanders to Catholicism.[2] The fifth Crusade threw away the advantages of the capture of Dimyāṭ (Damietta) in 1219 by stupidity and fanaticism which forbade the acceptance of favourable terms offered by the Muslims. Even the proferred return of Jerusalem was spurned. The diplomatic triumph of the excommunicate Frederick II which obtained Jerusalem once more for Christianity in 1229 was short-lived. The Muslims led by the Egyptian Ayyūbids had now the upper hand, and but for the appearance of an entirely new factor, the advance of the Mongols, must have ended the Frankish kingdoms when they retook the Holy City in 1244.

Christians of the East had some excuse for wishful thinking regarding the Mongols—the new invaders. The latter had for centuries been in contact with Nestorian missionaries and among the queens of the Mongol princes were Kerayt princesses who were staunch Nestorians. Between their first arrival in the Middle Eastern world in the 1230s to the Īlkhān Ghāzān's conversion to Islam in 1295 there appeared even chances that this enormously powerful and savage kingdom might be persuaded to act in the interests of Latin Christianity. After all, Clovis the Frank had done no less. The Mongol advance against the Muslims and the terrible massacre that accompanied their capture of Baghdad in 1258 seemed to corroborate this view.

Such were among the hopes that inspired the furthest ranging missionary effort undertaken by the Mediaeval Church. Already during the Fifth Crusade in 1219 St Francis had journeyed to Egypt and preached before the Sultan, and two years later he added the stipulation

[1] *Ibid.* p. 232. [2] See H. Magoulias, *art. cit.*

to his Rule that "whosoever of the brothers, inspired by God, shall desire to go among the Muslims and other unbelievers, let them go..." One of his disciples, the Dutch Franciscan, William of Rubruck, sent by St Louis, went to the Mongol capital at Karakoram in 1254 and had an audience with Qūbīlāy Khān. Though he failed to make any headway there against the powerfully placed Nestorians, he opened the way to further missions in the next decades.[1] In 1271 the Pope, Gregory X, appointed two Dominicans to accompany the merchants Nicolo and Maffeo Polo to the court of Qūbīlāy Khān, but the latter, despite an interest in Christianity which prompted him to ask for further missionaries in 1289, remained a pagan eclectic equally tolerant of Latins, Nestorians and Muslims.[2] It was the last-named that ultimately prevailed. Continued long intercourse with Muslim populations and merchants convinced the Mongol leaders as it had convinced the Seljuks over two centuries before, that Islam offered the best security for their people. In 1295 the Īlkhān Ghāzān accepted Islam as his own faith, and though he did not persecute the Christians these were reduced once more to the status of a minority overshadowed by Arabs, Turks, and now the Mongols, all Islamic peoples. No wonder the Latin Christian "Society of Pilgrim Friars" accomplished little in the fourteenth century except the conversion of some of the Armenians to Roman obedience. Even so, the legend of Prester John, and a great Christian kingdom somewhere in the East survived into the fourteenth century to inspire later Western missions.[3]

The native Christians also placed their faith in ferocious Mongol deliverers. For a generation or so between 1240 and 1280 this faith seemed well placed, and the Monophysite Church in Syria flourished, inspired especially by the activity of the great monasteries of Bar Saumas and Ṭūr 'Abdīn. The great writer and administrator Bar Hebraeus (d. 1286) (Gregor Abu'l-Faraj) shows that his Church could still claim in the West twenty metropolitans and a hundred bishops, including one in Cyprus, and eighteen bishoprics in the East (i.e. eastern Syria and Mesopotamia). The tradition of learning on which he and his disciples drew reached back to the great era of Greek theology represented by the Cappadocian Fathers, and led on from them

[1] A. S. Atiya, *The Crusade in the Later Middle Ages* (London, 1938), pp. 243–6, and R. W. Southern, *Western Views of Islam* (1962), pp. 47 f.

[2] Atiya, pp. 247 f.

[3] The provenance of the "Christian Kingdom" gradually became transferred from "India" to the Nile valley and Ethiopia. See V. Slessarev, *Prester John, the Letter and the Legend* (Minneapolis, 1959), pp. 84–7.

to Dionysius the Areopagite, Severus of Antioch and their followers. Bar Hebraeus claimed for the Monophysites the effective heritage of the whole Hellenistic and Syriac traditions.

Bar Hebraeus did not live to see his dreams shattered by the victory of the Muslim Mamlūks over the Christians in 1290–1. From that time on, the Monophysites were again isolated, and, bereft of outside support, began to decline. Bar Hebraeus had already pointed to idleness in the monasteries and simony and nepotism among the ecclesiastics. These defects seem gradually to have sapped the vitality of the Church. The final blow was the invasions of Tīmūr Lang in 1400.

In the later Middle Ages the future of Christianity in Syria lay with the Maronites and the Orthodox. The latter continued to exist in western Syria and were reinforced during the later Middle Ages by members of emigrant Armenians. Meantime, however, the success of Innocent III in bringing about the submission of the Maronites was gradually bearing fruit. Lebanon retained its Christian majority and provided a point of entry to Western cultural influence after the military settlements had collapsed. The Maronites were represented at the Council of Florence/Ferrara and they reaffirmed their union with Rome on 7 August 1445.[1]

That the Christian minority survived at all outside the Lebanon in the Ottoman period may be due to the introduction by the Turks of the *millet* system.[2] This system was applied throughout the Ottoman Empire. In essence it was a continuation of the view prevalent under the Arab dynasties that the "People of the Book", that is, the Jews and Christians, though outside the community of Islam had the right to their own laws and religion. The Ottoman Turks had long had to deal with Christian minorities in Anatolia who naturally still looked to the Patriarch of Constantinople as their religious leader. On the disappearance of the Byzantine emperor, however, Sultan Meḥmed, the conqueror of Constantinople, conferred upon Patriarch Germanos the civil as well as the religious headship of the Orthodox "nation", or "*millet*". Subsequently *millet* status was conferred on other Christian communities within the Ottoman dominions, and the Jews also constituted a *millet*. As in the past, the leaders of each community had to be approved by the Sultan, but once approved his position was

[1] The Bull *Benedictus sit Deus*. See J. Gill, *The Council of Florence* (Cambridge, 1959), p. 337. It concerned the Maronites in Cyprus in the first place.

[2] See A. H. Hourani, *Minorities in the Arab World* (Oxford, 1947), pp. 20–1.

fortified by an Imperial decree (*berat*) which alone enabled Ottoman officials to assume their offices and stipends. The head of the community had a senior position in the State and was the channel by which the affairs of their communities were represented to the Sultan and his advisers. The head of the *millet* was assisted by a council and had jurisdiction over the community not only in matters directly concerned with religion, such as clerical discipline, but in a large range of activities, including education, wills, divorces, church property and civil rights. Judicial decisions of the *millet* council could be executed by the State on their behalf.

The system made it possible for the Jews and Christians to maintain something of their communal life and social position. For good or for ill it formalized and fossilized existing religious and social patterns. Thus in the Syrian towns Christians and Jews continued to have a considerable role in the administration and commerce. In Egypt the Copts dominated finance. In northern Syria the feudal structure of society was preserved and with it a minority of Christian landowners and peasants. The existence too of an elaborate administrative apparatus in each community enabled the weaker as well as the stronger to maintain their separate identities. Without their own *millet* it seems evident that the scattered Jacobite communities would have been absorbed either into Islam or into the Latin-Maronite community.

The price, however, was a heavy one. The Christian *millets* remained at the mercy of the Sultan. He was not bound to listen to their representatives. They could not fall back on the safeguards of religious law open even to heterodox Muslim communities. They were condemned to the permanent status of second-class citizens with no avenue of escape except conversion to Islam. Through the Maronites the Syrian Christians maintained contact with the Christian West, and thereby hope of ultimate relief. The Copts were not so fortunate, and for all the "blight of Ottoman rule" was reality. From the sixteenth to the eighteenth centuries the Christians in the Middle East have little history worth the telling.

The Armenian Church

The story of the Armenian Church has been told elsewhere in this volume, and here only the briefest outline is necessary. The kingdom, christianized as early as the first decades of the fourth century, found itself perched uneasily between the empires of Rome and Persia. In the latter part of the fifth century, partly because Christianity in Persia was represented by Nestorianism and partly from conviction, Armenia accepted Monophysitism. This, together with the evolution of a national script and Christian literature, gave the kingdom a sense of independence against both Persia and Byzantium, though there was a tendency to ally with the latter against the former. In 591, however, after a long period of Persian domination, most of the kingdom was ceded to Byzantium by treaty.

The seventh century was one of the stormiest in the history of the Armenian Church. For more than twenty years Armenia was once more annexed to the Persian kingdom. In consequence, Heraclius' campaign starting from the Armenian border was regarded as a war of liberation and his subsequent attempt once more to restore religious unity in the Empire was welcomed. Already since about 580 the client kingdoms on the Black Sea and the Caucasus which had previously favoured Monophysitism had been edging towards Orthodoxy. The Armenians were prepared to give the victorious Greeks another chance. At the Council of Theodosiopolis (Erzurum) in 640 the Catholikos Ezr accepted the *Ecthesis* and its Monothelete formula of faith, and the Armenians fought valiantly if unsuccessfully in Heraclius' armies against the Arabs.

The emperor's death in February 641 brought hopes of permanent reunion to an end. The Byzantine garrisons in Armenia were unpopular and even the dramatic intervention of the new emperor, Constans II, in proclaiming unity in the cathedral of Dvin in 654 was without lasting effect. As in Syria and Egypt relations between the Byzantines and their erstwhile subjects grew worse as the century wore on. The Muslims established themselves in Dvin, but though they maintained garrisons in the country and sometimes raided as far as the Caucasus they made no attempt to proselytize. In 719 a synod held at Malazgirt (Manazkert) confirmed Monophysitism as the national faith of Armenia.

The ninth and tenth centuries saw Armenia relatively prosperous and gradually reasserting its national independence in face of the weakening power of the 'Abbāsid Caliphs. The ruling dynasty of the Bagratids received recognition from the Caliphs of Baghdad as "Prince of Princes", and a treaty of friendship signed in 886 marks the emergence of the kingdom once more as a sovereign state, or rather as a group of self-governing principalities. Meantime, the Byzantines had been consolidating their frontiers with Islam and once more sought agreement with the Armenian Church. In *circa* 870 the Patriarch Photius sent a long letter to the Catholikos Zacharias inviting agreement on the basis of acknowledgement of the canonicity of the Council of Chalcedon. In fact, there was little to differentiate the two Churches. The Armenians were partial to animal sacrifices, began Lent at Septuagesima, fasted on Saturdays, and used unleavened bread for the Sacrament.[1] These practices were Judaistic, but with good will agreement could probably have been reached. This was lacking, however, and Photius' move was rebuffed.[2] Indeed for another century the mood of Church and people was strongly anti-Byzantine.

The confused years that followed the further Seljuk invasions had another important result. The Bagratid dynasty ended in 1079 with the murder of King Kahug II. To escape the resultant anarchy a relative of the late king named Roupen moved into the valleys of the Taurus mountains with his followers and from there passed into Cilicia, where the Byzantine governor handed over some fortresses to him. This was the beginning of the kingdom of Lesser Armenia which was to last for three centuries until its fall in 1375.

Enemies of the Muslims and deeply distrustful of the Byzantines, the Roupenians were from the outset supporters of the Crusaders. They enabled them to occupy the Cilician plain rapidly and after the establishment of the principality of Antioch in 1097 Roupen pledged fealty to Bohemond and received his kingdom back as a barony. Further east the Armenians accepted Baldwin of Boulogne as ruler of Edessa and Tall Bashīr. In the next generation they continued to give loyal service in the Frankish armies in northern Syria. In 1124, for instance, the self-sacrifice of an Armenian band rescued Baldwin II and Jocelin from the hands of Kharpūt and they lamented the death of Baldwin, ruler of Marash, bitterly.[3] Despite some deviations the Armenians remained the one ally on which the Frankish princes could rely.

The panoply of the Third Crusade demonstrated that despite Muslim victories the Latin principalities could still count on aid from the west. The lesson was not lost in Lesser Armenia. During the long reign of King Leo II (1185–1219) Latin influence increased. On 6 January 1198, the eastern Christmas Day, the king accepted his crown at the hands of

[1] See S. Runciman, *The Eastern Schism*, p. 41.

[2] See S. Der Nersessian, *Armenia and the Byzantine Empire* (Harvard University Press, 1947), pp. 40–1.

[3] R. C. Smail, *Crusading Warfare* (Cambridge, 1956), pp. 46–8, also gives instances of Armenian disloyalty in this period.

the Archbishop of Mainz, who was also papal legate. Soon after the Catholikos Gregory IV opened relations with Rome. Innocent III could claim justly that a second heretical Church in the East now accepted Latin suzerainty, and through the thirteenth century the Armenians of Lesser Armenia could be regarded as in some sense a Uniate Church. But unlike with the Maronites, dogmatic questions were never fully settled. When in 1248 a papal legate put fifteen questions of dogma including those concerning papal authority, sacramental teaching and Christology to the Armenians, the latter rejected the papal point of view, and twenty years later rejected the Western insistence on the "Double Procession" of the Holy Spirit.

Meantime, the great clashes for supremacy in the Middle East between the Mongols and the Mamlūks were rendering these doctinal disputations irrelevant. The Armenians had seen the danger and striven their hardest to bring about alliance between the Latins and the Mongols. King Haytun of Lesser Armenia himself visited Möngke Khān at Karakoram in 1254, and acted as their ally against the Muslims in the great campaigns of 1255–60.[1] Greater Armenia had also signed a treaty of protection with the Mongols. The Muslim victory however, at 'Ayn Jālūt in 1260, followed by the generation of conquest of the remaining Crusader outposts involved the Armenians in the permanent hostility of the Mamlūks. Lesser Armenia was the first target. Hromkla fell to the Mamlūks in 1292 and the Catholicate was transferred to Sīs the next year. With Cyprus this fragment of the Cilician coast remained the sole outpost of the Crusaders after the fall of Acre. The Armenians maintained a precarious existence until Sīs fell to the Mamlūks from Syria in 1375.

The story of the centuries that followed the ending of Armenian independence is one of the great effort at survival by separated and dispersed communities. During the Crusading era Armenians had established themselves in the towns of Syria and the Lebanon. By the middle of the fourteenth century many had emigrated to Europe, while others moved south-east into Persia.

The rapid advance of the Turks overran many of the isolated Armenian settlements. Under Turkish rule the Armenians constituted a *millet* or "nation" with their Patriarchate at Bursa. Though the majority of those in Europe outside the Ottoman Empire accepted

[1] For this period see J. J. Saunders, *Aspects of the Crusades* (Canterbury University, 1962), pp. 39–49.

Uniate status, the remainder, especially those in Persia grouped around Iṣfahān, remained true to their Monophysite traditions. There was an Armenian Patriarchate in Jerusalem, which maintained contacts with Orthodoxy and the West through the sixteenth and seventeenth centuries. There the situation rested until the Ottoman decline and the Russian advance at the end of the eighteenth century awoke the Turks to the danger of a Christian nation in their midst which was tending once more to regard the successors of the Byzantines as their natural protectors.

Christianity in Egypt and Nubia, 642–1798

The story of the Coptic Church in Egypt under Muslim domination resembles that of the churches in Syria and Palestine. In all three territories the Muslims found Christianity the religion of the people. Alexandria was the hub of a great Monophysite domain, giving intellectual and administrative leadership to the forces opposed to Chalcedon throughout the Greek-speaking provinces of the Empire and beyond. In all these territores the Muslim conquest, if not actually welcomed, was accepted as the will of God, and the intense hatred of the people was reserved for the former Chalcedonian overlords. But by 700 the era of good relations between the Muslim military caste and the Christian subjects had ended, and in Egypt Islam, now revealing itself as a proselytizing creed, had begun to make steady progress at the expense of the Copts. This was aided by the continuous arrival of new bands of Muslim nomads in the Nile valley. In the eighth and ninth centuries Coptic revolts were suppressed and neither the Byzantine counter-offensive of the tenth century nor the Crusades brought the Copts relief. Ayyūbid Egypt was the power-house of Muslim resistance to the Crusades. No Coptic rising coincided with the Christian landings on Egyptian soil in 1219 or 1250. In the fourteenth century the sultans were able to heap further humiliations on the Copts, and gradually suppress the once-prosperous Christian kingdoms of Nubia. In these conditions the decline of the Coptic Church was continuous. In 640 there were perhaps six million Copts and two hundred thousand Chalcedonians. At the end of the eighteenth century Christians could hardly have numbered more than a hundred thousand.[1]

When in 646[2] Egypt finally capitulated to the forces of ʿAmr b.

[1] See M. Jugie, "Monophysite (Eglise copte)", *D.T.C.* vol. x, pt. 2, cols. 2256–7. The figure of 100,000 Christians is that for the year 1820.

[2] For the vexed chronology of the two sieges of Alexandria and final defeat of the Byzantine forces, see A. J. Butler's *The Arab Conquest of Egypt* (Oxford, 1902), pp. 465 f.

al-'Āṣ, the Coptic Christians were given the same status as *ahl al-dhimma* as had been granted to their fellows in Syria. In the final phase of the conquest many of the Copts had helped the Arab forces, and they were treated as favourably as any non-Muslim community in the Arab empire. This was not purely a matter of expediency. A text of al-Kindī, *Kitāb faḍā'il Miṣr* states that Muhammad had said that "the Copts are the noblest of the foreigners, the gentlest of them in deed: the most excellent of them in action and the nearest of them in kinship to the Arabs generally and to the tribe of Quraysh in particular". 'Amr was told that when he went to conquer Egypt he would find among them useful auxiliaries against his enemies and helpers in his religion.[1] In return for a poll-tax of two dinars a head from which monks and clergy were at first exempt, complete freedom of worship was guaranteed, and the property and churches of the Chalcedonians were handed over to them *en bloc*. This is made clear *inter alia* from a dispute in the next century over the property of the Church of St Menas between the Copts and the Chalcedonians, which was judged by the Amir 'Abd al-Malik. The Chalcedonians claimed, "In the beginning the power was in our hands, and the churches with all their property were ours. But the Muslims after their conquest of Egypt handed them over to the Copts". The Copts won the case.[2] Soon, the Patriarch Benjamin who had been in hiding returned to Alexandria for a hero's welcome. "Chalcedonian heretics" were reconverted to Monophysite orthodoxy. The ravages of the rule of Cyrus "the Caucasian" were soon repaired, a great monastery in honour of St Macarius was built, and canons drawn up for it by the Patriarch himself. When he died in 661 after a rule of thirty-nine years, Benjamin was mourned as "the great champion and maintainer of the faith in the Lord Jesus Christ and teacher of the orthodox creed".[3]

For another generation the Copts prospered. The strength of feeling against the Chalcedonians is well illustrated by two writers towards the end of the seventh century. John, Bishop of Nikiou, writing a history of Christianity down to his own day, states, *circa* 670, "And everyone said, the expulsion [of the Romans] and the victory of the Muslims is due to the wickedness of the Emperor Heraclius and his persecution of the orthodox through the patriarch Cyrus. This was the cause of

[1] Abu Saleh, *Churches and Monasteries of Egypt and Some Neighbouring Countries*, tr. B. T. A. Evetts and A. J. Butler (Oxford, 1893), pp. 97–100.

[2] *History of the Patriarchs*, pt. I, ch. XVIII, ed. Evetts, *P.O.* vol. V, p. 123.

[3] *Ibid.* pt. I, ch. XVI, *P.O.* vol. V, p. 3.

the ruin of the Romans and the subjugation of Egypt by the Muslims."[1] Elsewhere he adds, that the reason for the defeat of the Romans was that "they did not walk in the Orthodox Faith but divided the indivisible".[2] Another writer of the time, Theophilus of Alexandria, openly supports the Arabs against the Byzantines, announcing the arrival of "a powerful nation that will have care for the welfare of the churches of Christ".[3] So at this period it seemed. The Patriarch of Alexandria was extending his influence far beyond the bounds of Egypt. He had the right of appointing the Ethiopian patriarch and the metropolitan in the Nubian Christian kingdoms. In 687 Patriarch Isaac acted as intermediary in a quarrel between the Nubians and the Ethiopians.[4] The remnants of the Church in North Africa were depositing their lists of bishops in Alexandria and there were links between the Egyptian Monophysites and Christians in India.[5] Within their own territory of Egypt successive patriarchs after Benjamin had weakened the Chalcedonian opposition, and we read of the conversion of a large number of Melkites in the nomes of Choe and Agharwah about A.D. 680.[6] New bishops were being consecrated without let or hindrance, and new monasteries, like that of Anba Samuel in the south-west Fayyūm built and peopled with 120 monks.[7] The figure of 140 ecclesiastics on the staff of a single church in Alexandria, that of the Angels, also indicates the flourishing condition of the Coptic Church at this time.[8]

The position, however, of the "national Church" was becoming more precarious. It rested on the goodwill felt by the Muslim military aristocracy towards the Copts. So long as the former were engaged in wars of apparently limitless expansion westwards, the services of the Coptic bishops and educated leaders in the administration was necessary, and favour to the Coptic Church was not too high a price to pay. This situation, however, was changing and already during the Patriarchate of John III (677–86) the Amir ʿAbd al-ʿAzīz was beginning to assert his arbitrary powers to the detriment of the Christians. Soon Christians were obliged to possess an identity card under pain of a fine, and in the primitive administrative conditions of the time this led

[1] John of Nikiou, *Chronicle* (ed. R. H. Charles, 121. 2). [2] *Ibid.* 123. 5.

[3] Ed. H. Fleisch, "Une Homélie de Théophile d'Alexandrie", *Revue de l'Orient Chrétien*, vol. XXX (1935–6), pp. 374–5.

[4] *History of the Patriarchs*, pt. I, ch. XVI, *P.O.* vol. V, p. 24.

[5] *Ibid.* ch. XVI, pp. 36–7. [6] *Ibid.* ch. XV, pp. 18–19.

[7] J. Simon, "Le monastère copte de Samuel de Kalamon", *Orientalia christiana periodica* vol. I (1935), pp. 46–52.

[8] *History of the Patriarchs*, pt. I, ch. XVI, p. 26.

to injustice and exactions.[1] John himself incurred the Amir's suspicion through his far-flung contacts with Ethiopia and Nubia, and in a moment of fury the Amir ordered the "destruction of all crosses in the land of Egypt, even the crosses of gold and silver, so that the Christians of the land of Egypt were troubled".[2] He summed up his attitude towards the Copts by inscriptions attributed to him which read "Mahomet is the great Apostle of God and Jesus is also an Apostle of God. But verily God is not begotten and does not beget".[3] His were among the first of the long series of anti-Christian acts by avaricious or fanatical *amīrs* against which neither appeal nor redress was possible.

Moreover, the Church's hold on popular loyalty was not as strong as it seemed.[4] While the Armenians were protected from infiltration by their high mountain barriers which allowed each Christian principality to exist on its own in security, the Nile valley was open to continuous penetration by Islamized Arab tribes coming in from the east who settled down as privileged neighbours among the Coptic villagers. In the time of the Patriarch Michael (744–68) no less than 30,000 tribesmen moved into the mountains in eastern Egypt between Bilbays and al-Qulzum. Moreover, the long tendency towards obedience to a single centralized government favoured the Muslims once they were established and obviously victorious over the Byzantines, while hatred felt by the Chalcedonians and other minority Christian sects such as the Gaianites, Julianists and Eutychians for the Copts often influenced adherents of these to become converts to Islam rather than submit to the Copts. Thus quite early in the Muslim domination John of Nikiou refers to numbers of converts to Islam. "And now," he says, "many of the Egyptians who had been false Christians denied the holy orthodox faith and the life-giving baptism and embraced the religion of the Muslims, the enemies of God."[5] In particular John refers to one, "John the Chalcedonian" of the convent of Sinai, who embraced the faith of Islam, and quitting the monk's habit took up the sword (of the persecutor).[6] Moreover, towards the end of the century the Muslim authorities were tending to satirize the often obscure differences between the various Christian sects, relics of ancient controversies, and to treat all as potential supporters of the Byzantines and enemies of Islam. Despite this there remained more than sixty dioceses in Egypt

[1] B. Spuler, *Die morgenländischen Kirchen*, p. 287. For chicane in connexion with the administration of the pass laws, *circa* 715–20, *History of the Patriarchs*, pt. I, ch. XVII, *P.O.* vol. V, pp. 69–70. [2] *History of the Patriarchs*, *loc. cit.* p. 25. [3] *Ibid.*

[4] Spuler, *op. cit.* pp. 286–8. [5] John of Nikiou, *Chronicle*, 121. 10. [6] *Ibid.* 121. 11.

at the end of the seventh century, as well as a considerable number of sectarian bishoprics.[1]

The stage was set for the repression of Christianity that characterized the first half of the eighth century, and did far more harm to the Copts than the corresponding measures did to the churches in Syria. In about 706 the Amir 'Abd al-'Azīz appointed his son al-Aṣbagh as his deputy (*wālī*). Both are described as fanatical enemies of the Church, and along with the progressive Arabizing of the administration, they with their officials were responsible for measures designed to humiliate and impoverish the Christians. Taxes were increased, churches and monasteries were forbidden to carry on charitable work, churches were pillaged, and artificial dissension contrived by the Amir among the Christians.[2] Monks too were now forced to pay the poll-tax. Later they were ordered to be branded with the sign of a ring.[3] Churches were forbidden to display Christian symbols and Christians were supposed to have a lion tattooed on their hand. There was a serious effort to seduce prominent laymen from their religious allegiance. We hear of the more or less forced conversion of Peter, Governor of Upper Egypt, and the son of Theophanes, Governor of Mareotis, "and a body of priests and laymen not to be numbered on account of their multitude".[4] These measures continued at intervals as long as the Umayyad dynasty lasted. Under the Amir 'Abd al-Malik b. Marwān (*circa* 745) Bishop Wasim of Jīza (Giza) declared that the number of converts to Islam in the Miṣr (Cairo) district alone numbered 24,000.[5] In this same period the Patriarch Michael had to be rescued from imprisonment and humiliation by an invasion in force of Egypt by the powerful king of Nubia, Cyriacus. Michael then acted successfully as intermediary between the Nubians and the Amir and the persecution was halted.[6]

In Cyrenaica, too, which may have been largely Monophysite and where the Arab conquest had met with little resistance, Islam had won a complete victory. The documentation is as yet extremely slight but it would seem likely that here, as in North Africa, the Berber tribes converted from paganism to Islam direct, played a part in the transfer of allegiances. It is clear that the downfall of Christianity was relatively swift. Cyrenaican Christians shared the temporary relief from taxes

[1] *History of the Patriarchs*, pt. I, ch. XVI, *P.O.* vol. V, p. 34.
[2] *Ibid.* pp. 66–8. These acts seem to have taken place about 715.
[3] *Ibid.* pp. 51 and 68.
[4] *Ibid.* p. 52.
[5] *Ibid.* p. 117.
[6] *Ibid.* pp. 164–6.

secured by the Copts under the Patriarch Michael *circa* 750,[1] but by this time the churches in Apollonia may have already been destroyed, and excavations at Ra's Hilāl near Darna show that the village church there built in the sixth century had been abandoned and was being occupied by Muslims at this period.[2] In the ninth century Muslim houses were built across the nave of the principal church at Cyrene.[3] How much longer the monasteries and remote churches in al-Jabal al-Akhḍar survived is still a matter for conjecture. A great deal of research remains to be done.

During the remainder of the eighth and in the ninth centuries the sparse Coptic records preserved in the *History of the Patriarchs* leave the impression of the Church continuously more absorbed in its internal affairs and of a Christian population progressively more demoralized by extortion. Some Copts died as martyrs, but the names of only fifty such "new martyrs" (i.e. post-Diocletian) are recorded in the Coptic *Synaxarium*. Between 725 and 773 there were six Coptic risings; all failed. The same fate overtook the fierce revolt against over-taxation of the Christian tribe of Bashmurites in 829–30, in which both the Patriarchs of Alexandria and Antioch united in vain efforts to restore peace.[4] As a reading of the *History of the Patriarchs* shows, there was no real will to resist, only a passive acceptance of the inscrutable decrees of God.[5]

In this period, to the hostility of the Muslims was added dissension among the Christians themselves. Memories of old controversies dating to Byzantine times were far from stilled. Moreover, Muslims now seem to have formed the majority in the Delta and with this development, Arabic began to replace Coptic as the language of the ordinary people.[6] Most of the judges and administrators were now Arabic-speaking and on occasions the Coptic dignitaries had to speak to them through interpreters.[7] The Coptic Church was beginning to stand outside the main stream of Egyptian life.

[1] *History of the Patriarchs*, pt. I, ch. XVIII, p. 197.

[2] See R. M. Harrison, "A Sixth Century Church at Ras-al-Hilal in Cyrenaica", *Papers of the British School at Rome*, vol. XXXII (1964), pp. 15 and 19–20.

[3] Information from R. G. Goodchild, late Director of Antiquities in Cyrenaica who will be publishing this site.

[4] *History of the Patriarchs*, pt. I, ch. XX, *P.O.* vol. X, pp. 488–96. The futility of the protest against extortion made by the highest Christian authorities in Syria and Egypt shows how little the Muslims were caring for Christian susceptibilities.

[5] See O. F. A. Meinardus, "The Attitudes of the Orthodox Copts towards the Islamic State from the 7th to the 12th Century", *Ostkirchliche Studien*, vol. XIII (1964), pp. 153–70.

[6] B. Spuler, *op. cit.* p. 289. The last purely Greek papyrus is dated 780/1.

[7] *History of the Patriarchs*, pt. I, ch. XX, *P.O.* vol. X, p. 525.

As in Syria, the middle of the ninth century was a period of severe pressure for the Christians, and looking back on the evidence it would seem that the persecution of this period marked a decisive stage in progressive Muslim predominance. "Of what is the Church of God guilty that He shall bring down upon it this great trial?"[1] lamented the Patriarch Schenute I (859–80). He himself found comfort in the traditional Jewish theory of martyrdom and persecution as atonement for sin. All thought of rebellion against the tyrannical power of the Muslim rulers had been given up. Many Christians, however, had by now lost hope in the age-long traditions of the liturgy and ascetic life that were still current at this time and were ready to throw in their lot with their conquerors. The humiliation of the special clothes they were obliged to wear, and the wooden gargoyles they were ordered to put up outside their doors, was too great. Thus in the reign of Caliph al-Mutawakkil (847–61) we are told of numerous Christians who "denied the Lord Jesus Christ. Some denied on account of the worldly possessions which they loved, and others on account of the poverty which they suffered".[2] There were local schisms and cynicism concerning the value of following the traditions of Cyril. Even the great monasteries, the core of the Coptic Church, were caught up increasingly in a struggle for survival. The *History of the Patriarchs* records disastrous raids by the bedouin on the monasteries of Scete, *circa* 871.[3] The famous Dayr al-Suryān was among the houses sacked. From now on the monasteries tended to become fortresses,[4] safeguarding indeed their inmates but also creating a barrier between themselves and the ordinary people.

The outlook for the Coptic Church at the end of the ninth century was indeed dark. Its intellectual life was declining, as was its power to retain its adherents. There was little originality in its secular and religious literature. The moulds were still those of the heroic age of the fourth and fifth centuries, ever more elaborate *Lives* of Antony and of Pachomius, and apocryphal stories of the world of angels. Contact with actuality had been lost. Nonetheless events in the tenth century secured for the Copts welcome if temporary relief. The inter-

[1] *Ibid.* (ed. al-Masih and colleagues, Cairo, 1943), vol. II, pt. I, p. 37.

[2] *Ibid.* p. 6 and cf. *ibid.* pp. 8–9, and p. 39.

[3] See H. G. Evelyn White, *The Monasteries of the Wadi Natrun*, vol. III (New York, 1933), pp. 178 ff., 236 ff. and *History of the Patriarchs*, vol. II, pt. I, p. 45.

[4] H. Torp, "Murs d'Enceinte des monastères coptes primitifs et couvents-fortresses", *Mélanges de l'Ecole Française à Rome*, vol. LXXVI (1964), pp. 174 ff.

necine conflicts between rival claimants to the caliphate weakened the authority of the Egyptian Amir. Persecution became more sporadic, until in 969 the displacement of the Ikshīdids by the North African Fāṭimids opened up a period of greater mutual understanding between adherents of the two faiths. With one break marked by the savage, irrational persecution of Caliph al-Ḥākim between 1009 and 1017, in which great damage was done to the Copts and no less than 3,000 of their churches said to have been destroyed,[1] there was an era of toleration lasting until 1171. Then, the Fāṭimids were replaced by the more militantly anti-Christian Ayyūbid sultans.

Under the Ikshīdids and Fāṭimids we read of Muslim notables visiting the monasteries of Egypt and Muslim poets romanticizing them.[2] The ordered life of the monks and the peace of their surroundings awoke the wonder of Abu 'l-Faraj al-Iṣfahānī (d. 967) and al-Shābushtī in the tenth century, and not perhaps surprisingly, for this epoch marked the last renaissance of Coptic literature and arts. The paintings in the Church of al-'Adhrā' in Dayr al-Suryān date to this epoch.[3] Bohairic tends to supersede the traditional Sahidic as the ecclesiastical medium, but the monasteries produced magnificent illuminated manuscripts of the Gospels and patristic texts in both dialects.[4] In the same period Coptic writers also were active. Severus b. al-Muqaffa' who wrote a "History of the Councils" upholding the repute of Dioscorus and refuting the Melkite *History* of Sa'īd b. al-Baṭrīq is an example. Even so, these and other Coptic authors were already using Arabic as their medium. Despite the emergence of a Bohairic literature Coptic as the spoken language of the Egyptian people was doomed,[5] and with it any possibility of the Coptic Church remaining a serious rival to Islam.

In Upper Egypt, however, the middle of the tenth century brought about temporary union with an established Christian population. Just as the weakness and confusion of the affairs of the caliphate were facilitating the Byzantine reconquest of northern Syria, so similar disorder and consequent decline of Muslim military power in Egypt

[1] *History of the Patriarchs*, vol. II, pt. II, pp. 188 ff.

[2] Examples cited from R. R. Farag, *Sociological and Moral Studies in the Field of Coptic Monasticism* (Leiden, 1964), pp. 43–5.

[3] Farag, *op. cit.* p. 57.

[4] W. H. Worrell, *A Short History of the Copts* (Ann Arbor, 1945), pp. 65–7. The vellum MSS in Sahidic produced at the White Monastery are a notable example.

[5] For instance, the *Panegyric of Abu Samuel* written by a monk of the monastery of Kalamon in the tenth century, contains an eloquent plea for the retention of the Coptic language and customs, but this has survived only in Arabic translation. See J. Simon, "Le Monastère Copte de Samuel de Kalamon", *Orientalia Christiana Periodica*, vol. I (1935), pp. 46–52.

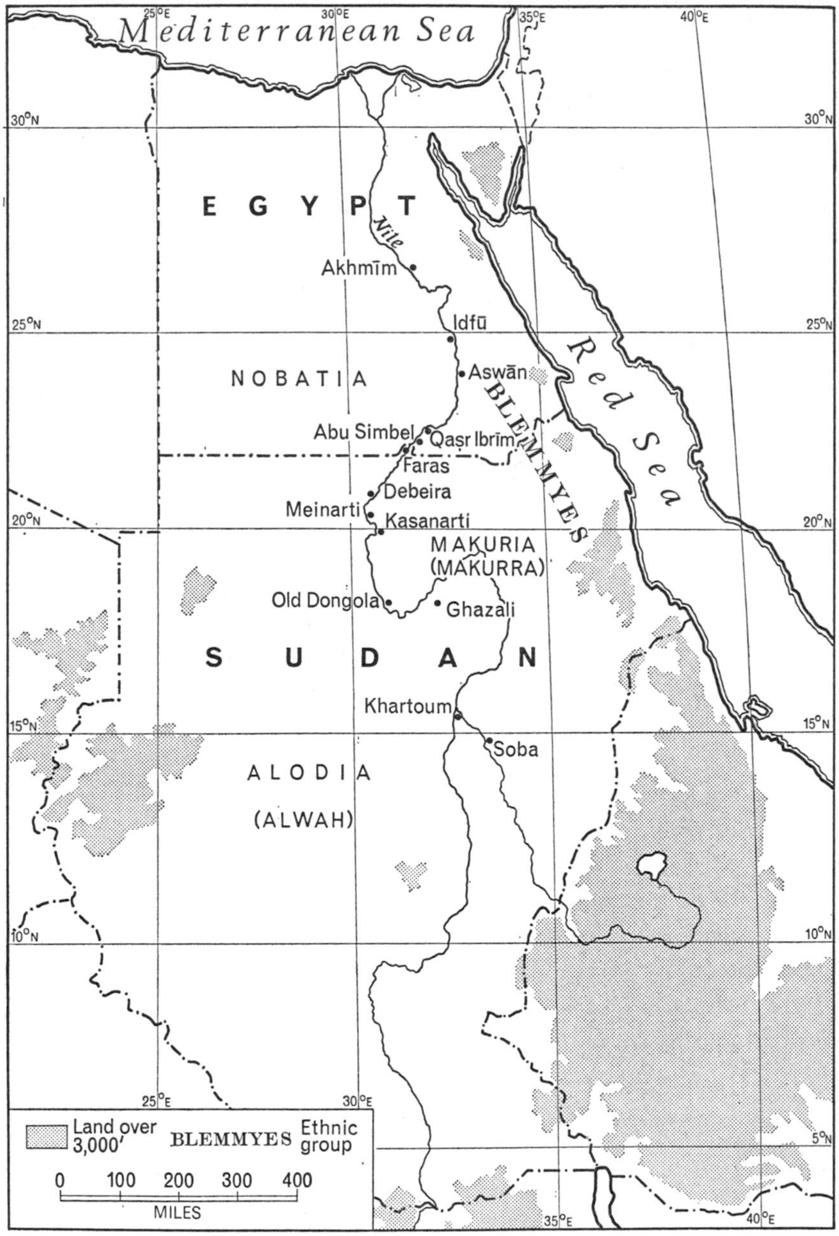
Mediterranean Sea
25°E
30°E
35°E
40°E
30°N
25°N
20°N
15°N
10°N
5°N
E G Y P T
Nile
Akhmīm
Idfū
N O B A T I A
Aswān
Red Sea
BLEMMYES
Abu Simbel
Qaṣr Ibrīm
Faras
Debeira
Meinarti
Kasanarti
MAKURIA
(MAKURRA)
Old Dongola
Ghazali
S U D A N
Khartoum
Soba
A L O D I A
(ALWAH)
Land over 3,000′
BLEMMYES Ethnic group
0 100 200 300 400
MILES

Nubia.

laid the southern frontier open to a massive attack from Christian Nubia. By 967 Akhmīm had been reached and for some years the Nubians continued to control the country as far north as Idfū. A discovery of Nubian manuscripts in the monastery of St Mercurios near there suggests that this had become a centre of Nubian culture.[1]

It is now time to discuss developments in these Nubian Christian kingdoms and give a brief survey of their religious history. The story of the great effort made by the Nubian people down to the fourteenth century and even later to preserve their heritage from destruction at the hands of the Mamlūks can now be pieced together more clearly, thanks to the results of the salvage work performed by archaeological teams, brought together by UNESCO to save what could be saved of the Nubian areas of settlement before these were drowned by the waters of Lake Nāṣir.

Three Nubian kingdoms seem to have arisen out of the ruins of Meroitic power towards the end of the third century A.D.[2] Piecing together the evidence of John of Ephesus with the results of excavations, it would appear that there was a northern kingdom (Nobatia) extending down the west bank of the Nile from the Egyptian frontier at Aswān as far as the Third Cataract, and peopled by Nobatae. Its capital was at Faras (Pachoras). Further south lay the kingdom of Makuria stretching as far as a site known to Arab writers as al-Abwāb ("the doors"), perhaps near Kabushia, and whose capital was at Old Dongola. Beyond this was Alwah whose capital, Soba, was near Khartoum. In the vast, waterless tracts east of the Nile were the Blemmyes, one of whose principal strongholds was the cliff-fort of Qaṣr Ibrīm (Primis).

The evangelization of the Nubians was the work of Justinian and Theodora, utilizing a favourable political situation which arose in the middle of the sixth century. In 453 the Roman general Maximinus had defeated the Nobatae and Blemmyes and forced them to sue for peace. One condition, however, had been granted, namely the right of these two tribes to visit the temple of Isis at Philae just below Aswān, and borrow the statue of the goddess for use in their own territories. The treaty was for 100 years and was kept remarkably well. The southern

[1] F. Ll. Griffith, "The Nubian Texts of the Christian Period", *Abhandlungen der kgl. preuss. Akad. der Wissenschaften* (1913), pp. 4 ff. One was accompanied by a Coptic MS dated to A.D. 985.

[2] A useful account of the Christianization of Nubia is given by P. L. Shinnie, *Medieval Nubia* (Sudan Antiquities Service, Khartoum, 1954), pp. 2–4.

borders of Egypt enjoyed a long period of quiet, and then the Byzantines were the aggressors. In 541, alleging the expiry of the treaty, Justinian sent his general, Narses, to destroy the temple of Isis and end the cult. He also sent an Orthodox mission to the Nobatae, but at the same moment, Theodora dispatched her confidant, the presbyter Julian, to convert them to the Monophysite cause, and with the support of the Coptic bishop of Philae, Theodore, he was the more successful. In 543 the king of the Nobatae was converted, and Theodore remained at his court.

The next step seems to have been a successful war against the Blemmyes. An inscription dating to about 560 in rustic Greek cut on the walls of a temple to Augustus at Kalabscha proclaims how Silko king of the Nobatae defeated the Blemmyes thanks to the aid of the Christian God, and expelled them from the Nile valley between Shallāl (Telelis) and Ibrīm (Primis). Silko claimed to be "king of the Nobatae and all the Ethiopians", though how far south his rule extended is not known.[1] The conversion of the Blemmyes seems to have followed soon after and Ibrīm was to become a great Christian centre. Meantime, in 569 the kingdom of Makuria was converted by Justinian's emissaries to Orthodox Christianity. The southern kingdom of Alwah however was destined to follow Nobatia into Monophysitism. The presbyter Longinus, agent of the Coptic (Monophysite) Patriarch Theodosius, visited Nobatia in 569, and after returning to Alexandria was commissioned with the more difficult task of winning Alwah for the Coptic faith. With the aid of the Blemmyes he evaded traps set for him by the ruler of Makuria and by 580 Alwah also was a Christian kingdom.[2] The whole of the Nile valley from the Delta to Lake Tana was now Christian, and predominantly Monophysite.

Muslim raids between 641 and 652 did nothing to shake the Nubians from their religious allegiance, although the Muslim armies reached Old Dongola and forced the Nubians into a treaty relationship with them. Indeed, the threat from the north seems to have consolidated the spirit of Nubian independence. Sometime between 650 and 710 Nobatia and Makuria came together to form one kingdom perhaps under king Mercurius (*circa* 700), and Monophysitism became the religion of the whole territory. Mercurius is referred to as "the new

[1] See W. B. Emery, *Egypt in Nubia* (London, 1965), p. 239.

[2] The story is told in John of Ephesus, *Historia Ecclesiastica* (ed. E. W. Brooks, *Scriptores Syri*, 2 and 3), IV, ch. vii ff. (pp. 138–41).

Constantine" in the *History of the Patriarchs*[1] and it is possible that the introduction of a Nubian Era about this time had a connexion with the reconstitution of Church and State on the basis of Monophysitism.[2] This Mercurius may be he who is named "famous and great" on the Aswān graffito referring to the fourteenth-century Nubian king, Kudanbes.[3] From now on Egypt had a comparatively strong Christian kingdom on her southern border. The effect of this was shown, as we have seen, in 745 when King Cyriacus invaded Egypt in strength and reached Cairo, forcing the Amir to release the Coptic patriarch together with a large number of Nubians he was holding as slaves.

By now the Nubian kingdom had entered on a long period of relative prosperity. The initiator of this era may indeed have been King Mercurius. It would seem that he was the monarch under whom a monastery and cathedral church at Faras was dedicated by Bishop Paulos in 707.[4] The ruins of the city, covering an area of some five square miles, testify to the existence of urban life amid a teeming Nubian population, and the hundred and fifty or so ruins of churches and monasteries so far identified in Egyptian and Sudanese Nubia, proclaim the strength of their religion. Excavations have now brought to light something of the magnificent achievement of this civilization. The frescoes of the cathedral at Faras can be dated to well-defined phases from the early ninth century (the "violet" period of the frescoes) to the eleventh century for the representations of some of the more vivid polychrome scenes taken from the Bible.[5] Further north, at Qaṣr Ibrīm, the stone-built church was constructed with a care and building-technique the equal, if not superior, to anything prevailing in western Europe until the twelfth century.[6] Not unreasonably it was described by the traveller Abū Ṣāliḥ "the Armenian" early in the thirteenth

[1] *History of the Patriarchs*, pt. I, ch. XVIII, p. 140. See also U. Monneret de Villard, *Storia della Nubia cristiana* (Rome, 1934), pp. 80 and 159.

[2] F. Ll. Griffith, *Abhandlungen*, pp. 61–2.

[3] F. Ll. Griffith, "Christian Documents from Nubia", *Proceedings of the British Academy* (1928), pp. 18–30.

[4] K. Michalowski, "Polish Excavations at Faras, 1962–63", *Kush*, vol. XII (1964), pp. 196–200.

[5] K. Michalowski, "Polish Excavations at Faras, Second Season, 1961–62", *Kush*, vol. XI (1963), pp. 250 ff. The excavators leave a liberal time-bracket for the "Biblical" murals, of "end of the tenth to twelfth centuries", *ibid.* p. 255.

[6] Preliminary reports have been published by Rev. Professor J. M. Plumley in the *Illustrated London News* of 11 July 1964, Archaeological Section 2191, and the *Journal of Egyptian Archaeology*, vol. L (1964), pp. 3–5, and by the present author who was Associate-Director with Professor Plumley on the 1963–64 Egypt Exploration Society Expedition, in the *Acta* of the 7th International Congress for Christian Archaeology, Bonn, 1967.

century in glowing terms as "large and beautiful, finely planned and named after Our Lady".[1] Primis too was a big centre of population, and if the figure of 700,000 inhabitants enslaved by Shams al-Dawla in 1173 was a gross exaggeration, there is evidence of a thickly occupied site spilling over on to the flatlands below the fort bordering the Nile. The pottery in ordinary use was also decorated with delicate designs derived from both Coptic and Meroitic traditions and shows the prevalence of high standards of taste and craftsmanship at this period.

Nubia remained culturally a Byzantine outpost.[2] It has been observed how the frescoes of Faras in the formal and serene cast of their features, the proportions and arrangements of the figures, the legends in Greek, and the range of colour, reflect a tradition inherited directly from Byzantium rather than from Coptic Egypt.[3] The churches themselves, usually small buildings, are of the same basilica type surmounted by a cupola common in the rest of the Byzantine world. The same may be said also of the liturgical manuscripts recovered from the silt above the floor of the church at Qaṣr Ibrīm. Most were in Nubian or Greek.[4] Coptic seems to have been confined largely to biblical and Patristic texts. The presence of Nubian liturgies may reflect a definite policy, for such state documents as have been recovered, including the nine leather scrolls found by the present writer in a sealed pot in the debris of a Christian house at Qaṣr Ibrīm are in Nubian. Greek, however, was occasionally used. Also, the high-sounding titles granted to officials at the Court of the Nubian kings, such as *eparchus* or *primicerius* or *protodomesticus*, all point to a powerful and long-continued fidelity to a Byzantine cultural tradition.[5]

In religion, however, the link was with Coptic Egypt, though there may also have been some ties with the surviving Christians of Ḥijāz.[6] The absence of a Chalcedonian Patriarch in Alexandria from 641–743 effectively prevented any revival of Orthodoxy. The bias of religious life was monastic, though the great cathedral at Qaṣr Ibrīm does not seem, like Faras, to have been immediately associated with monastic buildings. The monasteries, however, that clustered round the churches at Faras, Ghazali and Debeira were vast, complex buildings which

[1] Abu Saleh (tr. Evetts and Butler), pp. 266–7.

[2] Note Abū Ṣāliḥ's comments on the Nubian bishops saying prayers "in Greek" (ed. Evetts and Butler, p. 272).

[3] K. Michalowski, "Polish Excavations at Faras, 1961", *Kush*, vol. x (1962), pp. 230–1.

[4] To be published by Professor Plumley and the present writer.

[5] Noted by F. Ll. Griffith, *Christian Documents*, p. 17.

[6] See P. L. Shinnie and H. N. Chittick, "Ghazali—a Monastery in the Northern Sudan", *Sudan Antiquities Service*, Occasional Papers, No. 5 (Khartoum, 1961), p. 30.

must have housed hundreds of monks. Those at Debeira West comprised no less than eighty-six identifiable rooms.[1] Out in the desert, rock shelters which had once housed prehistoric man, now provided an abode for solitaries.[2] The Nubians drew inspiration, as did the Copts, from the martyrs of the era of Diocletian, by reference to whom Nubian dates were fixed. Epitaphs found at Qaṣr Ibrīm and Faras were dated by this era, as were those found in the large Nubian cemetery of Salimya. Here, the Saracen era was sometimes added also. In the ninth and following centuries, this religion was not static and on the defensive. Muslim settlers have left their trace in Faras but seem to have been absorbed, and the Muslim tribes and merchants prospecting for gold near the Red Sea coast were not as yet a serious menace. In contrast, Nubian missionaries worked for the evangelization of the western Sudan. Thus, a tenth-century Persian geographer has this to say about Christian monasteries in the far west. "Tari (Tahi?), a small province lying in the desert between the limits (territory) of Nubia and the Sudan: in it lies two remote (?) monasteries belonging to the Christians.... It is reported that in them...live 12,000 monks...and whenever one of them disappears...from Nubia, one of the Christians of Upper Egypt goes there."[3] Independent archaeological evidence suggests the existence of Christian communities at ʻAyn Faraḥ in northern Darfur in the twelfth and early thirteenth centuries.[4]

The end of the "classical age" of Nubian Christianity may be connected directly with the change of dynasty in Egypt. For reasons which are obscure war seems to have broken out almost directly after the fall of the Fāṭimids in 1171. At first the Nubians were successful, capturing Aswān and moving farther north, but in 1173 Saladin counter-attacked, and showed the military skill which he was to demonstrate a decade later against the Crusaders. An expedition led by his brother Shams al-Dawla took and pillaged Qaṣr Ibrīm. Abū Ṣāliḥ tells of the booty gained there, the destruction of pigs and the conversion of the church into a mosque. For two years the town was occupied by a Muslim garrison.

[1] P. L. Shinnie, "The University of Ghana excavations at Debeira West", *Kush*, vol. XI (1963), pp. 257–63.

[2] Examples were explored by Professor Plumley in the desert west of Mas-Mas and west of Abu Simbel, 1964.

[3] Cited from A. J. Arkell's notes on "The Influence of Christian Nubia in the Chad area between 800–1200", *Kush*, vol. XI (1963), pp. 315–21; at p. 320.

[4] H. N. Chittick, "The Last Christian Stronghold in the Sudan", *Kush*, vol. XI (1963), pp. 271–2.

Up to the time of the Egypt Exploration Society's excavations there in 1963–64, this was believed to mark practically the end of Christianity in this part of northern Nubia. This now needs modification. At Faras, the last dated burial, that of Bishop Tāmir, is 1181, but the cathedral seems to have been used for some time longer.[1] Two other sites, Kasanarti and Meinarti, south of Faras, indicate a long period of decline in which monastery buildings gradually decayed and fell out of use.[2] At Meinarti, significantly enough, the last Christian remains are those of a block-house. In the thirteenth century, however, the Nubians were still able to hold their own. In 1272 King David attacked the Muslims at 'Aydhab on the Red Sea, but this was the last offensive action undertaken by the Nubian Kingdom. At the turn of the next century dynastic quarrels broke out which the Muslims took advantage of. In 1323 or 1324 the last Christian king of Dongola, Kerenbes (Kudanbes), was defeated by his Muslim rival Kanz al-Dawla and the independence of the northern Christian kingdom of Nubia died with him.

There is some difficulty in interpreting the next piece of evidence. In 1928 Griffith published a long graffito in debased Greek found in the monastery of St Simeon at Aswān commemorating a long line of illustrious rulers of Nubia and ending with King Kuda[nbes] "a king worthy of three hundred years (reign)". The inscription is dated to 1322, and Griffith believed that "Kudanbes was the last Christian king and that his graffito was a last flicker of the expiring state religion of northern Nubia".[3] The tone of the graffito carried no indication of despair, and the excavations at Qaṣr Ibrīm have now established beyond possibility of doubt that Christianity remained a powerful force in northern Nubia for another three quarters of a century. Below the arch of the west crypt of the church at Qaṣr Ibrīm was found the body of a bishop, hunched up as he lay in the dust, but dressed in full episcopal regalia. Concealed in his clothing were two great paper scrolls recording in Bohairic and Arabic respectively that he, Timotheos, had been consecrated by the Patriarch Gabriel IV at Old Cairo, bishop of Libye (Primis?) and Pachoras (Faras).[4] The date of the

[1] From the Rivergate Church, see F. Ll. Griffith, *Liverpool Annals of Archaeology and Anthropology*, vol. XIII, p. 85, pl. LXIII.

[2] W. Y. Adams, "Sudan Antiquities Service Excavations in Nubia: Fourth Season, 1962–63", *Kush*, vol. XII (1964), pp. 218 ff.

[3] F. Ll. Griffith, *art. cit.* p. 28.

[4] These splendid scrolls are in course of study and publication by Professor Plumley, their finder.

enthronement was 1372. The church and see of Primis were still extant at this period and to judge from the remains of fine Greek and Old Nubian liturgical documents that littered the silt which formed above the floor of the church after its abandonment, it remained a cultural centre as well.

Islam however was gaining ground. Muḥammad had conquered Michael, and the mixed marriages between Nubians and the increasing incursions of the now victorious Arab tribesmen favoured the spread of Islam. Archaeologists have found Islamic graffiti and other evidence of Muslim occupation in the last phases of the occupation of Debeira West,[1] and Meinarti[2] both one-time Nubian monastic centres. These may betoken the change of religious allegiance. At the moment nothing Christian can be dated with certainty in the northern kingdoms of Nubia later than 1400.[3]

We know little about events in the southern kingdom of Alwah. Abū Ṣāliḥ describes its inhabitants as Jacobite Christians, and Alwah itself as having a large and spacious church.[4] There were "four more hundred churches in the kingdom", he adds. Excavations on the site of Soba in 1950–51 confirm the size, Christian character and general well-being of the town. It seems, too, that it survived for a century or more after the northern Nubian kingdom had fallen. Local tradition and the Funj Chronicle both state that Soba fell as a result of an alliance between ʿAmāra Dūnqas, king of the Muslim Funj, and the local Arab leader ʿAbdallāh Jammāʿ.[5] The date may be as late as 1500, for the reports of the Portuguese missionary in Ethiopia, Alvarez, in 1524, of a Christian kingdom somewhere to the north in the last stages of decline can hardly refer to anywhere else but Soba.[6]

[1] P. L. Shinnie, "The University of Ghana Excavations at Debeira West", *Kush*, vol. XI (1963), p. 262.

[2] W. Y. Adams, *art. cit. Kush*, vol. XII, especially his conclusions, pp. 240–1.

[3] The dating of the scrolls found in the pot discovered in the ruins of the house above the podium at Ibrīm is uncertain. The pot itself is of a type which could date to the middle of the fourteenth century, but the mention on one of the scrolls of a King Joel recalls the Joel recorded on the Kudanbes incription at Aswān, and might therefore be earlier than 1320.

[4] *Churches and Monasteries of Egypt* (tr. Evetts, p. 263). The Funj Chronicle adds the details that the books of the people of Alwah were in Greek and that they had a bishop appointed by the prelate of Alexandria like the Nubians before them.

[5] P. L. Shinnie, "Excavations at Soba", *Sudan Antiquities Service, Occasional Papers*, no. 3 (Khartoum, 1955), p. 14, and H. N. Chittick, "The Last Christian Stronghold in the Sudan", *Kush*, vol. XI (1963), pp. 264.

[6] Edited by C. F. Beckingham and G. W. B. Huntingford under the title of *Prester John of the Indies* (Hakluyt Society Publications, 2nd ser., vol. CXV, p. 129).

Nubian Christianity lasted just long enough to save Ethiopia from a similar destruction by Islam. It may have added substance to the legend circulating in the courts of Western Europe during the fifteenth century of the Christian kingdom of Prester John transferred from Asia to the Nile Valley. Early in the fifteenth century the traveller, Lannoy, refers to the ban on Christians travelling down the Nile or the Red Sea to India for fear that they might stir up Prester John against the Muslims.[1] From 1415 onwards the Portuguese were beginning to feel their way south of Sabta (Ceuta) down the African coast searching for a "western Nile" which would bring them to their Christian allies. Western interest came too late to save Soba but contributed to salvage what remained of Coptic Christianity.

For the Copts the age of the Crusaders were not years of great activity. In particular, there seems to have been no renaissance of spiritual life and no return to social and political influence. This was not perhaps accidental. In the two generations that preceded the arrival of the Franks the Coptic Patriarchs and the Fāṭimid Amirs seem to have been on the best of terms. The Copts accepted their situation and were prepared to co-operate with their Muslim masters.[2] Ibn al-Muqaffa', bishop of al-Asmunin, the continuator of the *History of the the Patriarchs* to 1102, remarks that the fall of Jerusalem merely prevented the Monophysite Christians making their pilgrimage "on account of what was known of the Franks' hatred" of them.[3] Even so, the continued success of the Crusaders down to 1140 aroused Muslim suspicions of the loyalty of the Copts. There were isolated acts of persecution, such as when the Church of St Michael on the Island of Cairo was destroyed *circa* 1130. The Copts, however, did not rise in support of the Latin Christians. There is no evidence that they actively supported Amaury when the latter invaded Egypt in the 1160s to aid the Fāṭimids. Their final chance of deliverance by the West in 1219 when John of Brienne captured Dimyāṭ (Damietta) and the Sultan al-Kāmil offered terms, passed them by. All they gained from the Crusades were heavier taxes and fresh disabilities.[4] In addition, owing to their insistence on appointing their own metropolitan in Jerusalem, instead of accepting the Jacobite metropolitan, relations with the Syrians deteriorated.

[1] Cited from A. S. Atiya, *The Crusade in the Later Middle Ages*, p. 196.
[2] O. F. A. Meinardus, *op. cit.* p. 169.
[3] *History of the Patriarchs*, vol. II, pt. III, p. 399 of translation.
[4] S. Runciman, *History of the Crusades*, vol. III, p. 170.

All this time, too, the cultural life of the Church was failing. Corruption and simony were endemic; the latter the evil result of Muslim extortion which compelled the Coptic Church to increase its funds by this means.[1] Monasteries and even centres of pilgrimage like the shrine of St Mena[2] near Cairo were declining. The leadership itself no longer required a high standard of learning. In 1145, for instance, the 71st Patriarch, Michael V, was a monk and completely illiterate.[3] Coptic was now rapidly giving way to Arabic. Even the teachings of St Anthony were being translated into that language. The last known Coptic document which is not a formal religious exercise is a poem called the *Triadon* or Triangle, written in the fourteenth century by a monk in Upper Egypt taking up the cause of the Coptic language:

> Come brethren, hearken to this sweet tongue,
> Let us savour its simple expression
> I wish you could see
> The worth of our Coptic language.[4]

In vain. Even then the author regards his ability to write Coptic as a miracle. In the seventeenth century even in Upper Egypt the language was practically dead.

The fourteenth century brought the final blows. Rid of the Crusaders and increasingly victorious over both Mongols and Armenians the Mamlūk sultans had little cause to spare the Christians in their midst. In the years following 1321 and 1354 respectively there were severe persecutions. Copts were expelled from public offices and from the employ of Muslim dignitaries. The Sultan forbade the Copts to ride horses or mules, and when riding donkeys they must ride backwards. A bell had to be rung if a Copt entered a public bath-house, and once again a special, and humiliating, garb was forced on them. These measures resulted in the destruction of churches and widespread lapses to Islam, and even in Upper Egypt the Muslims now became preponderant.[5] At the same time the Coptic monasteries on the edge of the deserts were coming under pressure from the bedouin tribes. Their attacks and the onset of plagues thinned down the numbers of monks, despite efforts like that of the Patriarch Benjamin (1327–40) to restore the monasteries.[6] The settlements in the Wādi 'l-Naṭrūn became

[1] B. Spuler, *op. cit.* pp. 292–3.
[2] O. F. A. Meinardus, *Monks and Monasteries of the Egyptian Deserts* (Cairo, 1961), p. 363.
[3] M. Jugie, "Monophysite (Eglise Copte)", *D.T.C.* vol. x, pt. 2, p. 2256.
[4] R. R. Farag, *Sociological and Moral Studies in the Field of Coptic Monasticism*, p. 135.
[5] W. H. Worrell, *A Short Account of the Copts*, pp. 47–8.
[6] Farag, *op. cit.* p. 53.

almost deserted, as did even the great fortified houses such as St Simeon's, at Aswān. Though travellers[1] in the early fifteenth century reported meeting with considerable scattered groups of Christians, it was also clear that by now they were a depressed and demoralized community, perhaps only about one-fifteenth of the population. The power of the Mamlūks, embracing both Egypt and Syria in one centralized government, had won the day.

The meeting of the Council of Florence-Ferrara 1437–42 had some importance for the Copts as it did for other Christians in the Middle East, though the Latins were less successful in their effort to bring about Unity than they were in Syria and among the Armenians. In 1440 the Coptic Patriarch John (1428–52) appointed Abbot Andrew to go to Rome and attend Eugenius' Council. His speech in Arabic hailed the Pope as "God on earth, and his vicar on earth and successor of Peter, the father, head and teacher of the universal Church". By February 1442 the Coptic delegates were sufficiently instructed to be ready to sign a Bull of Unity, *Cantate Domino*, in which "the heresies of Dioscorus were condemned" and the Councils legitimately convened and confirmed by the authority of the Roman Pontiff were accepted.[2]

There, however, the matter ended. The Bull was quietly forgotten. A tiny Uniate community established itself, but had no appreciable influence, until in 1741 Rome attempted to organize a hierarchy round the person of Athanasius, Patriarch of Jerusalem, who at this period in his life had accepted Uniate status. The Copts, though incapable of making head against Islam, were determined not to become satellites of the Latins.

So matters rested until the modern period. The Copts remained on the outer periphery of Christendom. The West was conscious of their existence, but that was all. The rule of the Turks from 1517 was a long period of stagnation. The *millet* system allowed the Copts to look after their own affairs in relative peace. The patriarchs in the sixteenth and seventeenth centuries often ruled for very long periods but in complete obscurity. A few western travellers report the existence of small communities of monks clinging to their vocation in the ancient monasteries. In 1712, for instance, Père Sicard found three or four monks surviving

[1] Ghillebert de Lannoy, "Item, est à sçavoir qu'en tout le pais d'Egipte, en bonnes villes ou aux champs, il y a grant quantité de Cristiens desquelz fay peu de mencion pour ce que peu de prouffit pourroient faire aux Cristiens servans à la matière". Cited from Atiya, *op. cit.* p. 195, n. 5.

[2] J. Gill, *The Council of Florence*, pp. 321–6.

in the monastery of Anba Bishāy in Wādi 'l-Naṭrūn, though this had been the centre of a flourishing settlement in the fifteenth century.[1] Only the landing of Napoleon in 1798, and the consequent destruction of Mamlūk power was to break the silence. From then on the Copts, like their Eastern co-religionists, were to experience the pros and cons of a more active Western interest in their fate.

The Church in North Africa and Ethiopia

It may seem strange to be treating the story of the Church in North Africa and Ethiopia from the seventh century onwards as a sort of appendix to that of the Egyptian and Nubian Monophysites. The Church in North Africa was Latin-speaking. It had been the home of Tertullian and Cyprian, of the Donatist movement and of the Augustinian theological tradition. In the sixth century its leaders had upheld Chalcedon against the attempts of Justinian to undermine its decrees at the Fifth General Council and they had condemned the vacillations of the papacy in the affair of the Three Chapters.[2] Though Donatism never regained the ground it had lost, it remained a powerful movement in Numidia in the latter part of the sixth century and the African Church itself represented a strongly dissenting element in the predominantly Monophysite world of Byzantium. Almost the last official act of the African Church of which record survives shows an African Council at Hadrumetum (Sūsa) in 646 condemning the Monothelete *Typos* of Constans II. To the very eve of the Arab invasions the North African Church remained true to its anti-imperial past and its concept of Latin orthodoxy.

Strong links, moreover, seem to have developed with Christian Spain in the sixth century. Prominent martyrs like Vincentius of Tarragona and Salsa of Tipasa were venerated in both territories, and after the Muslim conquest the Mozarabite liturgy seems to have retained a good deal of North African influence, even to the formula for reconciling converted Donatists.[3] Perhaps already by the end of the seventh century, however, the remnants of the African Church seem to have come under the authority of the Alexandrian patriarchate as its tenth

[1] R. R. Farag, *op. cit.* p. 54.

[2] R. A. Markus, "Reflections on Religious Dissent in North Africa in the Byzantine Period", *Studies in Church History*, vol. III (Leiden, 1966), pp. 140–9. Also L. Duchesne, *L'Eglise au VIème siècle*, pp. 643–5.

[3] See J. Gagé, "Nouveaux aspects de l'Afrique chrétienne", *Annales de l'école des Hautes Etudes de Gand*, Tome I (1937), Etudes d'archéologie romaine, p. 187.

province.[1] A list of African bishoprics was being kept in the archives of the see of Alexandria, and one may presume that some appointments to vacancies were made from Alexandria as in the case of other dependent Churches like Nubia and Ethiopia. How did this curious situation come about?

In contrast to the Coptic and Syrian Churches, the Church in North Africa was already in decline in the latter part of the Byzantine period. The process was slow and probably originates with the persecutions which the Africans suffered from the Vandals.[2] Some churches, as that at Thabraca[3], were destroyed and the numbers of bishoprics and the wealth of the Church declined, though here and there fine churches like those at Ḥaydara (Ammaedara) in south-western Tunisia seem to date to the Vandal period.[4] On the restoration of Roman authority by Belisarius in 534 the African Catholics could still muster 220 bishops in a council, though even this show of strength may be deceptive.[5] After that time, however, a change takes place. No other assemblies were held on such a scale and the quality of Christian buildings declines. The bishops of Carthage become shadowy figures and the papacy emerges as the great ecclesiastical landowner in Africa. African Christianity was going down. Even at Timgad the church built by the Patrician Gregorius in 645 was a miserable structure made entirely of re-used materials,[6] while in the Numidian countryside a significant little inscription dated 8 February 637 from a chapel near Telergma shows that while episcopal organization was still intact, Latin was becoming forgotten.[7] Some of the churches of this period were scarcely distinguishable from native huts. Of the scores of churches investigated by French researchers not one shows signs of being built in post-Byzantine times.[8] Moreover, North Africa failed to develop a popular

[1] See H. Gelzer's pioneer article, "Ungedrückte und wenig bekannte Bistümerverzeichnisse der orientalischen Kirche II", *Byzantinische Zeitsschrift*, vol. II (1893), pp. 22 ff., and William Seston, "Sur les derniers temps du Christianisme en Afrique" *Mélanges de l'Ecole française à Rome*, vol. LIII (1936), p. 119.

[2] See J. Mesnage, *Le christianisme en Afrique. Déclin et extinction* (Paris, 1915), for a survey of the evidence.

[3] H. Leclercq, "Thabraca", *DACL*, vol. XV, pt. 2, p. 2155.

[4] L. Poinssot and G.-L. Feuille, "Inscriptions chrétiennes d'Ammaedara (Haidra)", *Bulletin archéologique du Comité des Travaux historiques* (1941–2), pp. 619 ff.

[5] At the Council held by Bonifatius Bishop of Carthage in 525, thirty-seven bishops gathered from Proconsular Africa, compared with 164 in pre-Vandal days. C. Courtois, *Les Vandales et l'Afrique* (Paris, 1955), p. 307; cf. L. Duchesne, *op. cit.* p. 641.

[6] P. Monceaux, *Timgad chrétien* (Paris, 1911), p. 22.

[7] See A. Berthier and colleagues, *Les Vestiges du christianisme antique dans la Numidie centrale* (Algiers, 1942), pp. 120 and 172.

[8] For Numidia, see A. Berthier, *op. cit.* p. 172, and in general, W. Seston, *art. cit.* p. 101.

monastic tradition which could have preserved Christianity in the rural areas after episcopal government based on the towns had collapsed.

The agents for this phenomenon were not primarily the Arabs. Towards the end of the Vandal period, a great confederation of Berber nomads, known as the Lawāta, began to move westwards from Cyrenaica along the edge of the Sahara desert.[1] These tribesmen, we learn from Procopius, were pagan, "ignorant of the Christian god",[2] and by 520 they had defeated the Vandals and established themselves in Tripolitania and in southern Tunisia. The Byzantines held them in check, but damage had been done. The great plains of southern Tunisia were ideal country for nomadic tribesmen, and already by the end of the sixth century much of this territory had been abandoned by the native cultivators. Moreover, the independent Berber kingdoms that had grown up in the Awrās (Aurès) and Kabylie massifs in the latter part of the Vandal era had become progressively paganized. If their rulers were not hostile to Christianity and were sometimes anxious to retain some of the outward trappings of romanization, there is little doubt that many had reverted to ancestral paganism by the time Corippus left an account of the campaigns of John Troglita and Soloman against them in his *Iohannidos* (*circa* 550).[3]

Thus, when the Arabs defeated the Patrician Gregorius at Subayṭila in 647 in central Tunisia, Christianity had already taken on some of the characteristics of a "Melkite" Church. It was the religion of the surviving romanized townsfolk of the areas protected by the Byzantine *limes* and of the Romano-Berber cultivators in the same areas. In Mauretania also there were scattered but sizeable Christian communities, especially in the surviving towns. At Volubilis, for instance, a Christian inscription dated as late as 655 has been found.[4] The forces, however, whether Berber or Arab, which were to struggle for the domination of north Africa after the Byzantine defeat of 647 were not Christian. To judge by Ibn Khaldūn's account of the famous Aurès Berber queen, the *Kāhina*, who fought the Arabs in the last decade of the seventh century, there may even have been a Jewish admixture

[1] See C. Courtois, *op. cit.* pp. 340 ff. and the author's study, "North Africa and Europe in the Early Middle Ages", *Trans. of the Royal Historical Society* (5th ser.), vol. v (1955), pp. 61–80.

[2] *De Bello Vandalico*, III, 8, 18.

[3] For Berber pagans in the mid-fifth century, see Victor Vitensis, *Historia Persecutionis*, I, 35–7. In the mid-sixth century, *Iohannidos*, VI, lines 116, 147 ff.

[4] J. Carcopino, "Note sur une inscription chrétienne de Volubilis", *Hesperis* (1928), pp. 127 ff. Other Mauretanian Christian inscriptions dating from A.D. 450–650, see E. Diehl, *Insc. Lat. Christ. Vet.* (1961 ed.), vol. III, pp. 270–2.

in their religion.[1] In addition, North African geography began to assert its influence against the romanized Africans. The central plains of Numidia proved to be as much to the liking of nomads as those of southern Tunisia. What had previously been a vast olive-forest thickly interspersed by Christian villages, was gradually transformed into an arid corridor linking the centres of Muslim power in Egypt and southern Spain. Even before the successful invasion of the latter, Arabs and Berbers had fought for the control of the desert routes and wells along the edge of the Sahara. The old centres of civilization in the northern and central river valleys, even Carthage itself, were neglected. North Africa had turned its back on the Mediterranean, and its demography had begun to take the shape it was to preserve down to the French conquest in 1830.[2] It is not altogether surprising that the scattered Christians in this remote part of the Umayyad dominions should have been placed under the aegis of the Patriarch of Alexandria.[3] Carthage had no longer any significance.

Once they had been defeated, the Berber nomadic tribes tended to abandon paganism for Islam. Ibn 'Abd al-Ḥakam implies that the desert tribes accepted Islam rather than pay the *kharāj* and see their womenfolk seized by the Arabs.[4] In 703, after the defeat of the *Kāhina* her army is also stated by Ibn Khaldūn to have embraced the creed of their victors.[5] The same author describes the important nomad tribe of the Ṣanhāja in the neighbourhood of Sūsa as never having been christianized.[6] Yet Sūsa and its surroundings had once been completely Christian.

As might be expected, the process of decline and extinction was slower among the settled tribes and the remnants of Romano-Berber society. The terrible harrying of Numidia in the Khārijite wars of the eighth century probably destroyed much that had survived up to then. However, Arab historians down to the twelfth century allude to the *afāriq* or latinized Berbers as Christians and of a broad division between the sedentary Barānis who were mainly Christian and the nomadic Butr who were not. Near the end of the ninth century an

[1] For this confused period in North African history, see E. F. Gautier, *Le Passé de l'Afrique du Nord* (Paris, 1937), pp. 270 ff.

[2] See E. F. Gautier, *op. cit.* p. 280.

[3] See J. Mesnage's note "Une page de l'histoire de l'ancienne église d'Afrique", *Revue Africaine* (1903).

[4] *Conquête de l'Afrique du Nord et de l'Espagne* (Futuh' Ifriqiya wa'l-Andalus), ed. A. Gateau (Algiers, 1942), pp. 31 and 59.

[5] Gautier, *op. cit.* p. 277.

[6] *Histoire des Berbères* (tr. de Slane), vol. I, p. 212.

'Abbāsid official, Ibn Ya'qūb drew up a report on a visit to North Africa for his masters. He shows the country still in transition between its Christian past and Islam. Amidst the nomadic tribes which had infiltrated the hitherto cultivated areas were prosperous villages and olive farms owned and peopled by the *afāriq* and even a few who claimed to be descendants of the Byzantines. There was, however, little sign of growth or renewal, and even the foreign communities Ibn Ya'qūb met were mainly Muslim Persians and Arabs.[1]

Christian communities continued to exist for another century or so, and surprisingly, Christian inscriptions of the tenth and eleventh centuries have been found. Two inscriptions from Qayrawān dating to the period 1048–53 suggest the possibility of a monastery in this very centre of Muslim North Africa, where there is also known, from the *History of the Patriarchs*, to have been a bishop.[2] In Tripolitania the cemetery at En-Gila has yielded memorials of Christians between 945–1003, who were using the Alexandrine era for dating.[3] In the far west, the traveller al-Bakrī describes finding a community of Christians at Tlemcen in 1068,[4] and the Christian community in Africa was evidently large enough to stir Popes Leo IX and Gregory VII into trying to prevent it falling wholly under Coptic domination. Yet, all in all, the empty and ruined churches at Algiers and near Bāja in Tunisia which al-Bakrī also saw, probably provide a truer insight into the state of North African Christianity in the eleventh century. Moreover, on the analogy of Sicily under the Muslims in this period, one suspects that the Christians simply gave up the unequal struggle against Islam. It hardly needed the great Hilālian invasions of the second half of the eleventh century to extinguish the dying embers.

With the revival of Christian power in the western Mediterranean during the Crusading era, the re-christianization of North Africa became an obvious idea. The reconquest of Sicily from the Muslims and the progress of the Christian armies in Spain led to hopes that the struggle could be carried over into Africa. In 1219 five Franciscans were martyred trying to preach the Gospel in Morocco, and their example inspired St Francis to add to his Rule the aim of converting the

[1] See G. Marcais' analysis of his statements in "La Berbèrie au IXème siècle d'après el-Ya'kubi", *Revue Africaine*, vol. LXXXV (1941), pp. 42 ff.

[2] William Seston, *art. cit.* pp. 103 ff.

[3] M. Paribeni, "Sepolcreto cristiano di En-Gila pressó Suani beni Adem", *Africa Italiana*, vol. I (1927), pp. 76 ff.

[4] *Description de l'Afrique septentrionale* (ed. de Slane, 2nd ed. Paris, 1913), pp. 155–6.

Muslims and other unbelievers. The career of Ramon Lull, a Spaniard born in Majorca when memory of Muslim rule there was still strong, was dedicated to the same end. He was an Arabic scholar and made three missionary journeys in North Africa between 1292 and 1315 where he was killed by a mob at Bijāya (Bougie). Though he gained respect from Muslim leaders and a few converts, his work died with him.[1] Neither missionary zeal, nor the more direct crusading warfare of Louis IX availed. Neither Aragonese nor Castilians, nor Portuguese nor the Imperial forces of Charles V were able to make any perceptible impression on the Muslim hold on North Africa.

The complete disappearance of Christianity from North Africa is one of the problems of Mediterranean history. It may one day be possible to establish the existence of a Christian legacy within the framework of Islam in North Africa. The cult of saints and marabouts whose little white-washed shrines were so much part of the North African landscape as late as the Second World War, may owe something to the intensive cult of martyrs characteristic of Christian North Africa. But the sites of the two cults by no means coincide, nor is there convincing evidence as yet for the continuation of sites sacred to a particular saint or martyr from Christian into Muslim times. Similarly, the fanatical zeal and dissenting fury of the Khārijites in the eighth and ninth centuries has been seen as a possible prolongation of the Donatist spirit. Martyrdom, the Holy War and the vision of Paradise in the moment of death and victory had their place in both movements, but the links between them have still to be established. For the time being, the historian is on firmer ground when he points to the vast demographic changes that took place in North Africa between the end of the fifth and the end of the seventh century. The substitution of the nomad and transhumant for the cultivator, the disappearance of the Roman towns, and the victory of the desert over the Mediterranean as the prime cultural influence were surely powerful factors making for the end of African Christian civilization.

Geographical factors also influenced the religious history of Ethiopia, this time to the advantage of Christianity. Physical remoteness and a mountainous terrain enabled Christianity to take root and, as in Armenia, to become the national religion of the Amharic people. By the end of the fifth century Monophysite missionaries from Syria, the "Nine Saints", had established monastic Monophysite Christianity

[1] See A. S. Atiya, *The Crusade in the Later Middle Ages*, pp. 74–94.

in the northern part of the country and given the Ethiopian Church its permanent features though, as also was the case in Armenia, mingled with a great many purely Jewish characteristics.[1] Ecclesiastically, however, the Church continued to depend on Alexandria whence it had received its first mission in the time of Athanasius.

The Muslim conquests deprived the Ethiopians of their outlying sphere of influence on the Arabian peninsula but the existence of the Nubian Christian kingdoms to the north preserved them from direct attack. Only when the last of these fell early in the sixteenth century was the national religion in serious danger. By this time, not only were the areas to the north of the kingdom islamized, but Islam had penetrated the Galla tribes dwelling on the plain inland of Massawa to the south. Once again, Islam conquered steppe and desert, but failed to oust the Christians from the mountain massifs of the Middle East. This time the West came to the Christians' aid.

The Ethiopians sent an embassy to Rome in 1441 at the time of the Council of Florence, and afterwards contacts with western Christendom were strengthened. The existence of this surviving Christian kingdom in Africa with which was now associated the strange legend of Prester John, spurred on the Portuguese pioneers to find routes to the Indies and take the Muslim threat to Christendom in the rear. For the Ethiopians this interest came just in time.

The decisive victory over Muslim invaders was won in 1542 with the help of the Portuguese. Twenty years before, a Portuguese mission led by Alvarez had been received at the emperor's court. From now on, the Ethiopians had to struggle as much against Latin attempts to persuade them to accept a Uniate status as against Muslim attempts at outright conquest. Between 1559 and 1663 the Jesuits made two attempts to bring about the submission to Rome of the Ethiopian Church, the more successful led by Father Paez who gained great influence over the emperor Susenyos (1607–32), and for a few years the Ethiopian Church was reconciled with Rome. A reaction set in, however, and though the Emperor was victorious over domestic rebels the union did not last. In the eighteenth century Franciscans arrived in the country with the same aim, but with no greater success. Despite, however, its appearance of fossilization and its curious blend of the barbaric and the Christian, the Ethiopian Church maintained itself, and for the Copts at least provided a hope of survival amid a hostile Islamic world.

[1] See B. Spuler, *Die morgenländischen Kirchen*, pp. 191 ff.

The Nestorians in Mesopotamia, Persia and farther East

The study of the Nestorians confronts the historian with an entirely different set of problems from those represented by the Monophysites and Orthodox communities. This is a gripping story of how a tradition persecuted within the frontiers of the Empire and not truly accepted by the Persians among whom it took root became one of the great missionary movements of all time and nearly changed the history of Asia and the Middle East.

Towards the end of his reign the emperor Constantine had written to Shāpūr II, the king of Persia (309–79), commending to him the considerable numbers of Christians that existed in his domain.[1] Christian origins in Persia probably go back to the second century A.D., and the main missionary centre was Edessa whose combination of Christianity, Syriac speech and Semitic culture was to influence profoundly the course of Christianity among the Syriac-speaking peoples beyond the Roman frontier. As in the Roman empire, however, the Christians in Persia found themselves confronted by an organized state religion which brooked no rivals. The Zoroastrian *mūbadhs* were as hostile to the spread of the Church as had been their pagan counterparts in the Roman Empire. In addition, the Christians were regarded with some justice as pro-Roman and inimical to Persia. Thus, under the Sāsānid kings they were never more than a minority, alternately persecuted and tolerated as the mood of the monarch or the political situation dictated. These vicissitudes, however, bred a power of survival which was to serve them well in the centuries of Muslim rule.

The long conflict between Shāpūr II and successive Roman emperors was an era of persecution for the Christians. We are told by the fifth-century historian Sozomen that the Christians were subjected to intolerably heavy taxes and then forced to apostasize or risk death.[2] Certainly a great many were slain. Not until 410 did the Persian monarch (Yazdajird I, d. 420) summon a council of Christian leaders to his capital Seleucia, which in fact guaranteed the Church a tolerated status. At this Council the creed of Nicaea was accepted as the symbol of the

[1] Eusebius, *Vita Constantini* (ed. Heikel), IV, 13. The best modern work on the Church in Persia under the Sāsānids remains J. Labourt, *Le Christianisme dans l'Empire Perse* (Paris, 1904). See also, L. Duchesne, *The Early History of the Church* (tr. Claude Jenkins), vol. III, pp. 378–94, and F. C. Burkitt, *Early Eastern Christianity* (London, 1904), Lectures III and IV.

[2] Sozomen, *Hist. Eccl.* II, 9, 1–6.

Church in Persia, and a scheme of discipline formulated in line with the Nicene ordinances. The bishop of the royal city, Seleucia-Ctesiphon, was acknowledged as catholicus, or head of the Church, to whom the metropolitans of five ecclesiastical provinces into which Persia was divided owed obedience.[1] Most of the metropolate of Nisibis, however, lay beyond the Persian frontier in the Roman Empire and links with the school of Edessa and the patriarchate of Antioch therefore remained strong. However, in 424 a controversy involving the catholicus Dadiso resulted in a break between Seleucia and Antioch. It was agreed at a meeting of metropolitans and bishops held at "Markabta of the Arabs", that the Easterns (i.e. Christians in Persia) would not be permitted to carry complaints against their Patriarch before the Western Patriarchs.[2] The Christians in Persia were launched on a career of ecclesiastical independence.

The influence of the school of Edessa, however, remained. After the death of Bishop Rabbula in 435 only a minority of its pupils continued to uphold the Cyrillian theology that he represented. The majority became avid disciples of his successor Ibas (435–57) who was himself a pupil of Theodore of Mopsuestia. Thus, though they took no direct part in either of the two Councils at Ephesus or at Chalcedon, the Persian Christians found themselves divided between a majority who favoured the teaching of the Antiochenes and a Cyrillian minority. The rancorous rivalry between the two groups was to persist for centuries. In 482, however, the promulgation of the *Henotikon* by Zeno and the political need of maintaining at least an appearance of loyalty to their Persian overlords, forced the Christians to a decision. According to a tradition preserved by the Monophysite, Bar Hebraeus, the metropolitan of Nisibis, Barsauma (d. 495) told King Fīrūz that unless the Christians proclaimed a doctrine different from that of the Roman Empire, they would never be sincerely loyal to him.[3] Barsauma who may have become metropolitan of Nisibis as early as 435, was a firm disciple of Ibas of Edessa and a lifelong adversary of Cyrillian doctrine. Sure of Fīrūz's benevolence, he convoked a Council at Bēth Lāpāt (Jundayshāpūr) in April 484 and declared against the *Henotikon* on the grounds that it was Monophysite.[4] He also declared in favour

[1] Duchesne, *op. cit.* p. 380.

[2] The Synod of Dadiso, ap. J. B. Chabot, *Synodicon Orientale*, pp. 285–302.

[3] *Chron. Eccl.* vol. II, col. 66 (ed. J. B. Abeloos and T. J. Lamy, T. III).

[4] Regarding this Council and the subsequent dispute between Barsauma and the Catholicus Acacius, Labourt, *op. cit.* pp. 143 ff.

of permitting clergy and monks to marry.[1] His views carried the day. Two years later at a larger Council at Seleucia, the catholicus Acacius defined the belief of the Church in Persia: "Our faith must be as regards the Incarnation of Christ, in the confession of the Two Natures of the divinity and the humanity. None of us must dare to introduce jumbling, commixture or confusion between the diversities of the two natures. But the Divinity remaining and persisting in its own properties, and the humanity in its own, we reunite in a single majesty and a single adoration the diversities of the natures, because of the perfect and indissoluble cohesion of the Divinity with the humanity."[2] There was no *communicatio idiomatum*. Thus, the Council rejected not only the *Henotikon* but the *Tome* of Leo. The majority of the Persian Church had opted for Nestorius.

The emigration of the remaining students of the Antiochene school to Nisibis after the closure of their centre at Edessa by Zeno in 489 reinforced these tendencies. Through the sixth century the "Great Church" in Persia, presided over by the catholicus at Seleucia remained Nestorian. It was, however, confronted by an active Monophysite minority whose centre was at Takrīt on the Tigris and who were able to make a number of converts, including Philoxenos, later Bishop of Manbij (Maboug) in Syria (d. *circa* 523). By the end of the sixth century Takrīt had ten bishoprics depending on it, and the Monophysites were strong in the most christianized of the Persian provinces, Adiabene. Though this division weakened the Church's threat to the national Iranian religion, its missionaries began to spread the Gospel among the outlying tribes on the northern and north-eastern frontiers of Persia. Thus during the 480s a Nestorian monk named Saba preached to the Kurds with considerable success,[3] and set the pattern for the missionary activity of the Nestorian monks in later generations. Christianity was also being preached to the Huns. In about 498 when King Kavādh took refuge among them he found Christians there who helped him reconquer his kingdom,[4] and in 549 the great catholicus, Aba I, sent a Bishop to the Huns inhabiting Bactria and those on both banks of the Oxus river.[5] Thus by the middle of the sixth century the Nes-

[1] *Chronicle of Séert* (ed. A. Scher, *P.O.* vol. VII, pp. 100–1) and Bar Hebraeus, *loc. cit.* col. 64.

[2] Text cited from L. Duchesne, *op. cit.* p. 392.

[3] Labourt, *op. cit.* p. 187.

[4] *Chronicle of Séert*, XIV (*P.O.* vol. VII, p. 128).

[5] *Life of Mar Aba* (ed. Bedjan), pp. 266–9. See the texts on Nestorian missionary expansion in Central Asia collected by Dr A. Mingana, "The Early Spread of Christianity in Central Asia and the Far East", *Bull. of John Rylands Library*, vol. IX, pt. 2 (1925), pp. 297–371.

torians were following the Manichees as missionaries in central Asia. They had already taken Christianity far along the Silk Route which crossed the continent and had marked out the line for the sensational advances of the next two centuries.

In Persia itself, however, Christianity was no more than a tolerated religion during the sixth and early seventh centuries. The long wars between the Persians and the Roman Empire stretched the Christians' loyalty to their Persian overlords. Between 608 and 628 the Nestorians were without a catholicus, and not surprisingly during Heraclius' victorious counter-attack on Persia (627–30), both Monophysites and Nestorians showed pro-Roman sympathies. The Arab invasions of 637 onwards found them once more the object of suspicion in Persia. Where they did not actively aid the invaders, they stood aside from the fighting as they did in the Byzantine empire. We are told, indeed, that Maruthas the celebrated Monophysite Metropolitan of Takrīt, opened the citadel of his episcopal town "to the sons of Ishmael".[1] Like their brethren beyond the Persian frontier, Christians were ready to accept the Arab victory as the will of God, and the Arabs, for their part, were prepared to accord them toleration on terms.

The relations between the Muslim caliphs and the Nestorians were similar to those governing the Christians and Muslims in other parts of the Arab empire. Among them too, the Arabs in the seventh century were not reckoned as enemies, and the memorable sentence of the Nestorian catholicus Ishō'yāb III (650–60) is recorded: "The Arabs to whom God has given at this time the government of the world...do not persecute the Christian religion. Indeed they favour it, honour our priests and the saints of the Lord and confer benefits on churches and monasteries."[2] Church life seems to have continued normally enough, though there is a record of a trickle of educated converts to Islam.[3] In fact, only in the ninth century, under the Caliph al-Mutawakkil (847–61) was there an openly anti-Nestorian policy on the part of the caliphate, and in this instance the Nestorians were suffering from the general anti-Christian fanaticism which characterized this Caliph's reign. The storm was soon over, Nestorians once more held high positions at the Caliph's court, and later, a remarkable document,

[1] Bar Hebraeus, *Chron. Eccl.* vol. II, col. 125.

[2] Ishō'yāb III, letter to Simeon, Bishop of Riwardisir (ed. R. Duval, *Scriptores Syri*, 2nd ser., vol. LXIV, p. 182 of translation).

[3] See S. M. Stern, "Apocryphal Gospels in 'Abd al-Jabbār", *J.T.S.* N.S. vol. XVIII (1967), p. 36, for the influence of these converts in shaping Muslim propaganda.

dated to 1138, shows the Caliph al-Muktafī II (1136–60) conferring on the Nestorian catholicus Abdisho III the prerogatives of head of all the Christians "whether Greeks, Jacobites, or Melkites" in his dominions, and guaranteeing the Christians under his protection freedom of worship and property, on payment of the capitation tax. The catholicus had become a recognized officer in the Arab state service. As the editor, Dr A. Mingana, points out, it is an astonishing document for the age in which it was written.[1] No ruler in Europe would at this time have been asking for the prayers of a non-Christian leader.

As in Egypt and Syria, however, it was impossible to prevent Islam as the religion of the conquerors from gaining ground.[2] But in the Nestorian centres in northern and western Iran the process was slower than elsewhere in the Arab Empire, except Armenia. Islam rapidly won converts among the adherents of the old national religion of Zoroastrianism, and among the mixed Arab–Iranian population on the Persian Gulf. Here, as among the desert tribes of North Africa, economic pressure brought conversion. The Christian bishopric in Bahrain had ceased to exist by the eighth century, and the same fate gradually overtook Fārs in southern Persia,[3] but in the Aramaic-speaking areas where Nestorianism was deeply rooted Islam was less successful.

The Nestorians showed themselves far more flexible in their organization than their Monophysite rivals. The synod of Seleucia in 486 had accepted the marriage of clergy, and the vast expanses over which they had to operate had driven the catholicus to the commonsense decision in the next century that bishops of distant sees need not seek his confirmation of their elections, nor attend synods in the capital. This led to a welcome devolution of authority and allowed energetic local leaders to extend their missions to the heathen without let or hindrance. Married clergy working as merchants were able to supplement the efforts of the monks.

Their great success is shown by the advance of Christianity into China by the mid-seventh century. The well-known inscription

[1] A. Mingana, "A Charter of Protection granted to the Nestorian Church by Muktafi ii, Caliph of Baghdad", *Bull. of John Rylands Library*, vol. xx, pt. 1 (1926), pp. 126–33.

[2] See the letter of the Patriarch Ishō'yāb III to his Bishop Qamiso and others, telling them not to be deceived when heretics tell them that "by the order of the Arabs what happens, happens" (*Letters of Iso'yahb*, ed. R. Duval, *Scriptores Syri*, 2nd ser. vol. LXIV, p. 73 of translation). Also, Ishō'yāb's letter to Simeon, bishop of Riwardisir, cited above, where the Mazunaei tribesmen were being mulcted half their goods in return for being allowed to remain Christian, and many had apostatized.

[3] B. Spuler, *Die morgenländischen Kirchen*, p. 144. The province of Fārs did not become completely Muslim until about 1000.

found in 1625 at Sinanfu shows that in 635 missionaries had arrived at the court of the Emperor and had received permission to establish a monastery in his capital.[1] Thereafter Christianity was a tolerated religion down to the time of the erection of the inscription (February 781) which commemorates the annual synod of the Church in China. Linking the Chinese Christians with those in Persia were scattered communities beyond the Oxus extending through central Asia governed by two archbishops and twenty bishops, the archiepiscopal centres being probably at Kashgar and Samarkand.

At this moment the Nestorian Church produced one of the few great leaders of eastern Christianity under Arab domination, the catholicus Timotheos I (780–823). This remarkable man, whose term of office spans the climax of ʿAbbāsid power at Baghdad under Hārūn al-Rashīd (783–809), both galvanized the internal life of the Nestorian Church and put its missionary movement on an organized footing.[2] The catholicate was moved from Seleucia to the ʿAbbāsid capital, Baghdad—a significant change indicating the relationship which the Nestorians aimed at achieving with the caliphs. Bishops were chosen with care, bonds were strengthened with the scattered Nestorian communities in Syria, and a scholarly tradition founded which proved to be one of the main means for the preservation of the Classical heritage via the Arabs and ultimately to the West. These measures coincided with a great period of Nestorian missionary activity. In 780 a change of dynasty had taken place among the Vignur Turks, and this brought the Christians considerable gains. Timotheos was invited to send a "metropolitan" to them.[3] Many of the tribe were converted, though Manicheism still retained some foothold among them. In 797 a metropolitan was also appointed for Tibet.[4] Meantime, Nestorians had established themselves as merchants and missionaries in the Panjab, southern India, Suquṭrā and even at Ṣanʿāʾ in the Yemen. As the catholicus himself wrote "many crossed the seas towards India

[1] On this monument see P. Y. Saeki, *The Nestorian Monument in China* (S.P.C.K., London, 1916), and the short description and commentary see E. Tisserant, art. "Nestorienne (l'Eglise)" in *D.T.C.* vol. XI, pt. I, pp. 199–207. For a second Christian inscription containing some words of Psalm 24, verse 6, and a cross, see F. C. Burkitt, "A New Nestorian Document in China", *Journ. Theol. Studies*, vol. XXII (1920–1), p. 269.

[2] His letters have been edited by O. Braun, Timothei Patriarchae I, espitulae, *Corpus script. christ. orient. Scriptores Syri*, ser. II, vol. LXVII. See also J. Labourt's thesis, *De Timotheo i Nestorianorum patriarcha (778–823)*. One of his reforms was to publish rules intended to remove all excuses for Christians to have recourse to Muslim courts in case of civil disputes.

[3] A. Mingana, "The Early Spread of Christianity", p. 310. [4] *Ibid.* p. 310.

and China carrying only a stick and a bag".[1] In contrast to his predecessors, however, Timotheos attempted everywhere to give his converts a hierarchical government. We hear of the ordination of some eighty monks in charge of missions as bishops.[2] Six archbishoprics were created for communities stretching from India to central Asia and China, and to these archbishops was delegated authority for appointing lesser clergy. Yet the success of these enterprises depended very largely on the organizing ability of the catholicus himself. The distances over which the missionaries had to operate were vast. Even without Muslim interference, it would have been difficult to sustain a largely monastic Christianity among semi-nomadic populations. Nestorian missions rested on fragile foundations, emphasized by the fact that even among the Turks no really powerful ruler was converted. The Shī'ite Muslims had penetrated as far as Kashgar and Samarkand by 720 and ultimately the military prowess of the Muslims proved a trump card in favour of Islam. The choice of the Seljuks in the eleventh century was to be followed by others.

The crisis, however, was long delayed. The Nestorians still represented a higher level of culture than most of the Muslim inhabitants of Mesopotamia and Persia. Their value to the caliphs was proved by the numbers who became physicians and apothecaries at their court and, like the Coptic Christians of this period, exercised a wide influence as bankers and traders. Moreover, this cultural eminence was reinforced in the ninth, tenth and eleventh centuries by the development of a scientific literature based on study and translation of the manuals of the Ancient World. Aristotle and many of his commentators, Euclid, Hippocrates and Galen were among the writings translated into Syriac and Arabic by the Nestorians. In addition, the schism in the Muslim ranks between the Shī'is and Sunnīs provided a further protection for the Christians. Nisibis (Naṣībīn), Jundayshāpūr (Bēth Lāpāt) and Merv all flourished as Nestorian centres. With some exaggeration the Arab writer al-Bīrūnī stated in the early eleventh century that "the majority of the inhabitants of Syria, Iraq and Khurasan are Nestorians".[3]

[1] Letters of Timotheos I (ed. O. Braun), p. 70 of translation. For India see J. N. Farquhar, "The Apostle Thomas in South India", *Bull. of John. Rylands Library*, vol. XI (1927), pp. 20–50. Dr Farquhar believed that the effective founding of the Church in south India was due to Persian Christians fleeing the persecution of Shāpūr after A.D. 343 (p. 45).

[2] Thomas of Marga (ed. Bedjan), *Liber Superiorum*, pp. 261–2.

[3] al-Bīrūnī, *The Chronology of Ancient Nations* (ed. E. Sachau, 1879), p. 282.

The Crusading era affected the Nestorians less than the other Christians in the Middle East. The onset of the Seljuks in the 1050s caused some damage to buildings and property, but the fighting between Muslim and Christian took place west of the Nestorian centres. Indeed, the charter already alluded to, granted by the Caliph al-Muktafī II to the Nestorian catholicus in 1138 indicates that relations at Baghdad between Christians and Muslims remained tolerably good.

In central Asia meantime, the Nestorian missionaries and travelling merchants continued to win successes. The Keravts, a Turkish tribe numbering about 200,000 all told, dwelling in northern Mongolia became Christian in about 1009.[1] Their example was followed by the Namians and Merkites. In southern Siberia the presence of numerous Christians is attested by the discovery of two Nestorian cemeteries in the province of Semiyechensk,[2] and in the Turfan oasis Nestorian writings were found alongside Buddhist and Manichaean works.[3] Western travellers in the thirteenth century were unanimous concerning the large numbers of Nestorian Christians they encountered on their way to Cathay.[4]

As a result of these successes there is no doubt that the Mongol armies that pressed westward into Muslim territory in the thirteenth century contained many Christians. Güyük Khān (d. 1248), the grandson of Chingiz Khān, had a Christian vizier and is called by Bar-Hebraeus a "true Christian", in whose days the "prestige of the numerous Christian bodies in his dominions was very high. His camp was full of bishops, priests and monks."[5]

As we have seen, when Hülegü captured Baghdad in 1258, Christians and Shīʿī Muslims were spared the slaughter. Hūlāgū's wife was a Kerayt and a Christian, and his brother, Möngke Khān, had a Christian mother.[6] For a generation Christians exercised an appreciable influence on the policy of the khāns. In 1264 Qūbīlāy Khān whose uncle was a Christian accorded Christian (Nestorian) clergy the same freedom from taxation he had already granted the Buddhists and Tao'ists, and in 1289

[1] Bar Hebraeus, *Chron. Eccl.* vol. II, col. 279. See also A. Mingana, "The Early Spread of Christianity", pp. 308–9.
[2] A. Mingana, *op. cit.* pp. 333–4.
[3] F. W. K. Müller, "Handschriften-funde in Estrangelo-Schrift aus Turfan", *Abh. der Kgl. preuss. Akad. der Wissenschaften* (1904), pp. 1–117.
[4] Examples cited by Mingana, *op. cit.* pp. 314–17.
[5] Bar Hebraeus, *Chron. Syr.* (ed. Bedjan), p. 481.
[6] Also, Mingana, *op. cit.* pp. 312–13, and for Nestorian written remains from Turfan and Hara-Hoto dating to the thirteenth and fourteenth centuries, see N. Pigoulewsky, "Fragments syriaques et syro-Turcs, de Hara-Hoto et de Tourfan", *Revue de l'Orient chrétien*, vol. XXX (1935–6), pp. 1–46.

instituted a special office to supervise the affairs of the Christians throughout his entire empire. Indicating, perhaps, their hopes in the Mongols, in 1281 the Nestorians elected as their catholicus the Mongolian monk named Marcus (1244–1317). He took the title of Yabalāhā III and was to govern his Church through the reigns of six khāns (1281–1317)—a period of great initial promise followed by eclipse.

The decisive year was 1295, when the Īlkhān Ghāzān, a young man aged 24, declared himself a Sunnī Muslim. His example was followed by the overwhelming majority of his Turkish and Mongol subjects. Christians lost influence rapidly, though at the turn of the fourteenth century there were still twenty-five metropolitans, and Nestorian Christians all the way from Cyprus to Cathay.

The fourteenth century brought the same irredeemable decline to the Nestorians as it did to other Christians in the Middle East. Bishoprics remained unfilled, monasteries became deserted, many of the faithful either lapsed into the predominant Islam or continued to live out a sectarian existence mingled with the remnants of the Manichees, and in China, secret societies. In central Asia Islam advanced at the expense of both Buddhism and Christianity.[1] The final blows were struck by Tīmūr Lang (Tamerlane) (1360–1405). By then, however, Islam had won for itself the position of heir to the Classical heritage in the Middle East. The Nestorians had become, as they had been in Persia a thousand years before, a small, precarious group.

The remainder of the story is that of the relations of the scattered surviving communities with the Latins.[2] The final phase of Nestorian expansion had brought their Church into contact with the Crusaders, not least in Cyprus where they had been able to set up a bishopric. The first reactions of the Latins had been to treat them simply as heretics, and a bull of Honorius III dated 12 February 1222 instructed the Latin ecclesiastical authorities in the Outremer to take measures to enforce their acceptance of the supremacy of the Latin archbishop of Nicosia and his suffragans. It was over two centuries before these isolated Nestorians were prepared to accept Latin protection in 1445. With them, however, the "Chaldaean" Church in communion with Rome had been founded. Another century passed. By this time, the main body of the Nestorians had found refuge in the Hakkārī mountains in Persian

[1] E. Blochet, "La conquête des états nestoriens de la Asie centrale par les Shiites", *Revue de l'Orient chrétien*, vol. xxv (1925–6), pp. 1–133, especially 52 ff.

[2] See J. Joseph, *The Nestorians and their Muslim Neighbours* (Princeton, 1961), pp. 29–39, and E. Tisserant, *art. cit. D.T.C.* vol. xi, pt. 1, pp. 228–43.

Azerbayjan and around Lake Urmia, though scattered communities remained in Mesopotamia. Since 1450 the catholicate had come to be hereditary in the family of Bar Mama, descending from uncle to nephew.

In 1551, however, there was a schism between the adherents of Simon VIII Dinha and a rival group led by the Monk John Sulāqā. The latter was encouraged by Franciscan missionaries in the Mosul area where most of his adherents lived to travel to Rome. There in exchange for recognizing the Roman primacy he was accorded the title of Patriarch of the East, and his "Chaldaean" Church given Uniate status. Though John was imprisoned by the Turks on his return and died in 1555, the "Chaldaeans" survived and the schism between the two branches of the Nestorian Church was perpetuated.

The doctrinal differences between the Latins and the Chaldaeans took a long time to remove. Letters were exchanged in a desultory manner between successive popes and patriarchs through the seventeenth century until in 1692 the Sulāqā Patriarch renounced Catholicism. However, by this time a Latin Catholic community had been built up by Jesuit and Capuchin missionaries around Diyarbakîr (Amida). In 1672, Yūsuf, the Archbishop of the town also accepted Uniate status and for some years there were two separate Uniate communities among the Nestorians. In the eighteenth century the Chaldaean cause was sustained through the succession of Yūsufite Patriarchs at Diyarbakîr. It is doubtful whether the total number of Nestorians amounted to more than the 40,000 divided into twenty-eight districts as reported to Rome in 1653.[1]

CONCLUSION

It is not easy to sum up this long period. As Westerners we are used to thinking in terms of the differences and traditional hostility between Christianity and Islam. The situation looked far different in the eastern provinces of the Roman Empire in the seventh century. Here the real division of peoples and religions had taken place at the time of Chalcedon. To the Syrians and Copts, the Greeks were the enemies, and the Arabs the friends. How deeply the outcome of Chalcedon was felt may be seen from the example of Dionysius Bar Ṣalībī writing towards the end of the twelfth century against "the pride of the Chalcedonians",[2]

[1] Spuler, *op. cit.* p. 164. For the story of Nestorian relations with Rome, see E. Tisserant, *art. cit.*

[2] See A. Mingana and Rendel Harris, "Woodbrooke Studies; editions and translations of Christian documents in Syriac and Garstunu", *Bull. of John Rylands Library*, vol. XI (1927), pp. 110 ff.

as though he were participating in the fate of Dioscorus and Severus of Antioch centuries before. The Arabs brought nothing like the turmoil of the final years of Byzantine rule. Moreover, as John of Damascus shows, native Christians did not regard Islam as other than a powerful, and indeed noxious, Christian heresy. It could be weighed therefore in the balance against the admitted evil of the Chalcedonians.

With this in mind the march of events becomes intelligible. The Arab conquest was followed by a long period in which relations between native Christian subjects and Muslim rulers in the Middle East remain good, and the higher cultural level represented by the Christians wins the respect of the Muslim warrior aristocracy as well as rendering them indispensable in the administration of the conquered territories. Only gradually, at the turn of the eighth century, does this situation change. By then the attraction of Islam on economic and probably social grounds also is becoming irresistible. Even so, two more centuries pass before Islam becomes the predominant religion even in the Nile valley. In Mesopotamia and Persia it is hard to see any serious decline in Christianity at this period.

The revival of Byzantine power from 940 onwards brings a change on the eastern Mediterranean seaboard. Antioch falls, and Christianity becomes again the predominant religion in northern Syria and the Lebanon. The treaty between Michael IV and the caliph in 1036 marks the point of equilibrium between the two faiths in the Middle East.

No sooner established, however, than this equilibrium is shattered first by the Turks, then by the Crusades, and finally by the Mongols. The fourteenth century was catastrophic for the Churches in the Middle East. This period saw Islam completely in the ascendant with the Byzantine Empire all but destroyed, and the Muslims embarking on a missionary movement in East Asia which dwarfed that of the Nestorians. In all this turmoil, the Westerners appear as interlopers, interfering like Pope Leo, in matters which they did not understand and were not their concern. In the last act of the drama, we see the stunted but surviving Eastern Churches resisting the attempts by the Latins to absorb them into a world-wide Latin Church with the same dour obstinacy as for centuries they had demonstrated in the face of Islam. The catastrophe of the Synod of Diamper in south India in 1599 was not forgotten. Their long history of survival against all efforts from outsiders to disunite and destroy them has some relevance to ecumenical thought today.

CHAPTER 6

THE ORTHODOX CHURCH

By the Orthodox Church in the Middle East is meant the four ancient patriarchates of Constantinople, Alexandria, Antioch and Jerusalem. These are autocephalous churches, each independent and self-governing. The independence is only administrative; there is no visible head over them all ordering their affairs as in the Roman Catholic Church; and the pre-eminence given among them, as indeed among all Orthodox churches (Russian, Greek, Serbian, etc.), to the ecumenical patriarch of Constantinople is only one of honour and not of authority, each patriarch having his own metropolitans and bishops and his own holy synod. But in doctrine and in liturgy they are not independent: they all go back in doctrine to the Greek Fathers and to the original seven Ecumenical Councils of the Church, and they all have the same liturgy of Saint Basil the Great and Saint John Chrysostom. Their unity is not one of rule; it is the identity of their patristic roots, their tradition, their faith and their liturgy. Thus they are the preservers and continuers of the glorious religious tradition of Byzantium in the Middle East. They should therefore be distinguished, on the one hand, from the non-Byzantine and non-Catholic churches of the Middle East (the Coptic church, the Syriac church, the Armenian "Orthodox" church, etc.) which were excommunicated by the early Ecumenical Councils of the Church Universal, and, on the other, from the Roman Catholic Church with which they were in communion and with which they formed one Universal Church up until the tragic events which culminated in the separation of East from West and West from East in 1054. Orthodoxy in the Middle East is what is left of the original native Church of the Orient which was in communion with the Church of the Occident for a thousand years. It is what has survived from the original Greek branch of the Church Universal after thirteen centuries of Muslim–Arab and Muslim–Ottoman conquest and domination in the Middle East. We should probably use the phrase "Greek Orthodox Church" to distinguish this original Church of the Orient from other churches, such as the Coptic and Armenian, which also use the term "Orthodox", but in the plan of this work the term "Orthodox

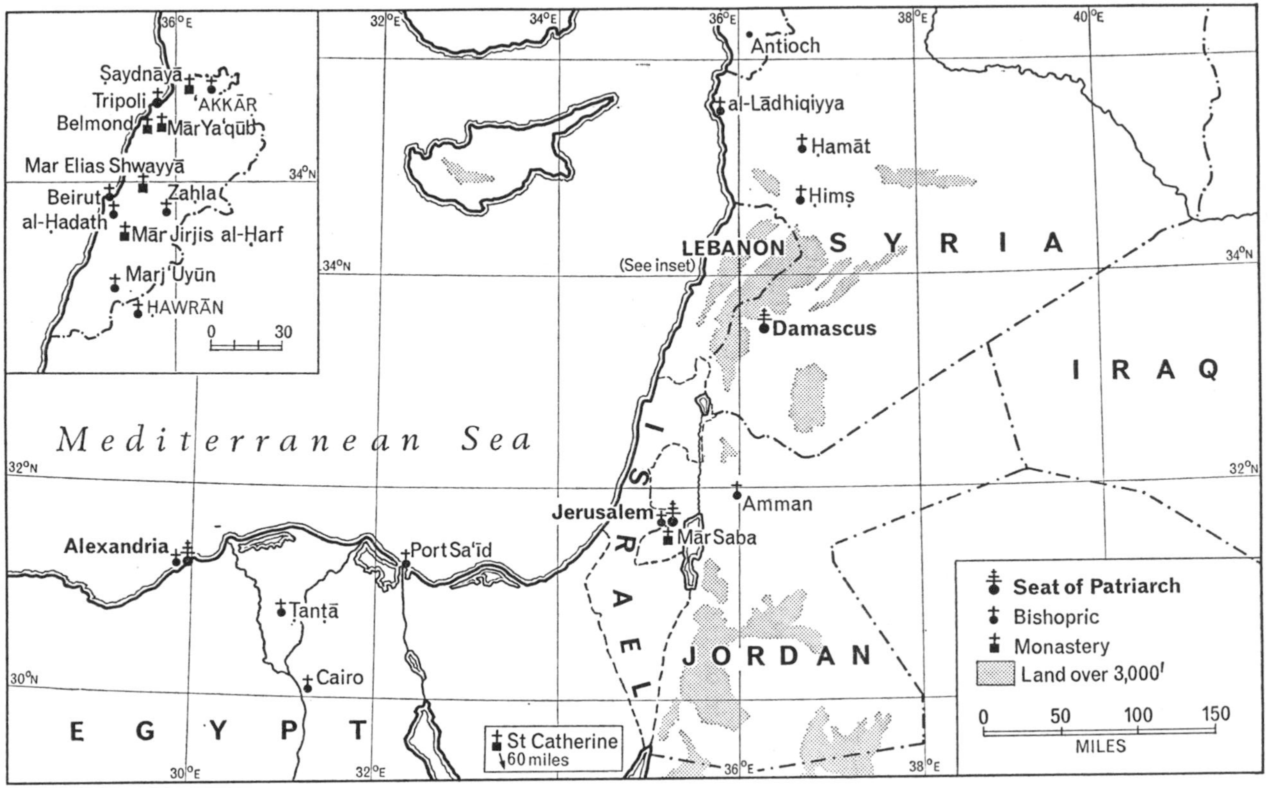

The Orthodox Church.

Note. Istanbul is also a patriarchal see; there is an Orthodox monastery at Mt Athos; Damascus is the seat of the patriarchate of Antioch.

Church" is clearly intended to signify only the Church of which we here speak.

The inner life of Orthodoxy in the Middle East, both as a corporate church and as individual believers, is known in its fullness only to God. In that great and final Day when Christ shall judge all men, those who will be asked to "inherit the kingdom prepared for them from the foundation of the world" should not be surprised if they should find there a few Orthodox from the Middle East. There has been suffering for His name, there has been faithfulness to His word, there has been intense devotion to His mother, there has been the sweetest piety from love for and attachment to His person—all this could produce some merit which, in His mercy, could count for righteousness in His eyes.

But it is the outer life of Orthodoxy in the Middle East during the nineteenth and twentieth centuries that can be clearly delineated in its broad outline. The Orthodox lived under concrete historical-social-political conditions to which they had to adjust and within which they realized whatever human and spiritual existence they could muster and conserve. While these "external conditions" doubtless determine the life of the spirit, they determine it only "externally": certainly it is not determined by them alone. In defiance of all "external" determination, there is always an independent determination rooted in the freedom of the spirit itself and ultimately in its ground in God. But the external determinants, such as they are, are real and important and should be carefully noted. They are seven: (1) relations to Islam in its Ottoman and Arab forms; (2) relations to Russian Orthodoxy and the Russian State, both tsarist and soviet; (3) relations to Rome and Roman Catholicism; (4) relations to Protestantism, European and American; (5) relations to the Western powers, principally France, Britain and the United States; (6) friction and conflict among the four sees; and (7) the problem of the relations between the Greek clergy and the faithful natives. Orthodoxy in the Middle East has been struggling for its existence, living its life, and realizing its being, under the banner of these seven concrete circumstances, combining and interlacing among themselves into a bewildering variety of patterns.

Orthodoxy in the Middle East has been living ever since the fall of Constantinople in 1453 in a predominantly Muslim world. The Muslim spirit encompasses it. It is free only within this spirit. Except for the extensive Greek colonies in the Ottoman Empire and until recently in

Egypt, the Orthodox of the Middle East belong almost wholly to the native populations of these lands. In the sees of Antioch and Jerusalem (apart from the Greek hierarchy in the latter), and among the remaining non-Greeks in the see of Alexandria, the faithful are all Arabic-speaking. The Orthodox are keenly conscious of their existential status as a Christian minority group in a vast Muslim sea, although in Lebanon this sense, so far as Lebanon thinks only of itself, namely, so far as Lebanon is independent from the rest of the Middle East, is considerably mitigated by the knowledge that they belong to a total body politic which is itself a community of minorities, some of which indeed are themselves Muslim.

Under the Ottoman Turks the Orthodox became part of the Muslim *dhimma* system. According to this system there is a distinction between Muslim and non-Muslim subjects; the former, constituting the *umma* (i.e. the nation) of Islam, enjoy privileges which the latter, being only *dhimma* (i.e. held under or protected by the dictates of the conscience of Islam, which includes the legal and political status allowed them by the Qur'ān), are not entitled to enjoy. They were thus distinctly second-class citizens. As *dhimma*, the Christians have their own religious, social and political status wherby they may practice their own religion "freely", but they cannot seek or accept the conversion of Muslims to Christianity, they cannot serve in the armed forces, they cannot hold high governmental office, their men cannot marry Muslim women, and they must pay special tribute to their Muslim rulers. If you wanted to remain Christian, you had to submit to this system. That is why the predominantly Christian Near East became with the passage of time predominantly Muslim.

Meḥmed the Conqueror into whose hands Constantinople fell, saw to it that the new ecumenical patriarch belonged to the anti-Rome party. In recognizing him, the Sultan addressed him as follows: "Be patriarch; may God keep thee; I grant thee my favour and support; and thou shalt enjoy all the rights practised by thy predecessors." An imperial edict was later issued guaranteeing the person and freedom of the patriarch, exempting him from all taxes, safeguarding his security in his throne, assuring the transmission of his prerogatives to his successors, recognizing his jurisdiction over all the prelates under him, and granting him some temporal authority. The precedence of honour accorded the ecumenical patriarch among the four patriarchs of the Orient ever since the fifth century was continued and formalized by the new regime.

The Orthodox had considerable though not unchequered influence in Constantinople under the Ottoman Turks. Often the Sultan would issue edicts or *fermans* in their favour against Catholic missions from the West. Thus in 1725 two such edicts were promulgated whereby Western missionaries were forbidden to enter the homes of the Christian subjects of the Sultan. And in 1774, a most important treaty (confirmed in later treaties) was concluded between Russia and the Ottomans, from which Russia emerged as a sort of protector of the Christians of the Ottoman Empire. In this treaty, the Sublime Porte pledged permanent protection to the Christian religion and the Christian churches, assured Russia that the Christian subjects of the Sultan would live under a just government and would enjoy religious freedom, and recognized Russia's right to make complaints about the rights of these subjects whenever she deemed that necessary.

The ecumenical patriarch was for centuries recognized by the Sultan as the ultimate Christian authority in the empire. But when large numbers both of Orthodox and Armenians established communion with Rome, a conflict of allegiance arose in their mind as between patriarch and pope. The Christians quarrelled bitterly among themselves, and often the sultan had to assume the role of umpire. Thus in 1828 Maḥmud II abrogated any authority that the ecumenical patriarch may have had over the Armenian Catholics and appointed a Muslim overseer to look after their temporal problems, reserving their spiritual affairs to the care of the Apostolic Nuncio himself; and in 1831 this same Sultan recognized in an imperial edict an Armenian bishop as the head of the Armenian Catholic *millet*, and authorized all Catholics, Armenian, Maronite and Greek, to regard him as their ultimate court of appeal, alike in spiritual matters and in those temporal transactions in which he could mediate between them and the Porte. It was thus by an edict of the Ottoman Sultan, the Caliph of the Muslims, that the uniate church of the Armenians and Greeks was formally legally established in the Middle East.

The treaties between Russia and the Porte concerning the Orthodox subjects of the Sultan signify that Orthodoxy was not dead in the Ottoman world (Greece and the Balkans were then under Ottoman rule) and that it had co-religionists in the realms beyond who were interested in it and who were prepared to "protect" it, whatever their ultimate motives may have been. But when feelings run very high, the binding character of these treaties is usually set aside. Such was the case in 1821 when, upon the outbreak of the Greek revolution in which both Russia and Britain played competing and counteracting parts, the Turks seized the ecumenical patriarch, Gregory V, while he was celebrating the Easter Divine Liturgy and dragged him from inside the church to the gate of the churchyard, where they hanged him in his ecclesiastical vestments. We have here a dramatic illustration of the precarious worldly conditions under which Orthodoxy lived.

In theory the Church under the Ottomans was free to elect its own patriarchs according to its own laws and procedures, but the electing bodies (bishops and laymen) had to submit candidates to the authorities from among whom the Porte could eliminate whomever it considered unacceptable. The electing bodies would then choose one from those allowed by the government, but even this choice required the further endorsement of the Porte. Only after a *berat* is issued confirming a patriarch does his election become legal. Thus the Ottoman authorities could, and often did, intervene at four levels: among the electing bodies prior to the submission of names of candidates, at the point of eliminating some of these candidates and allowing only some of them, at the time when the electing bodies make their final choice, and when the decision is made confirming the person elected.

The Eastern Question is a phrase expressing the jealousies and rivalries of the European powers with respect to the Ottoman Empire. Adjustments were successively worked out among themselves and with Constantinople. Because of chronic instability, a sort of power vacuum was created in the empire, into which the other nations rushed, and as they entered, they clashed. The Christian subjects of the Sultan were often the excuse, whether pretended or real. After the Crimean War, the pattern of adjustment arrived at in the Treaty of Paris of 1856 established a policy of non-intervention in the internal affairs of the Ottoman state, and required that no unilateral action be taken by any of the Christian powers with respect to the solution of any problems that might arise between them and the Sultan. To remove the possibility of using his Christian subjects as a pretext for intervention on the part of the powers, the Sultan issued an imperial edict, *khaṭṭ-i hümayun*, appended to the Treaty of Paris, in which he decreed equality between all his subjects, Muslim and Christian.

The examination of the character and causes of the bloody events of the sixties of the nineteenth century in Lebanon and Syria falls outside the scope of this study. There was a bewildering interpenetration and mutual determination of a maze of factors and actors: Egyptian pitted against Turk, Arab against Ottoman, French against British, European against Oriental, Maronite against Druze, Christian against Muslim, Catholic and Orthodox against Protestant, nationalist against imperialist. From the point of view of Muslim–Arab and Muslim–Turkish conditions under which Orthodoxy lived, which is the point of view of the present section of this essay, we need only note here that the outcome of this weird Levantine world of multiplicity, intrigue and clash, in which everybody was the agent or client of somebody, was the massacre of several thousand Christians, the burning of the seat and the church of the patriarch of Antioch in Damascus, and the setting up, within the Ottoman Empire, of a special autonomous regime for Lebanon guaranteed alike by the Porte and by the powers.

There are genuine elements of tolerance in Islam: the mere survival of Christian minorities under the "protection" (in the *dhimma*) of Islam may be looked upon as objective proof of that. The concrete atmosphere that prevails depends not only on the teachings of Islam, but principally on the climate of thought at the time and on the mentality of the rulers. These could conjure up tolerance and freedom or intolerance and persecution almost at will. Thus from moment to moment and mentality to mentality the *dhimma* idea could change from peaceful association and co-existence to one of persecution (spoken or unspoken) and radical intolerance. In the heat of the latter spirit, *dhimma* simply means that the Christians exist on sufferance, that so long as they continued to exist they are under the wing of Islam, that they are an alien and unassimilable element in the body politic of the *umma*. All this breeds mutual suspicion and fear. When on top of that there is in the background a whole heritage, going back to the Crusades, of political intervention by Christian powers in the name of religion, one understands how the Church could not be too prudent or too circumspect in its relations with the civil authorities. Under the Ottomans, patriarchs and bishops always prayed for the Sultan, and always reminded the faithful that they should respect, obey and serve their temporal lords. But they carried their prayers often to ridiculous extremes of obsequiousness and servility; and in the present epoch of independence extravagant language of congratulations, good wishes and prayer can be cited, language used by the same prelate of two deadly enemies overturning and succeeding each other in a matter of months.

The constitution of 1908 established equality among the subjects of the Sultan regardless of their religious affiliation. Christians would serve in the armed forces on an equal footing with Muslims. There was rejoicing as a result among the Christians throughout the empire. In 1910 many Orthodox soldiers from Constantinople and Izmir came on a campaign against the Druzes in Syria; special Orthodox services in Greek were held in the Cathedral of Damascus to which these soldiers used to come on Sundays and where they used to make confession and take holy communion. The ecumenical patriarch had submitted to the government the request that, now that Orthodox subjects would be enlisted in the armed forces, no religious conversion be allowed while the men were away from home and special clergy be assigned to the forces to attend to the needs of Christian soldiers. He asked also for other privileges, and the mere fact that he could make such requests reflected the liberal, indeed the revolutionary and unprecedented, atmosphere which the Young Turks brought with them.

Gregory IV of Antioch established good relations with the Sultan, which stood him in good stead with the Ottoman authorities in Damascus during World War I. But the war was desperate so far as the fate of the Ottomans was concerned. They vented their despair upon the Armenians in Asia Minor and the Christians in Lebanon and Syria. Tens (perhaps hundreds) of thousands of Christians perished in Lebanon from sheer starvation. Because of Gregory's good relations with the Turks, the Orthodox suffered less than the Maronites and Catholics in general. After the war this same Gregory cultivated the finest relations with the Arab authorities, and he was among the first to join in declaring Fayṣal I king of Syria.

So far as the relations of the Orthodox to their Muslim–Arab and Muslim–Turkish environments in the Middle East since World War I are concerned, we may here only note the following topics: (1) The Graeco-Turkish war in the early twenties and the massive exchange of populations between the two peoples as a result. (2) The displacement of tens of thousands of Orthodox from the present territory of Israel into Lebanon, Jordan, Syria and overseas as a result of the Israeli–Arab war of 1947–8. (3) The virtual liquidation of the Orthodox community in Egypt, and the emigration from Egypt to Lebanon since 1955 of tens of thousands of Orthodox of Lebanese or Syrian origin. (4) The migration of perhaps a hundred thousand Orthodox from

Syria into Lebanon in recent years. (5) The fact that Arabic-speaking Orthodox played a leading role in the Arab nationalist movement and in the renewal of Arabic literature and Arab culture in general. (6) The attack upon the Orthodox churches and cemeteries of Constantinople in 1955. (7) The ordeals which the present ecumenical patriarch, Athenagoras I, has been going through in his relations with the Turkish government, largely owing to the dispute between Turkey and Greece over Cyprus.

As selected sketches characterizing the way the Church has been kept inserted in its immediate Muslim environment, the preceding paragraphs yield a fairly adequate picture of the Church's relations to its socio-political world. The four ancient sees of Constantinople, Alexandria, Antioch and Jerusalem still exist, each having its own venerable patriarch and each counting still some faithful under its care; but Orthodoxy in the Middle East is practically reduced today to the see of Antioch, with the seat thereof in Damascus, and with its jurisdiction extending over Syria and Lebanon and the Lebanese and Syrian Orthodox emigration overseas; and even here the Orthodoxy of Lebanon *vis-à-vis* that of Syria is by far the more secure and free, even though the Orthodox in Lebanon are a minority relatively to the uniates. Everywhere therefore theirs is a minority status. Due to many causes, principally their rootedness, which anteceded Islam, in the soil and race and culture of the Near East, they survived thirteen centuries of Muslim–Arab and Muslim–Turkish domination. Their relations to Islam over the centuries may be characterized, in one word, as existentially chequered, morally subservient, and spiritually tragic, although, in the Arab world at least, they worked more closely with their Muslim compatriots on civic, social, cultural and national problems than any other Christian group. Religiously, all that can be said of them is that the little remnant to which they are now reduced has nevertheless managed to keep the faith, at least formally through the doctrine and liturgy of the Church, and considering concretely what they had to face and what existentially they went through, this in itself is a tremendous achievement, in fact nothing short of miraculous. So much for the past. The burden of the future we shall go into later.

Russia has always throughout history been deeply interested in the Orthodoxy of the Middle East. Russia therefore belongs to the external environment of this Orthodoxy. The Christianizing of the Slavic peoples was effected through Byzantine missionaries beginning with the ninth century, and an intimate relationship with Byzantium and its culture, thus established, has been maintained since then. Until the setting up of the independent patriarchate of Moscow in 1448, Russian Orthodoxy recognized the ultimate jurisdiction of the ecumenical patriarch, and even after it attained the autocephalous status it always looked upon itself as the child and heir of Byzantium. If the Russians called Moscow the third Rome, it was because, in their view, the first had lapsed into heresy for centuries, and the second had fallen into the hands of the infidels. In the seventeenth century the patriarchs of Alexandria and Antioch travelled to Russia seeking the spiritual, moral and material support of Moscow for their many problems.

On religious–cultural and political–military grounds, the Russians fought the Ottomans for centuries. They had always been lured by securing some firm foothold in the warm waters of the Mediterranean, and considering themselves the spiritual heirs of Byzantium, they looked upon the recapture of Constantinople as part of their national destiny. Europe, and especially England, stood in the way of their fulfilling this dream. We noted above the treaty of 1774 which recognized Russia's interest in the freedom and welfare of the Christian subjects of the Sultan. In the controversy between the Orthodox and uniates, Paris and Rome ranged themselves with the latter, while Russia consistently intervened with the Porte on the side of the former. In 1842 a delegation from the see of Antioch was sent to Russia to plead for assistance against the mounting activity of the Protestants and Catholics. In the nineteenth century, in opposing French and Russian influence in the Ottoman Empire, England patronized the non-Christians (Muslim and Druzes), and among the Christians, the Protestant missionaries; France supported the uniates (Maronites and Melkites); and Russia, the Orthodox.

The laying of the cornerstone of the Russian church of the Holy Trinity in Jerusalem by Grand Duke Constantine took place in 1859, and in 1881 the Princes Sergius, Paul and Constantine made their pilgrimage to the Holy City, where they were warmly received by the patriarch and clergy. The intention was that prayer was never to cease in the chapel they founded in the Garden of Gethsemane in memory of their mother. Upon their return to Russia, a Holy Land society was established in 1882; its headquarters was to be Nazareth and its purpose the promotion of elementary education and the provision of free medical service.

Of the four sees, particularly intimate relations developed during the nineteenth and twentieth centuries between the see of Antioch and the Russian Orthodox Church. Greek influence and interest concentrated more on the other three sees. In 1848 the Holy Synod of Moscow proposed, and the Tsar approved, that the church of the Ascension near the Kremlin be given to the see of Antioch, to the intent that its revenuc go to the education of the clergy and people of that see. In 1945 this church was replaced by another church whose ownership and the revenue therefrom have been retained by the Church of Antioch until this day. Missions were sent during the nineteenth century soliciting alms for the impoverished Church of Antioch from its more fortunate Russian sister, and the response, in characteristic Russian fashion, was always generous. Scores of men from Syria and Lebanon were sent to Russia, either for their higher theological or clerical education or to serve in the Antioch church of Moscow. Some of these men occupied very important positions in the Church of Antioch afterwards. One became patriarch (Alexandros III). Several became bishops. George Iṣbir Yārid taught in Russian schools and wrote what appears to be an important Russian work on Photius, on which Dvornik commented: "Ce travail n'a pas été assez pris en considération par ceux qui ont traité le problème."[1] Raphael Hawāwīnī was elevated to the episcopacy and appointed the first Syrian bishop over the Syrian Orthodox of America by the Holy Russian Synod itself. The Syrian Antiochian Orthodox Church of North America was thus founded by the Russian Orthodox Church. Gregory IV visited Russia before World War I, and the two patriarchs who succeeded him so far, Alexandros III and Theodosius VI, visited Russia several times with many bishops as guests of the Russian Orthodox Church. Patriarch Alexey of Moscow visited Beirut in 1945 and all four sees, together with Beirut, in 1960, and established special relations with Antioch, by having a representative (now a Russian bishop) near the patriarch in Damascus. He also sent a Russian priest to serve the Russian community in Beirut. Many generous gifts came from the Russian Church in recent years, including icons and vestments, extensive medical equipment for the Orthodox hospital in Beirut, and a beautiful golden altar for St George's Cathedral.

[1] François Dvornik, *Le Schisme de Photius* (Paris, Cerf, 1950), p. 36.

The Imperial Russian Orthodox Society for the Holy Land opened towards the end of the last century more than twenty schools, both for boys and girls, mostly in Lebanese towns and villages, but also in Damascus and Ḥimṣ. It sponsored the translation of numerous school textbooks into Arabic. Many Russian monks were sent to Lebanese and Syrian monasteries. The "Eastern" character of the Orthodox Church in the Middle East is demonstrated by the fact that if any language is written on icons or walls or other objects or pieces of furniture inside an Orthodox church, this language is always Arabic or Greek or Russian, but never, so far as I know, French or English or any language using the Latin script.

Russian consuls maintained close contacts at least with the see of Antioch. In a pastoral visit to the diocese of Ḥawrān (the church of Philadelphia of the Book of Revelation) in 1911, Gregory IV of Antioch was accompanied by Prince Boris Chakhovsky, the Russian consul in Damascus. In the service which he celebrated in a church named after St George, the patriarch spoke of "this ancient and venerable church" which had been so battered and ravaged by time, until God came to her succour through the providence of "the Tsar who with the eye of an eagle looked from the remote north upon her low estate".[1]

The year 1913 was the 300th anniversary of the establishment of the Romanoff dynasty. The Tsar invited Gregory IV of Antioch to visit Russia and be at the head of the religious celebrations planned for the occasion. The patriarch arrived in St Petersburg in February of that year. The Russian press warmly welcomed him to the soil of Russia, and praised his character, eloquence and piety, especially his firm stands in the face of the Catholic, Protestant and Masonic currents in the Middle East. In one of the ceremonies, Anthony, a Russian archbishop, addressed the patriarch of the Church of Antioch in the name of the Church of Russia as follows:

For 250 years the defenders of ecumenical Orthodoxy have not visited us. It is with veneration and happiness that we look upon you today, seeing in you the gladness of the Christian Church at her most beautiful, because in your Apostolic Person you occupy her highest summit. With utter spiritual joy we honour in your Person the supreme authority of the Church. While your throne no longer boasts of its former riches and external glory, nevertheless it is full of glory incorruptible, the glory of ever preaching the word

[1] Asad J. Rustum, *The Church of the City of God Great Antioch*, vol. III (Beirut, 1963), p. 349.

of salvation, the glory of struggling, in all prudence and with a heart pure and a resolve unmovable, for our divine faith. We do not honour the episcopacy for its riches and pomp, but for its spiritual struggle and self-denial. That is why we behold in your Person the splendour of Peter, the first head of the Church of Antioch, of St Ignatius the great...and of many others of God's elect. The Russian people, who revere the Apostolic struggle which has come down uninterrupted in your holy Church from the first disciples until now, perceive in you the bearer of this church glory, the glory of the harmony of earth and heaven, of the Church and Christ; and lift their voice with thanksgiving because they have been deemed worthy to behold the Person of your Beatitude.

Then, falling on his knees, Anthony added: "And here, prostrating themselves at your feet, the Russian people welcome you, rejoicing on their knees because you have entered the Holy Monastery of the capital of the north."[1]

On another occasion the Tsar received the patriarch in royal splendour. Sitting in his throne with the patriarch on his right, Nicholas turned to Gregory and said:

"I have heard for a long time of your intention to come here and I have much longed to see you. I know fully your uprightness and your piety, so I ask you to beseech and pray to the Lord God for me." Gregory answered: "I am a sinful man, my lord; nevertheless, may the Lord grant thee according to thy heart and faith; may He fulfil all the longings of thy bosom; and may He 'build up thy throne to all generations'." When the Tsar heard these words of David coming from the venerable prelate of the East, he was deeply moved, and descending from his throne he kissed the patriarch's right hand for the second time.[2]

It was on this trip that Gregory was asked by the Holy Russian Synod to elevate a certain archimandrite Alexey to the episcopacy; this he gladly did. It was this same Alexey who was destined to become metropolitan of Leningrad in 1933 and patriarch of Moscow in 1945, and who is still the head of the Russian Church until today. So intimately have the fates of Moscow and Antioch been intertwined in recent years that first Moscow ordains for Antioch its first bishop in North America, and then Antioch ordains a bishop who later became the patriarch of all the Russias.

The burden of this section has not been to provide a "history" of the relations between the Orthodoxy of the Middle East and the

[1] *Ibid.* p. 368.

[2] *Ibid.* pp. 368–9.

Orthodoxy of Russia; we have only illustrated in general how the latter Orthodoxy constitutes a sort of external environment within which the former Orthodoxy lives and with which it interacts. There are underlying affinities between the two Orthodoxies, stemming in part from their common Byzantine heritage, in part from the fact that both are "Eastern" or "non-Western". How may we characterize this Eastern and Byzantine type of Christianity as to its essence? There is a certain indefiniteness about its formulations, quite unlike the severe and clear-cut definitions of the romanized and aristotelianized West. In Orthodoxy much is left unsaid and undefined, and the attempt at defining it is often considered a provocation and a sin, much as God judged when Satan provoked David to number Israel. Orthodoxy is somewhat informal and democratic despite its hierarchical ecclesiastical order. Authority and tradition are thus accepted as a matter of course. The stress is on love and freedom, although a certain amount of phyletism is apparent in the identification of church and culture. The Fathers and the early Councils play the controlling role. There is thus a certain amount of existential discontinuity owing to the tragic discontinuities which afflicted the history of Orthodoxy itself. Despite this, the whole man is affirmed, without chopping him up into aspects and distinctions and functions and levels and rules. A certain degree of anarchy is also apparent, alike in thought and in the relations between flocks and shepherds and among the shepherds themselves. This anarchy is at times delightful and refreshing, but usually it helps only to enfeeble the soul. An educated Orthodox of the Middle East understands and appreciates a Dostoyevsky or a Berdyaev much more than an Aristotle or an Aquinas. The very soul of Orthodoxy breathes mystery, otherness, transcendence. Morals are considered important, but Orthodoxy is not moralistic: its intention is to bring out the mystery and freedom of Being. The moral-puritan ingredient in the Divine Liturgy is virtually nil: it is all about the real, existing, transcendent God. A sinner forgets his sin and obtains release therefrom because he is wholly absorbed in God. Besides the absolute reality of God and the efficacity of His mother's intercession, nothing is more striking in the Divine Liturgy of St John Chrysostom which the faithful know by heart than the repeated call to trust the mercy and loving-kindness of Christ. With respect to this dimension of transcendence Orthodoxy is at one with Islam, although of course it tempers it with God's humanity which Islam does not. The spirit of Chrysostom dominates the spirituality of Orthodoxy, and so to understand Orthodoxy one must steep oneself in the incomparable homilies and the magnificent liturgy of this Saint. Nay, to understand a good deal of the characteristic Russian spirit, even under communism, the knowledge of Chrysostom is indispensable.

But for the Russian Orthodox Church, Orthodoxy in the Middle East would have been an orphan. The Churches of the West come to it as to something alien: they want to change and convert it. Russian Orthodoxy comes to it as to bone of its bones and flesh of its flesh. It is not another, it is the same, at least in liturgy and in spirit. The Russian Church comes to share with it its trials and its blessings. People glibly speak of the Russian Church being used by the Soviet State in the Middle East. Thank God for the Orthodox Church in the Soviet State, and thank God for any contact with that church. Who is using whom remains to be seen at the end of time. Paul did not despise his Roman citizenship: he used it to the glory of Christ. When one sees a Russian patriarch with the cross on his breast standing in the royal gates and blessing the people with another cross in his hand, and when one attends a two-hour service in which a Russian bishop officiates and a Russian deacon assists, one is profoundly moved. Such witness to Jesus Christ cannot be altogether insincere, no matter who is using whom. For Jesus Christ is such that insincerity with respect to Him cannot long endure. Therefore, give me a witnessing person, in any system and under any circumstances, and I am immediately sure there is some sincerity there. For it must never be forgotten "that no man can say that Jesus is the Lord, but by the Holy Ghost". One can therefore say that the relations between the Russian Orthodox Church and the Orthodox Church of the Middle East have been so intimate that the former in truth belongs to much more than the external environment of the latter. In historical issues affecting the character and destiny of the Church, Middle Eastern Orthodoxy waits for the guidance and lead of the Russian Church.

Islam, with its laws, beliefs and religious outlook, is Orthodoxy's immediate world in the Middle East. The Russian Orthodox world has been perhaps its most important external environment. But the Orthodox of the Middle East are also in daily contact on every level of existence with other fellow Christians, principally with those in organic communion with Rome (the uniates). The important uniates of the

Middle East are the Maronites, the Melkites or Greek Catholics, the Chaldeans, the Copts, the Syrians, and the Armenians. Of the last four there are still many who are not in communion with Rome, but the term uniate would apply to them only when they are in such communion. All these groups have their own non-Latin rites and their own patriarchs, and all of them profess the identical faith of the Roman Catholic Church. The Melkites, following the identical Byzantine rite of the Orthodox, are descendants from Orthodox bodies which at some point since 1054 re-established communion with Rome. The Catholics of the Middle East include also Western Catholic missionaries (Jesuits, Franciscans, Dominicans, Carmelites, and others) and many Western Catholics engaged in business, education or diplomacy. The total life of the Orthodox in the Middle East must be interpreted, not only in relation to Islam and the larger world of Orthodoxy beyond, but in relation to the Roman Catholic world, both native and Western.

The relations of the Orthodox with the non-Catholic Christians of the Middle East have been frozen ever since the latter were excluded by the early Councils (principally that of Chalcedon) from communion with the Church Universal. Outwardly, relations are friendly and cordial, and there could even be intermarriage subject to conversion, but there is no doctrinal or liturgical or communal fellowship. These non-Catholic non-Orthodox Christians are good citizens wherever they are, although they have sustained many persecutions. They usually make common cause, wherever they can, with the Orthodox and Catholics on broad issues affecting the fate and freedom of the Christian community in the Middle East. There have been lately contacts and conversations between them and the ecumenical patriarch Athenagoras with a view to examining if fundamental points of doctrine, especially those which originate in the definitions of Chalcedon, may not be adjusted to the full satisfaction of the Orthodox Church so as to enable this Church to accept them back into full communion with it. The attitude of the Orthodox Church in this regard appears to be that any re-examination of position is welcome, but the Church obviously cannot alter the intent of dogma as handed down from the early Councils and as understood and interpreted by the doctors of the Church. There is also a general feeling that the correct approach to the problem of unity in this ecumenical age is for the non-Catholic non-Orthodox Christian bodies in the Middle East to reconstitute, if possible, with the Orthodox Church the Church of the East, and then in this corporate form to explore with the Church of the West what can be done to bring about the unity of East and West in the Church Universal. I think the Church of Rome itself is no longer interested in creating splinter uniate bodies in the Middle East, so that it would probably bless this approach of the East first consolidating its own ranks, while it keeps extending the hand of fellowship to all, in the spirit of comprehension and charity. There is an underlying spiritual–cultural affinity between the Orthodox and the non-Orthodox non-Catholics of the Middle East beyond and above any doctrinal differences congealed in the anathemas of the Councils, an affinity that brackets them together as quite apart from the Roman Catholics. It is this extra-dogmatic "Eastern" affinity that may help considerably in bringing them together, although the Orthodox Church cannot "buy" agreement with them at the expense of wider disagreement with Rome. All of this of course is human reflexion; the exact intention of the Holy Ghost may be quite different.

If relations between the Orthodox and the non-Catholic Christians in the Middle East have been frozen for centuries, and there is nothing moving or creative about them, the situation is entirely different with respect to the relations between the Orthodox and the Catholics. Here the confrontation is most active, most challenging, and most dynamic. There is real movement here, and things are really happening.

Present-day relations between Orthodox and Catholics in the Middle East must be viewed against the background of four basic developments which have, in varying degrees of relevance and potency, produced a peculiar legacy of attitude and feeling: the great schism of 1054; the Latin Crusades which were attended by most unfortunate acts against the Orthodox and their culture, acts which led the Orthodox of Constantinople to prefer, if it were a question of strict choice between Latin-Catholic domination (or assimilation) and Ottoman-Muslim domination, "the turbans of the *shaykhs* to the crowns of the cardinals"; the uniate movement, especially that of the seventeenth, eighteenth and nineteenth centuries, which culminated in the establishment of the Greek Catholic (Melkite) Church in the Middle East with its own parallel hierarchy to that of the Orthodox Church; and the proselytizing activity of Catholic missions.

The schism and the Crusades fall outside the proper scope of this study. Both ultimately involve the human difficulty of reconciling East and West, Greek and Latin, the claims of the particular and the claims of the universal. The Church, *to be* the Church, must rise above, by including and accommodating itself to, all particularisms, subject to the ineluctable proviso that all that does not accord with the will of Jesus Christ in any particularism, be it Eastern or Western, Greek or Latin, cannot be tolerated or risen above, nor can it be included or accommodated in the universality of the Church. Thus, if any particularism contains beliefs or practices condemned by Jesus Christ, they must be given up. But this is the metaphysical problem underlying both the schism and the Crusades.

The student of the events of the seventeenth, eighteenth and nineteenth centuries which brought about the establishment and consolidation of the Greek Catholic (Melkite) Church in the Middle East is struck by four things: (1) the utter disorder, decay and corruption in the Orthodox Church itself; (2) the intense activity of the Catholic missionaries, principally the Jesuits; (3) the fact that the Porte helped in causing the Orthodox people to fall out among themselves; and (4) the fact that the truth about many of these events is very difficult to ascertain, so that contradictory stories could be shown to be historically equally plausible.

On the role of the Ottomans, one or two observations must be made. Despite (or perhaps because of) Russia's influence with the Porte, and despite (or perhaps because of) the presence of large and influential Greek colonies throughout the empire, it was the fear of the Ottomans lest the Orthodox Church, under the protection or with the support of the Russian government and the Russian Church, might increase Russia's influence in the empire and might subvert it, that conduced the Porte to look with favour upon splitting up the Orthodox people among themselves and having some of them re-establish their allegiance to Rome. At the time of their capture of Constantinople in 1453, the Ottomans were more afraid of the West than of Russia, and so they opposed all projects of Orthodox communion with Rome; from the seventeenth century onwards they became more afraid of Russia than of the West, and so they favoured the splintering westwards of as much of the Orthodox Church as possible. This is the essential meaning of the Eastern Question: the rivalry of the non-Middle-Eastern world with respect to the Middle East, the division of Europe (including Russia) about the Ottoman Empire, the inability of the West (including Russia) to make up its mind once and for all concerning "the sick man of Europe", the cynical letting this "sick man" remain sick rather than curing him or letting him die, the perpetual dragging of the Eastern Question from indecision to indecision, the ability of Turkey to play off and balance East against West and West against East from generation to generation. All these phenomena repeat themselves today to perfection, albeit under different circumstances and with different actors. There is thus an eternal character about the Middle East: its destiny appears to be never to belong once and for all to one master, whether the master be itself or someone else. The Middle East is always an undecided question.

The documents reveal an incredible amount of intrigue, malice, spitefulness, meanness, mercenariness, venality, pettiness, feuding, vengefulness, and violence. Neither the uniates nor the Orthodox were free from any of these traits. They also instigated or sided with non-Christians against each other. They did everything that St Paul condemns in his epistles. There simply was no Christian charity. This is what happens when utter corruption and rottenness supervene. The indisputable outcome of all this confusion and decadence, however, is that there are today two hierarchies of one and the same rite stemming from the same trunk—the mother Orthodox Church and the Greek Catholic (Melkite) Church. This is the result at once of the decadence of Orthodoxy, the active alertness of Rome, the support by the French and Austrians of the uniate movement, and the successful playing off by the Porte of Christian forces against each other, forces existing within the empire and forces impinging upon it from without. The fact that Orthodoxy still exists betokens that it was not altogether decadent and that Russia was not altogether ineffectual. The fact that two hierarchies now exist betokens that neither Orthodoxy nor Russia was powerful enough to prevent part of Orthodoxy from splintering off into the bosom of Rome, even if that meant turning its back on the other part. It does nobody any good now to dwell on this whole sad episode. That is the task of the "pure" historian. But there is before us today a far higher task than "pure" historical research, a task attested alike by the three great men of our times, John XXIII, Paul VI and Athenagoras I: to heal wounds, to pray and work for the regeneration of rotten human nature, to bring hearts closer together, to forgive all, past and present, to ask forgiveness for all, past and present, to press hard towards the prize of the unity of love in the bond of peace in Jesus Christ.

I shall touch only on one or two points to illustrate some of the factors involved. In his instructions to his new ambassador to the Porte in 1728, Louis XV made it clear that the French government had three aims in spreading the Roman Catholic faith in the Ottoman Empire: the Christianizing of the Muslims, the conversion of the schismatics, and the uprooting of the seeds of heresy. The first was most delicate, as was proven by the fact that Rome herself had forbidden her missionaries to preach the Gospel to the Muslims. Western Christian missionary effort, then, was to concentrate on wooing the Christians not in communion with Rome back into communion with her. Western missionaries and native Catholics intervened with the French ambassador to support the uniate party among the Orthodox, but after he had time to study the situation and despite the instructions of his sovereign, he came to the opposite conclusion, and he wrote back to Paris in 1730 that the overzealous Catholic missionaries should be curbed, that the extreme uniates among the Orthodox should not be supported, and that, in the interests of concord and amity among the Christians, it was better to work with the moderate Orthodox elements. In another report in 1740 this same ambassador stressed the point that the spectacle of Christian fighting Christian in the world of Islam encouraged the Ottomans both to play the Christians off against each other and, by thus weakening them, to be more harsh and repressive in their treatment of them. He concluded that the only prudent policy was the promotion of love and forgiveness among the Christians themselves.[1]

Maximus Maẓlūm was the Greek Catholic patriarch in the first half of the nineteenth century. Under his energetic and determined leadership his Church attained its status as a uniate Church wholly independent from the Orthodox Church. He was made a French subject in 1822, thus enjoying French legal protection under the system of capitulations. There was active participation both by France and by the Latin clergy in the process of consolidating the Greek Catholic Church and separating it from the Orthodox Church. Maximus remained under the direct jurisdiction of the Armenian Catholic patriarch of Constantinople until 1837, when the sultan granted him a *berat* whereby, while still under the ultimate jurisdiction of the Armenian patriarch, he acquired virtual autonomy over all the three sees of Alexandria, Antioch and Jerusalem. In 1848 a second *berat*

[1] Père Antoine Rabbath, *Documents inédits pour servir à l'Histoire du Christianisme en Orient* (Paris, 1910), tome 2, pp. 388–9 and 561 f.

recognized him as completely independent from his former Armenian chief, while the other uniates remained subordinate to him. With this act of the sultan the establishment of a thoroughgoing parallelism (except for the external fact that whereas the Orthodox had three separate patriarchs for the three sees, the Greek Catholics combined all three under one patriarch) between the Greek Catholic hierarchy and that of the Orthodox was finally solemnized. The reaction of the four Orthodox patriarchs of the Middle East to the establishment of this parallel hierarchy was to issue a statement in 1838 rejecting and condemning this latinizing activity and repudiating the separation of the Greek Catholics from jurisdictional unity with their Orthodox brethren.

The Catholic shock helped to awaken the Orthodox Church. Without this shock Orthodoxy might have slumbered and decayed further. The response has been to open many schools, publish much Orthodox literature, renovate the music, found many new societies, educate the clergy, exhibit some concern for the material conditions under which they live, and in general fall back upon Orthodoxy's rich inner material and spiritual resources. The Orthodox Youth Movement is part of this response. We shall examine the promise of some of these manifestations later in this essay.

You cannot stop individual conversion; you cannot prevent individual change of allegiance; nor are you morally permitted to do so. Freedom of conscience is ultimate and sacred. Until the end of time there will be fluidity between the confessions on an individual basis. The methods of proselytizing may be repugnant, but when you come upon a corrupt scene (corrupt, not in the light of subjective criteria, but as judged by the objective norms of the Gospel, and by the wonderful flowering that occurred in these parts in the early centuries) and try to salvage as much out of it as possible, awakening people to the infinite riches and boundless grace of Jesus Christ, you cannot be blamed. You will be blamed if you looked upon it and did nothing. The Catholics and the Protestants came to the East and found, relatively to what obtained in the West, death there; it was the Holy Spirit in them that moved them to blow some life into this desolation. Thank God for that. The Orthodox Church can blame only its death for this. Christianity was all but snuffed out of existence under Muslim rule; in North Africa it disappeared altogether; it was a miracle it did not disappear in the Near East. What will you do, then, if you are in the shoes of the Christians of the West? Here they come and they find remnants, relics, barely moving corpses. They try to resuscitate them as best they can; they use the best methods they know; many individual stupidities are committed, but there is exigency, urgency, impatience in historical decision; they cannot look upon death and do nothing, especially in a region which was once so alive and to whose life the rest of the Christian world owes so much; they cannot wait until death so to speak moves itself. In the case of Maximus Maẓlūm, for instance, he was undoubtedly torn between two things: his profound desire for unity with Rome which every Christian must feel, and his attachment to the Greek Church which would not move with him. In a crisis of this order one goes through the agony of hell. How does he resolve it? Nobody knows what happens in a man's soul caught in the vice of such a conflict of allegiances; he himself probably does not know what is happening within him; God alone knows; God alone finally judges. Even his mixed motives are not important; God makes use of everything, mixed motives and everything, even the devil. Finally everything conduces to the glory of the Holy Trinity.

But while individual conversion can never and should never be stopped, *after a certain point two lines of policy* can be adopted by a more virile church descending upon a relatively dead one: to discourage change of allegiance, throwing people back upon their own spiritual resources, working with them all the time as closely as possible, and always assuring them of your love and fellowship; and when the church, the corporate body, the hierarchy, as such, shows signs of reawakening, of rediscovering its own proper heritage, of letting the Holy Spirit creatively and gloriously blow upon it, of assuming and pushing on with its responsibilities, then the line of policy should be to work and collaborate with it directly, in the bond of fellowship and love, on a footing of equality, letting the Holy Spirit itself gradually and freely open the eyes of both churches to the right *order of relationship* between them according to the will of Christ. There is no general rule by which one can decide in advance and as it were mechanically when that "certain point" is reached; that can only be left to the responsible decision of the more virile church under concrete circumstances.

There is not only a difference in approach and method, but a radical difference in tone and spirit, between the attempts at church unity made by Rome in the nineteenth century (by Pius IX in 1848 and Leo XIII in 1894) and the Orthodox replies thereto, and what has been happening lately under the aegis and with the inspiration of John XXIII, Paul VI and Athenagoras I. There is in the new climate a minimum of the old spirit of "we have always been right and you have always been wrong". With the apparently sincere abandonment of all polemics and all mutual recrimination, we seem to be on the threshold of a new era in the relations between Orthodoxy and Catholicism. The gentle pressure must be maintained; the sisterly challenge must not relent; and the aim should always be the glory of God and the overcoming of all human limitation and sin.

Thousands of Orthodox youth have studied in American schools, in the United States and in the Middle East. Athens College, Sofia College, Robert College in Istanbul and its sister women's institution, Smyrna College, Aleppo College, the American University of Beirut, the American University at Cairo, Asyūṭ College, and scores of American, British and German missionary secondary schools throughout the region, all number important Orthodox men and women among their graduates. At least three Orthodox bishops in the see of Antioch are former students at the American University of Beirut.

Whatever the causes, the fact is that the Protestant missionary activity over the last century and a half in the Middle East cannot boast of many recruits from Islam or Catholicism: Protestant converts in the Middle East stem overwhelmingly from Orthodox origins.

Who can forget the Holy Land? Who can forget Jerusalem, Bethany, Bethlehem, Nazareth, Joppa, Caesarea Philippi, Jordan, Galilee, the Dead Sea, Tyre and Sidon, Lebanon? People's right hand would sooner forget her cunning, and their tongue would sooner cleave to the roof of their mouth, before they forget these names and places. From now until the end of time, namely, until the Second Coming of Christ, and even beyond, these names will evoke in the heart of the Christian who loves Jesus Christ above everything else the deepest longing and the purest tears. So missionaries *had* to come from the Protestant world of the North and West to the Catholic and Orthodox lands of the Middle East. No power on earth can deny them this right. No limitation on their part or on the part of the Christians in these lands can prevent them from coming. They wanted to share with the remnants of Christianity here their own experience of Jesus Christ. Those of us who live in the Near East (I am now distinguishing between the Near and the Middle East), whether Christian, Muslim or Jewish, must understand and accept this eternal lure of our land: Jesus Christ, the Son of God, was born, lived, taught, talked to the woman from Samaria at Jacob's well, suffered, and was glorified *here*—not in Poland or Peru, not in the Cameroons or Korea, not in Florida or France. Therefore Protestant missionaries *had* to come to the Middle East, and a thousand million years from now, Christians from China, or from Mars or some planet in the Betelgeuse system, will come here too, to witness and to worship, and to share with the inhabitants of these hallowed lands their new and different experience of Jesus Christ. Let no Arab nationalism, let no Jewish Zionism, let no Middle Eastern Christian fear or sentimentalism, let no Western materialism, let no Christian secularism anywhere, beguile any man into believing that the Near East will ever cease to be a cosmic magnet for all those who know and love Jesus Christ. This is its unalterable destiny. We did not create it, we had nothing to do with it; in fact many of us, scared and limited as we are, wish it and have wished it otherwise: it was all determined by Jesus Christ himself.

So Christian missionaries *had* to come from the West. They were most sincere and dedicated. They were as human as the rest of us. Let no man judge them by their humanity alone, although by this scale they would still stand above most of us. They can only be fairly judged by their burden and their witness. They were bursting with something they wanted to say. Behind every limitation and ambiguity, what they really were saying was this: that they *too* had known the Lord Jesus Christ, and drawn by His star, they were coming here, this time from the West, to offer Him in the land of His birth and passion the gifts of their hearts. They struggled, they suffered, they fumbled, they served, they were tried, but here it was where they fought the good fight, here it was where they witnessed, and above all here it was where most of them died. And a crown is doubtless reserved for them at the hands of the Just Judge, at the hands of Him who sees all and understands all and in His lovingkindness rewards all way beyond their expectations or merits. Such were the Jessups and the Porters, the Blisses and the Van Dycks, the Websters and the Adamses, the Wests and the Crawfords, the Browns and the Dodges, the Closes and the Dormans, the Nickoleys and the Seelyes, the Days and the Dodds, the Nicols and the Stoltzfuses, the Watsons and the Smiths, the Quays and the Leavitts; and countless others. They established schools, founded hospitals, tended the sick, educated the uncouth and ignorant, trained the mind to see in the laboratory and observe in the field, taught youth to gird up their loins like men, imparted to the children of the Middle East new dignity and self-reliance, translated the Bible, published books, preached the Gospel, shared the deepest in their heart and in their life. They challenged the older churches and roused them from their sleep. If they somewhat misunderstood Mary, the Sacraments, the Saints, the Eucharist, the holy images, the liturgy, the hierarchy, the sign of the Cross, the holy feasts, the monastic life, the continuity of the tradition—all authentic marks of Near Eastern spirituality—that was their limitation, no doubt brought about by their honest zeal, and by that blinding impatience which often attends an effulgence of light. And now after a century and a half there is humility and tolerance, there is understanding and thankfulness, all around, on the part of the older churches for the immense labour of love thus conceived and thus lavished, and on the part of the comers from the North and West for seeing that the older churches did not lack the fullness of the deposit of faith, though they were wholly unworthy and at times wholly unaware of it.

Greek Orthodox existence in the Middle East cannot be fully understood apart from the total impact, both direct and indirect, of the great American and European Protestant missionary movement of the past century and a half.

The "presence" of the Western powers is part of the external environment in which the Orthodox of the Middle East live and have their being. The Middle East was opened up to the West in recent times first through the impact of Napoleon. French envoys often worked hand in hand with Catholic missionaries, as well as with the native Catholic clergy. This close collaboration with Catholics was guaranteed to the French by juridical instruments concluded with the Vatican, and after the fall of the Ottoman Empire a new concordat was signed in 1926 according to which the French Republic and her representatives would receive special honour in special high Masses celebrated in particular Catholic churches in the Asian territories which formerly belonged to the Ottoman Empire.

Nor does France yield to any Western power in the primacy of her interests and privileges in the Holy Places in Palestine, as was demonstrated in the debate over the fate of Jerusalem and the Holy Places in the United Nations in 1947, 1948 and 1949. There have been and there still are most vigorous French schools, both lay and religious, throughout the Middle East, principally in Egypt, Syria and Lebanon. In sheer numbers, both of schools and of students enrolled therein, and in intensity of cultural influence exerted thereby, France surpasses any Western power in the Middle East. There is a traditional friendship between France and Lebanon, repeatedly affirmed in history, most recently by the Presidents of Lebanon and France when they met in Paris in May 1965. The Maronites of Lebanon (the largest single religious bloc and by far the most influential element in the country) have always had closer relations with France than with any other Western power, and it was on the strength of these relations that the Maronite patriarch right after World War I asked in the name of Lebanon for a French mandate over the country. The sense of independence and distinctness in Lebanon is principally fostered by the immense cultural and political influence of the Université St Joseph, a French Jesuit institution in Beirut. If the "presence" of France in Lebanon is so dominant and decisive, and if, as we shall see later, Orthodoxy in the Middle East is being increasingly squeezed into Lebanon, it is impossible to exaggerate the importance of Catholic and lay France as an external determinant of this Orthodoxy.

Orthodox existence is determined by this massive presence, both directly through the many Orthodox who study in French schools or are otherwise impregnated with French culture, and indirectly through the many Catholic communities to whom France accorded preferential treatment, both political and cultural, and with whom the Orthodox have to associate and interact, both as fellow citizens and fellow Christians. It was fear of this preferential treatment, as well as other causes (both Arab-national and Orthodox-international), which led the Greek Orthodox Patriarch, Gregory IV, when the fate of Lebanon and Syria was being deliberated by the victors of World War I, to express disapproval of France being granted a mandate over Syria and Lebanon.

The meaning of France is not exhausted by the foregoing. Right after World War I Paris became a world Orthodox centre, both through the Russian Orthodox seminary that was established there and through the writings of many Russian thinkers, notably Berdyaev. Some Middle Eastern clergy studied in the Paris seminary, and some Orthodox thinkers in the Middle East have been influenced by Berdyaev.

Because of her Indian empire, Britain viewed the Middle East as strategically vital to her. It is this strategic necessity which explains at once Britain's stubborn opposition to the penetration of the region by Russia, her nineteenth-century policy of "safeguarding the integrity of the Ottoman Empire", the firm hold which she retained on Egypt and the Suez Canal, and her demanding and obtaining a mandate over Palestine. All this was reinforced after World War I by the extensive and—to her industry—absolutely vital oil interests which she developed and consolidated in the Persian Gulf area.

In opposing Russia (the Crimean War was only one instance) Britain helped to weaken the influence of the principal protector of Orthodoxy in the Middle East. Nor did she supply an alternative protection herself, for example, through the solicitude of the Anglican Church. For more than a century and until after World War II, no Western power had the pervasive and decisive influence that Britain enjoyed in the Middle East, and the Orthodox, no less than everybody else, were quite conscious of and had to adjust to this all-encompassing *Pax Britannica.* Her rivalry with France, ever since Napoleon's adventure in Egypt, led Britain to oppose French influence in the Middle East; and if this meant also opposing, or at least not encouraging, Catholicism, the motive was more political than religious, more to avoid further complications than to spread a rival religious persuasion; although Britain did show sympathy towards Protestant missions in the Middle East.

We thus see how the meaning of Britain in Orthodox existence in the Middle East consisted, negatively, in setting limits to Russian Orthodox help and protection and curing the Orthodox of any extravagant and therefore false expectations of succour from outside on religious grounds; and positively, in encouraging the Orthodox to identify themselves—what they were otherwise prone to do—with native nationalist movements (this was the principal effect of Lawrence upon Orthodox leaders), in thinking realistically in terms of peaceful co-existence with their Muslim fellow citizens, in opening the world of the West to them through the English language and through education in English schools, as well as the general order that the *Pax Britannica* promoted and vouchsafed.

America determines the Orthodox of the Middle East, temporally, through the Greek, Syrian and Lebanese emigration to the United States, through the preponderant political role which the United States has been playing in the affairs of the Middle East since World War II, and through American commerce and enterprise; and spiritually, through American schools in the area, through the many students who have studied in the United States, through American films, books and magazines, through the flourishing Orthodox churches in the United States, and through the American Protestant missionary movement.

Practically all the Middle Eastern emigration to the Western Hemisphere, as well as to Australia and New Zealand, is Christian (in the case of Lebanon, as many people of Lebanese origin live abroad as in Lebanon, and they are overwhelmingly Christian), with the result that there is hardly a Christian family in the Middle East (outside the Copts) that does not claim some relative in the United States, and this has tended to some extent to "Americanize" Christian, and (owing to the relatively greater French influence on the non-Orthodox Christians) especially Orthodox, existence. Although not in the same style nor with the same motives, the United States has nevertheless exerted in recent years the same dominant influence in the Middle East as did Britain formerly, although Britain has never been quite absent from the scene despite her reverses in Suez and Iraq. The policy of the United States is to ensure what it calls the stability of the area, and when broken down into its elements this phrase means the security of Israel, the prevention of change of frontiers by force, the protection of the vast American oil investments, and the exclusion, or at least the limitation as much as possible, of communist influence in the area. In the American enterprises in the Middle East many Orthodox have been earning their living. Taken as a whole, there is thus a marked American economic, political and cultural presence which makes itself significantly felt in Orthodox existence in the Middle East.

The very word "East" in the phrase "the Near and Middle East" proves that this region is intimately related to "the West". This is true historically, geopolitically and economically. In so far as there is a trace of religious content (or at least of humane–cultural–liberal content) in the West's dealings with the Middle East, the Christians and therefore the Orthodox receive some sustenance. Speaking of the West without Russia, this religious content, if it exists, can only be Catholic or Protestant; in that case the Orthodox are relatively at a disadvantage. In so far as the dealings of the West, with or without Russia, are purely secular–political–economic (which is pre-eminently the case today), the Christians and therefore the Orthodox are culturally and religiously submerged. The Orthodox Church must struggle alone today, expecting only such indirect sympathy and help as she may manage accidentally to glean from the Church of Russia, the Church of Greece, the Church of England, and the World Council of Churches.

The relations between the four Orthodox sees of the Middle East were often troubled. What saved them from falling out completely with each other was their identity of liturgy and doctrine, their common traditions, the fact that their flocks constituted small minorities in the Middle Eastern world of Islam and therefore they had no alternative but to cling to one another, the recognition by the sees of Alexandria, Antioch and Jerusalem of a primacy of honour to the ecumenical patriarch of Constantinople, and of his being preceded in this respect in the Church Universal only by the patriarch of Rome, the fact that the Ottoman Turks from the beginning accorded a certain legal status to the primacy of the patriarch of Constantinople over the other patriarchs, a status which enabled the ecumenical patriarch to exercise real authority, always of course within limits, over the other sees in moments of crisis, and the appearance now and then of wise and forgiving patriarchs who helped to heal whatever breaches happened to exist at the time.

Two outstanding cases of inter-see friction may be cited: the quarrel over the successor to Athanasius V, patriarch of Jerusalem, in 1844, when Constantinople tried to extend its influence in that see, and the quarrel over the Bulgarian question in 1872 when Constantinople convened a Council which excommunicated the Bulgarian exarch on grounds of phyletism, and either the clergy or the laity of the sees of Jerusalem and Antioch did not go along with the findings of the Council. A third case concerned the see of Antioch. During the nineteenth century this see fought for its independence from Constantinople. Ottoman intrigue, Greek nationalism, Arab nationalism, and Russian Orthodox (and even political) interests, all had a hand, of course in different ways, in this fight. Independence was finally won in the last year of the century when Meletius II succeeded the deposed Spiridon. Meletius was then recognized by the entire Orthodox world except by the three patriarchs of Constantinople, Alexandria and Jerusalem, and this isolation of Antioch persisted until the ascent of Gregory IV to the throne of Antioch in 1906 when amity and concord were once again restored between the four sister sees.

The risk of being afflicted by such frictions, jealousies, and divisions is exactly the price which the Orthodox Church pays for not adopting the Roman principle of strict centralization. (I am not thinking here of the dogmatic-canonical character of this principle; I am here only speaking rationally.) In a predominantly Christian world, such as the world of Byzantium or the world of Russia or even the world of Greece, such a risk may be worth taking, in view of the local independence and responsibility thus assured, without loss of Christian freedom and anchorage. But in an overwhelmingly non-Christian world, such as the Middle East, in which Christian freedom and anchorage are already considerably circumscribed, the risk tells tragically upon the soul of the faithful. Here the communion is superficial and the sense of unity abstract and sentimental. Here reigns dreadful solitude and there is pathetic drift. You cannot expect great spiritual heights from four orphans quarrelling miserably like children in a totally alien world. That they survived at all under such conditions is indeed a miracle, but it is not of their making. It is false to conclude from the foregoing that the norm in inter-see relations was feuding and quarrelling; this was rather the exception, and the rule was concord and co-operation. But quarrelling and feuding did mar their relations, and did determine externally Orthodox existence in the Middle East

Recent years witnessed no occasions for friction, as the four sees are now completely independent in the conduct of their internal affairs. Relations between them have therefore lately been smooth and friendly. While in the pan-Orthodox gatherings which have lately taken place at Rhodes no decision could be taken against the wishes of the churches of Greece and Russia, especially with respect to Orthodoxy's attitude towards the ecumenism of Rome, and while Antioch has at times humbly mediated between these two great sister Churches, Athenagoras of Constantinople has been playing a leading role, and the other three sees of the Middle East have tended to show complete solidarity with his position. This is a very precarious matter, as the whole thing has depended on the outstanding personality of Athenagoras who is now fairly well advanced in years.

Two of the cases of inter-see friction to which we referred in the preceding section—the Bulgarian question and the controversy, which raged in the last decade of the last century, as to whether it should be a Greek or an Arab who should occupy the throne of Antioch—raise the question of the relations between the faithful natives and the dominant Greek clergy. The Greeks fought tenaciously to maintain their supremacy. It is easy to see the virus of nationalism in all this, both on the part of the Greeks and of the faithful, but the thing cannot be so glibly interpreted. The Greeks were actuated by a most praiseworthy sense of responsibility; they hated wantonly to leave the tremendous divine treasure entrusted to them in unworthy or immature hands; and the natives were naturally unhappy for having to deal with superiors who did not understand their language and did not quite appreciate their customs and culture; and the Meletius solution of 1899 was perhaps inevitable. This is the problem of all struggle for independence, and while in the case of individuals the age of eighteen or twenty-one may be rationally assigned for the "attainment of reason", when it comes to political or cultural or religious "independence", no such natural rule commends itself. Only the actual struggles and decisions of history determine the issue. Phyletism may be hurled at both the Greeks and the Arabic-speaking faithful, because both were racially conscious and culturally determined; and it is always the case, where the Holy Ghost does not intervene and subdue and sober, that one phyletism provokes and calls forth another. It redounds to the enduring glory of the Greeks, such as patriarchs Methodius and Hierothius of the last century, that they preserved the priceless jewel of which they were custodians absolutely pure and untarnished, despite the unworthiness of individuals here and there, and that they were big enough to train and raise and sponsor such men as Gerasimos Yārid, Gerasimos Masarra, Gregory Ḥaddād, Alexandros Ṭaḥḥān, and others, who later became bishops and patriarchs, and who acquitted themselves most worthily in the office with which they were charged. The credit that is justly due to the Greeks is all the more apparent when one reads the abject slavishness with which the natives attacked their Greek superiors before the Ottoman authorities. Faced with such depths of corruption which recur again and again in the history of Middle Eastern Orthodoxy, one praises the Lord for the incredible wonder with which he has enabled his Church to surmount and survive all human rottenness and folly.

We thus see how concrete Orthodox existence in the Middle East was determined throughout the nineteenth century by a struggle, now and then erupting from hiddenness and subtlety into open crudeness, between the dominant Greek hierarchy and an emerging native hierarchy, supported by a nascent Arab nationalism which was itself in turn, both for good and for bad motives, encouraged if not incited by the Russians. The sees of Alexandria and Jerusalem are still Greek-dominated, while it is difficult to conceive of the ecumenical see as being ever controlled by non-Greeks. Only the see of Antioch, with the election of Meletius in 1899, has been since wholly in the hands of Syrians and Lebanese. And in the see of Jerusalem there are rumblings of uneasiness between Greeks and Arabs, muffled and mitigated by the state of relative helplessness and lethargy in which Orthodoxy finds itself in Jordan and Israel.

Orthodoxy in the Middle East lives in a Muslim world. It has had intimate relations with Russian Orthodoxy and Russian culture. It has been in daily creative contact with Roman Catholicism. The Protestants descended upon it in the nineteenth century, and it has had to react and adjust to them. The Western powers have had separate policies in the Middle East, often conflicting with one another, and almost always at variance with Russian policy, whether Tsarist or Soviet; this whole tangle, in relation both to the Ottoman Empire and to the successor states after the decline and fall of this empire, constitutes what is called the Eastern Question, and Orthodoxy had to accommodate itself to the changing exigencies of this Question. Jealousies and quarrels have not been absent from the relations subsisting between the four Orthodox sees. And the Greeks have had their own cultural–political problems with the non-Greek populations of the Middle East, and there has been real tension between the dominant Greek clergy and the non-Greek faithful natives, certainly in the see of Antioch and to a lesser extent in the sees of Alexandria and Jerusalem. All these constitute what we have called "the external determinants of Orthodoxy in the Middle East". The Orthodox Church has lived and struggled and survived under the external determination of these seven factors.

Having ascertained "the external environment" of this Church, we now ask: what is this Church in itself? What is *it* that is so externally determined? A thing is principally its own being, *and then* it enters into and undergoes all sorts of relations with *others*. Nothing that is not something in itself can have any relations with anything. It is only because Orthodoxy is already something in itself that one can speak of the Muslim world, the Russian world, the Catholic world, the Protestant world, the Western world, and the Greek world, as variously bearing upon *it*, and of troubled or smooth relations prevailing between *its* four sees. What, then, is this something-in-itself which we call the Orthodox Church in the Middle East? What is it made up of, what is its life, what are its problems, what are the challenges that face it, what are its prospects? The following tabulation explains itself.

The Orthodox Church in the Middle East

1. Sees	Istanbul (Constantinople)	Alexandria (data relate to Egypt only)	Antioch (actual seat in Damascus)	Jerusalem
2. Patriarchs (July 1965)	Athenagoras I	Christophorus II	Theodosius VI	Benedictus I
3. Bishops	16 6 titular	5	12 3 titular	11 4 titular
4. Archimandrites, priests and deacons	61	41	25 archimandrites 485 priests 10 deacons	60
5. Churches	89	55	500	120
6. Number of faithful	45,000	35,000	450,000	70,000
7. Number of faithful *c.* 1920	2,500,000	250,000	450,000	50,000
8. Monasteries and convents	8	3	19	45 mostly deserted
9. Monks and nuns	10	5	10 monks 90 nuns	50 Greek monks, Brotherhood of the Holy Sepulchre 50 Russian and other nuns in 3 convents, on the Mount of Olives, at Gethsemane and at Bethany 17 monks, of different nationalities, mostly old, in the Monastery of Mār Saba

The Orthodox Church in the Middle East (cont.)

	Istanbul	Alexandria	Antioch	Jerusalem
10. Sources of income	Property, Greek government, Greek Orthodox in America, World Council of Churches, gifts, and religious services	Property, Greek government, gifts, and religious services	Property, Russian Church, Greek government, Lebanese government, religious services, gifts, Orthodox Church in America, and possibly World Council of Churches	Property, Greek government, pilgrims, gifts, and religious services
11. Income of clergy	Salaries, services	Salaries, services	Salaries for city clergy and for most village priests, services, personal property	Salaries, teaching, services, personal property
12. Degree of education of clergy	Fairly high, every clergyman has some theological degree	10% theological degree	Theological degree / University degree: Bishops 50% 15% Archimandrites 50% 5% Deacons 20% 0% Monks and nuns 0% 1% Priests 0% 0%	8% theological degree 10% some university education
13. Schools	1 theological 7 secondary 23 elementary	10 secondary and elementary	12 secondary 25 elementary	10 secondary 30 elementary
14. Societies and clubs	57	150	200	25
15. Orphanages	1	10	10	Undetermined number
16. Hospitals and clinics	1 hospital	10	1 hospital 5 clinics	1 clinic
17. Homes for aged and disabled	1	4	3	1
18. Services in every church	4 Liturgies weekly 2 services daily	3 weekly plus feast days	In city Cathedral, at least 1 Liturgy and 1 service daily; for some of other churches, 2 Liturgies and 1 service weekly; for all, Sundays plus feast days	Churches in Holy Places, Liturgy and service daily; as a rule, 3 weekly plus feast days

The Orthodox Church in the Middle East (cont.)

	Istanbul	Alexandria	Antioch	Jerusalem
19. % of faithful attending services	25 to 30	10 to 15	At most 10	At most 10
20. Age distribution of those attending services	Undetermined	Undetermined	50% above age 40 30% between age 20 and 40 20% under age 20	60% above age 40 30% between age 20 and 40 10% under age 20
21. Confession and communion	90% of faithful at least once a year	80% of faithful at least once a year	50% of faithful at least once a year	50% of faithful at least once a year
22. Sunday schools	40 schools	Several thousand students	30 schools, 3,500 students; in Syria and parts of Lebanon religion also is taught in non-confessional schools	1,500 students
23. Bible and other religious reading	Very few	Very few	Very few, but on the increase	Very few
24. Baptisms	All Orthodox children are baptized	All Orthodox children are baptized	All Orthodox children are baptized	All Orthodox children are baptized
25. Marriage of Orthodox in other than Orthodox Church	0% of marriages	0% of marriages among Greeks, 15% among non-Greeks	4% of marriages	6% of marriages
26. Converts to Orthodoxy	Very few; not for religious reasons but because they marry Orthodox	Very few; not for religious reasons but because they marry Orthodox	Very few; not for religious reasons but because they marry Orthodox	Very few; not for religious reasons but because they marry Orthodox
27. Converts from Orthodoxy	Very few, mostly for marriage reasons	Very few, mostly for marriage reasons	Very few, for marriage reasons, or under non-Orthodox educational influence, or through proselytizing	Very few, for marriage reasons, or under non-Orthodox educational influence, or through proselytizing
28. Social classes of faithful	Mostly middle class; good standard of living	Rich and middle class, richer than in sees of Antioch and Jerusalem	A few rich both in city and country; majority in city middle class; in country almost wholly peasants and labourers but relatively with a decent standard of living	A few rich both in city and country; majority in city middle class; in country almost wholly peasants and labourers but relatively with a decent standard of living

The Orthodox Church in the Middle East (*cont.*)

	Istanbul	Alexandria	Antioch	Jerusalem
29. Education and culture	Above average in Turkey; in intimate touch with European culture	Above average in Egypt; in intimate touch with European culture	At least as advanced as any other native group; part of local culture; in touch with Western culture, especially in Lebanon	Above average; part of local culture; in touch with Western culture
30. Political orientation	Greeks, fully Greek in sympathies	Greeks, fully Greek in sympathies; Lebanese and Syrians, somewhat ambivalent; played important role in economic development and in intellectual and literary revival	Nationalists; played a leading part in Arab, Syrian and Lebanese awakening	Nationalists; played active part in political awakening

A few comments are called for.

These data have been difficult to compile. Reliable statistics on some of these matters do not exist. When you ask authoritative people to supply you with information, they fumble, either because they do not know (and if they do not know, then nobody else does), or because they are ashamed of what they know or afraid of disclosing it to you. Some think that the whole business of scientific investigation is a form of spying. I combined three methods: reliance on direct personal knowledge; the use of available published material; and gathering information through a questionnaire. I put in the hands of a score of authoritative people in a position to know a questionnaire of fifty items. I then tried to reconcile their answers in the light of what I know and what is published, and by checking with others who know. The result is the information tabulated above. Although future research will doubtless refine these data further, I believe their margin of error is negligible for the purposes of this study. Moreover, the Middle Eastern scene, as is evident, is changing rapidly, so that much of any further refinement will only mean that the objective situation has itself in the meantime changed.

The bishops under Istanbul refer only to those who live in the Middle East; in addition, there are a score or more bishops under Constantinople's jurisdiction with dioceses in Europe or the Western

Hemisphere or Australia and New Zealand. Similarly, the bishops under Antioch do not include the four bishops under the jurisdiction of that see whose dioceses are in the Western Hemisphere.

There are, then, only 600,000 Orthodox in the Middle East. This is about one-half of one per cent of the total population of the region, Christian and Muslim, and about ten per cent of the Christian population. The Orthodox of the Middle East are reduced today to about one-fifth of what they were half a century ago. We are therefore before what I might call "the phenomenon of the squeeze". This phenomenon manifests itself in two ways: the Orthodox have been squeezed, outwardly into Greece and into wherever they have been able to immigrate, and inwardly for the most part into Lebanon. The Orthodox immigration into Lebanon is part of the general Christian emigration from Turkey, Egypt, Syria and Israel. And even Lebanon is treated by many of these Christians as only a stopping station on their way out. The virtual liquidation of Orthodoxy in Turkey and Egypt is more a cultural–political phenomenon than a religious one, as the Orthodox in these two countries were overwhelmingly Greek, while the Orthodox of the sees of Antioch and Jerusalem belonged almost wholly to the indigenous population. The natural increase in the Orthodox population in these two sees during the last half a century was certainly comparable to that of any other segment of the population; this means that we can consider that during the last fifty years the Orthodox population was doubled; this increase does not appear in items 6 and 7 in the tabulation above because it was all absorbed by Orthodox emigration overseas, principally to North and South America. This emigration is part of the general "phenomenon of the squeeze". Orthodoxy will never be wholly squeezed out of Lebanon, Syria, Jordan and Israel, because it antedated and survived Islam, because it has lived with Islam for centuries and knows it inwardly very well, because it is existentially and historically thoroughly rooted in the soil and blood of the country, and in Arab culture and the Arabic language (e.g. the liturgy is all in Arabic), and because Orthodox leaders and thinkers have played and are playing an important role in economic, political, cultural and intellectual affairs. The see of Antioch is the irreducible and immovable bastion of Orthodoxy in the Middle East. This fact is of the greatest possible significance, not only for the future of Orthodoxy in this region, but at once for the future of Muslim–Christian relations and, in view of Orthodoxy's special historical relations to the Russian

Church, the future of the Pan-Orthodox movement and the ecumenical Christian movement in general.

With the phenomenon of the demographic squeeze there has been also an economic, social and political squeeze. In Turkey and Egypt, where Orthodoxy has been physically virtually liquidated, all the affluence that characterized Orthodox life forty or fifty years ago, in Izmir, in Istanbul, in Alexandria, in Cairo, is now gone, and therewith Orthodox social and political influence. But even where Orthodox remain, in Beirut, in Jerusalem, in Amman, in Damascus, in Aleppo, their former wealth and position have been markedly reduced. Still, the Orthodox Church in the Middle East, both as hierarchy and people, is a rich church. On the whole, the Orthodox people are well to do, and some of them are very rich; nor is there really abject poverty among them. Church property (*waqf*) is extensive, but it has not been properly administered or exploited. With scientific planning and upright management, the revenue of the Church from its own property could increase many times. But all these prospects would come to nought if the present socializing and nationalizing tendencies in the Middle East should also extend to Church property. Then the Church would be reduced materially to the destitute state to which it has been reduced in eastern Europe. Concerning Russian Church assistance to the see of Antioch, this takes the form mostly of gifts and payment of expenses of the clergy and some of the laity who study in Russia. While this assistance has not been substantial (except for the complete fitting out of the Orthodox hospital in Beirut), and while it is precarious and sporadic, I am sure it will continue, and may even increase. On the whole, the clergy, despite their grumbling, enjoy a higher standard of living than the average standard of their flock. Greater revenue from expanded judicious exploitation of Church property would not only benefit the clergy further; it would enable the Church to renovate churches, build new ones, open new schools, improve existing ones, undertake new projects of publication, found new intellectual and spiritual centres, and sponsor a possible revival of iconography and music.

That in the sees of Antioch and Jerusalem at most ten per cent of the faithful attend religious services on the average at any given time is a point to ponder. This certainly represents a drop from conditions obtaining a generation or two ago. The cause of this drop is partly the modern secular spirit which has also to some extent infected the Middle East, partly the greater economic and social demands upon parents to maintain a steadily rising standard of living for their family. If you ask those who do not attend regular eucharistic services in Europe about the state of their faith, you will find that most of them simply do not believe. This is not the case with those who do not attend the Divine Liturgy in the Middle East. They will emphatically tell you that they are Orthodox believers despite their non-attendance; they were all baptized in the Church, the married among them were all married in the Church, and all of them expect to die in it; and they regularly attend baptismal, marriage and funeral services. All this is not true of those who are not church goers in the West. Church attendance is some kind of an indicator, but in the Middle East it is not an accurate measure of the state of faith. Among the Catholic population the percentage who attend religious services is much higher. While it does not follow from this that there is greater sanctity among the Catholics than among the Orthodox, I believe it is most important for a man, whatever his state of sin or sanctity, to present himself before the Lord in the Church as often as he can, whether to beseech his mercy or simply and humbly and self-forgettingly to adore his truth and his beauty. This is also most important for the honour of the Lord and the integrity of His body the Church. There is in addition in the case of the Orthodox Liturgy such wealth and depth of spirit, and such incomparable drama, that no man who has any taste for these things can wilfully afford to miss this wonderful experience. Thanks to the Orthodox Youth Movement and to other causes, the number of young men and women who believe and pray and regularly attend religious services is annually on the increase.

Conversion from Islam to any form of Christianity is virtually unknown. Because of the enormous doctrinal and social hostility to such conversion, the very few known cases of converts from Islam have been most remarkable, alike in the depth of their conviction, in the clarity of their mind as to what it is all about, and in the intensity of their love for their fellow men. They have put many born Christians to shame. Nor is there any real conversion from Christianity to Islam based on conviction. The lines between the Christian communions have also been frozen: the uniate movement and the Protestant proselytizing movement, both aimed at Orthodoxy, have now practically spent themselves. There is therefore no fluidity, no movement, between the religions and between the Christian confessions in the Middle East. There is of course perpetual mutual determination of mind and manner and attitude, but there is no change of social–political–religious identification, no change of allegiance, even where (perhaps precisely because) the allegiance has ceased to have any genuine, inner, spiritual meaning. In the Middle East everybody is publicly tagged with his religion (in most instances, his very name betrays his religious affiliation); with the advent of Islam, the tags were changed on a vast scale; with the uniate movement of the seventeenth and eighteenth centuries and early nineteenth, there was some change of tags at the expense of Orthodoxy; and with the coming of the Protestant missions another slight shift occurred, again at the expense of Orthodoxy. The tags now are almost wholly fixed, nor does there appear any prospect for a new shuffling of them. People in the Middle East change their dress, their manners, their political and social ideas, their parties, their classes, their political masters, even some of their beliefs, *but not their religion.* This is a most significant fact. It means that religion is the chief historical product of the Middle East, of any universal–human significance; that is why everybody is publicly tagged with it. But it means also that the Middle East has ceased to be creative, that it is no longer interested in propagating its greatest creation, that the great products of the spirit which move men on their deepest level are no longer coming from it. Thus it cannot deny its greatest (possibly its only) product, for if it did it would deny itself, it would have nothing else to affirm about itself, and the very roots of its own self-confidence would then wither away. That is why it pertinaciously clings to religion and tags everybody with it. On the other hand, it is invaded from every side by modernism, scientism, socialism, nationalism, industrialism, and a host of other forces, and it is these—none of which of its own making—that produce movement and fluidity among its ranks. Religious demarcations are frozen but not obliterated in the Middle East, because there are mighty competitors to religion which take people's mind completely off the greatest product of their heritage.

Education among the Orthodox in the Middle East is distinctly above the average. They are in intimate touch with Western thought and culture, without—in the case of the non-Greeks—losing any of their organic rootedness in the indigenous culture. One can name a score of Orthodox thinkers who made a deep mark upon literary, intellectual and political developments in Egypt, Lebanon and Syria over the last three generations. Proportionately to the total Orthodox population, this group of thinkers perhaps stands out unique among all confessions. Among the dead, the following names may be mentioned: Adīb Isḥāq, Jurjī Zaydān, Faraḥ Anṭūn, Ilyā Abū Māḍī, Anṭūn Sa'āda [Antoun Saadeh], 'Īsā Iskandar al-Ma'lūf, and Asad Rustum. Mikhā'īl Nu'ayma [Mikhail Na'imy] is perhaps the greatest living literary figure in the entire Arab world, and Georges Shiḥāda [Georges Shehadeh], a playwright in French, has had some of his plays performed in Germany, Paris and the United States. As to the clergy, in Constantinople their theological formation is high, but in the other three sees it is very spotty. The village priests have no theological or university education; all that can be said of them is they are literate, and if they have a little theological sophistication, they acquired it, not formally, but as it were by nature and instinct, and from the intimations of the liturgy which they know by heart. There is room for immense reforms here. In the matter of university and theological training, there is a sharp hiatus between the younger and older bishops and deacons. It is hoped that when the new generation takes over in ten or twenty years, Orthodoxy at least in the see of Antioch, which, as we saw, is the decisive see, will present a new face to the world.

It is not an accident that some of the principal nationalist leaders, in the realm both of theory and political action, and both in the "Syrian" as well as the wider "Arab" sense of nationalism, have been Orthodox. This is due to Orthodoxy's deep indigenous roots. Soil, land, people, language, community and tradition are decisive in Orthodoxy. Anṭūn Sa'āda and Michel 'Aflaq are the most prominent names that may be mentioned. Both developed nationalist philosophies, the first on a "Syrian", the second on an "Arab", basis; and both founded, organized and led political parties. And while Sa'āda's party attempted unsuccessfully at least twice to seize power, 'Aflaq's *Ba'th* party rules Syria today. The fact that in some of the foundations of their thought they are diametrically opposed to each other, although perhaps they are equally sincere, is not inconsistent with the fact that their Orthodox background probably played a decisive part in the formation of their minds, no matter how strangely and obscurely. Nationalism, whether Syrian or Arab, hankers back to something more natural and more inclusive than religion; it has the effect, at least in theory, of equalizing between Muslim and Christian, and this is a great relief to both: to the Christian, because he thereby overcomes his minority status; and to the Muslim, because he is impressed by the relative superiority of the Western world which is identified in his mind with

Christianity, and because in working with his Christian brother on a non-religious basis, the religious irritant is thereby removed. The examination of this whole theme of the political and nationalist implications of Orthodoxy in the Middle East calls for a separate and much deeper treatment.

The iconography is all Byzantine. The Syrian school is decadent and the good icons come from Greece or Russia. The treasure of old icons throughout the land has suffered many depredations. The music is all Greek, or Greek-based, even where the liturgy is sung in Arabic. A veritable revolution has been accomplished by Mitri 'l-Murr who perfected the Arabic text so as to fit exactly the Greek tunes.

Three special Orthodox institutions of world renown can only be mentioned here: Mount Athos under the jurisdiction of the ecumenical patriarch, the Brotherhood of the Holy Sepulchre in Jerusalem, and the autonomous Monastery of St Catherine in Mount Sinai. Athos and Sinai contain ancient manuscripts and icons of great value.

The Orthodox in North and South America who trace their origins to the Middle East have flourishing churches under able bishops. Their number is of the order of 300,000 and their churches are at least 150. Spiritually, materially, and from the point of view of active participation in the life of the Church, this community is far superior to what obtains in the Middle East. Although these churches fall under the jurisdiction of Antioch, it appears that Orthodoxy in America is destined to constitute an autocephalous Church.

The Orthodox Youth Movement is one of the principal hopes of the Church. It was founded in 1942 by two young Lebanese Orthodox, Albert Laḥḥām and Georges Khiḍr [Georges Khodr], and was later joined by a similar group founded at about the same time in al-Lādhiqiyya (Latakia), Syria, by Marcel Murqus [Marcel Morcos] and Gabriel Sa'āda [Gabriel Saadé]. Educated in Catholic schools and religious by nature, these men felt that there was a peculiar original spirituality in Orthodoxy which was in danger of being lost if Orthodoxy were completely romanized or westernized. They therefore sought in total self-abandon to resuscitate Orthodoxy from within, both in their own lives and in the life of the Church. The historical development of this vision reveals the authentic workings of the Holy Ghost. Today the influence of this Movement is felt among all Orthodox in the see of Antioch. One of the founders of the Movement, now Father Khiḍr, helped also to launch the idea of Syndesmos, the World Organization of Orthodox Youth Movements, in 1953; and the other founder, Maitre Laḥḥām, was elected president of Syndesmos (whose headquarters are now in Beirut) in 1964. Murqus is now the superior of the monastic community of Dayr al-Ḥarf. A dozen clergy, including three bishops, are either members of the Movement or have been deeply touched by it. It inspired two monastic communities, one of nuns at Dayr Mār Ya'qūb and one of monks at Dayr al-Ḥarf, both in Lebanon.[1]

One can only mention here the meeting of Ecumenical Patriarch Athenagoras I and Pope Paul VI in Jerusalem in January 1964.[2] For Middle Eastern Orthodoxy this was most historic. It was preceded and followed by many exchanges of visits and letters between Constantinople and Rome. The relevant addresses and documents are published in *Osservatore Romano*. They make remarkable reading. A wholly new spirit of dialogue and openness prevails between Orthodoxy and Catholicism today. For years before Orthodoxy had been "meeting" and actively co-operating with Protestantism at the World Council of Churches. This is a wonderful ecumenical age, although only the Holy Ghost knows where it will lead in the end. Nor need we be too curious about this. Our duty is never to relent in loving, and praying, and forgiving, and working, and expecting miracles.

Whatever the past and the present, unless there is a real future, all is vain. Whatever the past and the present, if the future is only a repetition of the past and present, all is vain too. Being is the hope and lure and call of a real, possible, *better* future. Being is working hard in the present with whatever can be salvaged from the past for the sake of a future closer and nearer to God. Being is self-dedication in love with the faith and the hope that what has been and is being missed of the fulness of life which is God will somehow be made up for in a real future. He cannot live who has no such hope, and he alone knows the joy and creativity of the spirit whom God has granted such a hope, calmly, soberly, really, and without illusion.

[1] For an account of this important fresh breeze of the Holy Ghost, see *Orthodoxy, A Pan-Orthodox Symposium*, ed. The Brotherhood of Theologians "ZOE", Athens, 1964, pp. 265–79, by Father Khiḍr; and *Syndesmos* (November, 1958), pp. 10–13, by the Superior of the Dayr al-Ḥarf Monastic Community.

[2] Since then there has been a mutual lifting of excommunications between Rome and Constantinople; the Pope and the Ecumenical Patriarch met again in Istanbul in July 1967, and the Patriarch visited Rome in October 1967 to return the Pope's two visits to the Near East.

At the heart of every Orthodox in the Middle East is the feeling that things cannot continue as they have been. Orthodoxy is doomed unless it can realistically look forward to a better future. Quantitatively, it has been reduced to one-fifth of what it was half a century ago. Qualitatively, the bishops of the Holy Synod of at least one see physically hit and wounded each other in a recent session, and one faction sued the other before the civil authorities; the amount of intrigue and gossip that goes on is incredible; fasting, communion, church attendance, taking part in all the life of the Church, were much more widespread and serious fifty years ago than they are today; and while sanctity, morality and faith among the Orthodox are certainly not in worse shape than among the Catholics, the clergy of the former are on the whole much shabbier theologically and educationally than the clergy of the latter. This state of affairs cannot go on. One loves God, adores the liturgy, lives the life of the Church, is certain that Jesus Christ is everything, listens to the Holy Ghost, honours the Virgin, but one is not edified by what one sees in his Church. One is pained and discouraged.

In another essay,[1] I set forth what I considered to be the tasks facing the Christians of the Middle East if they are to move from the merely preservative function which they have been performing so admirably for centuries to something more creative. Everything I said there applies to the Orthodox Church. Here I want to sharpen a few matters.

The future of Orthodoxy in the Middle East appears to depend for the most part on the see of Antioch. The other three sees have their own formidable problems. One prays that they hold out under all their trials. The position of Athenagoras of Constantinople is especially critical. All men of good will, Orthodox and non-Orthodox, Christian and non-Christian, should see that only good can come out of strengthening his hands. All men therefore should support him and pray for the lengthening of his days. Equally critical is the question whether it is in the design of God to send a successor to Athenagoras (he is getting along in years) on this greatest of all Orthodox thrones of the stature of this good and incomparable man. In this ecumenical age, Constantinople alone can guide and lead and moderate, not only among the Orthodox but in their relations to the Catholics and Protestants as well.

The Orthodox Church is called upon to identify itself wholly with the indigenous culture. It must suffer all the stresses and problems

[1] M. Searle Bates and Wilhelm Pauck (eds.), *The Prospects of Christianity throughout the World* (New York, Scribner's, 1964), chapter 5, "The Near East", pp. 83–103.

of this culture from within. There can be no question about its not taking orders, politically, socially, and even culturally, from without. It is wholly native, wholly rooted in the soil and spirit of the land. In a nationalist epoch, the Orthodox can be politically nationalist to the core. There is every indication that the Middle East is heading towards a great renaissance; the very formidableness and intensity of its problems prove this. The Orthodox Church and the Orthodox people should be joyously and freely and confidently at the very forefront of every creativity and participation in the coming age, no matter at what cost and with what measure of suffering. God alone calls and God disallows, but no other spiritual agency in the Middle East is more humanly fit for this task.

Some kind of a dialogue with Islam is going to be opened. The Pope presaged that, and the ripening of intellectual and spiritual conditions will conduce to it. This is a very difficult and serious matter. Three distinct levels ought to be discriminated: all that science and reason can reveal to Muslim and Christian equally; all that Islam and Christianity as Abrahamic religions have in common about the nature of the one and transcendent God and the nature of man; and the areas of faith and doctrine in which they frankly differ from each other. Nothing but good can come from complete clarity on all three matters. Both the Orthodox Church, co-existing with Islam for centuries and knowing it from within, and Orthodox thinkers, sharing with their Muslim brethren every economic, political, social and intellectual concern, ought to be in a position to create an atmosphere of complete mutual trust and eager search for the truth in all these realms. Already attempts towards that end are being made in Lebanon. God alone calls and God disallows, but it appears that the Orthodox community is best suited to undertake this historic task.

The non-Chalcedonian Churches of the Middle East have an honourable and integral place in the final harmony of the Church Universal. The first step appears to be a genuine adjustment with the Orthodox Church. The conversations that took place in August 1964 in Aarhus, Denmark, and the Addis Ababa conference of January 1965 were in the nature of preliminary explorations of this matter. The spirit prevailing on all sides is excellent. The point is to be absolutely clear on the Christological issue which divided the Christian world at Chalcedon in 451. Precisely because the Orthodox Church is exactly as bound by the definitions of Chalcedon as the Catholic Church, the Orthodox

Church cannot proceed with any adjustment on this matter with the non-Chalcedonian Churches without agreement with Rome. God alone calls and God disallows, but the Orthodox Church appears to be in a unique position to bring together the entire Eastern family of Churches into a new unity of faith and love, on the basis of the truth, in preparation for the great day of universal Church unity ahead.

It is not difficult to dream, but hope and prayer have at times the character of dreaming. The Greeks and the Russians did not always see eye to eye with each other. The Church of Antioch is on good terms with both. Its very poverty, its very desolateness, its glorious name, the fact that it is rooted in the very existential soil from which our Lord sprang, all this may enable it some day to play an integrating role in the Pan-Orthodox world. There has been a faint glimmer of this in recent Pan-Orthodox gatherings. God alone calls and God disallows, but I pray that there be in the divine economy a deeper meaning to the reduction of Orthodoxy in the Middle East to the Church of Antioch than appears on the surface.

Again, the Orthodox of the see of Antioch have had more intimate contacts—indeed have wrestled more—with the Roman Catholics than any other Orthodox, certainly than the Greeks and Russians. The uniate experience belongs to their background more than to any other background. They are neither afraid of the Catholics nor by now are they prejudiced against them. Who knows therefore what active role God may be holding in store for them, despite their insignificance and despite their poverty, in the inevitable ecumenical confrontation between Orthodox and Catholics in the future? God alone calls and God disallows, but one nevertheless is not prevented from dreaming and hoping and praying that the Orthodox of the Middle East be more "understanding" ecumenically than other Orthodox, never of course at the expense of the truth or of their abiding solidarity with their Orthodox brethren all over the world.

Nor can their experience with Protestantism be in the eyes of God altogether a waste. The Protestant thrust fell upon them more heavily than upon any other community. Add to this the emigration of many of them to America and the influence of the American schools and especially of the American University of Beirut upon them (among the Christians who attend this University, the Orthodox constitute by far the largest bloc), and the result is a distinct Protestant spirit impregnating their soul. By right, every Christian experience everywhere will sooner or later establish for itself some foothold in the Middle East, for this is the one region in the whole universe where there can be no monopoly for any group counted on the Cross of Christ. God alone calls and God disallows, but the greater "understanding" which the Orthodox have acquired of Protestantism and the Protestant spirit may, despite their poverty and despite their insignificance, prepare them for some role in the great ecumenical feast of the future.

The Orthodox should rediscover and relive their wonderful tradition. How much will be left of Christianity if you remove the witness and conviction and vision of the early Greek Fathers of the Church? It is enough for the Orthodox to realize who St John Chrysostom and St John of Damascus were and what they believed and did. It is enough for them to contemplate the liturgy. It is enough to appreciate the monasticism and asceticism and anchoritism of the golden days. Here is a wealth of suffering and love which can transform the whole world. God alone calls and God disallows, but the mere fact that a thing was possible once proves that it is not impossible again.

The Orthodox today are unworthy of their possibilities. Perhaps it is sin of me to reason in this fashion, for certainly "God is able of these stones to raise up children unto Abraham". This we cannot control. But so far as the human intellect can go, I do not see how anything I have been dreaming here is going to come about tomorrow, or even the day after. The moral and venal corruption, the spiritual degeneracy, the empty bragging, the absence of a genuine sense of responsibility, the indifference to wonderful opportunities missed, the squabbling and backbiting that goes on, the false sense of satisfaction, the complete neglect of pastoral care, the political, social and ideological forces overwhelming the soul, the fear and distractedness, the escapism and flight from the truth—all this is humanly too much for honest hope, as distinct from dreaming and hoping and praying in general, to take root and develop. I do not say that God cannot overcome these things; but these things are precisely the things He *must* overcome. And if He does not intervene and the situation continues as it has been, many Orthodox will turn to uniatism or Protestantism or communism in sheer disgust and rebellion. It is entirely possible that the heyday of uniatism and Protestantism is not behind us.

A theological seminary at the Belmond Monastery in North Lebanon is absolutely needed and will considerably help. When the half a dozen younger clergy, who constitute part of the hope of the Church, come to positions of real responsibility, a new day may dawn upon us. The Orthodox Youth Movement has been a great leaven, but lately it appears to have slumped and wilted. The challenge is simply too much for it, and it must shake itself out of its amateurishness and become tenfold more serious. It can still do wonders. The contemplative seeds at Dayr al-Ḥarf and Dayr Mār Ya'qūb are great seminal hopes for the future. Fifty such contemplatives are needed, and then there will be a flood of grace and spirit. And the light should shine as well in the home and the parish, in the school and market place, in the office and bedroom, in the work of art and in the solitude of the soul. Something more than monastic contemplation therefore is needed in this utterly parched scene, something akin to the Catholic *Opus Dei*, where a group of absolutely dedicated men and women are sworn to invade the whole of human life, under God and for his glory alone. Sainthood is not to be achieved in monasteries alone; the question today is whether an engineer, a tennis player, a politician, an actress, a newspaperman, a housewife, a farmer, a merchant, can be a saint, recognized as such and canonized by the Church itself. Let there be fifty monastic contemplatives joined to fifty active ones, and you have the council of one hundred who will transform the entire Middle East.

I wish to close with two translations from the Arabic literature of the Orthodox Youth Movement, one a simple address by the Father Superior of the new Monastic Order of Dayr al-Ḥarf made on the occasion of four monks taking their First Vow, and the other a prayer by a Greek Orthodox priest. They are redolent of the best in classical Antiochian spirituality.

We thank God who hath called us unto Himself and confirmed us in the way of His patience unto the end. We thank Him because He hath overlooked our weaknesses and accepted and continues to accept us as we are. We thank Him because He is the ever-present cause of our faithfulness to Him.

As we take the First Vow we become consecrated to God for the rest of our life. We are pledged to put aside through His grace the pleasures of the world and to seek and pray for Him always.

We know we are unworthy of this wonderful grace; we know that the way ahead suits neither our nature nor our powers; we know we shall stumble on the way. But God visits His slaves, whoever they are, and the imperfection of those who surrender to Him he is able to heal.

Have we chosen a strange way by separating ourselves from others? But God Himself brought us to this strange and unknown way, and no doubt He is the author of the plan. And the Holy Church our mother hath approved it from the beginning, and it is she, in the person of his Lordship, our Venerable Father and Bishop, who clearly first encouraged us and tended our early steps...

The Church yearns in us all for the mercy of her Lord and needs to be filled with His grace.

In our opaque world the Church needs members who long for the face of the Lord above everything desired and longed for.

From the heart of the beloved Church of Antioch we draw near to the Lord, and there before Him we confess our sins, and through patience, blood and the ascetic life we beseech the dew of His great mercy and the shining of His love and light.

The Church is the bride of the Lord. How can she therefore forget her love and His love?...

The Church is the beloved bride of Christ. How can she therefore not seek Him with fervour? How can she not await His coming in the night, with the lamps burning strong and bright, to receive His salvation, and His resurrection in its dazzling light?

Will the Lord accept our burnt offering? Will He grant us to rise above ourselves and cleanse our hearts? Will He make our whole life a petition, pure and undefiled, in the mouth of the Church our Mother, bearing to Him with fidelity the longing of her heart?...[1]

I thank Thee O God for Thou hast visited me in my anxiety and sought me in my despair. Thou hast come down to the abyss and I ceased to feel that I am in it. In it Thou hast come to me with a new vision, taking off from Thy face the veil of my sin. Thou hast deigned to exchange Thy love with mine, and when Thou coveredst me with forgiveness, it was as one intoxicated though prefectly sober that I met Thee. And before Thy face thou liftedst me a brother beloved.

O Thou my companion in the sorest of trials and my mate in the sweetness of yearning. O Thou who when temptation reaches its utmost bounds causest Thy face to shine upon me, with tenderness and compassion. O Thou who only after I meet Thee I come out of my distress, to know Thee more and more. O Thou who in my choking and darkness makest Thy way Thyself to me. And as I behold Thee, Thou becomest my hope, and I know that I am then beyond death, having climbed the mount where Thou wast transfigured.

This is Thy story with me day after day. Thou hast thus become a law and a norm unto me, and Thy ways with mankind became perfectly clear. I then reconciled myself to what became only too familiar to me. I learned that I am powerless to save myself, but Thou acceptest me in my weakness though this weakness ever remains the same. This is what Thou hast willed from the beginning, and this is how Thou lovest. Thy mercy hath so amazed me that I spend all my life, between one fall and another, singing praises about it.

[1] The Publication of the Monastery of St George at Dayr al-Ḥarf (*Nashrat Dayr Mār Jirjis al-Ḥarf*), no. 14 (December 1962), pp. 1–2.

I sing these praises because Thou transformest my stumbling always to meditating on why I did not walk in Thy statutes. And so love captivates me anew; so I penetrate to the awful depths of my sin; so my misery and Thy mercy disclose themselves equally to me; and so I am assured, moment by moment, in victory and in defeat, in doubt and in certainty, that Thy dealings with me are dealings of compassion.[1]

[1] *al-Nūr*, 15 May 1963, p. 138. Prayer by Archimandrite Georges Khiḍr.

CHAPTER 7

THE ROMAN CATHOLIC CHURCH AND CHURCHES IN COMMUNION WITH ROME

INTRODUCTION

At the the beginning of this survey of "Catholics in the Middle East from 1800 to the present day" it may be helpful to make some preliminary observations designed both to show the spirit in which it is undertaken and to define its precise terms of reference.

In the first place, the survey is conducted in an essentially ecumenical spirit; in a spirit, moreover, which is seeking for the premises and psychological conditions necessary for an effective exchange of views with those who do not share the Catholic faith or, at best, do so only to a limited extent. At a time when the second Vatican Council is still sitting, it could hardly be otherwise. No longer do Christians of different communions anathematize or even turn their backs on one another. Considerable progress has been made since the celebrated "Conversations at Malines" between Cardinal Mercier and Lord Halifax. On the side of the Eastern Church, many prejudices have been abandoned, ancient conflicts appear to have died out and the brethren of a single faith are inspired by the "ethereal" spirit of a John XXIII to long for a more perfect communion in common reverence for their inalienable spiritual, religious and cultural heritage. The meeting between Paul VI and Athenagoras in the Holy Land, in the very place where the founder of Christianity lived, died and rose again from the dead, enjoining his disciples to dwell together in unity, is both the symbol and, to some extent, the prototype of the relationship in which Christians of different communions ought henceforth to be united. For this reason the decision to treat the Eastern Catholics as a separate subject, probably dictated by practical considerations, is perhaps to be regretted. Their fate is so closely linked with that of their brethren; they have, over the centuries, lived in such close proximity with them, enduring the same persecutions, fighting the good fight to preserve their faith and their legitimate customs, that it seems quite artificial to attempt,

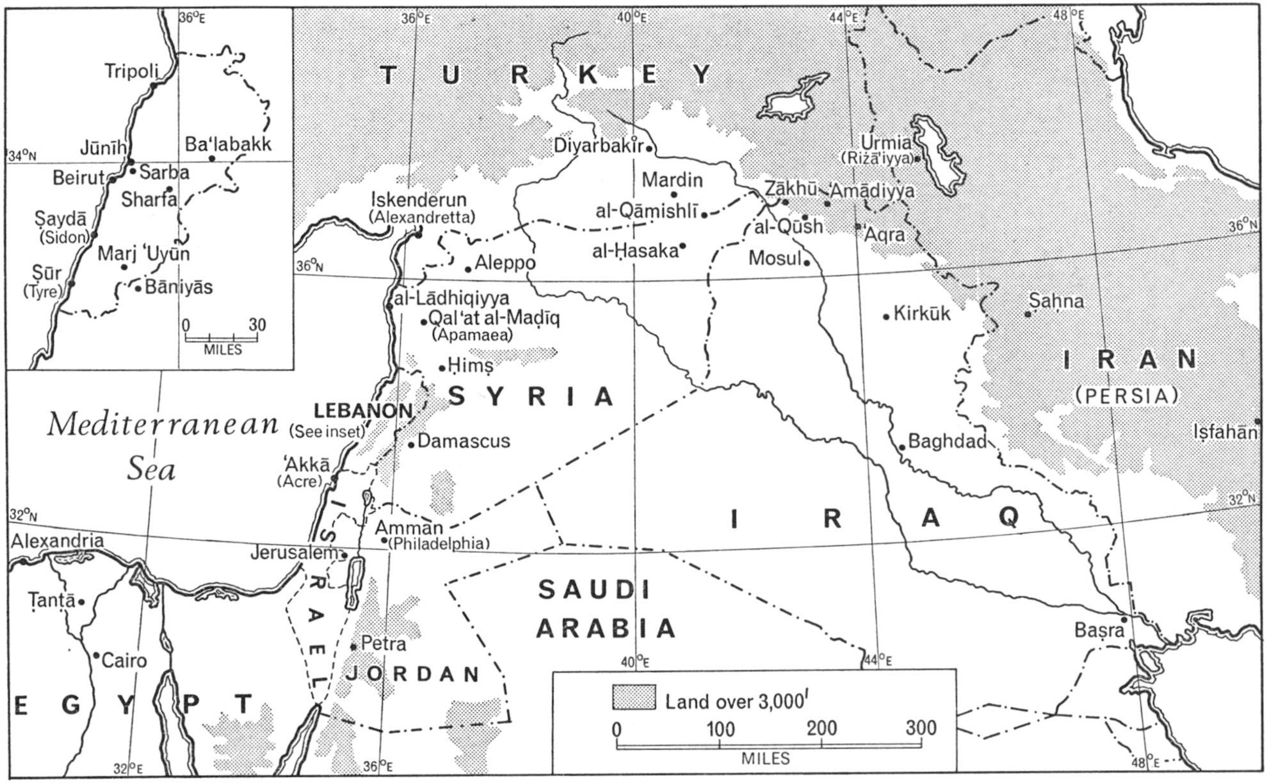

The Roman Catholic Church.

even in an academic survey, to speak of one section of the Church without the other. Accordingly, reference will often be made simply to "Christians" in considering the fate of the various communities which, up to the outbreak of the First World War, lived and carried on their struggle within the heart of the Ottoman Empire. In the movements for national liberation and intellectual renaissance Christians of different communions have also united their efforts, and such facts should be borne in mind throughout the ensuing discussion.

It is necessary, however, to accept the challenge offered and to deal specifically with the Catholic Church in the Middle East. How does the problem present itself?

Clearly a start must be made with the present state of affairs, that is to say, with the Catholic communities which are in existence today. Their history will be discussed only in so far as it assists the understanding of present problems and future trends. These Catholic communities are as follows: Melkites (or Greek Catholics), Coptic Catholics of Egypt (whose rite is akin to that of the Ethiopian Catholics), Armenian Catholics, Maronites, Chaldaeans (to whom the Malabar Catholics of India belong), Syrian Catholics (with the Malankars of India, who share their rite) and finally the various Latin communities which are distributed in greater or lesser numbers throughout the different regions of the Middle East.

In order to bring all these communities within the permitted scheme, the following plan has, after careful reflexion, been devised with the object of providing as much detailed information about them as possible within the fewest pages, while at the same time preserving the organic links which exist between the various communities and the countries to which they belong. After a short paragraph designed to establish the origin and the essential character of the different communities up to the beginning of the nineteenth century, the first part will deal, in rather more detail, with their history from 1800 to the present day. In the first sub-section it will be necessary to indicate the background, that is, the political context in which these communities have developed during the period under review. This constitutes in fact a study of the disintegration of the Ottoman Empire within which these communities existed, their struggle for survival, the reforms which the Sultans, under constant pressure from the nations of Europe, were obliged to concede in favour of the Christians and, finally, the fate of these communities during and after the two World Wars.

This common history was shared by all the communities alike; in the second sub-section each of them will be described separately—its origin, its development through the centuries especially during the nineteenth century, and its position at the present day. Statistics taken from *Oriente Cattolico* make it possible to determine exactly their respective importance in relation to one another.

In the second part the question will be treated more synthetically, with a study of the part played, both in the past and now, by Catholics in civil life—their religion activities (training of clergy, universities, seminaries and institutes), social, political and economic activities and finally intellectual and literary activity.

In conclusion, an attempt will be made to examine how Catholics are reacting to the tasks for the future from the point of view of organic integration in civil life, of ecumenical work with their Christian brethren of other communities and, finally, of Islamic–Christian discussions with their Muslim compatriots.

For the present purposes it may be said that, up to the beginning of the fifth century, there was only one Church in the East. The Council of Nicaea (325) defined, in opposition to Arius, the eternity and the consubstantiality of the Word. Schisms occurred when an attempt was made to define the union of the two Natures in the Person of Christ. In contradiction of the statements of Nestorius, Ephesus, where Cyril of Alexandria played a predominant part, insisted on the unity of the Divine Person in Christ. The Nestorians or Assyrians rejected the definitions of Ephesus and seceded from the main Church; some of them were later called Chaldaeans, or Syrians of Malabar. (For details, see the section dealing with the individual communities below.)

Some years later there was a reaction in the opposite direction. In the fight against Nestorianism (two Natures and two Persons in Christ) Eutychius adopted St Cyril's formula of a *single* Nature, which had been observed by Alexandria, but he expressed it in a unilateral form. He imagined the union of the two Natures, human and divine, as an intermingling in which the human Nature would be entirely absorbed by the divine Nature (hence the name Monophysitism given by Catholics to this doctrine). The Council of Chalcedon (451) condemned this argument and those who refused to accept the decisions of Chalcedon were called by Catholics Monophysites. They constituted three distinct communities: (1) Syrian Jacobites. Those of them who subsequently went over to Catholicism were called Syrian

Catholics, and the Indians among them Malankars. (2) Orthodox Copts of Egypt, and those of Ethiopia associated with them. Some went over to Catholicism and constituted the Coptic (and Ethiopian) Catholic Church. (3) Orthodox Armenians or Gregorians, from whom stemmed the Armenian Catholics.

To sum up, the main body of the Eastern Church is the Byzantine Church. Throughout the first ten centuries A.D. there was friction, misunderstanding, even temporary schism between Rome and Byzantium, particularly in the ninth century under the Patriarch Photius. It was in the eleventh century, under Michael Cerularius, that the final schism occurred. The Church which was thus separated from Rome was called in the Arab countries the Orthodox Melkite Church, and those of its members who went over to Catholicism formed the Melkite Uniate Church or the Melkite Catholics.

The Maronite Church, as has been already mentioned, appears to have remained continuously united with Rome since its foundation in the fifth and sixth centuries.

CATHOLIC COMMUNITIES: HISTORICAL BACKGROUND AND INDIVIDUAL CHARACTERISTICS

General Political Background

1. *From the beginning of the nineteenth century to the First World War*

At the beginning of the nineteenth century the Ottoman Empire was only a shadow of itself. National unity had never really been achieved under an Empire which was a kind of Muslim Austria-Hungary composed of a hotch-potch of twenty hostile races. Under the impact of various external factors, particularly the principles of the French Revolution, these various nationalities became ambitious for greater freedom, even independence. There occurred the phenomenon of centrifugal disintegration which gradually transformed the Empire into that "sick man" so carefully watched over by the European Powers, sometimes in order to bolster his precarious stability, in the fear that if he collapsed serious conflict might break out between the heirs, greedy for a share of his estate. What enormously complicated the situation was the existence of Christian minorities all over the Empire. From the very fact of their Christianity, these minorities remained in contact with their co-religionists. In time of peace, they were the perfect intermediaries between Europe and their Turkish compatriots, but in wartime they were suspected of having dealings with enemy Intelligence and subjected to measures of extortion and confiscation, if they were not actually massacred. The endemic massacres of Armenians, in particular, were to disturb the Christian—or simply the humane—conscience of Europe and led to intervention by the Western Powers to stop the carnage.

From the time of the Capitulations France had assumed the role of protector of Catholics in the Levant: her friendship for the Maronites had a long history. The Russians, for their part, were concerned with the Orthodox Christians, both in the Balkan Peninsula and in the Arab territories of Syria and Palestine, making it in particular a point of honour to uphold the Orthodox Christians in the Holy Places. If it be remembered that in addition Russia long cherished the ambition to establish herself at Constantinople and, moreover, that England was firmly resolved to safeguard the route to India by preventing any other European Power from taking possession of the Turkish "boulevard" which led to it, it may be possible to understand something of the inextricable tangle of interests which constituted the "Eastern Question" in the nineteenth century.

The nineteenth century was, for Turkey, a century of disintegration; of the two main reasons one was internal, arising from the archaic and theocratic conception of the state, which attempted to apply in full the principles of the Qur'ān to a society exposed to the influence of modern progress. The other, external, reason resulted from the infiltration of the ideals of the French Revolution, of liberty, equality and brotherhood. Subject peoples, and especially Christian peoples, longed to gain their autonomy and tried to shake themselves free of the Ottoman yoke.

The Serbs were the first to revolt and the insurrection which began in 1804 lasted for eleven years. They were led at first by Kara George and won a striking initial victory. Some years later, however, the Turks rallied; in 1813 they attacked the Serbs and crushed them.

In 1815 a fresh revolt under the leadership of Miloch Obrenovitch succeeded in defeating the Turks at Takor. The support of the Tsar, the protector of Orthodox Christians in the East and particularly of the Slavs, was instrumental in inducing the Sultan to grant the Serbs partial autonomy. Thanks to a flexible and cautious policy of neutrality, Miloch eventually succeeded, in 1830, in becoming the hereditary prince of the Serbs. All Muslims were required to leave Serbia and the nucleus of the new Serb state was formed: the vassal principality of Serbia.

From 1821 onwards Greece, in her turn, was trying to achieve emancipation. It is well-known that the Greek War of Independence was one of the fairest chapters in the struggle for liberty. During the first period (February 1821 to October 1827) the Greeks carried on the struggle alone against the Turks, a struggle which was fierce on both sides. In Constantinople on Easter Sunday 1821 the eighty-four old patriarch, in pontificial vestments, was hanged in the doorway of his cathedral. Christians were massacred. The Greeks, for their part, slaughtered 12,000 Muslims in cold blood after taking Tripolitza, the capital of Morea. The Turks responded with the massacre on the island of Chios in which 23,000 were slaughtered, 50,000 sold as slaves. These massacres give an idea of the hatred which existed between the two populations, based on the inbred contempt which the Muslim Turk had for the *giaour*, the Christian infidel, who was scarcely tolerated in the Ottoman Empire even as a third-class citizen.

The European Powers decided to intervene. The Egyptian-Ottoman fleet was destroyed by the Anglo-French fleet at Navarino on 20 October 1827. The Russians in their turn declared war on Turkey and seized first Silistria and then Adrianople in August 1829. The Treaty of Adrianople sanctioned the independence of the Kingdom of Greece, which was guaranteed by the three Powers, France, England and Russia.

The opportunity for intervention by the European Powers occurred in connexion with the Holy Places. Since the Crusades they had been in the joint possession of the six Christian communions—Roman Catholics (i.e. Latins), Greeks, Armenians, Syrians, Copts and Abyssinians. The three last communions were under the protection of the Armenians, who were also regarded by the Turks as representing financial power in the East. The Greeks, however, with the might of their ten million compatriots living in the Ottoman Empire, looked to Russia for support. The Latin clergy, of Spanish and Italian origin, enjoyed the privilege of extraterritoriality and French diplomatic protection.

A struggle for influence thus arose between the French and the Russian governments, and not a single occasion was missed for the assertion of alleged historical rights. In 1853 the Russians seized the opportunity afforded by litigation over the Holy Places for presenting an ultimatum to the Turks. Ostensibly they claimed that they were defending the rights of the Orthodox Christians, but what they really wanted was to obtain from the Turks an alliance conferring on them the "right of protectorate over all Orthodox Christians in the Turkish Empire".

After consultations with the French and English Ambassadors, the sultan refused, with the result that the Eastern Christians, who had become the subject of litigation, were the involuntary cause of a murderous war between three *Christian* European Powers. Ultimately the Russians were obliged to capitulate and to sign the Treaty of Paris (February–March 1856), by which the Powers guaranteed the territorial integrity of the Turkish Empire. Once more the Christians had to accept their lot as the unfortunate subjects of a drifting Empire, in which they were the poor relations.

It is true that, to salve their own consciences, the Christian European Powers made insistent demands on the Sultans, even requiring them to reform the laws so as to confer full civil rights on their Christian subjects. The precarious nature of these reforms became apparent in 1860 when a massacre of Christians broke out in the Lebanon. In order to check them the European Powers were once more obliged to intervene.

In the midst of all the confusion of a disintegrating Empire the Lebanon had remained an oasis. It was governed by the stern rule of the Amir Bashīr al-Shihābī (1789–1840), who in fact behaved like an independent sovereign. He maintained order and security throughout the country and at the same time preserved its character as a refuge for men in love with freedom. He extended its frontiers and encouraged the trade of Beirut. The change in equilibrium between the different elements of the population, Maronites, Catholics and Druzes, has already been noted. Hitherto north Lebanon had been inhabited by Maronites and other Christians, while the southern regions had been entirely occupied by Druzes. When the Christians increased in numbers they began to move southward, so that in the south the population became mixed.

As a result tensions greatly increased, aggravated by the weakness of the governors. In 1857 the peasants of the north, which was a purely Maronite region, rose against the landowners. The revolt, which was led by priests, by the younger sons of landowners and by leaders like Yūsuf Karam, succeeded in establishing a government of peasants, thus putting an end to the prerogatives of the nobility.

In the central and southern districts of the Lebanon where there was a mixed population of Druzes and Maronites, the conflict developed more slowly and was more complex, being at the same time religious (Druzes against Maronites) and social (Maronite peasants against Druze landowners).

In 1860 the events occurred which had a decisive effect on the fate of the Lebanon. The Druze peasants, in joint action with their overlords, launched an attack on the Maronites and on Christians in general; more than ten thousand Christians were savagely massacred in the Lebanon by the Druzes, with the connivance of the Turkish authorities. The anti-Christian feeling spread to Damascus where thousands more were killed by infuriated Muslims, in spite of the heroic attempts of some prominent people to prevent it.

Matters had come to a climax. Public opinion throughout Europe and especially in France was outraged. By international agreement a decision was taken in favour of military intervention. The Lebanon was separated from the rest of the country and placed under a privileged regime, on a widely autonomous basis. The unity of the country was strengthened by an increase in the powers of the governor, who was required to be a Christian. In administrative and magisterial affairs this governor was assisted by a council, elected by means of proportional representation. This statute, which was adopted enthusiastically by the Lebanese, is splendidly in character with Lebanese institutions and shows how the Lebanon, although a part of the Middle East, is strongly influenced by its Maronite population and is quite different from the other Arab countries.

The events of 1860 had important consequences. Inside the country a serious blow had been struck at the feudal system, and the clergy who had concerned themselves too actively with politics were somewhat discredited. From the international standpoint a precedent had been created which could be used to justify subsequent intervention by foreign powers to safeguard the religious and political liberty of the Lebanese. The Lebanon had acquired a political regime well suited to its structure, which was to some extent guaranteed by the European Powers. The confidence placed by Lebanese Catholics in Western, especially French, support is one of the most striking elements in the Lebanese character, as has recently been reaffirmed. When all the Arab countries had broken off diplomatic relations with France, the Lebanon alone maintained them; again in July 1958, when the Lebanon feared that her religious and political liberty might founder under foreign pressure, she appealed to the American Army for help.

The crisis of 1860 was of even greater importance in the history of ideas in the Arab Middle East, being described by the historian quoted above as "the decisive event of the nineteenth century".[1] It was in fact at this juncture that the Lebanese became aware of the moral stagnation into which they had fallen, the result mainly of a sectarian hatred based on ignorance. There followed a period of great enthusiasm for the founding of schools and for the removal of every obstacle which stood in the way of unity and peace. 1864 was also the starting-point for the first disciples of Yāzijī and Bustānī, who realized that freedom would not be assured until the day of their deliverance from the Turkish yoke. A sense of Lebanese and of wider Arab "patriotism" was born which was not to be satisfied until after a long and murderous struggle all the countries of the Middle East achieved their full political autonomy.

2. *From the 1914–18 War to the present day*

With the 1914–18 War the Middle East was to undergo a radical political transformation which was to give it, structurally, the appearance which it presents today. The Ottoman Empire, already moribund, had thrown in its lot with Germany and collapsed with the German defeat. Its former Arab provinces were about to gain their independence, by slow degrees and at the cost of prolonged effort. The famous "Eastern Question", whether it was "necessary or not to have a share in the division of the Sick Man's property", gave rise by its disappearance to an inextricable medley of "Eastern problems", new aspects of the "Question" of former times.

It remains to conclude the first part of this survey by considering briefly, with constant reference to the condition of the Eastern Christians, the growth of Eastern nationalism from 1920 to 1930 and the subsequent confrontation of Judaeo-Israelite nationalism and pan-Arabism between 1936 and 1955, as well as the effect of Soviet penetration in this explosive region which has enabled a renewed and dynamic Arabism, unified and socialist, to find forcible self-expression.

As a result of the First World War and the dismantling of the Ottoman Empire, the Arabs were able to take the first steps towards realizing their ambitions, to shake off the Turkish yoke and to rebuild

[1] G. Antonius, *The Arab Awakening* (London, 1938), p. 59.

the Arab Empire of former times. Great Britain, for her part, hoped to take over the remains of the Ottoman Empire, regarding it as the natural environment for the birth and development of Arab nationalism. Colonel Lawrence was to organize the "revolt in the desert", a revolt of Arabs against Turks, despite their common religion. The British indeed promised to "recognize and support the independence of the Arabs" and they set up Fayṣal, son of the Amir Ḥusayn, as head of this movement. However, in addition to the MacMahon–Ḥusayn conversations which ratified these promises, British policy had devised additional measures as a precaution against being taken unawares. Agreements concerning the Arab world and the mandates were signed by France and England, in particular the Sykes–Picot agreement, which provided that after victory Iraq and Palestine should be under a British mandate, while the Lebanon and Syria should be under a French mandate. According to the League of Nations definition of a mandate, the mandatory nation should, by its advice and by its guidance in internal affairs, assist the progress of the mandated state towards that full autonomy which it was to attain when it was capable of acting independently. It was obviously a form of tutelage of which nationalism would seek to rid itself as soon as possible, as well as putting up a determined resistance to such a parcelling out of Arab territories which it wished to see united in one bloc.

Even more serious, however, and destined to be the most persistent cause of discontent in the Middle East was the Balfour Declaration communicated by the British to Lord Rothschild on 2 November 1917, by which the British government stated that it "views with favour the establishment in Palestine of a national home for the Jewish people and will use its best endeavours to facilitate the achievement of this object".

Great Britain was to employ all her political resources, sometimes with liberality, sometimes with impassive severity, according to whether she judged it necessary, in her own interests, to favour one country or check the development of another. Thus Egypt's awakening to emancipation at first met with formal opposition from the British government and it was only after the demonstrations of 1919 that the British were induced to receive the *Wafd* of Egyptian negotiators. Christians and Muslims in a kind of holy alliance vied with each other in patriotic fervour. Father Sargios, an Orthodox Copt, delivered impassioned speeches from the pulpit of the Azhar. Finally in 1922 preliminary agreement was reached and Egypt was declared a sovereign state subject to four reservations: security of Imperial communications, defence of Egypt against aggression, protection of foreigners and maintenance of the *status quo* in the Sudan. It was a mere gesture, designed to have a calming effect on Egyptian nationalism.

On 19 April 1923 King Fu'ād promulgated the "Constitution", which established parliamentary government and recognized the freedoms of the individual, including freedom of conscience. Islam was, however, declared to be the state religion and the king was required to be a Muslim.

The long and laborious negotiations between Britain and Egypt from 1924 to 1935 were settled by an adverse circumstance and it was necessary for Ethiopia to be annexed by Mussolini for them to be brought to a conclusion, since Egypt felt herself to be threatened. The occupation was converted into a friendly alliance with Great Britain within the framework of the League of Nations; British troops withdrew to the Canal Zone; the British renounced their rights for the protection of foreigners and the *status quo* was maintained in the Sudan. In the following year the Convention of Montreux abolished the Capitulations.

Egypt, which had hitherto been contemptuous and even suspicious of Pan-Arabism, began to appreciate it and to move in its direction. In 1930 there was a recrudescence of Muslim religious feeling which was followed by a sense of unity arising from the Arabic language and its related culture and leading the way to an Arab solidarity which was soon to become decisive. It was based on the idea of resistance to imperialism and on the exaltation of Muslim principles.

Playing to the limit the card of Arab nationalism, which had become the axis of their policy in the Middle East, the British tried to make a pilot-state of Iraq, the champion of Pan-Arabism, while continuing at the same time to exercise a discreet but effective guardianship over her. Fayṣal, who had been expelled from Damascus after his conflict with the French, was set on the throne on 23 August 1921, and Nūri 'l-Sa'īd, the faithful friend of Lawrence, was for many years to be the skilful interpreter and manipulator of Anglo-Arab policy. In 1930 the British gave complete emancipation to Iraq, without heeding the legitimate protests of the anxious minorities. *De minimis non curat praetor.*

The example of Baghdad gave encouragement to Arab nationalism throughout the Arab world and was followed in Saudi Arabia and in

Egypt by other focal points which aimed to be the centre of it. In the Levant States the Hāshimite dream of a "Great Syria" was effectively fostered, as well as the struggle against local groups. Unfortunately the West sacrificed the minorities to its own interests, including Christians as well as Kurds. From 1920 the American Senate declined the mandate over Armenia, which passed, exhausted by war, within the Soviet orbit. The Nestorian Christians, called by the press of that time Assyrians, suffered an even worse fate. Great Britain, urging them in 1917 to fight against the Turks, had hailed them warmly as "our smallest ally". In order not to alienate the friendship of the Iraqi government, however, on which their whole Arab policy was based, they did practically nothing to save them. Many Assyrians fled in despair to Syria and on 11 August 1933 the relations they had left behind were savagely massacred in the region of Mosul with the complicity, if not by the actual instigation, of the Iraqi government.

The attitude of France towards the Lebanon was inspired by a different policy. France was faithful to the Christian minorities whose guardian she had been over the centuries and conceived of the Mandate as a labour of planned and progressive preparation, of long-term administrative and political education which would respect local minorities. From the outset she distinguished between the two political entities of the Lebanon and Syria. The former, which had become Great Lebanon, was divided into several sectors: in addition to the region of Beirut it comprised in the north the district of Tripoli and the plain of 'Akkār, and in the south, particularly, the rich plateau of al-Biqā'. The new state had a population of a little over a million, in which Christians and Muslims were practically equal. In 1925 one of the first decrees of the Tribunal of Conflicts established by Weygand proclaimed the principle of the equality of the communities. On 22 May 1926 Great Lebanon became "the Lebanese Republic", still under French Mandate. The constitution was promulgated and Charles Dabbās, a Greek Orthodox, became President of the Republic; in 1934 the presidency of the Republic was by tacit agreement restricted to Maronites and the presidency of the Council to Sunnite Muslims. Since, however, the Franco-Lebanese treaty, which had been drafted in 1936 and whose fate was linked with the Franco-Syrian treaty, had not been concluded, the country found itself on the eve of war in 1939 under French Mandate. The weakness of this mandate, as Rondot noted, was "undoubtedly a failure to observe that the rate of development in the

Lebanon and its ready acceptance values and friendships would have justified a speedy emancipation". Such a step would have given the mandatory Power an exceptional opportunity of dealing on a sound basis with an eastern nationalism which was not hostile to it. "Unfortunately this nationalism was almost completely ignored by the agents of the French mandate."

With regard to Syria, the misunderstanding was even more serious. The Mandate opened with a show of force, since it was necessary to expel King Fayṣal, who had been set up in Damascus by the British. It was not an ideal beginning to a relationship with the nationalists. The country was divided into four autonomous states: Aleppo, Damascus, the 'Alawites and the Druzes, who had been federated in 1922. The Sanjak of Alexandretta had its own special statute. Since the Lebanon had refused to join the federation of Syrian states, it was passed over by General Weygand when he formed Damascus and Aleppo into the new state of Syria in 1923. The 'Alawites and the Druzes remained independent of the Damascus government and came directly under the control of the mandatory Power. The nationalists instigated the Druze rising of 1925, which lasted a year before being suppressed, and the city rioting, of decisive importance, in 1936. All the concessions offered by the mandatory Power were of no avail. The expedients, many times repeated, of closing Parliament, holding new elections and starting negotiations merely aggravated the nationalist fervour. When stable conditions had been restored, negotiations were resumed and at one point it seemed as though agreement were about to be reached between Jamīl Mardam and Bonnet, the President of the Council. French opinion, however, a slave to certain conservative prejudices, was not in favour of ratification. At this juncture war broke out in 1939 and everything had to be postponed.

Yet another storm-centre was about to come into being in the Middle East. While the Balfour Declaration was bearing its bitter fruits for the Arabs, Great Britain, in an attempt to reconcile her contradictory promises, was trying to restrict Zionism in Palestine and to exclude it from the political sphere. She created Transjordan as a buffer-state between Iraq, Palestine, Saudi Arabia and Syria and appointed the Amir Abdallāh as its ruler, described by Rondot as "an Arab prince who was astute, subtle and probably self-interested".

Soon, however, the Jewish National Home in Palestine was acquiring para-government machinery, by means of which immigrants were beginning to stream in from all quarters. The effect of such an influx was to upset the political balance of the different communities in Palestine and it was inevitable that sooner or later there would be a clash between the British administration and the Zionists, out of which terrorism would be born.

The Arabs were conscious of the danger and at first confined themselves to protests, while refusing to co-operate with the administration. The first major incident, resulting in 249 dead at the Wailing Wall, demonstrated the gravity of the situation. An Islamic congress met in Jerusalem in December 1931 to organize the struggle against Zionism which was beginning to appear as pre-eminently a *national* movement. There followed an implacable struggle with the Arabs, who were defending *their* country; the past thirty years have shown how deeply rooted is this conflict.

The British then took stock of the whole problem. An inquiry was made by the Peel Commission, which in its report of 8 June 1937 proposed partition: in addition to a mandated territory which would be responsible for the neutrality and protection of the Holy Places, there would be two sovereign and independent states, one Arab and the other Jewish, allied by treaties to Great Britain. Neither the Jews nor the Arabs would accept these proposals and Great Britain announced, in exasperation, that she would leave the country on the expiry of the mandate.

Meanwhile the clouds were gathering and a second World War seemed inevitable. Great Britain and France made their preparations, signed treaties and, in an attempt to win Turkey to their side, ceded to her the Sanjak of Alexandretta. This cession may have been necessary for the purpose of gaining time, but it was deeply wounding to both Syrians and Arabs: the mandatory Power, instead of defending the interests of the country entrusted to it, was exploiting it for the purposes of self-defence. There was a growing contempt for the West. A gradual but deep-rooted conviction was taking hold in the minds of the Arab peoples that the West was playing the Jewish game. Accordingly, when war broke out, their sympathies were at first with Nazi Germany because of her attitude towards the Jews: a German victory would allow them to rid themselves of all trace of "colonialism", open or disguised. The whole situation was regarded from a viewpoint at once narrow and inflexible: Zionism, the paramount danger for the Arab peoples, must be destroyed.

This attitude was apparent from the very beginning of the war. Even in Iraq, which had been the pampered child of Britain, there occurred the insurrection of Rashīd 'Alī al-Gīlānī, who attempted to overthrow the pro-British administration of the Regent. The British, thanks to their military advantages, were able to restore the situation, but they realized that the battle to win over the Arab world must be fought seriously, if necessary by a change of tactics. Their first move was to land forces in Syria and the Lebanon, where Vichy troops had taken their stand. They occupied these two countries, as well as Iran. In Egypt, where there was no lack of pro-Axis demonstrations and where the government had refrained from declaring war on Germany, Great Britain took drastic measures. An ultimatum was presented to King Fārūq, the Palace was surrounded, on 4 February 1942, and the king was compelled to take as head of the government al-Naḥḥās Pasha, Chief of the *Wafd*, who had rallied to the side of the British after the treaty of 1936.

Untiringly Great Britain pursued her policy of uniting the Arab countries under her protection in order to be able to come to a better understanding with them. The Eden declaration of 29 May 1941 is of prime importance in this connexion.

> The Arab world has made great strides since the settlement reached at the end of the last War, and many Arab thinkers desire for the Arab peoples a greater degree of unity than they now enjoy. In reaching out towards this unity they hope for our support. No such appeal from our friends should go unanswered. It seems to me both natural and right that the cultural and economic ties between the Arab countries and the political ties too should be strengthened. His Majesty's Government for their part will give their full support to any scheme that commands general approval.[1]

The idea of the Arab League was launched. Iraq, under her Prime Minister Nūri 'l-Sa'īd, was to be in charge of the "Fertile Crescent"—Palestine, Syria, Iraq and the Lebanon. It was to be a centralized or federal structure dominated by Baghdad in which both the Maronites of the Lebanon and the Zionists would take their place as protected minorities with limited autonomy. What has been said above of the Lebanese Maronite love of freedom will explain why the Lebanon was always opposed to this plan. Egypt for her part had no intention of allowing Iraq to take the lead in Pan-Arab affairs. By the Protocol of Alexandria, dated 7 October 1944, the Arab League was founded,

[1] Quoted in Rondot, *Destin*, p. 138.

comprising Iraq, Egypt, Syria, Lebanon, Transjordan, Saudi Arabia, Yemen and Egypt; Egypt was soon to take advantage of it for the realization of her immediate objective: the expulsion of the British from Egypt.

At the end of the war the Palestinian problem once more became acute. When attempts to control the Arab-Jewish conflict had failed, Great Britain submitted the question to the United Nations and announced that she proposed to leave the country on the termination of the Mandate, on 15 May 1948. On 28 November 1947 the General Assembly of the United Nations decreed a plan for partition. In addition to the zone of Jerusalem which was to be under permanent international protection, two independent states were to be created, linked economically and each composed of three territories sharing common frontiers. It was a solution which took into account only the economic and material aspects of the problem; it overlooked the fact that the Holy Places were sacred for three religions and that discussions should have been based pre-eminently on spiritual considerations. "All that was needed, indeed, was to have listened to the grave and long-standing warnings given by the Holy See", declared a well-informed observer.[1]

The Jews accepted the plan for partition; the Arabs rejected it. Great Britain, in accordance with her declared intention, left Palestine on 15 May 1948, "not without having, very discreetly, provided the Arabs with the means of exploiting this decision to the full".[2] The Jewish State was proclaimed. "Sixteen minutes later it was given *de facto* recognition by Washington. The Arab world will never forgive America for its sponsorship."[3]

The course of events is well known. Arab troops entered Palestine; the Arab Legion took Nābulus, Samaria and Hebron and came within a few miles of Tel Aviv. They seized the Old City of Jerusalem, but modern Jerusalem was well defended and resisted them. Other Arab troops joined the conflict, but without any co-ordination, and by the time that the Egyptian Army intervened it was too late. "Its units, poorly supported by their supply columns, ill-directed by the High Command, fought to no avail."[4]

The Arab–Israeli conflict has been discussed at some length because the whole course of political events in the Arab countries, as well as

[1] Rondot, *op. cit.* p. 144.
[2] *Ibid.* p. 145.
[3] *Ibid.*
[4] *Ibid.* p. 146.

the repercussions among the Christian elements, has been dominated by it. There is no need to proceed further with the recital of events which are known to everyone, but it may be noted that among those officers who fought in Palestine and felt the bitterness of defeat most deeply was Jamāl 'Abd al-Nāṣir. It was during this period that he first resolved to bring about a radical change in the state of affairs which had led to this abyss, to sweep away the conservative and feudal Arab governments, minions of the Western Powers, and to discard all influence, not merely political, but economic, military and cultural, from the West.

Little by little, with tireless determination, he set about furthering his plans. As a result of the revolution of 26 July 1952 King Fārūq was overthrown and the Republic established shortly afterwards. There followed a programme of agrarian reform which was designed to remedy injustices, but which could not endow with fresh resources a country where the population-increase presented a desperate problem. Hence it became necessary to construct the High Dam at Aswān as a means of securing the irrigation of many thousands of barren hectares. It was for Egypt a matter of life or death. At the same time it was also necessary for the country to be armed against Israel, not so much, perhaps, for the sake of military revenge as in preparation for the ever-present possibility of attack. Money for such armaments and the immense financial aid required for the construction of the Dam was refused by the West, which was incapable of understanding the innermost state of mind of the Eastern world, long frustrated and excessively sensitive. 'Abd al-Nāṣir turned to Soviet Russia and her satellites and obtained unconditional supplies of arms; he then nationalized the Suez Canal, causing concern and discord in the Western camp. The United States, as newcomers to the Middle East whose real problems they did not understand, vacillated and hesitated. The Baghdad Pact of 1955 was violently denounced by 'Abd al-Nāṣir and his allies. Israel, unknown to the Americans and acting in agreement with the British and French, launched an attack on Egypt, while the British and French attacked. In the eyes of the Arabs Israel appeared more than ever as the spearhead of a new form of Western imperialism, unwilling to lose control. When the United States intervened to stop the conflict and force the British and French to take to their ships, they earned themselves no gratitude from the Arabs, whose resentment and distrust were too deep-seated. The struggle continued between

Pan-Arabism, which wished to remain neutral, and the Western Powers, and the efforts of the United States to join with the Middle East in a defence against communism were in vain. The Eisenhower plan for aid to the Middle East also miscarried. Although the intervention of the Sixth Fleet was successful in restoring order in the Lebanon, the Americans, on the other hand, failed completely in Syria. The dictatorships which followed, after many years of disturbances in that country, confirmed its anti-American policy (refusal of Point IV) and achieved a measure of social progress, but above all associated the revived Syrian nationalism with the Pan-Arabism of ʿAbd al-Nāṣir, which was increasingly united and victorious. At one time the swing towards Soviet Russia was so violent that the distracted rulers of Syria fled to Cairo begging ʿAbd al-Nāṣir to save them. Almost in self-defence he consented to the formation of the United Arab Republic. Once more peoples and ideas were in a state of upheaval, and collisions occurred resulting in political rupture. In spite of disagreements which were sometimes acute, however, the Middle East at least continued to present a united front to Israel, with a common distrust of the West.

In these feverish conditions the Christian communities of the Middle East, which had been shaken by continual crises since the end of the First World War, were pursuing their way, sometimes gropingly, towards an increasing degree of autonomy; they also continued to take part in the national struggles and to join the various parties which came into being (*Baʿth* Syrian Popular party, Lebanese Falangists, National Socialist Union, etc.), sharing in the general anxiety, in the sorrows of war and in the sacrifices demanded by social legislation, nationalization and sequestration. It is possible that in certain countries some groups of Christians suffered more from these last measures than others. Especially in this last decade social and economic upheavals and uncertainty regarding the future have driven many Christians, particularly Catholics of Syro-Lebanese origin who had for a long time been settled in Egypt, to emigrate either to the Lebanon or even, in considerable numbers, to Canada and the United States. Many others have remained behind, however, and become involved in the birth-pangs of a new world. The history of these various Catholic communities, their present conditions, their numbers, the structure of their churches, the part which they played in the last century and continue to play at the present time, will be described in the next section.

Individual Communities

Each individual community will now be considered separately, in the following order:

1. Melkites.
2. Catholic Copts (Egypt and Ethiopia).
3. Armenian Catholics.
4. Maronites.
5*a*. Syrian Catholics.
5*b*. Christian Malankars of India.
6*a*. Chaldaeans.
6*b*. Christian Malabars of India.
7. Latin Catholics.

In this section reference is frequently made to *L'Oriente Cattolico*, the official work on the subject, issued by the Congregation for the Eastern Church (Vatican). The statistics given have been taken from this work.

1. *Melkites*

This word is derived etymologically from the Syriac *malka* (Arabic *malik*) meaning an emperor or king. It was the Monophysite opponents of the Melkites who gave them the name contemptuously by way of stigmatizing their devotion to the Emperor of Byzantium.

Melkites (also written Melchites) are, strictly speaking, the Christians of the Byzantine rite, whether Catholic or not, belonging to the patriarchates of Alexandria, Antioch and Jerusalem. The word was employed for the first time in Egypt in 460 as a nickname for the followers of the legitimate Orthodox Patriarch. It is now usual to restrict its application to the Middle Eastern Catholics of the Byzantine rite.

This Melkite Church will now be considered only from the time when the first attempts at union to take shape, since this Church as it exists today is essentially composed of Orthodox Christians of the Byzantine rite who accepted membership of the Catholic Church.

Attempts at union. Between 1583 and 1587 the titular bishop of Sidon, Leonard Abīlā, was sent to the Orient by Pope Gregory XII in an attempt to win over to the Catholic faith the old Patriarch Michael VII, who had then resigned and retired to Aleppo. A small nucleus of Catholics was formed in Aleppo which probably dated from this period, and it increased in size when the Capuchins and Jesuits came to the city in 1625, followed a year later by the Carmelites. Further submissions took place in the seventeenth century, and before long conversions to Catholicism were sufficiently numerous for the Propaganda to consider appointing an administrator with the duty of looking after their interests. The choice fell on Euthymus Ṣayfī, metropolitan of Tyre and Sidon, a former pupil of the Jesuits, who had become a Catholic in 1684. It was he who founded the Salvatorian Basilians and who worked actively to extend Catholicism in Aleppo and Damascus.

In 1716 the Patriarch Cyril, a great friend of Pouillard, French Consul at Sidon, yielded to his persuasion and sent his profession of faith to Rome, together with that of Gerasimos, bishop of Daydnayya. After his death and the death of Athanasius III Dabbās who succeeded him, his nephew Serafino Tanas was elected to the patriarchate by the practising Catholics of Damascus and took the name of Cyril VI. The Greeks of Constantinople immediately set up a Cypriot in opposition to him, Mgr Sylvester, who took the name of Jeremy. There followed a desperate struggle between the two prelates. Cyril VI was driven out of Damascus and took refuge in the Lebanon in the Monastery of the Holy Saviour near Sidon where he worked to unite the Lebanese Melkites with Rome.

Cyril VI (1724–59) was followed by an uninterrupted succession of Catholic Melkite patriarchs of Antioch, but until 1819 they were not officially recognized by the Ottoman authority as the political leaders of their community. In this year civil emancipation was granted by the Ottoman authorities to all the Catholics of the Ottoman Empire enabling them to form themselves into communities under their respective patriarchs. The conquest of Syria by the Egyptians in 1382 inaugurated a period of religious toleration. The Patriarch Maximus III Maẓlūm (1833–55) took advantage of this lull to establish his residence in Damascus, where it has remained to the present day.

The precipitate introduction of the Gregorian calendar in 1857 caused a minor schism, to which other differences also contributed. Fortunately the rule of Gregory II Yūsuf (1864–97) which was at once cautious, wise and energetic, restored order and gave an active stimulus to the community. It was he who founded in 1882 the Seminary of St Anne in Jerusalem, which Cardinal Lavigerie agreed to put under the administration of the White Fathers (see below).

The work of union with Rome continued in the regions of Tripoli and Judayda–Marj 'Uyūn, extending also into Palestine (eparchy of Acre) and in the region of Ḥimṣ. At the present day the work of the Council and the vigorous ecumenical efforts made in the Orient have brought about a marked change in perspectives (see below).

The patriarchates of Alexandria and Jerusalem. The majority of the Melkite Catholics within these patriarchates came from Syria or the Lebanon. After being originally in the care of the Franciscans of the Holy Land, they were transferred to the authority of the Melkite Patriarch of Antioch, then residing in the Lebanon, by the Propaganda decree of 13 July 1773.

In 1838 the Patriarch Maximus III Maẓlūm obtained from Gregory XVI a privilege which was personal to himself but which would also be available to his successors of assuming the titles of the two other patriarchates of Alexandria and Jerusalem and also of administering them. In 1856 the titles and duties of these two patriarchates were appended by Rome to the see of Antioch.

Leo XIII in 1894 extended the jurisdiction of the Melkite patriarchate to all the Melkites of the Ottoman Empire. A continuous stream of Melkite immigrants from Syria and the Lebanon into Egypt had raised the total number there to 30,000. As has been shown above, however, this community began to disintegrate in 1956. The majority had settled in Lower Egypt, but there were also five parishes in the Sudan.

During the first decades of the twentieth century the movement for union with Rome spread from Jerusalem into Transjordan. In 1932 the eparchy of Petra and Philadelphia was founded, with its residence at Amman, capital of Transjordan. The eparchy of Jerusalem was administered by a patriarchal vicar in the name of the patriarch.

Finally, it should be mentioned that after the First World War a large number of Melkite Catholics emigrated to Egypt, to the United States, to Brazil and to the Argentine.

The Patriarch Maximus IV Ṣā'igh was elected in 1947. On 19 March 1962 Father Gabriel Acacius Kūsā, Assessor to the Eastern Congregation, who had for a long time been Professor of Oriental Canon Law to the Propaganda was appointed Cardinal by John XXIII. Unfortunately he died quite suddenly in the following year. In February 1965 the Patriarch Maximus IV Ṣā'igh was appointed Cardinal with two other Eastern patriarchs.

2. *Catholic Copts*

The foundation of the Orthodox Coptic Church as a result of the Council of Chalcedon, which it did not accept, has been described above. It remains to consider how this Orthodox Church gave birth to the small Catholic Coptic Church united with Rome.

In 1237 the Patriarch Cyril II showed some interest in union with Rome. During the Council of Florence, 1439–40, the Patriarch John XI wrote to Pope Eugenius IV, but without result. Attempts made during the second half of the sixteenth century and the first years of the seventeenth century were similarly unfruitful. It was not until the eighteenth century that Athanasius, the Coptic bishop resident in Jerusalem, declared himself in 1741 to be a Catholic. Pope Benedict XIV committed to his care some scattered Catholic Copts in Egypt who had embraced Catholicism in the seventeenth century, under the influence of the Franciscans from the Holy Land. Athanasius, however, was afraid of being attacked by the Orthodox Church and did not dare to go to Egypt in person, but contented himself with the appointment there of a Vicar-General.

Among Catholic Copts who were studying in Rome at this time, a certain Raphael Ṭūkhī distinguished himself by his editorial activity. He had in fact been given the task of editing Coptic liturgical books in the Coptic and Arabic languages. They were published in Rome after their revision during the years 1736–64. On 11 April 1761 he became *prelato ordinante* and was promoted to the titulary see of Acante; in 1764 he was transferred to the see of Arsinoe and he died in Rome in 1787.

Athanasius, the first Apostolic Vicar of the Catholic Copts, like several of his successors residing in Egypt, could not receive consecration as a bishop because there was no other Catholic bishop in Egypt who could perform it and the voyage to Europe was difficult. Having no churches of their own, the Catholic priests celebrated their liturgy in the churches of the Franciscans. It was not until 1829 that they were able to build their own churches, when Maḥmud II allowed Catholics of the Ottoman Empire to become independent of the Orthodox Patriarchs.

Coptic Catholic patriarch. In 1824 it was rumoured in Rome that Muḥammad 'Alī was very anxious for the Catholic Copts to have their own patriarch in the person of the Apostolic Vicar Maximus

Zuwayya. By the letter *Petrus Apostolorum princeps* of 15 August 1824 a Coptic Catholic patriarchate was actually created. The anomaly soon came to an end, however, and there was a return to simple vicars until the reign of Leo XIII.

On 15 March 1895 Father George Macaire was raised to the position of Apostolic Vicar and he took the name of Cyril with the title of Bishop of Caesarea Philippi. The Catholics, whose numbers had increased, expressed the desire to have a patriarch. Immediately after his election Mgr Macaire took his flock on a pilgrimage to Rome and conveyed this desire to the Pope, who, on 26 November 1895, by the letter *Christi Domini*, re-established the Catholic patriarchate of Alexandria. In addition to the patriarchal eparchy with its seat at Cairo, the patriarchate had two suffragan eparchies: (i) Hermopolis Magna, with its seat at al-Minya, and (ii) Thebes or Luxor, with its seat at Ṭanṭā, then at Sūhāj.

By the same apostolic letter Mgr Cyril Macaire was appointed apostolic administrator of the patriarchate. The number of Catholics increased rapidly: in 1907 there were 14,000, in 1931 35,000, in 1950 57,000 and finally in 1959 80,000.

In order to provide a discipline for the new patriarchate, a synod met in Cairo in 1898 whose decisions were reviewed and sanctioned by Rome. Mgr Cyril Macaire was promoted patriarch at the consistory of 19 June 1899. Several years of successful apostolate were followed by difficulties which in 1908 caused the resignation of the patriarch, who went over to the Greek Orthodox Church. He returned to the Catholic Church in 1912 and died at Beirut in 1922. The Coptic patriarchate remained vacant; affairs were in the hands of an apostolic administrator until 10 August 1947 when Mgr Mark Khuzām was appointed patriarch. He died on 2 February 1958. During this patriarchate a fourth diocese was instituted, that of Lycopolis with its see at Asyūṭ. On 10 May 1958 Stephanos Sīdārūs succeeded His Beatitude Khuzām. He was elevated to the dignity of Cardinal in February 1965.

Ethiopian Catholics. The Ethiopian Church was originally attached to the Church of Alexandria and followed the Coptic Orthodox Church in refusing to accept the Council of Chalcedon. Its history will be dealt with in a special section, and only its attempts at union over the centuries, together with the present state of Catholicism in Ethiopia, will be considered here.

Attempts at union. The geographical expeditions of the Portuguese in the fifteenth century first made it possible to enter into communication with Rome. In the *Fatha Neghest* or Legislation of the King, a religious and secular book which is still in use, the primacy of the Roman Pontiff is openly recognized. The Negus Lebna Denghel (1508–40) sought to establish relations with Leo X and Clement VII.

A regular mission was agreed upon between the Portuguese court and the Holy See, with the active support of St Ignatius Loyola. A change of attitude in the sovereign, however, and the scarcity of information available at this period on the ecclesiastical institutions of the Orient, impeded the success of the enterprises. It was decided to send a patriarch and two bishops, all Latins, to Ethiopia. The first patriarch, Nuñez Barreto, had to wait at Goa for a chance of making his way into Ethiopia, but he died in 1561. Only one of the two bishops, Andrea d'Oviedo, was able to enter the country secretly in 1557.

Although he was accepted only reluctantly, he was nevertheless able to exercise his jurisdiction over the Portuguese and, realizing the uselessness of direct attack, he devoted himself to a discreet and secret apostolate among the native population. He died at Fremona, near Aksum, in 1577 and his last two companions disappeared in 1577 and 1596 respectively.

In the seventeenth century the Neguses Yaqub Za Denghel and Susenyos were more sympathetic and the latter even embraced Catholicism publicly in 1622. His conversion was the achievement of the Jesuit Pedro Paez. Urbane VII thought the moment opportune for withdrawing the patriarchate which had already been granted to Nuñez Barreto. Alfonso Mendez was chosen in 1622, but in 1636 he was expelled and for many years from that date the Ethiopian Empire remained closed to all Catholic teaching.

It was not until the eighteenth and nineteenth centuries that new missions could be sent once more to Ethiopia. In 1788 the Propaganda sent the Ethiopian priest George Egziabeher; he was appointed titular bishop of Adulis and ordained in Rome according to the Byzantine rite. Father Michaelangelo Pocelli went with him; after some years however, in about 1797, the bishop was killed. A second mission in July 1840, under Theodore Abū Karīm, Apostolic Vicar of the Copts, does not seem to have finished its term. At the beginning of the nineteenth century the mission was reopened under a Lazarist father of the Syrian mission, Father Giuseppe Sapeto, who settled in Aduwa in 1838 with his French companion Antoine d'Abbadie. He studied the Ghe'ez language, and the monuments and history of the country. On his return to Rome Antoine d'Abbadie convinced the Prefect of the Propaganda, Cardinal Fransoni, of the necessity of instituting an Apostolic Prefecture in Ethiopia under the care of the Lazarists. One of the first priests to be sent was the blessed Giustino De Jacobis (1839–60), canonized on 25 June 1939, who in 1847 became the first bishop of the mission. He died in exile in 1860 after much suffering. Finally, mention must be made of the Capuchin mission directed by Guglielmo Massaia, who was appointed Apostolic Vicar of a vicariate instituted in 1846 for the Galla. When Italy took possession of Eritrea, the Holy See created a new Apostolic Prefecture there in 1911 and entrusted it to the Capuchins.

The increase in numbers of the Catholics in Ethiopia and of their priests led to the establishment, on 4 July 1930, of a native hierarchy under Mgr Chidané Maryam Cassa. He was constituted Ordinary for the Catholics of the Ethiopic rite in Eritrea.

After the Italian occupation of Ethiopia in 1936, a special commission of Cardinals studied the best means of promoting the Catholic apostolate in that country. The dioceses were reorganized by means of the institution of three vicariates and six apostolic prefectures. The Apostolic Vicariate and the Eastern Ordinary remained in Eritrea and an apostolic delegation was established. The Second World War upset these new arrangements, however, and the Latin missionaries were dismissed, while the native clergy and hierarchy became more important. In 1951 the Apostolic Exarchate of Addis Ababa was set up for Ethiopia; the Ordinary of Eritrea was raised to the rank of Apostolic Exarchate and both were entrusted to native clergy of the Ethiopic rite.

Two seminaries exist for the training of Ethiopian clergy, one at Asmara and the other at Adigrat, with pre-seminaries at Keren, Hebo and Atat, and in Rome there is an Ethiopian pontifical college in the gardens of the Vatican City, under the care of Capuchin fathers. In Ethiopia there are also the Cistercian monks of Casamari who have founded a monastic community of the Ethiopic rite. On 9 April 1961 an "Ecclesiastical Province" ("metropolia") was founded with its metropolitan see at Addis Ababa and suffragan eparchies at Asmara and Adigrat.

3. *Armenian Catholics*

The Catholic patriarchate of Cilicia does not, in fact, go back further than 26 March 1740, when Abraham Ardzivean, Catholic Bishop of Aleppo, was elected Catholicos of Sīs (Kozan). He came to Rome and was confirmed by Benedict XIV in the consistory of 26 November 1742. After leaving Rome in 1743 he was unable to return to Aleppo, since in the meantime an Orthodox Catholicos had been appointed there, but he settled at Kuraym, in the Lebanon. His successor transferred the patriarchal see to Bzummār, also in the Lebanon, which has since become the spiritual headquarters of the Armenian Catholics. After going to Rome Abraham Ardzivean took the name of Peter, a practice which was adopted thenceforward by his successors. Their jurisdiction extended at first into Cilicia, Syria and the Lebanon, then into Egypt and Mesopotamia and, after 1789, it included also the regions of Toka and of Pkernik in Asia Minor.

Groups of Armenian Catholics existed in various parts of Turkey as well as in Constantinople. There were almost 10,000 of them when, in 1707, the priest Ter Komitas Khlomourgean was martyred. By a decree of 9 July 1759 the Propaganda founded an Armenian Catholic Vicariate in Constantinople subject to the Latin patriarchal vicariate. It lasted until the institution of the primatial archbishop of the Turkish capital, effected by Pius VIII on 6 July 1830, as a result of the civil emancipation granted to all the Catholics of the Ottoman Empire in 1825.

In 1850 six new episcopal sees were founded in Turkey. Conflicts of jurisdiction between the two Armenian Primates, of the Lebanon and of Constantinople respectively, subsided after the consistory of 10 July 1867 had suppressed the primatial Armenian see of Constantinople and united it with the patriarchate of Cilicia. Antoine Ḥassūn, Archbishop primate of Constantinople (1860–7) was elected patriarch with his seat in Constantinople in the consistory of 13 December 1884, after having secured from Pope Leo XIII the establishment of the Armenian Pontifical College in Rome in 1883.

Although the ancient Armenian Church held several synods and promulgated many disciplinary canons, the documents have remained in manuscript.

A synod met at Bzummār in 1854, without the approval of the Holy See. In preparation for another synod, several episcopal conferences were held in Rome in July 1867, and in 1890 a synod was held at Kadîköy which did not itself receive approval, but which opened the way to the full synod held in Rome in 1911; it was reviewed and recognized by the decree of 14 September 1913. After having been thrown into disorder by the upheavals of the First World War and having lost several of its dioceses in Turkey as a result of the devastation, the Armenian patriarchate was reorganized by the synod of bishops which was held in Rome in May–June 1928 by invitation of the Oriental Congregation.

By a decree of 23 June 1928 the patriarchal see was transferred from Constantinople to Beirut, where a diocese was founded, under the special direction of the patriarchate, for Armenian immigrants. The archbishopric was re-established at Constantinople and of the eighteen pre-war dioceses there remained, in addition to Beirut and Constantinople, only Alexandria in Egypt, Aleppo and Iṣfahān. The archdiocese of Baghdad was founded in 1954 for the Armenians of Iraq and the diocese of al-Qāmishlī for those of Upper Jazīra in Syria. The number of believers coming under the patriarchate which in 1911 amounted to more than 100,000 now stands at about 52,000. For the Armenian Catholic refugees in Greece an Ordinary was instituted in 1925 which came directly under the control of the Holy See. In the same way an exarchate of episcopal status was instituted in 1960 for Armenian Catholics in France, which was considered as a suffragan of the archbishop of Paris.

Since the eighteenth century Armenian Catholics have had their own Mekhitarian monks, an order founded in 1701 by Mekhitar of Sivas which is composed of two branches: one in Venice, where it occupies the whole of the island of San Lazzaro, and the other in Vienna. This order has gained the respect and admiration of the learned world by its scientific, philological and literary works. The language of the liturgy is classical Armenian. The so-called modern language, spoken by the majority of Armenians today, also has its own literature.

The liturgical melodies of the Armenian rite are remarkable for their solemn beauty.

4. *The Maronites*

The Maronites are the only Oriental Catholic community which has no Orthodox equivalent detached from Rome. In fact, the Churches of the Maronites, Syrians (Catholic and Orthodox), Chaldaeans and Nestorians, as well as their off-shoots in Southern India, all spring from the same vigorous stock: the ancient Church of Antioch. As their name suggests, they belong to a monastery founded at the source of the Orontes (Nahr al-ʿĀṣī) near Apamaea (Qalʿat al-Maḍīq) above the tomb of a holy anchorite, Saint (Mārūn) Maron, who lived at the end of the fourth century and beginning of the fifth century in the region of Ṣūr (Tyre) and whose life has been described by Theodoret. This monastery, which became a centre of monastic life, was important by reason of its struggle against the monophysite heresies of the fifth century.

The struggles between the different religious communions, however, and the destruction caused by the Muslims (the convent of St Maron was laid in ruins) obliged the Maronite monks, towards the end of the ninth century, to emigrate with their flock to the Lebanon, which offered almost inaccessible mountain slopes as a refuge to those who desired to escape from Muslim domination and to preserve their liberty. For centuries the Maronites were able to maintain their independence both against the caliphs and, from 1526 onwards, against the Ottomans.

Two features which have distinguished the Maronite community over the centuries and which it has preserved up to the present day have been its unshakeable fidelity to the Holy See and its long-standing friendship with France. Relations were established with Rome at the earliest possible date: in 1215 the Patriarch Jeremy II al-ʿAmshītī was present at the 12th Ecumenical Council, Lateran IV, and was confirmed by Innocent III (Bull, *Quia divinae sapientiae* of 4 January 1216). From that time onward contact with Rome continued without a break. Moreover, Rome showed a special interest in the Maronites and was concerned both to encourage their spiritual life and to remedy their grievances. In the sixteenth century certain liturgical books were examined and printed in Rome. The first Lebanese synod was held at Luwayza in 1736, and was specifically approved by Pope Benedict XIV (1740–58). Others synods followed, but they were of less importance.

The second characteristic of the Maronite community is its friendship which has become traditional, with France. Even during the monarchy, the kings of France became recognized protectors of the Maronites and, when the Republican government supervened, the Maronites still found in the French friends of unshakeable loyalty. It has been noted above that French troops were in 1860 directed by the Powers to go to the aid of the Christians who were being massacred in the Lebanon. When the question of a mandate arose after the First World War, France was welcomed enthusiastically as the mandatory Power. This secular friendship is apparent not only in cultural exchanges, but also in the marked dependence of the Lebanese economy on the French economy, and explains why the Lebanon alone did not break off relations with France during the Suez crisis, when all the Arab countries did so.

The Maronite patriarch. At the head of the Maronite community is the patriarch, the undisputed leader who enjoys unrivalled prestige. He is elected by the metropolitans and the bishops meeting in a synod and is always a Maronite prelate at least forty years of age; the successful candidate must gain two-thirds of the votes. Subsequently he receives from the Pope the *pallium* which marks his union with the see of Peter. The patriarch is appointed for life and he has jurisdiction over all the Maronites of the former Empire Ottoman and of Egypt. The following are the most important of the many privileges conferred on him by custom and by the Lebanese synod of 1736: consecration of Maronite bishops; sole right to appoint perideutes (*baradūt*, visitor), archpriests and chorepiscopi (rural bishops); he alone consecrates the Holy Chrism and he reserves the right of absolution of certain sins. No translation from Syriac into Arabic may be published without his permission. Every three years he summons the bishops to a synod. Although the Maronite patriarch no longer retains ethnarchic rights in relation to his subjects, he nevertheless holds a position of great dignity in the Lebanon. For many centuries the Maronite patriarchs had their residence at Qannūbīn, and with them the bishops of the community. The synod of 1790 instituted the residence at Bkirkī. Some bishops living far away, in Damascus or Cyprus, for example, preferred to reside in the Lebanon, even after the allotment of sees by the Lebanese synod of 1736.

After the foundation of the Lebanese Republic, the territory of certain dioceses was redefined so as to extend across the frontiers. To assist the pastoral work, the Holy See in 1954 approved the decision of the synod of Maronite bishops to entrust the administration of the parishes of the eparchy of Tripoli, in Syria, to the Archbishop of Aleppo (under the title of apostolic administrator of Laodicea), as also of the parish of the eparchy of Damascus, situated in the Lebanon but separated from it in 1960 and converted into the eparchy of Ṣarbā.

The Maronites, although most numerous in the Lebanon, are

distributed throughout Syria and have colonies of varying importance in Cyprus, Palestine, Egypt (where the eparchy of Cairo was founded in 1946), in North and South America and elsewhere. The vernacular language of the Maronites, formerly Syriac, has been Arabic since the eighteenth century, but French is also used extensively. The rite is essentially Antiochene, with some additions of its own. The liturgy is celebrated in Syriac, and the texts are written and pronounced in the same way as in Syria. Some passages have an Arabic version added or even substituted, written in ordinary Syriac characters which for this purpose are called *karshūnī*.

5 *a*. *Syrian Catholics*

The Syrian Catholic Church was formed by Catholics who, after the Jacobite schism of the sixth century, returned to union with Rome.

It is clear that when the Byzantine Emperors, whom the fortunes of war had temporarily restored to possession of their former territories, tried to resolve the discord provoked by non-acceptance of the Council of Chalcedon, their efforts, based as they were on force, met with very little success. The Jacobites, on the other hand, were on good terms with the Crusaders: Franciscan and Dominican missionaries sent by the Pope in the thirteenth and fourteenth centuries achieved considerable results in 1237 and 1247, especially with the bishops and patriarchs, but were not able to win over the clergy and their flocks.

The Council of Florence in 1439 led to a wide movement for union in the East. In 1444 the Jacobite Church entered briefly into communion with Rome. Communications were difficult, however, by reason of the hostilities between Christians and Muslims and the necessity which faced the Pope of resisting a Turkish invasion. The Ottoman conquest of 1516 did nothing to change the situation. Towards the end of the sixteenth century, however, the Jacobite patriarch of Antioch, Niʿmat Allāh, admitted the possibility of a mass return to Catholicism. This consideration and the desire to see the Eastern Church accepting the Gregorian Calendar induced Gregory XIII to send the Maltese Leonard Abīlā, who had been consecrated titular bishop of Sidon, as a legate from Rome in 1583. Abīlā had several discussions with the leaders of the Jacobite Church, the results of which were not lost, since the lasting recollection of them made a more direct apostolate possible subsequently, in 1626: Jesuits and Capuchins settled in Aleppo, which was then a trading centre.

In 1781 the Jacobite Archbishop of Aleppo, Michael Jarwa, who had been converted to Catholicism in 1774, was chosen by the Jacobite Patriarch as his successor. After his election as patriarch on 4 January 1782 he was enthroned in his residence at Dayr Za'farān, but before long he was obliged to contend with a rival Jacobite. He was thrown into prison, but succeeded in escaping and after much persecution was able to find refuge in the Lebanon, where he settled on the hill of Sharfa and founded the monastery of St Mary the Liberator. With him began the unbroken line of Syrian Catholic patriarchs.

Subsequently, in about 1831, the patriarch transferred the patriarchal residence to Aleppo and in 1843, by the decree of that year, became the official head of his community. After the rising of the Aleppo Muslims against the Christians in 1850 the patriarch deemed it wise to transfer the patriarchal residence to Mardin, the centre of the Jacobite community. The Patriarch Raḥmānī (1898–1929), who had personal reasons for wishing to reside in Beirut, obtained a concession to do so which has become permanent.

His successor, Mgr Ignace Gabriel Tappouni, who was elected in 1929 and appointed cardinal on 16 December 1936, reorganized the Syrian Church. He built the new patriarchal see at Beirut and set up patriarchal vicariates—that of Upper Jazīra was made an eparchy (al-Ḥasaka) in 1957. Other vicariates exist in Jordan, in Egypt and at Mardin. Cardinal Tappouni brought back to the Catholic Church numerous Jacobites living in the Sudan, together with their bishop Mār Ḥannā Ghandūr, who died in 1961. The uniate movement is active all the time.

Syrian Catholics are numerous in Syria, in the Lebanon and in Iraq. They have colonies of varying importance in Jordan, Egypt and North and South America. Their common language is now Arabic. Spoken Syriac (*sūreth*) no longer survives except in certain districts of Ṭūr 'Abdīn and in Iraq, around Mosul.

Since the union with Rome three synods have been held: at Sharfa in 1853, at Aleppo in 1866 and again at Sharfa in 1888. The Acts of this last synod were published in Rome in 1896.

5 *b. The Malankars*

Malankar, which is synonymous with Malabar, denotes the south-western region which today forms the state of Kerala. The name Malankar was used to designate the Indian Catholics of the Syro-

Occidental or Antiochene rite, and distinguishes them from the Syro-Orientals or Chaldaeans called Malabars, who have the same origin.

How did this community come into being? In 1653 a group of Malabar Catholics became dissatisfied with the growing latinization of their rite and their traditions under the civil and ecclesiastical authority of the Portuguese and dissented. The leader of the schism was Thomas Parampil, who, since he could find no bishop willing to consecrate him, devised a kind of investiture by means of the laying on of hands of twelve priests. The efforts of the Carmelites and of the bishop Alexander Parampil, cousin of Thomas, succeeded in bringing back to the Catholic Church eighty-four churches which retained the name Chaldaean and called themselves Malabars. Thirty-two churches, however, remained in a state of schism and adopted the Syro-Antiochene rite.

Thomas Parampil was too well-informed not to realize that his pretended consecration as bishop was invalid. He made several approaches to the Nestorians of Mesopotamia for recognition, but his attempts failed. He then turned to the Jacobites of Mesopotamia and in 1665 Gregory, Jacobite metropolitan of Jerusalem, came to Malabar and consecrated him bishop under the name of Mār Tommas I. Gregory introduced a certain number of Jacobite heresies and eventually Thomas Parampil and his followers adopted the Antiochene rite. They were popularly referred to as "the new party" as opposed to the Catholic Malabars who were called the "old party".

Attempts at union. As early as 1868 the desire for union with the Catholic Church was evinced by the Jacobites and particularly by their metropolitan Mār Dionysius IV, who was known for his Catholic tendencies, his piety in relation to the Holy Sacrament and the Blessed Virgin. He delayed union for a little while, however, in the hope of being able to bring with him some of his suffragan bishops and a considerable element of the clergy, and he died without having taken the decisive step. The movement continued to gain strength, being directed towards the spiritual reform of the Jacobite Church.

In 1919 a Jacobite priest, Father Ghiverghis (George) Panikerveetil, who was already rector of the principal education centre for the clergy, founded in a place called Bethany a religious fraternity of the Imitation of Christ, followed shortly afterwards by a similar institution for women devoted primarily to education. He was ordained bishop in 1925, under the name Mār Ivanios (Giovanni) and with the title of Bethany. In 1928 he was promoted to Metropolitan, and one of his monks, Mār Teofilos, received in 1929 the title of Tiruvalla. At the synod of Jacobite bishops of the group attached to the catholicos in November 1926, Mār Ivanios insisted on the necessity of putting an end to the schism, since Christ had founded one single Church and the liturgical books in use among the Jacobites acknowledged the primacy of Peter. The synod allowed Mār Ivanios to undertake negotiations for union with Rome, on condition that the rite was preserved and that the bishops, who were five in number, retained their sees and their episcopal office. The Holy See agreed, with reservations, to confirm the validity of their baptisms, ordinations of priests and, for prelates, of their episcopal consecration.

When the affirmative reply came from Rome, only two of the five bishops resolved to take the decisive step: Mār Ivanios and Mār Teofilos. On 20 September 1930 they professed the Catholic faith, together with a priest, a deacon and a layman, and received the blessing of Mgr Benzinger, O.C.D., Latin bishop of Quilon.

Shortly afterwards other groups, including the two communities (male and female) of the Imitation of Christ, joined this small nucleus and an active uniate movement came into being. In 1937 a third bishop, Mār Severios, was converted to Catholicism and in 1939 a fourth, Mār Dioscore. The same rapid rate of increase was apparent in the number of lay conversions: in 1930 only five such came back to the Catholic Church: in 1932 5,150; in 1950 65,000; in 1955 85,000; in 1957 100,000 and in 1962 124,000.

6a. Chaldaeans

The designation "Chaldaean Church" is Western in origin and came into use only in the fifteenth century. Here discussion will be confined to Catholic Chaldaeans from the time of their first inclinations towards union. These in fact began at the time of the Crusades, which inspired a great missionary movement, chiefly undertaken by Franciscans and Dominicans. Thus, for example, Giovanni da Montecorvino took with him on his journey to China in 1289 a letter from Pope Nicholas IV for the Catholicos Yabalāhā III (1281–1317), who was of Mongol origin and well disposed towards the Catholic Church. When he arrived in China Giovanni made contact with the Nestorian community and achieved some measure of success.

In the Middle Ages only isolated cases are recorded of Nestorian bishops professing the Catholic faith. The Nestorians of Cyprus, on the other hand, in 1340, underwent a mass reconversion to Rome. At the Council of Florence in 1445 the union was re-established, but the whole of this community subsequently disappeared.

In modern times the first of the Eastern communities in separation to become united with Rome was the Chaldaean. The office of the Nestorian catholicos became hereditary in 1450, passing from uncle to nephew. In 1552 some of the flock opposed the appointment of Simeon VIII Dinha and elected as patriarch Giovanni Sulāqā, the Superior of the Rabbān Hormizd monastery near al-Qūsh. He came to Rome in 1552 and on 20 April 1553 was confirmed by the consistory as Chaldaean patriarch under the name of Simeon VIII. On his return to his own country he settled at Diyarbakîr, in Turkish territory, but was assassinated two years later. His successors resided at Siirt, Salmas and Urmia, but their links with Rome became increasingly weak. The Catholicos Simeon XIII (1661–1700) also reverted to Nestorianism and established his residence at Kuchanis, in the mountains of Kurdistan; it is from him that every Nestorian Catholicos in modern times is descended.

Some of the Chaldaean Catholics, however, remained faithful to Rome. At Diyarbakîr, thanks to the missionary activity of the Capuchins, a new group of Chaldaean Catholics was formed, and the metropolitan of this city, Joseph, became a Catholic in 1672. He obtained a special *ferman* from the Sultan conferring the title of patriarch, but the Holy See was reluctant to give him recognition: his sincerity did not appear to be beyond question and there was no desire to endanger the attempts at union begun with the Nestorian catholicos. Eventually, however, ratification was given on 23 June 1681, but without the grant of any see. Thus was founded a line of Chaldaean patriarchs, all of whom bore the name Joseph and lived at Diyarbakîr, down to Joseph IV who resigned in 1870 and finished his days in Rome after having entrusted the administration of his patriarchate to his nephew, Augustin Hindī, a pupil of the Propaganda and at that time merely a priest. He was consecrated bishop in 1804 and assumed, on his own authority, the title of Patriarch Joseph V. Rome refused him recognition and he died in 1827 as metropolitan of Diyarbakîr.

The Nestorian catholicos of Rabbān Hormizd, Elias XII Dinha (1722–78), after half a century in power, finally in 1771 signed a profession of Catholic faith. The great distance of Mesopotamia from Rome made communications difficult and negotiations were still in progress when Elias XII died. His nephew Elias XIII Ishō'yāb (1778–1804) had signed a profession of faith at the same time as his uncle, but after once becoming catholicos he showed by his conduct that his sincerity was not to be trusted. A second nephew of Elias XII, Giovanni Hormizd (Hormez) who had been ordained bishop at the age of sixteen by his uncle and put in charge of the metropolitan see of Mosul, became a Catholic in 1778. Many of his flock, with the encouragement of the Dominicans of Mosul, followed him, but he was opposed by his own brother Elias XIII and by Augustin Hindī, who wished to be the sole patriarch.

The Holy See, still hoping ultimately to win over Elias XIII, refused to give Giovanni Hormizd any better treatment than Augustin Hindī and allowed him only the title of Metropolitan of Mosul. Although poorly educated and without any ecclesiastical training, Giovanni Hormizd was nevertheless a devout man. In 1812 and again in 1818 his enemies succeeded in bringing him under suspicion: in 1818 they obtained from the metropolitan jurisdiction the nomination of the priest Giorgio d'Alqoch (al-Qūsh) in his place; he was to be subordinate to Augustin Hindī who had become apostolic delegate. To the astonishment of his enemies, Giovanni Hormizd submitted. Conditions became more favourable to him and he was absolved from the censure which he had incurred in 1826. Eventually, on the death of Augustin Hindī, he received from Pius VIII on 5 July 1830 the ratification of his appointment as sole patriarch of all Chaldaean Catholics, with his see at Mosul.

In order to abolish the principle of a hereditary catholicos, the Holy See in 1838 appointed Nicolas Ḍiyā' (Zeya), bishop of Salmas, as co-adjutor, with the right of succession. The patriarchal family renounced its ancient privilege and from this period onwards the election was made in accordance with fixed rules.

The Dominicans of Mosul worked zealously for the return of the Patriarch Joseph 'Awdū (1847–78) and of his successor Elias XIV Abu'l-Yūnān (1878–94). The efforts of the Catholic missionaries were checkmated, however, by the activities of other missionaries, notably American and Anglican Protestants in 1834 and 1876 respectively and Russians in 1898.

Nevertheless under the patriarchate of Mār Emanuth II Thomas (1900–47) the majority of the Nestorians rejoined the Catholic Church. During the First World War Chaldaeans and Nestorians, like all the other Christians of the Ottoman Empire, suffered greatly. The patriarch Simon XIX, elected in 1903 at the age of sixteen, had to leave Kuchanis with his flock. He was treacherously assassinated in 1918 when he was fleeing from the country.

The Nestorian refugees in Iraq who had settled in the cities, especially Baghdad, had no difficulty in finding the way to Catholicism and nearly 70,000 were converted. The Chaldaean Catholics, who had been reduced to 50,000 after the First World War, now increased to 190,000, and in consequence the Patriarch Joseph VII Ghanīma (1947–58) transferred his residence from Mosul to Baghdad.

For the Chaldaeans in the South of Iraq, the archdiocese of Basra was founded in 1954; in 1957 the diocese of Aleppo was created for the Chaldaeans of Syria, and the diocese of Beirut for those of the Lebanon. Two new eparchies were instituted in 1960, one at Mosul and the other at al-Qūsh. Baghdad is a patriarchal diocese.

The Chaldaean rite. The Chaldaean rite, like their evangelism, originated in Edessa, but developed independently. The liturgical language is Eastern Syriac. In the cities the common language is Arabic, but in the mountains north of Mosul modern Syriac or *sūreth* is spoken.

6*b*. *The Syro-Malabar Catholics*

Although India is not a part of the Middle East, it is nevertheless necessary to include the Syro-Malabar Catholics of India, since in fact they belong to the Chaldaean Church. They are Indians inhabiting the South-Western coast of the Indian peninsular called Malabar, which, since 1 November 1956, is largely equivalent to the federal state of Kerala, but there are also Christian Malabars in other states. Ethnically they are of Dravidian–Aryan stock and speak Malayalam. They are also called "Christians of St Thomas".

Kerala is the region of India which contains most of the Christians. Out of 13,550,000 inhabitants, there are 3,300,000 Christians, or 24·3 per cent. Of the 5,360,000 Catholics of the whole of India, Kerala accounts for 2,200,000 or 42 per cent. Adherents of the three rites are as follows: Malabars, 1,350,000; Malankars, 112,000; Latins, 750,000.

The Portuguese on their arrival in Malabar found four bishops of the Chaldaean rite who had been sent from Mesopotamia. The principal episcopal see was Angamala. Relations between the Portuguese and the Malabars were at first quite friendly. St Francis Xavier relates that in 1549 he saw one of the four bishops, Mār Jacob, in retreat in the

Franciscan monastery of Cochin. Contact with Rome was spontaneous and seems at no time to have been interrupted.

When Julius III confirmed Giovanni Sulāqā as Chaldaean patriarch in 1553, he also recognized his jurisdiction over India. Accordingly Sulāqā's successor Mār Abdisho in 1556 sent a metropolitan there to represent him.

Meanwhile in 1534 Paul III had founded the diocese of Goa, promoted in 1558 to the status of archdiocese and metropolis for all Portuguese possessions, with the sees of Cochin and Malacca as suffragans. A dispute soon broke out between the Metropolitan Mār Giuseppe, sent by the Chaldaean Patriarch to Malabar, and the Portuguese, who by reason of the royal "padroado" did not acknowledge any independent jurisdiction in India. Giuseppe, however, wished to vindicate his rights with the Pope. He left for Lisbon and after being confirmed by Pius VII in 1564 he returned to India. During his absence the Chaldaean patriarch, fearing that he would not return, invited to Malabar another Catholic bishop named Mār Abraham, who died in 1597. With him perished the last of the legitimate Catholic bishops sent to India by the Chaldaean patriarch.

After the death of Mār Abraham, Alession Menezes, the archbishop of Goa, came to visit the Malabar community which then numbered about 70,000. He made the archdeacon and the other leaders promise on oath never again to accept any bishop who was not under mandate from Rome. He had already obtained, in 1599, the appointment of a Spanish Jesuit, Father Francesco Roz, to the Malabar episcopal see of Angamala. In the same year Archbishop Menezes convoked a synod at Diamper (Udayamperur) which suppressed many traditional Malabar customs and replaced them with Latin practices. The archdeacon, although retaining his administrative functions, gradually declined in importance and soon even this Malabar institution disappeared. On 22 December 1608 Paul V converted the Malabar diocese of Angemala into an archbishopric subject to the Portuguese "padroado" and transferred its see to Cranganur, changing even the name of the archdiocese. Meanwhile opposition was increasing among the Malabar clergy and people to the synod of Diamper and to the Latin hierarchy in general, an opposition which in 1653 flared into actual revolt; it resulted in the schism of the Indian Jacobites (cf. Malankars).

Pope Alexander VII, on being informed of these events, in 1656 sent the Carmelite Giuseppe Sebastiani with other colleagues to quell the revolt, and in 1659 he founded an apostolic vicariate for pastoral work among the Malankars under the authority of the Propaganda. When the Dutch conquered the Malabar coast in 1663 the Carmelites had to leave the country. Before leaving the apostolic vicar Sebastiani consecrated as bishop a Malabar priest, Alexander Parampil (cousin of Thomas Parampil, leader of the schismatic movement) who attempted successfully to reduce the extent of the schism. Three-quarters of the Malabars resumed their obedience to the legitimate bishop. On the death of Alexander Parampil, a Carmelite of the Latin rite was chosen as his successor; he had his residence at Verapoly and was in 1700 appointed apostolic vicar of the Malabars of St Thomas "for as long as the sees of Cranganur and Cochin have no bishops of their own".

When Cranganur had its own Ordinary, a section of the Malabars did not wish to submit to him. The Propaganda accordingly decided to retain the apostolic vicariate with jurisdiction over those places where the Ordinaries of Cranganur and Cochin were not able fully to exercise their jurisdiction. There was thus in Malabar a twofold Latin hierarchy, that of the "padroado" and that of the Propaganda. According to the famous missionary Paolini de S. Bartolomeo, O.C.D., there were at the end of the eighteenth century twenty Malabar parishes under Cranganur and sixty-four under the apostolic vicariate of Verapoly. The Jacobites had thirty-two.

The Malabars did not lose hope of having a bishop of their own race and their own rite. In 1778 they sent two of their priests, Joseph Kariatil and Thomas Paremmakala, to Rome. Kariatil was appointed archbishop of Cranganur, but died in Goa on the return journey in 1786. His companion Thomas Paremmakala succeeded him as administrator without being ordained bishop. All the Malabars wanted to come under his authority, with the result that the apostolic vicariate held by the Carmelites was at this time without Malabar subjects, or, as they were then called, *Soriani*. After his death in 1799 and that of his successor George Ṣunqurī (Sankuri), who was also a pupil of the College of the Propaganda, in 1801, the original state of affairs was restored. In 1838 Gregory XVI suppressed the archdiocese of Cranganur and the diocese of Cochin, and all the Malabars came under the administration of the apostolic vicariate of Verapoly which was held by the Carmelites.

About the middle of the nineteenth century several priests under the leadership of Antoine Thondanatta, who had appealed to Rome without success, entreated Giuseppe VI 'Awdū (1848–78), patriarch of the

Chaldaean Catholics, to take charge of them and to send them bishops of the Chaldaean rite. The patriarch, relying on historic precedents, acceded to their request and in 1860, against the instructions of the Holy See, sent them the Chaldaean bishop Mār Tommaso Rokos. The Holy See directed him to return to Mesopotamia, but the Catholic Malabars and the Patriarch 'Awdū would not give way. In 1874 the Patriarch sent the Chaldaean bishop Mār Elia Mallūs (Mellus), who also received orders from the Holy See to leave India. He refused and became the centre of a community excommunicated by Rome which today numbers about five thousand. They use the liturgy and the discipline of the Nestorians and are called "Mellusians", in spite of the fact that Mellus ultimately submitted to Rome and died a Catholic in 1908.

In 1886 Leo XIII instituted the ordinary hierarchy for the Latins of India by raising Verapoly to the dignity of an archdiocese, which brought to an end the see of Cranganur. In the following year the two apostolic vicariates of Trichur and Kottayam were established for the Catholic Malabars, but the proposed bishops were once more European Latins.

Not until 1896 were three Malabar bishops of the Chaldaean rite appointed; in 1911 there was a further bishop for the Catholics of the South. The ecclesiastical province of Malabar was founded by Pius XI in 1923; he raised Ernakulam to the position of a metropolitan see by giving to it Trichur, Kottayam and Changanacherry as suffragan eparchates.

The jurisdiction of these bishops remained, however, restricted to the territory bounded by the rivers Pamba in the south and Ponam in the north. In the course of the last few decades numerous groups of Malabar Catholics have left Malabar, with the result that in 1955 the Malabar jurisdiction was extended to cover the territory included in the Latin dioceses of Coimbator, Ostacamund, Mysore and Mangalou in the north and as far south as Cape Comorin.

In 1956 the ecclesiastical province was divided into two: Ernakulam (with Trichur, Tellicherry and Khotamangalam as suffragans), and Changanacherry which was raised to the status of metropolis (with the sees of Kottayam and Palais as suffragans). The Malabar Church is progressing steadily. Its members, which in 1877 numbered 170,000, now total 1,349,000. The ranks of priests and monks are extraordinarily flourishing. At the local seminary of Alwaye in 1959–60 there were 686 students taking courses in philosophy and theology.

The Malabar rite is essentially Chaldaean, but contains many Latin elements which were introduced in the sixteenth century. The Malabar liturgy is in course of being restored.

7. *Latin Catholics in the Near East*

In addition to the Catholic communities of the various Eastern rites, there also exist in the Middle East Catholics of the Latin rite of different origins, arising from four distinct sources:

(*a*) They may be descendants from the Crusaders. It is known that in the Middle Ages there were several Latin patriarchs in the East, who disappeared with the end of the Crusades. Only the Latin patriarchate in Jerusalem was re-established in 1847, with a congregation of more than 60,000 and sixty-five secular priests, the great majority of them being natives of the country.

(*b*) They may be descended from the early Italian navigators: Venetians, Genoese, Pisans, Amalfians and others who settled in the countries of the Levant. The Catholics of the Aegean Islands belong to this category and in general those of Greece and of Constantinople.

(*c*) Some of them are natives of the Eastern countries who were converted by Latin missionaries in recent times, especially in the nineteenth century; for example, the Latin Catholics of Eritrea, Ethiopia and the Holy Land.

(*d*) Finally there are Latin Catholics of the West who for various reasons such as trade, industry or administrative functions have settled temporarily or permanently in Middle Eastern countries; among these are the Latins in Egypt, Iraq and Iran.

These Latin Catholics are subject to the Latin bishops occupying vicariates which have been founded for the purpose. By reason of the *Motu proprio Sancta Dei Ecclesia* of 25 March 1938 it is the Sacred Congregation for the Oriental Church which has exclusive jurisdiction over the following countries: Southern Albania, Greece, Bulgaria, Cyprus, Turkey, Syria, Lebanon, Palestine, Jordan, Iraq, Iran, Egypt, Eritrea, Ethiopia, Northern Afghanistan.

CATHOLICS IN CIVIL LIFE

By definition, the Catholic is a Christian who professes union with Rome and who therefore intends to remain in close touch with the teaching and instructions of the Roman See. In return, the Roman

Church considers that its first duty is to concern itself with the maintenance of a living faith among the Catholics of the whole world, with their instruction, enlightenment, protection in times of persecution and help in need. If this relationship between the ecclesiastical head and the limbs is valid on the vast scale of the Universal Church, how much more should it apply to the ties of the Roman See with the Catholic communities of the Middle East. *Ex Oriente Lux*. The Saviour was born in the East; he lived there for many years and founded the Church there; it was at Antioch that the Christians originally received their name; it was in Egypt that monasticism began; it was from Mesopotamia that missionaries departed to evangelize India and the Far East.

It is understandable that thenceforward the Churches of the East occupied a special place in the interest of the Holy See and were the object of its affection and concern. "We desire" said Pope Benedict XV, when founding a new dicaster entrusted with the affairs of the Catholics of the Eastern rite, "that the benevolence of the Apostolic See towards the Orientals may be so evident that it will be impossible to doubt it." And to the Christians of the Middle East he expressed the wish that he might see them "restored to possession of their former prosperity and pristine glory".

For this reason Rome was always assiduous, throughout the centuries, in sending missionaries to uphold the Eastern Catholics and to work for the restoration of unity among all Christians. From the day in 1181 when the Maronites obtained a special statute from Pope Innocent III, the Church of Rome tried unceasingly to maintain relations with the Christendoms of the East, in spite of the difficulties which arose from the occupation of all these countries by Muslim princes and in former times by Mongols.

So long as the affairs of the Universal Church were dealt with by the consistory, no special body was required to supervise relations with the East. Before long, however, the need was felt for some specialization. In 1622 Gregory XV decided to create the Sacred Congregation *de Propaganda Fide*, designed to promote the conversion of pagans and to work for the reunion of all those Christians, whether in the East or in the West, whose forbears had broken with Rome. The Catholics of the Eastern rites came under the jurisdiction of this new Congregation. In 1862 Pius IX subdivided its functions, so that one section was concerned with Latin missions, the other with "affairs of the Eastern peoples", *pro negotiis Orientalium*.

The dismemberment of the Ottoman Empire, however, together with the altered situation of the Eastern Catholics and the unexpected change in the relations between the civil and religious authorities, induced the Church to adapt itself to the new state of affairs. On 1 December 1917 the Sacred Congregation for the Eastern Church created by Benedict XV came into operation. For all Catholics of the Eastern rite, in any part of the globe, it replaced all other Congregations of the Roman Curia, apart from those of the Holy Office and of the Sacred Penitentiary. Mixed cases also came within its jurisdiction. In 1938 Pius XI extended the responsibilities of this Congregation by entrusting to it the Latin Catholics of the Middle East.

The foundation of a central body of this kind for intensifying and co-ordinating religious work among the Eastern Catholic communities is a necessary condition for the true Christian life, which cannot come to birth, develop and radiate good works unless a trained and energetic clergy are putting their hearts into their apostolic task. Certainly, in the East, bishops had always been aware of the urgent need for training the clergy. Their delicate and precarious position in Muslim countries, however, and the even more serious difficulty of finding qualified teachers, had not lightened their labours. Moreover Rome, which insisted on preserving the traditions of the Eastern communities and in making allowance for their material circumstances, had for a long time taken the initiative in founding seminaries in Rome for them, such as the Greek College, founded in 1576, and the Armenian and Maronite Colleges, instituted by Gregory XIII in 1584. When the Congregation *de Propaganda Fide* was founded in 1622, Urban VIII annexed to it a college with an athenaeum for seminarists. Orientals are still accepted there.

During the nineteenth century the Holy See undertook the foundation of good local seminaries by providing funds and personnel recruited from among qualified Latin monks, such as Dominicans at Mosul, Capuchins in Istanbul, Jesuits in the Lebanon, White Fathers in Jerusalem, Lazarists in Ethiopia.

A detailed study of all these institutions would exceed the bounds of the present work, and only the most important ones can be considered, namely the Pontifical Institute in Rome, and the four principal seminaries of the Middle East—the St Joseph University of the Jesuit Fathers at Beirut, the Syro-Chaldaean Seminary of the Dominican

Fathers in Mosul, the Greco-Catholic Seminary of St Anne in Jerusalem under the direction of the White Fathers, and finally the Coptic Catholic Seminary of Ma'ādī in Egypt.

Pontifical Institute for Oriental Studies

The Oriental Congregation is essentially an administrative organization in the widest sense of the term. There was need of a scientific institution which could train priests who were intended for the East or the Eastern priests themselves, and which could also, by means of a first-class specialized library, provide the Congregation with the documentation which might at any time be needed.

The Pontifical Institute for Oriental Studies was created by Benedict XV for this purpose. The programme assigned to the Institute was designed to enable it to fulfil the functions which have just been outlined. Thus it included courses on the comparative theology of the Orthodox Churches, courses in patristics, in Oriental canon law, in liturgy for all the Oriental rites, in Oriental civil and religious history, in ethnographical geography, in Oriental sacred archaeology, in the constitutional law of the Eastern peoples, in Oriental literary history and finally in Oriental languages.

In the beginning courses were intended to last for two years. The Institute accepted not only Latin priests and Eastern Catholics, but also individual monks who wished to acquire an exact knowledge of Catholic doctrine. It also gave specialized training to the ecclesiastical personnel of the Holy See who had to deal with the problems of the Eastern Churches.

The first courses began on 2 December 1918 under the direction of Father Delpuch, a White Father who had a thorough knowledge of conditions among Oriental Christians and on whose original idea the Institute had been based. In the following year he was replaced by Father Schuster, O.S.B., who was subsequently to become the Archbishop of Milan and a Cardinal. By 1921–2 the number of students had risen to twenty-five. The teaching staff was composed of experts, such as Father Martin Jugie, A.A., Father Bonaventure Ubach, O.S.B., Fathers Theophile Spacil, S.J., de Jerphanion, S.J., and M. Gordillo, S.J. To achieve greater homogeneousness and easier recruitment of teachers, the Institute was in 1922 placed under the administration of the Society of Jesus, and Mgr d'Herbighy, who died in 1958, became the first director. He was succeeded in 1931 by Father Emilio Hermann, professor of Oriental Canon Law. From 1951 to 1957 the director was Father Ortiz de Urbina and he was succeeded by Father Alphonse Raes, who in 1962 became Prefect of the Vatican. The present director of the Institute is Father Gill, an historian of the Council of Florence.

The quality of its teachers made it possible for the Institute to inaugurate, in 1923, a collection of scientific works, *Orientalia christiana*. In 1934, after one hundred fascicules forming thirty-six volumes had been published, the collection was divided into two series: *Orientalia Christiana Periodica*, a weekly journal, and *Orientalia Christiana Analecta*, for scientific monographs. Between 1935 and 1960 fifty-three volumes appeared. The Institute also undertook the publication of the sources relating to the Council of Florence and the Syriac Anaphoras. In 1926 it was given accommodation near St Mary Major in the complex of buildings surrounding the Church of St Anthony Abbot, and it now possesses the finest library in the world for the study of the Eastern Churches, including, most notably, complete sets of journals which were put up for sale in Russia after the Revolution. A mission dispatched in 1923–4 by Pius XI and composed of Mgr Tisserant (who was later a Cardinal and was for a long time Prefect of the Oriental Congregation) and Father Cyril Korolevskij (= Charron) enriched the library considerably. In order to bring the Institute to the notice of the Catholic world and to encourage bishops to send students to it, Pius XI published in 1928 the encyclical *Rerum Orientalium*. In 1931, by application of the apostolic constitution *Deus Scientiarum Dominus*, the Institute was re-attached to the Sacred Congregation of Seminaries and Universities. The duration of the course was extended to three years, the first year being devoted to general culture and the two others to specialization in one of three branches: theology, history or liturgy and canon law. Courses were subsequently introduced on Islamic institutions in 1924, on Marxist ideology in 1936 and finally on Oriental sacred music in 1952.

The University of St Joseph at Beirut

This University is one of the most splendid Catholic achievements in the Middle East, both by reason of its rate of growth since its foundation and the number of its Faculties. As early as 1923 Maurice Barrès, in his *Enquête au Pays du Levant* (*Enquiry into the Land of the Levant*) called it the "lighthouse of the eastern Mediterranean". It arose from quite humble beginnings and was originally concerned with providing members of the various Eastern rites with a good secondary and ecclesiastical education. In 1843 several Fathers settled, rather hesitantly, at Ghazīr, the chief town of Kisrawān, where the entire population is Maronite.

From 1860 onwards Beirut began to experience an influx of populations: Christian refugees escaping from massacre, traders attracted by the opportunities of steam navigation and the opening of the route to Damascus. The Protestant mission settled there on a grand scale. In 1875 a seminary and college were founded and collectively given the name of the University of St Joseph. In 1883 Leo XIII granted it the power to confer the degrees of doctor of philosophy and of theology. On the eve of the First World War the Oriental Seminary of St Francis Xavier, a school of the University, had awarded thirty-seven doctorates in theology, thirty-one in philosophy. Among its graduates were twenty-four bishops and 216 priests of various rites.

Courses were resumed in 1918 after the war, but the foundation of seminaries restricted to a single rite, such as that of St Anne, in Jerusalem, for the Melkites, in Sharfa (Lebanon) for the Syrians, in Rome, for the Armenians, caused the proportion of Maronites in Beirut to increase steadily. The numbers of students in scholastic philosophy and in theology rose from twenty-eight in 1930 to sixty-seven (of which fifty-six were Maronites) in 1959.

In addition to religious instruction, the St Joseph University provides:

(1) A Faculty of Medicine and Pharmacy instituted in 1883 and frequented by students from all parts of the Middle East. Up to the present day it has conferred 1755 doctorates in medicine, 360 diplomas in pharmacy, 436 diplomas in dentistry (school founded in 1920), 411 diplomas in midwifery (school founded in 1922), 215 diplomas in hospital nursing (school founded in 1942) and some thirty other specialized diplomas.

(2) A Faculty of Law.

(3) An Institute of Political Science.

(4) A School of Engineering.

In 1902 an Oriental Faculty was founded for the purpose of teaching, by means of a three-year course, classical Semitic languages (Arabic, Hebrew and Syriac), Coptic and Ethiopian, local history and geography and finally archaeology and Oriental epigraphy. In 1906 publication was begun of the series *Mélanges de la Faculté Orientale de Beyrouth*

(*MFOB*) (*Miscellanies of the Oriental Faculty of Beirut*). The Faculty was converted in 1937 into an Oriental Literary Institute, under the patronage of the University of Lyons and it confers a certain number of certificates for the degree of literature of the French State.

The Syro-Chaldaean Seminary at Mosul

Originally small numbers of Syrians and Chaldaeans were sent to Rome to receive their education at the Urban College *de Propaganda Fide*, at a time when it was scarcely possible to open seminaries in Mesopotamia or Persia. In 1846, however, the Lazarists instituted a seminary at Khosrova in Persia; in Mesopotamia it was the Catholicos Nicolas Ḍiyā' (Zeya) (1839–47) who first decided to start a seminary and even then there was some question of whether it should be entrusted to the Dominicans. At the council which met in 1853 at the monastery of Rabbān Hormizd, near Mosul, under the presidency of the apostolic delegate Benoît Planchet, the Chaldaean bishops returned to the charge and won a decision in their own favour. The apostolic delegate was charged with the supervision of the seminary and the Dominican Fathers with its actual administration; they co-opted a certain number of Chaldaean priests to give instruction in special subjects and to celebrate the liturgy. Mgr Planchet at once set to work to put in order the ancient monastery of Mār Jawārjīs (Gewarghis), at a distance of an hour and a half from Mosul, but the prevailing lack of security made it necessary to move the seminary elsewhere. Mār Ya'qūb, in the mountains, was at one time considered, but in the end it was thought more convenient to establish the seminary in Mosul, where the existing day-school directed by the Dominicans would make it possible to economize in staff. Accordingly, towards the end of 1877, the seminary opened its doors, and it was decided to extend admission to Syrians, who were distributed in considerable numbers throughout Mesopotamia. Its canonical structure was defined by a decree of the Sacred Congregation of the Propaganda for Oriental Affairs on 7 September 1882. Syrians and Chaldaeans were allowed to follow the same courses apart from canticles and liturgy. During alternate weeks the liturgy was celebrated according to the Chaldaean and the Syrian rites respectively. In 1914 the Seminary was obliged to close its doors because of the War, but it reopened them in 1923. Thirteen former pupils, one of them a bishop, were massacred during the persecution of the Christians from 1915 to 1918.

The Chaldaean Patriarchal Seminary

This Seminary, which celebrated its centenary in 1965, developed naturally from a school for the instruction and training of Chaldaean deacons (sing. *shammās*), established near the Cathedral in Mosul.

Only Chaldaeans are trained in this Seminary, which is under the immediate jurisdiction of the patriarch and is administered by the Chaldaean clergy. Although originally founded in Mosul, it was in recent years transferred to Baghdad and its administration has now been entrusted to the American Jesuit Fathers of Baghdad. In addition to a large number of priests, several bishops and patriarchs are among its former pupils.

Greek-Catholic Seminary of St Anne

The education of the few Greek Catholic priests in the eighteenth century was conducted by means of instruction from older priests under the direction of the bishop, chiefly at Aleppo. At the beginning of the nineteenth century the bishop of Zaḥla, Mgr Ignace 'Azūrī, a man of Aleppine origin, started an ecclesiastical school in his own house, which was very successful. The results encouraged the Patriarch Agapius Matar to open a seminary in 1811 at 'Ayn Ṭirāz, in the Lebanon, but it had only a brief existence. It was reopened in 1831 and survived for about ten years, but it was destroyed in the upheaval of the civil wars. After being reopened once more in 1866 by the Patriarch Gregory II Yūsuf, it admitted pupils until 1898, when the Patriarch Peter IV Gregory sent all the seminarists to the Greek College in Rome. Such was the shortage of teachers for purposes of instruction and administration that the patriarch appealed to the White Fathers of Cardinal Lavigerie, who had settled in Jerusalem in 1878 and opened an Oriental Seminary there.

After the Crimean War the Sultan 'Abdülmejid, in recognition of French support, presented France with the Church of St Anne which had been restored by the first Crusades and was built on the site where, according to reputable tradition, the house of the mother of the Virgin had been located. The White Fathers were summoned to preserve this sanctuary and to celebrate their services there. The desire of the Patriarch Gregory was fully in accord with the ideas of Cardinal Lavigerie: the seminary was opened on 6 June 1882, and the first ordinations were conferred in September 1890. Although disrupted by the First World War, it was able to reopen its doors at the close of hostilities.

The full course of the seminary comprises two years of philosophy and four years of theology and is designed for clergy of all the Melkite eparchies, forty of whom can be admitted at a time. The seminary is under the direct authority of the Oriental Congregation and its administration and instruction are in the hands of the Missionaries of Africa (White Fathers). The first of the White Fathers to conduct the Byzantine rite was Father Abel Couturier, who died in 1931; he devoted himself for many years to the teaching of the Byzantine canticles and liturgy.

Since 1951 the directors of the seminary have published a very interesting journal entitled *Proche-Orient Chrétien* (*The Christian Near East*) which, side by side with general articles dealing with the Orient, regularly includes detailed accounts of the activities of all the Christian communities of the Middle East.

The Coptic Seminary of Maʿādī

In 1879 the Jesuits opened a small seminary for Copts in their College of the Holy Family in Cairo. The seminarists went on from there to Ghazir in the Lebanon and afterwards to Beirut for philosophical and theological studies. By this means it was possible to secure the regular training of a fair number of Coptic priests. In 1907, however, the seminary in Cairo was closed; one of the Fathers who had been consecrated there, Father Jules Blin, performed a great service for the best choristers of the Coptic churches in Cairo by writing down the liturgical melodies of the Alexandrian rite, which had hitherto been transmitted by ear alone.

Cardinal Langenieux, Archbishop of Rheims and papal legate for the Eucharistic Congress of Jerusalem, was concerned on returning from Palestine through Cairo in 1893 at the condition of the Coptic Catholic Church, which at that time had only a simple Latin Apostolic Visitor. He made known the grievances of the Copts to Pope Leo XIII and the latter, after restoring the hierarchy in 1895, founded a seminary at Ṭanṭā representing the whole of the restored Coptic patriarchate. The great institution was inaugurated on 25 November 1899, but unfortunately, for various reasons and in particular because of the difficulty of finding teaching staff, the seminary was not able to fulfil the hopes which it had aroused. For several years the only possibility was to continue to send some seminarists to the Oriental Seminary of St Francis Xavier at Beirut; subsequently, however, the Coptic bishops Mgr Ignace Barazī and Mgr Maxime Ṣidlāwī evolved a project which in 1917 was approved by Benedict XV: the reorganized seminary of Ṭanṭā was to be used for seminarists who, in view of the extreme need for priests, could follow reduced courses in philosophy and theology. The best of them would be sent to Beirut to the Jesuit Fathers and others to Rome. In Cairo the small seminary which had formerly been administered by the Jesuit Fathers would be reopened. This plan was put into effect in 1927.

The small seminary had been established in a building belonging to the College of the Holy Family in Cairo. The seminarists attended classes at the College, but the internal administration of the seminary was entrusted to a Coptic lay clerk. In 1947 the small seminary was transferred to Ṭanṭā, in the Delta, where the seminarists were able to attend the school of the Fathers of the African Missions (St Louis College). The preseminary remained, and still remains, at Ṭanṭā.

The Sacred Congregation for the Oriental Church, in its concern to give the Catholic community in Egypt a training establishment for clergy adequate to meet the demands of the modern world, authorized the construction of a very large seminary at Ma'ādī, a residential district near Cairo, which was opened on 2 November 1953 by Cardinal Tisserant. In the same building, but in different wings, were the large seminary (two years of philosophy and four years of theology) and the small seminary (four years). The lower classes and those of the middle school were held in the pre-seminary at Ṭanṭā.

The seminary was administered by the Lazarist Fathers until the end of 1955; it then came under the direction of the Coptic secular clergy under Mgr Stephanos who, on being promoted patriarch in 1958, passed on the administration to the Fathers of the Society of Jesus. The seminary is open to candidates of all rites, but hitherto the majority of the seminarists have been Copts and the rite used by the seminary as a whole is the Coptic rite.

Oriental religious congregations

In addition to these seminaries in which most of the teachers belong to the great Western orders, there exist in the Middle East congregations or convents composed solely of Oriental monks. Each rite has such congregations, some of which go back almost to the first centuries of the Church. Their apostolic activities, whether actually in Oriental countries or among emigrants, colonies of Eastern Christians who have remained faithful to their religious traditions, show the vitality of the religious feeling preserved in these communities.

The following is a systematic review of the principal congregations:

(i) *Maronites*

Monastic life has always been revered among the Maronites, and it has had considerable influence in sustaining the Christian faith in the Lebanon. Until 1757 there were only two brotherhoods, that of St Elisha or of St Anthony, and that of St Isaiah, but in 1757 this latter brotherhood split into two—the Aleppo Antonines and the Lebanese Antonines who at one time took the name of Antonine Baladites. The following are some statistics relating to their numbers and their work.

Lebanese Antonines:

Religious houses	53	
Votaries	465	
Parishes	110	with 53 monks
Missionary centres	8	with 17 monks
Schools	17	with a total of 2,151 pupils
Other activities:	1	printing-press
	4	periodicals
	3	hospitals with 50 beds each

Aleppo Antonines:

Religious houses	10	
Votaries	80	
Parishes	26	with 32 monks
Missionary centres	6	with 6 priests (Ghana 2; Egypt 4)
Schools	2	(Egypt 1, with 400 pupils; Lebanon 1, with 80 pupils)

Antonines of St Isaiah:

Religious houses	19	
Votaries	79	
Parishes	9	
Schools	7	with a total of 1,500 pupils
Colleges	1	

Mention must also be made of the Congregation of the Lebanese Missionaries of the Kuraym, founded in 1866 by Bishop John Ḥabīb on the model of the Redemptionist Fathers; its monks devote themselves to preaching in popular missions, to spiritual exercises and to teaching. Their apostolate extends to the Argentine (1902), the United States (1920), South Africa (1929) and to Brazil, and they are principally concerned with Maronite emigrants.

Religious houses	7	
Votaries	49	
Parishes	3	
Missionary centres	4	
Schools	3	with a total of 2,500 pupils

They have a Maronite ecclesiastical convent at Salamanca and a patriarchal seminary at Kafr Ḥayy (Lebanon) for older candidates; they have two printing-presses at Jūnīh in the Lebanon.

(ii) *Melkites*

In addition to the seminary of St Anne administered by the White Fathers, which has already been mentioned, the Catholic Melkites have four religious brotherhoods, three of which bear the name of St Basil:

1. *The Basilians of al-Shuwayr.* This congregation was founded in 1697 at Aleppo, but their parent foundation is the convent of St John the Baptist of al-Shuwayr (Khinshāra) in the diocese of Beirut.

Religious houses	4	
Votaries	100	
Parishes	39	(Lebanon 25, Jordan 2, U.S.A. 6, Australia 3, Argentine 2, Brazil 1) with 39 monks
Missionary centres	4	(Lebanon, Jordan, Argentina, Australia) with 10 monks

2. *The Basilians of Aleppo.* This congregation effected a final separation from the Basilians of al-Shuwayr in 1829 and they exercise their apostolate outside Aleppo. Their central see is at the Convent of the Holy Saviour, Ṣarbā, Jūnīh.

Religious houses	9	
Votaries	74	
Parishes	9	with 9 monks
Missionary centre	1	
Schools	2	with a total of 440 pupils

3. *The Salvatorian Basilians.* Euthymus Ṣayfī, Metropolitan of Tyre and Sidon, founded this congregation at the beginning of the eighteenth century. Their parent foundation was the great Convent of the Holy

Saviour at Sidon, which was destroyed by the Druses in 1860 and rebuilt. The Salvatorians have their own large and small seminaries there.

Religious houses	18	
Votaries	126	
Parishes	64	(Lebanon 43, Jordan 4, Israel 1, Syria 5, U.S.A. 7, Canada 2, Mexico 1, Brazil 1) with 51 monks
Schools	4	with a total of 900 pupils

Large seminary at Methuen, U.S.A. for the training of Melkite clergy
Small seminaries in Jordan and the Lebanon
Patriarchal college in Alexandria

4. *Pauline Missionaries*. They were founded in 1903 by Mgr Germanos Mu'aqqad at Ḥarīṣā, Lebanon, for popular missions, and spiritual training of clergy and apostolate by means of a printing-press and books. They have modelled themselves on the White Fathers and do not constitute a congregation in the true sense of the term, but a society with an oath of obedience to the Superior.

Religious houses	3	(Ḥarīsā, Beirut, Jerusalem)
Votaries	45	
Parishes	4	(U.S.A., Venezuela, Argentine) with 4 monks
Missionary centres	3	(in Syria) with 10 monks
Primary schools	10	with a total of 635 pupils
Technical school	1	(Jūnīh)
Colleges	2	(Syria) with a total of 1,200 pupils

An important printing press at Ḥarīṣā
A journal *al-Masarra* published from 1910 onwards

(iii) *Congregations of other rites*.

In the *Coptic Catholic* rite there is only one quite small congregation of the Preaching of St Mark, which was founded in 1959 by Mgr Ghattas and is still at an early stage. The first nucleus received its training from the Dominican Fathers in Cairo.

Monastic life in the *Chaldaean* rite is represented by the Antonine congregation of Rabbān Hormizd or Saint Hormisdas, which was founded in 1908 and so far consists of only fifty-one votaries and three convents, Rabbān Hormizd and the Immaculate Conception north of Mosul, near al-Qūsh, and Mār Jawārjīs in the neighbourhood of Mosul. They have fifteen parishes, seventeen missionary centres, sixteen schools and one orphanage and all their activities are conducted in Iraq. Reference will be made later to the Priests of Christ the King.

The *Syro-Malabars*, on the other hand, have had an astonishing burgeoning of candidates for the religious vocation, thus demonstrating the vitality of Christianity in the midst of populations largely composed of Hindus. There are six male congregations recruited solely among the natives: the *Tertiaries of the Carmelite Order*, which number 814 votaries, 352 of them priests, and manifest intense apostolic activity, with twenty-four parishes, sixteen missionary centres, nineteen schools with a total of 10,000 pupils, two hospitals, six orphanages, two reviews and one newspaper; the *Congregation of St Theresa of the Infant Jesus*, with fifty votaries; the missionary *Congregation of the Holy Sacrament* with twenty-seven votaries; the missionary *Union of Malabar* with thirty-one votaries, the *Congregational of St Vincent* with 102 votaries; the *Oblates of the Sacred Heart* with thirty votaries.

Finally, in the Armenian Catholic rite, the Dominican *Congregation of the Uniting Brethren*, which displayed great industry in the Middle Ages, has completely disappeared. The congregation of the *Antonines*, which was founded in the Lebanon at the beginning of the eighteenth century and flourished until 1871, has likewise been extinguished by the troubles of that time. The only religious congregation which remains is that of the *Mekhitarian* monks, founded in 1701 by the Abbot Mekhitar, which in 1717 proceeded to establish itself on the Isle of San Lazzaro in Venice. In principle they follow the rule of St Benedict. They have existed since 1773 in two completely independent branches. The Venice branch has fifty-four votaries and four monasteries and religious houses (Venice, Rome, Constantinople and Bikfaya). Their printing-press in Venice, which since 1956 has been able to produce typo-lithography, is world-famous. The Mekhitarists of Vienna have only thirty-one votaries, but administer three parishes (Budapest, Boston, Los Angeles), three colleges (Istanbul, Cairo, Beirut), a polyglot printing-press and a monthly journal in Armenian.

The *Syrian* rite is the one with the fewest monks. The congregation of the *Brethren of Saint Ephraim* was dispersed during the 1914 War. The Convent of Sharfa in the Lebanon houses the patriarchal seminary and a printing-press. Near Mosul there is the monastery of Mār Binhām, which is directly subject to the patriarch.

Mention must also be made of the *Priests of Christ the King*, a small society founded in 1963 in Mosul which is composed of both Chaldaean and Syrian priests. It intends to devote itself to extra-parochial apostolic work and already publishes an interesting little monthly review in Arabic, *al-Fikr al-masīḥī*, which has made a promising start.

Reference has already been made to the help given by the Latin missionaries to their brothers in the Orient. To convey some idea of what is meant by this important contribution, it is proposed to mention, very briefly, the names and activities of these Orders and Congregations. It should be noted also that, although these institutions belong to the West, many of them admit as members Eastern Catholics, whose work among their own compatriots is made easier by the fact that they are familiar with both the language and the living conditions of their country of origin.

In 1899 the French Benedictines settled at Cariathiarim, near Jerusalem, after the Patriarch Raḥmānī had entrusted them with the training of his clergy. A monastery of St Benedict and St Ephraim was founded on the Mount of Olives with an annex intended to be a Syrian seminary, in 1903. The large seminary was in 1930 transferred to Sharfa in the Lebanon and the small seminary was also moved there later. The Benedictines were in charge until 1953. In 1906 German Benedictines founded the Abbey of Our Lady of the Dormition (at present composed of seventeen priests, fourteen scholastics and four brothers) and in 1921 the seminary of the Latin Patriarchate was affiliated to it, though it was subsequently given up, in 1932, to the Fathers of the Sacred Heart of Betharram.

The Italian Cistercians of Casamari have two religious establishments in Ethiopia. The Trappists were the first to return to the Holy Land after the Crusades. In 1890 they founded the monastery of Laṭrūn, in Jordan, which is today an abbey with twenty-eight votaries.

The Dominicans in the Middle Ages sent travelling missionaries who came into contact with Eastern non-Catholic bishops. A number of Armenians were affiliated with this Order and founded the "Uniting Brethren", who displayed great apostolic activity and translated a large number of liturgical and theological works into Armenian. The Constantinople mission dates from 1228, but at the present day there remain in Turkey only the two convents of Istanbul and Smyrna. In Jerusalem the Convent of St Stephen for Biblical Studies was built on the direct instructions of Leo XIII and, under the administration of Father Lagrange, occupied a position of exceptional importance in the sphere of exegesis. In 1920 it received the name of the French Biblical and Archaeological School (École Biblique). The school gives specialized teaching in biblical studies and undertakes excavations, notably at Qumrān, where the famous Dead Sea scrolls were discovered. It has, since 1892, published the *Revue Biblique* and also a series of biblical studies.

In Iraq the Italian Dominicans founded a mission in 1750 at Mosul, followed in 1847 by another establishment at Mār Ya'qūb, in the mountainous region inhabited by the Nestorians. After being obliged to discontinue its activities owing to lack of recruits, it was taken over in 1856 by French Dominicans who founded the Syro-Chaldaean seminary at Mosul (see above). In Cairo an Institute of Oriental Studies (especially Arab–Islamic) was founded in 1928, and since 1954 it has published a specialized review *MIDEO* (*Mélanges de l'Institut Dominicain d'Etudes Orientales—Miscellany of the Dominican Institute of Oriental Studies*). In Jerusalem the House of St Isaiah was founded in 1960.

Since the advent of St Francis in Egypt, Syria and the Holy Land, the missions of the Franciscans in the Orient constitute one of the fairest flowers of his Order. The Custody of the Holy Land was, moreover, the first of the Franciscan missions and dates from the thirteenth century, embracing Palestine, Egypt, the Lebanon, Syria, Cyprus and Asia Minor. Its principal function is the custody of the Holy Places and the preservation of their international character. The brethren also work together in pastoral duties, in teaching, in the administration of several hospitals and the organization of pilgrimages to the Holy Land. They have eight houses by the name of "Casa Nova" for the reception of pilgrims of all nationalities.

A special mission was established in Egypt for the Copts of Upper Egypt and in 1666 a convent was founded at Akhmīm by Italian Franciscans. While the brethren of the Custody looked to France for protection, the Coptic missions put themselves under the care of Venice, and when Venice passed in 1797 to Austria the Hapsburgs inherited, until their empire came to an end, the protectorate over the Catholic Copts. In 1893 the Propaganda separated the apostolic vicariate of the Copts from the prefecture of Upper Egypt, the vicariate administering all the establishments whose members belonged exclusively to the Coptic rite. The Franciscan prefecture was declared *Missio copta sui juris* and, on 17 September 1958, was raised to a Provincial Commissariat, subject to the Franciscan Province of Florence. It already numbered many Egyptian monks of the Coptic rite. In 1937 the Oriental Seminary of St Cyril was founded, which in 1939 was moved to Giza, near Cairo. It provides courses in philosophy and theology. The following statistics demonstrate the activities of the Franciscan Fathers in the Middle East:

Religious houses	106	
Votaries	447	
Parishes	64	with 117 monks
Missionary centres	19	with 6 monks
Primary schools	80	
Colleges	12	with a total of 18,600 pupils
Dispensaries	25	
Orphanages	10	

The Minor Conventual Brethren have one convent at Constantinople and another at Damascus. The Capuchins have several establishments in Turkey (twenty-three votaries, ten parishes, an inter-ritual seminary at Constantinople); in the Lebanon two religious houses, twenty-three votaries, four parishes, two missionary centres, one college, one school, one Seraphic seminary, one orphanage), and in Syria two missionary centres and one school of 500 pupils.

The Carmelite order is Oriental in origin since it was founded in Palestine in the twelfth century. The foundation disappeared, however, with that of the Latin kingdom of Jerusalem. In 1605 the Carmelites reached Persia; in 1609 they opened a mission in Iṣfahān and in 1623 at Baṣra. They returned to Aleppo in 1626 and from there flocked into the Lebanon, settling at Bsharrī in 1643 and Tripoli in 1645. Their establishment in Baghdad was not earlier than 1731; that at Mardin was founded in 1747. At the beginning of the sixteenth century the Carmelites had reached India and founded the mission to the Malabars. Inspired by them two Indian Carmelite congregations were founded—one of the Syro-Malabar rite, the other of the Latin rite. At the present day the Carmelites have one religious house in Cairo, one in India, three in Iraq, three in Israel, four in the Lebanon, one in Turkey, with a total of ninety-one votaries.

Although more recent in date, the activities of the Jesuit Fathers have been intensive in the Middle East. Since its foundation the Society of Jesus has been particularly interested in the Orient, and the first coming of the Jesuits to Constantinople was in 1583. Like the Carmelites they settled in Aleppo (in 1625), which is the starting-point for caravans going to Persia and Central Asia. Thence they advanced towards Damascus, Sidon, Tripoli and ʻAyn Ṭūrā, and these five residences constituted the "Ancient Mission". In addition to the work of preaching, they translated into Arabic, chiefly with the aid of Maronite priests, classical works of Catholic theology and mysticism, such as the *Summa Theologica* of St Thomas, the *Praelectiones theologicae* of Tournély, and the *Storia ecclesiastica* of Cardinal Orsi (in twenty volumes). In 1696 a residence was established in Cairo where the celebrated Father Claude Sicard, an excellent observer of local sites and customs, worked assiduously for union. Mention has been made above of the origins of the seminary of Ghazīr and the St Joseph University. In 1932 the American Jesuits founded a large modern college in Baghdad where highly-placed Muslims sent their children; it became in 1956 al-Ḥikma University after the creation of several Faculties and a school of Arabic (number of votaries, seventy-six).

In 1939 a Vice-Province of the Near East was constituted which was at first subject to the Province of Lyons, but from 3 December 1957 became completely autonomous. It combined under a single Superior the former missions in Syria (1831), Egypt (1879) and Armenia (1881) and covered all the activities of the Society of Jesus in the following countries: Lebanon, Jordan, Egypt and Syria. It consisted of sixteen religious houses (six of the Eastern rite), 208 votaries, many of them of various Eastern rites. The Province of the Near East included among its activities the St Joseph University at Beirut, three colleges (Cairo, Jumhūr and Ḥimṣ), four middle schools (Cairo, al-Minya, Beirut and Aleppo), three seminaries and training establishments (Ghazīr, Bikfayyā, Maʻādī), one parish Jarajūs (Garagos) in Upper Egypt), six residences (Alexandria, Cairo, al-Minya, Taʻnāyil, Damascus and Aleppo), the Biblical Institute in Jerusalem, subject to the Biblical Institute in Rome.

The Jesuits have two establishments in Ethiopia and nineteen votaries, a college and the beginnings of a university at Addis Ababa.

The *Fathers of the African Missions* of Lyons, whose main function is the apostolate in Central Africa, came to Egypt in 1877 in order to devote themselves to the ministry alongside the Latins and Catholic Copts. After 1922 several of the Fathers adopted the Coptic rite. One priest of extraordinary activity who adjusted himself perfectly to Coptic life in all its forms was Father Yaʻqūb Muyser; he died in 1956. The Fathers have a house which uses the Coptic rite at Zifta, with a parish and missionary centres at al-Zaqāzīq and Shibīn al-Kawm. They administer nine parishes, one of them according to the Coptic rite, and have three colleges with a total of 1,930 pupils, the majority of them (1,133) Muslim.

The greatest contribution to instruction, however, has been made by the *Brethren of the Christian Schools*, since it is their special function. After beginning their Middle Eastern activities at Smyrna in 1841, they proceeded to Egypt, where they were actively encouraged by the Khedive, in 1847, to Palestine in 1878. They rapidly increased the number of their schools and colleges in almost all the Middle Eastern countries and educated generations of young people who were to be highly esteemed as civil servants and in banks and business houses, and among whom some became ministers and one even a President. At the present day their establishments in the Middle East are divided into two districts: the eastern district, comprising Greece, Jordan, Israel, Lebanon and Turkey, and the district of Egypt composed of Egypt and Ethiopia. Eritrea, where they have two schools, a college and a juvenate, comes under the district of Rome. It is interesting to compare the relative numbers of pupils belonging to the various religions in the two districts. In the eastern district, there are eighteen colleges and nine schools, with a total of 12,971 pupils as follows:

Catholics	7,510
Non-Catholic Christians	2,635
Jews	563
Muslims	2,263

In the Egyptian district, among 8,777 pupils there are:

Catholics	3,380
Non-Catholic Christians	2,723
Jews	312
Muslims	2,362

Religious houses in the two districts total thirty-three, with 353 votaries in charge of fifteen schools and twenty-eight colleges.

The *Lazarists* have been in the Orient since the eighteenth century; the first Latin Apostolic Vicar of Aleppo, Armand Bossu (1762–5), was in fact a Lazarist. When the Jesuits were suppressed in 1773, their missions in the East were entrusted to the Lazarists, the first of whom arrived at Salonica, Santorin and Smyrna in 1783, in Constantinople, Aleppo, Damascus and ʻAyn Ṭūrā in 1784. They reached Tripoli in 1834 and Beirut in 1844. During the same year they settled in Alexandria and in 1870 were at Akhbas in Northern Syria. In 1840 a mission was opened in Persia, which won the special esteem not only of the Chaldaeans but also of the Syrians of Mesopotamia, thanks to the extraordinary activity of Father Paul Bijān, who printed a large number of Chaldaean and Syriac works. After being devastated by the Turks in 1915, it was reopened in 1921. The Lazarists established themselves in Ethiopia in 1838 and Justin de Jacobis (1839–60) worked there with an intense apostolic zeal which won him the honour of canonization in 1939. In 1956 the small seminary of Hebo (Ethiopia) was committed to their care. The total number of their houses in Egypt, Ethiopia, Greece, Iran, Israel, Lebanon, Syria and Turkey is sixteen, with eighty-three votaries, seven parishes, two missionary centres, four primary schools, four colleges (2,000 pupils), a technical school, an apostolic school and the seminary of Hebo (Ethiopia).

The *Salesians* came to the Orient much later. They settled in Palestine in 1891, in Constantinople in 1903 and from there proceeded into Jordan, Israel, Iran, Lebanon and Syria. The religious houses of the Middle East, all of them of the Latin rite (apart from the Aleppo establishment which uses the Melkite rite), are grouped under an "Ispetoria del Medio Oriente" composed of twelve religious houses with 206 votaries. Their establishments are to be found in Alexandria, Cairo, Port Sa'īd, Bayt Jamal (Israel), Bethlehem, Cremisan (Jordan), Tehran, Ābādān, Beirut, al-Ḥusayn (Lebanon), Istanbul. They are mainly technical and agricultural schools.

The *Fathers of Verona* (Combodians), founded in 1867, established two institutes in Cairo in the same year, one for men and the other for women, for the reception of liberated slaves. In 1872 they went to the Sudan and in 1936 to Ethiopia, which they had to leave in 1943. They opened a college in Eritrea in 1947. In 1964, after the disturbances in the south, they were violently expelled from the Sudan. At the time of writing (1966) they have the following establishments in Ethiopia: a college at Asmara with sixteen Fathers and 1,250 pupils, and also a seminary at Asmara and three parishes. In Egypt they possess four convents with twenty-two monks, three parishes, three schools, a college of 1,036 pupils and a technical school for the production of Egyptian rugs.

In the field of teaching, the *Marist Brethren* make a considerable constribution. They came to Constantinople in 1893, to Syria in 1895 and to Egypt in 1899, but as a result of political developments they were obliged to leave Turkey and Egypt. In Syria and the Lebanon they have six schools and colleges with fifty-five monastic teachers. The pupils are distributed as follows:

Lebanon	2,614
Catholics	2,267
Orthodox	144
Muslims	203
Syria	1,969
Catholics	1,103
Orthodox	315
Muslims	551

The *Little Brothers of Jesus*, under Father de Foucauld, provide an element of meditation among manual workers. About ten Little Brothers are assigned to five brotherhoods in the Lebanon, Turkey, Jordan, Syria and Iran (at Tabrīz among the lepers).

Female religious congregations

For the sake of completeness, some mention must be made of the many female religious congregations or institutions which are devoted either to a life of meditation or to various teaching missions, hospitals, refuges, orphanages, etc. Since lack of space makes it impossible to describe them in as much detail as the male congregations, only their names will be given and, for Eastern foundations, the number of religious houses (H) and the number of nuns (N).

A. EASTERN SISTERHOODS

(*a*) Inter-ritual congregations
  Sisters of the Blessed Hearts of Jesus and of Mary (= Mariamettes) H: 73; N: 500
  Dominicans of St Catherine of Siena (Syro-Chaldaean) H: 15; N: 130
(*b*) Coptic sisterhood: Egyptian Sisters of the Sacred Heart (Egypt) H: 8; N: 85
(*c*) Antiochene rite:
  1. Malankar: Sisters of the Imitation of Christ (India) H: 15; N: 170
     Daughters of Mary (India) H: 9; N: 120
  2. Maronites:
    (i) Independent communities, for meditation H: 3; N: 60
    (ii) Lebanese Antonine H: 5; N: 100
    (iii) Order of the Visitation H: 2; N: 44
    (iv) Antonines H: 19; N: 150
    (v) Order of the Holy Family H: 48; N: 80
    (vi) Order of St Theresa H: 12; N: 80

(*d*) Byzantine rite
1. Salvatorian Sisterhood H: 7; N: 60
2. Basilian Choerites H: 20; N: 115
3. Our Lady of Perpetual Succour H: 13; N: 115

(*e*) Chaldaean rite
1. Chaldaean: Sisters of Mary the Immaculate H: 8; N: 62
2. Malabar:
Carmelites H: 80; N: 2000
Order of St Clare H: 80; N: 280
Sisters of the Destitute H: 23; N: 280
Sisters of Adoration H: 56; N: 1040
Assisi Sisters of Mary the Immaculate H: 5; N: 70
Sisters of Charity H: 7; N: 120
Medical Sisters of St Joseph H: 10; N: 135
Sisters of Nazareth H: 4; N: 85
Congregation of the Holy Family H: 15; N: 320
Sisters of the Sacred Heart H: 39; N: 595
Sisters of St Joseph H: 4; N: 50
Sisters of the Visitation H: 16; N: 175
Samaritan Sisters, founded in 1961
Caritas Diocesan Secular Institute, founded in 1962

(*f*) Armenian rite
Armenian Sisters of the Immaculate Conception H: 23; N: 174

B. WESTERN SISTERHOODS

Catholic International Female Auxiliaries (AFI)
Sisters of the Rosary of Jerusalem
Benedictines
Carmelites
Sisters of the Order of St Clare
Ladies of Nazareth
Congregation of the Mother of God
Daughters of Charity
Daughters of the Heart of Mary
Daughters of Our Lady of the Addolorata
Daughters of Mary the Auxiliatrix (Salesians)
Daughters of St Anne
Missionary Franciscans of Mary
Missionary Franciscans of the Heart of Mary (Egyptian Franciscans)
Oblates of the Assumption
Sisters of St Zita
Pie Madre della Nigrizia
Our Lady of Sion
Little Sisters of the Assumption
Little Sisters of Jesus
Little Sisters of the Poor

Sisters of the Sacred Heart
Sisters of Mary of Reparation
Sisters of Charity of Bésançon
Sisters of the Divine Saviour
Dorothy daughters of the Sacred Heart
Dominicans of the Presentation
Dominicans of the Deliverance
Franciscans of the Cross of the Lebanon
Franciscans of the Immaculate Lady of Lons Le Saunier
Missionaries of Our Lady of the Apostles
Missionaries of the Good Shepherd
Scholastic missionaries of the Third Order of St Francis
Missionaries of the Holy Family of Villefranche
Order of St Elizabeth
German Sisters of St Charles Borromeus
Sisters of St Joseph of the Apparition
Sisters of St Joseph of Lyons

The above brief description of the religious and social activities of the Catholic monks and nuns in the Middle East may perhaps make it possible to estimate how far Christian ideals have been able to penetrate certain levels of society, reaching even non-Catholic Christians by such means as catechism courses in the schools, religious services, masses, retreats in which all Christians usually take part (or at least used to take part), numerous youth movements such as Valiant Hearts, JEC (Jeunesse Etudiante Chrétienne), scouting, study circles. Moreover, the activities of Catholic monks and nuns also have an effect on some sections of Muslim society through schools, hospitals, public lectures, journals and books.

The influence of Catholic activity in all its various aspects appears to be threefold. In the first place, it is certain that the immense and concentrated efforts of the missionaries have contributed to the reinforcement of Catholicism, to developing it and keeping it in touch with the universal life of the Church, while preventing Catholics from living in a spiritual ghetto. It is possible that among some of the missionaries, especially before the First World War, there was a slightly exaggerated bias in favour of westernization in the cultural sense, somewhat to the detriment of national culture, and an imprudent latinization of the liturgy at the expense of piety and spirituality. It must be stated, however, that taking the work of the missionaries as a whole, it has succeeded in preserving that which is, in a word, the "precious pearl", indispensable to a lively and living faith, a readiness to face the urgent problems confronting the modern world. The Church in the West tries to respond to these "signs of the times", to ensure its "aggiornamento" by an increasingly enlightened adherence to evangelical principles. The Catholics of the Middle East, like their brothers throughout the rest of the world, have profited from this approach.

It may perhaps be possible to go further, however, and state that Christianity as a whole has also profited. In all the Christian countries of the Middle East, Orthodox Christians have never hesitated to entrust their children to the care of Catholic colleges, as will be confirmed by a glance at the various statistics given. This common Christian education, conscientiously imparted by missionaries, has been a means of strengthening the faith of all, and elucidating it without requiring the Orthodox Christians to be in any way disloyal to their ancient community and its traditions. There can be no doubt that it has prepared the way for the ecumenical movement of which we are now reaping the fruits.

Finally, and without paradox, it may be said that this missionary activity has also helped to awaken in our Muslim compatriots a more highly refined religious sense, a greater awareness of responsibilities towards society, towards the needs of the people and the wretchedness of the poor; in fact there has resulted from it a happy rivalry with Christians in the field of social work. The Catholic colleges, and the other Christian colleges too, have given education and not merely instruction to generations of Muslims, male and female, in reverence for their faith and also in the observance of their duty to God and to their country. Many of these Muslims, young men and women, have later occupied privileged positions in society and have thus helped to strengthen the spiritual forces of the nation. Certain basic principles concerning the rights of the individual, the demands of justice, the dignity of work, the ideal of woman, the love which should control human relationships have passed through some kind of osmosis into general public opinion as a result of the steady and unceasing labours of Christian teachers for more than a century. There are certain enlightened and courageous beneficiaries who do not fail to rejoice in this bounty and who are ready to express their gratitude when required.

The participation of Catholics and Christians in general in civil life is not confined to its religious aspects. It may be observed in political, economic and social life, and in intellectual life. The effects naturally differ from one country to another, depending on the number of

Catholics to be found there. It is certain, for example, that the political activity of the Catholics is much more apparent in a country like the Lebanon where the Maronites, in particular, have always fiercely championed national independence. Even in a country like Egypt, however, where it was some time before native Catholics were much in evidence, civic duty and devotion to the community have consistently been preached by educated Catholics with a sense of duty. At a time when knowledge of foreign languages was very limited and when all the machinery of state was in foreign hands, they knew how to take charge of public affairs and to devote themselves wholeheartedly to organizing public works, postal services, finance and communications, and have continued to do so since the gaining of independence. Egypt's first Ambassador to Washington is Sesostris Sīdārūs, the father of the present patriarch. The existence abroad of an intellectual Christian élite coming from Egypt, from Syria or from the Lebanon and displaying qualities of prudence, maturity and sincere patriotism while defending in an intelligent way the legitimate claims of their country, has not failed, on occasions, to make an impression on public opinion and to win it over to the national cause. Moreover, the history of the Arab nationalist movement shows that in the early stages the influence of the Christians was decisive. As Antonius has shown in *The Arab Awakening*, it was the former pupils of the American University, all of them Christian, who made the first attempts at "conspiring" to shake off the Turkish yoke. It was Ibrāhīm al-Yāzijī who composed inflammatory verses, with the line "Arabs, awake", an unmistakable call to revolt. And in public meetings organized in Paris at the end of the nineteenth century with the object of promoting the Arab cause, it was the Christians who spoke first and in the most unambiguous fashion. It was a Maronite Christian, Najīb 'Azūrī, a former Christian official of the Ottoman government in Jerusalem, who in 1905 wrote the first treatise on Arab nationalism: "The awakening of the Arab nation in Turkey in Asia, in the midst of the interests and the rivalries of the foreign Powers, of the Roman Curia and of the Oecumenical Patriarch." It was to be followed, in the course of a year, by the monthly journal *Arab Independence*.

Other evidence may be adduced. Shaykh Philippe al-Khāzin extolled in Cairo in 1910 the *Perpetual legislative and judicial independence of the Lebanon*. His courage and outspokenness cost him his life, for he died on a Turkish gallows. It was a Maronite, Shukrī Ghānim, who in the

Correspondance d'Orient (*Correspondence from the Orient*) detailed the injustices committed against the Arabs, who were debarred from public office and deprived of representation. In 1915 Nādira Muṭrān, of the well-known Greco-Catholic family of Zaḥla, set forth in a long chapter of his book *Syria Tomorrow*, the impressive list, by communities, of Lebanese Christians who were pioneers of the Arab renaissance. A Maronite, Khayrallāh T. Khayrallāh, was the author of a book, *The Problem of the Levant: The liberated Arab regions*, which appeared in 1919 and which has become, according to M. Rondot, "one of the sentimental breviaries of Arab nationalism". Finally, in order to justify the condemnation and execution of Syrian, Palestinian and Lebanese patriots on the grounds of "Arab conspiracies", the Command of the Fourth Ottoman Army published after the war a Red Book entitled *The Truth about the Syrian Question*, with the object of stigmatizing the conduct of these "conspirators". Two of the secret societies mentioned included among their members the names of all the great Christian families of the Lebanon: 'Aql, 'Ammūn, Arqash, Ghānim, Khayrallāh, Khūrī, Mukarzal, etc.

In the economic sphere the Christians, thanks to their knowledge of foreign languages and close contact with Europe, were able to establish important and successful trading relations and to found flourishing industries, thus contributing to the development of the country's resources. If, as a result of their initiative and hard work, some of them were able to make their fortunes, their country and their compatriots also profited from the rewards of their labours. To mention only Egypt, such names as Sidnāwī, Kaḥla and Matossian are famous not only for their riches, but also for the social benefits which they have conferred on their country.

Finally, on the plane of intellectual and literary activity, the contribution made by Christians in general and, more particularly, by Catholics, cannot be disputed; the essential part they have played in the Naḥda movement has been emphasized by all serious historians of the cultural renaissance of the Middle East during the nineteenth century and at the beginning of the twentieth century.

Indeed it might be said that the first modern Arab schools came into being in the shadow of the convents. In the Lebanon, apart from the seminaries of 'Ayn Ṭūrā and Ghazīr, which were founded by the Jesuits and have been described above, there already existed the School of 'Ayn Warqā', established in 1789, where, following the example of Rome, instruction was given in Syriac, Latin and Italian, in addition to Arabic language and literature. In 1823 Buṭrus al-Bustānī founded the National School, while the Patriarchal School of the Greek Catholics and the Maronite College of Wisdom date from 1855. These schools inspired young people with the desire to study and a great love of the Arabic language. It is said that Nāṣīf al-Yāzijī, who was born in 1800 at Kafr Shīmā and was the best Arabic scholar of his time, was determined to take up the challenge of the Muslim proverb: "The Arabic language cannot be converted to Christianity." It was again a Lebanese of ancient Maronite stock (turned Presbyterian), Buṭrus al-Bustānī, who, having been educated on sound, humanist lines and knowing, in addition to a complete mastery of his native language, Syriac, Latin, Greek, Hebrew, English and French, compiled the famous dictionary *Muḥīṭ al-muḥīṭ* and set himself to work on a vast encyclopaedia, of which he published seven volumes. A veritable literary dynasty has succeeded to his task and today his grandson, Fu'ād Ephrem al-Bustānī, Rector of the University of the Lebanon, follows in his footsteps: he is actively presiding over the publication of an immense *Arab Encyclopaedia* which has reached its fifth volume.

The foundation in Beirut of the American University (in 1866) and the St Joseph University (in 1875) have had the effect of impressing this renaissance with a more scientific and technical stamp.

Similarly the modern Arab press owes its origin to two Greek Catholic Lebanese, Salīm and Bishāra Taqla, who emigrated to Cairo in 1875 and founded the celebrated newspaper *al-Ahrām*. Their descendants, with the aid of another Lebanese literary dynasty, the Jumayyils, who were Maronites, "were" as Rondot says, "to make this newspaper, with its world news service, its illustrations, its inquisitions and its editorials, the flower of the Arab press". In December 1913 the old King Ḥusayn declared to the Turkish philosopher Rіżа Tevfiq: "I tell you to my shame that it is the Lebanese Christians, like al-Yāzijī, Bustānī and nowadays Jurjī Zaydān who have succeeded in bringing about the revival of classical Arabic."

This renaissance is continuing at the present time and the part played in it by Catholics is very creditable in relation to their numbers. A study of the Catalogue of the Catholic Press belonging to the Jesuit Fathers in Beirut makes it possible to estimate the variety and quality of the works published, and the names of Oriental Catholic writers are much in evidence, such as Father Shaykhū, Mgr Shiblī, Fathers

Khalīfa, Nuwiyyā (Nwya), Abū, Paul Khūri, Jabr; MM. Nādir Bustānī, Fattāl. One of the greatest contemporary Arab poets, Khalīl Muṭrān, was Lebanese, and a Greek Catholic; so too was 'Ādil Ghaḍbān, another celebrated poet.

The great publishing-house al-Ma'ārif, directed by the Mitri family who are Greek Catholics settled in Cairo, has produced splendid publications of a very large number of classical works of Arab literature. There are also Catholic publishing houses in the Lebanon and in Syria.

Finally it may be noted that Catholic teachers are also well represented in the university world. On the subject of philosophy in Egypt, the works of Yūsuf Karam, a Maronite belonging to the Lebanon, are used even in the University of al-Azhar. M. Yūsuf Murād, Professor of Psychology in Cairo University, has founded a school of "Integrating Psychology" which is doing serious work in this field. M. Najīb Baladī, a Greek Catholic and professor for many years in Cairo University, may be regarded as a "Christian philosopher" of Pascalian tendencies. In his last work (in Arabic) *Stages of Moral Thought*, he has not been afraid, though writing for a mainly Muslim public, to appeal to evangelical values or to quote *L'Annonce faite à Marie* (*The Annunciation*) by Claudel and *Au cœur des masses* (*At the Heart of the Masses*) by Father Voillaume. Lastly, M. René Ḥabashī, a Lebanese philosopher who spent the first part of his life in Egypt, has succeeded in integrating Christian and Muslim values in an openly existentialist philosophy which should stimulate discussion between Muslims and Christians.

CONCLUSION: THE TASK FOR THE FUTURE

In conclusion, a few observations may be made on what may be called "the vocation of Catholics in the Middle East" or, alternatively, on the task which confronts them for the future.

It is a future which presents three aspects, closely interrelated. The history of Catholicism in the Middle East, as described above, the present condition of a world in search of renaissance and of a Church which, in adapting itself to the times, declares its firm intention of holding discussions with other Christian sects, with Muslims and with the whole of mankind—all these combine to show that for Catholics in their overall task there are three distinct motives: organic integration in their surroundings, ecumenical orientation and, finally, discussions between Christianity and Islam.

To consider first organic integration into their surroundings: there is no doubt that in the Middle East society is in a state of evolution, if not revolution. Two World Wars have completely overturned the political, social and economic conditions of this society. The revolution of 1952 in Egypt, that of 1958 in Iraq and those in Syria, the course of events in the Lebanon, together with the war in Palestine, have shaken not only the material foundations of the Middle East, but also its ideology. The weakening of ties with the West and the constitution of a neutralist Third of the World, an increasingly advanced degree of socialization internally and an attempt at unifying the various elements of society—these appear to be the essential features of the present situation.

What is to be the standpoint of the Catholics in such a state of affairs? Some of them who are too much westernized or who, in their life and culture, are too lightly rooted in such countries as Syria, Iraq or Egypt may prefer to leave this "dangerous area where lethal winds are blowing". What are their reasons? "Christians", they say, "have no future in a country which is becoming all the time more socialist and totalitarian. Their children are indoctrinated in the schools where the syllabus is devoted more and more to Islam and their faith is in danger. Debarred increasingly from public office and from nationalized societies, robbed of the property of their parents and unable to engage in profitable business in a society where almost everything is under State control, how can they survive? To remain is to condemn oneself to death by suffocation. It is better to go in search of a milder climate."

These are serious problems which can certainly not be solved by evasion. One thing is clear, that any who, as a result of their earlier education, react in this way are quite unfitted to remain in the country. It is their duty to emigrate. The arguments which they put forward may be valid—for themselves—up to a certain point. But every serious social revolution must involve a radical change of economic structure, a rearrangement of the component parts, the appearance of new and unexpected factors. It is inevitable that the experiment must take time, that it is temporarily damaging to certain personal interests or even to certain rights. But so long as religious faith is not directly attacked, so long as the Christian has the support of the Law and the Constitution in defending his essential rights, so long as he is able, even at a sacrifice, to live, perhaps in poverty but respectably, then how, if he has the choice, can he hesitate to remain in his own country when it is in course of complete social reconstruction? How can he refuse to collaborate, to the best of his ability, in bringing about the success of this social transformation, so that it may be effective in securing greater justice for all people, so that the struggle against poverty, ignorance and misery may be crowned with success?

It is maintained, therefore, that Catholics, and Christians in general, ought not to resign from public affairs nor to ruminate their grievances and formulate vague acts of vengeance. They ought, without sacrificing their ideals, to integrate themselves into the society to which they belong, to be active in promoting the principles which their Christian Faith dictates to them, and to make an effective contribution to the real progress (moral, social, economic and cultural) of their environment. To use the expressive metaphor of Mgr Hughes, they must be drops of blood not on the sleeve but in the very flesh.

It is important to realize, however, that this serious Christian attitude towards the true well-being of the country can only have a permanent effect if it does not remain isolated, in separate particles. Christians must unite so that their message of peace may be effectively transmitted and heard. The minority, everywhere, only plays its true part if it preserves its purity, its vitality, its specific qualities which render it indispensable. It is not by watering down or sweetening their faith that Christians will fulfil their task as citizens, but by living it and being loyal to it, and the fact remains that Christians must continue to unite, actively and thoughtfully, so as to recapture the authentic meaning of the evangelical message, which has been eroded by dissension, and in brotherhood and peace convey it to their Muslim compatriots as a token of love. There is no doubt that, for Christians, the ecumenical work of recent decades which has made quite spectacular progress at the Vatican Council II has been the work of the Holy Spirit, of pity, peace and love which alone can be of service to man, to all men whatsoever their faith.

Finally it may be stated that Christians who are united among themselves ought, in those countries of the Middle East which have a Muslim majority, to make a point of entering into discussions with Muslims, to bear their witness of love and to struggle untiringly against prejudice, family opposition and passions dictated by considerations of background and inheritance. Such discussion indeed requires two parties, but it also requires that there should be a sense of conviction and a determination not to be discouraged by any difficulty. Faith, true faith, can move mountains because it is inspired and maintained by love. The relationship between Christian and Muslim must be based on the same respect for the individual and his civil rights, on liberty of cult and religion, on freedom of conscience assured to each individual, on conditions allowing the free expression of the preaching of the Word of God. Everything which stirs up passions of hatred and enmity and which ranges citizens of the same country on opposite sides against one another must be systematically eradicated.

There is nothing which brings men closer together than their faith in God. If Christians and Muslims were to work with all their hearts to overcome their egotism and to keep alive respect for vocation and for human dignity and the claims of God's Kingdom, the world would be spared many evils and, what is more, the very countenance of the God whom they worship would appear more clearly to his creatures.

Melkite Catholics, from *Oriente Cattolico*, pp. 257–68

	Parishes	Churches	Chapels	Secular priests	Monks	Nuns	Schools	Hospitals	Dispensaries	Orphanages	Laity
Patriarchate of Antioch											
Metropolises											
Aleppo	5	6	5	16	15	23	7	—	—	—	17,000
Beirut	51	56	19	26	32	31	26	—	4	1	50,000
Buṣrā and Ḥawrān	22	18	4	16	4	12	10	—	4	—	12,950
Damascus	14	21	55	21	8	25	14	—	2	—	13,800
Ḥimṣ	10	10	5	10	9	11	8	—	—	—	10,262
Ṣūr (Tyre)	11	11	1	8	5	—	9	—	—	—	7,635
al-Lādhiqiyya (Latakia)	18	14	2	5	9	57	16	2	1	1	8,000
Eparchies											
ʻAkkā (Acre)	42	38	4	25	3	23	5	2	—	3	21,000
Baʻlabakk	17	15	6	17	4	28	29	—	—	1	9,305
Bāniyās	15	16	—	6	4	—	5	—	—	—	3,800
Ṣaydā (Sidon)	29	— 60 —		13	15	12	10	—	—	—	18,000
Tripoli	10	7	1	9	2	4	11	—	—	—	4,000
Zaḥla and Furzul	35	42	5	10	9	70	21	1	—	1	26,789
Alexandria	15	15	4	24	5	6	4	1	1	—	25,000
Vicariate of the Sudan	5	6	—	5	—	—	—	—	—	—	1,000
Patriarchate of Jerusalem	10	8	1	—	8	12	1	—	—	1	4,070
Archbishopric of Petra	32	21	11	24	8	46	—	—	—	6	15,000
Argentina	—	—	—	—	—	—	—	—	—	—	40,000
Brazil	—	—	—	—	—	—	—	—	—	—	50,000
France	—	—	—	—	—	—	—	—	—	—	1,400
U.S.A.	—	—	—	—	—	—	—	—	—	—	50,000
Other Countries	—	—	—	—	—	—	—	—	—	—	150,000
										Total:	397,611

Chaldaeans from *Oriente Cattolico*, pp. 360–77

	Parishes	Churches	Chapels	Secular priests	Monks	Nuns	Schools	Hospitals	Dispensaries	Orphanages	Laity
Patriarchate of Baghdad	10	7	4	16	4	27	4	—	—	1	75,000
Metropolises											
Kirkūk	9	10	1	10	2	6	10	1	—	1	14,000
Ṣaḥna	7	— 6 —		—	2	1	2	—	—	1	8,500
Urmia	6	22	3	5	5	4	2	—	—	1	4,852
Archbishopric of Baṣra	4	6	2	4	1	5	1	—	—	2	8,800
Eparchies											
Aleppo	6	5	—	3	3	2	2	—	—	—	6,000
al-Qūsh	6	— 14 —		8	10	20	3	—	—	1	17,000
ʻAmādiyya	12	— 22 —		8	3	16	8	—	—	—	6,783
ʻAqra	6	6	2	4	1	7	4	—	—	—	1,630
Beirut	2	1	1	5	—	—	1	—	—	—	3,000
Mosul	10	— 19 —		17	3	9	26	—	—	1	34,000
Zākhū	14	12	14	14	1	9	15	—	—	—	11,234
Patriarchal Vicariates											
Turkey	7	5	—	2	—	—	—	—	—	—	1,524
Egypt	1	—	—	—	—	—	—	—	—	—	500
France	—	—	—	—	—	—	—	—	—	—	550
U.S.A.	3	—	—	4	—	—	—	—	—	—	2,000
										Total:	190,000

Armenian Catholics, from *Oriente Cattolico*, pp. 400–08

	Parishes	Churches	Chapels	Secular priests	Monks	Nuns	Schools	Hospitals	Dispensaries	Orphanages	Laity
Patriarchate Armenian Cilicia											
Archbishoprics											
Aleppo	7	7	4	12	6	20	12	—	1	1	15,000
Baghdad	3	3	1	4	—	9	4	—	—	—	3,000
Beirut	11	13	10	31	8	47	12	—	—	—	18,000
Istanbul	6	12	2	5	6	18	7	1	—	1	4,000
Alexandria	2	4	7	6	5	21	5	—	—	1 home	6,500
Iṣfahān	3	2	3	1	1	7	1	—	—	—	2,600
al-Qāmishlī	4	4	2	3	1	7	4	—	—	—	3,000
Armenians outside the Patriarchate											
Lwow (Poland)	—	—	—	—	—	—	—	—	—	—	5.000 (in 1943)
France	8	4	—	6	7	8	3	—	—	1	20,000
Greece	2	2	—	2	—	—	1	—	—	—	600
Rumania	—	—	—	—	—	—	—	—	—	—	5,000
Argentina	—	—	—	—	—	—	—	—	—	—	5,000
Brazil	—	—	—	—	—	—	—	—	—	—	2,000
U.S.A.	—	—	—	—	—	—	—	—	—	—	8,000
										Total:	97,100

Syrian Catholics, from *Oriente Cattolico*, pp. 166–74

	Parishes	Churches	Chapels	Secular priests	Monks	Nuns	Schools	Hospitals	Dispensaries	Orphanages	Laity
Patriarchate of Antioch											
Patriarchal Vicariates											
Beirut and Lebanon	6	— 6 —		14	—	9	6	—	—	1	14,500
Egypt and Sudan	2	3	—	4	—	—	1	—	—	—	4,000
Jordan	1	1	—	2	—	2	1	1	—	—	1,200
Mardin and Turkey	4	4	—	2	—	—	—	—	—	—	800
Archbishoprics											
Aleppo	6	2	2	6	—	—	4	—	—	—	7,000
Baghdad	5	5	1	11	—	—	1	—	—	—	8,750
Damascus	4	4	—	5	—	—	2	—	—	—	3,807
Ḥimṣ	12	12	—	12	—	—	6	—	—	—	4,735
Mosul	8	10	8	25	—	27	13	—	—	1	17,000
Eparchies											
al-Ḥasaka	7	8	—	9	—	5	5	—	—	—	4,000
America and elsewhere	—	—	—	—	—	—	—	—	—	—	15,000
										Total:	80,000

Catholic Copts from *Oriente Cattolico*, pp. 115–21

	Parishes	Churches	Chapels	Secular priests	Monks	Nuns	Schools	Hospitals	Dispensaries	Orphanages	Laity
Alexandria (Patriarchal Eparchy)	26	22	11	37	26	50	18	—	3	—	30,000
Asyūṭ (Eparchy)	24	42	3	23	6	72	42	1	26	—	21,644
al-Minya (Eparchy)	19	19	6	14	8	67	20	—	—	1	16,250
Thebes (= Luxor)	37	— 42 —		14	18	101	46	—	—	3	15,000
										Total:	82,894

Catholic Ethiopians from *Oriente Cattolico*, pp. 102–4

	Parishes	Churches	Chapels	Secular priests	Monks	Nuns	Schools	Dispensaries	Orphanages	Laity
Addis Ababa (Metropolis)	10	10	12	16	29	45	12	4	7	12,315
Adigrat (Eparchy)	12	12	4	32	—	—	13	—	4	6,900
Asmara (Eparchy)	83	—104—		110	90	—	—	—	—	40,000
									Total:	59,215

CHAPTER 8

THE COPTIC CHURCH IN EGYPT

INTRODUCTORY REMARKS

It was at the time when Gaius Turranius was Prefect of the Roman Province of Egypt, that, according to the Evangelist St Matthew, the Holy Family fled to the Land of the Nile. They would have crossed the narrow isthmus of al-Qanṭara, nowadays a small village at the Suez Canal, and following the ancient caravan-route from Judea to Egypt, they would have entered the fertile province of Goshen. Coptic, Armenian, Syrian and Islamic sources from the fourth to the fourteenth century mention numerous localities and incidents in the Nile delta and valley in connexion with the "Story of the Flight of the Holy Family into Egypt". These details are mainly legendary, but to a large number of Copts, the Coming of the Holy Family to the Land of the Pharaohs is an annual event of jubilation, which is commemorated in their *Synaxar* and celebrated in many communities.[1]

The next time that we hear of Egyptians in connexion with the Christ is in Jerusalem on the first Day of Pentecost, when, among the "nations" represented, Egyptians also received the Holy Spirit.[2] There is good reason to believe, that some of these Egyptian Jews returned to Egypt, where they established Christian congregations.[3]

The Copts trace the foundation of their Church to St Mark the Evangelist, who, according to Eusebius, came to preach the Gospel in Egypt, where he established the see of Alexandria. According to tradition, St Mark received the crown of martyrdom in Alexandria. The apostolic foundation of the Coptic Church is significant, in that to this day, the head of the Coptic Church, who has the title of pope and patriarch of Alexandria, is considered the successor of St Mark.[4]

The history of the Coptic Church is both glorious and tragic, glorious in the number of her illustrious sons such as St Athanasius, St Cyril,

[1] M. Jullien, "Traditions et Légendes Coptes sur le voyage de la Sainte Famille en Egypte", *Missions Catholiques*, vol. XIX (1886), pp. 9–12. O. Meinardus, *In the Steps of the Holy Family from Bethlehem to Upper Egypt* (Cairo, 1963). [2] Acts ii. 10.

[3] Jewish colonies existed in Alexandria, Leontopolis (Tall al-Yahūdiyya), Babylon and Phile.

[4] Cyril VI, the present pope and patriarch of the see of St Mark, is the 116th successor of the Evangelist.

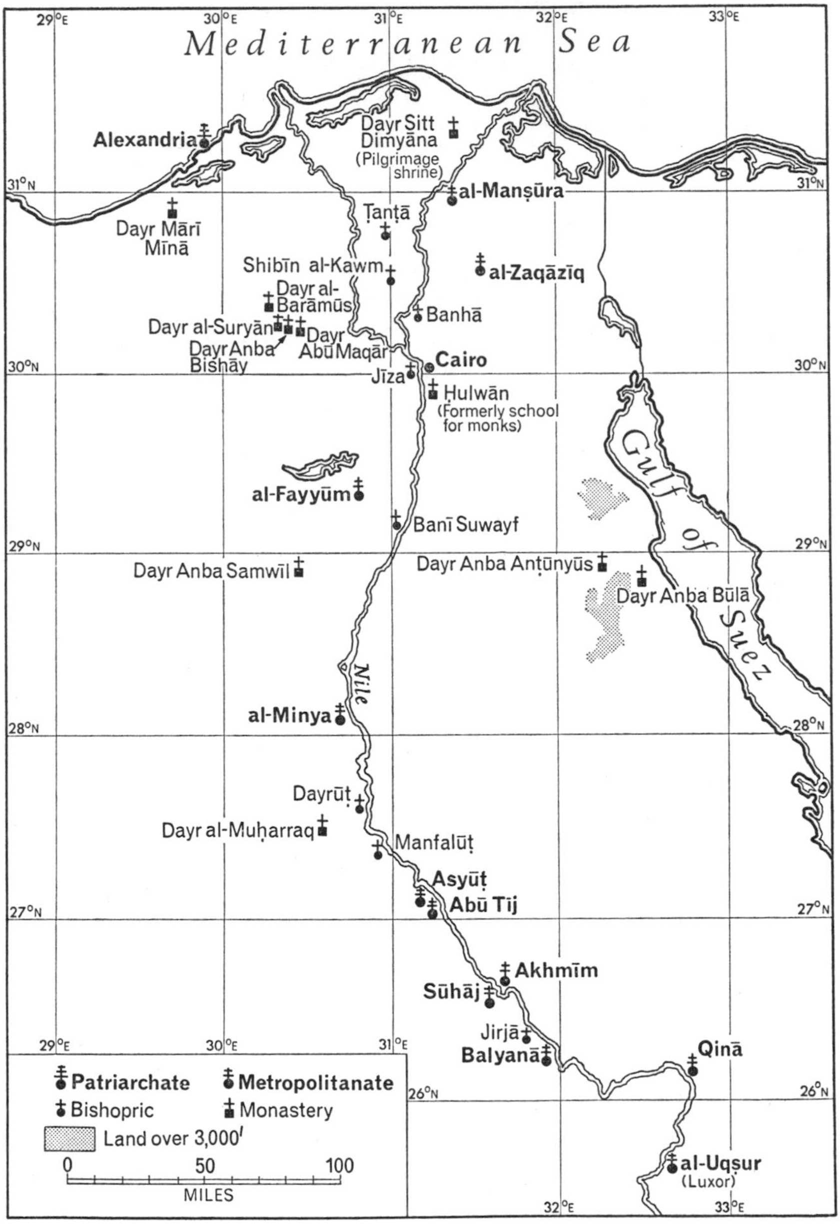

The Coptic Church in Egypt.

NOTE. The patriarch of Alexandria generally resides in Cairo; all the bishoprics which are marked were until recently metropolitanates; Omdurman, Khartoum and Jerusalem are also metropolitanates.

St Antony and St Pachomius, to mention but a few; tragic, however, in the vast number of her children who throughout the ages have suffered martyrdom for their adherence to the Christian Faith. Following a most severe persecution under Diocletian (303–10),[1] Egyptian Christianity emerged victorious, so much so, that its theology and christology were instrumental in determining much of the theological thinking of the Universal Church.

Two distinct contributions of the Coptic Church left a lasting impression. In the famous Catechetical School of Alexandria, scholars like Pantaenus, Origen and Clement of Alexandria endeavoured to relate Christianity to Greek philosophy, especially Neoplatonism, thus building a bridge between reason and revelation, while St Antony and St Pachomius, the fathers of anchoritic and coenobitic monasticism, transformed Egypt into one vast monastery. By the fifth and sixth century, Pachomian monasticism had penetrated the Churches of both the Orient and Occident, whereas Antonian monasticism flourished in the eastern and western deserts of the Nile valley.

The Chalcedonian Controversy (451), with Dioscorus I as the chief exponent from the Monophysitic point of view, led to the tragic schism, which alienated the Coptic Church from both the Eastern and the Western Churches. After the Arab conquest under ʻAmr b. al-ʻĀṣ (640), the Copts were gradually reduced from a majority to a minority, owing partly to immigrations from the Arabian peninsula, but chiefly to conversions to Islam. By the beginning of the eighth century, Arabic had become the official language, replacing Greek and Coptic. Direct and indirect pressure exerted upon the Copts, the confiscation of ecclesiastical funds and the periodic imprisonments of members of the hierarchy were largely responsible for the evil practice of simony, which for many centuries to come remained an outstanding reproach to the Coptic Church.

During the reigns of the Ṭulūnids (868–905), the Ikhshīdids (935–69) and the Fāṭimids (969–1171) the Copts were accepted on sufferance, though this relatively peaceful period was broken by the violent persecutions of al-Hākim. With the invasion of Egypt by Shirkūk, the Fāṭimid rule came to an end, and the Ayyūbid Dynasty (1170–1250) came to power. Although this period was not marked by major persecutions, none of the Ayyūbids showed any particular sympathy for the

[1] The Coptic Church begins its era on 20 August A.D. 284, the year Diocletian became emperor, thus commemorating the martyrs of the Diocletian persecution.

Copts. The rise of the Mamlūk Dynasties (1250–1517) gave cause for new persecutions and oppressions, so that by the fourteenth century the number of Copts in Egypt had decreased to one-tenth or even one-twelfth of the total population. Moreover, with the thirteenth or fourteenth century, recorded Coptic history, i.e. a detailed indigenous account as we find it in the *History of the Patriarchs of the Egyptian Church*, comes to an end. When in 1517 the Ottoman Turks conquered Egypt, an uneasy truce was established with the minorities which, however, was frequently interrupted by oppressive measures. From the early Middle Ages onwards, the Coptic Church declined sadly both in numbers and creative vitality.

THE NINETEENTH AND TWENTIETH CENTURIES

The French Invasion

When on 1 July 1798 Napoleon Bonaparte and his 37,000 soldiers disembarked in Alexandria, the Coptic Church had reached her lowest ebb, numerically and materially. Paradoxically enough, for the Christians of Egypt the situation steadily deteriorated during the three years of French occupation. In order to win the favour of his new subjects, Napoleon proclaimed himself a Muslim, though not a single Egyptian could possibly have trusted in his profession of faith. When the news of the French invasion reached Cairo, Copts and other Christians were in great danger; indeed, the suggestion was made in the *Dīwān*, that one of the first measures to be taken should be the extermination of all Christians in Cairo, and it was only the favourable intervention of Ibrāhīm Bey that saved the Christians from a general massacre. Having taken Alexandria, Napoleon marched towards Cairo, where he defeated the Mamlūk forces in the Battle of the Pyramids. Once established in Cairo, he commenced his administration by creating the General *Dīwān*, thus securing at least the outward support of the most influential and stable elements in Egyptian society. For the collection of taxes, he retained the hierarchy of the Coptic fiscal agents, which was headed by Mu'allim Jirjis al-Jawharī. For a brief period even, so al-Jabartī points out, Christians and Jews were seen riding on horseback, though the complaints of the Muslims forced Napoleon to order the Copts and the Jews to resume wearing their distinctive turbans, belts and shoes.[1]

[1] During the patriarchate of Cosmas II (851–9) the Copts were compelled to wear girdles as a mark of ignominy. During the reign of Qalāwūn (thirteenth century) the Copts were prohibited to ride on horses; instead they were made to ride on donkeys.

The most outstanding Copt during Napoleon's stay in Egypt was Mu'allim Ya'qūb Tadrus, who was officially in charge of tax-collection in Upper Egypt, but, in fact, served as Joint-Commander with General Desaix' expeditionary force in the Upper Egyptian campaign against Murād Bey's Mamlūks. In fact, there was hardly a decision Desaix made throughout the campaign without first consulting Ya'qūb. And when in the spring of 1800 portions of the Turkish forces under Naṣif Pasha overwhelmed the few French troops stationed in Cairo, and plunged the city into an apocalyptic nightmare and chaos, only the Coptic quarter under the capable leadership of Mu'allim Ya'qūb held out, and thus evaded the looting and raping of the invaders. After Napoleon's departure from Egypt, a Coptic legion was formed, and Mu'allim Ya'qūb became its commanding general. On his way to France, however, the Coptic general died.

The reign of Muḥammad 'Alī

In the wake of the departure of the French, the Turks seized control of Egypt, and again, as in the case of any governmental change in Egypt, the unfortunate Christians suffered severely. Turkish troops were stationed in the Christian quarters, where they were given the liberty to plunder and to rape. Many Christians were accused of co-operating with the French, and several Copts were put to death by the Turkish Pasha. Then, in 1805, Muḥammad 'Alī rose to power, and through a well-prepared revolt in favour of the Albanian usurper, the *shaykhs* of Cairo, in the hope of putting a stop to the intolerable anarchy which prevailed, elected him Pasha and implored him to assume the government. A year later an imperial *ferman* from the Sultan confirmed the choice.

During the reign of Muḥammad 'Alī, many Christians, Greeks, Armenians and Copts, reached high positions. He chose the most qualified men for his administrative posts regardless of their religion and nationality, and even bestowed upon several Christians the honorary titles of "bey" and "pasha". For many years, his financial adviser was Mu'allim Ghālī, a Christian, who at one time had served as secretary to Alfī Bey. Either because of false accusations or because of Ghālī's truthful reporting with regard to the financial state of Egypt, Muḥammad 'Alī issued an order for his assassination. In 1821, in the presence of Ibrāhīm Pasha and Tobias Bey, Ghālī's son, Mu'allim Ghālī was executed.

Muḥammad 'Alī's knowledge of Turkish led him to employ many

Armenian Christians in his government. Boghos Bey Yousoufian, an immigrant from Izmir, first served as economic adviser, and later as Minister for Foreign Affairs. The Egyptian Cabinet was largely composed of Armenians, the most noteworthy of whom were Artin Bey Cherakian, Garabed Noubarian and Arisdages Altoune Dūrī, while one of the important financiers was Yeghiazar Amira.

For the first half of the nineteenth century, the throne of St Mark was occupied by Peter VII (1809–52), the 109th successor of St Mark the Evangelist, who had one of the longest patriarchal reigns. Elected from the monks of the fifth-century Red Sea Monastery of St Antony, Peter VII displayed great integrity. As patriarch, he was much interested in the new developments of his time, always trying to raise the standard of his clergy and laity. The Coptic desert monasteries, which by this time had decreased to seven,[1] welcomed the rule of Muḥammad 'Alī, who stabilized the internal situation and restored order to the desert.

Many stories are still being related about Peter VII and Muḥammad 'Alī al-Kabīr. Muḥammad 'Alī had a daughter, named Zuhrā, who was possessed of a devil. The physicians, who had been consulted, were unable to do anything for her, and so Muḥammad 'Alī approached the patriarch with the request to heal his daughter. Peter recalled that he had a bishop, John of Minūfiyya,[2] who had the power to cast out devils. Bishop John was delegated to go to Muḥammad 'Alī's palace so as to pray over Zuhrā, and while he prayed, the devil came out from her toe in the form of a drop of blood.[3] Then Muḥammad 'Alī turned to the bishop and said: "What art thou in need of for thy troubles?" But the bishop replied: "I am not in need of anything." The Pasha, however, insisted on repaying the bishop. Then the bishop said: "If thou art really willing to give me what I ask, then I beseech thee that we may build our churches as we please, and that thou mayest treat our Christian sons equally in all positions in the Government and public life."

During the reign of Muḥammad 'Alī, the Copts acquired an increasing sense of identity, and many Christians were enabled to develop their skill in business, commerce and in the professions, and though they remained a beleaguered minority, the proportions of Copts among the wealthy and educated far surpassed their numbers.

[1] These are the Dayr Abū Maqār, the Dayr Anba Bishāy, the Dayr al-Suryān, the Dayr al-Barāmūs, the Dayr Anba Antūniūs, the Dayr Anba Būlā and the Dayr al-Muḥarraq.

[2] A similar story is told about Anba Sarābāmūn Abū Tarhā.

[3] To this day, the Copts engage in the apostolic practice of exorcism. Cf. O. Meinardus, *Christian Egypt, Ancient and Modern* (Cairo, 1964), p. 99.

The Coptic Englightenment

Following the death of Muḥammad ʻAlī and his son Ibrāhīm Pasha in 1849, ʻAbbās I, the grandson of Muḥammad ʻAlī, succeeded his uncle Ibrāhīm. Fortunately for Egypt, ʻAbbās Pasha ruled only for six years, and in 1854 he was strangled to death in his own harem. ʻAbbās was succeeded by Saʻīd Pasha, and, at least outwardly, the Copts continued to enjoy the same freedom and toleration, which had been accorded to them by Muḥammad ʻAlī. In many respects, the Copts were placed on the same level as the Muslims. Thus, for example, Saʻīd Pasha ordered that all Egyptians without distinction of religion should be liable to military service. This meant, that for the first time since the Arab Conquest, Christians were allowed to bear arms.[1] In Asyūṭ, a largely Christian town, all males were conscripted, and not one was being left for their families. Though Saʻīd Pasha had intended with his proclamation to put an end to discriminatory legislation, in reality the decree was used as an instrument of persecution. Once in the army, Christians were forced to accept the faith of Islam, and so great was the misery of the Copts, that Cyril IV, the 110th patriarch and successor of St Mark, intervened so as to have the Copts exempted from military service.

The patriarchate of Cyril IV, known as the Reformer, was one of the most significant milestones in the history of the Coptic Church. Committed to raise the educational standard of the Copts, he spent his short reign as patriarch in establishing schools. At the age of twenty-three, he had entered the Monastery of St Antony, where he was known as Abuna Dā'ūd al-Anṭūnī. After two years, he was elected *hegoumenos*, and soon afterwards he inaugurated a school for monks at the Antonian Dependency in Būsh near Banī Suwayf. In 1853, Dā'ūd was consecrated metropolitan of Babylon (Cairo) on the understanding that, if he proved himself worthy, he would be shortly afterwards elected to the patriarchate.[2] In 1854 Cyril ascended the patriarchal throne, and though his pontificate lasted only seven years, more than two of which he spent in Ethiopia, he initiated lasting reforms. In 1855, the Coptic Patriarchal College was opened, followed by two girls' schools in Azbakiyya and in the Ḥārat al-Saqqa'īn, and a boys' school in the same district. In

[1] During the Coptic insurrections between 725 and 773, the Copts acquired their arms clandestinely, while under Muʻallim Yaʻqūb they received their weapons from the French.

[2] This procedure was extremely uncanonical, since Coptic canon law prohibits the election of a bishop to the patriarchate.

addition to mathematics, geography and science, special attention was paid to the study of languages, which included Arabic, Coptic, Turkish, French, Italian and English. Moreover, Cyril IV was responsible for the first private Arabic printing-press in Egypt. The candidates for the Coptic priesthood were summoned by Cyril to the patriarchate, where either he or Qummus Jirjis, his assistant, taught them.

Throughout his pontificate, Cyril consolidated the Christian communities in Egypt, thus effecting some understanding between the Greek, Coptic and Anglican communions. His dynamic character and his efficient thoroughness soon attracted the attention of the authorities, who had him quietly removed. As R. Strothmann says: "In the Orient, poison was a governmental means to settling political issues, not seldom used."[1]

Cyril IV was succeeded by Demetrius II (1862–70), at one time *hegoumenos* of the Wādi 'l-Naṭrūn Monastery of St Macarius. His pontificate was uneventful, except for the rather widespread Coptic response to the Protestant (United Presbyterian U.S.A.) Mission in the Nile valley, especially in Asyūṭ and Minya. Dissatisfied with the ecclesiastical laxity and the political intrigues within the Coptic Church, many educated Copts joined the Protestant Mission Churches. Demetrius, realizing the potential danger in the rapid growth of the Protestants, excommunicated the members of the heretical Church. The result of this Mission was to create a division among the Copts, which prevails to this day.

The emergence of the Laymen's Movement

After the death of Demetrius II, Mark, bishop of al-Buḥayra, was appointed *locum tenens*, until the election of the new patriarch. Mark, in accordance with the thirteenth-century Coptic canons of Ibn al-ʿAssāl, selected several Coptic notables to help him in the administration of the financial and civil affairs of the Church. Moreover, the time for some radical administrative reforms had come, and the Coptic notables seized the opportunity to participate in the civil and legal affairs of the Church. The principal source of the Church-budget came from the *waqfs*, the religious endowments, which provided for the monasteries, and also assisted the destitute. The administration of these *waqfs* was to become one of the principal issues in the struggles and endeavours of the Laymen's Movement. There were those notables, who felt that the priests

[1] R. Strothmann, *Die Koptische Kirche in der Neuzeit* (Tübingen, 1932), p. 31.

and bishops should give their undivided attention to spiritual matters, and, therefore, leave the administration of the *waqfs*, the schools and legal affairs to competent and capable laymen. Others demanded a more liberal education for the priests and monks, and called for the formation of a council, which would initiate and supervise the establishment of a Theological Seminary, while others again proposed a lay participation in the administration of the "personal status" laws, which applied canon law in such matters as marriage, divorce and inheritance.[1]

When the idea of *al-majlis al-millī* (Community Council) became crystallized, Buṭrus Pasha Ghālī obtained a Khedival decree to establish the proposed Council by law, and the first *majlis al-millī* was elected in November 1874. However, it was soon dissolved because of disputes between the clergy and the notables. Immediately after his enthronement, Cyril V, the 112th Patriarch of Alexandria (1875–1927), rejected the idea of having a *majlis al-millī*, since he intended to be the sole authority in matters pertaining to the Coptic Church. The notables, however, succeeded in striving for their rights, and in 1883 the patriarch and the government authorized the election of a new *majlis al-millī*, and the first constitution was established in May 1883. It was stipulated that *al-majlis al-millī* should deal with matters of the "personal status", the supervision of the *waqfs*, the Coptic schools and the Theological Seminary. Moreover, *al-majlis al-millī* was to be responsible for the administration of the benevolent associations and to keep a record of the churches and monasteries. These new responsibilities of the laity considerably restricted the power of the patriarch and the bishops.

The long pontificate of Cyril V reflected the constant tension between the clergy and the laity. In the meantime, the Tawfīq Society for Reform among the Copts had stirred up public opinion, and the patriarch, who dreaded change, used every possible means to intrigue against it. By creating a rival society, called the Orthodox, Cyril only increased the existing tensions. At the time of the re-election of *al-majlis al-millī* in June 1892, the internal situation had deteriorated to such an extent, that the members of *al-majlis al-millī* appealed to ʿAbbās II to force the patriarch to resign from the chairmanship of the Council. Cyril refused, and consequently was exiled by *al-majmaʿ al-muqaddas* (Holy Synod) to the Dayr al-Barāmūs. In the meantime, Athanasius, bishop of Sanabū, who represented the reform parties, acted as *locum tenens*. After five

[1] The Ottoman rulers had established the *millet* system, which gave the non-Islamic minorities the right to employ their own laws in matters pertaining to the "personal status".

months, however, Athanasius quietly resigned from his vicarial office, and Cyril V entered Cairo in a triumphal procession. Yet, the disputes between the clergy and the laity continued. The *hegoumenoi* of the monasteries refused to allow their *waqfs* to be administered by laymen, and it was not until 1927 that *al-majlis al-millī* regained the rights and responsibilities which it had acquired according to the 1883 constitution.

After the death of Cyril V, the struggle for power between the patriarch and *al-majlis al-millī* abated for a short period, only to be resumed later. The pontificates of Macarius III (1944–45) and Joseph II (1946–56) were particularly clouded by serious conflicts and disputes. At the time of his election, Joseph II had promised to abstain from any interference in the administrative responsibilities of *al-majlis al-millī*. The patriarch, however, did not fulfil his promises, and refused the right of *al-majlis al-millī* to supervise the monastic *waqfs*. Finally in October 1954 *al-majma' al-muqaddas* decided to form a committee of three bishops to supervise the affairs of the patriarchate. The impatience among the Copts increased steadily, and the demands for the resignation of the patriarch became more and more expressive. Under pressure from *al-majma' al-muqaddas* and *al-majlis al-millī* the patriarch was deposed. At the same time, the responsibilities for the "personal status" laws passed out of the hands of *al-majlis al-millī* into those of the government, and the religious courts were abolished.

On the election of Cyril VI to the patriarchate, the responsibilities of *al-majlis al-millī* were even more curtailed. A government decree of 1960 stated that all Coptic *waqfs* were to be placed under the supervision of a special committee for Coptic *waqfs*. The principal functions of *al-majlis al-millī* were thereby assumed either by the government or by special committees. Today (1966) *al-majlis al-millī* serves in an advisory capacity to the patriarchate. Throughout its short history, the effect of the laymen's movement upon the Coptic Church was sadly vitiated by the continuous and unfortunate disputes between the clergy and the laity.

Among the many Coptic notables, who laboured for the cause of lay participation within the Church, mention should be made of the following. Yūsuf Sulaymān Pasha of Sindbis, Minister of Agriculture (1920) and Minister of Finance (1922), was an active member of *al-majlis al-millī* until 1920, when he became a minister and requested to resign. Murquṣ Ḥannā Pasha, a prominent lawyer and professor at Cairo

University, was elected to *al-majlis al-millī* in 1905, and Murquṣ Sumayka Pasha, the founder of the Coptic Museum in Old Cairo, served for many years in *al-majlis al-millī*. Iskandar Bey Masīḥa assumed in 1916 the financial responsibilities of the patriarchate. Three times he was elected and dismissed from *al-majlis al-millī*.

The English occupation: expectations and frustrations

In order to evaluate and appreciate the situation of the Coptic Church in the mid-twentieth century, it is imperative to understand the contributions, which her sons have made to the cause of freedom and independence. Throughout the nineteenth century and the first decades of the twentieth century, the Coptic notables played an important rôle in the political developments of Egypt. For that matter, the history of the Coptic Church in this period was largely determined by the devoted laymen rather than by the patriarchate.

In the summer of 1882 the British under Sir Garnet Wolseley landed their troops at Ismā'īliyya, and soon afterwards they defeated the Egyptian forces under the *fallāḥ* officer Aḥmad 'Urābī in the battle of Tall al-Kabīr. The Copts, who anticipated a new era of freedom, rejoiced in the coming of the British, a Christian nation. The financial chaos, the agitation and disorder under the reign of Ismā'īl Pasha, and 'Urābī Pasha's proclamation that Islam in Egypt was endangered by the increasing Coptic participation in government, caused the Copts to be well disposed to the arrival of the British. The Copts had hoped that the British would represent and safeguard their interests in the political field, thus providing here and there favourable treatment for their fellow-believers. However, the Egyptian Christians were soon to realize that the British were more concerned with a just and impartial administration than in engaging in a nineteenth-century crusade. Aware of the explosive atmosphere, the British no doubt felt that they had to pacify the Muslim majority, even at the expense of the Copts. For the British government officials who administered Egypt were not zealous missionaries and, in attempting to preserve internal peace, they frequently acceded to Muslim demands. The Copts in return became more and more impatient at seeing their position and influence deteriorating, in spite of the fact that their country was occupied by fellow-Christians. The Coptic grievances under Lord Cromer's, and later under Sir Eldon Gorst's administration increased to the point that in 1911 a Coptic Congress was held in Asyūṭ. The government, which feared that the meeting might agitate the public, advised Cyril V to publish a patriarchal proclamation, suggesting moderation and counselling the inadvisability of holding the meeting in Asyūṭ. Notwithstanding all difficulties, the Congress was held as originally intended. A committee of seventy representatives of the different provinces was formed, and George Bey Wīṣā was chosen as president, Khalīl Bey Ibrāhīm and Dr Akhnūkh Fānūs as vice-presidents, and Mr Andrāwūs Bishāra as treasurer. Other notables participating in the executive committee were Bushrā Bey Ḥannā, Tawfīq Bey Doss, Ilyās Bey ʻAwad, Mīkhā'īl Effendi Fānūs, Fakhrī Bey ʻAbd al-Nūr, ʻAbd al-Masīḥ Bey Mūsā, Murquṣ Effendi Fahmī and Murquṣ Effendi Ḥannā. The grievances were discussed under the following headings:

1. As a Christian body of people, the Copts are forced to violate the commandments of their religion by Sunday labour. The Congress requested that government officials be exempted from duty and students from study on Sunday.

2. A large number of administrative posts in the government service are entirely closed to Copts, and it is felt that in general they are not promoted in accordance with their capabilities and merit.

3. Under the existing electoral system in Egypt the Copts are left unrepresented on the Provincial Councils. They ask that a system similar to that at present in operation in Belgium should be introduced to secure the rights of minorities.

4. The Copts have no equal right to take advantage of the educational facilities provided by the new Provincial Councils.

5. The Copts claim that government grants should be bestowed upon deserving institutions without invidious distinction of race or creed.[1]

Throughout the first decade of the twentieth century, nationalist and anti-British feelings increased steadily. The Nationalist party under Muṣṭafā Kāmil (1874–1908) claimed that Egypt was ready for self-government. In 1907 Lord Cromer resigned from his post as British Consul-general, leaving Egypt in a state of unexampled material prosperity. He was succeeded by Sir Eldon Gorst, whose instalment of political freedom, however, was regarded as negligible. During the British administration, one of the most brilliant sons of the Coptic "nation" served his country, Buṭrus Pasha Ghālī. At first concerned with the liquidation of *al-dā'ira al-saniyya* (Ismāʻīl Pasha's debts), he

[1] Kyriakos Mikhail, *Copts and Moslems under British Control* (London, 1911), pp. 28–30.

later served as intermediary between 'Urābī Pasha and the Khedive. As Under-Secretary of State in the Ministry of Justice he reorganized the judiciary system. In 1883 he was appointed Minister of Finance, and in 1884 Minister of Foreign Affairs. Following the resignation of Muṣṭafā Fahmī, Buṭrus Pasha assumed the post of Prime minister. Though accused of having cherished pro-British sympathies, in each of his principal policy decisions, e.g. the Sudan question, the Dinshawāy incident and the Suez Canal concessions, he really had only Egyptian interests in mind. On 20 February 1910 Buṭrus Pasha was assassinated by a certain Wardānī, a prominent member of the Mutual Brotherhood, a Muslim terrorist organization.

Towards independence: the Wafd

The desire of "Egypt for the Egyptians" was always a cherished dream among the Copts. Inspired by the nationalistic sentiments of Muṣṭafā Kāmil and later by Sa'd Zaghlūl, Copts and Muslims joined in common purpose against the British administration. It was the first time in the history of Egypt that Cross and Crescent appeared on one and the same flag and that Coptic priests arm in arm with the Muslim '*ulamā*' paraded through the streets of Cairo, while Abuna Sargius, one of the most dynamic Coptic priests, preached for some time regularly from the pulpit of the tenth-century University Mosque of al-Azhar, the centre of Islamic learning and religion.

Again, it should suffice to mention some of the most outstanding Copts, who actively participated in the Wafd. Most prominent were Wāṣif Pasha Ghālī, Wīṣā Wāṣif, George Bey Khayyaṭ and Murquṣ Ḥannā and, though all four were sentenced to death by the British authorities, they were not executed. Other important Copts serving in the Wafd included Yūsuf Pasha Sulaymān, Ṣannūt Bey Ḥannā and 'Azīz Anṭūn. For many years, the Wafd was dominated by al-Naḥḥās Pasha, a Muslim notable, who together with the Copt Makram 'Abayd Pasha emerged as the leader of the nationalist movement. In 1922 the British ended their occupation, and Zaghlūl Pasha formed his first cabinet, in which two Copts served: Makram 'Abayd Pasha became Minister of Finance, and Wāṣif Pasha Ghālī became Foreign Minister. By 1940 al-Naḥḥās Pasha and Makram 'Abayd Pasha faced insurmountable difficulties in the leadership of the party, which subsequently led to its general disintegration.

The Wafd was a short-lived, yet highly significant movement, in which for the first time since the seventh century, the Copts could openly manifest their nationalist feelings and play a decisive rôle in the patriotic struggle for freedom and independence.

The patriarchates of Joseph II and Cyril VI

The middle of the twentieth century saw one of the major crises in the Coptic Church. From 1942 to 1944 Joseph II, at one time bishop of Jirjā (Girga) in Upper Egypt, served as *locum tenens* or acting patriarch. In May 1946 he ascended the patriarchal throne, beginning a pontificate, which was as turbulent and restless as his political environment. Often undecided and weak, Joseph II was unable to settle the many feuds and power-struggles within the Coptic Church. Corruption within the hierarchy had reached unimaginable limits. In the shadow of the patriarch there always stood Malik, an unlettered but shrewd Upper Egyptian *fallāḥ* (peasant), who served as the patriarch's valet. His political power increased as he managed all relations between the bishops, priests and laity on the one hand, and the feeble patriarch on the other hand. For all purposes, Malik was the "grey eminence", who, so it is reported, sold at least sixteen of the nineteen episcopal appointments that were made during the pontificate of Joseph II. The Coptic Church was sadly divided, and some of the enlightened members of the clergy and laity were agreed on removing the patriarch, while those who gained by simony and corruption sided with the patriarch. Accusations against the patriarch for his practices of simony and immorality appeared repeatedly in the local press, when in July 1954, a group of the people called *al-umma al-qibṭiyya* (Coptic Nation) demanded the patriarch's resignation. On 25 July 1954 the Coptic protest culminated in the kidnapping of the 115th successor of St Mark. When he refused to abdicate his throne, he was forced into a taxi and driven to the Coptic nunnery of St George in Old Cairo. However, the police intervened, and the patriarch returned to the patriarchal residence at Azbakiyya. Fourteen months later, Joseph II narrowly escaped assassination, and shortly afterwards he was officially exiled by the Holy Synod and *al-majlis al-millī*. On 21 September 1955 Jundī 'Abd al-Malik, the Coptic Minister of Supply, announced that the government had agreed to relieve the patriarch of his powers in response to the wishes of the Coptic people and the leaders of the Church, after all had agreed that His Holiness was no longer capable of executing his duties. A few days later, the sick and enfeebled patriarch was sent to the Dayr al-Muḥarraq, and a triumvirate of bishops was elected to administer the affairs of the patriarchate. On 14 November 1956 Joseph II died and Bishop Athanasius of Banī Suwayf was elected *locum tenens*.

Several times the Copts nominated candidates for the position of the patriarch, but each and every time the candidates did not fulfil all the requirements which were stipulated. Thus, for two and a half years the patriarchal see of St Mark remained vacant, when on Sunday, 19 April 1959, the altar lot was cast in favour of Abuna Mīnā al-Mutawaḥḥid al-Barāmūsī, now known as Cyril VI.

Cyril VI was born in 1902 in Tūkh al-Naṣārā, a small village in the Delta Province of Gharbiyya, where the Dayr al-Barāmūs has its dependency. As a young boy, he attended the primary school at Damanhūr and a secondary school in Alexandria. It was during his days in Alexandria, while working for Thomas Cook and Sons, that the present patriarch began reading "The Lives of the Desert Fathers", an experience which determined his course of life. At the age of twenty-five, he approached John XIX, the 113th Patriarch of Alexandria, with the request to enter the Dayr al-Barāmūs. Here, he became attached to and influenced by the famous monk Abuna ʿAbd al-Malik al-Masʿūdī, who was his spiritual father. In 1931 he was ordained to the priesthood and assumed the monastic name of Mīnā al-Mutawaḥḥid al-Barāmūsī. For two years he attended the former School of Monks at Ḥulwān. Believing that he was called to the solitary life, Abuna Mīnā again visited the patriarch with the request to be permitted to repeople the ancient White Monastery near Sūhāj in Upper Egypt. But, after a short stay, he was ordered to return, and so he moved to a cave in the vicinity of the Dayr al-Barāmūs, where he spent his most formative years. This cave had been previously occupied by Abuna Sarabāmūn, who was well known for his strict ascetic practices, and who had just died before Abuna Mīnā's arrival. In the desert, miles away from civilization, the present patriarch met the prophet of the desert, Abuna ʿAbd al-Masīḥ al-Ḥabashī, who still inhabits his cave in the Wādi'l-Naṭrūn.

In 1936 the anchorite again approached the patriarch, asking his permission to rebuild the ancient Shrine of St Menas in the desert of Maryūṭ. Permission was refused, and from 1936 to 1942 Abuna Mīnā retreated to Jabal al-Juyūshī, east of Old Cairo, where he inhabited one of the deserted Napoleonic wind-mills. The first few months he spent in building his cell and a small chapel. At night he would sleep on the floor on coarse sack-cloth. One day, John XIX climbed up the mountain to visit the hermit in his deserted wind-mill. On his way to the anchorite, he broke his patriarchal staff, the symbol of his office. When he arrived at the abode of Abuna Mīnā, the hermit offered to repair it, but the patriarch, after having given his staff to the monk, refused to take it back, thereby indicating that this staff would be his.

During the Second World War, the British, believing him to be a spy, forced the desert monk to leave his solitary abode. Abuna Mīnā came down from the hills, and for the following years he stayed in a room in Old Cairo. It was during this time, that he was appointed *hegoumenos* of the Monastery of St Samuel at al-Qalamūn. With the humble donations and gifts which he received from the many people who sought his counsel and advice, he bought a piece of land upon which to build the present Church of St Menas. A few years later, more land was added to the original establishment and a settlement-house was erected next to the church.

In April 1959, 765 electors of the Coptic Church from Egypt, Ethiopia, Jerusalem and the Sudan gathered in Cairo to select three out of the five candidates for the patriarchal throne. Disagreement and disappointment with the candidates caused considerable uneasiness among the electors, and twenty-two of the twenty-four members of the *al-majlis al-millī*, as well as five bishops abstained from voting. The three selected candidates were Damyan al-Muḥarraqī, Angelus al-Muḥarraqī and Mīnā al-Mutawaḥḥid al-Barāmūsī, and these names were placed on the altar of St Mark's Cathedral. On 19 April 1959 a five-year-old boy was led to the altar to select one of the pieces of paper on which would be written the name of the future patriarch. According to the Apostolic practice (Acts i. 26) the guidance of the Holy Spirit through a child's hand was about to end several years of turmoil for the Copts by electing a new patriarch. Immediately after his election and enthronement, Cyril VI devoted his attention to three major problems of the Church: the Ethiopian problem, the quest for greater unity among the Copts, and the issue of the *waqfs*, which had been a stumbling block in the life of the Church for seventy years. Moreover, a dream, which the patriarch had entertained for many years, was fulfilled, when on 27 November 1959 he laid the foundation stone of the ninth monastery of the Coptic Church, the Monastery of St Menas at Maryūṭ. Realizing that the future of the Church depends upon the integrity and spirituality of the monks, and believing in strict monastic discipline, Cyril VI ordered all itinerant monks to return to their respective monasteries in fulfilment of their monastic vows. While most monks obeyed the patriarchal order, some of the anchorites of the Western Desert disobeyed the command and thus incurred suspension from their ecclesiastical functions. Led by Abuna Mattā al-Miskīn, this group soon organized a religious community in the Bayt at-Takrīs (House of Sanctification) in Ḥulwān, which has become a bastion of conservatism, deep spirituality and other-worldliness.

In all fairness it should be said, that no patriarch can please all the Copts, and this is true also with regard to Cyril VI. There is no doubt, that he is a genuine *thaumaturgos*, a deeply pious and religious person with extraordinary spiritual gifts who, among other things, has stopped the evil practice of simony, at least with regard to the episcopacy. Many educated and sincere Copts, however, are sadly disappointed and even distressed on account of the inability of the patriarch to fulfil his administrative responsibilities; as Edward Wakin has so pointedly said: "Not only has a monk become a Patriarch, but the Patriarch has remained a monk."[1]

The revival of desert monasticism

Ever since the middle of the fourth century, many Copts were attracted to a monastic life in the eastern and western deserts, thereby following the example of the great hermit St Antony, the star of the desert, whom they often surpassed in their ascetic endurance. These are they, whose constant struggle against the Evil One has been so beautifully portrayed in the "Paradise of the Fathers" or the *Lausiac History*, of whom the best known are St Macarius, SS. Maximus and Domitius, St Bishoi, St John the Little, SS. George and Abraham, St Samuel and St John Kame.

The importance of our understanding and evaluation of Coptic monasticism in the mid-twentieth century lies in the fact, that, as in former times, the Coptic Orthodox leadership, i.e. the pope of Alexandria, the metropolitans and the bishops, are elected from the desert monks. Thus, it is not inappropriate to say, that the spiritual state of the desert monasteries determines in some measure the state and the spirituality of the Church.

In order to comprehend the significance of monasticism in the Coptic Church, we should remember, that pious Copts regard the monastic life as the "angelic life", and those who attain to the highest degree of

[1] Edward Wakin, *A Lonely Minority* (New York, 1963), p. 118.

monasticism are clothed with the *schema*, which is known as the "angelic garment". Moreover, the desert fathers are eager to point out that the image of Christ as portrayed by the Primitive Church displays many radical ascetic qualities; and it is this conviction that has led numerous twentieth-century university graduates to follow their Lord by "wandering in deserts, and in mountains, and in dens and caves of the earth" (Heb. xi. 38).

As in the case of Occidental Christianity, so also among the Copts, there are several motivations, which influenced and still influence men to become monks. Certainly, there are those, who like St Macarius the Great, are led into the wilderness on account of a dream, a vision or a profound religious experience. In other instances, a deep sense of guilt, as in the case of St Moses the Robber, has compelled men to a life of asceticism in the expectation that by good works, such as meditations, fasting and prostrations they may atone for their sins. Others are moved to this decision by the teachings of the Gospel. When one day St Antony heard the evangelical text: "If thou will be perfect, go and sell all that thou hast and give to the poor" (Matt. xix. 21), he sold all that he had, and retired to a cave. There is no doubt that the example of the great hermit has motivated many men throughout the ages to join the "angelic life". Those who are dissatisfied with the worldliness of the Church have withdrawn to the desert either in the pursuit of saving their soul or as a manifestation of their protest against the laxity and the lack of spirituality of the leaders of their Church.

Then, of course, there are those to whom the monastic life is a means rather than an end in itself. Since the canon law of the Church requires that the ecclesiastical leadership be chosen from the monks, there are instances where a man embraces the monastic life out of a desire for leadership. Yet, we ought to recognize that this is the exception rather than the rule. When I sent a letter of congratulation to a certain anchorite at the time of his consecration to the episcopacy, he replied: "...As a matter of fact, a letter of condolence rather than of congratulation would have been more appropriate. How may a monk be congratulated on leaving the calmness of the wilderness, so as to return amidst the disturbance of the city. For me it is a matter of shame. I remember the day of my consecration to the episcopacy with tears and lamentation. Indeed, the glory of solitude and contemplation is above measure. It may not be compared with that of the episcopacy or even that of the papacy. The true consecration, my dear friend, is the consecration of the heart as a holy temple for the Lord, Who on the Last Day will not ask us for our pastoral grade, but for our purity of heart... I write this letter from my beloved cave..." Written a few years ago, the spirit of this letter reflects well the attitudes which the early and medieval monks and hermits demonstrated whenever they received the call to the episcopacy or to the see of Alexandria.

Throughout the centuries ecclesiastical power and prestige was not confined to one or two monasteries. On the contrary, the history of Coptic monasticism shows a constant shifting of ecclesiastical influence from one institution to another. From the fifth to the thirteenth century, the Monastery of St Macarius in the Wādi'l-Naṭrūn supplied the Church almost exclusively with the candidates for the patriarchate. Well known for its library treasures and its distinguished history, the Monastery of St Macarius also served from the middle of the fifth century until the ninth century as a patriarchal residence, when the Melkites occupied Alexandria and thereby evicted the monophysitic Copts. Then, for a relatively short time, in the fourteenth and fifteenth centuries, the Coptic patriarchs were elected from the monks of the Monastery of the Holy Virgin, the Dayr al-Muḥarraq in the Nile valley. In the seventeenth, eighteenth and nineteenth centuries, the Red Sea Monastery of St Antony increased in importance and supplied not only the candidates for the patriarchate, but also the Abuna for Ethiopia and the metropolitan for Jerusalem. In the mid-twentieth century, the ecclesiastical leadership passed more or less into the hands of the monks of the Monastery of the Holy Virgin and St John Kame, also known as the Monastery of the Syrians. This was no mere coincidence, since this development was intimately related to the modern revival of desert monasticism, which centred in and around the Monastery of the Syrians. Here, for example, Abuna Anṭūnyūs al-Suryānī (now Anba Shanūda, bishop of Theological and Educational Institutions of the Coptic Church), Abuna Makarī al-Suryānī (now Anba Samwīl, bishop of Ecumenical, Social and Public Affairs), Abuna Mityās al-Suryānī (now Anba Dumādyūs, bishop of Giza), and Abuna Makaryūs al-Suryānī (now Anba Athānāsyūs, bishop of Banī Suwayf) had lived and prepared themselves for the episcopacy. Under the capable leadership of Anba Tawfīlūs, the monks of the Monastery of the Syrians also experimented in the revival of the coenobitic or Pachomian monastic life, which was so eagerly followed in the Byzantine East (St Basil) and the Latin West (St Benedict), but which after the sixth century never succeeded in impressing itself upon Coptic monasticism, At the same time, monks of the Syrian Monastery revived the classical anchoritic type of the ancient Desert Fathers. Around the Hill of Sarapamon, situated between the Monastery of the Syrians and the Monastery of the Romans (Dayr al-Barāmūs), there are several sandstone caves, which were inhabited by men like Abuna Mattā al-Miskīn, Abuna 'Abd al-Maryam, Abuna Mīnā and Abuna Istafanūs. To this day, whenever possible, Anba Shanūda delights in exchanging his office desk in the Theological Seminary in 'Abbāsiyya for his cave in the Baḥr al-Farāgh, some 11 km south-east of the Monastery of St Bishāy.

Besides the revival of the coenobitic and anchoritic forms of monasticism in the Monastery of the Syrians, several monks withdrew into the Inner Desert of al-Qalamūn, south of the Fayyūm, where ever since 1898 monks from the Wādi'l-Naṭrūn monasteries reinhabited the sixth-century Monastery of St Samuel. Here, many miles of sand and stone separate the utterly isolated desert monk from the fertile oasis of the Fayyūm and the overpopulated Nile valley. The young monks of this monastery are all university graduates, who see in the life of complete solitude the ideal of Christian monasticism. For several years, Cyril VI, the present Pope and Patriarch of Alexandria served as *hegoumenos* of the Monastery of St Samuel, which by every standard is the most isolated of all inhabited Coptic desert monasteries.

Whereas in the thirteenth and fourteenth centuries, the eastern and western deserts of Egypt were still studded with many monasteries and laurae, nowadays, there are no more than nine inhabited Coptic monasteries, the only survivors of a distinguished past. There are the four Wādi'l-Naṭrūn monasteries of St Macarius, St Bishāy, the monasteries of the Syrians (Dayr al-Suryān), and of the Romans (Dayr al-Barāmūs) with a total of approximately eighty monks. South of Suez, in the eastern desert of the Red Sea, there are the two monasteries of St Antony and St Paul the Theban, which are inhabited by some forty monks. The largest and at one time the wealthiest of all Coptic monasteries is the Dayr al-Muḥarraq, which is situated some 65 km north of Asyūṭ. About seventy to eighty monks are attached to this monastery, which for many years supplied teachers and financial aid to the Copts of Upper Egypt. The Monastery of St Samuel is inhabited nowadays by no more than nine monks. One of the first projects to which Cyril VI gave his attention after his enthronement to the see of Alexandria in the spring of 1959 was the rebuilding of the Monastery of St Menas on the ancient site of the desert of Maryūṭ. On 27 November 1959 the foundation-stone of the new monastery was laid, and, today, seven monks inhabit the newest of all Coptic monasteries. Several times a year, Cyril VI withdraws either from Cairo or Alexandria to the Monastery of St Menas for contemplation and prayer.

In addition to the inhabited monasteries, a brief reference ought to be made to the monastic dependencies, which supply the desert monks with food and material necessities. Situated in the Nile Delta (Tūkh Dalaka, Aṭrīs and Kafr Dā'ūd) and in the Nile Valley (Būsh and Zawāra), the dependencies are important administrative centres, since, in many instances, they also serve as the episcopal residence. In September 1952 a Republican Decree for Agrarian Reform was issued, which stated that no monastery was to possess more than 200 feddans. This law was applied in 1960 by the Republican Decree no. 264.

In comparison to the eighteenth and nineteenth centuries, mid-twentieth-century Coptic monasticism shows some definite marks of revival and reform. Since the future of the Church is so intimately associated with the spiritual life of the desert fathers, it is to be earnestly hoped that this monastic revival will some day be reflected in a more vigorous and dedicated life of the Church.

The question of the Holy Places

From the middle of the seventeenth century until the present day, the Coptic Church has been constantly involved in the arguments, disputes, violations and open fights pertaining to certain property claims and rights in the Holy Land in general, and in the Church of the Holy Sepulchre in particular. Whereas, in the Middle Ages the Copts still maintained some significant sites, rights and privileges in the principal churches of the Holy Land, for example, the Church of the Holy Sepulchre, the Church of the Sepulchre of the Holy Virgin, the Church of the Ascension, the Church of the Nativity of our Lord in Bethlehem and certain sites at the river Jordan, most of the ancient and medieval properties have been acquired by the Greek or Armenian Communions. During the seventeenth century, the various Christian Churches in the Holy Land suffered somewhat severely from the heavy taxes which they were forced to pay to the Muslim rulers. Poverty and economic pressure became conducive to ecclesiastical irregularities, and property violations, especially by the Armenians, constantly increased. Many ancient Communions, for example, the Nestorians, the Maronites, the Georgians and the Ethiopians, were forced out of their holdings because of their inability to pay the necessary taxes to their Turkish overlords. At the same time, the Copts were able to maintain some property rights even within the Church of the Holy Sepulchre.

Whereas, at one time, the Coptic holdings (joint properties with the Syrian Jacobites) in the Holy Land were quite significant, the seventeenth-century general penury among the Copts in Egypt reflected rather unfavourably upon their power and prestige in Jerusalem. Apart from the property on the roof of the Chapel of St Helena, the so-called Dayr al-Sulṭān with its adjoining passage leading to the parvis of the Church of the Holy Sepulchre and the Chapel of the Four Bodiless Living Creatures and the Chapel of St Michael, the *status quo* of the seventeenth century has been more or less retained, at least, with regard to the Coptic holdings. In this connexion it ought to be remembered that during the Ottoman rule and the British Mandate, no community was ever able to regain those sites, rights and privileges, which had been abandoned, either temporarily or definitely. In such cases, the community in question was replaced by those who were able and prepared to pay the rent.

Before commenting, however, on the highly complex and explosive issues pertaining to the Dayr al-Sulṭān, which have so sadly clouded the relationships of the Copts with their Ethiopian brethren, brief reference should be made to the undisputed Coptic properties, rights and privileges in the Holy Land.

In the Rotunda of the Church of the Holy Sepulchre, west of the *Kouvouklion*, the Copts possess the Chapel of the Holy Virgin, which they believe to be the holiest of all the sacred sites, since it is erected against the place where Christ's head rested at the time of His burial. The cells of the monks are situated between columns 9, 10 and 11 of the Rotunda, while another lodging is situated immediately west of the main entrance to the church. Though the Copts do not have the right to celebrate the Divine Liturgy in the Holy Sepulchre, they own four sanctuary lamps, which are suspended from the ceiling of the Holy Tomb. In the Chapel of the Angel east of the Holy Tomb they own one lamp, and of the eight lamps above the Stone of Unction, the third lamp from the left belongs to the Copts. Moreover, for many centuries, the Copts have been entitled to participate with the Greeks, the Armenians and the Syrians in the Holy Saturday Ceremony of the Holy Fire, at which occasion they receive the Holy Fire from the Armenian archimandrite.

During the sixteenth century the Copts still owned the altar of SS. Joachim and Anne in the Church of the Sepulchre of the Holy Virgin. Nowadays, however, they possess no properties in this church, though they are still entitled to celebrate the Divine Liturgy twice a week on the Armenian altar, west of the Sepulchre of the Holy Virgin. A similar agreement with the Armenians exists for the use of the altar of the Three Kings in the Church of the Nativity of our Lord in Bethlehem, where the Copts are permitted to conduct their service at Christmas.

His Beatitude Basilius IV, the Coptic Archbishop of Jerusalem, resides in the Monastery of St Antony, north of the Coptic Chapel of St Helena, near the 9th Station of the Via Dolorosa. Here also accommodation is available for the Coptic pilgrims, who once or twice a year flock to the Holy City. In addition, the Copts own the Monastery of St George, which comprises the Primary and Secondary Girls' School of St Dimiana.

The intricacies pertaining to the disputed Dayr al-Sulṭān belong to those unpleasant Jerusalem stories, which reflect the arguments and violations perpetrated by the representatives of the various Christian communions in the Holy Land. In this case, Copts and Ethiopians have argued and fought for this site. It is impossible to provide in this context a detailed and impartial account of the many property violations which have alienated Copts and Ethiopians from each other. Moreover, during the middle of the nineteenth century, the agents and representatives of England, Russia and the Ottoman Porte by supporting either the Egyptians or Ethiopians in Jerusalem elevated the Holy Land property dispute into the realm of international politics. Today, the situation with regard to the claims to the Dayr al-Sulṭān is substantially still the same as one hundred years ago, except that different nations are nowadays committed to the support of the contending churches. During the past few years, the United Arab Republic, the Hāshimite Kingdom of Jordan and Ethiopia as well as the Arab League became considerably involved in the monastic disputes of the sites on the roof of the Church of the Holy Sepulchre. In short, the issue whether the property belongs to the Ethiopians or the Copts depends largely upon the validity and legality of the *fermans* and documents which are presented by the two Communions to the Jordanian Ministry of the Interior. Unfortunately, Christians belonging to the same Apostolic See of St Mark compete in their overtures to the

Hāshimite Monarch so as to gain his interest and favour, thereby openly disobeying the Apostolic counsel to settle ecclesiastical disputes within the Church (I Cor. vi).

Towards new relationships with the Ethiopian Abunate

Ever since the days of St Frumentius, who was consecrated by St Athanasius as bishop of Axum, Ethiopia has been closely linked to the Alexandrian see.[1] The Egyptians used to base their right for nomination and consecration of the *abuna*, the head of the Ethiopian Church, upon the apocryphal and so-called Eighty Disciplinary Canons of Nicaea. Thus, it became an established practice, that the *abuna* as well as the bishops serving Ethiopian dioceses were to be always Egyptians, who were consecrated to their office by the Patriarch of Alexandria. From the fourth until the middle of the twentieth century, therefore, the ecclesiastical leadership of Ethiopia was vested in the hands of foreigners, either Egyptians or Latins, the majority of whom had little understanding of the ethos of Ethiopian Christianity.

The reign of Ras Tafari, however, marked the beginning of a new era in the Egyptian–Ethiopian ecclesiastical relationship. In 1926, on the death of Mathewos the Abuna, Ras Tafari approached Cyril V, the Coptic patriarch, with the request to consecrate a new *abuna* and several Ethiopian bishops. In May 1929 the Holy Synod of the Coptic Church agreed to the request, and for the first time in history, four Ethiopian bishops were consecrated for service in Ethiopia. In 1930, following the patriarchal visit of John XIX to Ethiopia, the *echege* was consecrated, being the fifth Ethiopian bishop.

During the Italian occupation of Ethiopia, beginning in 1935, the Italian government attempted to detach the Church of Ethiopia from the see of Alexandria. Cyril, the Abuna, was invited to go to Rome, from where he returned to Cairo. During his absence, the Italians appointed Anba Abraham, a new *abuna* of the Ethiopian Church as well as three archbishops and three bishops. However, the unilateral action of the Italians met with little success, and when the news of the separation of the Ethiopian Church from the see of Alexandria was related to Cairo, Anba Abraham and his self-appointed hierarchy were excommunicated.

After having regained independence, Haile Sellassie I requested the

[1] Except for two relatively short periods during the sixteenth and seventeenth centuries, when, on account of the missionary efforts of the Portuguese, the Ethiopian Church submitted to the see of Rome.

return of Cyril, the legitimate *abuna*. Subsequently, he sent a delegation to Cairo to study the possibilities of granting the *abuna* the right to consecrate Ethiopian bishops. This imperial demand marked the beginning of the efforts for ecclesiastical independence of the Ethiopian Church. Further demands included the right to nominate an Ethiopian *abuna* with the power to consecrate the Ethiopian hierarchy, the creation of an independent Ethiopian Synod which was to be responsible for the election of the Ethiopian bishops, and a seat in the Synod of the Coptic Church. In 1945 Macarius III, patriarch of Alexandria, convened the Synod of the Coptic Church, which absolutely refused to recognize the Ethiopian demands. In December 1945 the Ethiopian Church threatened to sever relations with the Coptic Church, if no satisfactory solution to the Ethiopian demands could be found. The tensions among the two sister churches increased steadily. In 1950, Cyril, the last Coptic *abuna* of Ethiopia died, and on 13 January 1951, Anba Basilius, the Ethiopian bishop of Shoa, was consecrated as the first Ethiopian *abuna* by Joseph II, patriarch of Alexandria. The same year, five Ethiopian bishops were consecrated by the *abuna* in accordance with the patriarch's order.

The unfortunate events leading to the unilateral deposition of Joseph II by the Synod of the Coptic Church in September 1955 caused profound resentment in the Church of Ethiopia. The ecclesiastical *coup d'état* was considered as being illegal, since it was accomplished without the consultation and participation of the Ethiopian Church. In June 1958 an agreement was reached between a Coptic and an Ethiopian ecclesiastical commission, which stipulated that the Ethiopian Church should participate in the election of the 116th Patriarch of the see of Alexandria.

In fact, after the election of Cyril VI, the Ethiopian question was seriously studied and, by the end of June 1959, a joint declaration of the two churches was published. The twelve articles provide administrative independence of the Ethiopian Church, though canonically attached to the see of Alexandria. The patriarch-catholicus, the head of the Ethiopian Church, is second in rank after the pope and patriarch of Alexandria. He is authorized to consecrate metropolitans and bishops. Exchanges of professors, students and monks between the two sister churches are recommended.

Up to recently, a few Ethiopian students studied in the Coptic Orthodox Theological Seminary in 'Abbāsiyya. Moreover, there are several Ethiopian monks in the Coptic monasteries especially in the Dayr al-Muḥarraq and the Dayr al-Barāmūs. To this day, however, the relations between the two churches are still sadly estranged on account of the respective Holy Land property-claims with regard to the Dayr al-Sulṭān.

The era of ecumenicity

The decisions of the 4th Ecumenical Council at Chalcedon in 451 tragically divided the unity of the Body of Christ. The deliberations of the Council pertaining to the christological issues of the nature or natures of the Redeemer resulted in the condemnation of the archimandrite Eutyches and in the banishment of Dioscorus I, 25th Patriarch of Alexandria. Later Eutyches was excommunicated even by the Egyptian Church for his erroneous beliefs. Out of loyalty to her patriarch, the Egyptian Church was forced to withdraw from the rest of Christendom, and for many centuries to come, the Coptic Church remained theologically and ecclesiastically isolated from both the Latin West and the Byzantine East.

Indeed, apart from the participation of John, the *hegoumenos* of the Monastery of St Antony, at the Ecumenical Council of Florence and Ferrara (1439–45), the Coptic Church retained her attitude of separation and isolation until the middle of the twentieth century.

In 1954, at the Second Assembly of the World Council of Churches in Evanston, Illinois, the Coptic Church was received into full membership of the World Council of Churches. Joseph II, patriarch of Alexandria, had requested membership of the Coptic Church in the World Council of Churches, and three Copts, Professor ʿAzīz Sūryāl ʿAṭiyya, Abuna Ṣalīb Sūryāl, parish priest of Giza, and Abuna Makarī as-Suryānī were delegated to represent the ancient see of St Mark. Since then, the Coptic Church has been regularly represented at the various councils and committee meetings; for example, Church and Society, Faith and Order, and Central Committee.

The involvement of the Coptic Church in ecumenical affairs in Egypt, the Near East and throughout the world increased steadily over the years, and by 1962 the need for a special office of ecumenical and social concerns became apparent. In September 1962 Abuna Makarī as-Suryānī was consecrated as Anba Samwīl (Samuel), bishop of Ecumenical, Social and Public Affairs of the Coptic Church, thus assuring the active participation of the Coptic Church in the ecumenical endeavours of the

World Council of Churches and the Roman Catholic Church. Ever since, Bishop Samwīl has tried to interpret the ecumenical movement to the Coptic Church and vice versa.

Since the 1956 Suez Incident, the Coptic Church has participated in the programme of the Egypt Inter-Mission Council Committee for Refugee Problems, and later in the "Ecumenical Advisory Council for Church Service" (EACCS). Moreover, it is hoped, that the Coptic Church will provide capable and imaginative leadership for the proposed "Ecumenical Council of Egypt" (ECE). In terms of ecumenical witness, the Coptic Church has joined with the Catholic, Anglican, Armenian, Greek and Protestant Churches in the annual observance of the Week of Prayer.

The Institute of Coptic Studies, which is situated on the second floor of the Dayr Anba Ruways Building at Shāri' Ramsīs, 'Abbāsiyya and founded by *al-majlis al-millī* in 1954, has become a centre of ecumenical studies and activities. Here, Orthodox, Protestants and Catholics meet together for study groups especially on social and educational affairs pertaining to all Egyptian Christians.

Although the Coptic Church is a member of the World Council of Churches, the Coptic Church has not so far joined the Near East Council of Churches, which grew out of the former Near East Christian Council. The fact that the Coptic Evangelical Church is strongly represented in this largely Protestant Council—the Syrian Orthodox Church is the only orthodox member in the Council—and the long association of the Near East Christian Council with the former International Missionary Council has made it virtually impossible, for the time being, for the Coptic Church to join this regional ecumenical council. And though the Coptic Church has been represented at the official meetings in an observer capacity, theological as well as non-theological factors have prevented the see of Alexandria from participating in the Near East Christian Council or the Near East Council of Churches.

Locally ecumenical relations between the Orthodox Copts and the Evangelical Copts are sadly impaired as a result of the missionary efforts which the United Presbyterian Church carried on among the Orthodox Copts throughout the past century. Since 1854 American missionaries have laboured in the Nile delta and valley, and established churches, hospitals and schools, thus alienating a small, yet significant, number of Christians from the Mother Church. Once known as the United Presbyterian Synod of the Nile, the Evangelical Christians gained ecclesiastical independence in 1957 with the founding of the Coptic Evangelical Church. The Orthodox Copts, however, have never forgotten the missionary zeal of the Protestants, and it is in the light of these historical circumstances that one should evaluate the ecumenical climate in Egypt. At the same time, when the application for membership in the World Council of Churches of the Coptic Evangelical Church was brought before the Central Committee at its meeting in Rochester (1963), Bishop Samwīl said: "The Coptic Orthodox Church warmly welcomes the membership of the Coptic Evangelical Church. We hope that their fellowship will bring us to a wider ecumenical spirit."

Ever since the days of St Francis of Assisi, Capuchin, Franciscan and Jesuit missionaries have attempted to unite the Coptic Church with the see of Rome. In fact, they succeeded in establishing a small but well-organized and dynamic Coptic Catholic Church. The Coptic Catholic patriarchate is divided into four dioceses, the patriarchal diocese of Alexandria which includes Lower Egypt and the Frontier Districts, the diocese of al-Minya, the diocese of Asyūṭ and the diocese of Sūhāj. Coptic Orthodox relations with this Uniate Church are generally friendly, though tinged with suspicion. For example, there are several instances, where Latin priests have been prevented from visiting some of the Coptic desert monasteries, because of their alleged proselytizing activities among the desert monks. In this connexion it is interesting to note that from the point of view of missionary strategy, Latin priests of the various orders have concentrated their missionary efforts on the Coptic monasteries, realizing that the conversion of the monks to Catholicism would eventually lead to the union of the Coptic Church with the see of Rome. Indeed, to this day, the Coptic monasteries supply the candidates for the Coptic hierarchy, and thus determine the future of the Coptic Church. In spite of the continuous and persistent efforts of the Latin fathers to influence and to win over the desert monks, it is noteworthy that none of the Coptic monasteries has joined the Roman obedience.

Like most Christian Churches, the Copts were represented at the sessions of the Second Vatican Council in Rome. Throughout the sessions, the Copts have repeatedly voiced their objections to the Vatican proposals for exonerating the Jewish people from the responsibility for the crucifixion of Jesus Christ. Several theological statements have been published to the effect that "since the Jews tormented and crucified Christ, they are generation after generation carrying the burden of responsibility for this brutal crime". This determined anti-semitic attitude, which is shared by the Orthodox and Evangelical Copts, should not be merely interpreted in terms of an opportunistic accommodation of the Christians to the political policies of the Egyptian government.

The relationship of the Copts towards the other Orthodox Churches in Egypt is cordial, though there are only few occasions for theological dialogue and ecclesiastical co-operation. The Pan-Orthodox Conference on the island of Rhodes (1961), which the Copts attended, accentuated in more than one way the theological differences which exist between the Greek Orthodox Church and the Copts. For the Byzantine Churches the Copts are still regarded as heretics on account of their monophysitic tenets. At the same time, both Coptic and Byzantine theologians begin to explore the numerous non-theological factors (e.g. political, ethnic, linguistic) which contributed to the unfortunate schism at Chalcedon. Yet, for all practical purposes, the importance of Byzantine Coptic relations has noticeably decreased on account of the steady exodus of the Greeks from Egypt. The decline of the Greek community in Egypt also strongly affects the image of the Greek Orthodox patriarchate of Alexandria, which, in time, will increasingly become more and more Arabophone (Arab–Greek Orthodox), especially on account of the absorption of the Palestinian refugees in Egyptian society. The present number of the Greeks residing in Egypt does not exceed 30,000.

Contrary to normal expectations, the Copts entertain virtually no relations with the monophysite Armenian Orthodox Church in Egypt. No doubt, this is largely due to the strong cultural and nationalistic sentiments of the Armenians, which so far have prevented any meaningful rapprochement of the two monophysite Communions. There are approximately 15,000 Armenians in Egypt, who are divided among the Armenian Orthodox, Catholic and Evangelical Churches.

Relations with the Syrian Jacobites, the monophysite sister Church of Antioch, are cordial. Although there are only small Syrian Jacobite communities in Cairo and Alexandria, the two sees (Alexandria and Antioch) have frequently exchanged patriarchal communications, and Ignatius XXXIX, Jacob III, Severus, the patriarch of Antioch, visited Cyril VI in May 1961.

In conclusion, it should be pointed out, that the idea of ecumenicity, which is genuinely cherished by some of the leading ecclesiastical administrators and theologians of the respective churches in Egypt, has hardly penetrated to the communities in the small towns and villages. To this day, ecumenical confrontations are largely limited to Cairo and Alexandria.

Some recent developments

Coptic archaeological and scholarly pursuits are undertaken by the Society for Coptic Archaeology, which was founded in 1935. The annual *Bulletin de la Société d'Archéologie Copte* is of high academic standard and is read by scholars throughout the world. In contrast to the Society for Coptic Archaeology, which is a private organization, there is the Coptic Museum in Old Cairo, which was founded by Murquṣ Sumayka Pasha in 1908, and taken over by the government in 1931. In 1947 the Coptic section of the Egyptian Museum at Mīdān al-Taḥrīr was transferred to the Coptic Museum.

In addition to the desert monasteries, the Coptic Church depends for its leadership largely upon the graduates of the Theological Seminary in Cairo. The first Theological Seminary was opened in 1893 by Cyril V at Mahmashā, and its presidents were Filūtāwūs Ibrāhīm, Yūsuf Macarius, Ḥabīb Jirjis and Ibrāhīm 'Aṭiyya. In 1953 the Theological Seminary was moved to its present building at Shāri' Ramsīs, 'Abbāsiyya. A new building was dedicated on the occasion of the centenary of Cyril IV in January 1961. About 50 per cent of the total number of candidates for the Coptic priesthood attend the seminary. In a Church in which the priesthood is largely hereditary, this, indeed, constitutes a remarkable advance. Those students, who have obtained the *al-thānawiyya al-'āmma* (university matriculation) follow a five-year course leading to the B.D. degree, whereas those who have only the preparatory certificate study in the Lower Section for a Diploma in Theology.

In Banī Suwayf, Anba Athanasius, one of the youngest and most capable bishops, has recently initiated the idea of holding diocesan conferences for the clergy with lectures and discussions on pastoral theology. There is good reason to believe that this experiment will be copied in the other dioceses in the Nile valley.

The Coptic Sunday School Movement, which began in 1908 under the direction of professors from the Theological Seminary, and was revised in 1930, ushered in a new era of concern among the Copts. Like no other attempt, this movement, which centred in Giza, provides capable leadership and dedicated parish-priests, of whom Abuna Būlus Būlus of Damanhūr in the Nile delta is an excellent example. Abuna

Būlus represents the efficient and responsible twentieth-century Coptic priest, who, in addition to maintaining the liturgical life of the Church, has initiated a social and community centre to meet the pressing needs of his parishioners.

Indeed, great changes within the Church must take place if she is to play her rôle in a society of rapid social change. Though it is true that the Coptic Church has successfully withstood the intellectual and religious challenges of the past centuries, she has now to face the problems of the new era, which is in the process of emerging in Egypt. It is the era of secularism and materialism, the era of religious indifference, the Kingdom of "no-God". Within the frame-work of a basically religious society, whether Chalcedonian or Islamic, the Copts were able to maintain their theological position by using the traditional theological arguments and attitudes. The twentieth century, however, raises questions which are not only entirely new, but which are even utterly alien to the Orient. Hand in hand with increased industrialization, and the subsequent social change, the Coptic Church will have to engage in theological encounters which lie beyond the traditional frame of reference. For the first time in 1,500 years, therefore, the Coptic Church with its four million or so believers will be forced to discover new means and methods of expression and communication in order to maintain her position in face of the revolutionary age. This encounter with a rapidly secularizing society can be only successfully met if the laity, the clergy and the theologians are dedicated to the task of reinterpreting the Eternal Divine Word in a manner which is both satisfying and acceptable to the new generation of Egyptian Christians.

CHAPTER 9

THE ETHIOPIAN ORTHODOX CHURCH AND THE SYRIAN ORTHODOX CHURCH

I. THE ETHIOPIAN CHURCH

Between Islam and the Christian West

Many of the Ethiopian Orthodox Church's current attitudes have their origin in her sixteenth-century experience. The issue then was not the Reformation, but rather the Islamic peril.

Expanding Islam has been a threat to Ethiopia's security from the days of the Prophet even until now. As early as the beginning of the fifteenth century King Yeshak (1414–29) had written to the "Kings of the Franks"[1] asking for assistance in defending the Christian faith against a feared Turkish invasion.

Meanwhile the righteousness and valour of the Christian Kings of Ethiopia had become the basis for the widespread legend of "Prester John". King John of Portugal sent Alfonso da Pavia and Pedro da Covilha in search of his mysterious but renowned namesake in Ethiopia.[2]

The West had its first full account of Ethiopia from Father Francisco Alvarez, the Chaplain to the second Portuguese mission to Ethiopia[3] (1520–7). They had come by request of the Ethiopian regent queen Elleni; but they had come too late to be of any real assistance in the war against the Muslim invaders from the lowlands of Ethiopia. King Lebna Denghel of Ethiopia had fought that war to victory without Portuguese assistance. It is understandable therefore that he was a little condescending towards the Portuguese mission.

Of course, Lebna Denghel was over-confident. The Muslim tribes of the Eastern plains soon found a leader of charismatic powers and consummate skill in Aḥmad al-Ghāzī. The second invasion was apo-

[1] "Frank" as a common name for all Europeans, has been assimilated into modern Amharic in the form *ferenc*.

[2] Elaine Sanceau, *Portugal in quest of Prester John* (London, 1943).

[3] See *The Prester John of the Indies*, ed. and trans. C. F. Beckingham and G. W. B. Huntingford, 2 vols. (The Hakluyt Society, London, 1961).

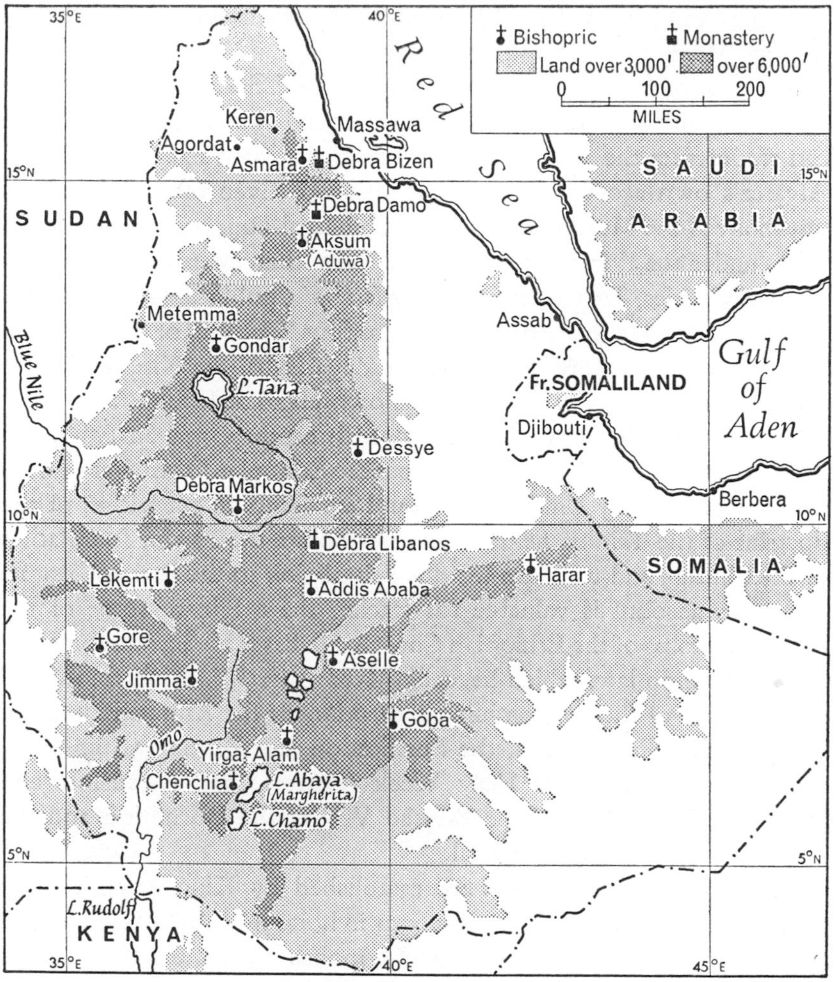

The Ethiopian Orthodox Church.
NOTE. Jerusalem is also the seat of a bishopric.

calyptic in its fury and catastrophic in its destructive power. The Portuguese Embassy had left in 1527. Immediately Aḥmad, called by his followers Imam Aḥmad and by his enemies Aḥmad Grañ (the left-handed), began leading campaign after campaign into the Christian highlands. For fifteen years (1527–42), he destroyed Ethiopian churches, monasteries and Christian settlements, plundering and pillaging, wiping out Christian populations with the fury of a whirlwind. Every historical monument was destroyed. All precious treasures were plundered.

Churches were burned to the ground. Christians were compelled to become Muslim or were put to the sword.

The glorious chapter of the history of the Ethiopian Church came to an end with that invasion. We have several sources from which we can reconstruct the state of the Church in the early sixteenth century. Alvarez's own account has been mentioned. Even more valuable as testimony is the Muslim chronicle of Shihāb al-Din, composed around 1560, under the title *Futūḥ al-Ḥabasha*.[1] Another interesting source is Michael Geddes, *The Church History of Ethiopia*, published in London in 1696. Contained in the latter work is a curious "account of the Habassin Religion, and Customs, composed by Zaga Zaba, the King of Ethiopia's Ambassador...written with his own Hand at Lisbon".

Zaga Zaba, who wrote in the sixteenth century, was an Ethiopian Roman Catholic. He therefore describes the Ethiopian Orthodox Church as if it were already Uniate, *filioque* and all. After an exposition of the doctrine of the Trinity, he goes on to elaborate the Petrine foundation of the Church, and to affirm his due submission to the Pope of Rome.

But his account is valuable for tracing the origin of some of the current customs of the Ethiopian Church. He bases his account on eight books of canon law, which he calls *Manda Abethlis*. Nine traditional annual feasts of the Incarnation are mentioned: the Annunciation, the Nativity, the Circumcision, the Purification, the Baptism (Epiphany), the Transfiguration, the Holy Week (Easter), the Ascension and Pentecost. Two feasts of the Blessed Virgin, the Dormition and the Assumption, are also traditional.

Certain additional feasts were established by King Zara Yaekob (1434–68). These are 33 days every year in honour of the Blessed Virgin (called Māryam today), a day every month in honour of Christ's Nativity (called *Liddatha* today, always the 25th of the month), and a day every month for Michael the Archangel.

The observance of both Sabbath (Saturday) and the Lord's Day (Sunday) is also traced back to the Apostolic tradition by Zaga Zaba. He insists that this is in obedience to the Scriptures, and "not therefore in imitation of the Jews, but in obedience to Christ". Recent research has lent weight to Zaga Zaba's argument. The observance of Saturday as a day of rest seems to have been common among most of the early churches.

[1] Edited and translated into French by R. Basset, *Histoire de la conquête de l'Abyssinie* (Paris, 1897).

Mortal sins are five in number, according to Zaga Zaba: sorcery, whoredom, murder, idolatry, and "loving and making a lie" (Rev. xxii. 15).

The six precepts of the Gospel are to be observed by the faithful: feeding the hungry, giving drink to the thirsty, entertaining strangers, clothing the naked, tending the sick, and visiting prisoners.

Circumcision, which Ethiopian Christians practise to this day, is traced back to Solomon and the Queen of Sheba; Zaga Zaba clearly asserts this is not necessary for salvation, which is only by faith.

The current custom of being "baptized" every year on the day of Epiphany, is also considered ancient by Zaga Zaba.

Women are to confess and communicate before childbirth, but are ceremonially unclean after childbirth, for forty days if the child is male, eighty if female.

Confession and Communion under both species according to Zaga Zaba, are frequent: "All among us, Layicks as well as Clerks, do receive the Sacrament at Least Three Times a Week." The Sacrament is not reserved. Confession and Extreme Unction are not regarded as Sacraments.

Each man has his own confessor (*yenafs abbat*), as is the case today.

The Scriptures are in eighty-one books, forty-one in the Old Testament, thirty-five in the new. (Zaga Zaba does not account for the remaining five—presumably the books known as the *Sunodos*.)

Priests and monks "live by their own Labour, for the Church hath no Tythes, it has Lands which are Cultivated by the Priests and Monks, either in Person, or by their Servants". Priests and monks are not allowed to beg.

The document, which is dated 24 April 1534, is in fact an answer to Roman Catholic charges of heresy and superstition against the Ethiopian Church. Zaga Zaba (*Tsegga Z-abo*, which means the Grace of God the Father) was an Ethiopian Catholic monk sent by King Lebna Denghel to Portugal.

Of course Zaga Zaba does not speak of any practice in the Ethiopian Church in the sixteenth century which is definitely culpable. To that extent he is not objective. Yet the accounts of Alvarez and the Muslim Chronicler alike point to a sixteenth-century Ethiopian Church which was in some ways superior to the European Church of that time in spiritual and cultural achievement.

There were two counts on which Ethiopian morality was sadly sub-Christian even in the golden age of Christianity—sexual morality and honesty in speech. All kinds of extenuating circumstances one could plead: the perennial state of war could serve as an excuse then, but hardly now.

Yet it was in the period of encirclement by Muslims that the Ethiopians built some of their most magnificent churches and produced countless saints whose names are unknown to us.

Aḥmad Grañ was finally beaten back, wounded, and later killed by a Portuguese musket. But the fifteen years of Muslim occupation, the atrocities of which were paralleled only in the Fascist occupation of 1934–41, have left scars hard to heal on the face of the complex religious picture in Ethiopia to this day. The Muslim chronicler gives the impression that nearly all the Christians of the country had become Muslim during the Grañ occupation.[1] The Ethiopian Chronicle says: "hardly one in ten retained his religion."

When the marauding forces receded, the Church was too weak spiritually to restore the people back to a deeper Christian faith. Certain re-consecration ceremonies were held by the Church, but little spiritual leadership was in sight.

The monarchy and the hierarchy, however, had never once given in to Islam. The great Islamic state of Harar on the Horn of Africa collapsed by the end of the seventeenth century. As Islam receded, the Church and the monarchy once again became rallying points for Ethiopian loyalty.

While the Islamic peril gradually faded away, Ethiopia's erstwhile allies, the Portuguese, themselves became a major peril, though not militarily. The remnants of da Gama's expedition had become assimilated into Ethiopian culture, but not into the Ethiopian form of Christianity. They had intermarried freely with Ethiopians, but their families remained Catholic. The Jesuit fathers who arrived, worked from this nucleus to spread the Catholic faith. They studied Amharic, the modern Ethiopian language, and began producing controversial literature in that language. The Jesuits were obviously better teachers than the Ethiopian Orthodox priests, and even the nobility and the royal household were susceptible to their charm and intelligence. Emperor Susenyos (1607–32) joined the Roman Church in 1613, though this was not publicly known till seven or eight years later.

[1] J. Spencer Trimingham, *Islam in Ethiopia* (Oxford, 1952), p. 88.

The Latin patriarch Mendez imposed measures, with the approval of the king, for the forcible conversion of all Ethiopians to the Catholic faith. Ethiopian Orthodox Christians were to be re-baptized, the churches were to be re-consecrated, the ancient Ethiopic liturgy was to be replaced by the Roman Mass in Latin. The relics of Ethiopian Saints were unearthed, desecrated, and discarded as "schismatic defilements" in the church. Dissenters were tortured, their tongues were cut, they were burned at the stake or hanged.

The situation was worse confounded by the fact that the Egyptian *abunas* who were in charge of the Ethiopian Church were as corrupt as corrupt could be.[1] They were living in drunkenness and debauchery of the worst kind, and the religious leaders of the Latins were by far superior to the Copts, despite the former's cruelty and fanaticism.

The people revolted. There was civil war in the country. The battle of Waina-Dega saw eight thousand dead. The king's son Fasiladas (Basilides, 1632–67) pointed out to his father that these had died in the defence, not of their motherland, but of a foreign faith. Susenyos saw the point, stuck by his religious convictions, and abdicated in favour of his son in 1632. His proclamation to his people before abdication is rather touching in its sincerity and pathos:

> Hear ye! Hear ye! We first gave you this faith believing that it was good. But innumerable people have been slain, Julius, Gabriel, Takla Giorgis, Sarsa Kristos, and now these peasants. For which reason we restore to you the faith of your forefathers. Let the former clergy return to the churches, let them put in their altars, let them say their own liturgy. And do ye rejoice.[2]

Basilides was kind to his father, but not to the Jesuits. They were to be interned and later deported. The patriarch Mendez bolted and fled to the enemy of the emperor, the chief of Eritrea (*Baher-Negash*). Basilides imposed firm measures to do away with Spanish Jesuit power. He executed all who resisted, including his own uncle, who had become a Catholic.

Thus came into being the second great fear of the Ethiopian Orthodox Church—the fear of Western Christianity.

The nineteenth and twentieth centuries can hardly be understood except in the light of these two fears—the fear of Islam, and the fear of Western Christianity.

[1] See Budge, *A History of Ethiopia, Nubia, and Abyssinia* (London, 1928), vol. II, pp. 389 f.

[2] Quoted by A. H. M. Jones and E. Monroe, *A History of Ethiopia* (Oxford, 1960), p. 98.

The Age of Theodore

When the nineteenth century opened, Ethiopia was in total chaos. The glory of Gondar had faded. The profligate and pleasure-loving monarchs of the Gondar interregnum could build "pavilions of delight" and "pools of pleasure" but not muster the strength and self-discipline necessary to hold the country together.

James Bruce of Scotland visited Ethiopia in 1770. He found Ras Mikhael of Tigre *de facto* sovereign and king-maker. The *de jure* emperor was Neguse-Negest Takla Hāymānot, a mere puppet in the hands of Mikhael. But his domain was limited. Feudal barons all over the country asserted their independence.

After Ras Mikhael's death in 1780, a chief of the Galla people, Ras Gugsa, came to power. He was a Christian, mainly because he knew that he had to be one in order to win the loyalty of the Ethiopian Christians. But the provinces were still ruled by independent chiefs.

Ras Wolde Sellassie ruled over Tigre from 1790 to 1815. Mr Salt, the British Consul in Cairo, visited his court at Antalo in 1804 and 1810, thus opening the first contacts between Britain and Ethiopia. On each of these visits he left with the Ras a young Englishman (Mr Pearce and Mr Coffin) who became his lieutenant.

Internecine wars split the country and reduced its wealth. The Galla people of southern Ethiopia marched as far north as Takkazie and were on their way to Adowa.

Mr Coffin went to England and came back with some muskets which he gave to the son of Walde Sellassie. Anglican Bishop Gobat of Jerusalem came to Ethiopia in 1830 and was well received by the ruler of Agamè.[1]

Dedjazmach Wubé ruled well in Tigre (1831–55). Ras Ali governed Central Ethiopia, Sahle Sellassie was King of Shoa, Gojjam was ruled by Goshu.

Europe was discovering Africa at this time and travellers of various ilks came to Ethiopia. Gobat went back to Europe and brought back three Protestant missionaries—Krapf, Isenberg and Blumhardt. Isenberg wrote a very useful Amharic dictionary (1841).

From Germany came a distinguished Austrian naturalist, Dr Rüppel who has left an excellent account of his visit (1834–7),[2] and a botanist Dr Schimper who remained in the country for a long time. The French

[1] S. Gobat, *Journal of a Three Years' Residence in Abyssinia* (1834).

[2] E. Rüppel, *Reisen in Abyssinien* (Frankfurt, 1838).

also came. The memoirs of their visit are elaborate and reasonably accurate.[1] In 1841 Father de Jacobis came from Italy as Vicar Apostolic and head of the Roman Catholic mission. He is said to have introduced the vine and the potato into Ethiopia.

Mansfield Parkyns came from England in 1843, and was joined by Walter Plowden and Bell. Meanwhile Major Harris had been sent from Bombay, and had left in 1843 after having concluded an Anglo-Ethiopian treaty of friendship with King Sahle Sellassie.

The Irish brothers Antoine and Arnaud Abbadie visited Ethiopia 1837–45, mostly in the Galla country, under the auspices of the Geographical Society of France. Under those of the French Academy of Sciences, M. Rochet d'Hericourt made two visits in 1839–40 and 1842.

It was more than normal curiosity and scientific or missionary interest that attracted these western visitors. The commerce of Ethiopia still had its reputation in Europe. And the West European powers were at least as interested in trade as in expanding the horizons of their knowledge. M. Lefebvre's report has more than scientific interest. He suggests to his government some clever means of capturing the Ethiopian market. It goes somewhat like this "Don't flood the Ethiopian market with all your goods at once. Start small and go steady. First import those articles which the Ethiopian is accustomed to. As they become more 'civilized' their needs will increase, and then new products can be introduced."

Lefebvre worked out a full scheme, with Massawa on the Red Sea Coast as port and warehouse, and a network of depots in the interior regulated from Gondar. In John Hotten's engaging but supercilious account of Ethiopia published in 1868 in London, there is a sentence in italics: "*It would be idle to speculate upon the hidden treasures that may be in store for that adventurous spirit who shall successfully perform the quest into these coy regions—for time and enterprise can alone reveal them.*"[2]

That significant sentence betrays the underlying motive of much of the great interest in Ethiopia on the part of the European nations. Hotten gives all the details he knows of the possiblities of economic exploitation of Ethiopia. After describing these possibilities, Hotten has another italicized sentence. "*A rich mercantile harvest is assuredly in*

[1] M. Lefebvre *et al. Voyage en Abyssinie exécuté pendant les années 1839–43*, 6 vols. (Paris, 1845). MM. Ferret et Galinier, *Voyage en Abyssinie dans les Provinces du Tigré, du Samen et de l'Ambara*, 3 vols. (Paris, 1847).

[2] *Abyssinia and its People or Life in the Land of Prester John*, p. 75.

store for those who shall unlock the portals of the Eastern Coast (of N. Africa), *and shall spread navigation upon waters that have heretofore been barren.*"

The rise of Kassa, known to the West as Theodore (Atsé Theodoros), can be understood only in the context of the prevailing anarchy in the country and the growing menace of economic exploitation and colonial subjugation by the powerful West.

The reign of Theodore is well-documented from Ethiopian as well as western sources.[1] In Ethiopia the condition of the Church is always closely allied to the situation of the State, and Emperor Theodore's attitudes and policies were just as much an expression of the Ethiopian Church's will as of that of the State.

The French Consul at Gondar, M. Guillaume Le-Jean (1860–2), published in the columns of *Revue des Deux Mondes* (November 1864) the memoirs of his stay in Ethiopia. The Egyptian bishops who led the Ethiopian Church seem to have been corrupt beyond measure. Emperor Theodore was crowned by Abuna Salama the Egyptian bishop on 7 February 1855. Soon after the coronation Theodore broke with Abuna Salama, and imprisoned him. Perhaps the reason for Theodore's contempt of the *abuna* can be seen from this account of M. Le-Jean:

> The present patriarch of Ethiopia (1864) is one of the most wretched specimens of the Coptic clergy. Haughty, violent, avaricious, and a meddler, he spends his time between usury, intrigue and commerce—and what commerce!...
>
> The character of Salama was so notorious that one day his confessor publicly disclosed his last confession, and informed the faithful that the Patriarch had nine mistresses, of whom two were nuns. His ignorance is so proverbial that the professors of theology occasionally submit knotty questions to him for solution, which he commonly does by excommunicating the inquirers.[2]

Emperor Theodore was born in 1818, son of a minor chief in Kwara, on his mother's side of royal lineage. Poverty and adversity hardened him from early infancy. Trained as a *debtera* or scribe, he later became a free-lance robber in the romantic tradition, with the whole village of Kwara faithful and obedient to him. He was intelligent and brave, well-versed in the Scriptures and yet ruthless in his treatment of enemies

[1] The main Ethiopian source is edited and published by Enno Littmann, *The Chronicle of King Theodore, Amharic Text* (Princeton, The University Library, 1902) and in the *Annali dell'Instituto Universitario Orientale di Napoli*, Nuova serie, vol. VI, 1957, vol. VII, 1958 and vol. VIII, 1959.

[2] English summary in John C. Hotten, *op. cit.* p. 93.

until they were vanquished, abstemious and continent, yet fierce-tempered.

By 1855 this fugitive leader of a band of robbers had become absolute monarch of most of Ethiopia. C. R. Markham has remarked:

> Theodore, the new king of kings of Ethiopia, was certainly the most remarkable man that has appeared in Africa for some centuries... At the date of his assumption of the regal title, Theodore was thirty-seven years of age, of medium stature, but with a well-knit muscular frame capable of enduring any amount of fatigue—a noble bearing and majestic walk—and he was the best shot, the best spearman, the best runner, and the best horseman in Abyssinia.[1]

The British Consul, Plowden, said of Theodore that he was generous to excess, free from all cupidity, merciful to his vanquished enemies, and strictly continent, but subject to violent bursts of anger and possessed of unyielding pride and fanatical religious zeal. He sought to break the power of the feudal chiefs, to abolish slavery, and to restore law and order in the country. His wife, Tewabetch, was his inspiring genius, beautiful and intelligent.

Theodore was a Jihādist in reverse, and that probably was his great mistake. He exhausted his strength in fruitless campaigns against the Muslimized Galla tribes. He declared that Muslims in Ethiopia would either have to be baptized as Christians or leave the country.

While he was engaged in campaigns against the Gallas, some chiefs in Gojjam and Semyen rebelled, with the support of Italian Catholics (Fr. de Jacobis) and French government officials (M. Belliard). Theodore's campaign against the rebels was swift, ruthless, and successful, but in these battles he lost his best friends and advisers, the two noble Englishmen Liqamakuas Bell and Consul Plowden, as well as his wife Tewabetch. These were replaced by ignorant sycophants. Theodore became cruel and heartless, suspicious and cynical.

When British Consul Cameron arrived (1862) at the camp of King Theodore with gifts from the British Queen, he was well received and, found himself in the company of several European missionaries. Six of these, Flad, Waldmeier, Saalmüller, Bender, Meyer and Keinzlin were laymen sent by old Dr Krapf. King Theodore wanted them to work for the country rather than to preach. They were set to making weapons and roads. There were several other missionaries, mostly from the German-speaking lands. Several of these had married Ethiopian wives.

[1] *A History of the Abyssinian Expedition*, p. 65.

Emperor Theodore's letter to Queen Victoria carried back by Consul Cameron, has now become famous:

In the name of the Father, of the Son, and of the Holy Ghost, God Three in one, Elect of God, King of Kings, Twodros of Ethiopia to Her Majesty Queen Victoria, Queen of England.

I trust that Your Majesty is in good health. By the power of God I am quite well. My fathers the Emperors had forgotten our Creator, and so God gave their Kingdom to the Gallas and the Turks. But He has created me, lifted me up from the dust, and granted this Empire to my rule. He has endowed me with power, and enabled me to stand in the place of my fathers. By His power I have put the Gallas to flight. I have asked the Turks also to leave the land of my forefathers, but they are refusing. I will soon have to wrestle with them.

Mr Plowden and my late Grand Chamberlain, the Englishman Bell, used to tell me that there is a great Christian Queen who loves all Christians. When they told me that they are able to introduce me to her and to establish friendship between us, then that made me very happy. I gave them my love, assuming that I had found Your Majesty's goodwill. All men are mortal, and my enemies, hoping to injure me, killed my friends.[1] But by the power of God, I have avenged them, exterminated these enemies, leaving not one alive, even those of my own kin, in order that by the power of God, I may gain your friendship.

I was prevented by the Turks who occupy the sea coast from sending to you an embassy during my difficult times. Consul Cameron came then with a letter and presents of friendship. I was happy, by the power of God, to hear of your welfare, and to have the assurances of your friendship. I thank you very much for the presents I have duly received.

I am afraid that if I send envoys with valuable presents of friendship,[2] even by the hand of Consul Cameron, they may be seized by the Turks. It is my desire that you will arrange for the safe passage of my envoys all along the way.

I would like to have a reply to this letter by the hand of Consul Cameron, and that he can go with my embassy to England. Behold how Muslims oppress the Christians!

Cameron sent the letter and gifts to Victoria through Aden; they reached the Foreign Office on 12 February 1863. Queen Victoria's failure to answer the letter was taken as an insult by Theodore. Poor Cameron, who returned to Theodore, was embarrassed when questioned about the reply from Victoria. He could not explain that there was a recent change in the Foreign Office in London, that Earl Russell

[1] I.e. Bell and Plowden.

[2] According to the Ethiopian chronicles the gifts sent to Queen Victoria were a gold decorated saddle, a gold decorated shield and gold shoes.

was interested only in trade and not in protecting Ethiopia against the Turks. Theodore became convinced that both Britain and France were insincere, and that they favoured the Turks.

To confirm his suspicions of the British, the news reached him that in 1863 the Turkish government of Jerusalem had unjustly given the Abyssinian Church and convent to the Egyptian Copts. The British are reported to have tried to intercede with the Turks, but the Pasha refused to listen, on the ground that Ethiopians were Turkish citizens. The news that reached Theodore was that the British had failed to help the Ethiopians in Jerusalem.[1] Theodore began to suspect the *bona fides* not only of the western governments but also of Consul Cameron himself. The missionary Stern had meanwhile written a book[2] on the Falashas which contained adverse references to Theodore.

In an outburst of temper Theodore had Cameron and Stern arrested and tortured to elicit information as to who had given Stern the stories he had published. They were imprisoned along with the Italian Pietro and the Irish lad McKilvie in the fortress of Magdala.

The discourtesy of Queen Victoria and her government was to cost both nations great expense and the loss of their mutual friendship. Theodore had seen the Foreign Office letter to Cameron asking him not to meddle in Ethiopian affairs.

From this time on Theodore became violent and irresponsible.

He began to lose control of his own affairs. Menelik, the heir of Shoa, escaped from the prison of Magdala and joined the Gallas, the enemies of Theodore. Theodore's tyranny provoked rebellions in all parts of the Empire. Shoa became independent again under Menelik. Kassa of Tigre conquered Tigre and became sovereign in the North.

When power was thus slipping from Theodore's hands, England decided, tardily enough, to send a reply to Theodore's letter. In June 1864 Mr Hormuzd Rassam, a native of Mosul in Iraq, was chosen to carry Her Majesty's letter to Emperor Theodore and negotiate the release of Cameron. Lieutenant Prideaux of the Bombay Staff Corps, who accompanied Rassam, has left us a full and vivid account of the mission to Theodore's Court.[3]

A clever trick was played on the British Embassy. Cameron and com-

[1] For a historical account of this controversy see Otto Meinardus, *The Copts in Jerusalem* (Cairo, 1960).

[2] H. A. Stern, *Wanderings among the Falashas* (1862).

[3] See chapter III of Markham, *History of the Abyssinian Expedition*. This chapter was written by Prideaux himself.

pany were ostensibly released. They joined the Embassy which had been received by Theodore and sent to Kuarata, where they were to stay. The Embassy was soon joined by a large number of missionaries and other foreigners. They were treated badly and moved from place to place. Theodore was testing them to see if they were allies of the Turks.[1] Rassam tried to tell Theodore that he was mistreating the embassy of the British Queen. Obviously the warning was not heeded.

Soon the Embassy found itself in prison in the fortress of Magdala, along with some of the prisoners whose release they came to secure. They were treated well. They had their Indian servants to cook for them. Their money was not taken away from them. They cultivated the yard with garden vegetables. Abuna Salama was in prison with them.

The sequel to the story is well-known. The expedition of Sir Robert (later Lord) Napier landed in Ethiopia in December 1867. On 15 April 1868 Theodore shot himself at Magdala which had been captured by the British. Before he committed suicide, he sent a letter to Napier, who had demanded the surrender of his person, in which he said:

> Believing that all power had been given to me, I had established my Christian people in this heathen spot...God has given you the power. See that you forsake not these people. It is a heathen land...His [God's] will be done. I had intended, if God has so decreed, to conquer the whole world, and it was my desire to die if my purpose could not be fulfilled. Since the day of my birth till now no man has dared to lay hands on me. I had hoped, after subduing all my enemies in Ethiopia, to lead my army against Jerusalem, and expel from it the Turks. A warrior who has dandled strong men in his arms like infants will never suffer himself to be dandled in the arms of others.[2]

What was the state of the Ethiopian Church during the reign of Theodore? The documentation here is quite limited. Markham's book describes some of the church buildings,[3] but gives little information about the religious life of the people.

We know that during Theodore's reign the patriarch Kyrillos IV of Alexandria came to Ethiopia and stayed for two years.

The contemporary account of Hotten, though highly prejudiced, gives a few glimpses:[4]

> When Theodore gave Hotten an audience, the Egyptian Abuna and the Ethiopian Etchegue (Chief Abbot) sat to the right and the left of the king,

[1] As a matter of fact, Britain had signed a treaty with Turkey against Russia.

[2] Markham, *op. cit.* p. 331.

[3] *Op. cit.* pp. 193 ff.

[4] Hotten, *op. cit.* pp. 239 ff.

while all the nobles stood. Hotten describes the trial of an Ethiopian Roman Catholic monk before the king, who asked him to dispute with the Egyptian Abuna. The monk said he would dispute only before the Pope of Rome, since he did not recognize the authority of anyone present. This was insubordination to the Sovereign and he was sentenced to death by the King. But Hotten claims he was able to get the sentence commuted to life imprisonment.

Hotten thought that the priesthood was generally more influential in the country than the feudal gentry. The clergy, according to him "holds in chains the mind of the people; moulds at will customs, morals, and all the social ties, which have consequently remained almost unchanged, amidst the change of dynasties, the ruinous shocks of international war, and the gradual crumbling away of a wide and Christian Empire".[1]

Hotten thinks that "the spirit of Protestantism, or free inquiry is not more welcome in Abyssinia than in other primitive churches"; but it is no great temptation to the people, and so the Government has not imposed any severe measures against it. The Church teaches only one book to the children of the Laity, namely the Psalms of David.[2] They do not forbid the learning of other books, but only discourage it, limiting the study of theology as far as possible to the priests and the *debteras*.

The larger towns are all sacred cities of refuge, and attract all sorts of dissolute and dangerous characters. The priests hold absolute sway in such towns. This, and the power of excommunication, make the priests powerful.

As a Protestant, Hotten thinks the Ethiopian Orthodox Church "a stumbling-block to improvement", and feels that while hating the Roman Church, the Ethiopian Church uses its methods to secure the blind submission of the people. "No one save the priest himself is ever instructed in the Gospel in any tongue. Great adoration is paid to the Virgin Mary, and to numberless saints and angels. Their Churches are filled with pictures, to which, when unveiled, the multitude bows with reverence. Fasting is rigidly insisted on."

Churches are numerous, and the buildings themselves are revered as residences of the Saint in whose name they are consecrated. The anti-Catholic Hotten sees the Ethiopians manufacturing miracles to increase the revenue of the churches.

Priests with their white turbans are highly revered. Each man has a priest-confessor, a *nafs-abbat*, or spiritual father. The confessors of the nobility are indulgent. There are many monasteries and more solitary

[1] *Op. cit.*, p. 158.

[2] This does not appear to have been the case, as shown by other sources.

monks, but Hotten thinks the life in the monasteries is very corrupt. Nunneries do not exist. The solitary monks, according to Hotten, "dwell in gloomy forests, feeding on roots, and exposed to ferocious animals". To Hotten's Protestant mind, they "are sometimes as sincere as they are useless".

Hotten is severely critical of the moral standards of the people:

> Thus it is not wonderful if lying, sexual intercourse, intoxication, or manslaughter, are regarded as venial...Their present immorality does not argue a bad nature in the Abyssinian; on the contrary, I am astonished that good and moral men are still found, and it is certain that Christianity, even thus debased, has hitherto saved them from wantonness of crime and excess of cruelty that stains the records of almost all African races, and of some in other quarters of the globe.[1]

Hotten thinks that the early English Protestant mission was "unceremoniously ejected" because they failed to be sensitive to the Ethiopian's horror of violating the fast, disrespect to a priest, or eating with Muslims.

The *echege* or chief abbot lived in Gondar, in Hotten's time. The Coptic *abuna* is almost worshipped by the people. Abuna Salama is the 118th in succession, and for each new Egyptian *abuna*, the Ethiopians have to send "some thousand dollars". He should be living in Gondar, but he has for the present been banished to a place near Adowah. The *abuna* has to consecrate all churches and ordain all priests and deacons. Crowds of pilgrims gather in his court, waiting for blessing, absolution or ordination.

French Catholic missions, with three bishops, are using money to establish themselves. The *abuna* is fighting them.

Priests are permitted to marry one wife, but not a second time. The *abuna* and the *echege* are of course celibate monks.

Priests receive no pay. They have the income of the Church land, as well as dues from those to whom they are confessors. The pious rich give them gifts. Dues have to be paid also on the occasion of births, baptisms, weddings, funerals and occasions of commemoration of the dead (*tezkar*). The priests are "numerous as the locusts" according to the Ethiopians themselves.

Hotten recognizes that the Church has preserved whatever learning, culture and civilization there is. But the priesthood is getting progressively more indolent and corrupt.

[2] *Op. cit.*, pp. 161–2.

Hotten describes the Church literature, which includes besides the canonical and apocryphal books of the Old and New Testaments, "some monkish legends, a code of laws, and the chronicles of their kings, containing in a mass of rubbish a few sentences worthy of notice". Painting, which once flourished, is now on the decline. Illuminated missals can be bought cheap, since there is very little demand. Hotten says "there are about four hundred works in the country, of which eighty-one relate to the Bible". Pilgrimages to Jerusalem are annual and popular.

The *debteras* are more learned than the priests. But they also exploit the people by writing amulets and charms against disease and evil. The *debteras* practice magic as well as medicine.

There are some Jews, despised, but not persecuted.

That is as much as we can glean from Hotten, who published his book while the British captives of Theodore were yet to be released.

Theodore died in 1868. Napier left in May, with a gold chalice, the crowns of Theodore and the *abuna* and the Imperial copy of the *Kebra-Negest* (or the chronicle of Kings).[1]

Anarchy reigned for four years. In 1872 Ras Kassa of Tigre was crowned Emperor of Ethiopia, to be known as Johannes IV.

The Twentieth Century

Johannes was able and brave, but the scramble for Africa became his constant headache. And the scramblers were not all Europeans. Khedive Ismā'īl of Egypt drove the Turks out of the Red Sea Coast and occupied even Berbera and Harar. Johannes managed to rout his forces in 1875 and 1876.

The Suez Canal had been inaugurated in 1869. This opened the door for Britain, France and Italy, and Johannes (1872–89) did not have sufficient experience to know how to handle these ambitious and enterprising strangers. But his suspicion of missionaries, both Catholic and Protestant, was complete. This is understandable. In Ethiopia, a priest is as much concerned about the welfare of his nation as of his Church. In the case of foreigners as well, the missionaries must be just as much in league with the plans of their nations.

In 1880 he issued an edict on Islam, ordering all Muslims to accept Christianity or leave Ethiopia, as some of his predecessors had done.

[1] The chalice is still in the Victoria and Albert Museum, London. The Imperial Crown was returned by King George V to the present Emperor in 1925.

But now as then, it was not enforced. In 1883 he issued another declaration granting toleration to Muslims in certain districts. In 1884 Johannes bargained with the British and regained the city of Keren and the use of Massawa as a port. He died at Metemma in a campaign against the Dervishes during which he is said to have slaughtered 60,000 Muslim followers of the Mahdī of the Sudan.

Emperor Johannes wanted very much to liberate the Ethiopian Church from the Egyptian yoke, as a preliminary to its reform. To this end, he petitioned the Armenian Patriarch in Constantinople to send Armenian bishops to Ethiopia, but public opinion in Ethiopia was against this proposal.[1] Then the Emperor requested the patriarch in Alexandria to consecrate one Archbishop and three bishops for Ethiopia. It is strange indeed that no Ethiopian bishop had been consecrated by the Egyptian Church up to that time.

Johannes caused the chief of the Wallo Galla, Muḥammad 'Alī, to be baptized a Christian. Many in Wallo followed their chief in becoming Christian; Islam never had very deep roots in Wallo.

When Johannes died, King Menelik of Shoa was crowned Emperor (1889–1913). He succeeded where Theodore had failed, in welding the warring tribes into a single nation and starting the process of modernization. His campaigns against the Gallas led to the expansion of Ethiopia right up to Khartoum and Lake Victoria.

Meanwhile the scramble for Africa was taking on new proportions. The Italians bought the port of Assab in 1882, and were infiltrating in large numbers into the surrounding country. In 1885 they took Massawa. The British in the same year, took Berbera and Zeila. The French took Djibouti. Johannes had struggled against this, but to no avail. Menelik played it wisely with the foreigners.

In Menelik's reign the Italians kept advancing into Ethiopian territory, and by 1895 had taken Agordat and Aduwa. In the famous battle of Aduwa in 1896, Menelik's 70,000 troops put the Italians to flight. Ethiopia's prestige in the West ran high.

Menelik consolidated his Empire and began using European technicians for the modernization of the country. In 1893 he founded Addis Ababa (*New Flower*) as his capital. Addis Ababa was surrounded by many famous monasteries[2] and the choice pleased the Church leaders. He was friendly to the French, and the French language became the

[1] H. M. Hyatt, *The Church of Abyssinia* (London, 1928), p. 46.
[2] Zuquala, Debra Libanos, Yerrer.

fashion among the educated nobility. The French built for him a railway from Djibouti to Addis Ababa.

Menelik subdued all the Muslim tribes, but did not attempt any forcible conversions. Harar was occupied and placed under the Governorship of Ras Makonnen, the father of Emperor Haile Sellassie. The 'Afar and Somali tribes, which had once carried out their *jihād* against Ethiopia under Aḥmad Grañ, were now peaceful though somewhat discontented citizens of Ethiopia.

Before Menelik died he nominated his grandson Lij Iyasu as his heir, and entrusted him to the safe keeping of the Egyptian Abuna Mathewos. Menelik had obviously more confidence in the *abuna* than in his grandson, and had ordered that if Iyasu failed to obey the *abuna*, he should be excommunicated.

So when Menelik died the *abuna* proclaimed Iyasu as Emperor. Iyasu's father was Negus Mikhael of Wollo, and his mother Shoa-Aregash, the favourite daughter of Menelik. Iyasu soon showed Muslim leanings. He had a genealogy made up for him showing descent from the prophet Mohammed rather than from King Solomon. There was an attempted Muslim coup, with the support of the Galla and Wollo Muslims.

Meanwhile World War I had broken out in Europe (1914). German and Turkish diplomats encouraged Iyasu's plans. He put away his Christian wife Romane-Worq and started a harem of the daughters of 'Afar and Galla chiefs around Harar, and a daughter and a niece of the Muslim chief of Kaffa.

Iyasu finally betrayed himself when in 1916 he officially placed Ethiopia under the religious authority of Turkey and had a crescent embroidered on to the Ethiopian flag. He called his fellow-Muslims to another *jihād* against the Christians of Ethiopia.

Abuna Mathewos now began mustering a powerful revolt against Iyasu and his father, Negus Mikhael. The Shoan chiefs revolted under the leadership of Ras Tafari, the present Emperor, and Iyasu was deposed by public proclamation of the *abuna* on 27 September 1917. Menelik's other daughter, Iyasu's aunt, Zowditu was proclaimed Empress with Ras Tafari Makonnen as regent and heir to the throne.

In 1926 when Abuna Mathewos died, Ras Tafari asked the patriarch of Alexandria to send an Egyptian *abuna* and at the same time to consecrate several Ethiopian bishops. This had been requested earlier on by Emperor Johannes. But only now did the Egyptian Church give heed.

In 1929 Kirillus was consecrated *abuna*, and also four Ethiopian bishops were consecrated. In 1930, the patriarch of Alexandria[1] visited Ethiopia and consecrated the *echege* or chief abbot as bishop. Thus for the first time in sixteen centuries of Ethiopian Church history there were five Ethiopian bishops.

Though Haile Sellassie I (the name which Ras Tafari assumed at his coronation in 1930, means "the power of the Trinity") is a devout Christian, he has always been tolerant to non-Christians, especially to Muslims. In principle, there is religious liberty in modern Ethiopia, though the social prejudices are still powerfully operative. The Constitution promulgated in 1931 does not mention any established State religion, though the Emperor is the chief and most active patron of the Ethiopian Orthodox Church. There have been Muslims in high ministerial and ambassadorial posts for quite some time now.

For anyone with some awareness of the Ethiopian Church's glorious past, her present state can be attributed, at least in part, to the administrative difficulties under which she has lived for centuries.

With thousands and thousands of churches and at least five times that many clergymen, the Ethiopian Church has had only one bishop for the whole country for centuries. And that bishop, the *abuna*, was always a Copt from Egypt. This is supposed to be based on the "Eighty Disciplinary Canons of Nicaea" (a seventh-century forgery?).[2] An Ethiopian Archbishop was consecrated for the first time on 13 January 1951.

During the sixteen centuries of Egyptian domination, the Coptic *abuna* was unable to care for the spiritual needs of the multitude of believers in the vast, rugged, mountainous country of Ethiopia.

He was not authorized to consecrate bishops. He could only ordain priests, deacons, and choristers, which he did in large numbers and without much discernment of their qualifications for the ministry. Candidates for ordination travelled weeks and weeks on foot to meet the *abuna* and be ordained by him. There was no adequate machinery for examining the qualifications of the candidates. Large numbers were ordained, on payment of the required fees, with little adherence to the traditional form of priestly ordination in the Eastern churches.

Another factor which led to the corruption of the Ethiopian clergy was the system of land grants as the remuneration of the clergy. Most

[1] Anba Yuhannes XIX (1928–42).

[2] It is hardly conceivable that Nicaea in 325 could have said much about the jurisdiction over Ethiopia, when according to our evidence, the Christian Church in Ethiopia had its first bishop only in 330.

of the clergy never received any salary. Quite often a priest would be given a large tract of land as his means of subsistence for life. All too often the possibility of securing the land has been the main incentive in seeking ordination. The laity paid some dues to the clergy only on such occasions as baptism, funerals and memorial services for the departed. But in general the clergy were more interested in ploughing the land than in preaching the Gospel or leading the people in worship.

The conflicts between the monks on one side and the *debteras* on the other have also been a source of trouble. The monks despised the *debteras* who were married and therefore "unholy". The *debteras* who were both religious teachers and choristers were generally better educated than the monks and therefore despised them.

The development of an educated clergy whether married or monastic with adequate ability to care for the spiritual needs of the parishioners is still something to be achieved in the Ethiopian Church.

The Church today

There are many popular misconceptions about the Ethiopian Orthodox Church. Its size is in dispute; estimates vary from 3·5 million to 15 millions. There are no census figures on which to base our estimate. If the population of Ethiopia could be estimated at 22 millions, the number of Christians would be about 12 millions. According to official figures released by the Orthodox Church there are 835 monasteries, 1,032 chapels, 12,000 parish churches.

Too many authors indulge their fancy in estimating the number of clergymen in the Orthodox Church. A recent book mentions varying estimates of the number of the clergy from one quarter of the Christian population to one fifth of the number of male Christians.[1] In other words it ranges from one priest to every three laymen, to one to every four males in the laity. These estimates have in fact no basis at all. However unreliable the official estimates may be they are certainly much closer to the truth. These estimates gives the figures as below:

Number of priests	73,563
Number of deacons	52,552
Choristers	39,040
Total	165,155

[1] George A. Lipsky, *Ethiopia* (New Haven, 1962), p. 107.

Another popular misconception is that the Emperor is the Head of the Church.[1] This is not true. The Head of the Church is at present the patriarch. The Emperor is the first layman. He still has considerable temporal authority over the Church. The Constitution of 1955 says: "The Ethiopian Orthodox Church founded in the 4th century on the doctrines of St Mark, is the established Church of the Empire and is supported by the State. The Emperor shall always profess the Ethiopian Orthodox faith. The name of the Emperor shall be mentioned in all religious services." The Emperor has also the power of final veto over the appointment of archbishops and bishops elected by electoral colleges consisting of representatives of the clergy and laity.

Yet another popular misconception is that the Church owns one-third of the land of the country. According to official figures land directly owned by the Church comes to 54,892·128 *gashas* of land which works out to 5 million acres. This is about 2·1 per cent of the total land area of the country. In other words the land owned by the Church is one fiftieth of the total rather than one third.

The total income of the Church is also often over-estimated. Revenue from land comes to about 1 million U.S. dollars per year. There may be an income of about half a million more from other sources. The central offices of the Church employ some 394 office staff, about 1,000 teachers and 150 evangelists. The Church operates 539 primary schools with a total enrollment of about 50,000.

The Church runs three theological schools. Unfortunately these have produced very few priests. The Holy Trinity Theological School established in Addis Ababa by the Emperor in 1944 has been remarkable in its failure to produce vocations for the Christian ministry. The Haile Sellassie I University has now a theological faculty with a very small number of students, few of whom are likely to choose the priesthood as their vocation. This fact of the poverty of educated clergymen does not augur well for the future of the Ethiopian Church. At present there are almost no clergymen with a proper university degree. The educated laity in the cities generally regard the Church as reactionary and outmoded. There are many educated laymen devout in their faith, but the Church seems unable to make use of them in its spiritual leadership. Even in the villages there is great discontent with the low moral standards and the avarice and ignorance of the clergy.

[1] J. Spencer Trimingham, *The Christian Church in Ethiopia* (World Dominion Press, 1950), p. 17.

The Church now has thirteen dioceses with their own archbishops and in some cases with suffragan bishops. One archbishop is the head of the Ethiopian community in Jerusalem. The patriarch is also the archbishop of the dioceses of Shoa and abbot of the monastery of Debra Libanos. Very few of the archbishops and bishops speak any foreign language. They are in general unable to deal with the problems posed by the spread of Western education and civilization.

It is true that all Orthodox Churches in the world have had to pass through a similar critical stage in confronting the modern world. They have all with the exception of Ethiopia begun to deal with the problem in one form or another. The break-through has always been in the form of a few priests who have been trained in modern universities. The Ethiopian Church may take another thirty years before it is able to develop even a nucleus of such educated leadership. It is likely, however, that by that time the Church will have lost the loyalty of many of its educated members.

The Emperor has understood this problem and has sought to develop such leadership, but his efforts so far have been largely unsuccessful. With the declining influence of the Emperor among the educated people of the country he may find it more difficult than ever to achieve his purpose. Even the young men whom he has sent abroad for theological studies have shown little inclination, on their return, to be ordained as priests.

Whatever new life there exists in the Church seems to find expression in lay organizations. These organizations have as their goal the strengthening of the spiritual life of the Church and the propagation of the Gospel. Their names are impressive:

1. *Sewasewa Berhan* (Spreading of the Light) Society for the Preaching of the Gospel.
2. *Haimanote Abew* (The Faith of our Fathers) College Students' Association.
3. *Mahbere Hawariat* (The Apostolic Society).
4. *Yewengel Malaktennoch Mahber* (Apostles of the Gospel Society).
5. *Mahbere Sellassie* (Holy Trinity Society).
6. *Fenote Berhan* (Dissemination of Light) Society.
7. *Fere Haimanot* (Fruit of the Faith) Society, and so on.

Several of these societies are extremely active, running night schools, preacher-training courses and programmes of radio broadcasting. These are supported by voluntary contributions of the laity.

The bishops, especially in those dioceses with large numbers of pagans, have been active in evangelism. It is estimated that about a million pagans have been baptized by the diocesan clergy in the last ten years. However, due to lack of adequate catechetical instruction and pastoral care the spiritual nurture of these newly baptized people has been in a regrettable state of neglect.

The early Roman Catholic missions, because of their close connexion with West European political expansion and their lack of sensitivity to Ethiopian patriotic feelings, came to nothing. Only in Eritrea did Roman Catholic and Protestant missions succeed in securing an adequate foothold. In 1866 Swedish Evangelical missionaries landed at Massawa and began work among the pagans. They founded schools and hospitals, learnt the local language and won the affection and trust of the pagan people. The United Presbyterian Church of U.S.A. began work among the Gallas in 1918. In 1914 the British and Foreign Bible Society secured permission for the sale of Scripture. The Sudan Interior Mission came in 1927. They have at present forty stations in the country. They run thirty-four schools, four hospitals, forty clinics and two leprosaria. They have 250 missionaries in the country. Unfortunately their exclusivism and fanaticism have prevented them both from co-operating with other Protestant missions and from winning the confidence of the Ethiopian people in general. The three main Ethiopian Protestant groups are (*a*) the Makane Yesus Church (Swedish origin), (*b*) the Bethel Church (American Presbyterian), and (*c*) the Sudan Interior Mission group. These Christians are mainly fundamentalist in their theological orientation and generally incapable of a sympathetic understanding of the Ethiopian Orthodox Church.

Roman Catholics are few in number. Their main strength is in Eritrea which had been under Italian influence for a considerable length of time. The Ethiopian Roman Catholics now have their own bishops, but the political associations of Roman Catholic missions in the past preclude any possibility of a large-scale spread of Roman Catholicism in Ethiopia. Even today to become a Roman Catholic is more of an act of disloyalty to the nation than to become a Protestant.

The foreign missions are under the administrative control of the Ministry of Education and wherever they do educational and medical work they are appreciated by the government.

The Mission of the Church can hardly be carried out by the foreign missions in Ethiopia. In the last analysis it has to be the task of the Ethiopian Orthodox Church. The churches outside Ethiopia would be more loyal to the missionary command and more effective in bringing the light of the Gospel to the people of Ethiopia if they would concentrate their efforts in assisting the Church of Ethiopia to fulfil her God-given mission.

This assistance can hardly come without an initiative springing from within the Ethiopian Church itself. As in all Orthodox Churches, this initiative has to manifest itself in four main areas: University Student work, theological training of the priests, participation of the laity in the mission of the Church, and the revitalization of the monastic movement for quickening the life of the Church and for the proclamation of the Gospel among Ethiopia's many millions of pagans.

II. THE SYRIAN ORTHODOX CHURCH IN THE MIDDLE EAST

In the fourth and fifth centuries the Syrian Church of Antioch extended over the Oriental and Asian provinces of the Byzantine Empire as well as over large areas of the Persian Empire to the East.

In the latter half of the fifth century the Syrian Church faced two crises. Following the Council of Chalcedon in 451, large numbers began to defect to the King's (Melkite) party which accepted that Council. At the same time worsening tensions between the Persian and the Byzantine empires made Eastern Christians in the Persian Empire suspect as sympathizers with or agents of Byzantium. This led to an autonomous jurisdiction being formed in the Eastern Syrian Church with Ctesiphon (present Baghdad) in Babylonia as its seat. The Western Syrian Church thus became in effect much smaller.

The autonomy of the Persian Syrian Church, which the West later called Nestorian, gave the spur to a missionary expansion which embraced vast areas of central and southern Asia including China and India. The Syrian occupant of the primatial See of Antioch styles himself to this day as "Patriarch of Antioch and all the East". In the thirteenth century there seem to have been more than 230 dioceses grouped in twenty-seven metropolitan areas in this Asian Church outside the Byzantine Empire.[1] But their relation to Antioch was, to put it mildly, without much cordial or concrete expression.

[1] R. P. Janin, *The Separated Eastern Churches* (Eng. tr.; London, 1933), p. 201.

With the rise of Islam, the Church of Antioch faced its third and most severe crisis. The Christian peoples of the Middle East, restive under the dominance of a Hellenic culture, soon accepted the living semitic religion of the Prophet of Mecca. Only in rare moments did the leaders of Constantinople see the perennial fact that enforced uniformity is always an enemy of wide-ranging unity.

Muslims were culturally well ahead of Byzantium and Rome, and surpassed all in vitality bordering on fanaticism.

Muslim law did for Christian Asia and Africa what the Code of Justinian (529) had earlier done for a pagan empire. Jacob Baradeus (*c.* 500–78) after whom the Greeks named the Syrian Christians as Jacobites, had reinvigorated the Syrian Orthodox Church in the face of repressive measures adopted by the Byzantine authorities who persecuted the Syrians on the charge of Monophysitism. Anti-hellenism and coerced conversions to Islam combined to decimate the Church in the Middle East.

The eleventh-century Crusades from the West finally resulted in Bohemond the Norman's capture of Antioch for himself. Navies from Venice, Genoa and Pisa co-operated in the siege, thus paving the way for a Roman Catholic missionary campaign.

The Arab conquest of Syria in 640 and the Mamlūk Turk conquest of 1291 were therefore warmly welcomed by Middle Eastern Christians. Many accepted Islam as bringing relief from Byzantine or European dominance.

Internal divisions continued to reduce the numbers of the Syrian Orthodox throughout the centuries. In 1656 Roman Catholics established a Uniate Church which first had many followers, but when the Syrians saw that Roman dominance was in no way to be preferred over Byzantine or Muslim hegemony, the Uniate Church also began to dwindle, at least soon after 1700. Though this Uniate Church has produced illustrious leaders like Patriarch Ignatius Ephrem Raḥmānī (1898–1929), its members today number less than 50,000.

The zenith of the Syrian Orthodox Church's achievements coincided with the peak period of the flourishing Muslim culture.[1] The thirteenth century, when the Renaissance had hardly begun to shine through the Dark Ages in the West, produced among the Syrians an erudite and encyclopaedic mind like Patriarch Gregory Bar Hebraeus (1226–86).

The decline, however, that started with the invasion of Tamerlane at the end of the fourteenth century, shows no signs of letting up even

[1] P. Kawerau, *Die Jakobitische Kirche in Zeitalter der Syrischen Renaissance* (Berlin, 1955).

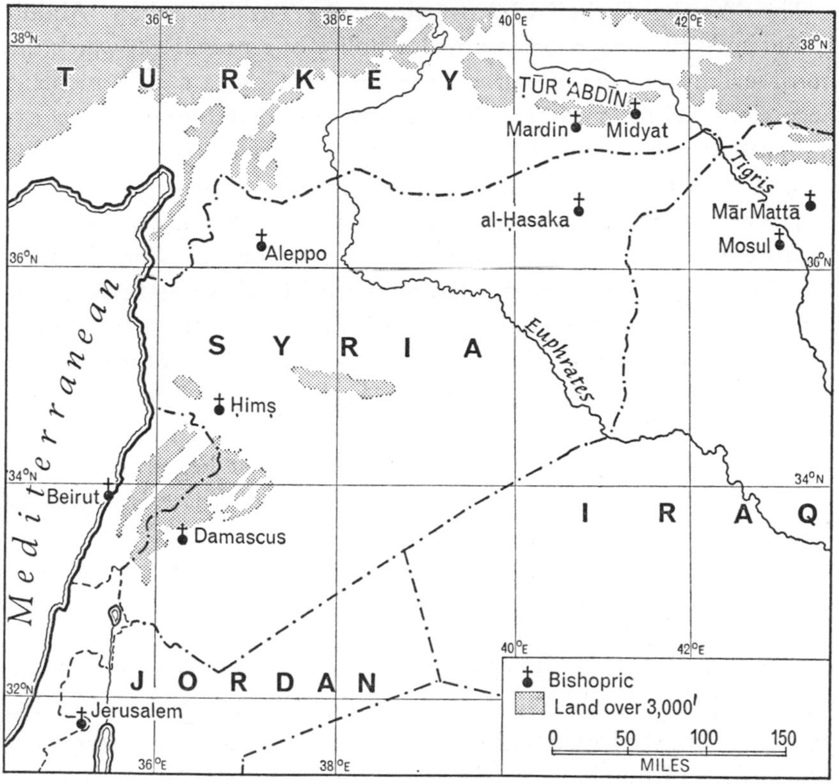

The Syrian Orthodox Church.

to this day. The Syrian Christians retreated from the scourge of the Turks into the mountains of Kurdistan. The Kurds were hospitable to them in the beginning. The economic experience and cultural advantages of the Syrians soon led to domination and exploitation of the Kurds, who retaliated in 1843, 1846 and 1860 with large-scale massacres of Syrian Christians.

In the nineteenth-century Turkish empire all Christians, whether Greeks, Latins, Syrians or Armenians, were always suspected of being in sympathy with the Western powers and with Russia. It was these latter that put pressure on Ottoman Turkey to grant independence to several Christian peoples in the great empire which once extended from Arabia to the Balkans. Thus Serbia became independent in 1812, Greece in 1829, Roumania in 1856, Bulgaria in 1878. The Levant came under French protection in 1861.

The "Young Turks" who overthrew the Turkish Sultan 'Abdülḥamid in April 1909, soon assumed a policy of repression towards the non-Muslim elements in Turkey, the Syrians, Greeks and Armenians becoming the main targets. The Armenians and Syrians were exterminated in large numbers. Those who could escape went to the Levant and later sought immigration to the Americas.

The census of 1905 showed the population of Syria, Lebanon and Jerusalem as 31·25 million of whom about a million were Christians. At the beginning of our century, Maronites and Melkites numbered about 300,000 each, with some 220,000 Uniate Catholics from the oriental rites. The estimated figures of 1905 show the number of Syrian Orthodox in these three countries together to have been 45,805, while there were already 21,520 Protestants.[1]

Modern Protestant missions to the middle East began in January 1819 under the initiative of the American Board of Commissioners for Foreign Missions, and were joined by the Irish in 1843, the British in 1829, and the Germans in 1860. By the beginning of our century there were thirty-five Protestant missionary societies operating in Syria.

Following World War I Syria and Lebanon were placed under French mandate, a period which favoured the activity of Roman Catholic missions. Many of the Syrian Orthodox capitulated to the attractive prospects, both spiritual and temporal, offered by a better-disciplined and wealthier Church.

There are about 200,000 Syrian Orthodox Christians today (not counting the Malabar Christians, who number 1·2 million today), of whom about 80,000 are in Syria.

The present patriarch, Mār Ignatius Ya'qūb III, has had his seat in the capital of Syria, Damascus, since 1959. Since the First World War the patriarch had his residence at Ḥimṣ (Emessa) and before that in Mardin in Turkey.

A considerable number of Syrian Orthodox live today in Iraq (Mosul) and Turkey (Ṭūr 'Abdīn). Some 30,000 live in the Americas.

The Church is divided into eleven dioceses, four in Syria (Damascus, Ḥimṣ, Aleppo and al-Ḥasaka), two in Iraq (Mosul and Mār Mattā), two in Turkey (Mardin and Midyat), one in Lebanon (Beirut), one in Jordan (St Mark's Convent, Jerusalem) and one in the U.S.A. (Hacken-

[1] See article on *Syria* by H. H. Jessup in the New Schaff-Herzog Encyclopaedia of Religious Knowledge. The article, though revised, is still very much out of date.

sack, N.J.). The patriarch has an episcopal Vicar (ecumenical or *tibeloye*) who resides with him in Damascus.

Syrian monasticism once flourished and gave the lead to the whole Asian Church. Today a few struggling houses survive, Mār Mattā near Mosul, Ṭūr ʻAbdīn in Turkey and St Mark's in Jerusalem being the best known. The number of monks in the whole Church is not very large.[1] They follow the order of St Antony and quite often are solitaries.

Liturgically the Syrian Church may claim credit on two counts—on having the widest liturgical variety (sixty-four different Syriac anaphorae are known, though only less than a dozen are in actual use), and for its closeness to the Jerusalem tradition of the primitive Church. Their present liturgical language, Syriac, was the Eastern dialect of Aramaic, so close to our Lord's own mother tongue. A few of the ancient Syrian families around Ṭūr ʻAbdīn in Turkey and some villages in Syria still speak a dialect of Aramaic or Syriac at home.

Since 1954 the Syrian Orthodox Church has adopted the Western or Gregorian Calendar, except in Jerusalem and Bethlehem where the Julian Calendar is still followed.

[1] For an engaging account of Syrian monasticism, see O. H. Parry's *Six Months in a Syrian Monastery* (London, 1895). A more up-to-date, historically oriented and less encouraging picture is in Jules Leroy, *Monks and Monasteries of the Near East* (Eng. tr.; Harrap, London, 1963).

CHAPTER 10

THE ARMENIAN CHURCH

The nineteenth and twentieth centuries as seen in the whole context of Armenian Church history have a crucial importance for the understanding of the present-day situation of the Armenian Church spread all over the world. This is not due simply to chronological proximity. These two centuries have marked the most decisive events related to the Armenian Church's life and mission to the Armenian people and to the Christian world at large. They are of a complex nature. On the one hand rapid developments in international relations and political upheavals in the whole Middle East extending from the Balkan countries to Transcaucasus, and, on the other hand, internal, national movements and achievements on social, cultural, educational and economic grounds deeply affected the life of the Armenian Church and shaped its present status. Therefore, the material is so rich, varied and complex that omissions and generalizations are unavoidable as one tries to compress the whole content of these two centuries into an intelligible presentation in the limits allotted to this study.

First of all, it is important to draw the picture of the political situation and indicate those events that have affected the life of the Armenian Church. When one realizes that the Armenian Church has continually been, but especially in the nineteenth century, most intimately, and almost inseparably, associated with the Armenian Nation, then a look at the political situation becomes necessary for a fuller understanding of the Armenian Church in modern times. Arnold Toynbee is quite justified in his comment referring to the Eastern Churches in the Ottoman Empire: "In the Near East a church is merely the foremost aspect of a nationality."[1]

THE POLITICAL SITUATION

At the beginning of the nineteenth century, the Armenian people lived under two major political allegiances: the Persian and Turkish rules. With the destruction of the Armenian Kingdom of Cilicia

[1] Arnold Toynbee, *The Treatment of Armenians in the Ottoman Empire* (London, 1916), pp. 617–18.

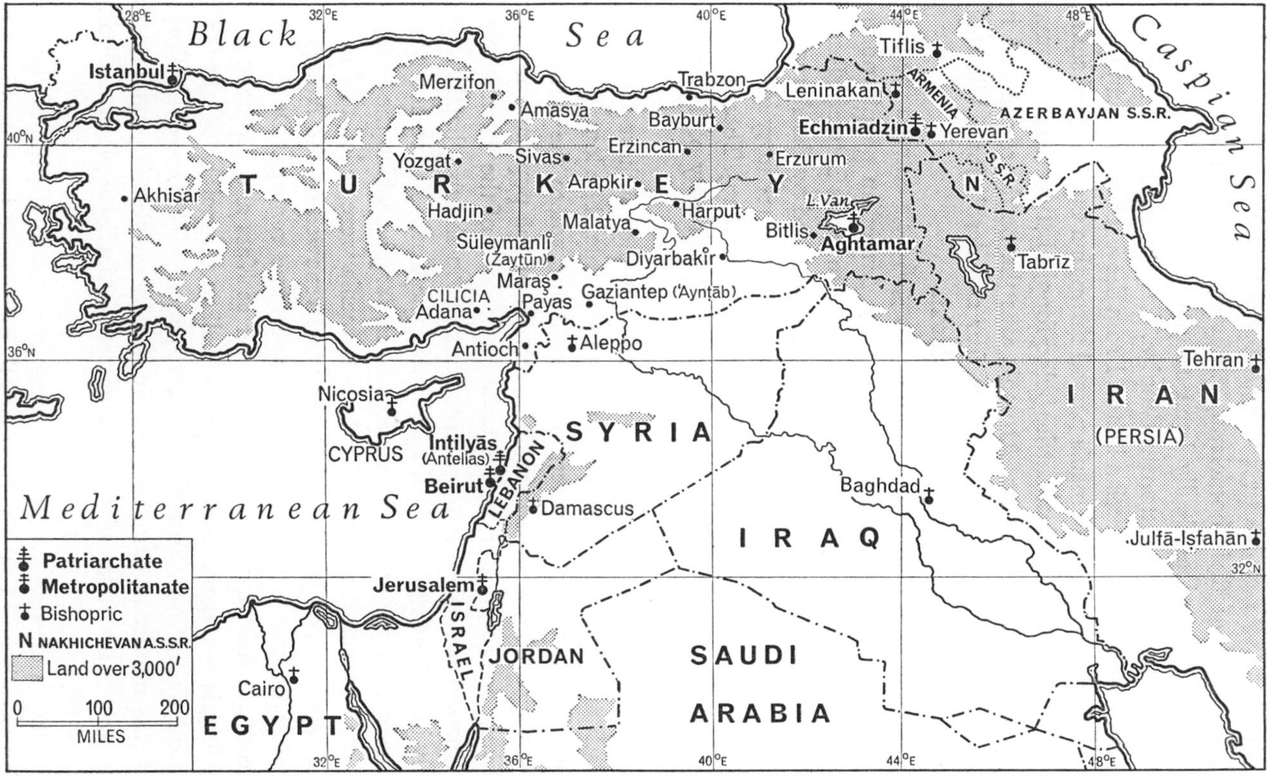

The Armenian Church.

(A.D. 1375), the Armenian people had lost their independence and in the largest part of their homeland, generally described as "Western Armenia", they had gradually been subjugated to the Turkish rule which soon became the Ottoman Empire. Eastern regions of Armenia fell under the rule of the Persian khans. From the fifteenth century to the eighteenth, the people of Armenia passed through a time of hard suffering because of the continuous battles being fought between the Ottoman sultans and the Persian shahs. Armenia was the battleground and its Christian population lived in constant fear and desolation while their country was being devastated and plundered.

In the beginning of the nineteenth century, Russia entered the Caucasus and consequently the situation of the Armenian people underwent considerable changes. Thus, after a series of wars between Russia and Persia, the Russian armies, being largely assisted by the Armenian volunteer corps, captured vast regions of Armenian territory including the plain of Ayrarat with Echmiadzin and Yerevan (1827). These regions were finally ceded by the Persians to Russia in the Treaty of Turkmanchay (1828).

As Russia had now secured a firm foothold in the southern Caucasus, the clash with the Ottoman Empire was inevitable. The long prepared policy of Russia was to penetrate Asia Minor where the Armenian people constituted a most influential section of the population. They had lived for centuries under the unbearable yoke of the Turkish rule. The Russian advance was quite considerable on the two battlefronts, namely in Asia Minor and in the Balkans. The Turks had to accept the terms of a Treaty signed in Adrianopolis in 1829 by which the bordering areas between Russia and Turkish Armenia were ceded to Russia.

The war between Russia and Turkey was renewed on the Armenian territories on two other occasions in the same century. During the Crimean war the Russians advanced as far as Kars and captured it in 1855. Russia was again successful in its Balkan campaigns of 1877–78. Her armies once more entered Turkish Armenia. This time the Turks ceded very important parts of Turkish Armenia to Russia by the terms of the successive treaties of San Stefano (3 March 1878) and Berlin (13 June 1878).

The effects of such events were very great upon the life of the Armenian people and Church. First of all, there were large numbers of Armenians who migrated from Turkey to Russia thus increasing the Armenian population in Eastern Armenia, which was soon to achieve a remarkable renaissance in educational, cultural, intellectual, social and economic fields. Secondly, the Russian rule was felt to be not as oppressive and humiliating for the Armenians as the Persian and Turkish dominations had been. Of course there was bitter resentment and disappointment among the Armenians when their hopes for an autonomous Armenia even within the boundaries of the Russian Empire were not fulfilled. The Russians, once established in the Caucasus, did not tolerate any autonomous community on the basis of national distinctness. Russia proved to be imperialistic to the great disillusionment of the Armenians.

But in spite of this disillusionment in Eastern (Russian) Armenia and the vain hopes that the Russian domination arose in the hearts of the Armenians in Western (Turkish) Armenia, the Armenians under Russian rule experienced a period of ecclesiastical, national and cultural awakening which should be considered the great benefit of the Russian occupation.

The Church had a direct participation in the emancipatory movement of the Armenian nation and naturally sympathized with the Russian penetration into Caucasus and Armenia. Particularly the Archbishop of Tiflis, Nersēs Ashtaraketzi (later to be elected Catholicos of Echmiadzin, 1843–57) became a heroic figure in the Russian army which liberated the Armenian territories from the Persian rule in 1827. But soon he also was to be eliminated because of his patriotic spirit and aspirations for an autonomous Armenia. The Church was to pass through difficult times towards the end of the nineteenth century and in the beginning of the twentieth as we shall see in due course.

Turkish Armenia

All historians agree in stating that Turkey was on the edge of its decadence and downfall in the nineteenth century. The Christian peoples had been suffering for centuries from the insupportable Turkish oppressions. Unless this situation is outlined the struggle of the Christian populations in the Ottoman Empire can never be well understood.

Pasdermadjian's description is both comprehensive and concise, and can be appropriately quoted in this context:

> As to the position of Christian peoples under the Turkish yoke, these were a people reduced to servitude, stripped of their elementary human rights, their property and lives constantly exposed to the arbitrary will of the government and the attacks of Moslem subjects of the Empire.

And if these Christian peoples enjoyed a sort of autonomy by virtue of their community constitutions those were subject to arbitrary treatment in their relations with the state and the Moslem subjects.

This industrious segment of the population (chiefly the Bulgarians and the Greeks in the European provinces and the Armenians and the Greeks in the interior provinces of Anatolia) were subject to perpetual vexations and were stripped of all guarantees of elementary human rights.

. . . The Christian population was also subject to the attack of armed Mohammedan bands (consisting of Turks, Albanians, Circassians and Kurds) and the sublime Porte, whose authority had declined, could not insure for them the least protection which the Christians were wont to enjoy in former times when the authority of the sultans was effective on all the subjects of the Empire.[1]

The European Powers could not remain indifferent towards this situation of the Christian communities in the Ottoman Empire, particularly at this time when the Russians were already entering Asia Minor. As the Christian peoples were protesting against the inhuman treatment they had been subjected to, the Western Powers tried to compel Turkey to undertake certain reforms in its traditional patterns of administration and thus to affect certain changes in the situation of its Christian population. Their rights for human justice and social equality should be recognized and respected.

And indeed, in 1839, Sultan ʿAbdülmejid promulgated an edict known under the name of *khaṭṭ-i sherif* of Gülhane as a basis for reforms by which he proclaimed the principles of equality of all Ottoman subjects without discrimination of race or religion. But all these principles remained mere principles recognized only on paper.

A second edict called *khaṭṭ-i hümayun* was promulgated in 1856. Again it was done under the pressure of Western Powers and re-established the same principles without envisaging any concrete measure to implement them in actual life.

In short, there was no real change in the situation of the Christians, particularly of the Armenians, who lived in the heart of Asia Minor and were more fully integrated in the structure of the Ottoman Empire than the Balkan countries. Whereas the latter were gradually regaining their independence, the Armenians were being subjected to even harsher treatment.

With the Russian victory in the 1877–78 wars, whereby a considerable part of Armenian territory in the Ottoman Empire was occupied by the

[1] H. Pasdermadjian, *Histoire de l'Arménie*, ch. XI (English translation in the *Armenian Review*, vol. XV, no. 4, 1962, pp. 72–3).

Russian armies, the Armenian Question came to the forefront of political negotiations between Russia and Turkey. The European Powers also were involved directly or indirectly since they were concerned with the Middle Eastern situation. Upon the request of the Armenian patriarchate of Constantinople, the headquarters of the Armenian Church in the Ottoman Empire, the case of the Armenians was put on the agenda of the negotiations in San Stefano which resulted in the well-known San Stefano Treaty (3 March 1878). Here official promises were given by Turkey to undertake the urgently needed reforms in view of ameliorating the situation of the Armenians in the Ottoman Empire (article 16). Three months later, however, owing to the intervention of the Western Powers, particularly of England, the San Stefano Treaty was revised in the Berlin Congress (13 June 1878) and article 16 was converted into article 61. This runs as follows:

> The Sublime Porte undertakes to carry out without further delay the improvements and reforms demanded by local requirements in the provinces inhabited by the Armenians, to guarantee their security against the Circassians and Kurds. It will periodically make known the steps taken to this effect to the Powers, who will superintend their application.

The Armenian delegation to the Berlin Congress was sent by the Armenian patriarchate of Constantinople. It was composed of two archbishops and two laymen.

But again these promises given so solemnly in such an international context were never meant to be implemented. On the contrary, they made the life of the Armenian Christians harder and harder, to such an extent that the Armenians tried to organize their own forces to defend themselves against the ill-treatment at the hands of the Kurdish tribes. Turkish irregulars and government officials. Hence, political parties came into existence. The first by the name *Henchak* (Clarion) was formed in 1885 and the second by the name *Hay Heghapokhagan Dashnaktzoutiun* (Armenian Revolutionary Federation) in 1890. Sultan ʿAbdülḥamid made a pretext of such movements to justify his dreadful plans for wholesale massacres with a sordid determination to eclipse the numerical and moral strength of his Armenian Christian subjects whose existence was causing difficulties for his government.

The massacres of 1894–95 in the province of Mush, particularly in the mountainous regions of Sassun, produced a terrible shock in both national and international circles. Soon they were extended to other regions in Turkish Armenia touching even the city of Constantinople in 1896. "The Sultan's organized brigands 'worked' quite satisfactorily, and Armenian blood flowed in rivers everywhere in Akhisar, Trabzon, Erzincan, Bayburt, Bitlis, Erzurum, Arapkir, Diyarbakîr, Meratia, Harput, Sivas, Amasya, Gaziantep ('Ayntāb), Merzifon, Marash, Caesarea, and other places, ending with Urfa, where 1,200 Armenians were burnt alive in the Cathedral at Christmas 1895."[1] More than 2,500 villages were devastated and buildings were put to ruins. The number of Armenians who took refuge in Russian Armenia, the Balkans, and America exceeded 100,000. Gladstone was right in saying: "The powers of language hardly suffice to describe what has been done and exaggeration is almost beyond power."[2]

The First World War and the Armenians

In 1895, with the accession of Archbishop M. Ormanian to the patriarchal see of Constantinople, a rather peaceful period followed the tribulations that fell upon the Armenian Christians during the period just outlined above. In 1908 the tyrannical rule of Sultan 'Abdülḥamid was overthrown by the Young Turks. It was replaced by a new government established on a constitutional basis. The Armenians had taken an active part in the revolt of the Young Turks. Almost all the leaders of the new liberal, progressive political party acted in close association with the Armenian intellectuals and political leaders. There was great rejoicing among the Armenians who thought and hoped that the old days of hardship and persecution had ended and that a new era was opened with promising prospects for a better future as the principle of equality among the Turkish subjects was firmly established.

But in the meantime the Young Turks were carefully devising their policy of *pan-Turanism* by which they understood the creation of a monolithic Empire of purely Turkish origin, character and tradition. This new pan-Turanian empire was to extend from the Eastern shores of Europe to Central Asia. The Armenians did not fit into this scheme because they were a distinct nation with a different racial origin and with a degree of civilization higher than the cultural status of the Turkish population. Turkish authorities sensed this very easily. Their policy of turkization of all the Ottoman subjects could not be applied to the Armenians except by force. It was this policy that led them to their

[1] Fridtjof Nansen, *Armenia and the Near East* (New York, 1928), p. 288.
[2] Quoted by H. Pasdermadjian, *Histoire de l'Arménie*, p. 388.

final determination to exterminate the Armenian people and put an end to the Armenian Question.[1]

The Armenians, unaware of all these plans, cherished certain hopes for the fulfilment of their national dream of an autonomous status of life when, after 1912, a genuine interest in the Armenian Question was shown by the six Western Powers which had signed the Berlin Treaty of 1878. Now, they designed a programme of reforms which was accepted by the Turkish authorities on 8 February 1914. It provided for the Armenians a kind of autonomous life under international supervision.[2] Two European governors were even appointed to carry out the scheme. But when they arrived in Turkish Armenia the First World War broke out and the whole situation was changed to the detriment of the Armenian people. For the Young Turks seized the opportunity to put into operation their well-planned scheme aiming at the extermination of the Armenian people who by their sheer existence constituted an obstacle for the realization of their pan-turanian policy.

It is impossible to describe the wholesale massacre of the Armenians during the First World War, particularly in 1915 and 1916. It has been called the "blackest page" of modern history. The Armenian massacres have drawn the attention of a great number of Western historians, ambassadors, diplomats, missionaries and travellers in the Ottoman Empire. We can only borrow the words so vividly and movingly uttered by Lord Bryce in his speech delivered in Great Britain's House of Lords on 6 October 1915. In fact, this passage gives in broadest lines an idea of the kind of inhuman action which cost the life of more than one million Armenians:

> The whole Armenian population of each town or village was cleared out, by a house-to-house search. Every inmate was driven into the street. Some of the men were thrown into prison, where they were put to death, sometimes with torture; the rest of the men, with the women and children, were marched out of the town. When they had got some little distance they were separated, the men being taken to some place among the hills where the soldiers, or the Kurdish tribes who were called in to help in the work of slaughter, despatched them by shooting or bayonetting. The women and children and old men were sent off under convoy of the lowest kind of soldiers—many of them just drawn from gaols—to their distant destination, which was sometimes one of the unhealthy districts in the centre of Asia Minor, but more frequently the large desert in the province of Der el Zor, which lies east of Aleppo, in the direction of the Euphrates. They were driven along by the soldiers day after

[1] See A. Toynbee, *Treatment of Armenians in the Ottoman Empire*, pp. 633–5.
[2] *Ibid.* p. 635.

day, all on foot, beaten or left behind to perish if they could not keep up with the caravan; many fell by the way, and many died of hunger. No provisions were given them by the Turkish Government, and they had already been robbed of everything they possessed. Not a few of the women were stripped naked and made to travel in that condition beneath a burning sun. Some of the mothers went mad and threw away their children, being unable to carry them further. The caravan route was marked by a line of corpses, and comparatively few seem to have arrived at the destinations which had been prescribed for them—chosen, no doubt, because return was impossible and because there was little prospect that any would survive their hardships.

This was the worst Calvary that the Armenian people experienced in their history. This was a genocide committed deliberately.

There is direct evidence for the truth that these massacres were ordered, directed and executed by the Turkish government. The texts of the orders given in telegrams sent by the Minister of Interior to the governors of several districts or regions have been preserved. We quote here one telegram which illustrates our point:

To the Government of Aleppo

Sept. 16, 1915. It was at first communicated to you that the Government, by order of the Jemiet (the Ittihad Committee) had decided to destroy completely all the Armenians living in Turkey. Those who oppose this order and decision cannot remain on the official staff of the Empire. An end must be put to their existence, however criminal the measures taken may be, and no regard must be paid to either age or sex nor to conscientious scruples.

Minister of the Interior
TALAAT[1]

In the course of the First World War, particularly after these horrible atrocities, the surviving Armenians both in the Russian front and in the Allied Forces fought fiercely and heroically against the Turks. Large groups of volunteers sacrificed their lives for the cause of the Allied Powers and for the emancipation of Armenia from the yoke of the Ottoman rule.

The descent of the Armeno-Russian combined forces in Turkish Armenia in 1915 liberated large regions to which the Armenians, who earlier had found refuge in Russian provinces, returned and started rebuilding their homes. But the Bolshevik Revolution of October 1917 caused anarchy in the Russian army and the soldiers abandoned the war

[1] *The Memoirs of Naim Bey* (Turkish Official Documents relating to the Deportations and Massacres of Armenians compiled by Aram Andonian, with an Introduction by Viscount Gladstone, reprinted in Boston, U.S.A., 1964, p. 64).

and went to Russia. The Armenians once more remained alone in their hard struggle against the Turkish armies. They actually delayed the latter's entry into the Caucasus. But they could not resist alone the far greater numbers of Turkish forces which soon recaptured the territories occupied by the Russians.

On 28 May 1918 the Armenians declared their country independent. A few days later, on 4 June, the Turks recognized this new, independent state having its centre in the city of Yerevan. The two years that elapsed between the beginning and the end of Armenian independence (28 May 1918–2 December 1920) were years of national recovery and consolidation. This was accomplished through heroic efforts of endurance and dedication.

The Treaty of Sèvres (10 August 1920) between Turkey and the allies recognized Armenia as a free, independent and sovereign state. In fact, Armenia was one of the signatory states. Upon the request of the same Treaty the President of the United States, Mr Woodrow Wilson, defined the western frontiers between Turkey and Armenia. Thus Armenia was entitled to cover an area of 127,000 square kilometres.

But once more what was decided on paper did not touch the real life. The allies did not make any serious effort to ensure and safeguard the territory won by Armenia and recognized as such by them. And when the new Turkish army, strengthened as it was under the leadership of Mustafa Kemal, advanced towards Armenia, again the Armenians found themselves alone in their life-and-death struggle. The Soviets now had established a friendship with the new regime of Mustafa Kemal and did not extend any help to the Armenians. The new master of Turkey, after the penetration of his soldiers in Armenia, inflicted new trials upon the Armenian people through new massacres. Finally, on 2 December 1920 the Armenian independent Republic was forced to sign in Alexandrapol a treaty of peace with Turkey. The same day it was transformed into the Soviet Republic of Armenia which soon was incorporated into the Soviet Union as one of its constituent Republics.

In Western Armenia, after the victory of the Allied Forces, more than 200,000 Armenians returned to Cilicia which had come under the protection of French Forces. In 1920 they also were attacked by Mustafa Kemal's army and new massacres ensued which cost the lives of more than 30,000 Armenians. In October 1921 the French abandoned the Armenians by signing a Treaty with Turkey by which Cilicia was evacuated by the French Forces and the Armenians were once more forced to leave their newly rebuilt homes and disperse all over the world. The great majority of them found refuge in the most hospitable countries of Syria and Lebanon where the Arab people, themselves having often been victims of Turkish atrocities, welcomed them.

After the First World War the situation of the Armenian people took a new shape. Now they lived in two distinct spheres: (*a*) In Soviet Armenia, and (*b*) in almost all the continents of the world outside Armenia, a state of Diaspora of most varied character. No substantial political changes have occurred in their situation since this dispersion. Therefore, our survey of the political events, which directly affected the life of the Armenian people and Church ends here. Now we turn to look into the situation of the Armenian Church.

If we have dwelt upon the political aspects of modern Armenian history it has been because of their strong and permanent impact upon the whole life and witness of the Armenian Church which, as stated at the very beginning of this survey, was integrally involved in the whole life of the nation as such.

In order to make our point even clearer, I would like to indicate at this juncture the scope of the disastrous effects that the tragedy of the Armenian People left on the present situation of the Church. According to the official ecclesiastical statistics quoted by Ormanian, one of the most influential Armenian patriarchs of Constantinople (1896–1908), there were 3,722,00 members of the Armenian Church before the First World War with 100 dioceses, 3,909 parishes and 3,788 churches.[1] With one third of the Armenian population having been massacred, forcibly converted to Islam or having perished due to the loss of their national identity during and after the First World War, forty years later, in 1954, the membership of the Armenian Church reached and even slightly surpassed its former number. Thus, in the new statistics compiled by Bishop T. Poladian, the number of the Armenian Church members appears as 3,674,757, but this time only with 26 dioceses, 446 parishes and 417 churches.[2] The simple comparison is more eloquent about the consequences of the massacres than any comment made by the most highly gifted historian.

Now we must turn to the Church and try to discern the main features and significant aspects of both the nineteenth and twentieth centuries.

[1] See Ormanian, *The Church of Armenia* (London, 1955), pp. 205–9.
[2] *Ibid.* pp. 211–12.

THE ARMENIAN CHURCH BEFORE THE FIRST WORLD WAR

The life of the Church in the nineteenth century revolves around five church centres situated in both Eastern and Western Armenia:

(*a*) The Catholicosate of Echmiadzin, being often described as the Mother See, in Russian Armenia.

(*b*) The Catholicosate of Cilicia in the Western regions of Turkish Armenia.

(*c*) The Catholicosate of Aghtamar in the province of Van (southern regions of Turkish Armenia).

(*d*) The Patriarchate of Constantinople.

(*e*) The Patriarchate of Jerusalem.

Of these five centres the weakest was the Catholicosate of Aghtamar which in fact was only a relic preserved from ancient times, beginning from the twelfth century when it was established in opposition to the Mother See which was located then in Cilicia.[1] The last catholicos, Khachadour, passed away in 1895. The see was governed by a *locum tenens* until the First World War which put an end to its existence, its people being massacred and dispersed.

The Patriarchate of Jerusalem by its very nature has had the character and scope of a monastic institution. The main task has been the preservation of the religious rights and privileges of the Armenian church in the Holy Land. During the whole course of the nineteenth century, the patriarchate was administratively related and subordinate to the patriarchate of Constantinople. And indeed, one of the thorny problems that stirred the life of the patriarchate concerned this very link with Constantinople which at several points hampered the work of the patriarchate. It was only after the First World War that the independence of the patriarchate was finally established on the basis of a new constitution which gave the Religious Community, or the Monastic Order itself, the authority to govern its own affairs. It was again after the First World War that the patriarchate of Jerusalem came to a prominent role in the life of the Armenian Church.

The Catholicosate of Cilicia as a distinct, autonomous centre existed in the Armenian Church since 1441 and fully shared the tribulations of the Armenian people in the Ottoman Empire. The patriarchate of Constantinople, established in 1461 by Sultan Meḥmed II Conqueror, eventually became the centre of the Armenian Church in the Ottoman

[1] *Ibid.* p. 43.

Empire and was recognized as such by the Ottoman authorities. The position and role of the Catholicosate of Cilicia was very much reduced on the ground of civil rights and in the field of religions and secular activities.

Having its seat in Sīs, the capital of the Cilician Kingdom, sometimes referred to as Lesser Armenia, the Catholicosate of Cilicia extended its jurisdiction over the dioceses of Adana, Hadjin, Payas, Peria (Aleppo), Marash (Germanicea), Süleymanlî (Zaytūn), Fernouz, Gaziantep ('Ayn-ṭāb), Antioch, Melitene, Yozgat, Gurun (Kurin) and Cyprus; in fact, over all the major cities and main regions of Cilicia and the surrounding areas such as Syria and Cyprus.

It was only after 1930 that the Catholicosate of Cilicia, being now transferred from Cilicia to Lebanon—due to the evacuation of Cilicia in 1921—was given such conditions that enabled it to render greater services to the Armenians now dispersed all over the world, a matter we shall take up later on.

Therefore, the two active centres of the Armenian Church before the First World War were the Catholicosate of Echmiadzin and the Patriarchate of Constantinople.

The Armenian Church in Eastern Armenia

The whole course of the nineteenth century in Eastern Armenia, as was already shown, was marked by a strong link of the Armenian people with the Russian Tsarist Empire. While accepting the political sovereignty of the Tzarist government, the Armenians never made concessions in the realm of their ecclesiastico-national distinctness. Their national identity was even strengthened by the religious and cultural awakening that they experienced during the nineteenth century.

The Russian policy first touched the life of the Church by bringing her under the closest supervision of the Russian authorities. They drafted in 1836 a rule under the name of *Polojenye*, that is to say, a "Supreme Regulation for governing the Affairs of the Armenian Church in Russia" which was signed by Emperor Nicholas I and communicated to Catholicos Hovhannes Karpetzi for application.

Polojenye is a regulation composed of ten chapters and 141 articles by which the procedure of the administration of the Armenian Church Affairs is defined. Of course this measure provided the Armenian Church with a well-established pattern of government officially sanctioned by the Russian State. Two major criticisms were levelled against it: In the first place by the provisions of the *Polojenye* the government of the Church was put in the hands of the clergy and the participation of the laity was much reduced. Particularly the Armenians in Constantinople were opposed to this provision considering it contrary to the tradition of the Armenian Church in whose administration laymen occupied a considerable place. No doubt the synodal system so characteristic of the Byzantine and Russian Orthodox tradition had a strong impact on the preparation of *Polojenye*. Secondly, the State interference in Church Affairs became conspicuous. In the case of the election of the Head of the Church the Armenians had to present to the Tsar two candidates chosen by an electoral assembly in which the clergy had the majority, and the Tsar had the right to nominate one of them (articles 11–19). A *procurator* was appointed by the Russian government with the charge of supervising, and often directing, the work of the Catholicos and the Synod in Echmiadzin (articles 45–46). Again, all the diocesan bishops, the number of dioceses stated in the *Polojenye* (article 56) being six, had to be nominated by the Tsar himself (article 57). Thus, on the one hand the status of the Armenian Church as a distinct institution was officially recognized, but, as Lynch puts it in such a poignant way, "on the other hand, in true Russian fashion, what is given with one hand is taken away with the other".[1]

The *Polojenye* was abolished with the downfall of Tsarist Russia.

The integrationist policy of Tsarist Russia was expressed in a more direct way through drastic measures after the Turko-Russian wars of 1877–78 when a new strategy was devised which aimed at the russification of the Armenian people and the integration of the Armenian Church into Russian Orthodoxy.

The Russians realized that the source of strength for the Armenian Church lay in the parochial or community schools. It was there that the Armenian learned his own language, religion and culture. It was the Church which ran these schools both financially and administratively. Therefore, the implementation of this new policy of russification started with the schools. An official edict was promulgated in 1884 which forced the Armenian schools to use only Russian as teaching language. The Ukase (edict) of 1884, says Lynch, "may be branded as an infamous document. It provided that church schools with more than two classes should be placed upon the same basis as private schools in Russia, that

[1] H. F. B. Lynch, *Armenia, Travels and Studies* (London, 1901), vol. I, pp. 233–4.

is to say, that the whole of the instruction should be conducted in the Russian language. This was tantamount to closing such schools."

Yet the most outrageous measure which revolted the Armenians was the edict of 1903 by which all the church properties—the source of revenue for the schools and cultural institutions—were forcibly confiscated by the government. Victor Bérard, an expert on the modern history of the Middle East, writing in 1905 says:

These properties which belonged to the Armenian Church of the whole world, and not only to the church in Russia, had been accumulated in the course of centuries, but especially during the nineteenth century, the proceeds of the bequests not only of Russian Armenians but the Armenians of Persia, Europe and America. These properties served only to promote the cultural work and the maintenance of the Church. Orthodoxy and the policy of russification now added them to the budget of the Russian church and Russian schools.[1]

The Catholicos of the time, Mkrtich Khrimian, a most popular figure in the Armenian Church, together with his bishops, clergy and people, vehemently protested against this new order. The Armenians all over the world made appeals to the Russian government and to other world Powers in Europe, and raised a serious campaign against the Russian confiscation of Armenian ecclesiastical possessions. The Armenians in Russian Armenia from the Catholicos to the simplest man in the street resisted in an unyielding spirit of self-defence to this new attempt which was meant to uproot the foundations of the Armenian Church and people. All felt that this was a life-and-death struggle. Finally, the Russians gave up this policy. The Church continued to serve the nation on spiritual, educational and cultural grounds in the line of her historical mission.

Religious and Cultural Awakening

The brightest pages of nineteenth-century Armenian Church history are those pages which describe the great spiritual and cultural renaissance that the Church experienced particularly in the last few decades. The outstanding figures in this respect were the Catholicos Nerses V Ashtaraketzi (1843–51), Kevork IV (1866–82) and Mkrtich I Khrimian (1892–1907).

The main task of Nerses Ashtaraketzi, who still as a bishop had already distinguished himself as a champion of Armenian emancipation

[1] Pasdermadjian, *Histoire de l'Arménie*, pp. 387–8 (*Armenian Review*, vol. XVII, no. 2, p. 74).

from the Persian rule (1827–28), consisted in securing a firm financial ground for the Catholicosate of Etchmiadzin and in establishing a harmonious and efficient order in the Religious Community of Etchmiadzin. He greatly contributed also to higher education by founding the Nersesian Secondary School in Tiflis and by constantly sponsoring its work which, indeed, proved of immense value for the whole Armenian people in the Caucasus. It was a centre which gave highly qualified and devoted servants to the Armenian culture.

Kevork IV's reign marked the most brilliant period in this century. First of all, the parish schools were given special attention. New schools were opened; a special commission was appointed to surpervise the whole educational work; a special regulation was drafted, on the basis of which all the schools had to carry on their work.

The most significant achievement in the field of education was the founding of a new Seminary in Echmiadzin which is known as *Kevorkian Jemaran.* Soon it became a centre of higher learning in theological and armenological studies. The largest number of Armenian intellectuals, clergymen, writers, historians, philologists, linguists, musicians and educators at the end of the nineteenth century and during the first half of the twentieth were graduates of this Seminary. Indeed, as many have pointed out, very few students entered the Church's ministry. Those who did, later on, became great leaders in the Armenian Church.

Catholicos Kevork's activities included the publication in 1868 of a new theological and armenological review called *Ararat*. In five months time it won 1,200 subscribers. In 1880 this number was raised to 2,200. *Ararat* was the official monthly organ of the Catholicosate. Gradually it reached the high standard of a scholarly review. It continued to appear until 1916.

Kevork IV showed a special concern also for the raising of the educational standard of the parish priests. He issued special orders to the bishops not to elevate to the order of priesthood any candidate without careful examination. He put in the hands of the Synod the right for final approval of the candidate's ordination.

Church music also was close to his heart. He invited capable Church musicians from Constantinople to unify the Church singing through musical notation and its uniform execution.

With all these positive achievements to his credit, Kevork's relationship with the Catholicosate of Cilicia was not a happy one. It caused resentment to many in his own time and created difficulties for the future. He wanted to bring all the Armenian Churches under Echmiadzin's immediate jurisdiction. He entered unnecessarily into a polemic with the newly elected (in 1899) Catholicos of Cilicia, Mkrtich Kefsizian by declaring the election as illegal and the existence of the Cilician See uncanonical. He even invited Kefsizian to resign. But the Catholicosate of Cilicia had existed since 1441 as an independent see and there was no justification for creating a conflict between the two major hierarchical sees of the Armenian Church. Fortunately, when Kefsizian was succeeded in 1902–03 by Catholicos Sahak II Khabayan, Catholicos Khrimian of Echmiadzin conveyed hearty congratulations and brotherly greetings which put an end to the unhappy situation created by Catholicos Kevork's unfortunate interference.

We have already spoken of Khrimian's period (1892–1907) which was marked by the struggle of the Armenians with the Russian policy of assimilation of the Armenian people and the confiscation of the Church properties. Khrimian's rule was characterized also by great cultural activities displayed by the students of the Kevorkian Seminary. Some had just returned from Europe, having pursued their higher studies in Germany on the university level in close association with such high ranking scholars and theologians as Harnack, Loofs and others.

The Armenian Church in Western Armenia

The whole life and work of the Armenian Church in Western Armenia, under Turkish rule, were centred in Constantinople. Here had been established in 1461 a patriarchate which served as the rallying point of all church activities undertaken by the Armenians in the Ottoman Empire. At first, the Armenians enjoyed here a comparatively peaceful situation which was, indeed, much happier than the state of life that was the share of their compatriots in the Eastern provinces of the Turkish Empire. Constantinople was a city where East and West met. The Armenians were in constant touch with European civilization. The nineteenth century marked the most brilliant period in which a national awakening was reached by the Armenians in the Capital with cultural, educational and literary achievements of great value and deep impact on all the Armenians in the Ottoman Empire.

The following are the major events which occured in the ecclesiastical realm and affected the life of the church.

In 1830 the Ottoman government recognized the religious autonomy of a group of Armenians who had accepted the Roman Catholic faith but had not yet acquired a separate status as a distinct community in the sense of a *millet* (nation) officially recognized by the Sublime Porte. In fact, in the first three decades of the nineteenth century, many attempts were made in view of a reconciliation of the Armenian Catholic sympathizers with the Mother Church. But all efforts failed and, through the intervention of the French ambassador in Constantinople, the Ottoman government issued in 1830 an edict by which the Armenian Catholics were recognized as a separate community with their own Church Head.

Later, in the same century, a controversy broke out between the two wings of the Armenian Catholic or Uniate Church. Thus, there were people who were closely attached to Latin Catholicism and others who strove hard to maintain a status of autonomy and national tradition of a greater degree than Rome would allow them at that time. The Roman Latin influence grew stronger and stronger in the Armenian Catholic tradition in the coming years.

The first contact of the Armenians with *Protestant* missionaries dates from 1821 when Parsons (a missionary sent by the American Board of Commissioners for Foreign Missions) met Armenians in Jerusalem and found among some of them a positive response to his preaching. Two Armenian clergymen were soon attracted by the Protestant beliefs and they were warmly received by the Syrian Mission in Beirut. But as the Mission was exposed to danger in Beirut because of staunch Islamic opposition, it was transferred to Constantinople.

With the adherence of some Armenians of Constantinople to this newly opened mission, the Protestant movement started to penetrate the life of the Armenian people. It soon expanded in the capital at the same time gaining ground in the neighbouring provinces.

One of the major incentives for the Armenians in their readiness to sympathize with the Protestant preaching was the fact that the missionaries were offering them opportunities for higher education by opening new schools or by sending some students to the United States for university studies. Thus, as early as 1834 they opened a school in Bera, the central and richest quarter of the capital, and another one called Bebek in 1840 on the Bosphorus.

The Armenian patriarchate could not stand indifferent to such proselytizing activities. The foreign missionaries together with their

Armenian converts and associates were teaching such doctrines and spreading such ideas that were not in harmony with the doctrines and Church practices held by the Armenian Church for so many centuries and at the cost of such great sacrifices. Those who adhered to the new preaching became alien to the tradition of the Mother Church and openly opposed such Church practices that could not be justified by Protestant standards of faith. The Church authorities, therefore, reacted to the expansion of Protestanism with the strong determination to hinder its advance. Various kinds of pressure were put upon those who followed the teachings of the missionaries. But in spite of these repressive efforts, and as a precedent had already been established with the recognition of the Armenian Catholic Community, so the Ottoman government being insistently approached by the British Ambassador at Constantinople, Sir Stratford Canning, recognized in 1847 the freedom of conscience of the Protestant converts. Three years later, in 1850, the Armenian Protestant Community was granted the legal status of a *millet*.[1]

The National Constitution

The greatest factor in bringing about the nineteenth-century Armenian national and cultural renaissance was the National Constitution which took its final shape in 1860 and was approved by the Ottoman government in 1863. The impact of the ideas which preceded and prepared the constitution and finally were introduced in it as basic principles, was far greater on the Armenians in Western Armenia than the impact of *Polojenye* in Eastern Armenia. For, in the case of the latter, it was the Russian (tsarist) government which imposed the *Polojenye*, and rather abruptly, as we indicated earlier; whereas the national constitution was the fruit of much labour undertaken by the Armenians themselves; in other words, it was the culmination of a long process of development in social thinking, of constant contact with the new trends in European history and of internal conflicts and struggles of a long time.

Since the first moment of its establishment, the Armenian patriarchate of Constantinople used to be governed by a patriarch who was assisted by *amiras*, high ranking personalities of the Armenian nobility. Generally speaking, these were wealthy persons who enjoyed a high position among the ordinary people and were held in high esteem in

[1] For the Protestant movement among the Armenians, see Leon Arpee, *A Century of Armenian Protestantism, 1846–1946* (New York, 1946).

government circles. Some of them occupied important posts as officials of the government. But their arbitrary actions combined with their personal ambitions soon provoked resentment particularly among the younger generation who were educated in the European ways of thinking and were affected by the social thinking in France as stimulated by the Revolution of 1789.

The promulgation by the Ottoman government of such edicts as the *khaṭṭ-i sherif* of Gülhane and *khaṭṭ-i hümayun* paved the way for the Armenians to organize their ecclesiastical-national life on the principles of the rights for equality of all the people. They had already established in 1847, two councils recognized by the government: the *Spiritual Council*, composed of fourteen clergymen, and the *Supreme Council*, composed of twenty laymen of all classes. These two councils worked under the presidency of the patriarch. The experience that was acquired through them served as the basis for drafting the constitution which was formulated in 1857, was given its final shape in 1860 and was approved by the government in 1863. This constituted the basic regulations of the Armenians in the Middle East after the First World War and until now it is fully maintained and officially recognized by the governments of Syria and Lebanon.

It is a regulation whereby the rights and duties of the Church authorities as well as the faithful are defined on administrative grounds. The fundamental structure of the administration as envisaged in the constitution presents the following pattern.

The supreme authority lies in the National General Assembly which is composed of 140 members: 120 laymen elected by the people (eighty representing the Armenians in the capital and forty representing the people in the provinces) and twenty clergymen elected by the Assembly of the ecclesiastics living in Constantinople. Thus, one seventh is composed of ecclesiastics and six sevenths of laymen.

The National General Assembly which meets once in two years elects the patriarch as well as the members of the Religious and Civil Councils which have an executive character and rôle.

These two councils carry on all the affairs of the patriarchate for a period of two years in the fields of religious and secular activities. The Civil Council has a field of action which is larger than the Religious Council's. All sub-committees are nominated by the Civil Council. It supervises education, finance, the eccelsiastical court, monasteries and other institutions and affairs related to the church. In certain cases where general and most important problems arise, the two councils meet in what is described as a "Mixed Council".

"The Patriarch of Constantinople is the president of all National Assemblies and the representative of their executive Authority" (article 1). He is elected by a National General Assembly and may resign or be deposed if necessary.

The system of administration in the dioceses is simply the reproduction in miniature of this central pattern.

As it may be seen very easily, the national constitution gives greater weight to the secular or civil aspects of the Church's activities rather than the spiritual and purely ecclesiastical. This is why the part of the laity is such an overwhelmingly dominant one that it reduces the role of the clergy to the minimum possible. Patriarch Ormanian who held office for twelve years (1896–1908) and had faithfully followed the regulations of the national constitution gives a well-balanced evaluation of it. He says:

> The Constitutional period, that is to say, half a century that elapsed since 1860, undoubtedly was a time of national progress and prosperity. But it would not be right to think that all this was the outcome of the Constitution of the Armenians in Turkey; for, many other factors, such as the demands of the century, the international contacts, the governmental regulations and the favourable conditions provided by foreign influences contributed towards the acquisition of this result. It should not be forgotten that the Armenians of Russian Armenia without the Constitution of the Armenians of Turkish Armenia today are found in a greater degree of progress and prosperity.
>
> ...It was necessary for the Nation to have a constitution; the superiority of certain classes over others due to hereditary factors or to financial advantages could no longer be tolerated by the spirit of the times; the participation of the laity in church affairs was a proper and dignified feature of the Armenian Church. All these principles had to be sanctioned in an official regulation or constitution. But those who tried to put these aims in practice were guided by influences they had received from their education in France rather than by the principles of their own tradition. In fact, they were stimulated by the French political ideas; they became enthusiasts for the same atmosphere which they had found in France and, thus, they tried to convert the community that had been constituted on religious and ecclesiastical basis simply into a form of a political community.[1]

The affinity between the ideas of the French Revolution (1789) and the principles of the constitution of 1848, on the one hand and the basic

[1] See Ormanian, *Azgapatoum*, vol. III, §2731, cols. 4072–3.

tenets of the Armenian national constitution, on the other hand, is an established fact.[1]

If I have dwelt upon the National Constitution at some length it is not only for the fact that it played a tremendous rôle in the past, but also because still in many countries of the Middle East, such as in Syria and Lebanon, it is used as the basis of the Armenian ecclesiastical and national life. Moreover, other regulations that have been drafted by Armenians living in other countries, in the Middle East and elsewhere, are influenced by the spirit and fundamental principles of the 1860 constitution. Indeed, it produced a whole mentality which still reigns in some sectors of the Armenian nation, particularly with the older generation.

In conclusion, one should accept that the National Constitution brought order, regularity and control in Church affairs; at the same time, however, it encouraged the secular element to such an extent that the purely spiritual aspects of the Church's mission were overlooked or brought to a lower position.

Religious Revival

Towards the end of the century, in 1889, a monastery situated in Armash, Nicomedia (North-west Asia Minor) became a centre of theological education, and played a decisive role in the religious revival of the Armenians in Turkey.

For many years the Armenian patriarchate of Constantinople needed a proper educational system whereby the priests, particularly the celibate, regular clergy could be well equipped for meeting the needs of a society which was gradually coming to a higher degree of education and to a new state of life due to influences from the West. The purely monastic type of theological training which existed here and there in the provinces was no longer adequate to the demands of the times. Therefore, it was generally recognized that a new pattern should be devised. This actually took place when Archbishop Malachia Ormanian, a man with a solid theological education, extensive erudition and an iron will, started a seminary in the monastery of Armash under the sponsorship of the patriarchate of Constantinople. The next year Vardapet Eghishe Tourian, a man of noble visions and deep spirituality, joined him and the school was soon converted into a centre of advanced theological and armenological studies.

[1] J. Etmekjian, *The French Influence on the Western Armenian Renaissance* (New York, 1964), pp. 115–24.

The students later occupied key positions in the life of the Armenian Church. A great number of them became primates or diocesan bishops in the remote provinces of Turkish Armenia looking after the spiritual needs of an oppressed people stricken at heart by the afflictions caused by the Turkish atrocities. Some of them perished as victims of the Turkish massacres in the First World War, thus giving the example of Christian martyrdom as the supreme expression of their faithfulness to Christ. Others, who survived, became highly respected figures of the twentieth-century Armenian hierarchy. Some of these displayed a literary activity which still constitutes the highest expression of Armenian religious literature. In one word, they were the key persons, the real leaders through whose devoted labour the recovery of the Armenian Church in the Diaspora was achieved in the twentieth century after the mortal blow of the First World War.

THE ARMENIAN CHURCH IN CONTEMPORARY TIMES

It has already been shown to what extent the situation of the Armenian Church was affected by the First World War. Two major factors played a most decisive rôle in the shaping of the present situation: first, the dispersion of the Armenians of Turkish Armenia almost all over the world; second, the subjugation of Eastern Armenia to the Soviet rule in 1920.

The evidence about the state of the Armenian Church in Soviet Armenia is indeed scanty and, to a large extent, inaccessible. The existing literature that is available needs careful reading as a considerable part of the evidence is controversial because of the excess of zeal in showing everything bright, or on the opposite side, describing everything in dark colours. We have to read in between the lines.

From the very first moment it was obvious that the new Soviet regime in Armenia was hostile to the Church, which it intended to eliminate from the life of the people. But the Church had been so deeply rooted in the history and the whole tradition of the Armenian people that a tactful and patient policy was needed in order to implement this objective of the Soviets. And, indeed, the first decade of Soviet rule in Armenia was a comparatively bearable period. The Catholicos, Kevork V Sourenian (1911–30) was an aged venerable Church figure who could not find any *modus vivendi* between the Church and the State. He carried on his activities along the lines of the ancient, pre-Soviet, tradition in which he had lived his whole life. Nevertheless, the Church actually did suffer from three kinds of measures taken by the Soviet State:

First of all, coercive methods were tried by which it was hoped that the Church was going to lose the grounds of its influence. The stage of persecution had not yet arrived. Heavy restrictions were imposed on the Church. As Matossian says:

Although freedom of worship was guaranteed, all activities of the Church, apart from conducting worship services, were curtailed or forbidden. The parochial schools were secularized and the Church was forbidden to interfere in education. All property of the Etchmiadzin Monastry was confiscated, including land, printing press, museum and library, except for forty desiatins of orchard land, the church, and the monastery quarters. Organized religious instruction of children under eighteen years was forbidden in church buildings. The exclusive jurisdiction of the Church over marriage and divorce was abolished; Soviet courts and the office of Registry of Acts of Civil Status were now in operation to legalize marital status.[1]

Secondly, the State created and supported in 1922 a Church movement which by its nature and specific aims was opposed to the official, established Church, her tradition and her authority. It is significant to note that this new Church movement was called "Free Church". Under the guise of a reformatory movement, it tried to undermine the official Church by attacking the central authority of Echmiadzin and by discrediting the centuries-old traditions of the Church to which the people were deeply attached. The movement was organized and directed by a small group of clergymen who had already gone astray from Church order and spiritual life. Some of them were even excommunicated by Catholicos Kevork V. Their periodical by the same name, "Free Church", made no impact on the religious mind and Church attitude of the people.

The third measure was the slowest but surest one: anti-religious propaganda on a well-organized basis. This in itself had two aspects, one being negative and the other positive. By the first, Christian beliefs, Church traditions and ecclesiastical personalities were bitterly criticized and shown as void of any value. Let us borrow the words of Matossian:

A special Soviet organization, the Union of Atheists, established a branch in Yerevan during the Twenties and began to publish *Atheist*. About two-thirds of each issue was devoted to satirizing pious Armenians, especially women of the older generation. The Union arranged for plays, evening gatherings, and lectures on anti-religious themes. Instruction in the natural sciences in Soviet schools was used to fight supernatural explanations of natural phenomena.

[1] M. K. Matossian, *The Impact of Soviet Policies in Armenia* (Leiden, 1962), p. 52.

The positive aspect of this anti-religious campaign consisted of efforts whereby the atheist views of man, world and life were propagated through teaching in schools or in public and through several publications.

By the end of this first decade, the strength of the Church was extremely reduced. The time was quite ripe now for more drastic measures to put an end to the story of Christianity in Armenia. If repression was the first step, liquidation was going to be the second. After 1929, stricter and more harmful actions were taken.

Catholicos Kevork V passed away in May 1930. Archbishop Khoren Mouradbekian conducted the Church affairs as *locum tenens*. He was a strong man with a new policy which amounted to a *modus vivendi*. In November 1932 he was elected Catholicos by an Electoral Assembly composed of seventy-three members of which fifty-three were laymen. The first years of his reign were quite peaceful. But the difficulties, started after 1936, and more openly in 1937, during the purge of all religious, national, cultural elements and influences which still kept alive the ancient, pre-Soviet tradition in the new world of communist ideology and social structure. The measures taken against the Church reached such a point that bishops, priests and simple believers came forward to oppose them and to defend the integrity of the Church. The Catholicos himself, who had been a man of compromise, could no longer bear this new attitude of hostility which was expressed through a new wave of persecution. Therefore, he had to be eliminated. And, indeed, Soviet officials of the secret police murdered him at his residence in Echmiadzin in 1938, when he was 65 years old but still an energetic person. The death was announced at the time as a natural one. Its true nature was only later disclosed. This was the climax of the anti-religious campaign.

It is highly significant to note that in those hard times of Church–State relationships, Catholicos Khoren could maintain his courage and find time to undertake positive activities such as the pan-Armenian celebration in 1935 of the 1,500th anniversary of the Translation of the Holy Scriptures into Armenian. His encyclical issued on this special occasion (1 October 1934, no. 1076) had a widespread echo in the Diaspora where all Armenian communities held special ceremonies, conferences, lectures and had books, brochures and articles published. It was at the same time a manifestation and renewal of the faithfulness of the Armenian people to the Word of God and to its saving power. A second encyclical issued on the 1st August 1937 (no. 419) officially sanctioned the idea and of the need for reform in the Armenian Church. For many years, leading Church dignitaries, simple priests and interested laymen had written articles and editorials emphasizing the need for certain changes in the Armenian Church, the main purpose of which being to render a more effective witness in the changing world of the twentieth century. Catholicos Khoren, being sensitive to this genuine need, officially put forward a scheme in which the major items were briefly presented. The Encyclical and the Schema were sent to the catholicos of Cilicia and the patriarchs of Jerusalem and Constantinople for comments. His sudden death in 1938 hampered the whole movement. The following were the items that appeared on the schema which was going to serve as the agenda of an Ecclesiastico-National Assembly for examination and final action:

1. *Liturgical problems*
   (*a*) Divine offices (daily worship in the Church).
   (*b*) Ecclesiastical feasts.
   (*c*) Sacraments and sacred ceremonies.
   (*d*) Lectionary.

2. *General problems*
   (*a*) The training of the clergy.
   (*b*) The case of celibate priesthood.
   (*c*) Marriage and divorce.
   (*d*) New calendar.
   (*e*) Change of ecclesiastical dress.
   (*f*) The financial security of parish priests.
   (*g*) Fasting.
   (*h*) Liturgical language.

Resuming now the presentation of the Church situation in Soviet Armenia, we realize that the Church–State relations took a new turn during the Second World War. In the life-and-death struggle, the Soviet authorities realized that Churches could render valuable service to them both within and outside the Soviet Union. With all the pressure and persecution that fell upon the Church, this latter still maintained a considerable influence in Armenia; moreover, holy Echmiadzin had a strong influence, a kind of mysterious power, upon the Armenians dispersed all over the world.

In 1941, an assembly was convened in Echmiadzin to elect a new catholicos. But as the required number for a quorum was not reached, those who attended were satisfied by accepting and confirming Archbishop Kevork Choerekjian as an elected *locum tenens*. It was only in 1945, just at the end of the war, that the election could take place. Choerekjian was now elected and consecrated catholicos, under the name of Kevork VI.

Having won the confidence of the Soviet State, Kevork VI worked hard to make his reign of nine years as catholicos a fruitful service to his Church. In 1944 he started the publication of an official monthly review by the name *Echmiadzin*. It gives a full account of the activities of the catholicosate at the same time containing religious articles and philological studies. In 1945 he opened the Theological Seminary in Echmiadzin where are trained the clergy for the Armenian Churches in the Soviet Union. Although the education does not reach a large number of students, the few who graduated from the Seminary are now holding important positions in Soviet Armenian Church life. He organized also the Community life in Echmiadzin and the administrative set-up of the catholicosate. In 1946–48 he encouraged the repatriation of more than 80,000 Armenians mainly from the Middle East (Syria and Lebanon), Greece and France. This was in line with the Soviet policy to strengthen the manpower of the country particularly in the aftermath of the war when the country needed new strength and new skills for its reconstruction. A few churches and monasteries were reopened for religious use and their administration was entrusted to Echmiadzin. He made plans for a complete restoration of the cathedral of Echmiadzin but he could not see the realization of his plans as he passed away in 1954 at the age of 85.

A young bishop, the primate of the Armenians in Roumania, Rt Rev. Vazgen Baljian, succeeded him in October 1955. He was elected by an Assembly which was the largest ever convened in Soviet Armenia (137 delegates: 98 from the Soviet Union and 39 from the Diaspora; he received 126 votes).

Catholicos Vazgen's reign (which had just completed its tenth year when this was written) has marked a considerable advance in the revival of the Church life in Soviet Armenia. His activities have included frequent pastoral journeys of quite long duration within and outside the Soviet Union. Hardly four months had elapsed since his election, when he undertook a journey (February–May 1956) to the Middle East and to

Europe. A second journey took him to the United States, South America, Portugal and France (May–October 1960). In June 1961 he visited the Armenian community in Istanbul and the Armenian community in Austria. Two years later, in October 1963, he made a pilgrimage to Jerusalem from where he proceeded to Egypt and India, there being the guest of the Syrian Orthodox Church of Malabar (South India). In January 1965 he went to Addis Ababa to attend the conference of the Heads of Oriental Orthodox Churches which was convened by His Majesty, Haile Sellassie I, the Emperor of Ethiopia. On his way back to Echmiadzin, he visited once more the Armenian communities in Cairo, Paris and London.

These pastoral journeys gave Catholicos Vazgen an excellent opportunity of getting closely and personally acquainted with the situation of the Armenian people scattered all over the world. He could also secure funds for the restoration of churches and monasteries that were returned by the State to Echmiadzin. These visits marked also high moments of spiritual and national awakening among the dispersed children of the Armenian church.

Catholicos Vazgen also undertook journeys in the so-called "internal" dioceses which are located in the Soviet Union such as the Armenian communities in Georgia and Azerbayjan. These also proved very useful in enhancing the importance of the Church in the life of men who live in a world which officially and formally denies for religion any place in the life of its citizens.

Besides the pastoral visits, which are so characteristic of Catholicos Vazgen's reign, the restoration of churches and ancient monasteries constituted a major aspect in his activities. Particularly the cathedral of Echmiadzin and the catholicosate residence together with other parts of the precincts of the monastery of Echmiadzin were restored and redecorated in the typically Armenian style of architecture, sculpture and painting. The community life in Echmiadzin and the theological education in the seminary received greater attention.

H. H. Vazgen I, still young (57 years old), is wholeheartedly devoted to his highly responsible and most delicate task as catholicos of all Armenians of Echmiadzin. No doubt he lives under difficult conditions. He has under his jurisdiction a large community of the widest variety: five dioceses within the Soviet Union: *Ayrarat* (Yerevan), *Shirak* (Leninakan), *Georgia* (Tiflis), *Azerbayjan* (Baku) and *Nor-Nakhitchevan and Russia* (Moscow). Those outside the Soviet Union are the following:

Egypt (Cairo), *Iraq* (Baghdad), *Western Europe* (Paris), *North America* (New York), *California* (Los Angeles), *South America* (Buenos Aires), *England* (London), *Rumania* (Bucarest), *Bulgaria* (Sofia), *India and Far East* (Calcutta). There are also vicariates in Milan, Vienna and Addis Ababa. The patriarchates of Jerusalem and Constantinople depend spiritually on the catholicosate of Echmiadzin.

Here is the numerical picture of Echmiadzin jurisdiction:

Soviet Armenia: 1,900,000

Other countries of Soviet Union: 1,400,000

Georgia:	500,000
Azerbayjan:	500,000
Other parts:	400,000

Diaspora: 663,000, of which 183,000 are in the Middle East
125,000 in Turkey
8,000 in Jordan
30,000 in Egypt
20,000 in Iraq

Since the takeover of Armenia by the Soviets and after the abolition of the *Polojenye*, there is no official constitution for the Armenian Church in Soviet Armenia. The ancient Synod is replaced by a Council which governs all the internal and external affairs of the Church under the name of Supreme Spiritual Council. It is composed of nine members, clergymen and laymen. This Council advises and assists the catholicos. A government official appointed by the State is in constant touch with the Church and supervises all the activities related to the catholicosate of Echmiadzin.

In concluding this brief survey of the Armenian Church in Soviet Armenia, it is important to underline the following points:

(*a*) The Church survived all the vicissitudes and tribulations, and now is growing, however slowly, and gradually gaining a larger ground in the life of the people.

(*b*) The Soviet authorities failed in their attempt to uproot the Christian faith and to disintegrate the Church in Armenia. Now, they have allowed her a restricted freedom. In doing so, they pursue a policy by which they hope to extend their influence on the Armenians living outside Soviet Union.

(*c*) The present situation can never be taken as a stable one. Because of the constant control by the Soviet State, the situation may change according to the changes that may occur in Soviet policy. The situation as described above impels us to recognize the constantly changing and, indeed, changeable character of the situation.

The great fact is that the Church continues to live and render her services to her Master Christ the Lord and to the Armenian people.

The Diaspora has been a permanent aspect of Armenian life throughout history. After the First World War it became a most important factor in the whole life of the Armenian people and their Church.

In the aftermath of the war, the situation of the Armenian people presented a picture of complete desolation. The people were migrating in all directions wherever they could find refuge: the Middle East, Europe (mainly France), the United States and South America. The first years were a period of settlement and adjustment. They lived now in new countries; they met new peoples; they began to speak new languages; they adopted new customs; they came in touch with new cultures. They had to find their way in a world-situation of most varied scope and character. Indeed, the recovery and revival of the Armenian Church in the Diaspora is amazing. A refugee people at the end of the First World War, the surviving Armenians soon rebuilt new homes in the countries which received them and which they considered as their second fatherland. They offered their wholehearted contribution to all peoples and countries with whom they shared their new life.

Where were now the centres of the Church?

The field work of the patriarchate of Constantinople was very much reduced as the Armenians of Turkish Armenia were partly massacred and partly dispersed. The new regime of Kemal, putting heavy restrictions upon the patriarchate confined the authority of the patriarch to purely spiritual activities. The catholicos of Cilicia followed the fate of his people who had come out of Cilicia and found shelter mainly in Syria, Lebanon and Cyprus.

In the immediate post-war period, the patriarchate of Jerusalem, which had not been so deeply affected by the massacres of 1915–16, became the most flourishing centre of the Armenian Church. Two great intellectual figures occupied the patriarchal see: Archbishop Eghishe Tourian (1921–30) and Torgom Goushakian (1931–39). The first had distinguished himself particularly in his educational, intellectual, and literary activities in the seminary of Armash and in the Armenian schools at Constantinople. The second was one of the most brilliant graduates of the same centre of theological and armenological learning. During their reigns the following were achieved:

(*a*) The patriarchate recovered its financial stability and soon reached the highest degree of its prosperity.

(*b*) The seminary was completely reorganized. High-ranking intellectuals, clergymen and laymen alike, joined the teaching staff. The number of the students increased; the syllabus of the courses was enlarged.

(*c*) The monthly review, *Sion*, reappeared in 1927. In the following fifteen years it was the leading periodical of religious, philosophical, historical and literary topics. In fact, it served as a meeting place for many scholars in the Diaspora. When one glances at the periodical referred to, one is deeply impressed by the richness and the high quality of its contents.

(*d*) The Publishing House became a most active institution. Various publications of liturgical, religious, historical, philosophical and literary character came out and were welcomed in the intellectual circles in the Diaspora. Up till now, the Jerusalem printing press provides most of the liturgical books in use in the Armenian Church.

(*e*) Students were sent abroad, particularly to England where they attended the courses of the Theological Colleges of the Church of England. Later, they assumed responsible duties in the patriarchate in Jerusalem and elsewhere. Today some of them hold high positions in the life of the Armenian Church all over the world from the United States to Europe, from the Middle East to India.

The past two decades, however, marked a considerable weakness and decline for two obvious reasons. First of all, after 1940, internal conflicts and quarrels within the Religious Community resulted in dissensions which broke down the unity and creativeness of the patriarchate. Some members even gave up their vows. Some left the patriarchate and went into the service of the Church at diocesan and parish levels. Secondly, the Arab-Jewish war of 1948 compelled a great number of Armenians living in Palestine to leave their homes and to find refuge in the precincts of the patriarchate or go abroad as refugees. The patriarchate devoted all its efforts to look after the afflicted people. But its financial and moral strength was very much reduced. In the last decade new rivalries in connexion with the election of a new patriarch shook once more the centuries-old patriarchate. At present, efforts are being made to heal the damage, to restore peace and confidence and to reorganize the seminary as well as the community life.

While the patriarchate of Jerusalem was thus entering a shadowy period, a new Church centre came to render valuable services to the Armenian Church in the Diaspora. In 1930 the catholicosate of Cilicia was established in Inṭilyās (Antelias), Lebanon. As new possibilities were now being created for the catholicosate of Cilicia, the Catholicos Sahak I Khabayan, already advanced in age and being deeply affected by the great sufferings of his people during the First World War, called Archbishop Babgen Guleserian—again one of the first graduates of Armash Seminary—to asist him in his efforts to rebuild a new ecclesiastical and national life in the new countries of the Diaspora. Archbishop Babgen was enthroned as coadjutor-catholicos in 1931. His five years as catholicos marked a time of intensive work which resulted in concrete achievements such as the establishment of a seminary directed by another graduate of the seminary of Armash, Vardapet Shahe Gasparian, the founding of a printing press, and the publication of a monthly review under the name of *Hask* ("Ear of Corn") which was accompanied by the publication of religious, educational and historical brochures and books. After his premature death in 1936 the archbishop of Cyprus, Petros Sarajian, was appointed vicar-general and later, in 1940, succeeded the aged catholicos Sahak, when the latter passed away in 1939. His short reign as vicar-general and as catholicos proved greatly beneficial in the sphere of building. The cathedral at Antelias, the memorial chapel of the Armenian Martyrs, and the seminary building together with the residence of the catholicos were built through his wise administration and tireless efforts.

The Second World War halted this constructive activity. But after 1945, when Catholicos Karekin I Hovsepiantz came to the throne, a new period of spiritual and intellectual awakening dawned upon the Armenian Church. During his reign of seven years, the catholicosate of Cilicia flourished primarily in cultural activities. The catholicos himself being a great scholar, encouraged the higher studies in the seminary and gave impetus to the publishing work. The monthly review, *Hask*, was enriched in content and was enlarged in scope. The number of theological students was increased. New items were added to the curriculum together with the addition of two years to the course of study. Well-qualified professors were invited to join the faculty. The scope of the catholicosate's work was extended as new priests were sent to various parts of the world to serve the parishes and dioceses.

Four years elapsed between his death and the election of his successor, Catholicos Zareh I (1956). The first graduate of the seminary of Antelias, he was an experienced Church leader in Syria having served as primate of Aleppo for sixteen years. During his short-lived reign many beneficial achievements were accomplished. The catholicosate's work was extended to those Armenian communities in the Diaspora which had been in desperate need of spiritual care for many years. Upon the urgent and eager request of the Armenian people in Iran, Greece and half of the Armenian community of the United States, he sent young bishops and priests to minister to them the Word of God and the Sacraments and keep them firm to the traditions of their forefathers. The seminary was given much encouragement. His personal insight and saintly life had a determining influence on all the students who readily entered the service of the Church by joining the religious community of the catholicosate. The relations of the Cilician see with other churches and governments of the Middle East were strengthened through his leadership. He can be rightly described as the ecumenical figure *par excellence* of the Armenian Church in the Middle East. He passed away, being victim of an heart attack, in February 1963, when he was only 48 years old.

His close associate, Archbishop Khoren Paroyan, the primate of the Armenian Church in Lebanon, succeeded him in May 1963 at the age of 48.

The jurisdiction of the Catholicosate of Cilicia extends to the following countries:

Syria (two dioceses, in Aleppo and Damascus)	100,000 faithful
Lebanon (Beirut)	135,000 faithful
Cyprus (Nicosia)	4,000 faithful
Iran (three dioceses, in Julfa-Iṣfahān, Tabrīz and Tehran)	180,000 faithful
Greece (Athens)	11,000 faithful
United States (New York)	150,000 faithful
Kuwait (Vicariate)	6,000 faithful

It is worth noting that the great majority of the Armenians in the Middle East depend on the catholicosate of Cilicia.

The catholicos is assisted by two Executive Councils: the Central

Religious Council composed of seven ecclesiastics and the Central Secular Council composed of seven laymen. Both councils are elected by the General National Assembly which convenes once every two years.

The constitution of the catholicosate is based on the national constitution of 1863.

PROBLEMS AND PROSPECTS

What are the most important problems that the Armenian Church faces at present, particularly in the Middle East? They can be recognized as follows in the remainder of this chapter.

The present situation of the Armenian people is a complicated one. With the fatherland being partly subjected to Soviet rule and partly captured and emptied by the Turks, still one million two hundred thousand Armenian Christians live scattered all over the world, half of them living in the Middle East. The link between the Church in the fatherland and in the Diaspora is a most natural and important one. At the same time, it is a most delicate and risky one. The hope and determination to recover the lost independence is alive in the hearts and minds of a great majority of Armenians. They believe that one day, in the near or remote future, justice will be done to their nation. Their rights are legitimate by any standard of human justice. They expect that Churches and Nations today should recognize their aspirations for justice. No one can predict what changes will occur in the international situation in the coming years which would create favourable conditions for the fulfilment of their expectations. They are conscious of the present-day imperative: to be constantly ready and watchful to take advantage of any opportunity that may be presented.

Besides her spiritual mission—the Christ-given message of salvation—the Armenian Church has a national mission which arises from her historical existence and is deeply rooted in her whole tradition. In the life-and-death struggle for the preservation of the Armenian people, the Church should be a rallying point, a centre of convergence, a ground for common action. But as the Church is deeply involved in the life of the nation as such, it is not always so easy to stay aloof and remain unaffected by the factors which operate in the national sphere of the life of the Armenians.

This difficulty was made manifest in a poignant way in a conflict which opposed the two Catholicosates of Echmiadzin and Cilicia in the last decade. After 1952, when the see of Cilicia became vacant, Echmiadzin tried by all means to bring under its authority the catholicosate of Cilicia. This latter resisted with unyielding determination to maintain its traditional independence which actually had assumed a more urgent importance because of the new situation of Armenians now living under the different allegiances of the Soviet Union and the Free World, which so often are in conflict with each other. The two catholicosates had existed in the Armenian Church as distinct, independent sees since 1441. They had recognized each other's status and respective jurisdictions. In 1956 when the election of a catholicos was going to take place in Antelias, the newly elected catholicos of Echmiadzin, Vazgen I, came to Antelias with an express wish to participate in the election and preside over the consecration of the new catholicos. This was, indeed, a historic event as no other catholicos of Echmiadzin had ever visited the catholicosate of Cilicia. But immediately after his arrival he intervened in the electoral affairs of the catholicosate of Cilicia; an intervention which was not canonical, had no precedent and, therefore, was refused by the Cilician see. H. H. Vazgen I left Antelias on the very day of the election (20 February 1956). In an episcopal meeting in Cairo (5–8 March 1956) he declared the election "defective and unacceptable". This was an open violation of the independent status of the catholicosate of Cilicia which ignored such pronouncements and endeavoured to defend its centuries-old independence against all the measures taken in opposition to the newly elected catholicos, H. H. Zareh I.[1]

The conflict went on for seven years. Gradually the tension was reduced. In 1963, after the sudden death of Catholicos Zareh I (18 February) and the election of his successor Catholicos Khoren I (5 May), Vazgen I during his pilgrimage to Jerusalem asked Catholicos Khoren to meet with him in brotherly love and thus to put an end to the existing chasm that was opened between the two catholicosates. H. H. Khoren I readily responded in the same spirit of brotherly love. Their historic meeting took place on 26 October and a requiem service was

[1] For a fuller treatment of the origin of the two catholicosates, the historical background of their relationship, their canonical status, the rights and privileges of the two catholicoi, together with the details of the recent conflict between the two, see *The Catholicosate of Cilicia: her Place and Status in the Armenian Church* (official publication of the Catholicosate of Cilicia), Antelias, 1961. Also J. Mécérian, S.J., *Un tableau de la diaspora arménienne*, part III, pp. 155–68; *idem*, "Le Catholocos Zareh I", in *Travaux et Jours, revue bimestrielle* (Beyrouth, Mars-Mai 1963, no. 9), pp. 31–44. Cf. Jean-Michel Hornus, "La Crise du Catholicossat de Cilicie", extract from *Proche-Orient Chrétien* (1956), Fasc. 3.

celebrated in memory of Catholicos Zareh I for whom Echmiadzin had refused until then to use the title of "Catholicos of Cilicia".

At present, the normal, regular relationship is re-established. However, there are problems which from time to time reappear and create difficulties. All these problems, taken in their very roots, arise from a divergence in understanding of each other's status and position within the Armenian Church. Whereas, the catholicosate of Echmiadzin recognizes itself as the supreme authority in the Armenian Church, having under its spiritual jurisdiction the catholicosate of Cilicia and the patriarchates of Jerusalem and Constantinople, the Cilician catholicosate considers itself as the supreme authority within its own jurisdiction having an independent status, but recognizing Echmiadzin's primacy of honour. Unless these two conceptions and attitudes are reconciled, conflicts may arise if other factors such as genuine Christian charity, real concern for the well-being of the Armenian Church, and a patient and understanding spirit, are overlooked. A solution is possible only when, on the one hand, Echmiadzin modifies its claims of absolute authority and adopts a more lenient, flexible and understanding attitude, accepting the independent status of the Cilician see, and, on the other hand, Cilicia respects the primacy of honour in a more concrete way. The antagonism should give way to mutual understanding and co-operation. They should not be opponents, nor competitors, but must function as co-workers, as has been the case in the past, in the same spirit of brotherly love, and sincere devotion to the work they share in common.

Unless such harmony is achieved, the Armenian Church cannot adequately fulfil her noble mission in its spiritual and national aspects. The preservation of the integrity, identity and unity of the Armenian Church and people is a sacred task that must not be neglected. In such harmony lies also the secret power for creative witness in the twentieth century.

Such harmony is necessary also for meeting an urgent need which the Armenian Church faces everywhere whether in the fatherland or in the Diaspora.

We have already referred to a reform movement which started in the second decade of this century and was officially recognized and encouraged by the Catholicos of Echmiadzin in 1937, having the support of other Armenian Church Leaders. But the movement faded away as the Second World War broke out. With the comparatively peaceful situation of the Armenian Church at present, the movement should be renewed because the need is becoming sharper and sharper as the gap between the Church and the people is getting wider and wider.

The preservation of the identity and distinctive characteristics of the Armenian Church is an absolute principle which cannot be compromised, minimized or overlooked. Particularly in the fluctuating situation of the Diaspora, the need of maintaining the national character of the Church is a highly important task which no one should disregard or disdain. Yet there are certain things in the existing traditions of the Church which need revision and adaptation. The spiritual side of the Church's mission cannot receive any impetus or stimulus if the spiritual needs of men in the twentieth century are not clearly discerned and adequately dealt with. The younger generation that is born and brought up in areas such as the Middle East, Europe, the United States or South America has to be cared for in different ways and by different methods from those to which their fathers and forefathers were accustomed. Attention should be given to the particular conditions in which they live today. But at the moment no diocese in such countries can, on its own initiative, engage in any serious activity with a view to changing certain things which have been integrated in or associated with the Church during the past centuries. Therefore, the gap between the Church and modern society remains unbridged.

In this respect, the Church as a whole should adopt certain principles and indicate certain general lines concerning Church reforms whereby the particular dioceses in different countries may be guided in their actions. It is not possible in this brief survey to identify the specific problems involved in the question of Church reforms. They are too many and too varied. The items that were suggested in Catholicos Khoren's encyclical and schema should be reviewed and seriously dealt with by the two catholicosates of Echmiadzin and Cilicia in joint study and through common action. In any case, the guiding principle in such action should be to cause no harm to the unity of the Church, on the one hand, and to enable the Church to render a more effective witness in the twentieth century, on the other hand.

The Armenian Church, as almost all the Christian Churches, has entered a new period of her history: the period of encounter or, to use a more common language, the ecumenical era. The situation of the Armenian Church provides her with favourable opportunities for a full participation in the Ecumenical Movement. In fact, the Armenian

Church, in the Diaspora, is present in almost all the corners of the earth. She is no longer confined to one, two or three countries. Therefore, the practical possibilities are genuine factors for her involvement in the present-day life of the Churches which are experiencing the happy moments of their mutual encounter in a new spirit of fellowship and openness towards each other.

Until recently, the Armenian Church took part in the Ecumenical Movement in an indirect way. Representatives in the capacity of observers, consultants or guests, attended the Ecumenical Conferences such as the World Conference on Faith and Order in Lausanne (1927), Edinburgh (1937) and Lund (1952). They were present also at the General Assemblies of the World Council of Churches in Amsterdam (1948), Evanston (1954) and New Delhi (1961). In August 1962 at the Central Committee meeting in Paris, the two Catholicosates were received as regular members of the World Council of Churches. Since then, the Armenian Church has been contributing her share to the activities of the W.C.C. in a direct and more active way.

But all this is still not sufficient. There is need for more lively and fruitful participation. The co-operation of the two catholicosates in this field can have a decisive role in increasing the contribution of the Armenian Church to world Christianity in its search for solidarity, unity, revival and faithful witness in the twentieth century.

Particularly important is the case of the ecumenical encounter in the Middle East where the Armenian Church is in constant contact with other Christian Churches of both Eastern and Western traditions. Three spheres of activity in this respect can be envisaged in the following ways:

First, solidarity and co-operation should be strengthened between the Eastern Churches which are in communion with each other, namely the Syrian, Coptic, Ethiopian and Armenian Churches. These are sometimes wrongly referred to as "Monophysite" Churches. In fact, they are non-Chalcedonian Churches which, having refused to recognize the Council of Chalcedon (451) as an Ecumenical Council, are not in communion with the Eastern Orthodox Churches of the Byzantine tradition. Recently, the Heads of these Churches met in Addis Ababa, in a Conference convened by His Majesty Haile Sellassie I, the Emperor of Ethiopia (15–21 January 1965). Here their unity and solidarity was deeply confirmed and a solid foundation was laid for closer co-operation in the future.

Secondly, the relationship with the Orthodox Churches of the Byzantine tradition is becoming a major concern particularly among the younger clergy of both branches of Eastern Christendom. Conversations should take place in a common effort to study the doctrinal differences, the historical difficulties which still stand in the way of rapprochement and recovery of Christian communion. A recent consultation between theologians of both traditions held in Aarhus, Denmark (August 1964), revealed once more the doctrinal and liturgical affinity between them. Plans are being made for a meeting between the theologians and, at a later stage, the Heads of these Churches. History is so deeply rooted in their present life that time and tact are required for paving the way to mutual understanding.

Thirdly, the Middle East needs co-operation on a larger scale. Orthodox, Catholic and Protestant groups of Churches should come together and study the specific needs of the Middle East and devise the appropriate means for meeting them. The Near East Christian Council is purely a Protestant organism with a very meagre influence in the area. The Churches of the Middle East should come out of their isolation and study their own conditions, look into their own histories and recognize the urgency of the ecumenical action for their mission. Polemics should be converted into dialogue, competition into co-operation, isolation into fellowship.

The Armenian Church with her traditional attitude of openness can serve as a constructive element in such a common endeavour. More specifically, the catholicosate of Cilicia in Lebanon and the patriarchate of Jerusalem in Jordan should lead the Armenian Church in the different spheres of ecumenical activity as outlined above.

Is the Church ready to cope with all these perspectives?

The real answer can be given only by a younger and devoted generation of clergy, together with enlightened young laymen, with new visions and readiness for self-dedication and genuine involvement.

CHAPTER II

THE ASSYRIANS

The Christians who are the subject of this chapter are often called the Nestorians. This name was used by themselves, as well as by others describing them, from the sixth century to the nineteenth century. In the last three generations they have ceased to call themselves the Nestorians, because that name seems to them to suggest that Nestorius was their founder or invented their doctrines. They prefer to be called the Assyrians, adopting the theory that they are descended from the ancient Assyrians. But they are not the only modern Assyrians; the Syrian-Orthodox or Jacobites and some Syriac-speaking Roman Catholics and Protestants are called Assyrian Christians. In this chapter the name Assyrian will be used with reference to the members of one particular Christian church. The official title of this church is "The Ancient Church of the East". *Ancient* is the word which now distinguishes the historic churches of the Middle East from groups of Roman Catholics and Protestants who left them, in modern times, to form Uniate and Reformed churches. This particular historic church is called *of the East*, because she grew up in the part of Asia which was outside the eastern frontiers of the Roman Empire in the first six centuries. In the theological controversies which arose within the Roman world, those who were condemned by the Roman churches were sometimes acquitted in the eastern regions. Thus in the fifth and sixth centuries A.D. most of the Christians of the Persian Empire refused to regard Nestorius as a heretic. Those among them who condemned him became attached to the Syrian-Orthodox Church of Antioch and were called Western Syrians. The Syriac-speaking defenders of Nestorius were described as the Eastern Syrians and, in the valleys of the Tigris and the Euphrates and elsewhere, they were regarded as the modern representatives of ancient Assyria and Chaldea.

It is important to notice that we are considering a church rather than a nation. There are Indian members of the Ancient Church of the East who are certainly not Assyrian by nationality. Especially between A.D. 800 and 1300 many Chinese, Tartar, Mongolian and other Asian Christians belonged to that Church. While all made some use of

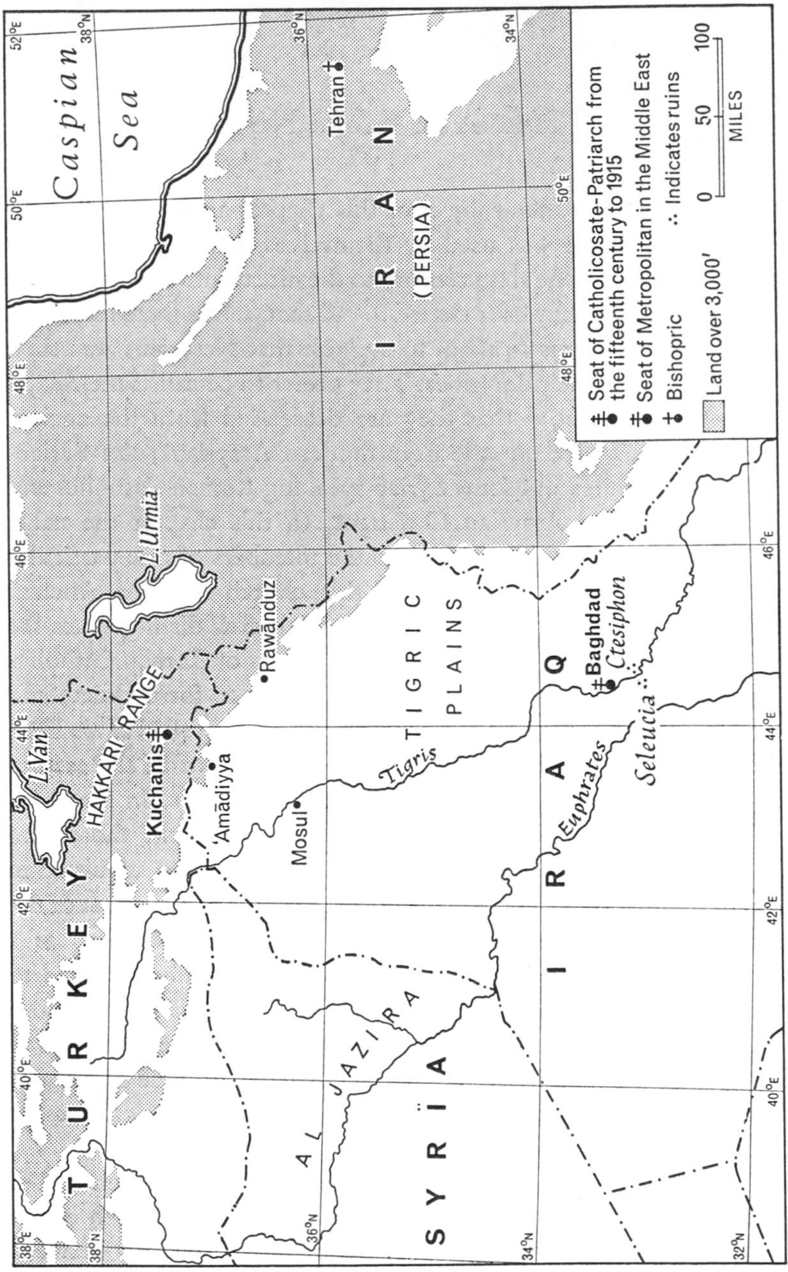

The Assyrians.

Syriac, it is clear that other languages were also used in prayer and teaching.

In the fourteenth century great disasters overtook the peoples of Asia. After the massacres of Tamerlane and other wars and plagues, in the resulting depopulation, the Church of the East, whose members were everwhere a minority, survived only in two regions. One of these was the Malabar Coast of south-west India; there, in the sixteenth century, under Portuguese influence, Roman Catholicism prevailed. In modern times she has returned to Malabar at Trichur, where she has a bishopric. The other region where she lived on, until the present century, was a mountainous area between Lake Van in Turkey and Lake Urmia in Persia, north of the plain of Mosul. In and around Mosul she had members until the sixteenth century when a conflict arose between the Christians of the plain and those of the mountains; the men of the plain were reconciled with Rome. There were Assyrian colonies farther west, in Damascus and Famagusta for example. These dispersed Assyrians began to submit to Rome as early as the fifteenth century. When in communion with Rome they were called Chaldeans; in Mosul this may have been partly due to the historical fact that Chaldea was south of Assyria, as the plain is south of the mountains which were the stronghold of opposition to union with Rome. But it is curious that in India those who have returned to the Nestorian doctrinal position are called Chaldeans, the Roman Catholics of Syrian rites being called Syro-Malabar and Syro-Malankar.

Early in the nineteenth century the Ancient Church of the East was almost entirely confined to the mountains north of the Mesopotamian plain, between Lake Van on the west and Lake Urmia on the east. Most of the inhabitants of this region were of the Muslim faith; they included Kurds, Persians and Turkish-speaking Azerbayjanis. There were Jews who spoke Syriac and Yazīdīs, a people with a strange religion of their own which has caused them to be regarded as devil-worshippers.

As we shall see, the Assyrians left Turkish territory after 1914 and have not re-established themselves there. In the villages of ʿAmādiyya and Rawānduz in Iraq they are indigenous; so they are in the Urmia district of Persia. But the great majority of Assyrians, in Iraq, Persia, Syria and the Lebanon, as well as in the West, are refugees. They have been forced to leave their ancestral homes. Before we come to the story of their dispersion, it seems necessary to give some account of their community life, as it was lived in their own mountain home. What follows is based mainly on the writings of British and American priests, teachers and doctors who settled among them or visited them during the nineteenth century.

There were six Assyrian Christian tribes in the Hakkārī region who claimed to be independent of the Turks. They recognized no temporal authority apart from their own chiefs or *maliks*; these were under the authority of the one patriarch of the Ancient Church of the East, called the catholicos. His see, originally at Seleucia-Ctesiphon, near Baghdad, had been moved to Kuchanis, a large village near Hakkārī. No Turks entered Hakkārī, although they came to Kuchanis to meet the Assyrian patriarch. The tribesmen were always armed. Kurds in Assyrian tribal areas were under the civil authority of the Assyrian chiefs; likewise Assyrians in Kurdish areas obeyed Kurdish chiefs who were independent of the Turks. There were often alliances between particular Assyrian tribes and Kurdish tribes near them. They also fought tribal wars, making peace when they were exhausted. Outside the tribal areas, the Assyrians were *râya* or subjects of the Turks and the Persians. Some were landowners and their church had much landed property. Many were tenants; but they had their customary rights. Disputes between them were settled, according to their own customs, by their clergy and their *maliks*. The patriarch was their temporal head.

Islamic respect for the community, both in Turkey and in Persia, was said by its members to be based on a tradition according to which the defenders of Nestorius were to be the most favoured church. As the main body of the Christians of the Persian Empire, they were a *millet* with their own institutions at the time of the Arab conquest; they gave advice and aid to the conquering monotheists in their conflict with the Magians or Zoroastrians. They were never associated with any political or military opposition to Islam, before or after the Crusades. They taught medicine and Greek philosophy to the Arabs. Even theologically they were considered to be closer to Islam than other Christians.

For many centuries the Christian neighbours of the Assyrian Nestorians were the Syrian Jacobites and the Armenian Monophysites. Jacobites and Nestorians spoke one Syriac language, even if they wrote it and pronounced it in different ways; they were one people in their history. The reason for their separation was a theological controversy which began in the Roman Empire in 431 and was carried into Mesopotamia and Persia during the fifth and sixth centuries. According to the Syrian-Orthodox or Jacobites and the Armenians, all defenders of Nestorius did not believe that Christ should properly be called our God. According to the Assyrian Nestorians, the Jacobites or Monophysites (Armenian and Syrian) did not believe that God the Word really took our nature upon Him. At the time when the controversy reached the Persian Empire full agreement with the views prevailing in Constantinople was unpopular there, for obvious political reasons. Thus hardly anyone in the Eastern regions treated both Nestorianism and Monophysitism as heretical.

The controversy may be briefly described as follows. Nestorius of Constantinople wrote in Greek and objected to a Greek word, *Theotokos*, meaning Bearer of God or Mother of God. He thought it wrong to speak of the birth, passion and death of God and of the miracles and resurrection of Man. He considered that Christ, rather than God or Man, should be the word used as the subject of the sentence in statements about the incarnation. Christ was born and died and rose again; His humanity was born and died and His deity triumphed over death. The refusal to say that God was born and died was heresy in the eyes of the opponents of the Nestorians. The Jacobites and Monophysites were the extreme wing of the opposition to this heresy.

The Ancient Church of the East thinks that this mode of speech and belief is falsely described as heresy; it existed long before Nestorius in her tradition. It may be possible to find individual expressions in her ancient prayers and hymns which Nestorius would have criticized; on that ground it has sometimes been contended that she is not Nestorian. But a comparison between her service books and those of all the other historic churches (especially in the Eastern half of Christendom) shows a clear mark of difference. It is not said in her prayers and hymns that God the Word was born and that Mary is the Mother of God the Word. In not using this type of language, the Assyrians seem to the rest of Christendom to be retaining and maintaining a distinctive Christological doctrine, whether this is to be called a heresy or not.

The Assyrians also have certain customs which are contrary to the practice of other historic churches. Their priests and deacons marry after ordination and re-marry on becoming widowers. At one period in their history their patriarchs, archbishops and bishops were allowed to marry. This custom prevailed in the fifth century and was abolished a century later. For nearly a thousand years after its abolition the bishops were drawn from the monasteries; but the disasters of the later middle ages swept away these foundations. The hierarchy had to take special measures to secure its own perpetuation. From the fifteenth century onwards each bishop had a brother and a sister-in-law who were ready to dedicate some of their children to the service of the church. These children were dedicated from birth; they ate no meat and (until released from the bond of their parents' vows) might not marry. One of the bishop's nephews was designated as the future bishop. One of his sisters was a celibate and was to be his housekeeper. A brother was married so that the family might go on. This was not a unique arrangement. In Montenegro from 1696 to 1851 the ruling prince was the Orthodox archbishop and was therefore a celibate; he was succeeded by his nephew. That the precarious freedom of the Assyrians might be maintained it was essential that their spiritual and temporal head should be appointed peacefully and speedily at each vacancy. Moreover, true vocations to celibacy were very rare in the mountains; peasant parents would not let their children remain unmarried, unless they saw their sons as future bishops. Between 1876 and 1914 the Anglican clergy and teachers living among them met only two or three celibate clergy not belonging to episcopal families. These were exceptional men, devoted to traditional learning and to the copying of MSS.; there were a few of them in each generation, living as hermits. It is doubtful whether they could have provided the episcopate.

All those who know how to read in Syriac sing the hymns and responses at the church services; this is not left to the choir, as it is or was until recently in the other historic churches of Eastern Christendom. The Eucharist, called the *qurbāna*, is celebrated only on the more important feasts. In the nineteenth century before each celebration of the Eucharist all the clergy and people fasted and attended special services of prayer for three days. Then all communicated; the people received both kinds separately, usually at the hands of two deacons. They communicated standing. Private confession was not customary; the priests either absolved the congregation as a whole after a general confession or gave absolution to individuals without any detailed self-accusation. The loaf to be consecrated was baked in the church with *the Holy Leaven*. This was believed to have come from Jerusalem; it was said that at the Last Supper the Beloved Disciple John took an additional piece of bread, to be used as leaven in baking in his own home. With this the bread was baked for the apostolic Eucharists after the resurrection; ever since a piece of dough from each baking of the Holy

Loaf has been kept for the next baking. It is not consecrated bread, being retained in the place of the oven and not placed on the Holy Table; but it links together all Eucharists and is an element in the conception of the Apostolic Succession, as held in the Ancient Church of the East.

Usually in their church buildings there are neither pictures nor statues. The cross is shown and is venerated; but it is generally without any picture of Christ upon it. There is no evidence of any formal or synodical prohibition of the use of pictures; their disappearance seems to have been due to poverty and lack of artists in an isolated community. But this austerity, in combination with the marriage of the clergy, congregational singing and the way in which communion was given, made a great impression on the American Protestants and British Anglicans who visited the Assyrians. They felt that they were meeting something essentially different from the religion to be found in the other historic churches of the Middle East. Actual lack of pictures also influenced the relations between the Assyrians and their Muslim neighbours. Western Christians living among them praised their family life and their loyalty to their community; but they noticed and blamed a tendency to quarrels between parties in that community.

The English-speaking friends of the Assyrians who visited them in the nineteenth century are conveniently divided into two groups, the men of the American Board of Missions and the Anglicans. The work of the American Board brought into existence the Reformed Churches in Persia and Iraq; but it was not begun with that intention. It was in conflicts between the pupils of the mission schools and the rest of the Assyrian community that local Protestantism emerged. Even after this the Americans continued to help the Ancient Church and her members; especially in Persia, they were associated with the Syriac-speaking community as a whole. They promoted the writing of books in modern Syriac. Anglican work took the form of a Mission of Help to the Assyrian Christians, sent by the archbishop of Canterbury at the request of the catholicos-patriarch, after preliminary inquiries. The name Assyrian was used and from that time forward the Nestorians were known as Assyrians in the English-speaking countries. The schools of the Anglican Mission of Help were church schools of the Ancient Church; the pupils went regularly to her services. On the other hand, the two churches, Assyrian and English, remained distinct; there was no inter-communion, although there are some indications that the

Assyrian clergy were anxious for inter-communion. It was repeatedly stated that, in the future, there was to be a dialogue between the two churches, on equal terms, aimed at unity on the basis of doctrinal harmony.

In the Roman Catholic view, the Assyrians needed reform in many ways; but the central issue was their attitude to the question of the visible unity of the church. The men of the American Board saw the justification for a Reformed Syrian or Reformed Nestorian Church in the rejection by the Ancient Church of what they called the Gospel. Only for the Anglicans was Nestorianism the principal issue. The Anglicans, wishing to improve their relations with the Greek Orthodox, the Syrian Orthodox and the Armenians as well as with the Assyrians, were anxious to avoid involvement in ancient controversies. Also they regard the Council of Ephesus as an authentic General Council, in terms of the Anglican tradition.

A very curious episode resulted from this. The service books of the Ancient Church of the East were printed by the Anglicans at Urmia; this was the first accurate printing of these liturgical texts in Syriac. The earlier printed editions had been Uniate and had been amended according to the requirements of Rome. In the Anglican edition a blank space was left wherever the names of Nestorius of Constantinople, Theodore of Mopsuestia and Diodore of Tarsus were found in the Syriac MSS. These three were heretics according to the decisions of General Councils recognized by the Anglican Church as well as by Rome and Constantinople. In the services of the Ancient Church of the East they were commemorated as faithful defenders of the truth. When each copy of the Anglican edition passed into the hands of the Assyrian ecclesiastical authorities, for use in church, the three names were inserted in the blank spaces by a scribe. There was a service in the course of which Cyril of Alexandria was anathematized for his attacks on Nestorius. I have not been able to find out whether the Anglicans actually printed this serivce; but I have no doubt that, if they did so, his name was omitted and reinserted in the same way.

In the last years of the nineteenth century a Russian Orthodox Ecclesiastical Mission appeared at Urmia in answer to an Assyrian appeal. A bishop and a large number of Assyrian clergy and laity declared for immediate union with the Orthodox Church, under Russian auspices. The Anglican Mission then moved from Urmia in Persia to Van in Turkey and much of their work was handed over to the Russians.

Prepared as they always were to defend the Assyrians in controversy with other Western Christians, the Anglicans were not ready for a controversy with the Orthodox about the conditions of a union between two Eastern churches.

Among the MSS. in the library of the catholicos-patriarch at Kuchanis was a book called *The Bazaar of Heraklides*, a Syriac translation of an autobiography of Nestorius written in exile after his condemnation. In 1908 an Anglican professor J. F. Bethune-Baker, published *Nestorius and his teaching*, a study based on this manuscript. He dedicated the book, in Latin, to the memory of Nestorius and to the Nestorian Church. It was not the only Anglican book published at that period which could well have created the impression that, among Anglicans, Nestorius was no longer anathema. The Assyrians could hope for union with Canterbury as Nestorians, without loss of face or change of doctrine. The Orthodox had to demand an anathema on Nestorius and the rehabilitation of Cyril of Alexandria. Rome had to demand submission. The American Protestants wanted a deep change of heart and mind; but they also wanted a fundamental alteration in the Assyrian conception of the Church. Desiring both reform and escape from isolation without dishonour and without a split in the community, the Assyrian leaders looked towards the Anglicans for support.

Then came their political catastrophe. The Ottoman Empire fell and the New Turkey arose. Orthodox Russia was swept away. The further growth of the Assyrian–Anglican relationship was frustrated by political complications.

Having been provoked by many Kurdish and Turkish attacks in 1914 and 1915, the independent Assyrian tribes severed their tributary relations with the Sultan, under the leadership of their catholicos-patriarch, Benjamin Mār Shim'ūn. In October 1915 the Assyrians of Turkey, including both the independent tribes and the *râya*, marched into Persia and joined the Russian forces there. In April 1918 their catholicos-patriarch was treacherously murdered by a Kurdish chieftain with whom he was negotiating. Some months later, as an army, accompanied by their families, the majority of the Assyrians marched in the direction of Iraq in order to meet the British forces. A minority took the other direction and went into revolutionary Russia.

Some 50,000 Assyrians, from Persia as well as from Turkey, were placed in a refugee camp at Ba'qūba near Hamadhān and were later moved to another camp at Mindān near Mosul. The brother of the murdered patriarch, Paul Mār Shim'ūn, was elected as his successor; but he died in 1920, to be succeeded by his nephew, Ishai Mār Shim'ūn, then a child of 11 years old. All the military operations in Turkey and Persia involved a great loss of life. This continued in the camps; the climate was unsuitable to mountain-dwellers and many children died. The men became an irregular fighting force, employed by the British army to operate against Kurds, Turks and rebels in Iraq. Later they were the guards defending the British R.A.F. stations. Between 1918 and 1924 it was thought likely that the final frontiers between the New Turkey, Iraq and Persia would leave a considerable part of Eastern Anatolia outside all three states. The Armenians, the Kurds and the Syriac-speaking communities might thus obtain some form of political independence. Some thought of the Syrian-Orthodox, the Assyrians and the Uniates using Syriac as forming a single Assyro-Chaldaean nation. Others considered that the Assyrians, as a nation, should have a country between Turkey and Persia. But neither diplomacy nor physical force had any success in these projects. The frontier between Turkey and Iraq, as it was drawn in 1924, left in Iraq only two small places which had been inhabited by Assyrian Nestorians before 1914, 'Amādiyya and Rawānduz. All Assyrians who returned to Turkey after 1918 were expelled by the Turks within a few months. Their hills and valleys in Turkey were given to others. A few places in Iraq which had been deserted by Turks or Kurds during the war were assigned to the Assyrians; but these did not form a homogeneous area. No one could displace people living normally in Iraq in order to settle the Assyrians; funds for buying land were not available in sufficient quantities.

A large proportion of the Assyrians in Iraq still thought of themselves as refugees who had not been settled on a permanent basis when the British Mandate came to an end. The Iraqis associated them with the Mandate; they had come into the country armed in order to fight on the side of the British and they had been in action against Iraqis. The Kingdom of Iraq was not unwilling to grant legal recognition to the jurisdiction of the Christian communities over their members, in such matters as marriage. But the Assyrians, especially the tribesmen from Hakkārī, wanted a different kind of autonomy. In particular, they wanted an area set apart for their own settlement, where they could be governed according to their traditional customs. Their young catholicos-patriarch went to Geneva to plead for this in 1932.

In 1933 there was a crisis; a body of armed Assyrians marched into

Syria to seek French protection. They were sent back into Iraq with their rifles; at the frontier they clashed with the Iraqi army. Fighting followed in various parts of Iraq. The catholicos-patriarch and several of his blood-relatives were deported. They were placed in Cyprus; seven years later the catholicos himself went to the U.S.A.

The Assyrians were dispersed. Between three thousand and four thousand of them are in America. About five thousand live in the Lebanon, where one thousand are now in the process of being settled in one village, on land bought for them under the auspices of the World Council of Churches. In the Jazīra district of north-eastern Syria several Assyrian and Syrian-Orthodox settlements were organized by the French, with the help of the League of Nations, during the thirties. But these settlements of refugees from Turkey on the Upper Zāb have not been a great success in the period of Syrian independence; many of their former inhabitants are now in the Lebanon. More Assyrians, perhaps as many as thirty thousand, are still in Iraq. But the political and military strife between Arabs and Kurds in the north of Iraq since 1958 has brought danger to all the minorities. Assyrians are moving southward into the larger towns and especially into Baghdad. Similarly in Persia the disorders which followed the Second World War made life in the countryside insecure. Attempts to create an independent Azerbayjan under Russian protection brought suspicion on Armenians and Assyrians who could be regarded as having historical links with Russia. Many have moved into the cities; there are now eight thousand Assyrians in Tehran. Under modern urban conditions questions of religion, race and community have less connexion with a man's chances of work than they have in rural areas. A modern secular life enables the minority to find a market for its talents.

In 1876 Canon E. L. Cutts in his book, *Christians under the Crescent in Asia*, estimated that the Ancient Church of the East had twelve bishops in addition to the catholicos, about two hundred and fifty priests and a larger number of deacons. The total membership of the community he thought to be about seventy-five thousand. At the present time the highest estimate of the number of church members given is a hundred thousand. It seems likely that seventy thousand would be more realistic; this would include six thousand Indians. It should be recognized that several Christian communities in the Middle East have doubled or even trebled their membership in the last hundred years, simply by natural increase. There are now five bishops in addition to the catholicos. Two of these are metropolitans, one in Iraq and the other in India. There is a bishop in Persia; the two other bishops are in Iraq. The catholicos is in the U.S.A. It has been estimated that there are sixty priests and that deacons are more numerous.

In the U.S.S.R. the Assyrians are no longer a church; as far as we know, they have no clergy of their own, although some of them are probably members of the Russian Orthodox Church. They are settled in the Caucasus and continue to speak Syriac. In the Arab countries it is difficult for the children of Syriac-speaking parents, educated in Arabic, to retain their grasp of Syriac. This has been easier where the predominant language is not Semitic. But nowadays in Persia life is making the retention of Syriac harder. The Assyrians have very few primary schools and in these the language of the country must be taught. There is no secondary education in Syriac and the only training provided for the future clergy is what the bishop can give in his own household. This is traditional; but a theological college is much desired by the Assyrians of the Middle East.

The Ancient Church of the East has her own English version of the Bible, translated from the Syriac; it is claimed that, at least in the Four Gospels, it is more accurate and less obscure, as an account of what was actually said and done, than translations from the Greek New Testament. An English translation of the liturgies of the church and an English catechism, dealing with doctrinal issues, have been produced in India. There the local language is also used and there is a small seminary; but Syriac is the only language of liturgical worship.

The catholicos-patriarch has been able to meet the other bishops on a few occasions. In 1962 he came to the Middle East, visited Beirut and Damascus and went to Persia, where he consecrated a bishop in Tehran. In 1964 he and the senior metropolitan met in the U.S.A. and wrote to all the bishops, announcing their acceptance of a new calendar. This meant that the Christmas and Easter of the Assyrians would coincide with those of Western Christendom. The same letter recommended certain modifications of the traditional church rules about prayer and fasting. A French translation of it was published in *Proche-Orient Chrétien*[1] in 1964. The catholicos has not designated his successor and has consecrated as a bishop at least one man not belonging to an episcopal family. It is evident that in India and elsewhere there are many

[1] By the White Father at St Anne's Church, Jerusalem, Jordan. Pp. 234–8 in the 1964 volume.

PART 1: JUDAISM

1 *a* *Hēkhal shelōmōh*, the seat of the Chief Rabbinate, in Jerusalem, Israel.

1 *b* Jews praying at the Wailing Wall in Jerusalem.

2 Scroll of the Law being shown to the congregation on *simḥaṯ tōrāh* (Rejoicing of the Law, the last day of the Feast of Tabernacles), in the ancient synagogue El-Griba (al-Gharība) on the Tunisian island of Djerba (Jarba).

3 *a* Old Jews reading Hebrew religious books in the synagogue al-Gharība on Jarba.

3 *b* Seven-armed candlestick—an example of contemporary Jewish religious art in Israel.

4 Ark (containing the scrolls of the Law) in a synagogue at Ṣafad, Israel. On the left is a modern painting of Rachel's tomb; on the right, one of the Wailing Wall.

5 *a* Young Jews reading from the Torah during service in an Israeli synagogue.

5 *b* Yemenite Jewess practising the traditional Jewish craft of damascene work.

6 Family from Yemen celebrating the Passover in Israel.

7 *a* Two Cochin (India) Jews discussing a passage in the Mishnah.

7 *b* From an illuminated Yemenite Pentateuch, folio 39*a* of the British Museum Codex Or. 2348, dated 1469. The contours of the fish in the centre contain verses from Psalm CXIX.

PART 2: CHRISTIANITY

8 St Catherine's Monastery, Sinai.

9 The Chair of St James in the twelfth-century Cathedral Church of St James the Great in the Armenian quarter of Jerusalem.

10 Interior of the modern Church of St Peter Gallicantu, Jerusalem.

11 *a* A silver cross from the Church of St Mary of Zion, Gondar, Ethiopia.

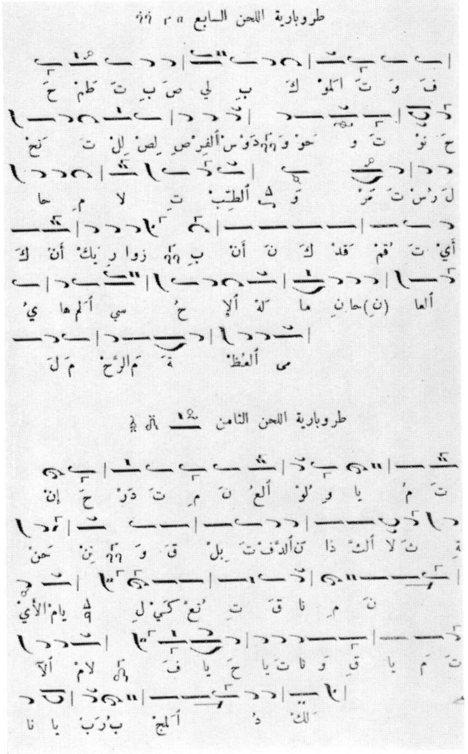

11 *b* A page from Mitri 'l-Murr's adaptation of Greek church music to Arabic—an example of Chrysanthine notation (a modern development of Middle Byzantine notation) in which Greek church music is usually printed. The signs indicate the nature and direction of the melodic movement within the framework of the mode (*laḥn*) indicated in the heading.

12 The Monastery of St Bishāy, Wādi 'l-Naṭrūn.

13 *a* The Cauldron of the Catholicosate of Cilicia in which the Holy Chrism is blessed.

13 *b* Illuminated fragment of a Nubian MS. from Qaṣr Ibrīm.

14 Interior of the Church of St Simon the Zealot, Shīrāz, Iran.

members of the Church who object to the system of episcopal families and want the hierarchy to be elective. An English pamphlet written by the Assyrian metropolitan of India on these lines, *The Assyrian Church and the Hereditary Succession*, was published in 1963.[1]

It has often been predicted that the Ancient Church of the East will disappear. It used to be said that in the Arab world and in India her members would become Roman Catholics, if in Persia and the Americas they became Protestants. A few years ago a number of Assyrian families near Mosul, whose candidate for the episcopate was not accepted, became Syrian-Orthodox; some of them say that they still want to belong to the Assyrian or Nestorian Church. No large group of Assyrians has become Roman Catholic in recent years. Protestant or Reformed Nestorians in the U.S.A. have joined the Ancient Church. It may be true that what the members of that church learn of their faith comes mainly from their grandmothers and great-aunts. But this is the only type of religious education available to Christians in a great part of the world today.

[1] At the Mar Narsai Press, Trichur, Kerala, India.

CHAPTER 12

THE LUTHERAN AND REFORMED CHURCHES

The subject of this chapter covers the whole field of Christian undertakings and activities which are of Western origin but which do not go by the name of Catholicism or of Anglicanism. Such a definition must be given at the outset, for one of the characteristics of the subject to be explored is the multiplicity of projects which have been accomplished there, almost independently of one another.

There are, nevertheless, three main communities, which have themselves sprung from three important and closely interdependent American societies: the Armenian Evangelical Union in the Near East, offspring of the American Board of Commissioners for Foreign Missions (A.B.)[1] which became in 1958 the United Board for World Ministries of the United Church of Christ; the Evangelical Synod in Syria and Lebanon, offspring of the Presbyterian Board (P.B.);[1] and the Coptic Evangelical Church, offspring of the United Presbyterian Church of North America (U.P.),[1] these two last societies being converted, by the fusion of their respective churches on 28 May 1958, into a Commission on Ecumenical Missions and Relations of the United Presbyterian Church in the U.S.A. The presence of the Lutheran element, for its part, has resulted from the employment of German and Swiss missionaries by the Anglican societies in the last century and also from that curious ecclesiastical adventure, the creation of the Anglo-Prussian bishopric in Jerusalem, an occurrence which serves as a reminder that, although the Anglicans are treated separately from the other Evangelical denominations in this book, relations between them all have always been very close in the Middle East. In Constantinople the British Ambassador always stood as the protector of the Protestants and was one of the promoters of Protestant influence. All the missionary societies had their origin in the Evangelical Revival, which disregarded confessional differences—a fact which over a long period and on many occasions has revealed itself both in their general policy and in the

[1] In this chapter these initials will be used from now on.

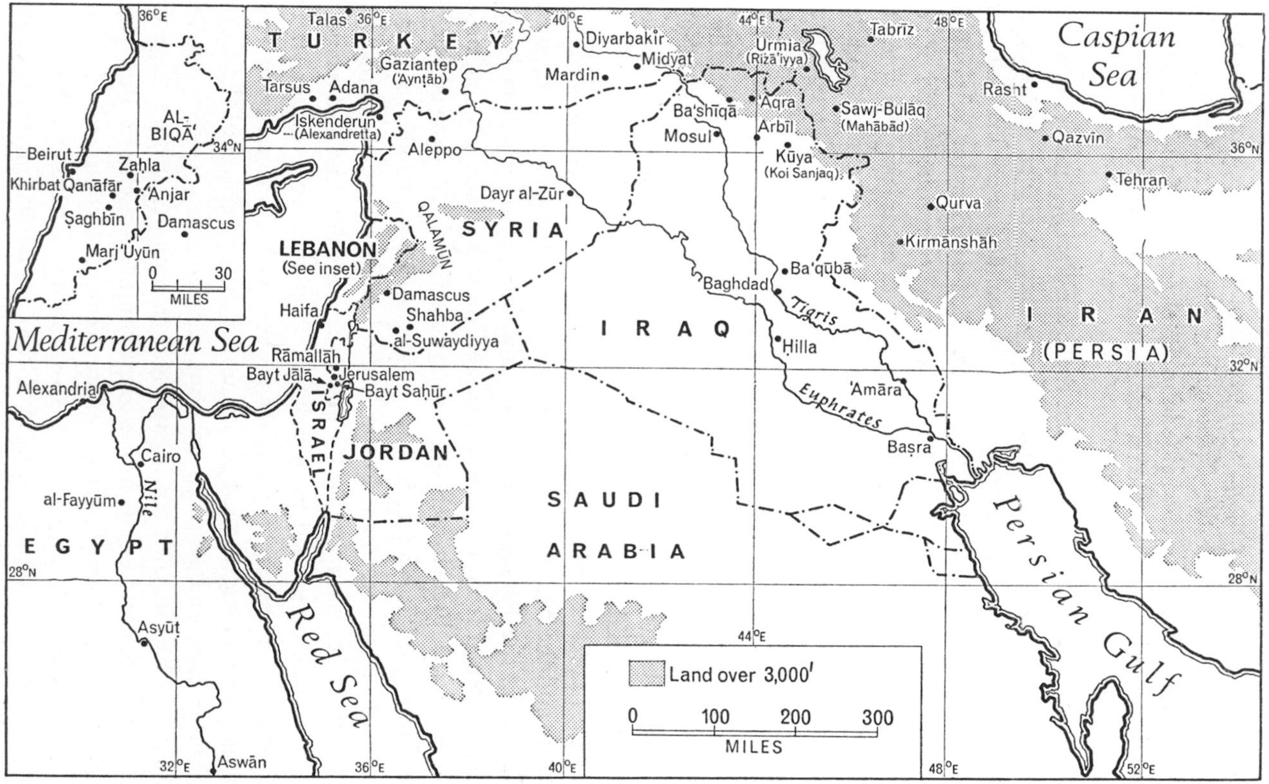

The Lutheran and Reformed Churches.

behaviour of their local representatives. The Anglo-Catholic renaissance, although laying more emphasis on points of difference, did not change deeply the outlook of the Episcopalian Arabs. Furthermore it has allowed the existence or even aided the development of a whole series of committees and councils which work for the co-ordination of effort and common witness.

More broadly, one may note that there are Protestant missions of all sorts and kinds organized almost everywhere, whether sectarian and separatist or, conversely, non-denominational and sometimes even inspired by purely philanthropic motives. This overlapping of good intentions, with its almost unbelievable wastage of resources and of personnel, and the efforts made to join together in organizing the common task, as well as the fissiparous tendencies which occur in each undertaking and the constant arrival of fresh missionaries, bringing with them their new variety of Protestantism, are the web on which is woven the story about to be told. It is necessary to keep in mind this unruly proliferation, even though the historian must dominate it intellectually in order to arrive at a view of the whole, and though the Christians who realise the demands of a sound ecclesiology are devoting their labours to the task of reducing it.

There have been many and varied points of contact between Protestants and the Middle East. From early times there were Protestants living under the Turkish Empire and subsequently in the national states which emerged from it, having been led there by their occupation or their fate: the French-speaking Protestant Parish of Constantinople stated in 1737: "It is a fact that no power in the world allows greater liberty of conscience than do the Mahommedans."[1] This parish had then already been in existence for more than one hundred and ten years and had been composed principally of craftsmen and traders. It included a fair number of French refugees, as well as refugees from Hungary and Transylvania, and was under the protection of the Dutch Embassy; each embassy had its own chaplain, just as each trading community had its own small parochial community. Hence there existed, and often still exists, in the great commercial cities a Protestant element which, although settled there, remained completely foreign, such, for example, as the English-speaking, French-speaking and German-speaking colonies in Constantinople, Izmir (Smyrna), Beirut, Alexandria and Cairo. These communities would lie outside the scope

[1] *BSHPF*, vol. XI (Paris, 1862), p. 75.

of the present subject if they had not repeatedly played an important part in the relationship between the Eastern Churches and Protestantism. The first missionaries were also in many instances their ministers and blended together the existing community with their new converts. This foreign Protestant element at the same time both materially assisted and often seriously compromised the native Protestants.

The interest shown in the Middle East by Protestantism was not originally nor solely a missionary interest aiming at the conversion of Muslims and Jews, but a theological and polemical interest which sought to base the standard of criticism applied to the Western Church on a better knowledge of the Church in the East. It may be said that this theological propensity dominated the sixteenth and seventeenth centuries,[1] whereas the missionary trend took the lead at the beginning of the nineteenth century. It may also be stated, however, that the theological interest itself acquired a missionary tone, for it was soon observed that Eastern Christianity was far from being ideal and the desire ensued to set in motion there a Reformation similar to that which had purified one section of Western Christianity. On the other hand, those who were subsequently to associate themselves with the missions to the Jews and to the Muslims were to see in the Eastern Churches chosen tools for this work, seeing them at first as auxiliaries and later aiming at reforming them so that they would at last become equal to this missionary task. In the end, by an ironic turn of events, it was from these Eastern Churches that almost all the Eastern Protestants were to be wrested, so that the great mission aimed at the conversion of non-Christians was not only diverted from its objective, but it even contributed to the still further weakening of the ancient Churches which it first had wished to support. It is only during the course of the last half-century and particularly since the growth of the ecumenical spirit that this state of affairs has begun to be remedied and that there have been signs of the beginnings of mutual disinterested help between the Reformed Churches and the ancient Eastern patriarchates.

As early as 1808 the London Missionary Society had sent several emissaries to Malta which, after its occupation by the English in 1800 and its definite annexation in 1811, was the starting-point for Protestant expansion in Eastern Mediterranean countries. It was, however, only

[1] On this question, which goes beyond the present survey, see the writer's article "Contacts entre l'Eglise orientale et le Protestantisme avant le début de l'ère missionaire", *IIIe Cahier d'études chrétiennes orientales* (Paris, 1965).

in January 1820 that the two first missionaries of the American Board reached the Middle East, landing at Smyrna. After a period of exploration, where centres of work changed frequently, in part because of the troubled political conditions of the time, from 1830 on the work settled in two distinct sections: one, with its centre in Constantinople, was directed toward the Armenians of Turkey; the other, from Beirut, dealt with the population of Mt Lebanon.

As a result of the work among Armenians and in spite of the massacres of 1895, which chiefly affected Eastern Turkey, and of 1909, which decapitated the Union of Cilicia, Armenian Protestantism at the outset of the 1914 war was full of vitality, with 140 churches, 100 pastors and 50,000 full-members. In the course of the war, however, it disappeared from Turkey, falling a victim to the genocide which afflicted the whole of the Armenian people at that time. It was only in Istanbul that a small Armenian population was able to continue, with the remnants of a Protestant community which today numbers three churches and fewer than 2,000 members.

The fate of Armenian Protestantism, as re-formed in the countries of refuge, Soviet Armenia, France and the United States, cannot be followed here, but it is necessary to mention those groups which re-established themselves in the Middle East. In Iran the refugees came to reinforce an already existing Armenian population and Armenians represent about half of the Iranian Protestants in the organization of which they have been more or less integrated. In Egypt, Armenian Protestants have one church in Cairo and another in Alexandria, with perhaps a thousand members altogether. It was in Syria and the Lebanon, however, that the most numerous and active community was reconstituted, with a total of twenty-five churches and 6,000 members in Syria, and seven churches and a further 6,000 members in the Lebanon. They organized themselves into a new union of Armenian Evangelical Churches, at first confined to Syria and the Lebanon and then extended, about ten years ago, over the whole of the Middle East.

The disaster of 1920 compelled the A.B. to revise its plan of action completely. After a moment of hesitation, it abandoned to their fate the Armenians who had been uprooted from Turkey and decided to continue its missions on Turkish territory and in the same buildings as before, though what had originally been intended to serve primarily the former Christian populations was now put at the disposal of Muslims alone. There are three medical foundations: the hospital at Gaziantep

('Ayntāb) and the clinics of Talas and Adana. The sixty-four primary schools which had been reopened were closed by government decree in 1942. Four secondary schools continue to function, however: two for girls at Usküdar (Scutari), a suburb of Constantinople, with 500 pupils, and at Izmir with 560 pupils; two for boys, at Talas, and at Tarsus with 170 and 300 pupils respectively. About 95 per cent of these children are Muslims, the remainder being divided about equally between Christians and Jews.

The only Protestant communities which remain in the interior of Turkey are composed of rather fewer than a thousand Christians of Syriac origin, in Kurdish country in the south-east of Anatolia; they are to be found at Diyarbakîr and Mardin and especially in five little village churches, the most important of which is Midyat, surrounded by Killit, Middih, Karburan and Hessena. There are also several families at Iskenderun (Alexandretta).

In addition the A.B. continues to share, on an equal footing with the P.B. and with the native churches, in the direction of the College of Aleppo which has 670 pupils and is the successor, in the country of refuge, to the former college of Central Turkey at 'Ayntāb. It also collaborates, on the same terms, with the Near East School of Theology at Beirut, established in 1932 by the amalgamation of the School of Religious Workers of the P.B. with the School of Religion created at Constantinople in 1922 by the A.B. to replace its three seminaries of Masovan, Marash and Harput which were destroyed by the war, and transferred almost at once to Athens under pressure of events.

The American Press, transferred to Beirut in 1834, was for several decades the most modern and almost the only Arab press of this region.[1] This Protestant press was the first to publish the works of the great Maronite scholar of the beginning of the eighteenth century, the Bishop Germanos Farat, from whose writings it produced three volumes between 1836 and 1841.[2] It also republished in 1834 a work of the no less famous Greek Catholic layman Abdallāh Ẓāhir, which had been originally published at the convent of Ẓuhūr al-Shuwayr in 1764 and for many years could not be traced.[3] The Press had an immense programme for the publication of religious treatises, cultural works and school-books. But its principal achievement was certainly the translation of the Bible into Arabic, which was begun in 1848 under the

[1] Bibliog. of the main Arab titles of the press at Malta and Beirut, in G. Graf (see below, p. 669), vol. IV, pp. 281–5. [2] Graf, vol. III, pp. 417–21. [3] *Ibid.* p. 195.

direction of Eli Smith, with the help of Buṭrus al-Bustānī and Nāṣīf al-Yāzijī, and was continued from 1857 onwards by Cornelius Van Dyck. After the publication of separate fascicles from 1846, the whole Bible was published in two volumes in 1864[1] and, from 1867, was produced by the electro-type method, making it possible to flood the market with copies at a low price.

Simultaneously with this important literary output, the missionaries were developing their teaching missions, not only at Beirut but throughout the whole region. There was a vigorous Catholic reaction and half of the nineteenth century was dominated in the Lebanon by this strong rivalry, from which the people themselves ultimately reaped considerable advantages since both faiths competed in serving the community through education and health-service. The Jesuits came to Lebanon for that explicit purpose and they were the most active opponents of the Protestants. The first to engage in combat was however the Maronite patriarch, Joseph Ḥubaysh, who, on 15 December 1826, had issued a decree of excommunication against those associating with the Protestants, and who renewed his censures after the return of the missionaries in 1830. Such opposition did not prevent the missionaries from gaining converts and on 31 March 1848 the First Arab Evangelical Church was officially established in Beirut. At the beginning Protestantism had made very little progress in the mountainous regions of the Lebanon. But the missionaries set to work to try to save lives and to alleviate the greatest hardships during the massacres of May 1845 and May 1860.

Their actions mitigated somewhat the existing prejudice against Protestantism and it was thus imagined that spectacular successes were about to be achieved. The illusion was soon dispelled, however, and although small Arab evangelical parishes were formed and maintained, chiefly around the mission schools, there was never a mass movement comparable with the progress of Armenian Protestantism in other areas.

In 1870 upon the reunification of the two principal branches of North American Presbyterianism, it was decided that the A.B. should transfer its missionary activities in Syria to the Presbyterian Board. The P.B. settled in Zaḥla in 1872, Aleppo in 1920 and had a very successful medical work in Dayr al-Zūr from 1924 to 1958. The Irish Presbyterians for their part had begun missionary work in Damascus in 1843. The Church set up as a result became completely independent

[1] On this publication see Graf, vol. I, pp. 98–9, and John A. Thompson, *The Major Arabic Bibles* (New York, 1956), pp. 20–7.

in 1948. Part of the work started by the Irish in the mountains north-west of Damascus was resumed in 1900 by the Danish *Orient Mission* which had been established by the efforts of the missionary Fox Maule in the region of the Qalamūn. It is noteworthy that this mission, although coming from a Lutheran country, adopted the Presbyterian system in order to work in harmony with the rest of Syrian Protestantism. The achievements of the Irish and Danish missionaries were thus able to be fused without friction with those of the American missionaries in the service of the Lebanese–Syrian Synod.

Farther south, in Palestine, an Anglo-Prussian bishopric had been founded in 1841 on the basis of the very peculiar theological conceptions of King Frederick William IV.[1] From 1846 to 1879 the titular holder of this bishopric was Samuel Gobat, a Swiss of German education and sympathies, who was appointed to the position by the King of Prussia. He was able to secure the help of Kaiserwerth deaconesses, who were soon reinforced by a German pastor. A *Jerusalem Verein* was founded in 1853 and, in 1860, the Anglican Bishop did not hesitate to put it in charge of the parish of Bethlehem. In 1879 a second Arab Lutheran parish was created at Bayt Jālā, quite close to Bethlehem. With the end of the Anglo-German agreement in 1886 the Lutherans acquired still more independence and established in 1899 a third parish at Bayt Saḥūr, in the same neighbourhood. Finally in October 1898 the Emperor William II came to Palestine in person. He made a triumphal entry into Jerusalem and inaugurated, on the day of the Feast of the Reformation, the Lutheran Church of the Saviour (*Erlöser Kirche*), built directly opposite the Holy Sepulchre, on the site of the Muristan which the Sultan had given to the King of Prussia in 1869. William was accompanied by his wife and it was as a result of their visit that the enormous *Stiftung Kaiserin Augusta Victoria* was built, a symbol of German influence in Palestine. The German Crown Prince also came to inaugurate its chapel in 1910. As a result of the two World Wars the building passed through many and various hands; today it is the property of the Lutheran World Federation and is administered by Kaiserswerth.

In 1854 Ludwig Schneller arrived in Jerusalem; he was to be in charge of the mission station in the Holy City of the "Apostles' Road", which Spittler, the founder of the St Chrischona Mission at

[1] See the writer's series of articles "L'évêché anglo-prusse à Jérusalem (1841–81)"; "Controverses autour de sa création (1841)"; *POC*, vols. XIII (1963), pp. 130–49 and 234–58; XIV (1964), 184–201 and 307–34. A complete basic bibliography relating to the German Lutheran mission in Palestine will be found there, p. 135, numbers 44 to 48.

Basle, dreamed of pursuing as far as Ethiopia. After Spittler's death in 1867 the project was abandoned, but at the end of 1860 Schneller (1820–96) had gathered together orphans who had escaped from the Lebanon massacres and had founded in the plain of Judea the Syrian Orphanage which was to continue an eventful but blessed existence under the administration of his son and then of his grandson. Large properties were rented in 1890 and subsequently purchased in 1906. These were confiscated by the State of Israel in 1948, but the Orphanage, which at first took refuge in Bethlehem with one hundred orphans, was finally re-established in the Biqā' at Khirbat Qanāfār, where its buildings were opened in 1952.

The deaconesses, on the other hand, opened a boarding-school for girls, Talitha Cumi, and a hospital in Jerusalem. In 1900 they numbered about one hundred and were also working in hospitals in Beirut, Constantinople, Alexandria and Smyrna. Only their missions in Palestine and in Egypt have been able to survive until the present day.

There was at one stage quite a German colonization of Palestine. In 1868 Christopher Hoffman started a colony of his "Spiritual Temple" at Haifa. On the eve of 1914, there were four such colonies, numbering 1,330 inhabitants.

Schneller, for his part, had established an actual settlement where his orphans, who had grown up and were provided with land, formed a community and continued to live there in a German Protestant atmosphere. As a result of the two World Wars, and more particularly the second, this attempt at population and settlement was completely swept away, though the German evangelical missions were allowed to continue in the service of the Arab population. There exists today an Arab Lutheran Church in Jordan, officially registered by the Jordan government on 17 May 1958 and comprising, in addition to the four parishes already mentioned, that of Rāmallāh created in 1956; the Lutheran influence secured by a German Probst, with the active support of the World Lutheran Federation, remains considerable.

As regards the region which forms present-day Iraq, Mosul was from time to time occupied by the American Board. But the first serious evangelical work was done in the southern part of the country by the Arabian Mission of the Reformed Church in America. In 1892 it occupied Basra, the gateway to Arabia; it then proceeded northwards and came to 'Amāra in 1901 and finally to Baghdad in 1919. But this little church was not strong enough for its mission to occupy the whole of Iraq single-handed after its constitution as an independent State. On the other hand, at the end of the First World War, almost the whole of the population looked after by the P.B. from Urmia had disappeared from this region and many had taken refuge in Iraq, whither the missionaries had followed them, reoccupying Mosul. Accordingly in 1923 a United Mission in Iraq was founded, uniting the forces of the two Societies with the addition of the A.B. and the southern Presbyterians.

Once organized, however, the United Mission was more concerned with evangelism farther afield than with the care of existing communities. In particular, it refused to allow itself to be identified with the Nestorian plans for political revenge which were to lead to disaster in 1933. Very soon the Mission effectively abandoned the Syriac schools in order to devote itself to three Arab schools, one for boys and one for girls in Baghdad, one for girls at Mosul, as well as an undertaking among the Kurds beyond Mosul. Further south, Ḥilla was occupied in 1926 and it was in 1929 that the Mission reached the peak of its development. Afterwards it was confronted simultaneously with internal difficulties, with the political troubles which started in 1931 and finally with the financial consequences of the world depression. Its decline during the ensuing seventeen years was such that the average number of missionaries working in Iraq was not more than four. By 1958, however, it had again risen to twenty-two. The political upheaval of 14 July 1958, although at the outset a source of vexation to all foreigners, at least helped the Mission to free itself from its antiquated structures and in order to mark its reorganization the name was changed to the Iraq Fellowship. The mission station at Baṣra, with its two schools especially designed for the poorer classes, and the station at 'Amāra, for the time devoid of staff, which until then had been included within the Arabian Mission, were officially incorporated into the Iraq Fellowship on 1 January 1962. The boy's school at Baghdad had to be closed in 1929; the girls' school at Mosul in 1941. The only large school to survive was the girls' school at Baghdad, which was opened in 1925. It once had up to 250 pupils, but since only the secondary classes have been retained the number has fallen to 150.

The American Board started work among the Nestorians of Persia at Urmia in 1835. It was officially decided to extend it to the Armenians on the one hand, to the Muslims on the other, in 1870, the very year where the field was transfered to the Presbyterian Board. Nevertheless in 1885, at the time of the Mission's Jubilee, virtually the only protestant organization was to be found among the Assyrians of the extreme north-west. They had twenty-five fully constituted churches with six thousand adherents. The First World War was to impose a terrible ordeal on the whole of this region. The Mission tried to alleviate the hardships of all and to protect by turns Christians and Muslim Kurds, who were alternately subject to massacre by the hordes of the other creed. After the mass exodus of the Nestorian people in 1917, Urmia became practically depopulated and it then assumed the new name of Riżā'iyya. The mission station nevertheless continued its work and even constructed a magnificent hospital in 1931, but two years later the station was finally closed by order of the government. Between 1920 and 1930 the Mission had made a special effort on the medical side. Hospitals, many of them excellent, were built or reconstructed at Rasht (1923), Mashhad (1924 and 1935), Kirmānshāh (1929) and Tehran (1930). In 1932 three quarters of the mission schools, all those designed for young children, were closed by order of the government. The remainder in their turn were shut by a new decree at the end of 1939. With the return of some Assyrians to their former territories after 1920, sixteen evangelical churches were re-established in this region and a presbytery was organized uniting them together and with the church of Tabrīz. These churches were ravaged afresh by the disturbances following the Second World War, when Azerbayjan came for a time under the authority of the Democratic party, supported by the Russians against the central government. Since then they have continued to decline as a result of unceasing emigration. At the same time, however, their activities developed especially in the region around Mashhad, where a church was established in 1921, and where there is a small but vigorous Christian community gathered out from a non-Christian background. In addition, the First World War brought in a flood of Armenian refugees, among whom were a fair number of Protestants; these have contributed materially to the reinforcement of the churches of the interior and to the foundation of new communities, particularly in Tehran, where there subsequently arrived also the Assyrian elements who had deserted Urmia.

In concluding this survey it remains to consider Egypt. The General Synod of the Associate Reformed Presbyterian Church opened a mission station in Cairo in 1854. In 1857 Alexandria was also occupied. In 1860 the missionaries were making extensive use of the *Ibis*, a pleasure-boat used for evangelical meetings as far down the Nile as Aswān. They then used several other boats for the same purpose. By this means evangelical influence extended along the whole course of the river. At the beginning most of the Protestants were to be found in the region of Asyūṭ, while the delta was almost untouched. But in recent years there has been a spectacular development in the delta, chiefly in Cairo. Today there are in Egypt eight Presbyteries, united in the Synod of the Nile which proclaimed its independence from the Mission in 1926. The relatively large number of its followers makes it a living and authentic reality, much more substantial than the Lebanese–Syrian Synod or, *a fortiori*, than Iraqi or Iranian Protestantism. In this respect it can only be compared with the former state of Armenian Protestantism. But, whereas the latter formed part of a different nation from that to which the Muslim majority belonged, the Egyptian Protestants are descended without any possible question from the most ancient stock of the Egyptian people.

Some information must also be given on the smaller Protestant missions working in the area, since the general public usually knows nothing about their history. The majority of them are missions for relief, which originated in the last century at the time of the great massacres of Christians under the Turkish Empire. The most important is the Lebanon Evangelical Mission, which was founded by Mrs E. Bowen Thompson in October 1860 under the name of the British Syrian Mission.[1] This is essentially an educational mission, but it has also developed a medical branch. It has been characterized throughout by the vigour of its evangelistic activities. Although a fair number of its workers have been Anglicans and it was at one time in close touch with the bishop in Jerusalem, this mission has always worked in agreement with the Lebanese–Syrian Presbyterians and has never engaged in disruptive activity. The same was true of the Knights of St John and of the Deaconesses of Kaiserswerth, who also came to the Lebanon in response to the massacres of 1860 and who, pursuing a different line from the one followed in Palestine, did not attempt to create separate Lutheran parishes. These German missions in the Lebanon were confiscated outright by the French after the First World War and the deaconesses had to leave in August 1920. An *Association des Œuvres protestantes françaises en Syrie et au Liban* inherited the property of the deaconesses in 1925 and set to work in 1927. At first it maintained

[1] See J. D. Maitland-Kirwan, *Sunrise in Syria* (London, 1930), and Frances E. Scott, *Dare and Persevere* (London, 1960).

dispensaries at Damascus and in the Jabal Druze, at al-Suwaydiyya and at Shahba, but they were closed at the termination of the French mandate and only the ophthalmological dispensary at Beirut has been carried on until the present day. The chief success of the Association has been the French Protestant College at Beirut. Where the German deaconesses had received 130 orphans at Christmas 1860, there were in 1956 more than 1,000 pupils, mainly girls belonging to the best Lebanese families. In the same year the existing premises in the rue Chateaubriand were discarded in favour of fine new buildings erected at Ra's Beirut on land belonging to the French Embassy. The number of pupils is now in excess of 1,300. This splendid educational undertaking has adopted wholeheartedly the official French government viewpoint and is thus forbidden all brotherly contact with the German societies whose spoils it has acquired. It is not primarly concerned to put itself at the service of Lebanese Protestantism, but has hitherto been more of a cultural than an evangelical mission.[1]

In the same way the Armenian massacres of 1895 gave rise to the *Deutscher Hilfbund für Christliches Liebeswerk im Orient* (D.H.L.) with its seat at Frankfurt on Main and an affiliated society in Switzerland. This organization has today only one mission in the Armenian village of ʿAnjar in the Lebanon; but on 6 December 1922 one of its former workers, the respected pastor Paul Berron, founded the *Action Chrétienne en Orient* (A.C.O.) which, in full agreement and fundamental spiritual communion with the Frankfurt Mission, took up the task which under the French mandate the latter was no longer able to continue in Syria and in the Lebanon. The A.C.O. now shares in the work in Jazira, at Aleppo, at Beirut and at Ṣaghbīn, in the Biqāʿ. Its principle has been not to have independent missions, but to work throughout with native Arab and Armenian Evangelical churches, and for their benefit.[2] The *Deutsche Orient Mission* was founded also in 1895 by Dr Lipsius. After he had left this first society his friends created the *Dr Lipsius Armenisches Hilfwerk* in order to carry on his work. Lipsius was an indefatigable founder of orphanages and of refuges for Armenian widows at Urfa, Urmia and Kūya (Koi Sanjaq); his missions have by now disappeared, but his name remains a symbol of Christian fidelity and clear-sightedness

[1] See on this subject the present writer's *Lettre concernant l'aumônerie du College protestant français de Beyrouth, adressé aux membres du Comité des Œuvres protestantes françaises en Syrie et au Liban*, 10 pp. roneographed (Beirut, 1958).

[2] Cf. Paul Berron, *Une œuvre missionaire en Orient et en Occident. Origine et développement de l'Action Chrétienne en Orient* (Strasburg, undated [1963]).

at a period when most people were blinded by nationalist emotions. The Christians of the Middle East were frequently made the playthings and victims of divergent interests among the Western Powers, and even the missionaries themselves were sometimes mere tools, fooled by the slogans of their respective countries, but in 1916 Lipsius had the courage to denounce by written and spoken word the Armenian massacres which were in the course of being perpetrated. Even though the reaction of German Protestantism which he awakened remained ultimately ineffective, it may at least be said that the honour of evangelical Christianity was thus vindicated.

It is in succession to the interest formerly aroused by Lipsius that a number of small Lutheran missionary societies carry on their work today, directing their efforts towards the remnants of the Nestorian people and the Kurds in the northern part of the frontier region between Iraq and Iran. They are to be found at Ba'shīqā and Arbīl in Iraq, at Sawj-Bulāq and at Qurva (Ghorveh), where the Lutheran Orient Mission has just opened a hospital in Iran.

In spite of the wide variety of conditions and localities, it may perhaps be possible to define several major problems. First there is the problem of Israel. The missionary urge towards the Holy Land had its origin largely in the attention paid by the revivalist movement to the prophecies concerning the return and the conversion of Israel, interpreted as messianic signs. To tell the truth, it appears that the first missionaries expected to find a Palestine which was already Jewish and were somewhat surprised to discover it to be mainly peopled by Arabs. There were however considerable Jewish communities through the whole of the Middle East and missionary stations were accordingly established in the Jewish quarters of Constantinople, Alexandria, Smyrna and Damascus. Today they have all completely disappeared, engulfed by the great upheavals of the twentieth century. On the other hand Jewish immigration to Palestine was intensified, particularly after the end of the nineteenth century, until it culminated in the creation of the State of Israel.

The situation was thus entirely transformed, not only with regard to the geographical distribution of missionary work, but from the ideological standpoint. Political Zionism developed in a way that was very different from the interpretation of the prophecies. But it is difficult to convey this difference and, even for the Church on the spot, to envisage it clearly when the same words, or very nearly the same, are used in both instances. Protestantism in the Arab World was thus particularly sensitive to the injustice inherent in the creation of such a State, established at the expense of a population which had done nothing to deserve that fate.

Zionism, both political and religious, had, of course, long anticipated the Nazi persecutions, but these have created in much of the Western world a sense of guilt which in turn has played its part in helping to create the State of Israel. This is something which the Arab peoples find it impossible to accept. As they see it there is no moral advantage in giving back a country to an uprooted people if, by the very same act, another people is uprooted from its country and now has a home no more. Acting on these considerations the Arab Church was unfortunately tempted to take the line of dissociating itself from everything which, directly or indirectly, was connected with the idea of Israel. In relation to human beings, such a position might lead to a serious lack of charity. The position of the convert has been and remains tragic. "In the bitter strife of Palestine today the Christian Jew finds it almost impossible to live at all. Among Jews because he is a Christian, and among Arabs because he is a Jew."[1] More serious still, however, is the danger of reaching a stage of no longer daring to read the Old Testament or of expunging from the hymn-books all such suspect terms as "Zion", "Jerusalem", etc. The Church is thus being menaced by a theological corruption similar to Marcionism or to that of the *Deutsch Christen*.

Conversely, there is a risk that those who work in Israel may develop a Judaeo-Christianity which could be equally heretical, forgetting that in Christ there is no longer either Jew or Greek. In effect, missionary work in the new State has become paralysed and there exists virtually no native evangelical church. But already in 1941 as important a writer as McDougall was speaking of the need for a Hebrew Christian Church,[2] a conception which has since acquired authority. In so far as the universal Church aims at becoming naturalized in Israel, as it should be in each country instead of retaining the particular characteristics of the missionaries' country of origin, there is obviously a need for it. But this process of naturalization must never be allowed to obscure the essential universality of Christianity. Protestantism in the

[1] W. H. Stewart, "Palestine Today", *The East and West Review*, vol. XIV (1948), pp. 67–71; quoted from p. 70.

[2] David McDougall, *In Search of Israel* (London, 1941), p. 171.

former Ottoman Empire had already encountered difficulties through being regarded as a single *millet*, whereas those to whom it was addressed belonged to different communities which were for them realities of a national rather than a religious character. Many people were under the impression that they would cease to be Armenians, Greeks or Assyrians if they became Protestants and the question presents itself afresh today with the absence of the Union of Armenian Evangelical Churches from the discussions held with a view to creating a United Evangelical Church of the Arab World. Although some of its reasons may be open to criticism, one of them is real enough: it is the desire to preserve a close relationship with the Gregorian mother-Church, a subject which will be discussed further. However, in the case of Judaism, it would be precisely this last aspect which would be heretical, for it is the whole Christian Church which claims to be the new Israel.

Certainly the use of scriptural texts for the purpose of asserting that politically Palestine belongs *de jure* to the Jews of today displays an exorbitant fundamentalism. Many "Arab" refugees, at least among those coming from Galilee, are descendants of those "true Israelites" who recognized in Jesus of Nazareth "the Christ of God". The author of this relevant observation states in conclusion: "Apart from the problem of prophecy, its diverse interpretations, or its being morally conditioned, there would seem a pressing need for an unequivocal statement as to what the Christian Church means by *Israel*. Is its connotation spiritual, political or geographical? How far do the respective interpretations of the *promises to Abraham* by Jews and Christians agree or conflict?"[1]

Another major problem has been that presented by *Islam*. It is certain that most of the believers whose generous gifts made it possible to maintain and develop the mission believed that its object, when it was not the conversion of the Jews, was the conversion of Muslims. It was pleasant to imagine a new, peaceful, crusade which, following in the steps of Raymond Lull, would bring the Light of the Gospel to the Islamic peoples. And it was quite often thought that Protestantism, which was devoid of all superstition and of all seemingly idolatrous practices, had a better chance than Catholicism of reaching souls which were dedicated to a strict monotheism, and of bringing them a pure

[1] Eric F. F. Bishop, "What is the place of the Old Testament in Christian worship?", *Hibbert Journal*, vol. LII (1954), pp. 134–40. Quoted from p. 139.

Christianity. Jessup went so far as to combine with these ideas some rather strange racial considerations when he stated at Saragota Springs on 18 May 1879, before the General Assembly of the Presbyterian Church which had just elected him as its moderator: "It is (my) purpose...to show the evident plan and providence of God in the past, present and future relations of the Anglo-Saxon Christian race to the Mohamedan world...The Mohamedan religion arose, in the providence of God, as a scourge to the idolatrous Christianity... and a preparation for the future conversion to a pure Christianity."[1] In fact, however, conversions of Muslims have always been extremely rare and the missionary societies were really committing an abuse of confidence, though perhaps unconsciously, when they omitted to specify in their statistics the religion to which their converts belonged before becoming Protestants. One obstacle was the complete identification of religious adherence with membership of the political community, which is still a characteristic of Islam as it was of medieval Christianity. It applied not only to Turkey, where the Sultan 'Abdülḥamid was to lay claim to the title of Caliph, but also to Shī'ite Persia and it remained largely true of Syria, Iraq, Jordan and Egypt when these countries had acquired their independence. Adherence to Islam, at first regarded as a unifying link in a multi-national state, was later often to be considered as a national characteristic, chiefly in relation to the West, from whose guardianship each of the States concerned was engaged in emancipating itself. A change of creed among persons who were already outside Islam was unimportant, but the defection of a Muslim amounted to political treason and any incitement to such defection on the part of foreign missions was a threat to the security of the State. It was tolerated by governments only when they were powerless to resist the demands of the Western Powers, a fact which aggravated still further their sense of wounded national pride. Besides, even when governmental assurances had been obtained, popular feeling gained the upper hand. It was his own social environment which repudiated the guilty one and often his own family which effected his disappearance. The same weakness which had obliged the government to admit conversions provided it with an excellent pretext for declaring itself powerless in the face of such events. Only in Egypt did the British protectorate guarantee a minimum of security and converts often sought asylum there. Most frequently, however, the missionaries shrank from the risk to the

[1] H. H. Jessup, *The Mohamedan Missionary Problem* (Philadelphia, 1879), p. 13.

mission itself and from the responsibility to be assumed for neophytes. "The missionaries abstained from trying to influence the Mohamedan population", states Richter, speaking of the A.B.[1] This remark is also applicable to most of the other societies. Only two of them were to aim expressly at the conversion of Muslims: the German *Orient Mission of Lipsius* in Turkey and in Persia, from 1900 until the upheavals which followed the First World War had come to put an end to its work, and the Egypt General Mission, operative from 1898 onwards. In the face of these hard facts, references to indirect Christian influence or to "secret believers" appear principally as escape-clauses. Forty years ago Richter was saying that "The Mohamedan missions in the countries round the Mediterranean are yet in the period of preparation. The end of the first period of the missionary movement is generally reached when the formation of Christian congregations has begun and is advancing. As long as Christian congregations are more or less impossible, we have not advanced beyond the period of preparation."[2] Except in Iran, there is not yet a single Protestant congregation which contains any significant proportion of members of Muslim origin, and the illusion that Protestantism could look forward to notable successes in this sphere is dead indeed. In the realistic words of an expert in a related field of activities, the Maghrib: "If statistics alone were the basis of judgment...missions to the Muslims would (then) be a large-scale waste of time, effort, intelligence and lives."[3] He thinks that the quest for numerous conversions is illusory and perhaps even dangerous. But he insists on the fact that the duty of the Church is to "lift high" Jesus Christ, to bear full and radiant witness before all men without paying too much attention to visible results which are, ultimately, the concern of the Holy Spirit itself. Protestantism in the Middle East has, in this account, been gravely burdened by its worldly "successes". The weight of responsibility for numerous premises and institutions has not only monopolized the attention of the Western missionaries, but has often caused them to shrink from the prospect of losing them if they deliver too clearly the message which it is their function to impart. Hence the author of an article which is severe but full of just observations[4]

[1] Julius Richter, *A History of Protestant Missions in the Near East* (London, 1910), p. 171.

[2] J. Richter, "The Present Situation in the Near East", *Moslem World*, vol. XIV (1924), pp. 114–17. Quoted from p. 116.

[3] W. N. Heggoy, *Fifty Years of Evangelical Missionary Movement in North Africa, 1888–1938* (University Microfilms Inc.; Ann Arbor, 1962), p. 14.

[4] E. M. Earle, "American Missions in the Near East", *Foreign Affairs*, vol. VII (1929), pp. 391–417.

quotes with legitimate surprise a letter written by H. O. Dwight in 1895, in which he represented the A.B., in whose name he was writing, to the American authorities "from the point of view of a business enterprise". After having strained the analogy to include even matters of detail, he concluded "$7,000,000 is a rough way of estimating the money value of the stock, real estate, equipment and other property provided by Americans for our present operations in Asiatic Turkey".

Similarly the relatively important native communities which were founded in one region or another from non-Muslim elements came to resent the chance arrival of Muslim converts as a foreign intrusion and something which was to be avoided at all costs as a very dangerous threat in the face of legal and social prohibition. There seem, however, to be important changes now in progress in this respect. The witness of Christianity before Islam is being regarded more and more as a bounden duty and a joyful calling, as much by native Christians as by missionaries. It is also becoming more of a concrete possibility. The struggle in terms of power and of conquest, even though limited to the spiritual plane, appears to be increasingly out-dated. Discussion between the men of different religions has at last become fairer. Neither tries to dwell only on the weaknesses of the other, nor does he regard himself as having the right to offer him anything less than the entirety of his own faith.

A third problem has been that of the *Ancient Churches*.[1] The Protestant missionaries of the nineteenth century found themselves in a spiritual world of which they were completely ignorant. And, even though they certainly had no premeditated plan for undermining the Eastern Churches, they did show a complete lack of understanding. The highly coloured but hopelessly negative account which the missionaries E. Smith and H. G. O. Dwight gave of their stay in Echmiazin, from 19 to 23 November 1830, is very revealing on this point.[2] Oriental hospitality had thrown open to them the doors of the residence of the catholicos, a reception which the travellers seemed, incidentally, to regard as theirs by right. Instead of showing the smallest gratitude, they thought only of surveying their surroundings with a critical and accusing eye. Their sole comment, after being invited to be present at the Holy Liturgy, was: "The Armenian Church turns into a solemn

[1] See R. Pierce Beaver, *Ecumenical Beginnings in Protestant World Mission* (New York, 1962), pp. 203–19.

[2] *Missionary Researches in Armenia* (London, 1834). (The original edition of Boston and New York, in 2 vols., is dated from the previous year.) Letters 15 and 16, pp. 280–311.

farce the celebration of that simple ordinance" of the Lord's Supper[1] and it was the Vartabet John Sourenean, secretary to the catholicos, who had to give them a lesson in practical ecumenism, from which, as it happened, they seemed to derive little profit. On the eve of their departure he told them "It is time that those who agree in the doctrines of the Trinity, the divinity of Christ and the atonement...should no longer be divided". Indeed such divisions have "hitherto weakened the Church and prevented the conversion of the world".[2]

Again, eighty years later, the same complete lack of understanding was manifested by Jessup, who did not hesitate to state that the immorality and idolatry of the Oriental Churches, Orthodox and Uniate alike, were the great obstacle to the conversion of Muslims to Christianity.[3] He rejected with indignation the idea, which had been upheld throughout the whole of the first century of Protestantism, that a capital distinction must be made between the Roman Church, with which organic collaboration would be impossible, and the Oriental Churches, on the other hand, with whom it should be sought persistently. Today, indeed, this partial ecumenicalism seems sadly unilateral, but Jessup, instead of surmounting it, took an appreciable step backwards and it was in fact as much with the Orthodox Churches as with the Roman Church that he refused to have any relations which were not polemical. Criticizing repeatedly "the hope of reforming the Church from within", which he attributed to the "high Anglicans" alone, he declared that the separatist movement from the Oriental Churches was necessary and inevitable: "the people themselves have demanded and compelled the organisation of a new Oriental Evangelical Church in Egypt, Palestine, Syria and Asia Minor."[4] It will be seen that this interpretation of the facts has been vigorously disputed by the native Protestants. But what must be emphasized first is the universality of the purely negative and unashamedly aggressive attitude of the missionaries towards the Churches which they sometimes declared they had come to uphold. Until the beginning of the twentieth century there occurs in their writings, for example, the expression "*corrupt* Eastern Churches" as a stereotyped linguistic term and almost an official title, conferred without even a pause for reflexion regarding what substance it might originally have had. Smith admits, with a disarming frankness,

[1] *Ibid.* p. 287. [2] *Ibid.* p. 310.

[3] H. H. Jessup, *Fifty-three Years in Syria*, 2 vols. (London, 1910), vol. 1, p. 85; see also the booklet by the same author, *The Greek Church and Protestant Missions* (Beirut, 1891).

[4] *Fifty-three Years in Syria*, vol. 1, p. 91.

that if he is particularly interested in the Armenians and in the Orthodox Christians it is only because they are defenceless: "While Papists are hedged around by inveterate prejudice, and Moslems by their intolerant law against apostasy, *those Churches are accessible*."[1] A contemporary Protestant historian gives "the pressure of a popular demand in the home churches for tangible results" as the first of all the causes which led "the missionaries to abandon the more obscure and intangible work of quietly enlightening the Oriental Churches, and to adopt a method and policy which promised results more easy to be tabulated".[2] The missionaries had from the beginning been well aware that if an Oriental received communion from the hand of a Protestant it must *ipso facto* mean a break with his own church.[3] Nevertheless, without even trying to reach any *modus vivendi* with the Churches which had welcomed them, they seized the earliest opportunity to incite such persons as were under their influence to take this decisive step. The first historian of the A.B. seems to have been almost the only one at that time to realize the unjustifiable nature of such behaviour. Immediately after the passage in which he describes the reception of the first Armenian converts at Beirut in 1827, he continues: "No one, so far as is known, then doubted the correctness of this policy; but it was probably a mistake." He recalls that the example of Luther cannot be invoked to justify such action. Indeed, the Reformer did not reject the Roman Church, but was rejected by it, and besides it is precisely from the time when, after the death of Luther, Protestantism became a separately constituted religion in Germany that it also ceased to make progress there. Then, reverting to the specific event which had inspired this reflexion, he concludes: "Foreigners had come to Beyroot, uninvited and undesired. There they dwelt and labored, under the consular protection of a foreign power. They sought, not merely the reform, but the destruction of the established Churches; and endeavored to draw away their members to a new organisation."[4] Thus, paradoxically, the Protestant attitude was exactly complementary, in Oriental eyes, with the action taken by the Roman Church on its own account. "The Western policy created among the Eastern Churches a widespread impression that both Rome and Protestantism were bent on their subjugation and destruction and were ready to spend limitless energy and money in order to achieve this

[1] *Missionary Researches*, p. lxiii.
[2] Leon Arpee, *A Century of Armenian Protestantism* (New York, 1946), p. 56.
[3] *Missionary Researches*, p. 289. [4] J. Tracy (see below, p. 670), p. 168.

aim. Such conviction was still prevalent among Eastern Christians on the eve of the First World War."[1] But the converts themselves were not always in agreement. In the course of painful explanatory discussions with the Mission in 1882, the Armenian Protestants did not hesitate to declare that the organization of their group into a separate community by the efforts of the missionaries in 1846 had been "a grave mistake".[2] At its assembly of 19 May 1881 in Constantinople the Meeting of the Union of Bithynia severely rebuked the missionary Barrows who had referred to the Armenian people as "pagan": "A nation which has borne the Christian name for centuries deserves not to bear so opprobrious an epithet."[3] Similarly, in an official letter of 15 June 1883, in which he recalled the case of eight hundred Gregorian Armenians at Caesarea who had recently undergone a spiritual reawakening, S. M. Minassian, addressing himself to the Chairman of the Prudential Committee of the A.B. and to his peers, urgently entreated them "to request their missionaries in Turkey, by cable or otherwise, to use all their influence in the case against the formal separation from the Armenian Church, and the uniting of the said eight hundred enlightened Armenians with the Protestant organisation". And, in accusing the missionaries of understanding nothing of the situation, he explained his own point of view as follows:

I know that the leading men in general in the Armenian Church do not oppose evangelical views entertained by their people. They rather favour it. Their opposition is wholly against the spirit of secession from the national organization into which state the enlightened men often fall, being led by outside influences and unwisely... That little body of Armenians holding Evangelical sentiments, if left to act and work in their mother church, may prove like the little leaven which will in time leaven the whole lump. Better, a thousand times better, it would be for vital Christianity in Turkey to have this body of Armenians remain in their Ancient Church and bear much persecution rather than to be cut off from connexion with their Church, kindred and people.[4]

In 1888 Dr Gabrielian launched, in the Armenian Evangelical press, the idea of recovering the elements which had perhaps been too lightly abandoned when leaving the Gregorian Church. The Synod of the

[1] Nicolas Zernov, "The Eastern Churches and the Ecumenical Movement in the Twentieth century", pp. 645–74, in R. Rouse and S. C. Neill, *A History of the Ecumenical Movement*, see p. 649.

[2] *Controversy between the Missionaries of the American Board and the Evangelical Armenian Churches* (New York, 1882). Quoted from Preface, p. 1.

[3] *Ibid.* p. 5.

[4] *Correspondence and other Documents Relating to the Troubles in the Turkish Missions of the American Board* (New York, 1883). Quoted from p. 24.

Union of Cilicia at ʻAynṭāb took up the question in the following year, and this gave rise between 1892 and 1894 to a series of studies by the pastors Terzian, Ignadiossian and Jamgochian, examining closely "in what way the Evangelical Church can, without betraying its fundamental principles, make use of the ancient traditions of the national Mother Church, of its liturgy, its hymnology, its religious literature, etc.".[1] The massacres which followed put an end to these academic inquiries, but on a practical level they drew the two communities closer together. For example, until the summer of 1896, Protestant worship and the Gregorian services at ʻAynṭāb were celebrated one after the other and in common. The same thing happened in other places and henceforward a brotherly relationship prevailed everywhere. From 1892 onwards the Protestant school of theology at Marash accepted as regular students young people who were studying for the ministry of the Gregorian Church. Finally, it should be mentioned that very favourable sentiments were expressed with regard to missionaries and to Protestants in general by Mgr Ormanian, patriarch of Constantinople from 1896 to 1908, and by the Catholicos Sahag, who occupied the see of Sīs for thirty-seven years from 1902. On the eve of the First World War the latter did not hesitate to preach a sermon in the Protestant church at Marash, in which he said: "To many of you it may seem extraordinary to see the Catholicos in a Protestant pulpit. But why should it cause astonishment? Is not the Catholicos the spiritual father of the whole Armenian people and are not the Protestants Armenians? The very names Protestant and Evangelical have been borrowed from the Gregorian Church." After speaking in very favourable terms of the witness borne by the Reformed Church in the sixteenth century, while asserting that this witness had already been borne by the Armenian Church a thousand years earlier, he concluded: "Therefore, when the question is to protest (bear witness) the Protestant and Gregorian Churches are one, alike and united, and they cannot be separated from one another in the realisation of this glorious purpose. The Armenian and Protestant Churches are also one and united in their aim of being evangelical."[2] In the same spirit, after similar attempts had been made locally, an Armenian Joint Council was set up in Constantinople at the end of the First World War. The three communities, Gregorian, Catholic and Protestant, were equally represented on it, with the

[1] Y. Kassouni, *Loussachavig* [The Way of Light] (Beirut, 1947), p. 180.
[2] *Ibid.* p. 312.

understanding that the spokesman for the Council should be the Gregorian representative. Again in 1921 the three communities jointly addressed a pathetic appeal against the evacuation of Cilicia to the High Commissioner of France in Constantinople. But what was achieved was more a uniting of efforts in the service of the national community than an association on a purely religious ground.

A similar alliance was formed in Egypt, but since it occurred in less tragic circumstances its inspiration was more purely spiritual. The man chiefly responsible for this development was an Anglican missionary, W. H. Temple Gairdner (1873–1928), who had the loyal support of Bishop Gwynne. The Fellowship of Unity started by Gairdner in 1921 contained, among others, Egyptians who had become Protestants under the influence of missionaries from the West. Some of these converts had been members of the Eastern Churches; the relations of such with their former co-religionists had not been at all friendly, and it was a real achievement to bring all these groups together into one society. As the result of the activities of this Fellowship of Unity the atmosphere of suspicion and even hostility existing among the Christian minorities in Egypt was to a large extent transformed into a spirit of trust and co-operation.[1] On this solid foundation it was later possible to establish actual collaboration, with the result that in 1944 a Liaison Committee was organized which also included Catholics and which dealt with questions of relations with the State as well as various practical schemes.[2]

On a broader and more official scale, the Near East Christian Council, which had been founded in May 1927 as a meeting ground for the Evangelical missionary Societies from the West, began in 1958 to change its structure so as to become a regional component of the W.C.C. able to embrace all the Churches. The difficulty is that a system of representation proportional to the number of believers would effectively cause the disappearance of the small groups of Protestants which originally constituted the Council, while representation based on a strict equality between religious communities, without taking into account the number of adherents, would be outrageously partial to Protestantism and would set a kind of premium on schism, since the more the original group disintegrated, the more numerous would be its representatives. However, such a declaration as was made by His

[1] Zernov, *op. cit.* p. 652.

[2] S. A. Morrison, "The Churches of the Near East and the World Council of Churches", *Ecumenical Review*, vol. 1 (1949), pp. 277–84.

Beatitude Athenagoras at Beirut in 1960 shows the distance that has already been covered: "The Orthodox Churches, in their response to an offer of union from Rome, cannot dissociate themselves from the Protestant Churches." This statement is the more important since the patriarch later had an opportunity of expanding it in a manner which leaves no room for tendentious interpretation.[1]

There remains to be presented the problem created by the relations of the missionaries with their converts and with the other Protestant denominations. The native Protestants have often reproached the missionaries with maintaining a paternalistic attitude towards them and on several occasions they have accepted or invited the support of new denominations whose behaviour towards the established evangelical Church resembled the earlier behaviour of the latter towards the Eastern Churches. The missionaries, when they became the victims, were greatly shocked by the methods which they themselves had formerly employed. Such was the dissatisfaction of the Armenian Protestants that they even appealed to the American public for a decision, in two resounding pamphlets.[2] This agitation gave a new lease of life to an Armenian episcopal church which the Archbishop Meguerdich Chahanian was administering at 'Ayntāb after having seceded from the Gregorian Church in 1865 and subsequently enrolled as a member of Bishop Gobat's clergy in Jerusalem. Meguerdich was officially received in England in 1879 and in the following year had an Armenian–Turkish translation of a part of the Prayer Book published there. Canon Tristram of Durham, secretary to the supporting committee, went on a visit to the whole of the south of Turkish Armenia from May to July 1881 and returned with an enthusiastic report, speaking of Armenian Anglican communities at Adana, Adîyaman, Diyarbakîr, Harput, Keshap, Marash and Sivas. At that time the movement was expanded somewhat and caused the A.B. some anxiety.[3] Meguerdich was a very limited personality, however, and, after Archbishop Benson had withdrawn from the movement all the support given to it by his predecessor, he eventually died completely abandoned in January 1904. Nevertheless, in April 1907 Archdeacon Dowling of Jerusalem and Parfit of Beirut reinstituted the scheme at 'Ayntāb itself and had a certain measure of success. It was only the First World War which put an end to this com-

[1] *POC*, vol. x (1960), pp. 61–3.

[2] *Controversy* and *Correspondence*, already quoted.

[3] Henry Marden (missionary in Marash), "The English Movement in Central Turkey", *Missionary Herald* (September, 1885), pp. 338–40.

munity, which had gathered its flock as much from the Gregorians as from the Armenian evangelicals.[1] From about the year 1884 Adventist, Baptist and even Mormon missionaries began to work among the Armenian Protestants, though without achieving very much. Movements of a fundamentalist order in the tradition of the Plymouth Brethren were started from about 1900, the most important of them being the one which, under the inspiration of Abraham Seferian, has split the Aleppo Church since 1924. In the samc way the Church which the Presbyterian Board founded in 1923 at Qazvīn (Iran), composed entirely of Armenian refugees, passed rapidly under the control of the Plymouth Brethren and the Pentecostalists, and it would be possible to give many other examples. In Egypt it was a former U.P. missionary, the Reverend B. Pinkerton, who originated the Plymouth Brethren movement which was very active in Egypt from about 1880. The Reverend W. L. McClenahan, who arrived in Egypt in 1898, exerted a similar kind of influence. After having resigned from the U.P. mission in 1914, he worked in the Middle East as an independent Baptist missionary until his death in Israel on 6 September 1953. Hence in Egypt there is still a total of fourteen small revivalist, Pentecostalist, Baptist and other denominations and a similar state of affairs exists in Jordan and in the rest of the Middle East. These various groups united in 1952 to form a Middle East Bible Council, affiliated to the I.C.C.C. of Dr McIntire and denouncing vehemently the N.E.C.C., which is accused both of modernism and of indulgence towards Rome.

More serious, however, than this attack by marginal groups was the need for Protestantism in the Middle East to reconsider its own internal development in passing from the stage of a foreign mission to that of a native Church. As early as 1882 the Armenian Evangelical Church was protesting strongly against what it called a "domineering *pro-slavery* mission policy".[2] In May 1883 a conference was held in Constantinople which was attended not only by representatives of the Armenian Evangelical Churches and of the mission to Turkey, but also by delegates of the Prudential Committee and of a special commission constituted by the A.B. At the close of this meeting it could be said: "Heretofore we have had foreign missionaries and native helpers. If the principles laid down by this Conference are consistently maintained and

[1] See *Armenian Reformation Church Fund, First report*, 10 pp. Nov. 1880; *Second report*, 18 pp. February 1882; *Third report*, 100 pp. February 1885; A. Dowling, *The Armenian Church*, (London, 1910), pp. 144–8.

[2] *Controversy*, p. 24.

applied, we shall have in the future native preachers and foreign helpers."[1] From the point of view of the organization, this implied that the indigenous Church would have full autonomy in questions concerning its own life, with the creation of a mixed committee for the administration of educational and medical missions. The difficulty, however, was always that the missionaries regarded themselves as chiefly responsible for the funds raised by the generosity of the American Churches, while the native Christians considered that they themselves were principally responsible for the application of funds in their own country.

A new period of serious misunderstanding between the A.B. and the Armenian Churches began in 1924. By its decision to remain in Turkey, the A.B. virtually resolved to abandon the Armenian community, which had been uprooted from there. Without even consulting them, the A.B. arranged for the Armenian Protestants who had taken refuge in Syria and Lebanon to be the concern of the P.B. and to mix with the Arab Presbyterians for whom the P.B. was responsible. The Armenian Evangelicals preferred independence and renounced practically all foreign support, except that of the Armenian Missionary Association of America. But they felt, especially with regard to the College of Aleppo, that they had been wronged by their friends, and in the hour of their greatest adversity.

In Egypt missionaries and native ministers had formed a joint presbytery which, as has already been noted, multiplied into a number of presbyteries united under the Synod of the Nile. It was not until 14 March 1959 that the Coptic Evangelical Church attained full autonomy and ceased juridically to be merely a regional subdivision of the United Presbyterian Church of North America. However, in addition to this ecclesiastical organization, where they sat with their Egyptian colleagues, the missionaries had instituted in 1870 a Missionary Association which alone administered the funds originating from America and in this way effectively controlled the distribution of the missionaries and the functioning of the different establishments. In Egypt also there were sometimes skirmishes, until in 1926, as a result both of the development of Egyptian Protestantism and of the American economic crisis, the financial independence and responsibility of the native Church were recognized. Three years later the Synod suggested that the time had now come for the positions to be reversed and that the representatives of the Church of Egypt ought henceforth to be present at those meetings

[1] *Correspondence*, p. 36.

of the Missionary Association which were concerned with the joint undertaking.

In Syria the organic separation between Mission and Church had been more complete at the beginning, since at the time of transfer in 1870, the Missionary Conference had stipulated, on the one hand, that the missionaries should be able to retain their membership of their home-presbytery in the United States, whatever it might be, and on the other that future Syrian presbyteries should be independent of the General Assembly in America. Thus officially the missionaries were not able to belong to the local ecclesiastical organization, but were merely invited by the presbyteries which were created from 1882 onwards and only voted there when the lawful members, that is to say the Arab Presbyterians alone, passed a decision, which had to be renewed on each occasion, inviting them to do so. The Lebanese–Syrian Synod, officially constituted in 1940, at first restricted itself to the internal affairs of the Church, while the Mission retained almost single-handed the responsibility for evangelism and education. Ultimately, however, it was observed that this work was liable to be effective only in so far as it was carried on by the native Protestants themselves. This trend, which had been perceptible from the end of the First World War, took an institutional form in 1949 with the organization of regular meetings between the executive committees of the Mission and the Church[1] and the constitution of co-operative parishes in the Biqāʿ, in Marj ʿUyūn and in Jazīra. But while this new structure was being formed the American mission suddenly decided on a much more radical policy and on 28 January 1958 proclaimed from its New York office its own dissolution and the integration of all its members as "fraternal workers" in the service of the native Church and under the latter's authority. This step did not resolve all the problems, for it remained to define the extent of the assistance in materials and personnel which the Churches of Europe and America had undertaken to continue to supply. It was, however, a true act of faith which allowed Protestantism in the Middle East to appear at last as a genuine national reality and not a foreign importation.

Since 1955 discussions have also been in progress for the foundation of a united Evangelical Church. A tentative plan involving the Evangelical Synod of Syria and Lebanon, the National Evangelical Union (i.e. the schism arising from the persistent refusal of the Beirut Church

[1] On this new orientation see the principal report prepared by Park Johnson and adopted by the N.E.C.C. in April 1952 "Certain new emphases in Missions policy", *News Bulletin of the NECC* (October 1952), pp. 24–8.

to submit to the Presbyterian organization of the Synod), the Episcopal Church in Jordan, Lebanon and Syria, and the Lutheran Evangelical Church in Jordan was published in 1964. At the same time a similar venture was attempted in Iran beween Presbyterians and Episcopalians, while the Coptic Evangelical Church also regarded herself as being concerned with the project.[1]

A further problem is that of *benevolent activities*, particularly medical and educational activities. Care for the sick was always regarded both as a practical demonstration of Christian love and as the only effective means of coming into contact with a population which otherwise remained inaccessible. Doctors and missionary hospitals certainly saved many human lives and contributed widely to the training of native practitioners. However, as the progress of science and the expansion of the relevant institutions demanded more substantial resources, the Mission became less and less able to carry such a burden. Moreover, with the development of the national conscience local authorities were required to assume an increasing degree of responsibility, with the result that today most of the great missionary hospitals have disappeared.

There was besides always a conflict between the respect owed to the principles of the sick person and the desire to bear manifest evangelical witness. In some centres attendance at religious services was compulsory; in others patients were simply invited to attend, but without any obligation. Elsewhere again the teaching depended mainly on personal contacts and on the systematic work of the Bible-women. It was realized to an increasing extent that the most important witness must be the example of devotion and of a dedicated life. This restraint was found to be even more necessary in missions of relief. The first large-scale operation of this kind was organized on the occasion of the Syrian massacres in 1860. The missionaries of the A.B. were then transformed into the executive agents of the Anglo-American Relief Committee which was created for the purpose and which distributed $150,000 in relief. The situation was the same after the Armenian massacres of 1895, when a Committee of Help for the Armenians was formed in the United States. In England the former Turkish Missions Aid Society, which had become the Bible Lands Missions' Aid Society, redoubled its efforts. In Switzerland a similar mission was founded, and the German contribution has already been mentioned.

During the First World War a new Armenian Relief Committee was

[1] Texts in *News Bulletin of the NECC* (Easter 1965), no. 84, pp. 7–16.

created, on 16 September 1915, the name of which was changed successively to Armenian and Syrian Relief Committee, American Committee for Relief in the Near East and finally Near East Relief (NER). The missionaries played an essential part in the organization and subsequent development of this great work and it is more than symbolic that the President of the NER, Dr Barton, should have been previously the Secretary-General of the A.B. But charity should know no frontiers and it was the policy of the organization to be non-confessional. It represented a great impulse of generosity on the part of the American people as a whole and brought its aid to all, without discrimination. It should be noted here that, even though the United States made the greatest effort in terms of quantity, the Protestants of all Western countries also formed similar missions up to the limit of their resources: first the Germans, so far as circumstances allowed, then the English, the Swiss, the Danes and even the small French Protestant community.

The plight of the Arab refugees from Palestine, from 1948 onwards, caused a new and urgent appeal to be made for the same goodwill. This time the work was organized on the basis of organic co-operation between the different churches and missions through the Relief Committee of the NECC. In 1951 a conference met at Beirut, under the auspices of the Division of Inter-Church Aid and Service to Refugees of the W.C.C. "to show that Christians are concerned about the plight of Arab refugees"[1] and in that very year the NECC distributed $550,000 in relief. In 1953 the total reached was $1,000,000; in 1955 $1,300,000; in 1957 $2,000,000 and in 1962 $2,500,000, about one quarter of these sums being distributed in cash and the remainder in supplies. This very considerable achievement does not include, however, the figures of the World Lutheran Federation, which wished to administer its relief fund itself and which must independently have reached an almost comparable total. In addition to the Augusta Victoria in Jerusalem which it administers with funds from UNRWA, it is responsible for several polyclinics in which more than 100,000 sick received attention in 1957 alone.

The Mission has certainly also played a pioneer role in education, and the rivalry between Protestant and Catholic Missions has even been beneficial, in that emulation has impelled each to try to do better than the other. There too, however, relations soon became strained between the upholders of the view that education was a means to the end of

[1] Elfan Rees, "From the First Beirut Conference to now. Service and disappointment", *Second Report from Beirut*, p. 21.

evangelism and those who regarded it as a disinterested service, an end in itself. The great institutions for higher education which originated as an aftermath of the Protestant Mission had in fact from the beginning an independent existence. The first of them, Robert College in Constantinople, was founded almost against the wishes of the A.B. since about the middle of the nineteenth century, there was serious controversy regarding the kind of education to be provided. The mission, whose most conspicuous spokesman was the secretary, Rufus Anderson, insisted on the necessity of adaptation to local conditions, on the use of the native languages and on adjustment to the average intellectual level of the country and to its real needs. The most philanthropic circles, on the other hand, believed in the universal virtue of Western civilization and wanted to found institutions of a higher standard where the teaching would be conducted in English. This conception had been initiated in 1857 by James and William Dwight, sons of the missionary who had contributed most to the implantation of Protestantism in Asia Minor, and met with no success at first. But one of the men whose interest they had aroused, the millionaire Christopher R. Robert of New York, secured the co-operation of the director of the seminary of the A.B. at Bebek, Cyrus Hamelin, who was completely opposed to the principles maintained by Anderson. Hamelin accordingly handed in his resignation to the A.B. in 1860 and in 1863 opened the new Robert College, in the very premises of the former Bebek Seminary. Over the years Robert was to contribute $400,000 to the institution which bears his name, and in May 1871 permanent premises were acquired, with Hamelin as president until 1877. His policy met with the most cherished ideals of Armenian Protestantism. Therefore, when the difficulties between the mission and the church came to light in 1882, it was at one time proposed that Hamelin should be sent to Constantinople to take charge of the Church of Pera, and to try to restore peace while developing mutual understanding. The Armenians welcomed this plan with jubilation, but the other side was sufficiently powerful to prevent its realization. The present President of Robert College, Dr Patrick Murphy Malin, has been in office since March 1962. The institution has adapted itself to the transformed conditions in the country. "With the founding of the Turkish Republic in 1923, the College came under the Ministry of Education of the modern Turkish Republic; and thanks to the close relations always maintained between the College and the Turkish education officials, Robert College has been permitted to share in the development and progress of the Republic."[1] Thus it appears to identify itself entirely with the ideology inspired by President Atatürk.[2]

The second institution, the Syrian Protestant College of Beirut which in 1919 became the American University, was on the contrary created in conformity with the express resolution of the Conference of Missionaries. Daniel Bliss, who had been a missionary in Syria since the beginning of 1856, was put in charge of the undertaking. But it was clearly indicated to him that the College was to be developed independently without reliance on direct support by the Mission. For this reason Bliss returned to the United States for four years, from 1862 to 1866, in order to muster the necessary support, and the College was opened on 3 December 1866; it was established in its present premises in 1873 when there were about a hundred students. In 1914 there were nearly 1,000, a figure which was again reached in 1920; it rose to 2,000 in 1942 and stands at almost 4,000 today. The relations of the A.U.B. with the Mission and the Protestant Churches have always been friendly, but they illustrate perhaps better than anything else the dogmatic laxity in which Middle Eastern Protestantism was in danger of losing itself. The living symbol of this period was Howard Bliss, son of the founder of the College, who had been a Congregationalist minister in New Jersey until his appointment to succeed his father as head of the A.U.B. in 1902, a post which he was to retain until his death in 1920. At the very end of his life H. Bliss published an article-programme which, though doubtless written in the spirit of the times, today appears somewhat surprising.[3] In it, he calmly explains that the modern missionary can dispense with the old disputes on matters of dogma and that he should urge the Church to put in the forefront of its message the ideas of reason and of rationality, of independent thought and of natural development.

In 1882 the Faculty of Medicine had been disturbed by a serious crisis; all the professors except one resigned as a result of the fact that one of their number had been prohibited from publicly teaching Darwinism. The Board of Trustees then demanded that all teachers should sign a very detailed confession of faith, even including, as a precaution against any oversight, adherence to "the whole body of evangelical doctrine as contained in the inspired Word of God, and

[1] *Robert College, Catalogue 1963–64.* Quoted here from p. 20. [2] *Ibid.* p. 21.

[3] "The Modern Missionary", *Atlantic Monthly* (May 1920), pp. 178–96, reproduced in full, Stephen B. L. Penrose, *That They May Have Life, The Story of the American University of Beirut, 1866–1941* (New York, 1941).

represented in the consensus of the Protestant creeds, as opposed to the erroneous teachings of the Romish and Eastern Churches".[1] On his arrival in 1902 H. Bliss caused this text to be abolished, but at the same time he proposed the "establishment of a *Church of Christ in the Syrian Protestant College*...absolutely undenominational, absolutely Christian and—in its conditions for membership—absolutely religious rather than theological, practical rather than metaphysical. It must seek to include all who are seeking to lead their lives as children of God, in the spirit of Jesus Christ. It must exclude all the others." In May 1907 the Board of Trustees requested that the Mission and the native Protestant Churches should be consulted on the establishment of an "independent, undenominational, evangelical College Church, whose members would be cordially recognised and received into fellowship by the Missions and native Protestant Churches".[2] This strange idea was not put into practice, but, on the contrary, after the Young Turk Revolution, a revolt actually broke out in 1908 among the non-Christian pupils, Jews and Muslims alike, who were not willing any longer to take part in courses of Bible study or religious exercises. The affair attained enormous proportions, with the Syrian and Egyptian newspapers supporting the rebel students, while the American and British governments upheld the College in its refusal to yield to pressure. Finally, however, after "alternative exercises" had for several years been provided for those who definitely refused to attend worship, the services were spaced out, made optional and, above all, carefully expurgated of any specifically Christian elements. At the time of the conflict in 1909 the Faculty was already declaring that "The aim and the purpose of the College is to develop character...the College believes that the highest type of character cannot be developed without the aid of religion."[3] But may this not have been the worst of all solutions, consisting as it did in representing by the name of the Christian Faith something which was no more than an insipid mixture of psychological remedies and rules of moral propriety? A disinterested devotion to Christian duty, a radical secularization accompanied by an unequivocal personal witness probably remain the only valid answer, the opportunity for which can be provided by institutions which are not directly connected with the Church. But is the position still the same in relation to missions which identify themselves as being missions of the Church? It has been seen

[1] Jessup, *Fifty-three Years*, vol. II, pp. 707–8; Penrose, *op. cit.* p. 47.
[2] *Ibid.* p. 132.
[3] *Ibid.* p. 135.

that the A.B. believed it to be so in Turkey and resolutely pursued this course. The Scottish Presbyterian Mission held exactly the opposite conviction and closed its scholastic missions to the Jews, first in Istanbul in 1930 and then in Alexandria after the Second World War, when it was forbidden any longer to bear unequivocal spoken witness to the full teaching of the Gospel.

The situation is confused in all the great teaching institutions which have been directly established by missionary work and which today declare their close adherence to the evangelical community. On the other hand, the position is clearer in the most recent of these establishments of higher education, the American University at Cairo, which began modestly as a secondary school in October 1920. In the following year it opened a School of Oriental Studies for the training of specialists in the languages and culture of the Near East. Finally in 1925 the secondary school, which was itself abandoned in 1952, gave rise to a University section. This University proceeded to develop rapidly, with the creation of a Department of Education in 1931 and of a Social Research Centre in 1953. Here it had been understood from the beginning that the proper function of the institution was educational and not missionary. Nevertheless, the first three presidents were ordained ministers: Charles R. Watson, founder and president until 1945, was a United Presbyterian missionary; John Badeau, who succeeded him from 1945 to 1953, was a Presbyterian minister; Raymond F. MacLain, President from 1955 to 1963 and, subsequently, Chancellor of the University, is a minister of the Church of the Disciples of Christ. In spite of having no organic connexion with the Church, therefore, the establishment shows signs of strong Protestant influence in respect of its personalities. It may be wondered, however, whether a private institution of this kind will not inevitably have some ideological colour and whether the religious aspect may not have been supplanted by political and national interests. This impression has been strengthened by the fact that Dr Badeau was also the American Ambassador to the U.A.R., and on a wider plane the impression is conveyed of a westernization of the intellectual ranks educated by these various institutions. There has been talk of a "new middle class—Orthodox in faith... nationalist in sentiment, and English...by adopted speech",[1] and the same author adds "Bitter and long experience has taught Eastern Christians, especially in the Near East, to look upon...Protestants as

[1] N. Zernov, *op. cit.* p. 646.

emissaries of Germany, and more recently, of the United States".[1] However, even if originally most of the students were Eastern Christians, the percentage of non-Christian elements, Jews and especially Muslims, has continued to increase.

It must not, however, be imagined that Western influence has been used only for Western ends. The part played in the renaissance of the various national cultures had indeed been of the greatest importance. When the missionaries first arrived, the Armenians had to a large extent abandoned their language in favour of Turkish or Arabic. Classical Armenian was little more than a liturgical language, remote from daily life, and the Protestant schools had a decisive influence on the stabilization and literary development of modern Armenian, which greatly assisted the awakening of the Armenian people and its acquisition of national consciousness. On many occasions the Turkish authorities even accused the American institutions and the Protestant Churches of being the nurseries of revolutionaries, and although the accusation is exaggerated it indicates a genuine influence. The American press of Urmia performed the same function for Syriac in the service of the Nestorian community. It may be wondered, in the light of the dramatic events which subsequently uprooted these communities, whether this course was well-advised and whether an attempt should not have been made to help Christians to become more completely integrated within the framework of the State to which they belonged, rather than, by encouraging their individuality, to make them appear as a foreign body to be eliminated. However, such a question was clearly beyond the scope of the missionaries and they can hardly be held responsible for the mistakes and transgressions of the Turkish government and of the great Western Powers.

Furthermore, the work of restoring national and cultural values was not undertaken solely for the benefit of Christian groups; Protestant impact also played a considerable part in the Arab renaissance and its historian has no hesitation in writing, of the Syrian Protestant College: "Its influence on the Arab revival, at any rate in its earlier stage, was greater than that of any other institution."[2] He also emphasizes the contribution made by Buṭrus al-Bustānī (1819–83), who was one of the founders of the Protestant Church of Beirut, and of Nāṣīf al-Yāzijī (1800–71) who, even though he never officially became a Protestant, worked, like Bustānī, in permanent association with the missionaries. In 1847 these men launched the first Society of Arts and Sciences, from

[1] *Ibid.* p. 669. [2] G. Antonius, *The Arab Awakening* (London, 1938), p. 43.

which sprang the various societies which spread the spirit of national independence among the Arabs. Antonius speaks of the members of the secret society of Beirut as "most of them pupils, all of them disciples, of Yazeji and Bustani",[1] having already written on an earlier page of the group of young Arab nationalists opposing the Turks that "they were the pupils of Yazeji and Bustani, the first generation to have been nurtured on the recovered cultural inheritance".[2] It is for this reason that he is entirely justified in saluting the native helpers of Smith and Van Dyck in the Arabic translation of the Bible, as "two great figures who dominate the intellectual life of the period".[3] They were not isolated instances, however. Other Protestants included Khalīl al-Khūrī, who in 1857 founded the first Syrian daily newspaper, Khalīl and Ibrāhīm Sarkīs, John and Iskandar Abkāryūs, Nawfal and especially the celebrated convert of the United Presbyterians of Damascus, Michael Mushāqqa (1800–88), whose literary output includes historical works, important studies of Arab music and treatises of Protestant controversy against Catholicism. A more recent name must be still added to this list of Protestant Arab scholars: that of Anīs Sallūm, minister of the Church of Damascus some years ago, who was a member of *al-Majma' al-'ilmī al-sūrī*, the most famous literary society in Syria. Protestants have likewise played a relatively important part in the political life of Syria and the Lebanon; it is sufficient to mention here Fāris al-Khūrī of Damascus and Ayyūb Thābit of Beirut.

Numerically the results of the Protestant penetration of the Middle East remain very small. The census of March 1947 gave, out of a total Egyptian population of 19 millions, 126,581 Protestants. At the same date they numbered 12,641 in Lebanon and 12,661 in Syria, at least half of them in each of these two countries being Armenians. The official census of 1955 in Turkey gave the number as 8,952. In Israel there are 200 Jewish Protestants, excluding 700 foreign Protestants and 900 Arab Episcopalians. For the other countries the figures are less certain. There are said to be about 1,500 Lutheran Arabs in Jordan, but this figure may be exaggerated, for the entire Protestant population is not estimated at much more than 2,000 and the Episcopalians, who are included in this total, are undoubtedly more numerous than the Lutherans. Protestants must amount to fewer than a thousand in Iraq and from 3,000 to 4,000 in Iran.

[1] *Ibid.* p. 88.
[2] *Ibid.* pp. 45–52, 60; Graf, *op. cit.* vol. IV, pp. 318–37.
[3] Antonius, *op. cit.* p. 45.

CHAPTER 13

THE ANGLICAN CHURCH

Jerusalem has consistently proved a maker and breaker of ideals. Its history has been a disconcerting touchstone of intentions, allowing their ardour yet outwearing their capacities. The habit of the Holy City is to match aspiration with attrition. So it happened in the most notable and well augured political enterprise of English history in biblical territory —the Palestine Mandate. When Allenby entered Jerusalem in December 1917 he was rapturously greeted by a liberated population. Aḥmad Shawqī, the most celebrated Arab poet of that time, who had himself suffered exile in Spain through the action of the British, pointed the meaning and paradox of the opportunity in his Arabic lines:

> O thou conqueror of Jerusalem,
> Lay the sword aside.
> The Cross was not of steel, but wood.
> When I saw the humiliation of the crucified One,
> His two hands outstretched to embrace the poles,
> I understood that beyond weakness lies strength,
> The victory is to right and not to power.

But thirty years later the tragic sequences of vision and frustration had concluded characteristically in a ruin of hopes.

The Anglican Church in the Middle East, with a near century of narrative antecedent to those years of Mandate, is closely involved with that climax of the Anglo and the Palestinian. Its story is inextricable from the Ottoman complexities which preceded and the partitioned embitterments that followed. Through all the chapters of political change runs a double thread of high endeavour and besetting infirmity. Jerusalem is no kinder to ecclesiastical ventures than to political: for the men of faith and ministry as for the men of affairs there are the same intractable external circumstances. But the Church, in the midst of them, has had its own brand of indecision and inward tension. The stresses within its own ethos are as evident in the history as the vicissitudes and complications of the outward scene. Jerusalem being what it is, the business of the perceptive historian, whether of bishops or of consuls, is as much with the springs of action as with the setting of events. The strains within the ecclesia were revealed, rather than created, by the exactions of the world in which it moved. Or, as Shakespeare might have counselled:

> ...survey
> The plot of situation and the model:
> Consent upon a sure foundation,
> Question surveyors, know your own estate,
> How able such a course to undergo,
> ...or else, like one
> Beyond his powers to build it...
> A naked subject for the weeping clouds.

There is no field which more tellingly presents the Church of England in "its own estate", both for good and ill, than its enterprise in the biblical East, from the concepts and controversies of the joint bishopric in 1841, to the inauguration of the archbishopric, as an organ of the whole Anglican Communion, in the year after the Suez tragedy of 1956. To explore the issues within that history is to move among the deepest tests of the spirit and the will. "There is no promotion" wrote one of its ablest servants during the Mandate and a devout Anglican, "after Jerusalem."[1] For the identical reason, within Jerusalem there is no unambiguous prosperity. Sanctities dissolving into sentiments, sentiments reaching rudely after sanctities, are too close at hand. Mankind, it has been said, is one large Pharisee, and not least in belabouring its prototype. Even Gethsemane and Calvary become the themes of an accusing, and so an excusing, which contravene their true temper in controversy about their culprits. So their sufferer is wounded again in the house of his friends. They defend his "Father forgive them" with a sort of "Hold it against them for we know well who they are". Of these perversities holy things are made at once the prey and the ground. Loyalties so readily become hypocrisies and fidelities unworthy when they have to do with sacred custodies.

The sacrament of geography is too much for our qualities of soul. Feeling becomes either sour or over-indulgent and in either case is religiously unreal. A score of temptations await the Christian in the precincts of his redemption and are multiplied again when he takes up his ministries in its meaning to the other religions which, in their

[1] Ronald Storrs, *Orientations* (London, 1937), p. 516. It is odd that so perceptive and masterly an analyst of the Palestinian Mandate as Christopher Sykes (*Cross Roads to Israel: Palestine from Balfour to Bevin*, London, 1965) should have failed so completely to understand the remark. See p. 157.

diversely passionate ways, possess the same territories. "Half friendships", as William Blake wrote, "are often bitterest enmities", a remark he worked out in his mystical epic of the union of Albion with Jerusalem, but which, transposed from those haunting yet perplexing subtleties of his *Jerusalem*, belongs with all the prosaic mutuality between English Christianity and the Near Eastern scene.

There is an old legend, often quoted, that when the last Jewish Temple was destroyed a splintered fragment of stone entered the heart of every Jew in succeeding time. The myth in its own way captures a wider truth of the Judean hills, looking, as many a traveller has noted, "clear into Arabia", yet casting their empire of reverence to the edges of the Western world. It is that lodgement of painful love in a diversity of peoples and an enmity of faiths which shapes the criterion for the Anglican, as for every other, intervention and measures both its paltriness and its integrity. To pray for the peace of Jerusalem is to live uneasily. For there is nothing so out of joint as "the city that is compact together".

The expository procedure here followed relies on a broad estimate of three interacting elements in the story—the impulses at work, the situations obtaining from external circumstances and the imaginative achievement, or the lack of it, emerging from their interplay. Since we are attempting an essay not a chronicle, no catalogue can be offered of places, dates and personnel and many worthy names must find no mention. India and Pakistan, though part of the scope of these volumes, are here by design allowed to be peripheral. Several of the leading figures, like Gottlieb Pfander, Thomas Valpy French and Edward Craig Stuart, happily belong both to the sub-continent and the nearer East. Our dedication here to the triangular relations of Judaism, Christianity and Islam justifies, in the present proportions, a concentration of concern on the Palestinian and the Arab core, with things Persian, North African, East African and Indo-Islamic corroborating and extending the features readily discernible, and powerfully symbolized, in the centrality of Jerusalem. It is believed that such a pattern of review is both practically necessary and poetically right.

IMPULSES: "THE ROAD TO JERUSALEM IS IN THE HEART"

When the Reformers taught so, they meant to deter pilgrimage as the likely ally of superstition. But their saying was ambiguous and sustains the very thing that they deplored. In truth, as Samuel Purchas observed in the ninth of his twenty volumes of *Hakluytus Posthumus* (1625) on pilgrimages and other travels by Englishmen and others, "the best pilgrimage is the peaceable way of a good conscience to that Jerusalem which is above". Much the same had been said of Mecca by al-Ghazālī. Yet what is in the heart may thereby take to the road, despite the Puritan notion that it is a Jewish thing to ascribe holiness to places. The pull of the biblical East in one form or another persistently drew the generations of the English Church. It was inseparable alike from the lore of their medieval sacrament and the impact of their Reformation Bible. Within either, for all their uneasy disparity, lay the common faith of the Incarnation. Whether shrines, or memories, it was one attraction.

In 1291 the last foothold of the Crusaders at Acre was relinquished. But through the rest of the medieval centuries, the pilgrim movement was sustained, with its John Mandevilles and William Weys, as well as the silent and the nameless who left no record of their privations and their destination. In 1517 came Richard Torkyngton, Knight and Rector of Mulberton in Norfolk, together with Thomas Toppe, priest from the west country, closing, as it would seem, the long sequence of the English Middle Ages in thrall to Palestine. Coincident with the Reformation at home, there supervened the Ottoman capture of Jerusalem and when, after an interval, the "pilgrim" reappears in the second half of the sixteenth century he is in the guise of chaplains to the new merchant venturers who came in the wake of Queen Elizabeth's successful diplomatic representation at Constantinople. A new temper appears in the Anglican contact with the Holy Places. Geographer-priests present themselves, like William Biddulph, chaplain at Aleppo, whose concerns anticipate, in less expert ways, those of the Palestine Exploration Fund of three centuries later. The pattern develops in the eighteenth century with travellers like Henry Maundrell, also chaplain at Aleppo (*Journey from Aleppo to Jerusalem*, 1697), Thomas Shaw, botanist and chaplain at Algiers in 1738, and Richard Pococke, author of a three-volumed *Description of the East* (1734–5). Their interests are erudite and their observation tireless, even when their impressions are sometimes naïve. They are the eighteenth-century form of the fascination of the Bible, territorial, enthusiastic, but not yet missionary.

In the closing year of the eighteenth century, Sir Sidney Smith at Acre extinguished Napoleon's dreams of eastern empire at the very point where the Crusaders made their last surrender exactly half a millennium before. Romantics like Lady Hester Stanhope and Byron, as well as painstaking scholars of the mettle of John Burckhardt, whose diary was published as *Travels in Syria and the Holy Land* and *Travels in Arabia*, came in the wake of that Napoleonic incursion and personify in their contrasted ways the longing for the East. Their generation overlaps with the first pioneers of mission proper.

The earliest protagonist, exemplar of many who followed, was Joseph Wolff, of the London Society for Promoting Christianity among the Jews (founded in 1809). Son of a rabbi, converted at Prague, he made a notable journey in 1821–3 through Gibraltar, Malta, Alexandria, Tyre, Jerusalem and Damascus. According to a contemporary he could "conciliate a pasha, confute a patriarch, travel without a guide, speak without an interpreter, live without food and pay without money...a comet capable of setting a whole system on fire".[1] By such intrepid travellers the beginnings were made and the patterns laid. Wolff later continued his journeys beyond the Oxus river to Bukhara and thence, via Afghanistan and the Khyber Pass, to India.

Initial ventures of the Church Missionary Society (founded 1799), based on Malta, in 1815, resulted three years later in the sending of a pioneer group of five to Egypt, two of whom went on to Ethiopia, the others attempting friendly but ill-received relations with the Coptic Church. It was not until 1851 that the C.M.S. entered Palestine. But its most revered Islamic pioneer, Henry Martyn, had already ensured both Persian and Arabic versions of the New Testament by his incessant labours, beginning at Madras in 1806 and ending in Tokat, Armenia in 1812. His achievement was literally a self-oblation, the life-in-death of an undauntable consumptive.

Hallowed in sacrifice by these beginnings, the mission to Jerusalem flowered in 1841 in the novel plan for an Anglican bishopric in the Holy City. The aegis was that of the London Society and the formal proposal the King of Prussia's, Frederick William IV. But the travailing spirit was that most famous of all nineteenth-century Anglicans, the Earl of Shaftesbury. The political context of the suggestion falls to be examined below, as well as the ecclesiastical contentions. For the present our concern is with its quality of incentive. The driving impulse was unmistakeably evangelical and its generating passion the biblical "mystery" of the Jews. It was the controversial product of a remarkable upsurge of interest in Jewish evangelization. Under Shaftesbury's pre-

[1] W. T. Gidney, *History of the London Society*, etc. (London, 1908), p. 105. The reporter was Lewis Way, who added: "He knows of no church but his heart."

sidency the London Society became a focus of lively hopes and energies as well as a liberal patronage.[1]

His character and convictions are the clearest index to the impulse giving birth to the Anglican bishopric. Biblical, ardent, prophetical, he was dominated by a compulsion both to deplore the obduracy of a continuing Judaism and yet love its recalcitrant people, as being, withal, a first debt of Christendom and a future clue to the Divine providence. It was a thrust capable of ignoring, even defying, appearances, eager for vindicating statistics, yet capable likewise of out-hoping the adverse ones. It was served, moreover, by outstanding scholarship. Alexander MacCaul, professor of Hebrew at King's College, London, and President of the Society's College, commanded a tireless erudition, while Michael Solomon Alexander, his successor as professor and the first bishop, and Joseph Barclay, the third bishop, were men of competence and energy. The cause, for all its intensity, was ably manned, and what its oversimplifications neglected its ardour spiritually redeemed. The establishment in Jerusalem was the child of a philanthropy its main architect was elsewhere to make proverbial: it was rooted in his understanding, in both Old and New Testaments, of the philanthropy of God.

Bishop Alexander's tenure lasted only four years. He laid the foundations of the Anglican Church in the Old City beside the citadel of David and founded the short-lived Hebrew College. In 1845 he succumbed during a journey to Egypt to the physical conditions of life in Ottoman Jerusalem, an insanitary warren of ruinous houses, enclosing at that time an ill-served population variously numbered at ten to twenty thousand. The leadership passed to another figure, a French-speaking Swiss, Samuel Gobat, whose long career included fifty-five years of missionary labour, thirty-three of them as bishop. He was born in the same year as the C.M.S. itself and his personality and episcopate epitomized its main qualities and problems. He was heir to the energies of Joseph Wolff and travelled tirelessly through the vast dimensions of his jurisdiction, from Ethiopia to Turkey. His zeal and industry were monumental and his journeys, when set against the conditions of his day, are a kind of epic of personal evangelism, illuminated with numerous incidents of patient, pastoral achievement, of which is the Kingdom of Heaven. Two of his Ethiopian "disciples", for example,

[1] The Lord Mayor of London chaired its annual meeting at the Mansion House and C.M.S. preachers, anxious for their prestige, were compelled to take as their text: "Is He the God of the Jews only?" See Barbara W. Tuchman, *Bible and Sword: England and Palestine from the Bronze Age to Balfour* (London, 1957), p. 118.

whom he had brought to Cairo, came in the street upon the very man who had earlier sold them into slavery, now in the deepest penury. They took him in their charge and for a whole year before his death maintained him from their slender resources.[1]

The concerns and postures of the evangelist were never lost, with Gobat, in the dignity and office of the bishop. By his interpretation of episcopacy and his practice of its pastoral meaning as he saw it, he became in retrospect a personal focus of a sharp dilemma. Bishop Alexander's work, brief as it was and in the main specifically Jewish, hardly served to define the latent issue. Gobat made it explosive.

From the beginning, Alexander's instructions had charged him with evangelization among those outside the churches and with a proper solicitude for, and recognition of, the Orthodox patriarchate and other oriental Christians. It was, of course, with this in mind that the Anglican bishopric was styled "in" and not "of" Jerusalem. Gobat's loyalty to the nature of his episcopal "writ" was not in doubt. Rather it was its pastoral fulfilment and interpretation. His robust evangelism in that time and context made an irenic solution wellnigh impossible. He preached his own understanding of Christ, the simplicities of grace, the openness of the Scriptures, the servant Church, the plain sacraments, the believer's assurance, the priesthood of all, the sole sufficiency of Christ and the communion of saints, not their merits. Inevitably, the places of his witness and the persons of his acceding hearers became the battleground of an entrenched and venerable Church tradition, suspicious of intrusion, fearful of molestation, uneasy at the scattering of the Scriptures, uncomprehending of the unfamiliar and beset, as both parties were, by the frailties and foibles of human nature, accentuated as ever by ecclesiastical causes.

The "mystery" of the sacraments, the venerability of the saints, the virginity of Mary, the careful identity of Orthodoxy, the assertion of tradition—all became strident and quarrelsome in their self-defence and militant in their dogmatic strongholds. And there were innumerable occasions of contrariety in practice, deriving from the very shape of church architecture, the habit of clergy, both in dress and mind, and the patterns of liturgy. Gobat's leadership precipitated the whole gamut of issues implicit in a venture of evangelical Anglicanism, albeit speaking with a strong French accent, within the Orthodox world. And it perpetuated them in the shape of the "Palestinian Native Church"—to use

[1] *Life of Gobat* (London, 1884), p. 156.

the title of its later council—resulting from this clash of evangelicalism and Orthodoxy. It may be doubted whether at that juncture either could have sustained its inner loyalties without collision. It is important for historians not to assess possibilities in terms of the temper of a later age. To a certain paradoxical degree, Gobat may be said in fact to have contributed substantially to later and more fraternal times by the steady fidelity of his own mission. Horatio Southgate, in his episcopalian ventures in Smyrna and Constantinople in 1830, had encountered similar tensions, as did also the Presbyterian and Congregational missions from the United States in several parts of Syria, Lebanon and Armenia.

That the innate controversy had been anticipated in the apprehensions the whole Anglican bishopric project had aroused in the Church of England should not obscure the tenacity or the devotion with which Gobat unflinchingly suffered it in his own person. It was one thing for remote ecclesiologists to feel misgivings, another for a pastoral episcopate to bear them in the brunt of an active commission which would have been betrayed in their avoidance. Theology, in the end, is always safest where it is in relation rather than in discourse. Risks and the "comfort" of the Spirit are frequently in company. That the four archbishops of Canterbury, York, Dublin and Armagh came to his defence at a critical juncture in 1853 is proof both of the intensity of the issues Gobat provoked and of the official solidarity of the English Church with his policy.

His own statement of it should perhaps be quoted, as it might, from any part of his stolid but never wearied diary. Setting out the paramount priestly and episcopal obligation in the Gospel on one occasion, he added:

> Nevertheless it ought never to be the preacher's aim to convert people to this or that Church, but to lead them to the source of all truth and life, even to the Lord Jesus. This having been effected, to let them remain in their respective churches. But if individuals are persecuted for their love to their Lord and their confession of the truth, if they are anathematised and cast out by their Church and therefore present themselves to us with the request that we would receive them, I do not see that we could refuse admittance to such without rejecting the Lord Himself.[1]

The stresses which the Ecumenical Movement is only slowly mastering a century on are there. In the person of its fourth bishop, the Anglican

[1] E. Headland, *Brief Sketches of C.M.S. Workers* (London, 1897), Each of the sketches is separately numbered. The extract is quoted on p. 15 of the chapter on Gobat.

temper emerged with a different emphasis. But the contrast between Gobat and Blyth only underlines an abiding debate within its ethos.

The former's long tenure (1846–79) saw the ordination of a growing number of Arab clergy, the multiplication of schools throughout the area, the opening of hospitals and orphanages at Nazareth, Jerusalem and Lydda, the building of churches at Nazareth, Nābulus, St Paul's in Jerusalem and chapels and clinics in sundry towns. In Egypt and Ethiopia, vigorous efforts were made from the 1850s to pursue Muslim evangelism. Henry Aaron Stern in 1856 spent several months in Arabia, just twenty years after Wolff's visit to Jidda. The assumptions within this ministry will be examined later. Robert Bruce, meanwhile, in the early 1870s laid the foundation of the Anglican Church in Persia. In Gobat's closing years the Lutheran partnership began steadily to break up and the German personnel withdrew to activities and ecclesiastical orders of their own.

After Joseph Barclay's short episcopate (1879–81), the bishopric remained in abeyance for six years. Prussian co-operation terminated and after lengthy deliberation Archbishop Edward Benson, encouraged by assurances from the Orthodox patriarch that a Church of England bishop ought to be resident in the Holy City, decided on a purely English establishment. In line with this approbation was the appointment of Bishop George F. P. Blyth, who held the see from 1887 to 1914, and whose temperament and training fitted him for a much closer sensitivity to the mind and ethos of the Eastern Churches. Yet, paradoxically, his independence of the C.M.S. traditions constituted him an alert and doughty champion of the Arab clergy, of Gobat's vintage, often against their own English "superiors". Bishop Blyth's episcopate in fact supplied the third strand in the Anglican "service for Jerusalem", complementing Shaftesbury's love for Jewry and the Bible, Gobat's active evangelism among all and sundry, with a sober, indeed, meticulous, discretion towards the ancient Churches. With these three motives remaining in sometimes uneasy unity, Blyth gave increasing substance to the "embassy" concept of the Anglican presence.

It was symbolized in the foundation (1894) and consecration (1898) of St George's Collegiate Church as his cathedral, token and sign of a new order. He emphasized, by the creation of episcopal canonries for Anglican primates in six different countries, the pan-Anglican nature of his tenure. He did not seek to undo the results of Gobat's régime nor its genesis of an Arab ministry and a council of Arab Churches, though he mystified many of its people by his insistent efforts to secure their abandonment of any practices, such as the enormity of evening Communion, which he calculated would offend or bewilder eastern Christians. He dreaded what he called "a policy of proselytism which might stamp the work with an uncatholic discredit". The resultant tensions were, in part, offset by his sturdy episcopal concern for the material well-being of Arab Anglicans and their proper recognition within the mission-council relationship. By his organization in London of the Jerusalem and the East Mission he aimed to ensure a continued supply of funds and personnel independent of the two major societies within his jurisdiction. This he considered necessary to a bishopric spiritually self-responsible.

A man of little stature (his stone mounting-steps may still be noted outside the porch of the Close on the Damascus road), he fostered a growing sense of Anglican integrity and by his personal qualities and the length of his years did for catholicity and propriety of Church relations what Gobat had done for the Gospel. Yet he too had his visions. "We stand" he declared in his Third Charge "in the rising daylight: the 'Eastern Question' of the Church and the prospect of the Church of the Hebrews gathers outline in the mists of daybreak." His conservation of the Eastern Church, at once bellicose and tender, was consistent with his expectation of recruitment from Jewry and Islam.

That hope takes our immediate narrative of impulses to its goal. "Embassies" have, by and large, an easier existence than missions. But they belong in one. The will to constitute both is set in relief by the contrasted activities of the Palestine Exploration Fund which, though not invariably Anglican in its personnel, merits, for all its remarkable achievements, a brief place in these themes. The archbishop of Canterbury was its president and it owed its initiation, in part, to the example of Stanley's *Sinai and Palestine* (1857). With the P.E.F. the biblical was an end in itself, without complication of church relations or missionary ambition. Its indefatigable response was to the holy terrain itself, in thankful neutrality about the theological liabilities of its biblical curiosity. As the Bible, in the familiar edition, was said to be "designed to be read as literature", so for the P.E.F. it was "taken to be explored by archaeology". "Appointed to be read in churches", be it confessed, can be an equally neutralizing phrase.

Yet the Palestine Exploration Fund has a striking place in the general scene. Its researches, in giving back the life of the past, tended to educate and excite the sense of Palestinian belonging in the existing population, as well as demonstrating for would-be advocates of immigration the ancient potential of the country for an enlarged one. Its exhaustive map-making was inspired by a military thoroughness and precision hardly surprising in that so many of its ablest field workers were army men, the most noteworthy being the surveyor, Lieut. Conder, companion of Kitchener. So valuable in the later campaigns of Allenby did these surveys prove that some have suspected a sinister connexion between archaeology and empire. At all events, the impetus to biblical imagination and to a sense of scriptural fact was neither conjectural nor unworthy. The very neutrality of the explorers *vis-à-vis* the religious tensions so often then manifest at the shrines, and later bitterly over the whole land, helped to objectify the meanings it elucidated and to enlarge the accessibility, not only of the land, but of its other secrets. It may not be immodest, as it is not inaccurate, to claim for this tribute of love and truth some Anglican responsibility.

SITUATIONS: "THE INTERESTS OF INDIA...AND THE SEPULCHRE OF CHRIST"

The phrase is borrowed from Eliot Warburton's *The Crescent and the Cross* (1844), a popular travelogue, whose author was an early caller on Bishop Alexander in Jerusalem. In approximate language the sentiment of imperial concern behind the "love" of Palestine runs through this whole story. Though doubtful of Mount Zion as a likely place of Hebrew conversion, Warburton was alert to the political possibilities belonging with the geographical location of the Holy Land. The potential of the religious interest for national ends was a connexion the Foreign Office was already making. Through all the generations from Palmerston to Eden, the Middle East, with Palestine athwart the life-lines to the Persian Gulf and India, has compounded "spiritual" and political concerns. Jerusalem, as of old for Hezekiah, has been a pawn on the imperial board. The whole tangled question of faith and power and of the integrity of mission amid the shifts and dictates of diplomacy belongs with it. It is evident that an essay on Anglican history has a special obligation towards this power motif. Other churches and missions, it is true, belonged with the same complexities, though some, the American in particular, enjoyed a near immunity from reproach even as late as 1940. But for the Church of England it was implicit in the very origins of the bishopric. Lambeth is only a river's breadth from Westminster and critics have always suspected the proximity. Shaftesbury, they noted, had the ear of Palmerston and even Lloyd George found biblical place-names kindling a title to sympathy in his calculations at Versailles. The enigma of Balfour, whose Declaration in November 1917 paved the way for the Mandate of 1922–48 into which it was written, is at least partly solved in the hypothesis of a vicarious nationalism on behalf of Palestine, and a mystical sense of obligation to the political legatees of scriptural "mystery". The ambiguities of faith, church and policy belong in one form or other with the whole reach of modern western Christian mission and Jerusalem, sharpening all things, stamps them with its own complexity.

Their full measure has been ill-taken in what is none the less a patient documentation of Anglican history in Palestine. A. L. Tibawi's *British Interests in Palestine: 1800–1901*[1] presents a harsh and prosecuting form of the matter, under a title which is perversely categorical. The reader might assume it to be a history of English foreign policy of the region and the period. It is in fact a painstaking survey of Anglican mission, with the sub-title: A Study of Religious and Educational Enterprise, and offers a detailed access to the inner workings and stresses of the episcopal and missionary administration, to some aspects of which we will return below. It does so, however, under the distorting insistence that mission was in fact throughout the tool of national policy. From the initial *ferman* under which Bishop Alexander's tenure was secured, Dr Tibawi interprets the Anglican presence as no more than the "front" for the diplomats and the empire-builders. The thesis collapses under its own weight, despite its commendable researches. For without a modicum of disinterested integrity in mission the parties could hardly have served the political ends alleged of them. Nor were the seats of power as self-seeking as he assumes. Indeed it is one of the marks of Palestinian policy in London that in its deepest crises it was confounded by transcendent intentions. It is idle, in this field, to believe that the effective factors were uniformly the political.

Yet "British interests" there were, if never in simple equation with the Church's presence. Oddly perhaps, it was the very form of Ottoman power and administration which required the alliance, to which Alexander owed his coming, between Church and State. No foreigners were permitted to reside in Ottoman Jerusalem, though allowed access as

[1] London, 1961.

visitors. Neither was it permitted them to build churches or initiate places of worship. The Islamic minority, or *millet*, system lent itself readily to the forms of external protection which powers like France (Latins and Uniates) and Russia (Orthodox) claimed to exercise on behalf of Christian communities, as a means to exerting influence in their own regard. It is doubtless idle to wish that the *modus vivendi* of the minorities, and the *modus intrandi* of western Christians with their stake in the Holy City, had been otherwise or to will the attitudes of this middle century upon the nineteenth. The Ottoman Islamic order, nevertheless, bears the initial responsibility for the shape of western initiatives. Consular protection and diplomatic démarche were inseparable, in the event, from "such a radical innovation as a Protestant church in Jerusalem".[1] It is not an evident Islamic consistency to disapprove operation for doctrinally obligated ends through politically enabled means, even if an Islamic reproach and a Christian regret are proper attitudes when it occurs.

The Anglican activities, then, had an admittedly political occasion. Bishop Alexander was named jointly by the Crowns of Prussia and England. He travelled on H.M.S. frigate *Devastation* and came to Jerusalem, escorted or escorting, in the company of H.B.M. Consul in Beirut, and accompanied by a hundred mounted guards. He was, we might say, a new sort of centurion in the Holy City. He and his "missionaries were obviously seeking to work, not merely with the force of their spiritual message, but also with the prestige and protection of their great nation".[2] By this means, and some subterfuge, the original church was erected. Through all the vicissitudes that followed there was a persistent duality about the Anglican and the British presence.

The Act of Parliament which established the Jerusalem bishopric without naming it, and created in doing so a notable precedent, in fact began the legal and constitutional possibility of the Anglican Communion. (Bishop Seabury in the United States had been consecrated by Scottish initiative.) For it empowered the archbishop of Canterbury to consecrate to sees outside the British realms persons of foreign citizenship, whom it absolved from oaths of allegiance and supremacy, without the royal licence for their election or mandate for their consecration. It limited the jurisdictions created under it, however, to British congregations and such other Protestant congregations as might be desirous of placing themselves under their episcopal authority. This

[1] Tibawi, *op. cit.* p. 39.

[2] *Ibid.* p. 15.

apparently circumscribing proviso was, in effect, surmounted, as under Gobat, by a free interpretation of "desirous" and "Protestant". Newman's comment, from what he called even before this "my death-bed as regards my membership of the Anglican Church", is worth recalling: "If England could be in Palestine, Rome could be in England." Yet that trespass, or overlapping, of diocesan rights, as Newman saw them, is the assumption of the whole Ecumenical Movement in the sense that there is no essential territorial monopoly in the Churches of the World Council.

"England could be in Palestine." There is neither space nor need to trace that presence in its political sequence. The general nineteenth-century theme, through Palmerston and the Crimea, Disraeli and the Treaty of Berlin, was to bolster the Ottomans in order to exclude the Russians from the vital imperial lines, and to outmanœuvre the French. The occupation of Egypt and the earlier purchase of the Suez Canal had the same intent. With the steady decline of the Ottomans, the slow emergence through the tyranny of 'Abdülḥamid II of a courageous Arab nationalism, and the growth, uncertain till Herzl, of Jewish aspirations after a Palestinian return, the narrative moves on to the First World War, and, beyond it, to the ideals, the frustrations and the tragedies of the Mandate. When the traditional Eastern Question had resolved itself, by collapse, into "What should fill the vacancy created by the Ottoman demise?", all too readily was the answer given: "The mandated 'empires'." Never was answer so tragically interrogated. For its Palestinian form precipitated two mutually aggravating problems—the rough denial of Arab fulfilment and the steady progression of Zionism towards statehood as Israel. Around it seem to hover those malevolent furies which Thomas Hardy imagined in *The Dynasts*, where there occur these stage directions: "Night...in the same summer. A lofty ridge of heathland reveals itself dimly, terminating in an abrupt slope, at the summit of which are three tumuli...In front are two ricks of fuel, one of heather and furze for quick ignition, the other of wood for slow burning." Passions, at once combustible and abiding, have accumulated across the ridges of the Holy Land. Their pathos is that they complement each other. It is the necessity of statehood as Zionism saw it—and so comprehensibly in the light of Jewish experience in Europe—which is the ultimate factor earning and ensuring the inflexible opposition of the Arab context. Whatever the Balfour Declaration could, or should, have meant by a "national home...in Palestine" it could only end for Jews as a "national state of Palestine", and the safeguarded "civil and religious rights" of the existing population had to be interpreted as rights consistent with reduction to minorities and aliens. For national states in populated territories can establish themselves in no other way. So Israel, within frontiers which do not satisfy, is in danger of being a sort of independent "quarantine" as far as the natural hinterland is concerned. The form of its acceptability to itself is the certainty of its rejection by its neighbours, who in their turn see its existence as a sort of perpetuation, in their Palestinian frustration, of the self-interested presence of western power—an instinctive conviction which Suez, 1956, did everything, seemingly, to justify.

The vicissitudes of these tragic events from 1920 to the present lie beyond our brief here. Our concern is only with their bearing on the gallant, if sometimes blundering, attempt to authenticate and maintain an Anglican partnership, through, with and despite them, and an Anglican ministry in Christ embracing effectively the Arab and the English elements and upholding its duty in Christ towards Jews also.

At the outset all was sanguine and expectant. Bishop Rennie MacInnes, Blyth's successor, appears in a photograph in Wavell's *Allenby* with the victorious General four months after the entry into Jerusalem. He had been appointed in 1914 but remained in Egypt through the war years. On his arrival in Palestine he set energetically about the immediate task of reorganization and the pressing business of co-operative Syria and Palestine Relief. The Arab clergy, like As'ad Manṣūr, and those of the Jamal, Mūsā and Marmūrā families—well-known names in Arab Anglican history—had quitted themselves manfully in the privations and distresses of the Turkish defeat and retreat. The Diocese of Egypt and the Sudan began a separate existence in 1920, under Llewellyn Gwynne, who remained its much-loved bishop until 1946.[1] Through the first decade of the Mandate, steady consolidation continued with new and vigorous ventures into higher education, notably the Jerusalem Girls' College, led by Mabel Warburton. Medical and evangelistic work centred around four C.M.S. hospitals in Nābulus, Gaza, Jaffa and Salt, together with that of St Luke at Hebron (already hallowed by the devoted work of Alexander Paterson of Scotland), a new private venture at Amman and the hospitals of the old London Society, renamed the Church Missions to Jews. It was sustained and informed by the programme of the Newman School of Missions, under

[1] See H. C. Jackson, *Pastor on the Nile* (London, 1960).

the gentle guidance, from 1927 to 1950, of Eric F. F. Bishop, a patient nursery of Arabic and Islamic "scholars" (in all senses of the word) for the whole area and the several missions.

Relations with the Jewish community were fostered through the presence of Herbert Danby, a distinguished Hebraist, on the staff of St George's Cathedral, where the idea of specialist canons, caring for the fields of Jewish, Islamic, Orthodox and educational study, though rarely realized in full at any one time, served to focus and undertake the several lines of obligation. The Cathedral fully reflected the Anglican image under the Mandate. It was the place of the mandatory power at prayer, graced on all formal occasions and many private ones by successive High Commissioners, a Palestinian version of the establishment familiar at Westminster and New Delhi, with the colourful and courteous dignitaries of eastern Christianity, and of the other faiths, in reticent or cordial attendance. The pattern continued, under increasing tensions, through the episcopate of Graham Brown (1932–42) and the first years of Bishop Stewart (1942–57) into the darkening shadows of the Second World War which, strangely, brought an uneasy truce among the troubled populations of Palestine. Yet only on the occasions of special solemnity, calling for prayers and proclamations in the three official languages, was the Cathedral the home of Arabic or Hebrew worship. The Arab and European Jewish congregations remained communally apart and constitutional pre-requisites for their integration were never surmounted.

Support for the bishopric gathered momentum through the inter-war years, bringing fruition to Bishop Blyth's hopes and ideals. After Bishop MacInnes's visit to the U.S. in 1922 the Good Friday Offering for Jerusalem grew apace. An American chaplain, Charles T. Bridgeman, attached to the bishop's staff from 1924 to 1944, made himself an effective liaison with the Greek and Armenian Churches. The archbishop of Canterbury's Assyrian Mission came fully in 1939 into the purview of the Jerusalem and the East Mission. The phenomenal rise of the oil companies in the Iraq and later in the Gulf brought increasing pastoral responsibilities within the jurisdiction. Since the nineteenth-century ventures in Damascus and Baghdad there had been no sustained Anglican Mission in those areas, save for personnel within enterprises independently organized, like the British Syrian Mission (begun in 1860). Anglican chaplaincies, however, have pursued their ministry in capital cities and commercial centres from Istanbul to Qatar, the most recent being that at Abu Dhabi, where the ruler donated land for the church building.

Meanwhile, ventures in Persia and the Sudan—two notable areas of missionary imagination and vigour—had been proceeding gallantly despite numerous obstacles. These two fields are closely linked with the names of two pioneer bishops, Edward Stuart in Iṣfahān and Llewellyn Gwynne in Khartoum. The former's service of sixteen years in Persia (1894–1910) saw churches, and hospitals or schools, established in four main centres, Iṣfahān, Shiraz, Kirmān and Yazd. The contacts made by Martyn, French and Bruce, in their generation, were now deepened into a more abiding impact on the Persian soul, which was later to blossom, particularly in Shīrāz and Yazd, into finely conceived architectural expressions of the faith. Mission experienced a much greater numerical success in this field than elsewhere in the Muslim east. Despite the vicissitudes of war and revolution the Anglican Church in Persia, though shorn of its finest educational ventures, has developed an effective Persian leadership and ministry, owing much to W. J. Thompson, bishop from 1935 to 1961.

Llewellyn Gwynne first arrived in Omdurman, in company with Harpur (founder of the Old Cairo Hospital), in 1899. Kitchener's forces had only lately defeated the Khalifa's armies. The new administration was averse to missionary activity and only reluctantly agreed to Gwynne's plans, first among Copts, in 1902, and then among the pagan Sudanese in 1905. Khartoum Cathedral was completed in 1912. Archdeacon Shaw gave the whole of his active life to the completion of the New Testament and the Book of Common Prayer in Dinka. Gwynne's labours were interrupted during the First World War. But he returned in 1920 to the Diocese of Egypt and the Sudan and for twenty-seven more years presided over its work with unflagging energy. The Cairo Cathedral, consecrated in 1938, became a pioneer centre of ecumenical action in those years, beginning with the first of the unity services in 1924. In the southern Sudan emerged one of the fastest growing churches of the Anglican Communion, with the Mundri Theological School, named after Gwynne, as its nursery of ministry.

The termination of the Second World War brought the *descensus Averni* to Jerusalem. With the surrender of the Mandate, the evacuation and the war, resulting in truce frontiers still wanting treaty sanction, the Anglican Church confronted a shattering situation. The jurisdiction was sundered. The promise and pride of the Mandate had become chaos and reproach. The bitterness of irreconcilability darkened every cause. Arab congregations were disrupted and transplanted, while Christian groups, including Arab minorities, in Jewry, faced the untried problems of existence within Israeli statehood. The urgency of the immediate refugee situation evoked a vigorous response from Christian sources, within the Near East Christian Council and by the energetic initiatives of Bishop Stewart.

But aside from this concrete, and for that reason "comforting", opportunity for action,[1] it was a day of small things and of a holding operation amid persistent uncertainties. Two trends in particular are to be noted: the first a steadily deepening desire among Arab Anglicans for a pattern of things more congruent with the realities of national independence; the other a growing sense of worldwide Anglican stake in the vocation of the Church in the Middle East. Both factors tended towards the same solution, namely the establishment of the archbishopric, with a constituent diocese created within it and entrusted to Arab leadership. Bishop Najīb Qub'ayn, of the Diocese in Jordan, Syria and the Lebanon, became the first Arab Anglican bishop. His appointment brought many deferred hopes to fruition. Archbishop Geoffrey Fisher presided over these changes, in line with his policy of provincial autonomies in several parts of Africa. The dioceses of Egypt and Libya, of Persia and of the Sudan, together with those of Jerusalem and Jordan, were grouped within the new unit with Campbell MacInnes, son of the fifth bishop, as metropolitan. In 1961, Persia, too, had its first "native" bishop, in the person of Ḥasan Dihqānī Taftī, consolidating the devoted quarter century of the leadership of his predecessor.

With these changes the narrative must conclude. They are more the opportunity for, than the substance of, the Anglican vocation. For the questioner, retrospect is a wiser direction than prospect. There are some searching questions.

There is first the burden for Christians, especially those of Arab allegiance, of Zion according to Zionism. What of the problems that lie beyond the necessary postures of political confrontation? Or the use of the Old Testament where emotion and solidarity find it hard to dissociate Joshua from Mr Ben Gurion or to sing: "Blessed be the Lord God of Israel", in the context of the neighbour and the enmity what is the answer? In a measure, the Arab Church is only in an acutely emotional form of a problem which is relatively present for all Gentile

[1] The story is well told in Stewart Perowne, *The One Remains* (London, 1954).

Christians, western, African or Asian, namely a right understanding of the integrity of the Bible and a proper discipline for the Old Testament under the New. But how adequate and clear has been the inter-Anglican effort after genuine partnership and lively understanding in the presence of this vexing issue?

The due Christian sense of being "children of Abraham" has critical duties in and with the State of Israel and that State's moral obligation to the Arab pain and cost of its creation. We must not be diverted by consideration of our biblical involvement in Jewry from the sure and steady assertion of there being in Christ "neither Jew nor Greek". For only in the strength of that final irrelevance of the distinction can we return rightly to its relative validity. "Male and female...Jew and Greek", the distinctions, indeed, persist. But we only have them rightly when we refuse to allow that the differences matter. And this works both ways. It commands our ultimate compassion; but it justifies no "chosennesses" to override moral realities. As part, intimately, of the history within which the present antagonisms of the Middle East were shaped, the Anglican Church can expect no exemption from their burden, defined and demanded by the mind of Christ.

For the Arab Christians within their own nationhood, there is a well-nigh insupportable ambivalence. What may be to other nations the merely sentimental, or the blindly racial, reaction to Jewry, or for other Christians an easy acknowledgement of spiritual ancestry, is for them a specific confrontation. It is a controversy about displaced populations, appropriated lands, military defeats and persistent fears. These stand in their own concreteness. They beset a people and a culture entirely innocent of the European enmities against Jewry and who in fact pay in their own estates such reparation for those enormities of Europe which the State of Israel may constitute. Within the archbishopric, the external Anglican participation finds itself ill placed to serve, still less to plead, the limits of resentment and the claims of the unities in Christ. For its nations—in the main the U.K. and the U.S.—have been party to the train of events producing the tragedy that concerns forgiveness. Pleas for reconciliation, here and everywhere, can so easily seem the work of an uneasy conscience wanting its own reproach removed. In any event, forgiveness can only arise where the injustices belong. It has no writ for other parties' wrongs. Yet the duty to forgive abides paramount. The question is whether the Christian fellowship, multinational as it claims to be, disciplines and enables its separate elements for their proper vocations of compassion, forbearance and peace within their own nationhood.

Retrospect of the imperial and post-imperial story provokes one further inquiry. The Anglican presence—has it been unduly pre-occupied with the interests of its own expatriates throughout its dispersion? The "Jerusalem Bishopric Act" (popularly so named) based itself on British congregations even in allowing alien bishops. Everywhere, its "chaplaincies" have been in the forefront, with their distinction from "missions" too little questioned and transcended. No doubt the "chaplaincy" concept has immensely served the faith, and in many situations it was the only feasible shape of things. Henry Martyn, we remember, achieved his monumental work from within the status of chaplain to the East India Company, a body whose Directors, in their official Minutes a few years before his appointment described "the sending of missionaries" as "the maddest, most extravagant and most unwarrantable project ever proposed by an enthusiastic lunatic".

But in the ecclesiastical assumptions of the imperial heyday chaplaincies were liable to be concerned unduly, if not exclusively, with the needs, or even the nostalgia, of exiled English. The spiritual claims, and indeed the witnessing potential—either way—of expatriate communities are unquestionably valid. The question nevertheless persists as to whether these aspects of Anglican presence overseas were sufficiently disciplined to an explicit universality in Christ and pastorally integrated into the wholeness of the Church. This issue is of shorter duration in the eastern Mediterranean world than in India and parts of Africa. Yet the British presence there was ample and prolonged enough to warrant the inquiry how far within its own ecclesiastical life it achieved a true "Communion" of its parts, in the day of its "English" opportunity. For beyond that is the sterner question of its viability in the day of its "English" eclipse. Through both runs the largest issue of all—whether Anglicanism, effectively and rightly transcending "Englishness", has the resilience to survive, or what, in truly multicultural openness, it might become. That theme, however, for all its fascination and urgency, we must forbear to pursue here, in duty bound to more immediate, though perhaps contributory assessments.

REFLEXIONS: "OUR FEET...WITHIN THY GATES..."

Impulses and situations—feet that went up to seek the house of the Lord and the gates that received them—these have been followed and described. Anglicans in the east had the purposes and encountered the occasions we have studied. What of the measure of their achievement? By what criteria should their history be judged?

Much outpouring of devotion would be the first, and perhaps in the end, the sufficient, answer. The story has its kindling quality of simplicity and is rich in consecration of life. As an essay in compassion, it was, no doubt, beset, as all mission has been, with the temptation to arrogance and patronage, to indulgence in self-esteem by the very exercise of superior skills in the name of mercy and for the commendation of faith. The mission hospital, or school, it must be confessed, ministers to egoism for the very reason that it ministers to suffering or to ignorance. Such is our perversity that even humility may be a matter of congratulation and sacrifice of pride. There is no natural immunity.[1] The steady validities of ministry abide, nevertheless, made sure and authentic in the cleansed intention. If the foregoing survey has followed episcopal sequence and organized its duties behind the names and dates of leaders, it had its substance only because it comprised an unfailing succession of obscurer folk giving their sustained loyalty without stint in every sphere. There were those well-loved doctor-figures whose names a grateful locality borrowed to denote their institutions—Carr in Iṣfahān, Harpur in Cairo, Sterling in Gaza, and a varied continuity of indefatigable women, resourceful, indomitable, who gave as much as half a century of life to obscure corners of the land they had taken for their heritage. There were, too, those with special *charismata* of imagination and sensitivity: Thomas Valpy French deliberately burning out his candle in the weeks between February and May 1891 at Muscat, architect of St John's College, Agra and for ten years the first bishop of the vast diocese of Lahore, a magnificent cathedral builder ill at ease for evangelism after a lifetime of institutional achievement; or Temple Gairdner, gifted Arabist and musician, bringing gaiety and zeal into the rigours of a Cairo mission and inspiring Constance Padwick, his biographer and colleague, to work out his legacy in the Central Literature Committee for Muslims; or Norman

[1] Arabic readers have a bitter, exaggerated, but still significant, indictment of this paradox in 'Umar Farrūkh and Muḥammad al-Khālidī, *al-Tabshīr wa'l-isti'mār* [Missions and Imperialism] (Beirut, 1953).

Sharp, still serving in the University of Shiraz and builder of the exquisite Church of St Simon the Zealot in that city; or Graham Brown, the sixth bishop, whose qualities of soul and tragic death wrote his name with tender emphasis into the Anglican memory. Selection is either random or invidious. But if the Epistle to the Romans is not in fact complete without an addendum of salutations and names, otherwise unknown, this chapter is improperly without one.

The decade in which Graham Brown was bishop saw the climax of educational endeavour. Conditions in places tended to the elimination of village schools, of which perhaps the most exceptional, and persistent, was that in the Druse village of ʻAyn ʻAnūb in Lebanon. But, despite them, the major "high" schools had their heyday. St Justin's House, as an Anglican Hostel at the American University of Beirut, was designed by Graham Brown to serve their graduates from Palestine. The hope through those years was that common school living and learning would symbolize and perpetuate co-operation in the new generation of Arabs and Jews. The tides of enmity proved too strong for these sanguine expectations. The kinships they fostered were too transitory and visionary to counter the tragic political causes. Nevertheless an education under Anglican auspices belongs with a remarkable proportion of the present-day leaders, merchants and professional classes within the Middle Eastern scene from Haifa to Kuwait. "The élite of the Middle East", wrote the Prior of the Benedictine Monastery at Toumliline in the Atlas Mountains of Morocco, "have been educated by Jesuits, Christian Brothers, Mesdames of the Sacred Heart and Franciscan missionaries of Mary."[1]

The more modest Anglican parallel raises a further reflexion about education, namely the degree to which Islam remained impervious to formal Christian recruitment through its impact. It is true that there were invariably factors, both legal and social, which militated against change in religious allegiance. The fact, nevertheless, remains that Muslim and Jewish households could send their sons and daughters without reserve, indeed with eager enthusiasm, to mission schools, drawn by English language, by standards of learning and ideals, by moral confidence, and yet did so with entire, and usually justified, equanimity, about their exposure to Christian tenets, principles and

[1] In *Crosscurrents* (a quarterly pub. Crosscurrents Corporation, 103 Van Houten Fields, West Nyack, New York 10994), vol. xv, no. 1 (1965), p. 27. Toumliline is a remarkable venture in the fulfilment of the "presence" concept of the Christian duty to Islam.

invitations. Whatever the abiding fruits of Christian education and its investments in successive generations of a sustained quality of dedication, they are not those of conversion, at least in the measurable senses of the word. In the light of this it is perhaps surprising that contemporary state controls should handle the Christian schools with increasing stringency, sometimes to the point of a harshness seemingly born of resentment or of fear. The bread, for all that, is on the waters.

What of the Anglican record in the field of inter-religious communication, as it is now customarily called (though the word suggests a sort of aloofness, still more implicit in "approach", which fits ill with the intention)? There is perhaps about all mission the danger perversely stated in the gibe about the old man of whom it was said that "no cause was irretrievably lost until he had made it his own". It is no reproach to the early pioneers if we have not yet fully found a way to a hearing through the deterrents set in train by seeking one. Situations even yet are not reciprocal enough and labour under all the liabilities of political complications and historical memories. Yet the materials of the Christian concern about Islam in the fields of scholarship and study were ably and laboriously gathered, through a century of endeavour, in which Anglicans had an honoured place. The most representative early name is that of Gottlieb Pfander (1803–65), master linguist and controversialist, tireless alike in travels through Armenia, Iraq, Persia, India, the North-west Frontier and Turkey, as in public disputation and writing. His most noted work was *The Balance of Truth* (1829), compendium of the intricate and iterated themes of Muslim–Christian debate—abrogation, Scriptures, prophecy, salvation, faith, works, Divine Names, free will and the Holy Spirit. There were striking examples of discipleship to Christ developing from Pfander's ministry, notably 'Imād al-Dīn, the *mawlvī* officially deputed to contest his message.

As the physical and cultural isolations began to give way in the first quarter of this century to new circumstances of inter-penetration and Islam emerged from traditionalism, the temper of Christian relationship changed. Its classic statement at the Jerusalem Conference of 1928 was given by Temple Gairdner and represented a new acknowledgement of the "mystery" of Islam, as well as its antipathy (a posture personified uniquely and within French Catholicism by Louis Massignon, d. 1962). Whether *vis-à-vis* the synagogue or the mosque, Anglican thinkers and workers have, within the counsels of the Ecumenical Movement, stood in the main for the temper of reverence and good hope in Christ, in the study and discharge of the Christian obligations. There is a growing sense of potential liberation from the dogmatic immunities which have foreclosed in the past so many transactions in truth and the Spirit between faiths. In this development, fragile as it is and precariously related to many factors outside religious control, Anglican Christians may claim to have served a modest role. Pfander, Muir, Stern, French, Flad, Sell, Tisdall, Thornton, Gairdner, Cash, Lilias Trotter, Danby, L. E. Browne, Eric Bishop, Guillaume, Trimingham, Watt and David Brown represent an impressive succession within the larger resources of the Churches in general.

On that ecumenical question as a whole, it would be fair to reflect that the Middle East has both notorious difficulties and substantial achievements. Its very sanctities have, of course, attracted, especially in this century, a wide variety of representation to add to the already vexed disunities of eastern Christendom. There seems in the biblical setting a chronically tenacious quality about these divergencies. Nevertheless the steady Anglican policy of constructive friendship with the Orthodox, since it began to be viable in practice under Blyth, has slowly won confidence and goodwill and therewith the opportunity to take theological and liturgical encounter seriously. For many years this determination had to be content with reciprocal courtesies and passive tolerance.

Within the Churches of the World Council membership with missionary presence in the area co-operation has been increasingly close. The Lutherans, as we saw, abandoned the formal partnerships of the 1840s after three decades. The polity of missions divided the whole region into agreed centres of concentration and these were faithfully observed. The United Missionary Council of Syria, Lebanon and Palestine and the larger Near East Christian Council were the local and regional bodies within the International Missionary Council, founded in 1910. Successive Anglican participants have played a vigorous role in their social, theological and ecclesiastical counsels. Cairo has been a prominent centre in the promotion of unity. The ministries of relief and rehabilitation, after both World Wars, helped to cement and vindicate ecumenical unity in practical action. The N.E.C.C. since the New Delhi Assembly of 1961 has become the Near East Council of Churches, though thus far only the Syrian, of the Orthodox Churches, is in full membership. Formal reunion negotiations have, however, been fitful and slow and there is nothing yet comparable to developments in South and North India, Ceylon, Nigeria and Ghana.

These questions belong with one final domestic issue. There is a measure of tension, which might be cynically described as confusion or worse, and hopefully, as, in a limited way, ecumenical, *within* the Anglican Communion. But this quality of comprehension has always had unfinished business with itself and needs to be made good as something more than nominal cohabitation. It is possible in fact, and futile in reality, to be both comprehensive and uncomprehending. The Jerusalem archbishopric is peculiarly involved in this Anglican characteristic for reasons arising, in part, from the unresolved issues within its history. There was a sense in which, under the policy of Bishop Blyth, the parishes constituted by his predecessors in many centres existed only by violation of his principles and were yet a living part of his jurisdiction and so properly of his obligation. How does one disavow the origins and still admit the claims of one's inheritance? Bishop Blyth, it is true, did not seek to ignore history: nor did he fail fellowship. But the living situation demanded a firmer persistence, and a larger will, for its integration than it has ever since received.[1]

For all Blyth's pastoral energies on behalf of the Arab clergy and congregations, they continued in the main within the patterns and traditions of their genesis, unaffected by the dialogue or interaction of churchmanships within their larger heritage. Anglican dichotomies were acquiescently suffered to remain, precluded by this kind of "tolerance" from effective integration. Particular characteristics, in fairly static order, simply co-existed within a wider potential of which all elements were seldom creatively one. The situation was accentuated by the factors of nationality and language which the political evolution made ever more crucial.

Part of this failure on all sides to be fully Anglican, by mutually acknowledged criteria, relates to the unhappy fact that all too little was done to bring the genuine worldwideness of the Anglican Communion into personal expression in the Mother City. Episcopal canons from Japan, India and Africa, in stalls which at best they once occupied, were no more than the token, never the substance, of such inter-racial fellowship. Resident clergy from these countries in positions of authority and esteem would have done much to mitigate the purely Arab, Anglo-Saxon equation.

Thus it was that when the diocese in Jordan, Syria and the Lebanon

[1] The Arab Anglican Evangelical Episcopal Community has been harshly analysed, with some errors of fact and more of temper, in Howard Johnson, *Global Odyssey* (London, 1963), chapter 14.

came into being, with an Arab bishop, it took over not only a sense of postponement but a perpetuation of the Church-Council approach and a temper not joyous or free enough to achieve all the potential latent in the opportunity it created and to surmount the heavy psychological and material liabilities with which it began after decades of communal life, nine years of refugeedom and fifteen months after Suez. It needs every encouragement to take its full place with the Persian and Sudanese Churches within the whole and to reach out into all levels of Arab life and culture. There is no essential reason why it could not assume much more of the "embassy" concepts towards Orthodoxy and take the brunt of relations in Christ by the Spirit with Islam. And there is every practical urgency that it should. Only then could it return, as in the foreseeable future it surely must, in critical freedom and loving dignity, to its English partnerships, both historic and contemporary. Only then will all the participants in Anglican Jerusalem have been true to the dimensions of their calling.

To search for a conclusion is impossible in Jerusalem. Her bulwarks were counted by the psalmist only that he might recite their condition to them that come after. "I was glad" he wrote elsewhere, "when they said to me: 'Let us go into the house of the Lord.'" For many reasons—brokenness, compromise, pathos, misery, frustration, unworthiness—he might well have rather written: "I was sad when they said..." But in the final reckoning it is these which are the possibility of joy. "Happy is he" wrote George Herbert, priest to the Temple and craftsman of Anglican psalmody—

> Happy is he whose heart
> Hath found the art
> To turn his double pains
> To double praise.